Intentional Perspectives on Information Systems Engineering

Selmin Nurcan · Camille Salinesi ·
Carine Souveyet · Jolita Ralyté
Editors

Intentional Perspectives on Information Systems Engineering

Springer

Editors
Selmin Nurcan
Université Paris 1 Panthéon – Sorbonne
IAE de Paris
21, rue Broca
75005 Paris
France
Selmin.Nurcan@univ-paris1.fr

Camille Salinesi
Université Paris 1 Panthéon – Sorbonne
Centre de Recherche en Informatique
90, rue de Tolbiac
75013 Paris
France
Camille.Salinesi@univ-paris1.fr

Carine Souveyet
Université Paris 1 Panthéon – Sorbonne
Centre de Recherche en Informatique
90, rue de Tolbiac
75013 Paris
France
Carine.Souveyet@univ-paris1.fr

Jolita Ralyté
University of Geneva
CUI, Battelle – bâtiment A
route de Drize 7
1227 Carouge
Switzerland
Jolita.Ralyte@unige.ch

ISBN 978-3-642-44236-0 ISBN 978-3-642-12544-7 (eBook)
DOI 10.1007/978-3-642-12544-7
Springer Heidelberg Dordrecht London New York

ACM Computing Classification (1998): D.2, H.1, I.6, J.1

Cover design: KuenkelLopka GmbH, Heidelberg

Printed on acid-free paper

Springer is part of Springer Science+Business Media (www.springer.com)

Preface

Colette Rolland, in the words of Arne Solvberg, one of her oldest and closest friends, "was introduced to the wider European research community during the process of establishing a Technical Committee for Information Systems – TC8 – of IFIP – The International Federation of Information Processing Societies. Professor Børje Langefors from Sweden led the effort. He and his colleagues brought with them upcoming younger researchers. Professor Langefors brought Janis Bubenko Jr., Mads Lundeberg and Arne Sølvberg. Professor Le Moigne brought Colette. Together with Janis and Arne, Colette was instrumental in establishing the IFIP TC8 working group WG8.1 on the Design and Evaluation of Information Systems. She quickly established herself as a driving force in information systems research with her REMORA project. She was deeply involved in organizing the annual working conferences of the working group, which brought together a growing number of researchers from Europe and overseas. The network of young researchers that was formed in IFIP TC8 became the nucleus of the scientific community behind the CAiSE conference series, where Colette had a central role. She is today the undisputed 'queen' of information systems research, as well as a good friend to everyone in the international research community of information systems engineering."

Amongst her numerous scientific qualities, Colette was able to abstract and formalize new and difficult problems, invent original concepts to deal with them, and develop methods, techniques and tools demonstrating how to use them in a very practical way.

Colette's original contributions to the information systems engineering discipline have been abundant. Among others, she established the behavioral paradigm to information system design in which she promoted the event-driven approach with her REMORA methodology. She pioneered object orientation in information systems analysis and design with her O* methodology. She developed an original approach to system prototyping. Being at the cutting edge of meta-modeling, she was one of the earliest to specify methodological processes and introduce guidance features in CASE tools and to propose the concept of method chunks and contextual models to engineering methods. She was one of the main actors in promoting method engineering as a discipline. She created the NATURE decision-driven process meta-model. She formalized the coupling of goals and scenarios in the CREWS-*L'Ecritoire* requirements engineering method. She developed an intentional basis for process modeling in the notion of a MAP expressing intentions. She brought the fitness analysis issue to the forefront. She was a strong supporter of dealing with services at the business level and explored service-based information systems. She developed many information systems engineering methods, CASE and CAME tools like REMORA, OICSI, RUBIS, MENTOR, and L'Ecritoire, to name but a few.

One of the most striking of Colette's numerous scientific contributions is that "intention" should be considered as a first-class concept in information systems engineering. Not only can it be handled in different ways and modeled with different languages. It is also fundamental to a number of application domains in performing various types of analysis and solving very different categories of problem: process specification, requirements engineering, service—oriented architectures, enterprise modeling, business IT alignment, COTS customization, etc. Indeed, as John Mylopoulos said, "Her plethora of contributions include novel concepts, methods and tools for building information systems, as well as dozens of young researchers who will carry the torch of her ideas for years to come. One of those ideas that has had tremendous impact on the field is the notion that system requirements are stakeholder goals—rather than system functions—and ought to be elicited, modeled and analyzed accordingly."

This book is a testimony of gratitude to Colette for her contribution to the concept of *intention*. The book was created with the idea of drawing a big picture of the different perspectives that exist today, in 2010, on this concept in the information systems community.

The book is a collection of 20 contributions in information systems engineering that were compiled on the occasion of Colette's retirement and will be distributed at the CAiSE conference in Tunisia. Even though Colette is General Chair of CAiSE 2010, we tried to hide this initiative from her, and she kindly pretended not to be aware of it. The contributions were written by friends and colleagues of Colette from around the world. In the difficult task of selecting who to invite, we decided to concentrate on those with whom she collaborated most closely, and some of those whom she took as examples for her young researchers, and referenced in her own papers. All those who were invited to be involved in this book were eager to participate, and have written original contributions on one of the numerous topics of interest to Colette. Some even wrote personal testimonies of friendship in their papers, which we found very touching.

We thank all the authors and the Springer editors for their support in the publication of this book. We also thank CAiSE organizers for agreeing to its presentation during the Conference. Last but not least, we thank the following for sponsoring this book for distribution to all CAISE 2010 participants: the Sorbonne's Graduate Business School (IAE de Paris), IFIP (International Federation for Information Processing) Working Group 8.1 on Design and Evaluation of Information Systems, RIADI (ENSI – University Manouba, Tunisia) and the Centre de Recherche en Informatique of University Paris 1 Panthéon – Sorbonne.

Paris, France Selmin Nurcan
Camille Salinesi
Carine Souveyet
Switzerland Jolita Ralyté

Short Biography of Colette Rolland

Colette Rolland was born on December 19th, 1943 in Dieupentale, Tarn-et-Garonne, in the southwest of France. She received her PhD Degree in Sciences (Applied Mathematics) in 1966 and her "Grand PhD" Degree in Sciences (Applied Mathematics) in 1971. Both degrees were under the supervision of Professor Legras at the University of Nancy.

In 1973, Dr. Rolland was appointed Professor in Computer Science at University of Nancy.

Colette Rolland joined the Mathematics and Informatics Department of the University of Paris 1 Panthéon – Sorbonne as a Professor in 1979. In 1992 she founded the CRI (Centre de Recherche en Informatique – http://crinfo.univ-paris1.fr), at the University Paris 1 Panthéon – Sorbonne and has been the center's Director since its creation. Today, she supervises a team of 8 full time Associate Professors and 25 research students.

Professor Colette Rolland heads the Master degree program in "Information & Knowledge Systems", at the Sorbonne Graduate Business School (IAE de Paris). A program she created thirty years ago.

In 1988, she launched the MIAGE curriculum (Méthodes Informatiques Appliquées à la Gestion des Entreprises, i.e. methods for informatics applied to the management of enterprises) at the University Paris 1 Panthéon – Sorbonne. The program was designed to train young engineers in informatics. Several years prior to the implementation in France, of the LMD Standards (Bachelor, Master, PhD or 3-5-8), she extended the MIAGE program to include an apprenticeship track leading to a master degree in "Information & Knowledge Systems".

Following on these successes, Colette Rolland created IKSEM (Information & Knowledge Systems Engineering and Management), an English Master Degree program at IAE de Paris in 2009.

Colette Rolland has led two Ph.D. programs in "Theory and Engineering of Data Bases" and "Intelligence, Information, Interaction". The University Paris 1 Panthéon – Sorbonne and the University Paris 11 Orsay jointly managed the two programs.

Professor Colette Rolland has *extensive experience in supervising research work* (see the Academic Tree); supervising more than 100 PhD, participating in multiple European research projects and collaborating extensively with industry. Her research work has been funded in France by CNRS (Centre National de la Recherche Scientifique), INRIA (Institut National de la Recherche en Informatique et Automatisme), MRT (Ministry of Research and Technology) and by the Commission of the European Communities (ESPRIT, STI and the Basic research program).

Colette Rolland is the inventor of the REMORA methodology for the analysis, design and realization of information systems, a precursor of object-oriented methodologies. She has co-authored 5 textbooks; edited 8 books and published over 300 referred papers in journals and conferences (see Bibliography). Colette Rolland has delivered more than 50 keynote talks in international conferences.

Colette Rolland is a member of various academic and professional committees, an IFIP officer since 1981, IEEE fellow, and the French representative to TC8 (IFIP Technical Commitee on Information Systems). From 1988 to 1999, she served as vice chairperson and then chairperson of WG8.1 (IFIP Working Group on Methods and Tools for IS Development). She is also a member of the European Commission's expert groups. She has been a member of various research evaluation committees in Sweden, Norway, Finland, Italy, Canada, Switzerland and Hong Kong, as well as a member of committees for the appointment of professors in Canada, USA, Japan, Malaysia, Venezuela, and Tunisia.

Colette Rolland has been honored by several awards including: the "Palmes Académiques" (French Educational System award – 1981), the IFIP service award (1988), the IFIP Silver Core (1992), the Francqui's Foundation award (a Belgium prize awarded annually to an outstanding scientist – 1991), and the European award of 'Information Systems' (2002).

In 1995, Colette Rolland was nominated a member of the Class of Exceptional Professors in France. She is Doctor Honoris Causa of the University of Geneva, Switzerland (2007). She is also a visiting professor at the University of Loughborough Business School (United Kingdom) where she cooperates with the research group on enterprise modeling and IT alignment.

Colette Rolland serves on the board of 15 international journals published among others by IEEE and Springer. She is a member of program committees of multiple international conferences per year, has been chairperson of 25 conferences, and editor of 25 conference proceedings.

Academic Tree

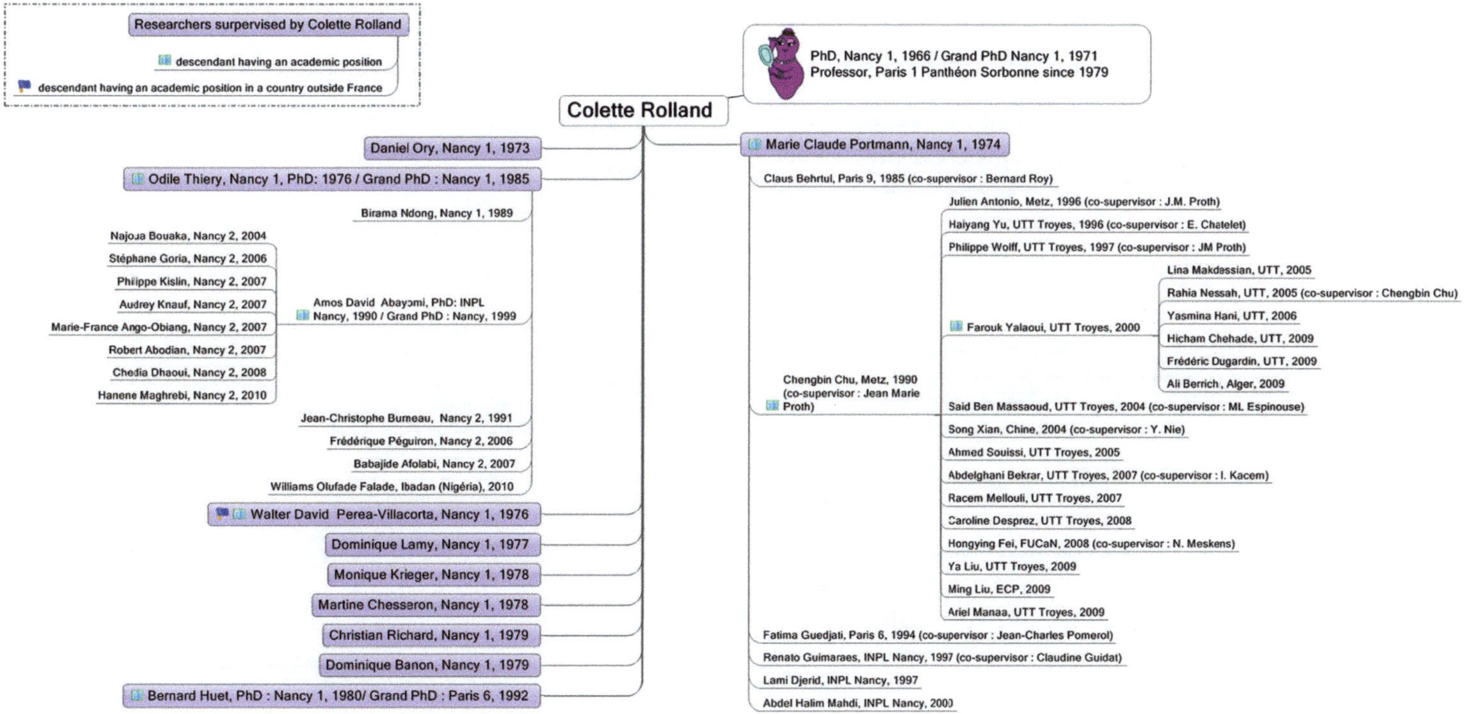

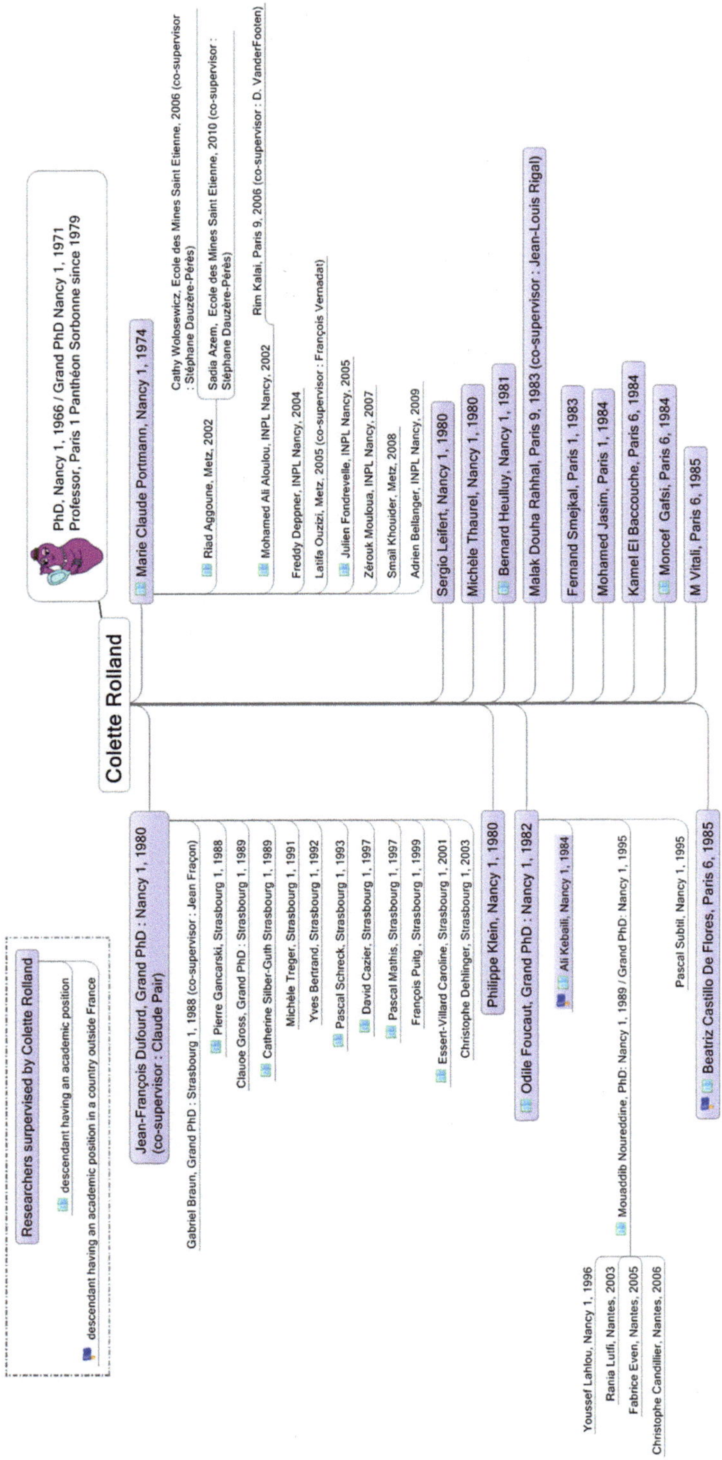
Colette Rolland
PhD, Nancy 1, 1966 / Grand PhD Nancy 1, 1971
Professor, Paris 1 Panthéon Sorbonne since 1979
Marie Claude Portmann, Nancy 1, 1974
Cathy Wolosewicz, Ecole des Mines Saint Etienne, 2006 (co-supervisor : Stéphane Dauzère-Pérès)
Riad Aggoune, Metz, 2002
Sadia Azem, Ecole des Mines Saint Etienne, 2010 (co-supervisor : Stéphane Dauzère-Pérès)
Rim Kalai, Paris 9, 2006 (co-supervisor : D. VanderFooten)
Mohamed Ali Aloulou, INPL Nancy, 2002
Freddy Deppner, INPL Nancy, 2004
Latifa Ouzizi, Metz, 2005 (co-supervisor : François Vernadat)
Julien Fondrevelle, INPL Nancy, 2005
Zérouk Mouloua, INPL Nancy, 2007
Smail Khouider, Metz, 2008
Adrien Bellanger, INPL Nancy, 2009
Sergio Leifert, Nancy 1, 1980
Michèle Thaurel, Nancy 1, 1980
Bernard Heulluy, Nancy 1, 1981
Malak Douha Rahhal, Paris 9, 1983 (co-supervisor : Jean-Louis Rigal)
Fernand Smejkal, Paris 1, 1983
Mohamed Jasim, Paris 1, 1984
Kamel El Baccouche, Paris 6, 1984
Moncef Gafsi, Paris 6, 1984
M Vitali, Paris 6, 1985
Researchers surpervised by Colette Rolland
descendant having an academic position
descendant having an academic position in a country outside France
Jean-François Dufourd, Grand PhD : Nancy 1, 1980 (co-supervisor : Claude Pair)
Gabriel Braun, Grand PhD : Strasbourg 1, 1988 (co-supervisor : Jean Fraçon)
Pierre Gancarski, Strasbourg 1, 1988
Clauoe Gross, Grand PhD : Strasbourg 1, 1989
Catherine Silber-Guth Strasbourg 1, 1989
Michèle Treger, Strasbourg 1, 1991
Yves Bertrand, Strasbourg 1, 1992
Pascal Schreck, Strasbourg 1, 1993
David Cazier, Strasbourg 1, 1997
Pascal Mathis, Strasbourg 1, 1997
François Puitg , Strasbourg 1, 1999
Essert-Villard Caroline, Strasbourg 1, 2001
Christophe Dehlinger, Strasbourg 1, 2003
Philippe Klein, Nancy 1, 1980
Odile Foucaut, Grand PhD : Nancy 1, 1982
Ali Kebaili, Nancy 1, 1984
Mouaddib Noureddine, PhD: Nancy 1, 1989 / Grand PhD: Nancy 1, 1995
Youssef Lahlou, Nancy 1, 1996
Rania Lutfi, Nantes, 2003
Fabrice Even, Nantes, 2005
Christophe Candillier, Nantes, 2006
Pascal Subtil, Nancy 1, 1995
Beatriz Castillo De Flores, Paris 6, 1985

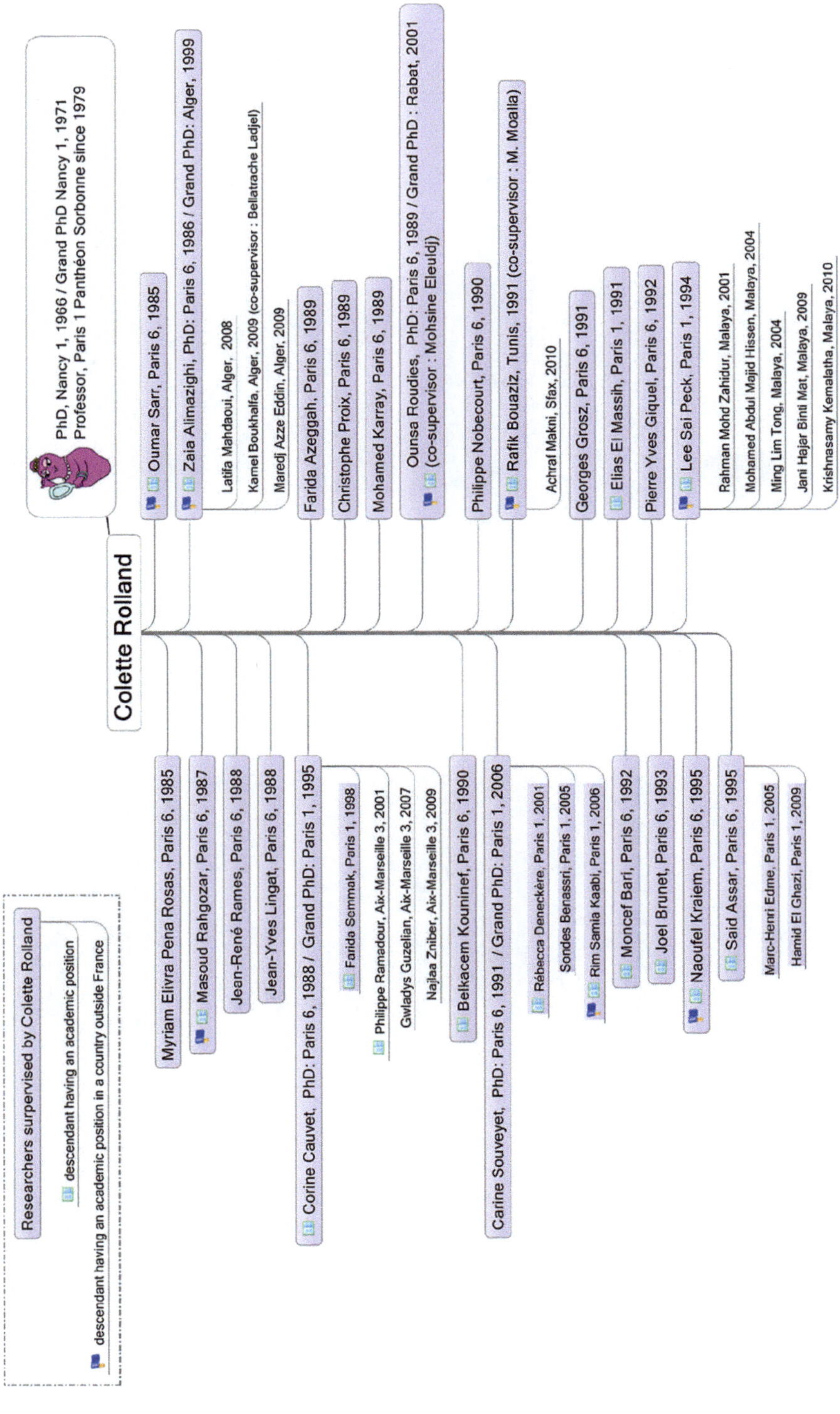
Colette Rolland
PhD, Nancy 1, 1966 / Grand PhD Nancy 1, 1971
Professor, Paris 1 Panthéon Sorbonne since 1979
Oumar Sarr, Paris 6, 1985
Zaia Alimazighi, PhD: Paris 6, 1986 / Grand PhD: Alger, 1999
Latifa Mahdaoui, Alger, 2008
Kamel Boukhalfa, Alger, 2009 (co-supervisor : Bellatrache Ladjel)
Maredj Azze Eddin, Alger, 2009
Farida Azeggah, Paris 6, 1989
Christophe Proix, Paris 6, 1989
Mohamed Karray, Paris 6, 1989
Ounsa Roudies, PhD: Paris 6, 1989 / Grand PhD : Rabat, 2001
(co-supervisor : Mohsine Eleuldj)
Philippe Nobecourt, Paris 6, 1990
Rafik Bouaziz, Tunis, 1991 (co-supervisor : M. Moalla)
Achraf Makni, Sfax, 2010
Georges Grosz, Paris 6, 1991
Elias El Massih, Paris 1, 1991
Pierre Yves Giquel, Paris 6, 1992
Lee Sai Peck, Paris 1, 1994
Rahman Mohd Zahidur, Malaya, 2001
Mohamed Abdul Majid Hissen, Malaya, 2004
Ming Lim Tong, Malaya, 2004
Jani Hajar Binti Mat, Malaya, 2009
Krishnasamy Kemalatha, Malaya, 2010
Myriam Elivra Pena Rosas, Paris 6, 1985
Masoud Rahgozar, Paris 6, 1987
Jean-René Rames, Paris 6, 1988
Jean-Yves Lingat, Paris 6, 1988
Corine Cauvet, PhD: Paris 6, 1988 / Grand PhD: Paris 1, 1995
Farida Semmak, Paris 1, 1998
Philippe Ramadour, Aix-Marseille 3, 2001
Gwladys Guzelian, Aix-Marseille 3, 2007
Najlaa Zniber, Aix-Marseille 3, 2009
Belkacem Kouninef, Paris 6, 1990
Carine Souveyet, PhD: Paris 6, 1991 / Grand PhD: Paris 1, 2006
Rébecca Deneckère, Paris 1, 2001
Sondes Benassri, Paris 1, 2005
Rim Samia Kaabi, Paris 1, 2006
Moncef Bari, Paris 6, 1992
Joel Brunet, Paris 6, 1993
Naoufel Kraiem, Paris 6, 1995
Said Assar, Paris 6, 1995
Marc-Henri Edme, Paris 1, 2005
Hamid El Ghazi, Paris 1, 2009
Researchers surpervised by Colette Rolland
descendant having an academic position
descendant having an academic position in a country outside France

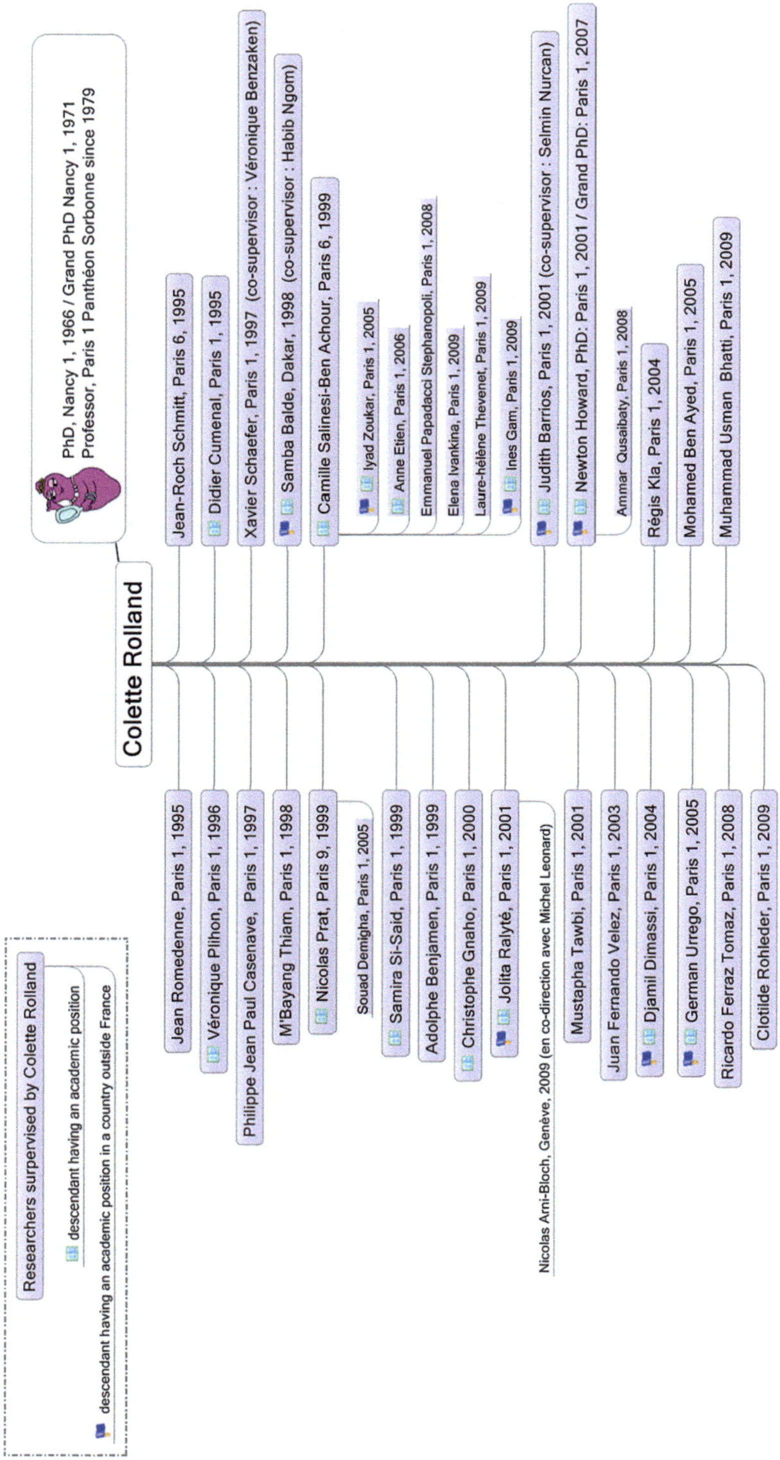
Colette Rolland
PhD, Nancy 1, 1966 / Grand PhD Nancy 1, 1971
Professor, Paris 1 Panthéon Sorbonne since 1979
Jean-Roch Schmitt, Paris 6, 1995
Didier Cumenal, Paris 1, 1995
Xavier Schaefer, Paris 1, 1997 (co-supervisor : Véronique Benzaken)
Samba Balde, Dakar, 1998 (co-supervisor : Habib Ngom)
Camille Salinesi-Ben Achour, Paris 6, 1999
Iyad Zoukar, Paris 1, 2005
Anne Etien, Paris 1, 2006
Emmanuel Papadacci Stephanopoli, Paris 1, 2008
Elena Ivankina, Paris 1, 2009
Laure-hélène Thevenet, Paris 1, 2009
Ines Gam, Paris 1, 2009
Judith Barrios, Paris 1, 2001 (co-supervisor : Selmin Nurcan)
Newton Howard, PhD: Paris 1, 2001 / Grand PhD: Paris 1, 2007
Ammar Qusaibaty, Paris 1, 2008
Régis Kla, Paris 1, 2004
Mohamed Ben Ayed, Paris 1, 2005
Muhammad Usman Bhatti, Paris 1, 2009
Jean Romedenne, Paris 1, 1995
Véronique Plihon, Paris 1, 1996
Philippe Jean Paul Casenave, Paris 1, 1997
M'Bayang Thiam, Paris 1, 1998
Nicolas Prat, Paris 9, 1999
Souad Demigha, Paris 1, 2005
Samira Si-Said, Paris 1, 1999
Adolphe Benjamen, Paris 1, 1999
Christophe Gnaho, Paris 1, 2000
Jolita Ralyté, Paris 1, 2001
Nicolas Arni-Bloch, Genève, 2009 (en co-direction avec Michel Leonard)
Mustapha Tawbi, Paris 1, 2001
Juan Fernando Velez, Paris 1, 2003
Djamil Dimassi, Paris 1, 2004
German Urrego, Paris 1, 2005
Ricardo Ferraz Tomaz, Paris 1, 2008
Clotilde Rohleder, Paris 1, 2009
Researchers surpervised by Colette Rolland
descendant having an academic position
descendant having an academic position in a country outside France

MIAGE Sorbonne – Information & Knowledge Systems master students, Graduation Ceremony, February 13th, 2009 Amphitheater Richelieu at Sorbonne with 67 Master Students

Colette with Arne and Janis at CAISE'2007, Porto, Portugal

Contents

Contributors

Mikio Aoyama Nanzan University, 27 Seirei, Seto 489-0863, Japan, mikio.aoyama@nifty.com

Maria Bergholtz Department of Computer and Systems Sciences, Stockholm University, Forum 100, SE 16440 Kista, Sweden, maria@dsv.su.se

Janis Bubenko Jr. Department of Computer and Systems Sciences, Royal Institute of Technology, Forum 100, SE-164 40 Kista, Sweden, janis@dsv.su.se

Corine Cauvet Université Paul Cézanne Aix-Marseille 3, Laboratoire LSIS, Campus Universitaire de Saint Jérôme, Avenue Escadrille Normandie Niemen, 13397 Marseille Cedex 20, France, corine.cauvet@lsis.org

Amit K. Chopra Department of Information Engineering and Computer Science, University of Trento, Via Sommarive 14, 38123 Povo, Trento, Italy, chopra@disi.unitn.it

Fabiano Dalpiaz Department of Information Engineering and Computer Science, University of Trento, Via Sommarive 14, 38123 Povo, Trento, Italy, dalpiaz@disi.unitn.it

Maya Daneva University of Twente, Drienerlolaan 5, P.O. Box 217, 7500 EA Enschede, The Netherlands, m.daneva@utwente.nl

Éric Dubois Centre de Recherche Public Henri Tudor, 29, avenue John F. Kennedy, L-1855 Luxembourg, eric.dubois@tudor.lu

Xavier Franch GESSI Research Group, Universitat Politècnica de Catalunya, UPC – Campus Nord, Omega building, c/Jordi Girona 1-3, 08034 Barcelona, Spain, franch@essi.upc.edu

Johny Ghattas University of Haifa, Carmel Mountain 31905 Haifa, Israel, ghattasjohny@gmail.com

Giovanni Giachetti PROS Research Center, Universidad Politécnica de Valencia, Camino de Vera s/n, 46022 Valencia, Spain, ggiachetti@pros.upv.es

Paolo Giorgini Department of Information Engineering and Computer Science, University of Trento, Via Sommarive 14, 38123 Povo, Trento, Italy, pgiorgio@disi.unitn.it

Sean Hansen Peter B. Lewis Building, Weatherhead School of Management, Case Western Reserve University, 10900 Euclid Avenue, Cleveland, OH, 44106-7235 USA, hansen@case.edu

Patrick Heymans University of Namur (FUNDP), PReCISE Research Center, Rue Grandgagnage 21, B-5000 Namur, Belgium, phe@info.fundp.ac.be

Matthias Jarke Information Systems, RWTH Aachen University, Ahornstraße 55, D-52056 Aachen, Germany, jarke@dbis.rwth-aachen.de

Paul Johannesson Department of Computer and Systems Sciences, Stockholm University, Forum 100, SE 16440 Kista, Sweden, pajo@dsv.su.se

Kim Lauenroth Software Systems Engineering, University of Duisburg-Essen, Gerlingstraße 16, 45127 Essen, Germany, kim.lauenroth@sse.uni-due.de

Michel Léonard University of Geneve, CUI, Battelle – bâtiment A, route de Drize, CH-1227 Carouge, Switzerland, Michel.Leonard@unige.ch

Kalle Lyytinen Peter B. Lewis Building, Weatherhead School of Management, Case Western Reserve University, 10900 Euclid Avenue, Cleveland, OH, 44106-7235 USA, kalle@case.edu

Raimundas Matulevičius Institute of Computer Science, University of Tartu, J. Liivi 2, 50409 Tartu, Estonia, rma@ut.ee

Nicolas Mayer Centre de Recherche Public Henri Tudor, 29, avenue John F. Kennedy, L-1855 Luxembourg, nicolas.mayer@tudor.lu

Andreas Metzger Software Systems Engineering, University of Duisburg-Essen, Gerlingstraβe 16, 45127 Essen, Germany, andreas.metzger@sse.uni-due.de

John Mylopoulos Department of Information Engineering and Computer Science, University of Trento, Via Sommarive 14, 38123 Povo, Trento, Italy, jm@disi.unitn.it

Hans W. Nissen Institute of Communications Engineering, Cologne University of Applied Science, Betzdorferstraße 2, D-50679 Köln, Germany, hans.nissen@fh-koeln.de

Antoni Olivé Department Enginyeria de Serveis i Sistemes d'Informació, Universitat Politècnica de Catalunya, Jordi Girona 1-3, 08034 Barcelona, Spain, olive@essi.upc.edu

Oscar Pastor PROS Research Center, Universidad Politécnica de Valencia, Camino de Vera s/n, 46022 Valencia, Spain, opastor@pros.upv.es

Mor Peleg University of Haifa, Carmel Mountain 31905 Haifa, Israel, peleg.mor@gmail.com

Barbara Pernici Politecnico di Milano, Piazza Leonardo da Vinci 32, 20133 Milano, Italy, barbara.pernici@polimi.it

Anne Persson Informatics Research Centre, University of Skövde, P.O. Box 408, SE-541 28 Skövde, Sweden, anne.persson@his.se

Klaus Pohl Software Systems Engineering, University of Duisburg-Essen, Schützenbahn 70, 45127 Essen, Germany, klaus.pohl@sse.uni-due.de

Naveen Prakash Department of Computer Science, MRCE, Sector 43, Delhi Surajkund Road, Faridabad 121001, Haryana, India, praknav@hotmail.com

Jolita Ralyté University of Geneva, CUI, Battelle – bâtiment A, 7, route de Drize, CH-1227 Carouge, Switzerland, jolita.ralyte@unige.ch

Thomas Rose Fraunhofer FIT, Schloss Birlinghoven, D-53754 Sankt Augustin, Germany, thomas.rose@fit.fraunhofer.de

Motoshi Saeki Department of Computer Science, Tokyo Institute of Technology, Ookayama 2-12-1-W8-83, Meguro, Tokyo 152-8552, Japan, saeki@se.cs.titech.ac.jp

Dominik Schmitz Information Systems, RWTH Aachen University, Ahornstraße 55, D-52056 Aachen, Germany, schmitz@dbis.rwth-aachen.de

Munindar P. Singh Department of Computer Science, North Carolina State University, 890 Oval Drive, Raleigh, NC 27695-8206, USA, singh@ncsu.edu

Pnina Soffer University of Haifa, Carmel Mountain 31905 Haifa, Israel, spnina@is.haifa.ac.il

Arne Sølvberg Department of Computer and Information Science, NTNU – The Norwegian University of Science and Technology Sem Sælands v 9, 7491 Trondheim, Norway, asolvber@idi.ntnu.no

Janis Stirna Department of Computer and Systems Sciences, Stockholm University, Forum 100, SE 16440 Kista, Sweden, js@dsv.su.se

Alistair Sutcliffe Manchester Business School, University of Manchester, Booth Street West, Manchester M15 6PB, UK, a.g.sutcliffe@man.ac.uk

Albert Tort Department Enginyeria de Serveis i Sistemes d'Informació, Universitat Politècnica de Catalunya, Jordi Girona 1-3, 08034 Barcelona, Spain, atort@essi.upc.edu

Roel Wieringa University of Twente, Drienerlolaan 5, P.O. Box 217, 7500 EA Enschede, The Netherlands, roelw@cs.utwente.nl

From Sustainable Information System with a Farandole of Models to Services

Michel Léonard and Jolita Ralyté

Abstract This chapter is an overview of the development of the information systems domain since its infancy. This domain is recognized as very important for the development of private companies and public organisations and therefore it more and more needs solid concepts and sharp ways of thinking. This chapter relates some breakthroughs and tries to place the IS domain in the centre of several worlds. From a simple mediator between the activities world and the informatics world, IS becomes a creator of values, in particular with the emergence of services. But, it requires a shift with several dimensions in the usual way of thinking about activities and informatics and this is the origin of the difficulty. IS complexity comes from its trans-disciplinary nature, which requires several different models to describe it. Besides, all these models must be articulated together to constitute a coherent IS – that is a farandole of models. When a model changes, due to its environment, the other models have to change too in order to keep the farandole coherent. The IS is then sustainable.

1 Introduction

While the domain of Information Systems (IS) is now recognized as very important for the development of enterprises and public institutions, the development of IS still struggles with the lack of dedicated skills and clear understanding of the IS role in organisations and Society.

Understanding challenges and opportunities in the domain of Information Systems (IS) means first of all understanding how this domain evolved from its beginnings to nowadays. This chapter aims to overview the growth of the IS domain

M. Léonard (✉)
University of Geneve, CUI, Battelle – bâtiment A, route de Drize, CH-1227 Carouge, Switzerland
e-mail: Michel.Leonard@unige.ch

S. Nurcan et al. (eds.), *Intentional Perspectives on Information Systems Engineering*,
DOI 10.1007/978-3-642-12544-7_1, © Springer-Verlag Berlin Heidelberg 2010

since its infancy throughout its advancement challenges until today's concerns by revealing its role in organisations and the difficulty to play this role.

Then, the chapter tries to position IS as a heart of several closely related and overlapping but also so different worlds: enterprise activities, information and informatics. The IS development has to deal with the overlap between these worlds. Such a way of thinking is not common in the IS development but it is necessary in order to attain IS sustainability. It requires a multi-dimensional shift in the usual way of thinking about activities and informatics. Besides, the trans-disciplinary nature of the IS increases the complexity and difficulty of its development and requires several different models to describe it. Creating several models for an IS means managing the risk of inconsistency between these models. All these models must be articulated together to constitute a coherent IS. We can call that a *farandole of models* [13]. When one model changes, due to different environmental factors, the other models have to change as well in order to keep the farandole coherent and therefore, to guarantee the sustainability of the IS.

Finally, the chapter concludes with a new perception of IS – IS as a creator of values. In particular this is possible with the emergence of the notion of service which gains a new perspective in the domain of IS. In this chapter information service is considered as a future of IS development.

2 IS Stakes

2.1 IS Origins

This section should be written by historians with their rigour of analysis of a terrain and with their way of making synthesis. Unfortunately, we do not have these talents. Nevertheless, the past gave the directions to the development of the IS domain around the world and these directions are important to be considered for planning strategic directions for the next future.

Hence, here is a vision of the past, which tries to be consensual but which cannot be objective.

Despite of the pioneering work of eminent researchers[1] who created the scientific IS domain, including its technological components, the IS domain had only to play a cameo role at the strategic level as for instance, in the Universities, in the Research funds, in the enterprises. The only domains considered as important were management science and computer science! Nevertheless, the IS domain was considered as sufficiently useful, and therefore, some curricula in the IS domain appeared. Indeed, enterprises had to hire people for IS engineering, but they were able to employ only specialists at the technical levels of engineering! IS domain was only an *application*

[1]Notably, the members of the CAISE advisory board: Professor Janis Bubenko Jr., Professor Colette Rolland, Professor Arne Solvberg.

of computer science to management situations, which were called "problems" to be solved thanks to informatics!

In the board of Management, Information Systems began to be the origin of new problems that the classic Management theories did not seem to take into account relevantly! How to teach persons IS? The MIS[2] movement claimed that it is possible to *teach* IS without any know-how in informatics. As a consequence, a lot of persons with such background were promoted as managers of IS developments in various countries. Obviously, they were not skilled to take into account not only informatics but also the subtle, complex differences and shifts between human activities and computerized tasks and processes.

The gap is great and no bridge can be built to cross it!

2.2 Shift

As soon as Information Systems became a main component of the enterprises, there was a *shift* from informatics oriented towards materialized objects – often called products like computers – to informatics oriented towards dematerialized objects – information. This shift has four main dimensions.

1. The *first dimension* concerns the quality of the result: in one side of the shift, the quality concerns the product, its performance, its feasibility, its reliability; in the other side of the shift the quality concerns the information, its accessibility, its accuracy, its consistency, its usability, its use, its security, its transformation. In one side there are technical aspects and generic usages to take into account when in the other side there are actors whose activities are strongly dependent on the quality of information. This shift is similar with the economic shift from the economy oriented towards goods to the economy oriented towards services.

   This shift does not destroy the first side oriented towards product. But, it builds a new conceptual space upon it and therefore, it constitutes a new complex where the first side can no more be considered per se, but only as a component of the complex, which has to be strongly related with the second one.

   To face this shift, two popular attitudes appear:

   - *A passive attitude*: the shift does not introduce any fundamental modification, any new knowledge, any new methods; the usual ones are always relevant – and so, IS stays only a domain of computer applications; specialists on management and informatics can continue to work as usual!
   - *An ethereal attitude*: a new domain emerges with new business models and new fruitful perspectives, *but* with still the same fundamental concepts: from management perspective the IS does not have to take into account informatics and from informatics perspective the IS does not have to take into account management!

---

[2]Management Information Systems.

The CAiSE community rejected these two approaches, because they were not relevant to explore and explain design situations, impacts, etc. It did not follow a grey approach – to stay in the middle. It created another approach, out of these lazy approaches.

2. In its *second dimension*, the shift has significant impact on informatics because it introduces subtle differences, too often neglected, which induced deep transformations in methods and knowledge. Before IS, software was recognized as a real discipline after a long and painful process of emergence. Software is a dematerialized object and the software industry becomes the industry, which gathered the most fruitfully know-how, technical knowledge, methods, in the engineering field of dematerialized objects. *But,* software is not IS engineering, even if the two domains share a lot of similar concepts and ways of reasoning. Even Information Technology (IT) is not IS engineering. Both, software and IT take into account only *generic* functions or uses. IS has to take into account *actors* who will use IS in the accurate situations of their responsibilities. Thus, IS must be flexible because situations of actors are not unchanging. Due to the IS stakes, informatics has to be re-invented, for instance to support effectively and efficiently the various situations of IS evolution.

   In the view to this second dimension, some approaches claim that the problem is only to *customize* generic software with parameterisation for instance: Other ones claim that there is no problem at all because users must only adapt their behaviour to the new IT products or the new software. Such approaches at the scientific level dodge the IS complexity.

   The CAiSE community worked explicitly or tacitly towards the emergence of IS knowledge related with software and IT *but* also different from them.

3. In its *third dimension*, the shift has significant impact on management. Indeed, if informatics is only composed with products, managers can continue to work as usually or eventually becoming users of some IS functions. But the shift induces another completely different position of managers: actors, who are able to mix their activities with artificial supports provided by the IS, and even authors, who are able to co-create some relevant IS parts. In both cases, there are great stakes at the personal level and the firm level: it is the question of creating new value by means of IS or maintaining activities at a sufficient level of efficiency, given the competition.

4. The *fourth dimension* of the shift considers the relations between human activities and information systems. The question is not to *translate* activities performed by actors into informatics – it is not a question to automate such a translation process. The question is much more interesting than only to find generic systems to *solve the problem*. In fact, there is *no* problem at this dimension. Actor is not a problem, *but* a person. The question is *not* to transform actors into conductors of robots *but* to support efficiently their activities. The main question is then how to assure *entente* between human capabilities and artificial information systems at the level of an organisation.

To conclude, the shift with its four dimensions constitutes a real complexity. The IS pioneers worked with no certainty, just with a creative intuition of their future utility, to discover how to deal with such unknown complexity. They were confident on the future relevance and usefulness of their research and developments. In fact, many resemblances emerged between their situation and that of pioneers of informatics. The IS pioneers discovered relevant models, combining management and informatics. Their master concept of their exploration was *information.*

2.3 Governance of Information Systems

Information systems introduce the complexity of mixing human activities and informatics, of designing this mix and of managing its evolutions. But the world of human activities and the world of informatics do not have the same properties, the same criteria of quality. Each one has its own autonomy in its transformations and its movements, which are greatly independent one from the other. Thus, the IS governance requires a much more sophisticated approach than *alignment*[3] of these two worlds. In fact, their alignment is impossible. A promising approach to pierce the IS complexity is to consider the *interoperability* of these two worlds and to discover the conceptual overlap between them by exploring their common concepts. The major concept is then concept *information* as it provides a hinge between the world of human activities and the world of informatics. In fact this overlap is a true domain by itself, often called the *conceptual world* (e.g. conceptual model)

Thus, the IS domain can be analysed as the combination of three worlds: the world of human activities, the world of information, and the world of informatics. In the following the chapter describes the interoperability between these three worlds. It presents the IS governance as the way to assure the *entente* between these worlds in a given period, *but also* to assure the entente when one of the worlds is in movement – for instance, at one side, introduction of a new strategic plan, or, at the other side, introduction of a new information technology. Finally, the chapter introduces the services.

3 IS Worlds

The aim of this section is to observe some main breakthrough issues that IS researchers have created and will continue to create. In this chapter, the IS domain is decomposed into three worlds: activities or enterprise, conceptual or information and informatics. But these worlds cannot be isolated from each other in the IS

[3]Align – to arrange in a line or so as to be parallel; to adjust (parts of a mechanism, for example) to produce a proper relationship or orientation; to ally (oneself, for example) with one side of an argument or cause; to adhere to a prescribed course of action; to move or be adjusted into proper relationship or orientation (http://www.thefreedictionary.com/align).

perspective, because the results obtained in each of them are interwoven in order to constitute an information system. In the following the principles of conceptual interoperability, interwoven aspects of these worlds, must be described in the perspective of conceptual overlaps between them.

These interwoven aspects are explained by following the principles of conceptual interoperability: they must be described in the conceptual overlaps, which have to be formalized. Therefore, this section is organised as follows: the conceptual world, which plays the central role here, is presented first following by the definition of the overlap between this world and the informatics world and the overlap between this world and the activities world. Then, a paragraph introduces the ontology world for the IS cohesion and finally, some aspects of IS governance and general principles of sustainable IS are provided.

The master concept of this section is *model*. An IS contains a huge number of aspects, which must be described by means of models in a formalized way: a *meta-model*. Since there are so many aspects to take into account for IS design, there are consequently several meta-models, each of them covering a particular IS aspect. This section is only at the level of meta-model and it replaces systematically the term *meta-model* by model.

3.1 The IS Conceptual World

There are many relevant papers and books [7, 12, 21, 23, 27] covering the IS conceptual models. In [22] Antoni Olivé provides a relevant description of this crucial domain. The master concept of this world is *information*. It comes in a variety of concepts. Nevertheless, there are main atomic concepts such as class, method, attribute, object, relation, integrity rule,[4] role, event, and also complex concepts defined upon atomic ones like hyperclass, hyperobject, process, set of integrity rules, hyper-role, complex event, IS component.

All these concepts are interrelated: a class is defined with attributes and methods; a method and an attribute is defined on a class; a relation is defined between two classes;[5] an integrity rule is defined over one or several classes and expresses a condition that objects must satisfy; a role determines a domain of activity in terms of access rights to objects of classes and to methods of classes; an event is defined by a condition expressed by means of the previous concepts. Hyperclass [34] is a complex class defined on several classes: it is a generalization of the class concept and so hyperobject is an *object* of a hyperclass. Process is defined over several methods and then of several classes, but also on several roles, on several events. A set

[4]Often called integrity constraint.

[5]For example existential dependency: a class A is existentially dependent on another class B if any object of A is related with an object of B permanently; another kind of relation is specialization: A is a specialization of B if A is existentially dependent on B and if an B object can be related to only one A object.

of integrity rules defined on a same class is another integrity rule defined on this class. Hyper-role is a combination of several roles, which can be assumed by a same person at the same time. Hyper-event is a combination of several events, which can occur at the same time.

Since all conceptual models have to be implemented, they must be written by means of a conceptual meta-model, which is interoperable with the informatics meta-model. In the IS infancy, the most appropriate informatics for IS was the database management system, and therefore, most of the concepts of the conceptual world were extracted of concepts of informatics and stripped of their technical aspects.

3.2 Overlap Between the IS Conceptual World and the IS Informatics World

As mentioned before, the stakes of the conceptual world and the informatics world are not the same: the first ones are centred on the concept of information when the second ones are focused around performance, reliability, distribution, concurrency, etc. Obviously, these worlds share concepts and, therefore, their interoperability can be assured. But, they use them in different contexts [31]. For instance, a class is used at the conceptual level to represent information when, at the informatics level, it is used to store data with a homogeneous internal schema. Thus, a class at the conceptual level can be decomposed into several classes at the informatics level in order to improve performance, to assure security, to distribute its objects on several internal layers.

The classic position is to consider that the conceptual meta-models must obey the informatics meta-model. Even if this way of thinking has its part of relevance, it becomes dogmatic if it argues that this is the only way of thinking. Another way of thinking is to consider that the IS domain discovers new generic situations, which have to be taken into account by systems. More generally, the creators of systems, which are used to develop IS, must take care of the generic situations, which IS developers face to, and these situations are described in the conceptual meta-model.

Let us consider some examples. At the time of the relational DBMS, the creators of DBMS were interested only by the attributes of classes (named relations or tables at this time). However, for some IS pioneers, it was obvious that the determination of methods obeys the same rules as the determination of attributes. And then they discover that an important part of the IS dynamics can be described with these *methods* and *events* (e.g. method Remora [8, 29]). After some years, the object-oriented approach "discovered" this relevant property and developed object-oriented systems. Another example concerns the concept of *specialization*. This concept is well known in several sciences such as botany for example. In the IS domain, the static specialization defined as in botany – an object takes a permanent place in a specialization hierarchy – is a particular case of the utility of specialization in the IS domain, because the object can move in the specialization hierarchy: a person can become a student and, after, can be no more a student. The dynamic specialization is not difficult to implement in a DBMS [10, 11]. Unfortunately, the creators of object-oriented systems preferred to implement the static specialization by means of the inheritance mechanism. Nevertheless, the dynamic specialization is the most interesting at the conceptual level for the IS domain, because the obtained models are much more rigorous. The situation is then not complex but complicated due to drawbacks of the chosen design by creators of systems.

The general rule is that it is impossible to automatically translate conceptual models into informatics models due to the complexity of informatics. But it is possible to assist the transfer of a conceptual model into a system if we develop a deep knowledge of the situations that the persons in charge of the activities have to overcome. This is also fundamental for another reason: the reverse way, from a system to a conceptual model, is also meaningful in the IS development. For instance, very often developers can find lacks in the conceptual model: they will be able to explain the lack if the reverse way is viable.

3.3 Overlap Between the IS Conceptual World and the Activities World

The stakes of the activities world and the conceptual world are completely different because in the first one the stakes concern strategies, organization, people, budget, etc. and in the second one the stakes concern information which can be efficient to support activities by means of information systems. The fourth dimension of shift presented in the previous section claims that it is not a question of translating activities into processes supported by an IS.

Nevertheless, these two worlds have a lot of common concepts: the major one is *information* but it does not have the same meaning in the two worlds. In the conceptual world *information* must be taken into account by the information system when in the activities world *information* can come from the IS but also can have many other origins. Another common concept is *decision*: one of the targets of the IS world is to improve the informational environment of decisions, when in the world of activities the main question is to take decision and to assume their consequences. *Activity*, *task*, *process* are well known concepts of the domain of management, of organization, of human resources, but they are also popular in the IS domain, where they refer to IS dynamic part such as workflows. Even some research papers are confusing, because they did not find necessary to precise the world they address. However these two worlds, activities and conceptual, don't obey the same criteria of quality and of rigour because their stakes are not the same.

The traditional position was to consider that the activities world has to decide what are the objectives of the IS development. So, the inputs of an IS development would be given by the activities world and then the IS conceptual world has to find a solution, which becomes a problem for the informatics world, which has to solve it by means of systems.

But, IS pioneers discovered that this schema was not fruitful for the enterprise itself and the overlap between the activities world and the IS conceptual world must be extended, in particular in the reverse direction from the IS conceptual world to the activities world. Therefore, they developed the domain of requirements engineering [28] oriented towards IS and their results became very useful for software engineering and information technologies too. The following steps are to release IS from too functional aspects and then to propose strategic approaches notably by introducing intentional approaches [25, 26]. In fact, the IS domain with its knowledge and its methods has a real and increasing influence on the activities world.

There are other exchanges and influences which go through the overlap between the IS conceptual world and the activities world, for instance, by means of schemas of business processes (e.g. [20]) and use cases [1] to study special situations of actors. More and more, the IS conceptual world plays the role of the basis of a large part of the activities world.

3.4 Ontology for IS

Implementing IS inside an enterprise transforms its organization and sometimes also its activities. Behind these transformations there are elements that stay stable. It is important to maintain cohesion between people, whose activities are involved by the new IS developments, but also to design the IS itself. Ontology for IS contains all these invariants, in particular knowledge but also some business rules, roles of persons, which are independent of the IS development. For example, in the domain of e-Government, the laws belong to this kind of ontology [18]. Ontology will play the same role for IS as the keel for a boat.

In the future, these invariants can change and these changes are often independent of the IS. But the IS must take into account them. For instance, laws can be modified and therefore, the IS for e-government, built upon these lows, must also be modified. Then, it is important to have the trace of these laws in the various IS parts to assure IS evolution.

The important question is to choose the meta-model of ontology: it must be interoperable with the conceptual meta-model and so the results of ontology can be transformed into conceptual models following a precise procedure to keep the trace of the elements coming from ontology. In the domain of ontology, the differences between static part and dynamic part become blurred. This fact has a possible impact of the IS conceptual meta-model itself because it opens the way to a new kind of meta-model, which fully integrates static and dynamic aspects of the considered domain [14, 16].

3.5 IS Governance and Sustainable IS

With all these worlds composing the IS domain, and with all their meta-models, an IS becomes a farandole of models. This farandole must be articulated around the conceptual model and such a result can be achieved if the underlying meta-models are interoperable at least with the conceptual meta-model. Therefore, one of the IS governance tasks consists to assure that these models are coherently articulated and to manage the IS development to achieve this result.

Furthermore, the IS governance has to face multiple factors provoking transformations of one or several models of the farandole. This situation can be overcome if the meta-models support the evolution of their models. A meta-model supports evolution if it includes a complete set of mechanisms to manage the evolution of its models. That means that a meta-model is described as a database schema with its integrity rules to assure the coherence of the facts to be stored and which constitute a model. The mechanism of evolution executes an atomic modification such as creating, deleting or updating of a stored fact and verifies all the involved integrity rules of the meta-model. The set of mechanism is complete if all the primitive actions on the database – creating, deleting, updating – are taken into account [2]. Consequently, the systems underlying IS must include a complete set of mechanisms of evolution, like [3].

After or during the evolution process of a model, the IS evolution process requires to analyse the consequences of its evolution on the other models, which are articulated with it. Indeed the general question of the IS evolution concerns not only the evolution of one model but also the evolution of the farandole of the models.

At the commencement of the IS domain, the pioneers tried to create a whole methodology to develop an information system (e.g. Merise [33]). Their results still provide a framework for IS development. Besides, some very substantial works were finalised by developing *computer assisted information system engineering* environments (e.g. Rubis [30]).

Nevertheless these methodologies became too imprecise to cover the whole life cycle of an IS development. That is due to the huge variety of situations that designers have to face to. A promising way is to use as a pivot the concept of situation (e.g. [19, 36]) for the investigation of which type of method, or rather an assembly of method components, is the most appropriate for a given IS development. Several approaches (e.g. [24] introduce the notion of method component (also fragment or chunk) and propose different ways to assemble them into a situation-specific method for IS development. Besides, there are also attempts to implement an information system to manage the activities around an IS [17].

3.6 Conclusions on IS Worlds

The IS world is in fact composed of several worlds: activities, conceptual, informatics, ontology, governance. These worlds have their own properties and their transformations are independent on each other. For a given IS, it is important to assure the entente between all the models obtained in all these worlds. That is the key role of the conceptual world to assure that all these models constitute an articulated and well-formed farandole. Moreover, this entente has to be dynamic: the evolution of one model must be coherent with the other models, which perhaps, also have to be modified in order to keep the articulated farandole consistent. The IS is then *sustainable*.

Furthermore, this decomposition of the IS world also shows the impacts of worlds on the IS conceptual world and reciprocally the impacts of the conceptual world on them.

4 Services

Many observations reveal a great change in the domain of information systems in firms and even in Society. Of course, information systems are widespread everywhere in the Society. In the enterprises, IS become larger and larger and its management becomes more and more difficult and imprecise. The whole IS architecture became obscure, only IS parts or aspects can be well described. Furthermore, we can observe for instance, that the domain of information technologies (IT) delivers more and more new systems, platforms, which are very interesting for IS, that IS becomes a real challenge at the strategic level of firms, and that a great number of persons are convinced that their professional future is in this direction even if they do not have IS skills.

In this section we present our understanding of this deep emerging transformation. First, IS can be decomposed into IS components. Second, the power of IS development will be distributed in terms of initiatives. Third, the conceptual world will be the hinge of trans-disciplinary efforts. Fourth, value becomes the central question, cost comes just after. Finally, the concept of service emerges from the IS domain and it has the potential to be the kernel of a real Science.

4.1 IS Governance Through IS Components

An IS component is defined over classes, methods, integrity rules, processes, roles, events, which constitute a *semantic unit* where several actors deal with the same goals to achieve, the simple principles to observe [35]. It is important for this concept to be a formal one. An IS component must verify integrity rules and consequently some operations are defined over it or over several well-formed components. The concept of hyperclass [34] is one option for such a formalisation.

The IS components have overlaps between them, because they are not isolated and in particular, they share classes. In these overlaps the coordination between the involved semantic units can be analysed [15].

As a consequence, another IS perspective is to consider IS as composed of IS components. The IS governance must assure that the IS component obtained by a development process or an evolution process is well-formed and consistent with the other IS components.

To summarise, the IS governance has to manage IS development in terms of development of IS components of the given IS, which is a deep transformation in IS development.

4.2 Initiatives, Value and Trans-Disciplinarity

Usually the power of IS developments in the enterprises is centralized, even if there are always lots of unofficial developments by means, for instance, of spreadsheets. But now the IS stakes are much closer to the professions and the analysis process suffers from the lack of the analysts' knowledge of the encountered situations, where IS can be efficient (the 4th dimension of shift). More and more professionals have pertinent ideas of what kind of efficient support they need. In this new perspective, they will have the opportunity to take initiative of new IS development, which in fact will concern an IS component rather that the whole IS. This situation offers several challenges. The professionals do not have sufficient IS skills. A real question of management of initiatives will emerge: an initiative could be a false good idea, several initiatives could be combined, all the initiatives could not be developed because of lack of means, etc.

One main criteria of a good initiative will be the value that the realization of the initiative will bring to the firm. The substantial approach [9] provides elements to face this question. This question of value must be added to the previous overlap between the IS activities world and the IS conceptual world.

Generally, such initiatives to create value have to be trans-disciplinary: then, the value comes from the communication between several partners, who are in charge of various tasks and who have different skills. The question is not only interdisciplinary but also based on various kinds of knowledge: addition of a new IS component can partially transform the activities of each partner and provide a new professional environment, unknown before. To do that, one possible way is to use the conceptual modelling approach as a *cross-pollination space* [37], where the interwoven elements of various partners will be discussed precisely.

4.3 Service

Based on the previous reasoning, a new concept – *service* – can be introduced [4]. This concept is built upon the concept of IS component with all the usual worlds of the IS domain, but also with *value* in a prominent place and with a completely different way of development, which lays on initiatives, agile developments, trans-disciplinary efforts around a cross-pollination space.

The concept of *service* exists in various disciplines like Economy, Marketing and Public Administration. Besides, it is also used in informatics with the services oriented architecture. Therefore, it is perhaps wiser to use the expression of *information service* as once suggested by Prof. Janis Bubenko Jr.

Nevertheless, the cross-pollination space needs to host people with different skills and in particular coming from informatics. The concept of service, built on input-output schema, is useful because a lot of services can obey this schema. Their *autonomy* can be defined easily. *But*, this kind of services is only a particular case in the theory of services. In the more general IS situation, information services will share classes, integrity rules, roles, events, processes. Their *autonomy* must be defined in a different way. The way of thinking that some specialists of SOA would like to impose, is dogmatic because it shuts the door to discovering new scientific fields.

IS appears to be the provider of information, which are used by services, even if services can also produce information. Two visions are possible (perhaps more): one is to consider that services are upon IS; the second is to consider that in the future IS will be composed only of services. But, one question will still emerge: how to integrate a new service into an existing IS [5, 6]?

This is a rather short and incomplete presentation of the concept of service, coming from the IS domain. Numerous disciplines will be interested by this concept, which can be defined more broadly, for instance: "the application of competences for the benefit of another, meaning that service is a kind of action, performance or promise that is exchanged for value between provider and client" [32].

5 Conclusion

This chapter gives an overview of the emergence and the development of the domain of information systems during these last decades. Nowadays, the IS domain becomes a real strategic domain for the development of firms but also of the Society. The aim of this chapter is to recognise all the efforts that the colleagues of the CAiSE community and also the Inforsid French community did in the past and continue to do in the domain of IS.

Colette Rolland played a major role in the emergence of this domain: in particular, she initiated very fruitful breakthroughs, as we mentioned along this chapter. She received the grade of Doctor Honoris Causa of the University of Geneva (2007).

References

1. Alexander I, Maiden NAM (eds) (2004) Scenarios, stories and use cases. Wiley, New York
2. Al-Jadir L, Léonard M (1998) Multiobjects to ease schema evolution in an OODBMS. In: Proceedings of international conference entity-relationship'98, LNCS vol 1507. Springer, Berlin/Heidelberg, pp 316–333
3. Andany J, Léonard M, Palisser C (1991) Management of evolution in databases. In: Proceedings of the international conference on very large data bases, VLDB, Barcelona, Spain
4. Arni-Bloch N, Ralyté J (2008) MISS: a metamodel of information system service. In: Proceedings of the 17th international conference on information system development (ISD), Springer US, pp 177–186
5. Arni-Bloch N, Ralyté J (2008) Service-oriented information systems engineering: a situation-driven approach for service integration. In: Proceedings of CAiSE'08. LNCS, vol 5074. Springer, Berlin/Heidelberg, pp 140–143
6. Arni-Bloch N, Ralyté J, Léonard M (2009) Service-driven information systems evolution: handling integrity constraints consistency. In: Proceedings of the 2nd IFIP WG 8.1 working conference, PoEM 2009. LNBIP, vol 39. Springer, Berlin/Heidelberg, pp 191–206
7. Boman M, Bubenko JA Jr, Johannesson P, Wangler B (eds) (1997) Conceptual modelling. Prentice Hall, Englewood Cliffs, NJ

8. Foucaut O, Rolland C (1978) Concepts for design of an information system conceptual schema and its utilization in the Remora project. In: Proceedings of the 4th international conference on very large data bases, pp 342–350
9. Gordijn J (2002) Value-based requirements engineering: exploring innovative e-commerce ideas. PhD thesis, Vrije Universiteit Amsterdam
10. Junet M, Léonard M, Tschopp R (1981) ECRINS/81. In Proceedings of IFIP 8.1 workshop, Sitgès
11. Junet M, Falquet G, Léonard M (1986) ECRINS/86: an extended entity-relationship data base management system and its semantic query language. In: Proceedings of international conference on very large data bases, VLDB 1986. Kyoto, Japan
12. Krogstie J, Opdahl AL, Brinkkemper S (eds) (2007) Conceptual modelling in information systems engineering. Springer, Berlin/Heidelberg
13. Léonard M (2003) The farandole of fancied conceived and shaped objects. In: Bodart F (ed) Utility, usability and complexity of emergent information system. Presse Universitaire de Namur
14. Léonard M, Luong BT (1981) Information systems design approach integrating data and transactions. In: Proceedings of 7th conference of very large data bases, VLDB Endowment, pp 235–246
15. Léonard M, Parchet O (1999) Information overlap. In: Proceedings of the international symposium on database applications in non-traditional environments – DANTE′99, IEEE Computer Society
16. Léonard M, Pham Thi TT (1999) Information System integration with the static and dynamic aspects. Swiss-Japanese seminar, Kyoto
17. Léonard M, Grasset A, Le Dinh T, Santos C (2001) Information Kernel: an evolutionary approach to integrate enterprise information assets. In: Proceedings of the international workshop on open enterprise solutions: systems, experiences, and organizations, OES-SEO2001
18. Léonard M, Khadraoui A, Ralyté J (2006) Regulation in information systems at the level of tunement. In: Proceedings of the CAISE'06 workshop on regulations modelling and their validation and verification ReMo2V ′06, Luxembourg
19. Mirbel I, Ralyté J (2006) Situational method engineering: combining assembly-based and roadmap-driven approaches. Reqs Eng 11:58–78
20. Nurcan S, Etien A, Kaabi R, Zoukar I, Rolland C (2005) A strategy driven business process modelling approach. Special issue of the Business Process Management Journal on Goal-oriented business process modeling, Emerald, 11:6
21. Olivé A (2000) An introduction to conceptual modeling of information systems. In: Piattini M, Diaz O (eds) Advanced database technology and design. Artech House, pp 25–57
22. Olivé A (2005) Conceptual schema-centric development: a grand challenge for information systems research. In: Proceedings of CAiSE 2005. LNCS vol 3520. Springer, Berlin/Heidelberg, pp 1–15
23. Olivé A (2007) Conceptual modeling of information systems. Springer, Berlin/Heidelberg
24. Ralyté J, Rolland C (2001) An assembly process model for method engineering. In: Proceedings of CAISE'01. LNCS, vol 2068. Springer, Berlin/Heidelberg, pp 267–283
25. Rolland C (2007) Capturing system intentionality with maps. In: Krogstie J et al (eds) Conceptual modelling in information systems engineering. Springer, Heidelberg pp 141–158
26. Rolland C (2008) Intention driven conceptual modelling. In: Johannesson P, Söderström E (eds) Information systems engineering: from data analysis to process networks. IGI Global, Hershey, Pennsylvania, pp 16–42
27. Rolland C, Cauvet C (1992) Trends and perspectives in conceptual modelling. In: Loucopoulus P, Zicari R (eds) Conceptual modeling, databases and CASE: an integrated view of information systems development. Wiley, New York, pp 27–48
28. Rolland C, Prakash N (2001) From conceptual modelling to requirements engineering. Annals of software engineering on comparative studies of engineering approaches for software engineering (ASE)

29. Rolland C, Richard C (1982) The REMORA methodology for information systems design and management. In: Olle TW, Sol HG, Verrijn-Stuart AA (eds) Information systems design methodologies: a comparative review. North-Holland, pp 369–426
30. Rolland C, Cauvet C, Nobecourt P, Proix C, Coligon P, Lingat JY, et al. (1988) The Rubis system. In: Olle TW, Verrijn-Stuart AA, Bhabuta L (eds) Computerized assistance during the information systems life cycle. North-Holland
31. Snene M, Léonard M (2003) From the design to the distribution of e-business system: the overlap knowledge pattern. In: Proceedings of IADIS 2003, Portugal
32. Spohrer J, Maglio Paul P, Bailey J, Gruhl D (2007) Steps towards a science of service systems. IEEE Computer 1:71–77
33. Tardieu H, Rochfeld A, Colletti R (2000) La Méthode Merise: principes et outils. Editions d'Organisation
34. Turki S, Léonard M (2002) Hyperclasses: towards a new kind of independence of the methods from the schema. In: Proceedings of the 4th international conference on enterprise information systems – ICEIS'2002, vol 2. Ciudad Real, Spain, pp 788–794
35. Turki S, Léonard M (2002) IS components with hyperclasses. In: Proceedings of the OOIS 2002 conference workshops. Advances in object-oriented information systems. LNCS, vol 2426. Springer, Berlin/Heidelberg, pp 301–307
36. van Slooten K, Hodes B (1996) Characterizing IS development projects. In: Brinkkemper S, Lyytinen K, Welke R (eds) Proceedings of IFIP TC8 working conference on method engineering: principles of method construction and tool support. Chapman & Hall, pp 29–44
37. Yurchyshyna A, Opprecht W (2010) Towards an ontology-based approach for creating sustainable services. In: Proceedings of the international conference on exploring service science – IESS 1.0, to be published in LNBIP vol 53, Springer, Berlin/Heidelberg

On Roles of Models in Information Systems

Arne Sølvberg

Abstract The increasing penetration of computers into all aspects of human activity makes it desirable that the interplay among software, data and the domains where computers are applied is made more transparent. An approach to this end is to explicitly relate the modeling concepts of the domains, e.g., natural science, technology and business, to the modeling concepts of software and data. This may make it simpler to build comprehensible integrated models of the interactions between computers and non-computers, e.g., interaction among computers, people, physical processes, biological processes, and administrative processes. This chapter contains an analysis of various facets of the modeling environment for information systems engineering. The lack of satisfactory conceptual modeling tools seems to be central to the unsatisfactory state-of-the-art in establishing information systems. The chapter contains a proposal for defining a concept of information that is relevant to information systems engineering.

1 Introduction

Information systems are built in order to support some other system by keeping track of its state-of-affairs, by supporting the exchange of information between the other system and its environment, and by providing information needed for changing the behavior of the other system, either through direct intervention or through making information available for other change agents [3]. When seen from the information system point of view, "the other system" is known by many different names, e.g., the user system, the user domain, the Universe of Discourse (UoD), the real world, the business processes. In particular during the development of an information system

A. Sølvberg (✉)
Department of Computer and Information Science, NTNU – The Norwegian University of Science and Technology, Sem Sælands v 9, 7491, Trondheim, Norway
e-mail: asolvber@idi.ntnu.no

S. Nurcan et al. (eds.), *Intentional Perspectives on Information Systems Engineering*,
DOI 10.1007/978-3-642-12544-7_2,

"the other system" is often seen to belong to "the real world" as opposed to the abstract plans and specifications of the so far intangible information system to be.

Information systems are closely intertwined with computer systems. Modern information systems are unthinkable unless based on computers, computation and communication technology. So we have to distinguish between the information system and its computer system, where the computer system is seen as a part of the information system which it serves. The computerized parts of information systems are often called application systems (or data systems) reflecting that they apply computer technology (to store and process data) in order to meet their aims. In the Nordic countries it is common to distinguish between infology (the discipline of information systems) and datalogy (the discipline of data systems).

In spite of having built information systems for half-a-century there is still much to be desired in improving the cost-effectiveness of building and maintaining information systems. The IT profession has attracted a vast talent pool over many years. In spite of this there is widespread concern that the methodological basis for building sustainable computerized information systems is too weak.

The dissatisfaction comes both from within the IT-profession and from the user side, both from those who engineer the systems and from those who pay the bill for failed projects. The IT-profession is not satisfied with itself. The self-criticism comes both from the information system side [19], and also from the data system side, e.g., from software engineering [47]. Much of the dissatisfaction is due to the profound technological changes of the last 10–20 years. Solutions to old problems are no longer relevant in the new reality [32]. The academic community translates the dissatisfaction into research agendas aimed at defining new problems and solutions [12, 19, 21, 23, 32].

The recent SEMAT initiative [47] calls for improving current software engineering method and theory. Of particular concern is the perceived lack of a sound, widely accepted theoretical basis for building and maintaining computerized systems of sufficient size. The SEMAT initiative calls for developing an approach to software engineering that is based on solid theory, proven principles and best practices, and that includes a kernel of widely-agreed elements, extensible for specific uses, which addresses both technology and people issues.

It is unclear why we have not reached further, why the dissatisfaction is so deep. Research has been going on for several decades aiming at developing a sound theoretical basis for information systems engineering, see [4] for an overview. Research results have come out both from the academic world and the industrial world. Even if much progress has been achieved over the years there is still some way to go before we can declare "mission accomplished".

Some elements in an explanation may be that

- domain issues are so different from computer issues that they demand different treatment, so that it is difficult to arrive to a unified theory;
- domain issues are so different from each other that the relationships between the computer sphere and the various domains are so different that there is not one solution for all, but separate solutions have to be developed for each computer-domain pair;

- technology develops so fast that as soon as a solution for a computer-domain pair has been found, it is outdated by new technological innovations;
- the problem is simply too difficult to solve, at least for us.

In spite of the above we shall propose a modest analysis of the situation, and hopefully come up with some recommendations for further work. Important requirements to a renewed approach to software engineering and information systems engineering are:

- the theoretical framework must make it possible to build *integrated models* of systems which consist of both digital and non-digital components;
- information models must represent the *meaning* of data, that is, data should be explicitly related to the phenomena they represent;
- system models must be *comprehensible* on every level of systems detail;
- system models must permit *specification in terms of solutions* on every level of detail, in order to provide for executable specifications;
- system models must support the need for *validation* of design proposals during their development;
- system models must support *different specification detail*, both formal and informal specifications;
- system models must encourage *systematic evolution of specification detail* from low level of detail to high level of detail;
- system models should support proven *engineering practice*.

These many facets of information systems engineering will be discussed in the sequel. Requirements to the information systems engineering approach will be suggested. It seems that conceptual modeling is central to finding good solutions for many of the unsolved problems.

2 Information Systems, Data Systems, Domain Systems and How They Relate

Information systems consist of collections of data, and of information processes that collect, store, transform and distribute data in forms that make sense to the receivers of the data. That is, *data* is seen to be *information* when the data is presented in a form that is understood by the receiver. In advanced societies almost all data are collected, stored, processed and distributed in digital form by computers. Almost every system in every domain has a sizable information system component. Communicating digital devices are everywhere. Software is everywhere. Digitized information (data) is everywhere.

We shall distinguish between the *information system* and the *domain system* ("the other system") which is served by the information system. We shall also distinguish between the *information system* and its *data system* (the computerized parts of the information system). We shall use the term *total system* for the "whole" formed by the information system and the domain system.

2.1 Information Systems and Domain Systems

The distinction between the information system and the domain system may change over time, and may differ among people who are involved in different parts of the interplay between the information system and its domain. So parts of the information system may sometimes by some be seen as being parts of its domain, and vice versa. Also the borderline between the total system and its environment may at times seem fuzzy. In practice it is sufficient that in the various situations it is made clear whether a particular system component is part of the information system, its domain or of the domain's environment.

Modeling the domain is an essential part of requirements elicitation in information systems engineering. Initially the large volume of computer applications were in the support of information processing in organizations, e.g., banking, finance, government, retail, industry. Those were the applications where the large volumes of data were found, and where data base technology found the largest markets. Conceptual modeling was initiated from these application types. Depending on the nature of the particular application domain these modeling efforts are called by different names, e.g., enterprise modeling [9], business modeling [13], agent modeling [7, 15], intention oriented information systems modeling [27–29].

The wide penetration of computers into most aspects of human activity has led to a need for relating information systems engineering to every domain where computers are applied. Information systems engineering "in the domain" usually goes far beyond the design of the information supporting role of the information system. The ambition is usually to re-engineer the domain in order to take maximal advantage of available technology, e.g., "business process re-engineering".

In order to re-engineer in a particular domain it becomes necessary to relate general IT-knowledge to the discipline knowledge of the relevant domain. So the conceptual modeling theory of information systems engineering and software engineering has to relate to all kinds of domain theories.

2.2 Information Systems and Data Systems

The distinction between digital and non-digital representation is not always used as a criterion for decomposing information systems into structures of smaller parts. Many information system components therefore is seen to consist both of computerized parts and of parts where information is stored in non-digital forms, e.g., paper, and where the information processing is not done by computers but, e.g., by people. In the computerized parts of an information system the information collections and messages must be encoded in some formal expression. The non-digitized information may very well be informal, e.g., expressed in natural language. The formalization of informally expressed information usually requires new details and complexity to be added to the informal form. The interplay between formality and informality often creates difficulties for the information exchange.

The first information systems appeared together with the databases during the 1970s. Information systems were specialized and self-contained. Software and hardware was built to support one and only one information system. Over the years we have learnt how to reuse software, and standard software packages are increasingly replacing the specialized solutions. For large organizations the transition from specialized to packaged software was over at the end of the 1990s. Almost all large companies by then used some form of packaged enterprise system [9].

Operating systems as well as central application systems in e.g., finance and auditing, evolved during the same period into software platforms for large application domains, e.g., banking platforms, Enterprise Resource Planning (ERP) platforms. Most of the software platforms are proprietary, in the sense that they are owned and controlled by large industrial actors, e.g., Microsoft Windows. The platforms provide a competitive edge for the companies that own them. The increasing reliance on software platform can also be seen in service oriented computing [24] and in workflow management [8].

A very interesting development is seen in the development of application platforms for mobile phones. The major vendors of "smart" phones invite the general public to develop applications ("apps") for their proprietary operating system platform. This represents a major "democratization" of application software development, see [14]. Virtually everybody with relevant knowledge can develop their own app and sell it via their smart phone producer.

The movement towards Open Source Software has made available large numbers of packaged solutions for a myriad of application areas [35]. Information systems engineering has moved towards becoming a "normal" engineering discipline were it is possible to shop for available software solutions in a way similar to what is done in "classical" engineering, where design is based on the effective assembling of available system components.

3 Central Issues in Information Systems Engineering

Some of the most important issues in information systems engineering are concerned with:

- managing information system projects,
- systems design approaches,
- modeling languages for information systems, domain systems and data systems,
- comprehension of specifications,
- modeling of the meaning of data,
- validation techniques,
- changes in the information systems domain and technological environment.

These will be discussed in the sequel.

3.1 Engineering Practice

Engineering projects follow a well tested and successful approach, which is the same for all kinds of engineering. Work is done in phases, each phase addressing different issues at different levels of detail. Each phase must produce well defined and well documented results, which are subjected to evaluation prior to being accepted as basis for further work. The first project phases are concerned with setting the objectives of the projects, e.g., what is the final outcome of the project, what is the budget (time, money, competences). That is, the first phases are concerned with developing the requirements to be satisfied by the project. The next phases are concerned with developing engineering designs that satisfy the stated requirements. Each new phase adds new detail to the design proposals from previous phases. The end-of-phase evaluations concern technical issues, as well as project economy and plans for the remaining work in the project.

Information systems engineering differs from classical engineering in the cost profile of the projects. In classical engineering, e.g., the building of roads and bridges, the lion's share of the costs are invoked during the last phase of the projects, when the actual realization of the engineering design is done. During this last phase many hands and machines are put to work, and components of considerable size and cost are assembled according to the plans developed in the previous phases.

In information systems engineering the project is essentially over when the software have been written and tested. There is no building phase which is comparable to the building phase of classical engineering. The lion's share of information systems engineering and software engineering is associated with the requirements development, the design, the programming and testing. These phases in classical engineering carry costs that are small compared to the total project expenditures.

The costs of making mistakes during the design are huge in most classical engineering projects because of the large investment of time and money in the last phase of the construction work, e.g., a bridge that falls down is a calamity. Therefore all project phases are subjected to strict control and management practices. These practices have been taken over in information systems engineering projects where the costs are large of making mistakes during requirement development and system design.

The classical engineering approach has been much criticized in the software engineering community and is seen by many as being both old-fashioned and traditional. The classical engineering approach is known by different terms in the software engineering community, the most common terms are *top-down design* and *the waterfall method* when the classical approach is used for information systems engineering. Several other approaches have been proposed. A common feature among many of the competing proposals is the early development of software prototypes, and a gradual expansion and continuous testing of a prototype, until the prototype has been developed into a final product.

The two major approaches to information systems engineering are the top-down "requirements-first" approach and the bottom-up "agile" approach.

- The “requirement first” approach recommends that solutions for the computerized parts of an information system should satisfy validated requirements. The approach also recommends that requirements and solutions should be kept separated, so that modified solutions can be validated relative to modified requirements, see [46].
- The “agile” approach recommends that specifications of the computerized parts of an information system are stated in terms of computer solutions, that is, in terms of executable specifications, see [37].

The “requirements first” approach is seen as an old-fashioned traditionalist approach by the “agile” community. The “agile” approach is widely seen by the “traditionalists” as a “program first – think later” approach which can only be used for systems of limited size and limited life span.

The classical engineering approach has in particular been criticized for a linear, heavy handed approach to project management. This is when the classical approach is compared to competing approaches which are claimed to rely more on iteration and gradual development of the systems. When subjected to analysis this claim does not seem to hold [2]. Iteration is basic to engineering design, independent of approach to project management.

3.2 Evolution of Detail

Most solutions to engineering problems are so complex that it is impossible for anybody to understand every detail at the same time. Information systems of this complexity are sometimes called unperceivable [16], but are more commonly called unsurveyable [31]. A basic problem in engineering is to find an approach to developing solutions to unsurveyable systems.

The most common solution strategy consists in breaking a problem into simpler subproblems, then to find solutions to each subproblems so that they together form a solution to the problem. Gabriel Krohn [40] developed this divide-and-conquer strategy into an approach for solving electrical engineering problems [41]. He called the approach The Method of Tearing, or Diakoptics (Greek: *dia*–through + *kopto*–cut, tear). The essentials of diakoptics is the splitting of physical problems into subproblems that can be formalized and solved independently of each other, then recombining to give an overall formal solution by taking into account the relations among the subproblems.

Krohn’s method was in the 1960s generalized and applied for information systems design by Langefors [42]. In the information systems field the approach is known as The Fundamental Principle of Systems Design [16]. A system is seen as a collection of subsystems with stated external properties, related through a system structure which relates the external properties of the subsystems. In order to be used to its full potential it takes that both the system structure and external properties of each subsystem can be formally stated, so that the external properties of the resulting system can be formally calculated. This is possible for some categories of physical systems, e.g., electricity networks, but is not generally possible. For software engineering problems the calculations are usually not decidable or even not semi-decidable.

The decomposition of systems into subsystems stop when existing solutions are found for the system, or the system is simple enough to be understood without further decomposition. For physical systems there are large offers of commercially available system components which are specified according to agreed standards. The most detailed level of physical system design is the level of standardized components. Solutions are developed as assemblies of available standard components. Knowledge of the properties of available standard components influence designers in formulating system requirements, so that there will be a preference for formulating requirements that can be met, rather than being unrealistic and reach for the moon.

The information systems field has traditionally been short of universal product standards. There are many proprietary standards competing for market share, e.g., the standard for writing apps for recent mobile phones. Some of the company standards succeed in becoming universal, e.g., the standard for offering Java code to the world. The lack of a standards regime which is comparable to engineering standards for physical systems makes software solutions more often to come in the form of complete solutions than in the form of components. There are large collections of software solutions available as Open Source Software, see [35] for discussion and overview.

3.3 Requirements and Solutions

Information systems have always been built in order to satisfy some purpose. The first information systems were built from scratch. Computers were expensive and the required software most often had to be built for one purpose alone. Faced with limited budgets most of the effort in the information system projects were spent on making programs, and too little was spent on clarifying the purpose which the system should serve. This "program-first-think-later" approach resulted in information systems of low quality that did not live up to expectations.

The user centric approach to information systems development which emerged during the 1970s came as a reaction to the many failed software projects of the time. The user-centric approach recommended that user requirements were thoroughly analyzed prior to building software. Requirements analysis became a standard part of every information system project. "Late binding" was often recommended, meaning that programming was deferred to the later project phases: first get the requirements right, then design and program the software and the databases. It followed from this that requirements specification and software specification is kept separate, and that software specifications should be derived from the requirements. This recommendation was at times overdone. Sometimes one became so obsessed with developing requirements specifications that one did not come down to programming. Many projects produced many requirements and few solutions.

There were two major approaches to information systems engineering and software engineering, the deductive approach [20] and the process oriented approach, e.g., data flow oriented techniques [6]. Basic to the deductive approach is the assumption that problem formulation can be separated from the problem's software solution, much in the same way that the solution of mathematical problem is separate from the problem formulation. This line of thinking is consistent with the recommendation of keeping requirements specification separate from the software specification (the "think-first-program-later" approaches). Basic to the process oriented approach is that problem formulation and problem solution are intertwined, that the solution to a problem at one level of detail serves as the formulation of a problem on the next level of detail.

During the 1980s and 1990s there were substantial efforts in the software engineering community in developing specification languages at the algorithmic level of detail, see [11]. Early successes in applying first order logic for problem formulations encouraged the ambition of being able to verify the correctness of problem specifications prior to programming. These "problem-oriented" approaches rest on the principle that designing effective solutions requires a detailed understanding of the problem. Only for problems of limited size is it possible to precisely and completely define the problems up-front. The problem oriented approaches did not sufficiently recognize the need for prescribing a gradual and continuous refinement of a problem description in order to identify new or previously missed context elements and requirements.

The problem specification languages that were proposed, e.g., Z and VDM, were based on set theory. They were not executable, that is, software that satisfied the specifications had to be expressed in appropriate programming languages. These specification languages did not enjoy success. There may be several reasons for their lack of success. One reason was that it was very time consuming to develop in parallel problem specifications and solution specifications to the same level of detail. The verification facilities of the problem specification languages were not powerful enough to defend the extra resources needed to develop the problem specifications. The executable solution specification was seen as being enough for most problem types. The only fields were verification approaches seem to have been used to any extent, is for system critical software, that is for software where the cost of breakdown is very large, e.g., for nuclear facilities, for airplane control systems. In the clear light of hindsight it may be said that these approaches were not enough concerned with the elicitation and validation of problem statements, and the transformation of problem statements into design solutions.

It is now widely recognized that for large and complex information systems architectural solutions and requirements need to be co-developed [25]. Large and complex information systems have to be stratified and described at levels of increasing detail. Increasingly it is necessary to specify both what the systems is expected to do as well as what it is expected not do [30]. Often the complexity demands that different facets have to be treated separately [22, 25]. At each level it is common to develop a system architecture that provides a solution to all of the required functionality of all of the facets at that level. Central to this are co-design processes for taking the different facets into consideration when proposing architectural solutions and associated requirements on the appropriate levels of specification detail [25].

The system architectures are usually expressed in terms of solutions to the stated requirements. Each part of a system solution at one level of detail serves as a requirement to the system architecture at the next level of system detail. At the most detailed level we should be able to formulate the system specifications in terms of executable specifications, or in terms of pre-existing solutions. Process oriented approaches seem to fit very well with this line of thinking.

3.4 Formal and Informal Specification

Data and data processes are usually associated with computer programming. Information and information processes are associated with the use of data by people. Information systems designers have to relate to both computers and people, to data as well as meaning. People mostly communicate through natural language but also through drawings and sketches of system structures. Computers communicate through binary numbers. To make sense out of messages, be they uttered in language or as numbers, the messages must be related to a model of what the messages are about. This model of "the real world" must be shared among the communicating parties if misunderstandings are to be avoided. Computer systems will break down if the various digital components do not share a common model of "reality" and a common model of data representation. People may be able to discover misunderstandings prior to a system breakdown and to take corrective actions, computers cannot.

During the initial phases of systems design the ideas about the system-to-be are usually both imprecise and vague. Requirements to the system-to-be are usually not well thought through. Desired system properties may be unrealistic. An important aim of the initial project phases is to develop a consensus among the interested parties about whether and how desired system properties can be achieved. The level of ambition for desired properties must be balanced with the availability of resources for building and operating the system-to-be.

The usual form of communication is through natural language, spoken and written, through informal sketches of various system architecture proposals, and through more or less formal descriptions of existing solutions to systems similar to the one being discussed. Only when "the dust has settled" and agreement has been reached on the major parameters of the system-to-be comes the time for adding formality to the systems descriptions.

Formality of systems descriptions is needed in order to understand every detail in the proposed solutions. When sufficient formality cannot be achieved for a reasonable cost one has to rely on designers' experience. When technology is not well enough developed one has to rely on handcraft. Even if formality is achievable there is a long way to go from the initial informal specifications to the formal expressions that make up the specifications of the final system details.

A desirable property of a specification language would be that it lends itself both to the informal and formal tasks. Unfortunately there is no such language. What we would like to have is a modeling language which supports increased formality of expression through systematic addition of specification detail, starting from an informal basis. An example would be that an initial informal natural language specification is systematically enriched with more and more detail until the most detailed specification can be transformed into a formal form, based on linguistic analysis. Another example would be a graphical language for, e.g., information modeling, which is as suitable for high level informal sketches of information objects as it is for describing detailed data structures.

An approach to formalization of natural language specifications is found in an extension to fuzzy set theory which is called computation with words [38]. The basic idea is to quantify words and sentences so that they can be given mathematical treatment. Another approach is to relate model fragments (semantic frames) to natural language sentences, see, e.g., [39] for a collection of semantic frames.

Graphical languages are usually used for sketching systems structures on the exploratory road from informality to formality. These languages are widely used, e.g., UML, ER-diagrams. Graphical languages for specifying every detail in a structure are far between [10]. A comprehensive analysis of graphical languages has recently been published in [17].

3.5 Comprehension

With the penetration of computers into all realms of human affairs comes the need for understanding what the computers do, to enable people to judge whether the software produce correct data. Both data specifications and software specifications must be comprehensible in the sense that they can be understood and validated by people that are not computer specialists.

The need for comprehension of system specifications is complicated by the necessity that somewhere in the development process system specifications are stated in executable terms, that is, in the languages of data bases and computer software, which are usually only understood by specialists.

A solution of the dilemma has been sought in *model driven development* (MDD), also known as *model driven architecture* [43] and *model driven engineering* [44]. The main idea of using the term *model driven* is that, in order to increase comprehensibility, software and data specifications are developed in a language that reflects the particularities of the domain. These specifications should later on be automatically translated into executable software.

The difficulty lies in the details. The current state of the art of expressing executable specifications requires the specification of so many details of the data system realm that the comprehensibility of the specifications suffers severely for those that are not software specialists.

3.6 Validation

Systems are composed of subsystems which are related to each other. The relations among the subsystems are called the system's structure. A concrete proposal of subsystems and structure is called a system design. High level designs are often called system architectures. Each design proposal is associated with a set of expected system properties.

The purpose of design is to propose systems which have a set of desired properties. Validation is the process of comparing the desired properties of a system to the expected properties of its design, and of determining whether the expected properties of a proposed design of system satisfy the desired properties.

Of central importance is whether we are able to state the expected system properties when we know the parts and the structure of a system. For some system types it is possible to formally calculate the expected properties of a design. A minimal requirement for this to be possible is that relevant properties of each system part can be formally expressed along with relevant properties of the system's structure. When formal calculation is not possible we have to resort to evaluations based on informal reasoning and previous experience in building similar systems.

Relevant system properties comprise many system features. Desired properties are usually expressed as requirements specifications. They are usually written in natural language. Expected properties of a system are implied from a design proposal. For some features this may be achieved through formal calculations and logical deduction, if the design is formulated in a formal language. Prototyping is an often used technique for system features where it is impossible or difficult to formally deduce the expected system properties. "Agile" software development approaches are often used in order to rapidly build software prototypes to support validation processes.

The comparison between expected and desired properties is mostly based on human evaluations of informally expressed statements of system properties. Some of the most important features are associated with economy: from the current state-of-affairs, are the available resources enough to develop a system with the desired properties? To answer this question requires that there is a plan for finalizing the system building project, and that there is a way of calculating the cost of developing the remaining parts of the project.

4 Modeling of Data, Information and the Domain

We distinguish among data systems, information systems and domain systems. Each of these has their own particularities. Concrete systems solutions are increasingly composed from both digital components and non-digital components, which are interacting among themselves as well as with people. We need to simultaneously model in the realms of data, domain and information. Current practices apply different modeling languages for data systems, information systems and domain systems.

Our aim is to find a way of modeling which makes it possible to interpret the meaning of data with respect to our understanding of the UoD. The approach is to view information as a relationship among data types and UoD concepts. The ambition is to provide for semantic preserving transformations, so that when new concepts of new world views are introduced and defined relative to previously defined concepts, new information which is relevant to the new world view may be produced from what is already present in the data bases.

The realization of the digital system components require that the appropriate domain models are expressed in the modeling languages of computers, in the form of data structures and computer programs. But the associated domain systems must usually also be expressed in the relevant domain modeling languages so that the system models can be understood in the domain culture. Data system languages are keys to realization of the digital system components and cannot be avoided. So we need to have parallel specifications, in three different modeling languages.

The mathematical basis and the modeling tradition of the various modeling cultures differ. For example, most modeling cultures in technology and science require mastering of differential equations, while the mathematical basis of data systems is discrete mathematics and mathematical logic. Information systems apply additional modeling approaches from linguistics and sociology, e.g., speech act theory, and rest on the associated mathematical basis.

There is no automatic translation among the modeling languages. So it is very labor intensive to maintain several specifications when the systems are changed. And change is the normal state-of-affairs: laws and regulations change, products have to be changed to meet competition in the marketplace, new system versions are made to meet the needs in new markets. The usual situation is that only the executable specification is maintained. That is, the details of a domain system model are found only in the data system specification. The negative consequences for comprehension and validation are obvious. Even for systems of medium size comprehension and validation is impossible. This is acceptable only when system failures are of little consequence.

The deep penetration of computers in all realms of society necessitates a change in approach whereby domain problems being expressed in domain oriented language can be made to co-exist with specifications of data systems and information systems without everything having to be translated into data system oriented specifications. IT concepts, tools and theory consequently have to be better integrated with the wide spectrum of domain specific modeling concepts and theories. In order to reconcile the various approaches to modeling it seems to be necessary that the different specification languages are based on similar ontology, and that there exist an understandable relationship between data and what the data stand for.

In information systems engineering we have three groups of concepts: for concept modeling in general, for behavior modeling, and for data modeling. The concepts of state, event and process are used for behavior modeling. These are separate concept classes and represent the evolution over time of properties of concrete systems. These concepts are used for behavior modeling in all three modeling realms.

Over the years many approaches to concept modeling and behavior modeling have been proposed. Some influential modeling approaches were proposed by Wand and Weber (the Bunge-Wand-Weber model) [34] and by Colette Rolland, first through her REMORA methodology [26] and later through her work on intentional modeling [27]. Central in much of the research in information systems modeling has been to achieve a cross-disciplinary approach to business process design. As the years have gone by the work on information systems modeling has become more and more central to information technology as a whole.

We shall, however, not discuss these concepts further. We restrict the rest of our discussion to a model ontology that is relevant to data and information.

4.1 Meaning

Digital data is always associated with meaning. Each data element represents some relevant property of the world. This is necessary in order for the data to be useful to the world outside of the computer, as well as for ensuring that systems provide for meaningful communication among their components. What meaning data convey depends on how the human receiver of data perceives the phenomena that the data refer to. More often than not there is no explicit model of the world for the human interpreter to lean to. In data systems the world models are usually implicit in the software, and are hidden to the human interpreters of the data.

Relationships between digital data and what the data refer to are seldom explicitly stated, but are usually informally indicated by the names given to the data elements, e.g., a data element named NAME-OF-PERSON is understood to represent information about the name of a person, and a data structure named EMPLOYEE usually represents information about persons who work in a company. The structure of a data base reflects the world view of the data base designer, and is expressed through the names of the data structures. This works well within each individual information system, but leads to difficulties when integrating several data bases representing different world views. The need for explicitly expressing the meaning of data was encountered in the data base field when trying to find approaches to data integration. The first approaches to data integration were concerned with structural integration. Recent research is concerned with semantic integration, see [36] for an overview of the research area.

Data on the World Wide Web are mostly natural language text. The meaning of a text is intuitive in the same way as every text is intuitively understood through the reader's association of terms and sentences to the reader's understanding of the world. Linguistic theory applies to most of the data on the web. The objective of having a "semantic web" is unreachable unless there is an explicit relation between the linguistic constructs and the appropriate world model, that is, between the data and the conceptual models of what the data stand for. So we are faced with the same problems for providing meaning to data independent of whether the data is structured or unstructured.

Information modeling is an approach to provide meaning to data. Information models relate conceptual models and data models. Conceptual models provide structure to the relevant world views and provide means to relate different world views to each other. Data models provide structure to digital data inside of the computer. Information models relate data models and conceptual models, thereby providing meaning to digital data.

4.2 Concepts for Modeling the UoD

The knowledge, which is represented in an information system, is entirely conceptual. The data, which are stored and processed by an information system, are linguistic units, which denote concepts and referents in the Universe of Discourse [18]. The linguistic units are represented by digital numbers. Concepts are grouped differently depending on users' needs. Linguistic concepts are different from facts and ideas. Information systems are concerned with data that represent facts in a Universe of Discourse. A fact is what is known -or assumed- to belong to reality. In science and technology one usually distinguishes the following kinds of facts: state, event, process, phenomenon, and concrete system e.g., a magnetic field [5]. Ideas are formally expressed as concepts, formulas (e.g., statements) and theories, which are systems of formulas. Conceptual models are the formal expressions of ideas.

Conceptual modeling in computer based information systems are most often concerned with phenomena where it becomes important to distinguish among individuals, and to deal with classifications of individuals, e.g., the concept of PERSON represents all persons, dead, living and unborn. Set theory is well suited to deal with discrete phenomena. This makes set theory to be well suited to deal with digital representations of facts. The relevant modeling ontology reflects the properties of mathematical set theory and is thus of considerable generality.

Unfortunately set theory is less suited to deal with phenomena of continuous nature. For example, take the concept of copper. Copper is part of bronze and it is part of brass. It feels somewhat artificial to view copper as a class concept, its extension being all things of copper [5].

4.2.1 Conceptual Modeling of Non-Discrete Phenomena

The deficiencies of set theory may be counteracted by introducing mereology – the theory of parthood relations – as a mathematical foundation of similar importance as set theory, see [45]. This makes possible within a respectable mathematical framework, the alternative, but still similar, classification of facts which is found in the American National Standard's guidelines for thesauri construction [1], which recommends that distinction is made among the following kinds of concepts (non-exhaustive list):

- things and their physical parts, e.g. bird, car, mountain;
- materials, e.g., water, steel, oxygen;
- activities or processes, e.g., painting, golf;
- events or occurrences, e.g., birthday, war, revolution;
- properties or states of persons, things, materials or actions, e.g., elasticity, speed;

- disciplines or subject fields, e.g., theology, informatics;
- units of measurement, e.g., hertz, volt, meter.

The classification above is accompanied by recommendations for how to construct the associated terminology, e.g., rules for when to use plural and singular forms, and rules for relating terms to each other, which may depend on the kind of concepts designated by the terms.

4.2.2 Conceptual Modeling of Discrete Phenomena

The most successful modeling approach for the UoD is found in science, where distinctions are made among individual concepts, class concepts, relation concepts, and magnitudes (quantitative concepts) [5]. These general concept types are tools for distinguishing among items and for grouping them. Individual concepts help us to discriminate among individuals. Class concepts are used to establish classifications. Ordering and comparison are made possible by relation concepts. Distinctions are made between specific (definite) concepts and generic (indefinite) concepts, e.g., "Obama" is a specific concept, but "x" is a generic concept and denotes an arbitrary referent.

The concept classification of science is independent of the concept classification made for thesauri purposes, and may be used for concept modeling within each group in the thesaurus classification as well as for building models to relate concepts that belong to different groups in the thesaurus classification.

Quantitative concepts apply to properties that reflect magnitudes associated with individuals and/or sets, e.g., the temperature of a body, the number of elements of a set. No distinct object is associated with a quantitative concept. Functions are the structure of quantitative concepts, e.g., weight, mass, heat, acceleration. For example, weight is a function W that maps the set of bodies (each of which has a weight) into the set of real numbers. Quantitative concepts are the conceptual core of measurement [5].

Let "b" be a generic individual concept that represents some physical body (the object variable) and let "w" be a generic individual concept that represents a numerical value (the numerical variable). Then "W (b) = w" reflects the functional nature of W, and is to be read "the weight of b equals w". The numerical variable w occurring in the weight function is equal to the number of weight units on a given scale, e.g., kilogram or pound. If scale and unit system is not fixed by the context we need to indicate it by a special symbol, say "s". In short, "W(b,s) = w" is to be read "the weight of b equals w measured in the scale s".

Domain models are structures of individual concepts, class concepts, relation concepts, and quantitative concepts. Class concepts apply to collections of individuals, e.g., "PERSON" refers to all possible persons, and "NORWEGIAN" refers to all Norwegians. That Norwegians are persons is stated in the domain model as NORWEGIAN is a subset of PERSON.

Relation concepts and class concepts are closely related. For example, "MARRIAGE" may be seen as a relation concept, where (it used to be that) each instance involves one man and one woman, but there is also a corresponding class concept of "MARRIAGE", seen as a legal entity. In mathematics, the concept of relation is not a primitive concept along with set and member, but is defined in terms of notions already available in set theory for defining set and set-membership. This is done in order to keep the number of irreducible concepts in set theory to a minimum [33].

4.3 Data Concepts

From a conceptual point of view there is no difference, in principle, between binary numbers and other referents. Binary numbers may be abstracted in class concepts and related by relation concepts as may every other collection of referents making up this Universe of Discourse. Computers deal directly with their referents (the data), and it becomes important to distinguish between a concept and its extension. Important concepts for data modeling are:

- data item: the specific individual linguistic concept, the term, the value;
- data record: a structured data item composed from other data items;
- variable: the generic individual linguistic concept;
- data type: a linguistic class concept, in programming languages usually called "type";
- data set: a set of data items, each data item being different from the others in the set;
- data collection: a collection of data items which need not be different;
- data base: a collection of data collections.

The names given to data types may used to distinguish among quantitative concepts and how they relate to other UoD concepts. Quantitative concepts are general in the sense that they apply to large numbers of referents, e.g., every physical body has a weight and a temperature. A generalization of the definition in the previous section provides us with the definition of a quantitative concept as a function $q:UoD \times S \rightarrow D$, where UoD is the set of referents, S is the set of scales, D is the set of linguistic units (the possible values), and consequently the set of quantitative concepts is $Q=\{q|q:UoD \times S \rightarrow D\}$.

Assume that we want to define three data sets, one to contain the weight values of Norwegians, one for Americans and one for the British. Assume further that weight is measured on the metric scale, but in units of kilograms with two decimals precision for Norwegians, in pounds with one decimals precision for Americans, and in stones with three decimals precision for the British. The corresponding (informal) definitions may look like

W: American x (scale lbs 1 decimal) → WAlbs1
W: British x (scale stone 3 decimals) → WBstone3
W: Norwegian x (scale kg 2 decimals) → WNkg2

where WAlbs1, WBstone3, WNkg2 are data types of positive real numbers.

The data types may now serve as names of different combinations of class concepts and the quantitative concept weight W, and may be used to define data sets, e.g., a table with the name WEIGHT-A and attribute WAlbs2 will denote a data collection with one record for every American, WEIGHT-B can be defined similarly for the British, and so on.

Unfortunately the usual situation is that the weight definitions and their relations to the data types are either not made as explicit formal statements, or they are soon lost in heaps of documentation, which are usually not well maintained. The weight definitions must be seen as part of the definitions of the data types. So the relevant data sets appear as undefined entities without explicit reference to what they carry information about. The "memory" of the definitions is imprinted only in the software processes where the variables of these data types are used.

4.4 Information Modeling

While data collections may contain several equal data items, information collections are sets, where all individual members are different. Information sets are defined by relating UoD concepts and data concepts. Langefors [16] introduced the concept of elementary message (e,v,t), where e is an entity in the UoD, v is a measurement value and t is the time of the measurement. We view information to be a relationship between a quantitative concept, a domain concept and a data type. A message is a relationship between an individual domain concept and a (quantitative concept, data type) pair, an information set is a relationship between a domain class concept (and relation class concept) and a (quantitative concept, data type) pair. The original definition of elementary message may need to be expanded to include spatial information in addition to time. We will not discuss this aspect further here.

In order for a data item to carry meaning it must be related to the appropriate quantitative function, to the appropriate referent in the UoD, to the scale of measurement s in the set of scales, and to the time and location, and to the data representation of the observed value. The precision of the unit system must be specified, e.g., whether the weight is represented with an accuracy of hundreds or thousands on the chosen scale, be it kilogram, ton or pound. When represented in a computer program, precision is defined by the data type of the appropriate numerical variable, e.g., integer, real, double precision, decimal number, or some other user defined data type, as shown in the previous section on data modeling.

Information sets must be defined relative to the conceptual model of the world that is represented by the data items. For example, an information set that contains the numerical values of the weights of all persons could be specified as a data collection containing one element for each member of the extension of the appropriate world concept. In order to qualify for an information set, each of the elements in the set must be a pair consisting of a unique label for each individual of the domain class concept and a value for the corresponding weight.

We illustrate this by continuing the example of weights of persons and Norwegians. For Norwegians the situation is straight forward. All Norwegians are associated with a unique label defined by the 1:1 mapping PID-N from all Norwegians to the data type PNO, which is called the person number, more formally expressed as PID-N: Norwegian ↔ PNO. We may now define the information set NOR-WEIGHTS = (PNO, WNkg2), and we may interpret the meaning of the corresponding data, as we have the complete semantic definition of every concept used.

This is admittedly a complicated way of defining the meaning of a data item. On the other hand there is a certain economy involved in specification volume because many of the concept definitions can be reused. Weight and age and person number are reusable, as are scales and types. Essential is that domain models may be modified without requiring a simultaneously modification of the corresponding information models and data models.

New domain concepts can be defined relative to already existing domain concepts. We don't have to modify already defined information definitions and data models. New information set definitions can be done as additions to already existing ones. Modifications of information systems can be done by replacing old information sets with new ones, both new and old information being properly defined. We can transform information sets and data structures while preserving their semantics.

The following is an indication of what a full specification of information about weights of Norwegians, Americans and British may look like at an early stage of information systems engineering. In order to be able to express information associated with individuals on the level of sets of these individuals, even if we don't know how to identify the individuals, we have to introduce a special quantitative concept which maps 1:1 from a class concept to an unknown data type. This special mapping is called label and serves as a surrogate for a unique name for the members of the class concept. Example: label(Person) stands for an unknown data type which could serve as a unique identifier for all persons on the planet. But label is a quantitative concept in its own right, and can be used to specify, e.g., PNO to be a unique identifier for Norwegians.

Example: The objective is to specify information as a relation between data concepts and UoD concepts. The data concepts are data types, and the UoD concepts are class concepts and quantitative concepts. Scale concepts including measurement units and precision come additionally.

First, the modeling in the domain:

C-concept Body, Person, American, British, Norwegian;
Q-concept weight: Body → *positive real*;
Body *includes* Person;
Person *includes* American, British, Norwegian;

Then, we have to introduce appropriate data types:

datatype real Aweight, *real* Bweight, *real* Nweight, *integer* PNO;
Q-concept label: Norwegian ↔ PNO;
Q-concept weight: American → wA(lbs.d)
Q-concept weight: British → wB(stone.ddd);
Q-concept weight: Norwegian → wN(kg.dd);

We may now define appropriate information sets:

informationset A-weight, B-weight, N-weight;
A-weight: *foreach* American (label, weight);
B-weight: *foreach* British (label, weight);
N-weight: *foreach* Norwegian (PNO, weight);

There is no properly defined specification language defined yet. For example, it should be possible to be somewhat vague in the specifications, e.g., in addition to being able to state *forall* also to state that *formost* American, *forsome* Norwegian, *forafew* British, and so on. Such possibilities should make the language more suitable for supporting increasing level of detail in the specification during the information system engineering process.

5 Conclusion

Our thesis is that a comprehensive theory of information systems engineering must comprise a clear definition of the concept of information. Such a definition should come as an addition to the modeling concepts of data systems domain systems, not as a replacement. To this end we propose a definition of information as a relationship between domain model concepts and data model concepts. The ambition is that the proposed definition of the information concept will permit semantic preserving transformations of data structures, and thereby provide the basis for comparing data collections on the web and in data bases with respect to the meaning that they carry. Much detailed work remains.

References

1. ANSI/NISO Z39.19-1993 (1993) Guidelines for the construction, format, and management of monolingual thesauri. ISBN 1-880124-04-1
2. Berente N, Lyytinen K (2007) What is being iterated? Reflections on iteration in information system engineering process. In: Krogstie J, Opdahl AL, Brinkkemper S (eds) Conceptual modelling in information systems engineering. Springer, Berlin, pp 261–278
3. Boman M, Bubenko JA Jr, Johannesson P, Wangler B (eds) (1997) Conceptual modelling. Prentice Hall, Englewood Cliffs, NJ
4. Bubenko JA (2007) From information algebra to enterprise modelling and ontologies – a historical perspective on modelling of information systems. In: Krogstie J et al (eds) Conceptual modelling in information systems engineering. Springer, Berlin, pp 1–18
5. Bunge M (1998) The philosophy of science. Transaction Publishers, New Jersey
6. DeMarco T (1979) Structured analysis and system specification. Prentice-Hall, Englewood Cliffs, NJ
7. Dietrich A, Lockemann PC, Raabe O (2007) Agent approach to online legal trade. In: Krogstie J et al (eds) Conceptual modelling in information systems engineering. Springer, Berlin, pp 177–194
8. Eder J, Lehmann M (2007) Uniform and flexible data management in workflow management systems. In: Krogstie J et al (eds) Conceptual modelling in information systems engineering. Springer, Berlin, pp 91–106

9. Gulla JA (2007) Using models in enterprise systems projects. In: Krogstie J et al (eds) Conceptual modelling in information systems engineering. Springer, Berlin, pp 107–122
10. Halpin T (2007) Fact-oriented modeling: past, present and future. In: Krogstie J et al (eds) Conceptual modelling in information systems engineering. Springer, Berlin, pp 19–38
11. Harry A (1996) Formal methods fact file VDM and Z. Wiley, New York, NY
12. Jeffery KG (2007) Systems development in a GRIDs environment. In: Krogstie J et al (eds) Conceptual modelling in information systems engineering. Springer, Berlin, pp 279–294
13. Johannesson P (2007) The role of business models in enterprise modelling. In: Krogstie J et al (eds) Conceptual modelling in information systems engineering. Springer, Berlin, pp 123–140
14. Krogstie J (2007) Modelling of the people, by the people, for the people. In: Krogstie J et al (eds) Conceptual modelling in information systems engineering. Springer, Berlin, pp 305–318
15. Kung D, Kavi K (2007) Conceptual modeling and software design of multi-agent systems. In: Krogstie J et al (eds) Conceptual modelling in information systems engineering. Springer, Berlin, pp 159–176
16. Langefors B (1066) Theoretical analysis of information systems. Studentlitteratur, Lund
17 Moody DL (2009) The "physics" of notations: towards a scientific basis for constructing visual notations in software engineering. IEEE Trans Softw Eng 35(5):756–779
18. Ogden CK, Richards IA (eds) (1923) The meaning of meaning. Kegan Paul, Trench and Trubner, London
19. Olivé A (2005) Conceptual schema-centric development: a grand challenge for information systems research. In: Proceedings of CAiSE 2005. LNCS, vol 3520. Springer, pp 1–15
20. Olivé A (2006) Conceptual modeling of information systems. Springer, Berlin
21. Olivé A, Cabot J (2007) A research agenda for conceptual schema-centric development. In: Krogstie J et al (eds) Conceptual modelling in information systems engineering. Springer, Berlin, pp 319–334
22. Opdahl AL, Sindre G (2007) Interoperable management of conceptual models. In: Krogstie J et al (eds) Conceptual modelling in information systems engineering. Springer, Berlin, pp 75–90
23. Pastor O, Gonzales A, Espana S (2007) Conceptual allignment of software production methods. In: Krogstie J et al (eds) Conceptual modelling in information systems engineering. Springer, Berlin, pp 209–228
24. Pernici B (2007) Adaptive information systems. In: Krogstie J et al (eds) Conceptual modelling in information systems engineering. Springer, Berlin, pp 295–305
25. Pohl K, Sikora E (2007) Co-development of system requirements and functional architecture. In: Krogstie J et al (eds) Conceptual modelling in information systems engineering. Springer, Berlin, pp 229–246
26. Rolland C (1988) An information system methodology supported by an expert design tool. Elsevier Science Publishers, University of Paris
27. Rolland C (2007) Capturing system intentionality with maps. In: Krogstie J et al (eds) Conceptual modelling in information systems engineering. Springer, Berlin, pp 140–158
28. Rolland C (2008) Intention driven conceptual modelling. In: Johannesson P, Söderström E (eds) Information systems engineering: from data analysis to process networks, IGI Global, Hershey, Pennsylvania, pp 16–42
29. Rolland C (2009) Exploring the fitness relationship between system functionality and business needs. In: Lyytinen K et al (eds) Design requirements engineering – a ten-year perspective. MIT, Cambridge, MA
30. Sindre G, Opdahl AL (2007) Capturing dependability threats in conceptual modelling. In: Krogstie J et al (eds) Conceptual modelling in information systems engineering. Springer, Berlin, pp 247–260
31. Sølvberg A, Kung D (1993) Information systems engineering. Springer, Berlin
32. Thalheim B (2007) Challenges to conceptual modeling. In: Krogstie J et al (eds) Conceptual modelling in information systems engineering. Springer, Berlin, pp 58–74
33. Wall R (1972) Introduction to mathematical linguistics. Prentice-Hall, Englewood Cliffs, NJ

34. Wand Y, Weber R (1995) On the deep structure of information systems. Info Systems J 5: 203–223
35. Wasserman A (2007) Methods and tools for developing interactive information systems. In: Krogstie J et al (eds) Conceptual modelling in information systems engineering. Springer, Berlin, pp 195–208
36. Ziegler P, Dittrich KR (2007) Data integration – problems, approaches and perspectives. In: Krogstie J et al (eds) Conceptual modelling in information systems engineering. Springer, Berlin, pp 39–58
37. http://agilemanifesto.org/. Accessed 15 Dec 2009
38. http://www-bisc.cs.berkeley.edu/ZadehCW2002.pdf. Accessed 15 Dec 2009
39. http://framenet.icsi.berkeley.edu/. Accessed 30 Nov 2009
40. http://en.wikipedia.org/wiki/Gabriel_Kron. Accessed 20 Oct 2009
41. http://www.answers.com/topic/diakoptics-mathematics. Accessed 20 Oct 2009
42. http://en.wikipedia.org/wiki/B%C3%B6rje_Langefors. Accessed 20 Jan 2010
43. http://en.wikipedia.org/wiki/Model-driven_architecture. Accessed 20 Sep 2009
44. http://en.wikipedia.org/wiki/Model-driven_engineering. Accessed 20 Sep 2009
45. http://plato.stanford.edu/entries/mereology/. Accessed 10 Sep 2009
46. http://en.wikipedia.org/wiki/Requirements_engineering#Requirements_engineering. Accessed 15 Dec 2009
47. http://www.semat.org/bin/view. Accessed 07 Dec 2009

Contemporary Challenges in Requirements Discovery and Validation: Two Case Studies in Complex Environments

Sean Hansen and Kalle Lyytinen

Abstract Requirements have remained a key source of difficulty since the dawn of computing. Complicating this fact, recent substantive changes in systems development and associated requirements processes – as reflected in reliance on packaged software components, off-shore development, and software-as-a-service – demand a reappraisal of requirements challenges. Yet, there are few empirical studies focusing on what current requirements challenges are, why they emerge and how they affect requirements engineering (RE) efforts. In the present study, we assess the cognitive, social, and complexity-based impediments to effective requirements discovery through two exploratory case studies of large, multi-party development projects. We develop a rich understanding of the requirements challenges facing these development efforts, how these challenges interact and affect the requirements engineering process and outcomes. The analyses reveal significant consistency in the primary challenges of large RE efforts and the profoundly systemic nature of requirements-related impediments. Several recommendations for research and practice of RE are developed.

1 Introduction

In their early seminal work, Ross and Schoman [47] stated that inadequate attention to system functions leads to "skyrocketing costs, missed schedules, waste and duplication, disgruntled users, and an endless series of patches and repairs euphemistically called 'system maintenance'" (p. 6). Since then researchers have continued to observe that major sources of project distress are related to a project's design requirements [1, 9, 54] and despite three decades of intensive research, the "requirements mess" persists [28]. Complicating this pursuit is the observation that

S. Hansen (✉)
Peter B. Lewis Building, Weatherhead School of Management, Case Western Reserve University, 10900 Euclid Avenue, Cleveland, OH, 44106-7235 USA
e-mail: hansen@case.edu

S. Nurcan et al. (eds.), *Intentional Perspectives on Information Systems Engineering*,
DOI 10.1007/978-3-642-12544-7_3,

the requirements research community has struggled to keep pace with developments in requirements practices [3, 25, 51]. With the rise of outsourcing, a shift toward commercial off-the-shelf (COTS) applications [44], and the widespread use of external consultants and third-party systems integrators, requirements processes are increasingly distributed and present a stark contrast to the traditional views of requirements engineering (RE) as orchestrated by a single team with respect to a standalone artifact [23, 24].

Given the changing nature of RE practices, prevailing development initiatives present a critical opportunity for re-assessing challenges associated with design requirements. In recent research, we developed a model of requirements challenges that integrates long-acknowledged impediments to effective RE with emergent challenges flowing from contemporary shifts in the systems development landscape [21]. The model outlines categories of RE challenges based on cognitive limitations, traction in social interactions, and the broader complexity of the development environment [21]. In addition, we argue for the systemic nature of these challenges in that they reflect dynamic interactions and feedback loops. In the present research, we seek to validate the degree to which these requirements challenges help us understand how RE issues emerge and evolve in situ. Specifically, we ask:

- What are the challenges that development professionals encounter in the elicitation and specification of requirements associated with large scale multi-stakeholder systems?
- How are various requirements challenges related to one another?
- To what degree are RE challenges recognized by professionals and how do they mitigate these challenges?

To address these questions, we conduct multi-site case studies involving multi-party software development projects, focusing specifically on their RE efforts. The remainder of the chapter is structured as follows: In Sect. 2, we provide an overview of the literature on challenges in RE and introduce the systemic model of requirements challenges [21]. Section 3 outlines the research design for the case study. In Sect. 4, we provide a detailed overview of the two projects studied. Section 5 provides primary findings related to RE challenges in the cases. In Sect. 6, we discuss the implications of findings for both information systems development (ISD) professionals and the research community.

2 Towards a Systemic Model of RE Challenges

2.1 Earlier Typologies of Requirements Challenges

In his seminal article, Davis [10] noted three causes for incomplete requirements: (1) cognitive limitations, (2) the variety and complexity of requirements, and (3) the patterns of interaction between users and requirements engineers. Davis proceeded to focus primarily on the first category by emphasizing the limits on the human short term memory and simplifications of information needs resulting from bounded rationality. The idea of cognitive limitations was later taken up by Loucopoulos and Karakostas [29], but now with an emphasis on users. They identify a host of impediments relating to the users' cognitive abilities: lack of a clear idea of what a new system should do, difficulty in articulating domain knowledge, and resentment of change (see also, Woolgar [56]). They consequently recognize a broad range of problems resulting from these limitation including the indeterminacy of requirements, the dynamic nature of the RE process, and the difficulty of identifying and integrating heterogeneous knowledge.

Several scholars have pursued the idea that social interactions form another significant source of requirement challenges. Impediments based on communication breakdowns and intergroup conflict are a natural byproduct of the inherently social nature of requirements activities (e.g., [13, 19]). While user participation has been widely advocated as a central element in a successful requirements endeavor, it may engender substantial challenges including: (1) animosity between analysts and users [31, 50], (2) the lack of interest or access to knowledgeable users [13], and (3) the increased diversity of user inputs creating conflicting requirements (e.g., [6, 18, 38, 53]). The social challenges of RE are acerbated further when information system development efforts correspond with broader business process change within an organization. The marriage of business process change and information systems development and the impediments that this pairing implies has been addressed by several RE researchers, most notably in a series of studies by Rolland and her colleagues [15, 40, 46].

2.2 A Systemic Model of Requirements Challenges

We recently conducted a field study to identify challenges IT managers experience in managing requirements associated with large development efforts [21]. Consequently, we proposed a framework for identifying and analyzing requirements challenges (Fig. 1). We briefly summarize its key features and implications for RE practice. The model identifies three broad categories of RE related impediments: (1) *cognitive challenges*, (2) *interpersonal challenges*, and (3) *complexity challenges*.[1] To some degree, these are consistent with those identified by Davis [10], but at the same time they reflect a number of novel challenges emanating from the changed landscape of contemporary RE. We also observed, unlike Davis [10] that these challenges are highly interactive and create systemic effects on the RE process. We will next briefly outline each challenge category and the specific impediments that they incorporate.

[1] This classification structure was determined through grounded theory coding of the data, rather than on an a priori schema.

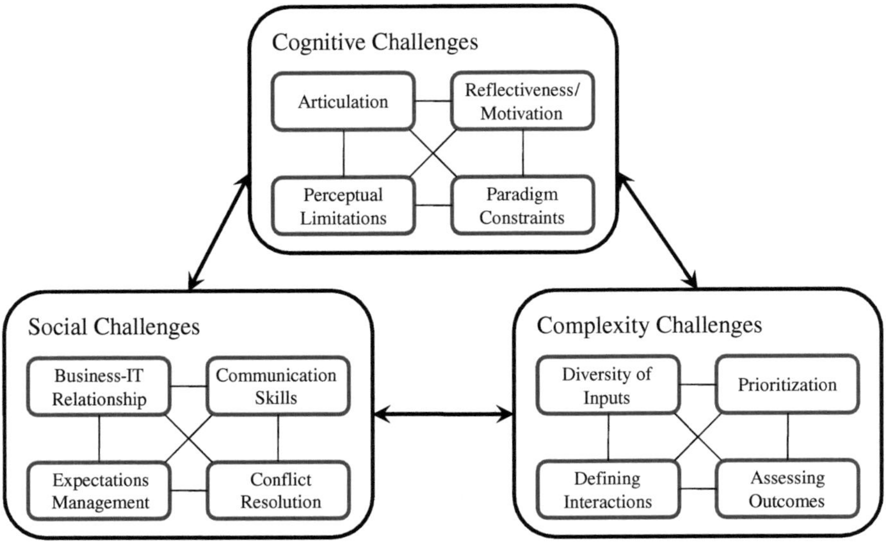

Fig. 1 A systematic model of requirements challenges (adapted from [20])

Cognitive Challenges. Overall, these challenges decrease stakeholder's ability to express needs explicitly, to overcome their conceptual "blind spots," and to envision a different future marked by new processes and IT capabilities. These challenges were observed in all stakeholders: users and managers, systems analysts and designers. *Articulation challenges* refer to the inability of individuals to articulate their needs concisely and concretely. To some degree, this inability reflects the limitations inherent in the distinction between tacit and explicit knowledge [32, 34]. Challenges associated with *reflectiveness and motivation* center on the unwillingness of professionals to be reflective about their activities and needs. This lack can again be partly traced back to the tacit-explicit dimension, in that design stakeholders often find it difficult to explicitly describe their domain. The motivational element underscores, however, the idea that stakeholders often simply forego a thorough analysis as it is painful or they fail to perceive its value. *Perceptual challenges* refer to difficulty of understanding the system landscape and functionality within the work environment. This inability often reflects the rising complexity of the environment within which designers and users interact. Finally, we refer to the vision generating limitations among stakeholders as *paradigmatic constraints,* in that stakeholders are limited in their imagination by the prevailing paradigms of their professional settings.

Social Challenges. Requirements activities represent an intense social undertaking creating a set of social challenges [22, 48, 49], including communication breakdowns or disruptions due to politics [2]. Not surprisingly, a range of interpersonal issues were identified as impediments to effective requirements determination. *Business-IT relationship issues* refer to the presence of an adversarial relationship between business units and IT personnel. This challenge is nowhere more relevant than in the requirements phase where users and IT professionals communicate about the needs of business. A second area is the lack of *communication skills* on the part of development personnel and users. Typically, however, respondents tended to emphasize the poor communication skills of development professionals. *Managing expectations* refers to the difficulties in fostering a realistic understanding of objectives and outcomes. Finally, *conflict resolution* refers to the increased demand to resolve discrepancies between distinct stakeholder groups.

Complexity-based Challenges. Recently, new interdependencies among components and broadened sets of stakeholders have increased socio-technical complexity [20]. From this perspective, complexity has shifted to higher levels of abstraction and span across highly heterogeneous elements complicating RE efforts. The first complexity-based challenge relates to difficulties with *prioritization*. Currently, designers struggle to develop heuristics to reduce requirements to a manageable set [27, 30]. *Diversity of inputs* refers to the expansion of socio-technical inputs into a design process including not only a larger number of stakeholders but also other information systems (e.g., legacy systems and vendor platforms) and regulatory regimes (e.g., HIPAA). *Defining interactions* refers to challenges encountered in articulating interactions between stakeholder groups, distinct business processes, and system components. This has become increasingly acute due to nested platforms and widespread customization of components, and it makes it more difficult to analyze requirements using static modeling approaches. Finally, *assessing outcomes* refers to the difficulty of assessing a system's adherence to the evolving requirements set (i.e., backward traceability).

Systemic Nature of RE Challenges. The challenges model calls attention to the interrelated nature of RE challenges [21]. While several requirements challenges have been discussed separately, the model integrates these challenges into a more dynamic framework to guide RE research. Importantly, interactions between RE challenges occur both within each category and across categories, and the model highlights ways in which the RE challenge categories build upon and contribute to one another. For example, cognitive challenges both contribute to, and are affected by, the socially-based challenges in how groups interact. At one level, the cognitive limitations are carried over into social processes. For example, the absence of *communication skills* is partially generated by the inability of the individuals to *articulate* their needs. In addition, the inability of users to effectively *articulate* their needs implies that conflicts between distinct groups remain unidentified, increasing the challenges of *conflict resolution*. Similarly, we can see that social issues are clearly embedded within complexity-based challenges in that social structures are one of the key sources of such complexity. Finally, cognitive challenges are interconnected with the complexity of the systems landscape as well, because cognitive limitations influence the degree to which IT and business professionals comprehend an increasingly heterogeneous IT environment.

The observation of the systemic nature of RE challenges suggests that it is fruitful to reconsider previously identified impediments in light of a contemporary development context. For example, although requirements conflict and conflict resolution have been addressed repeatedly in the RE literature (e.g., [5, 11, 37]), it would be erroneous to conclude that our understanding of associated mitigation strategies is complete. The increased prominence of challenges associated with broader systems complexity has in many ways changed the nature of the more fundamental impediments (i.e., cognitive and social) that the research community has addressed in the past.

3 Research Design

We conducted a multi-site exploratory case study of requirements processes and related challenges among two design teams involved in the design of large multi-party information systems. We felt that a case study approach was warranted to engage in a rich exploration of system designers' practices for theory generation, refinement, and validation related to RE challenges [12, 57]. In the past, similar case studies have been carried out in attempts to generate rich and theory-yielding insights about the broader issues within RE [17, 36, 42, 58].

In our data collection efforts, we employed a multiple-case study design. The unit of analysis was an individual design project. We focused on requirements-related activities in two project teams. The case inquiries were conducted in accordance with all prevailing case study field procedures, including the development of a case study protocol prior to data collection, triangulation using multiple sources of evidence, and the maintenance of a chain of evidence [57]. The data collection effort included interviews, direct observation of project meetings and the broader development environments, and documentary review (e.g., specification documents, customization requests, business process models, design mock-ups). Interview transcripts and observational field notes were then coded using Atlas.ti, a qualitative analysis tool. While the initial field study for formulating the framework followed a grounded theory approach [21], this later stage involving two rich multi-case analyses that drew upon the theoretical RE challenge framework as a preliminary coding structure. Additional codes were developed as they were identified in the coding process. Through this data analysis effort, we also sought to assess the generalizability and internal and external validity of the RE challenge model [21]. In the next section, we discuss the two ISD projects that form the core of the present analysis.

4 Research Context: Two Multi-Party Systems

The two projects studied in the present research effort – the University SIS and IPSI systems – experienced significant challenges related to the determination and management of requirements. In this section, we provide an overview of the two development processes and the issues encountered.

4.1 The University SIS Project

In 2006, a mid-sized Midwestern U.S. University initiated the acquisition, customization, and implementation of the PeopleSoft Student Information System (SIS) ERP. The SIS Project was intended to integrate all student information and student-facing administrative functions across the university's nine distinct schools. Key functions supported by the envisioned platform included admissions, financial aid, course selection and enrollment, grading, degree tracking, and transcript management. The initial roll-out of the system was completed in Fall 2008, with additional functionality rolled out over the course of the subsequent academic year. The installation of the PeopleSoft SIS platform was generally considered a successful effort, including the management of platform requirements.

Background. The studied university is a mid-size private university located in the Midwestern United States. The university serves nearly 10,000 students (4,200 undergraduate, 2,147 graduate, and 3,490 professional students) across nine (9) distinct schools. Traditionally, each school managed its own student records, with some aggregation of basic student information in the university's legacy information system, ISIS. Different administrative functions were managed using a collection of distinct software applications. The SIS Project was undertaken in an effort to integrate various student-related data sources and functions across the entire university.

The SIS was the third phase of a broader ERP installation program. The university had selected Oracle's PeopleSoft platform as the ERP package. In 2005 and 2006, the university had rolled out two installations of the platform, covering the Financial and Human Capital Management components. The SIS was the final major installation necessary for the achievement of a comprehensive enterprise-level information system serving the university.

Project Structure. Several roles and responsibilities were identified at the initiation of the SIS Project. An executive steering committee and executive sponsor position were established to provide oversight. The university's Vice Provost for Undergraduate Education was given the status of executive sponsor. The executive steering committee was made up of leading financial and administrative officers as well as the lead members of the project team. Leadership of the internal project team consisted of a Project Director, three project leads (i.e., covering Functional, Technical, and Project Management domains), multiple functional leads, and a training team. Functional leads for the project reported to the Functional Project Lead. The Functional Leads were responsible for coordinating the input of multiple functional subject matter experts (SMEs). The project's Technical Lead oversaw the work of a team of technical experts, who were responsible for the requirements elicitation and specification. In addition, technical experts were tasked with supporting the data mapping, system testing, and data conversion. The Technical Lead also managed a technical support team which was responsible for the development and implementation of the system. Specifically, the technical support team was assigned to provide database and network administration, application support, data warehouse development, and portal support. Finally, the Training team was tasked with the design, scheduling, and delivery of training programs to user groups. This role included identifying training needs; the development and maintenance of training materials, job aids, and tutorials; the management of help-desk functions; and the formulation of a communication strategy related to system implementation and roll out.

In addition, the university engaged the services of a consulting firm that specializes in enterprise system implementations within the higher education marketplace. The consulting team adopted a structure directly mirroring that of the internal project team. A Project Manager was appointed to oversee all project management functions in conjunction with the Project Director. Similarly, the company provided consulting personnel to fill the roles of Functional and Technical Consultants, supporting the efforts of their university counterparts. Finally, an Account Manager worked directly with the executive steering committee and made regular recommendations to the Project Director.

RE Processes. The determination of requirements on the SIS project reflected a diversity of efforts engaged by different project members. These team members did not adopt a single formal approach to the elicitation and specification of requirements. Rather, the team processes relating to requirements evolved over the course of the project. Furthermore, the processes and artifacts employed were often the product of collaborative development by multiple project team members.

Prior to the initiation of the project, several baseline functional and non-functional requirements had been established. In large part, this was a reflection of the vendor selection. Since the university had selected PeopleSoft for implementation and completed the installation of two of the three core modules, the vendor platform was established in advance. Thus, a large number of the requirements were embodied in the PeopleSoft system – both the SIS module itself and the existing Financial and Human Capital Management components implemented. In addition, several high-level requirements were determined during initial project planning through interactions with the executive steering committee. To some degree, these requirements reflected assumptions about the environments necessary to support an effective implementation. In the Project Charter document developed at the initiation of the project, these preliminary requirements are categorized as Technical, Functional, Financial (i.e., budgetary), and Personnel.

The central effort at requirements elicitation in the early stages of the SIS project was called the Interactive Design and Prototype (IDP) process. The IDP process sought to inform key stakeholders about the functionality of PeopleSoft and to elicit statements of needs for customization or modification. Thus, IDP was at its core what a gap analysis. The IDP process consisted of JAD-style focus group discussions scheduled with every one of the over 100 functional offices on campus.[2] Initiated by the Functional Leads (University and Consultant) and functional subject matter experts, the IDP sessions included the Technical Experts and focused on the input of office personnel regarding the appropriateness of the PeopleSoft system for their business functions. The result of each session was the articulation of desired modifications. Initially scheduled for a six-month period, the IDP phase of

[2]We use the phrase "JAD-style sessions" to convey the idea of engagement between the design team and user representatives around process design questions. However, the IDP sessions were oriented toward the gap identification rather than a formal design effort.

the project lasted for approximately nine months, forming the core of the initial requirements effort.

Throughout the duration of the project additional requirements were identified and explored. In general, this ongoing requirement identification was initiated by the project's Functional and Project Management Leads. Through communications with the users, the need for a functional or technical change was identified. Based on these conversations, the Functional or Project Management Leads would draw up a preliminary specification. The format for the specification documents evolved over the course of the project, but was generally text-intensive. Its main graphical component was the use of screen shots which were manually altered to convey a desired change without reference to the underlying data structure.

Consensus around specifications and change requests was achieved through walkthroughs. The walkthrough process was introduced roughly halfway through the project under the recommendation from one of the consultants. The walkthroughs were attended by the leadership of the project team, including the Project Director; Functional, Technical, and Project Management Leads; the consulting Project Manager and lead functional and technical consultants; and training team representatives. No users, functional SMEs, or technical experts were in attendance. During the walkthroughs, the spec developer would guide the participants through a detailed discussion of a requested change and process. Questions were raised and debated by the entire project team. The walkthroughs generally resulted in three outcomes: (1) the specification was accepted and the Technical Lead took responsibility for scheduling modifications, (2) the discussion raised sufficient problems with the current status of the specification so that a decision was made to revise the document, or (3) the specification was tabled for later discussion.

As noted, the training team was responsible for the determination and resolution of training requirements. Training requirements were determined through several sources. First, many of training requirements were outlined in the PeopleSoft documentation. Second, the IDP process highlighted several of idiosyncratic training requirements across the university. Finally, the training team identified a range of additional requirements through the mapping of business processes across the nine schools. Perhaps surprisingly, business process mapping was not undertaken at the initiation of the project. Rather, it was first begun by one of the consultants working with the internal training team. The business process maps were developed outside of the development platform using Microsoft Visio. The process maps turned out to be a critical asset, supporting not only the identification of training requirements but also functional requirements that had not emerged in the initial IDP exchanges.

4.2 Integrated Public Safety Initiative (IPSI)

The Integrated Public Safety Initiative (IPSI) was a multi-party project aimed at establishing effective information sharing across members of the law enforcement community within a one of the largest counties on the east coast of the

United States.[3] A regional software vendor, called Blue Systems, Inc. (BSI), was selected to provide the information sharing platform that formed the core of the initiative. In this capacity, BSI professionals acted as the primary managers of the overall project effort. The project was envisioned as a multi-year effort, with the four central law enforcement entities in the county adopting the system in 2008, while additional public safety entities migrated onto the platform over the next three years.

Background. In the wake of the terrorist attacks of the September 11, 2001, many federal, state, and local agencies began calling for more intensive information sharing among law enforcement and other public safety organizations. Indeed, the U.S. Department of Homeland Security had made *information sharing* one of the primary areas of focus for local and regional law enforcement agencies. In response to this trend, the County initiated the Integrated Public Safety Initiative, or IPSI, in the fall of 2007.

The County is one of the largest counties on the east coast of the United States. Located within the metropolitan region of New York City, the county includes the state's largest city. The founding members of the IPSI project, called anchor partners, were the four primary law enforcement agencies in the county, including the County Prosecutor's Office, the County Sheriff's Office, the City Police Department, and the County Corrections Department. These were the first four entities targeted for integration on the IPSI platform.

In addition to the broader public safety sector call for enhanced information sharing, the County anchor partners had significant operational justification for the IPSI effort. Despite constant interaction between the entities, much of their data transfer was still conducted through manual hand-off of paper. The foreseeable result was significant operational inefficiency. Nearly all arrest and incident data was subject to redundant data entry as it was passed from one partner's platform to another, greatly increasing data integrity concerns. In addition, the manual transfer process created potential for error and waste. For example, criminal defendants could not be transferred from one agency to another without the proper paperwork, and repeated trips between locations were common. Finally, the Prosecutor's Office was required to make a "Prosecute-Don't Prosecute" decision on all suspects within 72 hours of an arrest, giving all parties a vested interest in timely processing and transfer of information. Thus, the potential benefits of the IPSI effort were clear.

Blue Systems, Inc. After an extensive request for proposals (RFP) process, the IPSI anchor partners selected a local software vendor to provide the information sharing platform. BSI is a medium-sized software development and implementation firm headquartered in the state. Specializing in public safety software, the firm had made its reputation as a developer of operations and analytical support systems for local police and fire agencies. BSI's marquee brand was a computer aided dispatch and records management system (CAD/RMS), called *Shield*. In 2004, the firm began its foray into the information sharing domain with the development of

[3]Names and locations have been changed to comply with assurances of confidentiality.

an information sharing platform called *Enforce*^{3} (pronounced "Enforce cubed"). It was this platform that the County anchor partners engaged BSI to provide.

At a high level, the *Enforce*^{3} platform was designed to support the collection and normalization of incident and arrest data from multiple public safety agencies and to provide a uniform Web-based interface for browsing, search, analysis, and reporting by participating agencies. In addition, the platform created mechanisms for less formal communication between information sharing partners, such as discussion forums and chat. Other specific modules of the platform included GIS mapping of data, systems alerts (i.e., watch lists and incident tickers), crime forecasting and probability analysis, and free-form keyword search.

The BSI Project Team for IPSI was relatively small. The Project Manager held the central role in coordinating the four partner entities as well as a handful of other law enforcement agencies that were targeted for later adoption of the *Enforce*^{3} platform.[4] Because of the relative importance of the IPSI project for the local and regional reputation of the firm, the Project Manager was reinforced in his coordination and client support efforts by several of BSI's senior officers, including the Chief Operations Officer (COO), Senior Vice President (SVP), and Chief Technology Officer (CTO). The development unit for the initiative was a team of three to four developers led by a Senior Developer. Finally, there was an implementation team consisting of approximately three FTEs, who were responsible for all data conversion planning, installation scheduling, and platform training.

RE Processes. The IPSI project reflected a range of requirements processes, including those pursued by the anchor partners and vendor separately, as well their joint activity after the inception of the project. The majority of the requirements for the project were articulated prior to BSI's engagement in the partners' RFP document. Within the RFP, system requirements were laid out in an "Integration Platform Requirements" section. This section included the detailed requirements covering the areas of integration platform requirements, IPSI system overview requirements, technical IPSI system requirements, system implementation and support requirements, specific mandatory tasks and associated deliverables, and IPSI system documentation overview requirements. The requirements outlined in the RFP were almost entirely text-based, rendered in natural language. The 150-page RFP document contained only five graphical models, including business process or data flow diagrams for each of the four anchor partners and a simplified architectural diagram for the proposed system.

Interestingly, the requirements detailed in the RFP were in turn drawn from multiple sources. As a primary input to the RFP document, the anchor partners identified an RFP released two years earlier by a consortium of law enforcement agencies is another county. The IPSI RFP was largely modeled on this earlier RFP document. In addition, each of the anchor partners was tasked with documenting their internal

[4]It was envisioned that information from all of the law enforcement agencies within the county will eventually be integrated on the system.

business processes to establish integration and interface requirements. Finally, the RFP incorporated federal-level requirements for information sharing among law enforcement entities.

The anchor partners weren't the only parties coming to the table with established requirements. Since *Enforce*^{3} was an existing platform offered by BSI, the system itself embodied a broad range of functional and technical requirements. The *Enforce*^{3} system was initially designed as an add-on to the firm's *Shield* platform (i.e., CAD/RMS). Thus, the design of the system was largely driven by informal statements of need from BSI's existing clients. BSI clients discussed the desire for greater exchange of information with other municipalities in their local area, and *Enforce*^{3} evolved as the BSI developers "toyed around" with ways to expand their platform to address these needs. It was only after the system had been implemented as a pilot module with a number of their clients that the senior management of BSI recognized the value proposition of the *Enforce*^{3} distinct from its integration with the *Shield* offering. As a fully developed, independent module, *Enforce*^{3} met an array of technical requirements set by acquiring clients. These included network specifications, data submission requirements, and training expectations.

In addition to the operational objectives of the BSI clients, the *Enforce*^{3} system drew significant functional requirements from standards developed at the federal level. Specifically, *Enforce*^{3} was designed to be in compliance with the Global Justice XML Data Model (GJXDM), a standard developed by the U.S. Department of Justice to act as a *de facto* data reference model for information exchange within the nation's public safety communities.

Not all requirements were established prior to the initiation of the project. Several requirements had to be identified and clarified through the interaction of the anchor partners and the vendor. Specifically, these novel requirements centered on the areas of service level agreements (incorporating a range of non-functional requirements), forms definition requirements, and security policy requirements. The most intensive of these collaborative requirements-setting tasks was the determination of unified forms requirements. Because the four anchor partners were expected to employ *Enforce*^{3} for uniform reporting and exchange, the project team had to design data entry and reporting artifacts that satisfied the needs of all partners. Furthermore, additional law enforcement agencies from across the county had been engaged for this effort, because of their anticipated migration to the platform over the subsequent one to three years. To achieve the unified form designs, the BSI team pursued a two-pronged strategy: (1) collecting arrest and incident report forms from all law enforcement agencies within the county and completing a gap analysis to determine unique fields or classification differences, and (2) convening focus group sessions with user representatives to clarify reporting needs (e.g., determination actual usage of data fields and perceived criticality). In documenting the specifications for unified forms, the BSI team had foregone formal modeling techniques in favor of comparative checklists and iterative prototyping of data entry and reporting forms.

5 Alignment with the Challenges Model

We will next review requirements-related challenges encountered by both project teams and consider commonalities and differences. Overall, we note significant consistency with the challenges articulated in Sect. 2 [21]. Specifically, eleven of the twelve challenges outlined in the systemic requirements challenges model are also reflected in the case study findings.

5.1 Articulation Challenges

Not surprisingly, the idea that the envisioned users of a system cannot easily state their requirements for the software did surface in the cases. While there was no explicit discussion of these challenges within the University SIS project, the IPSI case included multiple references to the inability of users to state what they required. The following statement provides an example:

> So the intent now is we get the baseline [platform] in, we show them the capability, we start getting feeds in. And we'll see how they start working it and we'll evolve to it because they really can't come out and say, 'Here's a requirement' other than, 'We want to see indictables [offenses for which the Prosecutor's Office can indict an individual].' But they can't define 'indictables' because they don't want to see all indictables. It's really strange. We're going to have to evolve to a requirement. – IPSI Project Manager

As the comment reveals, the perceived difficulty of articulation on the part of users led the development team to place an emphasis on the evolution of the platform. Rather than emphasizing the need for all requirements at the outset, the project team simply acknowledged that requirements would emerge by involving the users with the initial adoption of the system.

5.2 Reflectiveness/Motivation

Challenges related to *reflectiveness and motivation* were more pronounced in the SIS project. In fact, the development team felt that several stakeholders lacked motivation and reflectiveness regarding their engagement with the development effort. As one project team member noted:

> It would be an interesting meeting [i.e., student and faculty committee meeting] should they show up. That's another problem. I don't think we've ever had a full attendance. The last student one we had there was one student . . . even though we offer all kinds of pizza to get them to attend. – SIS Communications Lead

Overall, engagement from various stakeholder groups varied widely. In addition to intermittent participation on student and faculty committees for the project, different schools had widely divergent rates of participation, with some schools providing several representatives and others providing only a single individual and limited communication. Further, the project team remarked that many requests for customization did not surface until users were actually using the system.

While the issues of reflectiveness and motivation were less salient in the IPSI project, the challenge was still apparent. The development team felt that the law enforcement stakeholders were highly motivated to participate because of the functionality promised, but ensuring reflection and feedback remained an issue. As the Project Manager observed:

> So we went into the first meeting, distributed this to everyone and said, 'This is the first cut at a report standardization. Take a look at it, see if it's different from what you have, and be ready to make some comments.' We went to a second meeting a couple of weeks later. Some people had looked at it and some people hadn't. This is not their main objective. Sometimes it's hard to get to cops [i.e., the law enforcement participants].

Overall, it was difficult to ensure that different users would reflect upon their existing environment to discern additional requirements.

5.3 Perceptual Limitations

In contrast to the field study of development professionals, the cases analyzed did not reflect a specific focus on the inability of stakeholders to apprehend their existing IT landscapes and functionality. Indeed, in both cases, the primary concern of users with respect to the proposed systems was maintenance of existing functionality and associated work practices. This tendency toward replication of existing practices is embodied in the theme of paradigmatic constraints.

5.4 Paradigmatic Constraints

The challenge imposed by stakeholders not being able to see beyond their prevailing paradigms was clearly discernible in both of the cases analyzed. For example, in the IPSI project, the development team struggled to foster openness to alternative reporting processes and structures among the participating agencies. Each agency felt that their existing reporting mechanisms were essential. However, given the multi-party nature of the project, some changes to the reporting processes were necessary. This need for alternative approaches created substantial challenges for the development team:

> They all have different reports. But at least twenty-five percent on each one is different ... All the reports follow a similar pattern just slightly different ... We would have been in much better shape had it not been for the Prosecutor's insistence on the fact that the report that's filled out has to be identical. It has to be the exact report.

The University SIS project revealed that paradigmatic constraints are not exclusive to end-users. In that project, the development team encountered significant challenges because of their consultants' insistence upon certain measures that had been encountered in earlier installations of the software at other universities. The following quote provides a salient example:

> I think the thing that worked against me the most in my goal to limit the changes was the consultants. Unfortunately they had been on other projects that either were not very disciplined about the changes they made or had bigger budgets or had larger IT teams behind them or for whatever reason went ahead and made a lot of these changes. Basically we were getting in situations where the consultants were saying, 'You've got to do this. Other schools do.' Really 'other schools do' meant one or two that they had just recently been at. – SIS Technical Lead

The experiences from both of the projects illustrate the fact that RE efforts are frequently impeded by the assumptions that users and developers alike bring to a design effort regardless of their applicability in the focal environment.

5.5 Business-IT Relationship

Despite the general perception of positive relationships between users and IT personnel in the cases the projects suffered from poor IT business relationships. In both projects, mistrust between users and IT arose to challenge the successful determination of requirements. In the SIS project, team members perceived distrust among some of the other stakeholders. As the Communications Lead observed:

> Some schools [within the University] don't want anything to do with it [i.e., the new platform]. They just are being really difficult. I just don't know. I still have not understood why. PeopleSoft is here and it's not going away.

On the IPSI project, although the IT team (i.e., the BSI personnel) was new to most of the agencies, several of the users came to the project with expectations of an adversarial relationship:

> We were looking through it [an interface mock-up] and trying to calm them down because they thought it was going to be one of these, 'You're going to do it and that's the end of it' situations ... [So their reaction was,] 'Don't tell us this is what you want because it's not good enough. It doesn't serve our purposes. You're not making our life easy; you're making it hard.' So we said, 'This is just a draft. It was just a start. Don't get excited ... Let's take it easy and come to some kind of compromise.' – Senior Developer

Thus, as with the paradigmatic constraints, challenges in the business-IT relationship reflect the importation of expectations of an adversarial relationship, even when no breach of trust has actually occurred.

5.6 Communication Skills

The communication skills of IT professionals and users was not a primary emphasis in either of the projects observed. However, some concerns over the effectiveness of communications between IT and business-oriented stakeholders did surface. In the

SIS project, the Technical Lead expressed concerns about the ability of his staff to engage with stakeholders:

> The title here is Programmer-Analyst. In this environment they're really more programmer than analyst. That's because they've worked for the university supporting the legacy systems ... So they didn't really have an opportunity to understand the whole business process through and through ... So they're somewhere along their learning curve and they're able to be effective programmers if we can point them in the right direction and figure out enough of the specs so that they can run with it.

Even within the development team, communication breakdowns occurred frequently. In some cases, developers initiated changes to the systems, but never communicated those to other members of the project team. As one participant noted:

> We found out that one of the schools had submitted a change and the technical team did the change, but no one ever told us about it. So we went out to do the training and they said, 'Wait that's supposed to have changed.' Well, it had changed, but we never knew it. – SIS Trainer

While communications issues were less prevalent on the IPSI project, some challenges were discernible. In working with the partner agencies, the BSI team encountered some differences in the interpretation of the project scope:

> In the RFP it says, 'The incident report and the arrest report.' It specifically states, 'Incident Report, Arrest Report.' However the sheriff's office was one of these anchor tenants and in one of the meetings came and said, 'Oh, by Incident Report I meant the Incident Package.' I was thinking, 'What does that mean?' It's about fifteen reports. I looked at the project manager. I said, "We'll see what we can do. We'll talk about it." So right now we've added a supplemental report. – BSI Development Manager

Overall, by comparing observations of this analysis with the previous field study [21], it appears that challenges based in the communications skills of project participants were less prevalent than anticipated.

5.7 Expectations Management

The necessity of managing expectations was repeatedly discussed in both projects. In the SIS project, several observed that requests for customization would be essentially limitless, if they were not tightly managed. Indeed, the project's Technical Lead noted that he perceived minimizing customization as his primary task. Accomplishing this objective required an open exchange:

> He [the SIS Technical Lead] is very low key. If someone wanted this major customization, he would say, 'Do you really need it? This could take a month of work. I'd have to take the programmers off whatever to do this.' So he didn't just say 'No,' but he had to set expectations. – SIS Development Consultant

A very similar pattern emerged on the IPSI project, with the BSI Project Manager seeking to limit changes to the existing platform, while still acknowledging the desires of other agencies. In one example, the Project Manager reflected upon his approach to minimizing the concerns of one of the partner agencies by delaying the discussion of an issue that was likely to arise:

> We didn't say anything about 'We're going to transmit your current reports just like we do in Springfield so we have two sets of arrest reports, incident reports.' No. The timing was not right to broach that subject in any of the executive meetings yet. I want to get them happy. I want the Prosecutor to say, 'This is great! I like the way it's working. I need this, this, and this.' Then we can maybe approach the subject and say, 'By the way one of the downsides is you're not going to get that report.' Then we can say, 'We're working on this. We're getting close. Why do it for a couple of months?'

Interestingly, on the IPSI project, the need for adjustment of expectations did not flow in only one direction. The development team was forced to revisit their vision of *Enforce*[3] platform as the expectations of the agencies became more apparent:

> We had big plans initially. Later what turned out was that departments – police agencies and the police departments and the owners of the data – were in fact a little bit reluctant to share the data. And that brought our expectations of what we wanted our program to be down a lot.

The management of expectations between all parties was a constant concern for the development teams in both environments. Interestingly, the discussion of expectations was frequently paired with a focus on the evolutionary nature of the system – perceiving the software as an evolving solution enabled parties to establish expectations that are more realistic while maintaining the hope for additional functionality.

5.8 Conflict Resolution

Not surprisingly, substantial conflicts over requirements were observed in both project settings. In the University SIS project, most conflicts were identified during project walkthroughs, which brought together all core project team members as well as representatives from the schools and functional departments:

> It [conducting walkthroughs] got people around a table. Some of them were pretty unpleasant ... Somebody would have an idea about how something should be done and Jack [the Project Manager] would totally disagree and they'd go at it for some time. [Q: How was that resolved?] Sometimes it didn't get resolved and we'd just schedule another walkthrough because time would run out. – SIS Communications Lead

When unresolved conflict persisted, it was generally addressed through an appeal to authority (e.g., relying upon the discretion of the Project Manager, Technical Lead, or University Registar's Office).

The IPSI project followed a similar pattern. When conflicts arose, the BSI project team adopted an expressly cooperative stance, seeking to generate a novel solution to satisfy all parties. A clear perception of the political ramifications of decisions guided the project team in determining whose positions required the most weight, while ensuring that decisions appeared to reflect the needs of all stakeholder groups. The following statement illustrates this sensibility:

> If we don't compromise with Springfield, it's not ever going to happen. So you have to play that game. But you have to be careful because it can't look like it's Springfield's project because then you have political problems with everybody else in the county. – BSI Development Manager

However, when conflicts did not allow for a mutually satisfactory resolution, an appeal to authority was invoked, specifically allowing the Prosecutor's Office to make the determination as to the path to be followed.

5.9 Prioritization

Indeed, the failure in prioritization was a significant source of tension within the SIS project team. An illustrative comment came during one of the requirements walkthroughs as one of the lead consultants remarked in exasperation, "As far as I can tell, we've spent about six months pouring over minutiae because some of us don't have the ability to say 'No!'." The need for prioritization was underscored by requests for customization that were essentially limitless:

> I think the challenges are to not go crazy with modifications, because you can modify the system so easily. We could do everything that everybody wanted but it would take us ten years. Essentially, from the users, there would be an endless stream of requests if it were allowed. – SIS Training Manager

Despite a clear recognition of the need for prioritization, the SIS project team had no formal mechanism for prioritizing changes. Rather, the primary mechanism for determining the necessity of various changes was the input of the Functional Leads and the discretion of the Project Manager and Technical Lead.

Within the IPSI project, the need for prioritization was widely acknowledged, but not perceived to be fundamentally problematic. As with the SIS project, the IPSI team lacked formal mechanisms for prioritization, but they did obtain some simple heuristics to guide the customization of the system. For example, returning the issue of reporting standardization, the BSI Project Manager explained his prioritizing approach:

> What I've done is I've taken all of that information in [feedback on desired fields], as much as I've gotten back, and I've come up with a matrix. We've got six or seven columns of responses. If we have five or more checked, that's going in a report guaranteed. It has to go in. If it's three to four, we'll consider it. If it's only one or two agencies, we're not going to do it. That's just a starting point.

In contrast to the SIS project, the IPSI project team felt comfortable that prioritization would emerge naturally. Again, this stance reflected the project's overall focus on requirements evolution rather than a priori clarity with respect to all agency needs.

5.10 Diversity of Inputs

Given the nature of the two projects analyzed, the diversity of inputs was relatively high in both settings. On the University SIS project, requirements were derived from a wide range of sources, including the vendor platform (PeopleSoft), multiple legacy systems, individual schools and functional departments, and the project consultants. While the challenges of integrating the consultants' requirements have been discussed above, the varied requirements of the individual schools and their associated legacy systems presented an equally acute challenge.

> All of the schools had different admission applications. They used Contact Manager, home-grown Access databases, CCC, and other applications. So there were lots of different processes and systems that we had to plan for. – SIS Trainer

The IPSI project encountered a similar diversity of voices to the customization and implementation of the information sharing platform. In addition to the requirements embodied in BSI's *Enforce*^{3} system, each of the anchor partners came to the project with distinct processes and legacy platforms that needed to be accommodated on the new system. The participation of ancillary agencies targeted for migration to the platform over the subsequent years expanded the range of consideration dramatically. As the project progressed, several new sources of requirements input were indentified, including the State Attorney General, the State Police, federal law enforcement entities (e.g., the U.S. Federal Bureau of Investigation), and national public safety information platforms (e.g., the National Data Exchange [N-DEx]). Balancing all of these inputs was a consistent challenge for the IPSI effort.

5.11 Defining Interactions

As the diversity of inputs outlined above suggests, capturing interactions between the vendor platform and other disparate systems was a recurring theme in both the University SIS and IPSI project. In the University SIS case, the project team encountered multiple issues because of inappropriate mapping to legacy applications. Even within the PeopleSoft suite (i.e., between SIS and the existing Financial and Human Capital Management modules), the project team struggled to define appropriate interfaces and maintenance processes:

> Actually PeopleSoft delivers the software intending you to run in a combined, shared environment of those systems. We decided to keep them separate here and then build the interface program between them because one of the main costs of these PeopleSoft systems is the maintenance. It's very difficult to get the two different business cycles on the same schedule to do maintenance. Now might actually be a good time in Human Capital management to be doing maintenance but it's a terrible time in the Student system with classes starting. The middle of the summer might be good for the Student system, but for Human Capital Management, that is when they enter all the performance reviews for people, so it's a bad time for them. – SIS Technical Lead

On the IPSI effort, the project team anticipated significant difficulty in converting the disparate CAD/RMS systems used by various partner agencies onto the information sharing platform. As the proposed number of agencies to be supported by the Enforce3 platform grew, so did the challenges in defining interactions between the various legacy systems. As the Project Manager observed:

> They'll be some coding issues. In one agency for example, you may have hair color: black, brown, red, yellow (1, 2, 3, 4). Well in my agency, we've got five colors. It's yellow, black, green, brown, blue or the numbers are different. You're sending me numbers. You can't send me numbers. I have to know what the color is. How are we going to work this out?

> So there's this mapping that has to take place with every client, including our own clients because every agency has slight differences when it comes to mapping because those are content, not context. We're going to have to do that. There's enough work involved in doing that.

Thus, the two project environments encountered significant difficulty flowing from the complexity of the broader systems landscape with which their focal systems had to interact. In both cases, project leaders reflected the perception that the appropriate solutions to these complexity-based challenges had not yet been identified, but that it would emerge over time as the system matured.

5.12 Assessing Outcomes

As with most of the challenges discussed, the difficulty of assessing outcomes with respect to meeting requirements of stakeholders was relevant in both cases. In the University SIS project, the initial implementation of the platform surfaced a number of necessary modifications that the project team had failed to identify and test for during the customization of the PeopleSoft platform. The project team members felt that their ability to predict the outcomes of the system would have been enhanced if the business stakeholders had assisted them in identifying possible user behaviors:

> I guess a lot of the challenge was the ownership in the process mostly from the business side. We talked about making a commitment to get the spec in on time, for example, and understanding that it would affect them down the road as much as the technical team. Anticipating how the system was going to work once it's been developed. Testing and finding things before we put the software into production and before it's critical and before we have no time to resolve the incidence. It was very difficult. – SIS Technical Consultant

In several cases, during the initial implementation of the platform, interfaces between the SIS system and a range of legacy platforms in use by individual schools failed to work as anticipated based on variation in data entry and reporting processes by the end users.

On the IPSI project, the multi-party nature of the project created some impediments to outcome assessment. Testing of the proposed system required receipt of sufficient data from all anchor partners, but the flow of data was intermittent As the BSI Senior Developer observed:

> We can operate now and he [the Prosecutor] will have easily seventy-five percent of his information coming in consistently exactly the way he wants it. That's a tremendous benefit to him. So we're close to schedule. But we're having some issues getting the database so we can test. I can't test anything yet because I don't have the database.

Thus, the complexity of the project context placed significant limitations on the ability of the project team to test the feasibility of various requirements that emerged. Here again, the project team expressed the hope that consistency would emerge as the platform evolved.

Table 1 Mapping requirements challenges in two cases

Challenges	Specific project issues
Individual cognitive challenges	
Articulation	IPSI: Acknowledgement that users are not able to state their needs
Reflectiveness/Motivation	SIS: Differing experiences in engaging students, faculty, and administrators in the RE process IPSI: Difficulty of eliciting feedback to preliminary design proposals.
Perceptual Limitations	No explicit discussion in the case projects
Paradigm Constraints	SIS: "Importation" of inappropriate requirements on the part of users and consultants. IPSI: Fostering consideration of alternative processes among all county law enforcement agencies
Interpersonal challenges	
Business-IT Relationship	SIS: Limited access to time and effort of envisioned users IPSI: Assumptions of an adversarial relationship among selected stakeholders
Communication Skills	SIS: Communication breakdowns with users and between team members; non-communication of substantive changes in requirements IPSI: Differing interpretations of project scope between anchor partners and the development team
Expectations Management	SIS: Need for minimizing customization to the platform and communicating the effort necessitated by specific requests IPSI: Difficulty managing the expectations of anchor partners
Conflict Resolution	SIS: Conflict visions emerging in the project walkthroughs; resolution through an appeal to authority IPSI: Managing requirements conflicts between anchor partners; resolving architectural conflicts
Complexity-based challenges	
Prioritization	SIS: Difficulty in prioritizing requirements of all users IPSI: Focus on prioritization through simple heuristics and platform evolution
Diversity of Inputs	SIS: Discontinuity in the role of project consultants; reconciling input from a wide range of stakeholder groups IPSI: Aggregating and reconciling agency needs, vendor requirements, and extra-project entities at the state and federal levels
Defining Interactions	SIS: Integration of a multiple legacy systems IPSI: Mapping impacts on the reporting systems and processes of individual law enforcement agencies
Assessing Outcomes	SIS: Receiving test conditions from business stakeholders during the identification of requirements IPSI: Obtaining adequate data to test the platform in a comprehensive manner

5.13 Summary of Challenges

Table 1 provides a summary of the challenges observed in the two cases. It is interesting to observe that many of the pressing challenges in the projects relate to the complexity that the design teams encountered, most notably in the diversity of inputs, difficulties in prioritization, and defining interactions. This observation underscores the perception of increased RE complexity [21]. This fundamental challenge is perhaps most concisely articulated by one of the respondents: "Our biggest challenge probably is the complexity of any new thing we want to do – they tend to get bigger and bigger."

6 Discussion

The analysis offers a number of key insights regarding the impediments to current RE processes. It also suggests that the systemic model helps effectively characterize many of the most pressing issues in systems development teams. Of the twelve core challenges we outlined [21], eleven are represented in various forms in the two project contexts studied. In addition, the cases underscore the fundamental interactions between these challenges.

6.1 The Systemic Character of RE Challenges

In both projects, the within-class interactions of various challenges are readily apparent. This is not surprising, as the classification reflects the conceptual affinity (shared variance) of these challenges. Within the category of cognitive challenges, the inability of users to *articulate* their needs contributes to, and is augmented by, their lack of *reflectiveness and motivation* in discerning the informational demands of their business environment and the difficulty they experience in envisioning alternative future states (i.e., *paradigmatic constraints*). While all of these cognitive limitations are intertwined, a couple of relationships are particularly salient. First, the *articulation challenges* originating from tacit knowledge clearly contribute to the lack of *reflectiveness/motivation* of the business professionals. Because rendering tacit knowledge in an explicit form is difficult, users avoid such an exercise unless they can be certain that it is worth the effort. Secondly, the difficulty of making one's needs explicit (*articulation challenges*) necessarily limits the degree to which those needs can be integrated into emerging paradigms of information management (*paradigmatic constraints*). In the same way, the absence of a clear vision for how a future state might be created contributes to the inability of users to describe clearly their demands for functionality.

Likewise, in the realm of social challenges, each challenge contributes to the others. For example, the assumption of an adversarial nature in the *Business-IT relationship* inhibits effective *expectation management* and *conflict resolution,* because the business-side stakeholders adopt a skeptical stance with respect to the requests of the technical project team. Focusing on the category of complexity challenges, the same systemic pattern of interaction emerges. For example, the difficulty of *defining interactions* between socio-technical elements is impacted by, and in turn impacts, the *diversity of inputs* that must be considered, the inability to effectively *prioritize* requirements, and the impediments to *assessing outcomes* of the requirements process.

While the within-class relationships between various RE challenges may be largely intuitive, impacts across categorical boundaries were equally prevalent. For example, the cognitive challenges contributed to, and were affected by, the socially-based challenges. Specifically, the inability of users to effectively *articulate* their needs leads to multiple conflicts between the requirements of distinct groups remaining unidentified, increasing the difficulty of *conflict resolution* when such discrepancies finally surface. In the opposite direction, the social dynamics between stakeholders affect the cognitive impediments of individuals. For example, on the IPSI project, the expectation of an adversarial relationship between business and IT stakeholders undermined *reflectiveness/motivation* of the anchor partners, because they failed to perceive the value of reflection on their own processes.

The relationship between socially- and complexity-based challenges is similar. At one level, we can see that the social issues are embedded within the complexity of the projects. This is illustrated by the fact that the diverse social project structures (e.g., multiple schools, distinct agencies) are one of the key sources of complexity in the form of a *diversity of requirements inputs*. In addition, the difficulties experienced in *managing expectations* and *resolving conflicts* significantly undermined the ability of personnel to establish requirements priorities (*prioritization*). Likewise, the *diversity of inputs* significantly impacted the capacity of designers for *conflict resolution*, because the potential for discrepant requirements grew with the increases in sources from which they were drawn. This dynamic affected the nature of the *business-IT relationship.* Similarly, the difficulty that business personnel and developers alike had in *defining interactions* influenced developers' ability to *manage expectations* and *resolve conflicts.*

Overall, the picture that emerges is one of broad systemic interactions. Each of the types of impediments affected, and were in turn affected by, each of the other types. One insight that we can draw from this is that it is important to consider these challenges from a systems based perspective. Focusing on any one challenge in isolation provides some solutions and improvements, but it robs us of a comprehensive view of systemic difficulties facing RE.

This point is particularly relevant in that not all challenges have received adequate attention. Much of the extant research has focused on challenges within the cognitive and social categories. Cognitive issues of articulation have been widely acknowledged since the earliest RE research (e.g., [7, 10, 16]). Similarly, nearly all of the challenges discussed at the social level have some precedents in the literature.

As such these reviews offer valuable insights into the impact and nature of each challenge. The challenges dealing with broader systems complexity have received less attention. Indeed, for those complexity challenges that have been addressed (e.g., prioritization; [30, 55]), few associated management techniques have made their way into community.

This observation suggests that it is fruitful to reconsider RE challenges in light of contemporary development contexts. For example, the challenges of requirements conflict have been addressed repeatedly in the RE literature (e.g., [5, 11, 37]), but it would be erroneous to conclude that our understanding of the issues and associated mitigation strategies is sufficient. The increased prominence of challenges associated with systems complexity has changed the nature of the some fundamental impediments (i.e., cognitive and social). Accordingly, there is significant opportunity for research on (1) issues that have emerged with the increased complexity of the environments and (2) the ways in which cognitive, social, and complexity-based challenges interact.

6.2 Implications for Practice

In addition to the implications for the RE research community, this study suggests a number of insights for practice. While the primary focus of our research was in assessing the validity of the model, the findings highlight a number of issues that need increased attention in practice.

Improving Ownership. A recurring theme in the cases is the question of individual responsibility and ownership of system and process elements. The perception of the project team members was that the complexity they experience makes it difficult to assign responsibility of requirements and design in a comprehensive way. The challenge was particularly acute on the SIS project, with significant concerns about a dearth of ownership. The following quote is illustrative:

> What I see as a big challenge here is the specific ownership of the different modules [by the business stakeholders]. I would say that Student Records is best represented ... but other areas that I worked in, like Academic Advisement, are kind of a gray area of who really owns this. So when the functional consultants left, it's kind of like it was just sitting out in the middle of the floor. Who owns this thing? – SIS Technical Consultant

The resulting perception is that with the rise in overall systems complexity a diffusion of responsibility occurs. The engagement of multiple parties leads individual participants to conclude that ownership will reside with someone else. In the end, the relevant module or process is orphaned, and when problems arise there is no clear-cut owner to guide the resolution. As the complexity of the environment increases, novel strategies must be developed to determine responsibility in a more holistic fashion. Hence, researchers and practitioners alike should focus on the development of enhanced collaboration tools and process measures to support improved ownership.

Focus on Platform Evolution. Another theme was the value of an evolutionary perspective on the development. The emphasis on iteration in the development was central to the IPSI project team's expectations. In contrast to the traditional RE pursuit of complete requirements at the outset of an ISD process [4] the developers held a belief that a set of comprehensive requirements was effectively impossible to reach and they had to nurture tolerance for ambiguity. Indeed, as Hansen et al. [20] observe, an emphasis on evolution has become a critical facet in effective expectations management.

To a significant degree, the focus on evolution reflects lessons drawn from agile methodologies, where a premium is placed on iteration, collaboration, and gradual clarification [8, 26, 33]. In addition, several RE researchers have explored the value of an evolutionary perspective in the monitoring of platform requirements [14, 39, 45]. The clear implication from the present case analyses is that a better understanding of software evolution is a clear necessity for effective RE practices.

Creating Opportunities for Open Exchange. While the projects we studied surfaced a wide range of RE impediments, they also revealed some mechanisms that can be pursued to mitigate these challenges. Most prominently, in both cases we observed benefit in creating arenas for broad exchanges across stakeholders.

In the University SIS project, the team adopted the practice of conducting walkthrough sessions for the project team's members to collectively review all requests for customization. Specifically, the walkthrough sessions routinely included the Project Manager, Technical Lead, all Functional Leads, the Communications Lead, members of the training team, several consultants, and one or members of the technical development team (in addition to the Technical Lead). The specifications discussed in the walkthroughs were generally directly relevant to the work tasks of only a few of those represented, with most discussions being driven by the exchange of two or three individuals. Despite the apparent inefficiency of expecting widespread representation at such sessions, the project team perceived the walkthroughs to be the most important process innovation with respect to the earlier PeopleSoft module implementations (i.e., walkthroughs had not been conducted during the Finance and HCM projects). While acknowledging that the sessions pulled several individuals away from their most pressing tasks, team members felt that the walkthroughs created an engine of creative idea exchange and helped ensure that key project stakeholders were "on the same page" regarding the overall project direction. As the Technical Lead noted: "I like getting everything on the table ahead of time before we spend time working on something and then find out it isn't right."

In the IPSI project, the BSI team enforced a similar structure for communications. While the sessions were not centered on walking through all customization requests, the IPSI project had weekly meetings with participation from all agencies, including the four anchor partners, representatives from the Phase 2 agencies (i.e., those targeted for migration onto the platform in years 2 and 3), and occasionally the State Police, or other ancillary stakeholders. Concerns about inefficiency were balanced by perceptions of value from the shared exchange and level-setting that the meetings enabled. Thus, both of the projects reveal the importance of creating opportunities for open idea exchange among project stakeholders despite the concerns over project efficiency and redundancy that these activities may engender.

As a final point, a critical element of the collective exchange sessions in both projects was the repeated generation of ad hoc scenarios which supported the exploration of application-in-use for the relevant platforms. The scenarios served as an effective mechanism for surfacing assumptions and creating productive conflict, in which stakeholders had to work through their differences. For several years now, the RE research community has recognized the importance of individual scenario generation [35, 41, 43, 52]. However, scenario-based RE has tended to focus on modeling approaches to scenario development, not their effective deployment. The two cases suggest that formal scenario generation needs to advance to situations where it can help direct requirements-oriented inquiries [35].

7 Conclusion

In this study, we have explored the cognitive, social, and complexity-based impediments to effective requirements discovery and validation through two exploratory case studies. The research has a range of implications for RE researchers and practitioners as we wrestle with increasingly complex and heterogeneous environments. The case studies provide an initial evaluation of the applicability of the systemic model of requirements challenges to the practical issues faced by project teams. In this regard, we find that many of the core challenges perceived by practitioners are readily observed in real-world development projects. In addition, the case studies serve to underscore the fundamental interrelatedness of requirements challenges. This finding suggests the need for a more system-based, holistic approach to the requirements challenges. Our case analyses also suggest a number of areas for process and tool innovation in support of multi-party ISD efforts. These include improved mechanisms for establishing task and process ownership in multi-party development, use of evolutionary approaches that allow for the iterative integration of requirements as an artifact comes into existence, and creating opportunities for comprehensive exchanges across organizational, functional, and task-based boundaries.

References

1. Aurum A, Wohlin C (2005) Requirements engineering: setting the context. In: Aurum A, Wohlin C (eds) Engineering and managing software requirements. Springer, Berlin, pp 1–15
2. Bergman M, King J, Lyytinen K (2002) Large-scale requirements analysis revisited: the need for understanding the political ecology of requirements engineering. Reqs Eng 7(3):152–171
3. Berry DM, Lawrence B (1998) Requirements engineering. IEEE Softw 15(2):26–29
4. Boehm B (1984) Verifying and validating software requirements and design specifications. IEEE Softw 1(1):75–88
5. Boehm B, Egyed A, Port D et al (1998) A stakeholder win–win approach to software engineering education. Ann Soft Eng 6(1):295–321
6. Boehm B, Grünbacher P, Briggs R (2007) Developing groupware for requirements negotiation: lessons learned. In: Selby RW (ed) Software engineering: Barry W. Boehm's lifetime contributions to software development, management, and research. Wiley, Hoboken, NJ, pp 301–314

7. Bubenko J Jr (1995) Challenges in requirements engineering. In: Proceedings of the Second IEEE International Symposium on Requirements Engineering (ISRE'95). IEEE, pp 160–162
8. Cockburn A (2002) Agile software development. Addison-Wesley, Reading, MA
9. Crowston K, Kammerer E (1998) Coordination and collective mind in software requirements development. IBM Syst J 37(2):227–246
10. Davis G (1982) Strategies for information requirements determination. IBM Syst J 21(1):4–30
11. Easterbrook S (1993) Domain modelling with hierarchies of alternative viewpoints. In: Proceedings of international symposium on requirements engineering (ISRE'93). IEEE, San Diego, CA, pp 65–72
12. Eisenhardt K (1989) Building theories from case study research. Acad Manage Rev 14(4):532–550
13. El Emam K, Madhavji N (1995) A field study of requirements engineering practices in information systems development. In: Proceedings of second IEEE international symposium on requirements engineering (ISRE'95). IEEE Computer Society, York, ENG, UK, pp 68–80
14. Ernst NA, Mylopoulos J, Wang Y (2009) Requirements evolution and what (research) to do about it. In: Lyytinen KJ, Loucopoulos P, Mylopoulos J, Robinson W (eds) Design requirements engineering: a ten-year perspective. Springer-Verlag, Heidelberg, pp 186–214
15. Etien A, Rolland C (2005) Measuring the fitness relationship. Reqs Eng 10(3):184–197
16. Goguen J, Linde C (1993) Techniques for requirements elicitation. Reqs Eng 93:152–164
17. Gotel O, Finkelstein A (1997) Extended requirements traceability: results of an industrial case study. In: Proceedings of third IEEE international symposium on requirements engineering. IEEE Press, Annapolis, MD, USA, pp 169–178
18. Grünbacher P, Seyff N (2005) Requirements negotiation. In: Aurum A, Wohlin C (eds) Engineering and managing software requirements. Springer-Verlag, Berlin, pp 143–162
19. Hall T, Beecham S, Rainer A (2002) Requirements problems in twelve software companies: an empirical analysis. IEE Proc Softw 149(5):153–160
20. Hansen S, Berate N, Lyytinen KJ (2009) Requirements in the 21st century: current practice & emerging trends. In: Lyytinen KJ, Loucopoulos P, Mylopoulos J, Robinson W (eds) Design requirements engineering: a ten-year perspective. Springer, Heidelberg, pp 44–87
21. Hansen SW, Lyytinen KJ (2010) Challenges in contemporary requirements practice. In: Proceedings of 43rd Hawaii international conference on system. Sciences (HICSS'10). Koloa, HI, USA
22. Hirschheim RA, Klein H-K, Lyytinen K (1995) Information systems development and data modeling: conceptual and philosophical foundations. Cambridge University Press, Cambridge
23. Jarke M, Bubenko J, Rolland C et al (1993) Theories underlying requirements engineering: an overview of NATURE at Genesis. In: Proceedings of IEEE international symposium on requirements engineering (ISRE'93), San Diego, CA, USA, pp 19–31
24. Jarke M, Pohl K (1994) Requirements engineering in 2001: (Virtually) managing a changing reality. Softw Eng J 9(6):257–266
25. Kaindl H, Brinkkemper S, Bubenko JA Jr et al (2002) Requirements engineering and technology transfer: obstacles, incentives and improvement agenda. Reqs Eng 7(3):113–123
26. Kovitz B (2003) Hidden skills that support phased and agile requirements engineering. Reqs Eng 8(2):135–141
27. Lehtola L, Kauppinen M, Kujala S (2004) Requirements prioritization challenges in practice. LNCS 3009, pp 497–508
28. Lindquist C (2005) Fixing the requirements mess. CIO Magazine, pp 52–60
29. Loucopoulos P, Karakostas V (1995) System requirements engineering. McGraw-Hill, New York, NY
30. Lubars M, Potts C, Richter C (1993) A review of the state of the practice in requirements modeling. In: Proceedings of IEEE international symposium on requirements engineering (ISRE'93). IEEE Computer Society, San Diego, CA, USA
31. Lyytinen K (1987) Different perspectives on information systems: problems and solutions. ACM Comp Surv 19(1):5–41
32. Nonaka I (1994) A dynamic theory of organizational knowledge creation. Org Sci 5(1):14–28

33. Orr K (2004) Agile requirements: opportunity or oxymoron? Softw IEEE 21(3):71–73
34. Polanyi M (1966) The tacit dimension. Doubleday, Garden City, NY
35. Potts C, Takahashi K, Anton A (1994) Inquiry-based requirements analysis. Softw IEEE 11(2):21–32
36. Ramesh B, Jarke M (2001) Toward reference models for requirements traceability. IEEE Trans Softw Eng 27(1):58–93
37. Robinson W (1989) Integrating multiple specifications using domain goals. ACM SIGSOFT Softw Eng Notes 14(3):219–226
38. Robinson WN, Fickas S (1994) Automated support for requirements negotiation. AAAI-94 workshop on models of conflict management in cooperative problem solving, Menlo Park, CA, USA, pp 90–96
39. Robinson WN, Fickas S (2009) Designs can talk: a case of feedback for design evolution in assistive technology. In: Lyytinen KJ, Loucopoulos P, Mylopoulos J, Robinson W (eds) Design requirements engineering: a ten-year perspective. Springer, Heidelberg, pp 215–237
40. Rolland C, Nurcan S, Grosz G (1997) A way of working for change processes. In: international research symposium '97 – effective organisations, Dorset, ENG, UK, pp 201–204
41. Rolland C, Souveyet C, Achour CB (1998) Guiding goal modeling using scenarios. IEEE Trans Softw Eng 24(12):1055–1071
42. Rolland C, Achour CB (1998) Guiding the construction of textual use case specifications. Data Knowl Eng 25(1–2):125–160
43. Rolland C, Grosz G, Kla R (1999) Experience with goal-scenario coupling in requirements engineering. In: Proceedings of the IEEE international symposium on requirements engineering (ISRE'99). IEEE Computer Society, Limerick, IRL
44. Rolland C (1999) Requirements engineering for COTS based systems. Inf Softw Tech 41(14):985–990
45. Rolland C, Salinesi C, Etien A (2004) Eliciting gaps in requirements change. Reqs Eng 9(1):1–15
46. Rolland C (2009) Exploring the fitness relationship between system functionality and business needs. In: Lyytinen KJ, Loucopoulos P, Mylopoulos J, Robinson W (eds) Design requirements engineering: a ten-year perspective. Springer, Heidelberg, pp. 305–326
47. Ross DT, Schoman KE Jr (1977) Structured analysis for requirements definition. IEEE Trans Softw Eng 3(1):6–15
48. Sawyer S, Farber J, Spillers R (1996) Supporting the social processes of software development. Inf Tech People 10(1):46–62
49. Sawyer S, Guinan PJ (1998) Software development: processes and performance. IBM Syst J 37(4):552–569
50. Senn JA (1978) A management view of systems analysts: failures and shortcomings. MIS Q 2(3):25–32
51. Siddiqi J, Shekaran MC (1996) Requirements engineering: the emerging wisdom. IEEE Softw 13(2):15–19
52. Sutcliffe AG, Maiden NAM, Minocha S et al (1998) Supporting scenario-based requirements engineering. IEEE Trans Softw Eng 24(12):1072–1088
53. van Lamsweerde A, Darimont R, Letier E (1998) Managing conflicts in goal-driven requirements engineering. IEEE Trans Softw Eng 24(11):908–926
54. van Lamsweerde A (2000) Requirements engineering in the year 00: a research perspective. In: Proceedings of the 22nd international conference on software engineering, Limerick, IRL pp 5–19
55. Wiegers KE (1998) Read my lips: no new models! IEEE Softw 15(5):10–13
56. Woolgar S (1994) Rethinking requirements analysis: some implications of recent research into producer-consumer relationships in IT development. In: Jirotka M, Goguen J (eds) Requirements engineering: social and technical issues. Academic, London, pp 201–216
57. Yin RK (2003) Case study research: design and methods. Sage Publications Inc, Thousand Oaks, CA
58. Zave P (1997) Classification of research efforts in requirements engineering. ACM Comp Surv 29(4):315–321

Semantic Requirements Engineering

Motoshi Saeki

Abstract Requirements engineering (RE) techniques play a crucial role in information systems development processes. There are many excellent techniques of RE to assist requirements analysts and stakeholders in producing requirements specification of higher quality, and some of them are put into practice in industry. However, one of the issues of these RE techniques is that they do not handle semantic aspects of requirements. If we can deal with the meaning of requirements by using automated techniques, we can get more effective RE techniques to produce requirements specifications of higher quality. In this chapter, we consider an ontology as a semantic domain so as to provide the meaning for requirements, and discuss the potentials of the RE techniques using an ontology as a semantic basis. Especially, we illustrate an extension of goal-oriented requirements analysis where this idea is embedded, i.e. we provide the semantics for goal descriptions written in natural language using a mapping from them to an ontology. The inference mechanisms of the ontology allow us to decompose a goal into sub-goals and to find missing goals. Furthermore, in this chapter we discuss the possibilities of the techniques to support the other activities of RE processes using this ontological technique, e.g. measuring quality metrics and controlling versions of requirements from a semantic view. Due to similarity to Semantic Web techniques, we call a family of these engineering techniques *Semantic Requirements Engineering* in this chapter.

1 Introduction

Requirements engineering (RE) techniques play a crucial role in information systems (IS) development processes. In usual IS development like waterfall style, the requirements for an information system are elicited in the early step of its

M. Saeki (✉)
Department of Computer Science, Tokyo Institute of Technology, Ookayama 2-12-1-W8-83, Meguro, Tokyo 152-8552, Japan
e-mail: saeki@se.cs.titech.ac.jp

S. Nurcan et al. (eds.), *Intentional Perspectives on Information Systems Engineering*,
DOI 10.1007/978-3-642-12544-7_4,

development process. If a requirements specification of lower quality was constructed in this process, it would be propagated to the latter steps and as a result, final products of lower quality, e.g. not satisfying customers or users, could be produced. In this worst case, developers should abandon all of the developed products and re-do their process from the beginning, i.e. requirements elicitation. It wasted much more money, human resources and development time.

Roughly speaking, a RE process can be divided into four activities; (1) requirements elicitation, (2) requirements specification, (3) requirements validation and (4) requirements management. There are many excellent techniques of RE to assist requirements analysts and stakeholders in producing requirements specifications of higher quality during each of the above activities, and some of them are put into practice in industry. However, one of the issues of these RE techniques is that many of them do not handle semantic aspects of requirements. If we can deal with the meaning of requirements by using automated techniques, we can get more effective RE techniques to produce requirements specifications of higher quality. As an example, consider a part of the model of a lift control system shown in Fig. 1. The model consists of a sequence diagram specifying a scenario of lift behavior. Although it is syntactically correct as a sequence diagram, it includes an incorrect part, i.e. a lift does not stop itself before opening a door, and the lift object should have sent a message "stop" to itself in the sequence diagram. We can find this missing message sending, because we understand the meaning of words "Lift" (object), "up", "open" etc. which figure in the diagram and know that it is very danger for passengers to open a door of a lift while it is moving. This point results not from the syntax of sequence diagrams but from the semantics of the description. To detect this kind of incorrectness, we should consider the semantics of a subject domain, i.e. domain semantics in our technology.

Note that we can have a wide variety of subject domains. In this example, we focus on the domain of lift control, where the information system to be developed operates, and it is termed the problem domain. Consider the reason why "up" and "open" are specified as messages in the sequence diagram of Fig. 1. We know that the concept of messages in sequence diagrams represents actions and that the words "up" and "open" also denote actions. As well as the meaning of these words, we

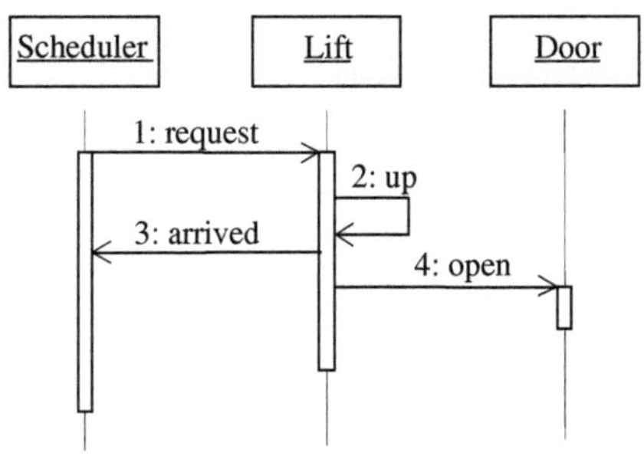

Fig. 1 A sequence diagram for a lift control system

should know the meaning of elements such as Message and Object included in sequence diagrams, in order to write the diagrams easy to understand. Thus, we can consider the semantics of elements of sequence diagrams, i.e. the semantics of a meta model of sequence diagrams, and this is the case where our subject domain is meta models, not a problem domain of lift control.

In this chapter, we propose one of the techniques to provide semantics to requirements and RE techniques. We consider an ontology as a semantic domain so as to provide the meaning for requirements and discuss the potentials of the RE techniques using an ontology as a semantic basis. More concretely, we adopt the technique of denotational semantics and consider mappings from artifacts (incl. requirements) to the ontology. An ontology consists of a thesaurus and inference rules on it, and the thesaurus includes the words and their relationships. Each word in the thesaurus is frequently used in a certain subject domain and it denotes an atomic semantic element that has a unique meaning in the domain. We can map artifacts to the words in the thesaurus and the meaning is provided for the artifacts by the mapped words. As a result, we can reason about semantic properties of the artifacts by using the inference rules on the words. This is a basic idea in this chapter. As a result, we can have a light-weight semantic processing of artifacts for assisting RE activities, e.g. semantic consistency checking of requirements, retrieving the requirements that are semantically similar as reusable components, etc. Our technique is inspired by the technique of Semantic Web [20], where HTML texts are annotated with semantic tags derived from ontological components. In Semantic Web, the meaning of information on the web is defined using the annotated semantic tags so as to make it possible to analyze and process the web contents by computer. The semantic tags represent the meaning of information where they are annotated. In our technique, any kind of artifacts related to RE process, including specified requirements with natural language sentences or UML diagrams, meta models, etc., are annotated with (mapped to) semantic tags (ontological components) so that the existing RE techniques can semantically process them by computer. Thus we can use the word *Semantic Requirements Engineering* by the similarity to the idea of Semantic Web.

The rest of the chapter is organized as follows. The next section presents the essential idea of our approach more concretely. As a concrete application, in Sect. 3 we show an extended version of goal-oriented requirements analysis (GORA) technique combined with ontologies. GORA techniques are for eliciting and specifying requirements and one of the major RE techniques supporting the first and the second in the four activities mentioned above. In Sects. 4 and 5, we illustrate the other applications of our technique in a different activity, requirements management. Section 4 presents metrics to measure the quality of requirements specifications considering their meaning, while we discuss the version control based on the meaning of requirements, so called semantic version control. We would like to show how our technique using ontologies can reinforce the existing RE techniques in each of the four activities, throughout the whole of RE processes.

2 Using Ontologies

Ontology technologies are frequently applied to many subject domains nowadays [3, 21]. As mentioned in [9], we consider an ontology as a thesaurus of words and inference rules on it, where the words in the thesaurus represent concepts and the inference rules operate on the relationships on the words. Each concept of an ontology can be considered as a semantic atomic element that has a unique meaning in a subject domain [14]. That is to say, the thesaurus part of the ontology plays a role of a semantic domain in denotational semantics as mentioned in Sect. 1, and the inference rules help semantic processing by computer [6].

Below, let's consider how a requirements analyst uses an ontology of a subject domain for completing a sequence diagram. During drawing the sequence diagram, the analyst should map its elements into atomic concepts of the ontology as shown in Fig. 2. In the figure, the ontology of a subject domain is written in the form of class diagrams. For example, the message "aaa" in the sequence diagram is mapped into the concepts A and B. Formally, the analyst specifies a semantic mapping F where F (aaa) = {A, B}. According to the notation of web contents, we can use the semantic tags which have the same names as the mapped concepts and write this semantic mapping like <A><B>aaa</B></A> in the sequence diagram. The sequence diagram may be incrementally improved, and logical inference on the ontology suggests to the analyst which parts she or he should incrementally improve or refine. In the figure, although the sequence diagram includes the concept A at the item "aaa", it does not have the concept C, which is caused by A. The inference resulted from "C is caused by A" and "A is included" suggests to the analyst that a diagram element having C, e.g. a message "ccc" should be added to the sequence diagram. Note that a meta model of sequence diagrams can define their abstract syntax and we can check any sequence diagram using the meta model. However, this check is on syntactical aspects only.

Figure 3 illustrates a semantic mapping of the lift control system shown in Fig. 1. Since we check the semantic aspect of the sequence diagram specifying a lift control system, we use an ontology of lift-control domain as shown in the right part of the

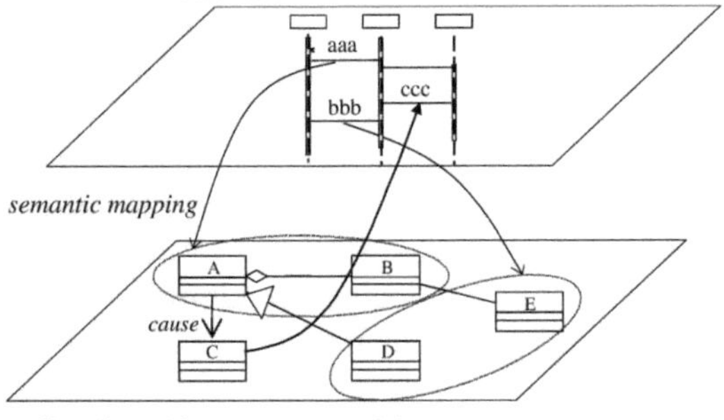

Fig. 2 Basic idea: semantic mapping

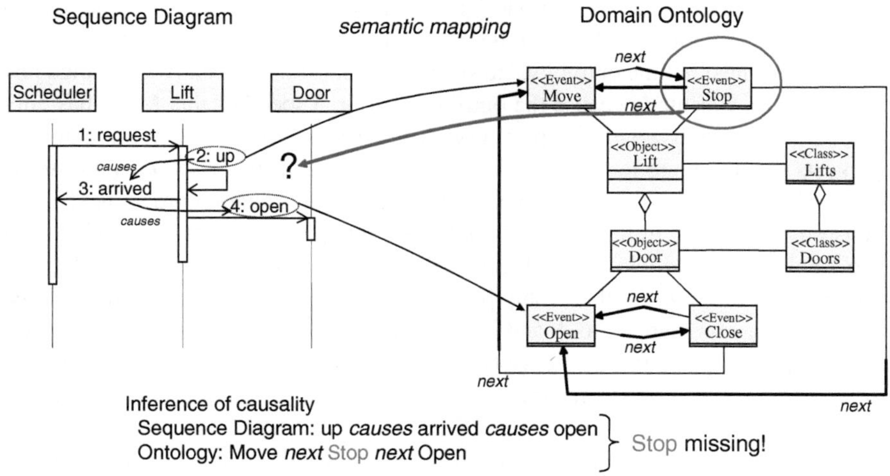

Fig. 3 A sequence diagram and a domain ontology

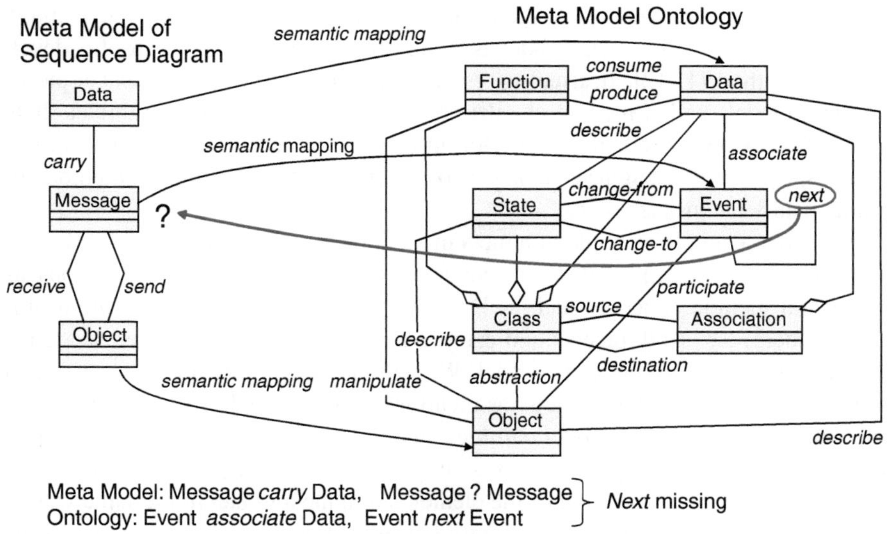

Fig. 4 Meta model and meta model ontology

figure. We will explain stereotypes attached in classes of the ontology in the next example of a meta model ontology shown in Fig. 4.

The analyst maps the messages "up" and "open" in the sequence diagram into Move and Open concepts of the ontology, when developing the diagram, as shown in Fig. 3. Suppose that the execution order of message sending in a sequence diagram is represented with the relationship "causes" between messages. This relationship would be included in the meta model of sequence diagrams. And she or he tries to map "causes" relationship between the messages "up" and "open" into the association of type "next" of the ontology. However, no events but Stop can be executed just after Move is executed because the ontology of Fig. 3 specifies that Move has only one outgoing "next" relationship to Stop. Thus the inference rule on the ontology suggests that there are no "next" relationships between Move and Open and some events should be added to keep semantic consistency of execution order "next" relationship. Obviously, in this case the analyst should add the message Stop between "up" and "open", which a Lift object sends to a Door object. The used inference rule is "If there is a *next* relationship between the concepts A and B in the ontology, then the elements mapped to A and B in the model, if any, should have the association mapped to *next* among themselves". Thus, we can solve the problems related to semantic incorrectness, illustrated in Sect. 1, using an ontology as a semantic domain.

We will show another example in a different subject domain below. In the above example, we used the ontology of lift control domain, i.e. a problem domain where the system to be developed operates. On the other hand, this second example needs the ontology of meta models to provide semantics of meta models to help a method engineer (engineer for developing meta models) in constructing a meta model of semantically higher quality. A meta model defines an IS development method, and the quality of the meta model is a significant factor to get a useful development method [1, 12]. In usual cases, a method engineer usually selects pieces of meta models called method chunks or method fragments, and assembles them into a development method suitable for an IS development project [2, 10]. In this process, the method engineer should avoid constructing meaningless methods or semantically inconsistent ones.

Consider a simple example of a meta model of Sequence Diagram of UML. The left part of Fig. 4 depicts the meta model of Sequence Diagram, and it consists of several method concepts such as Data, Message and Object, and relationships among them, e.g. send, receive and carry. Note that, for simplicity, we used Class Diagram to represent this meta model. We will check the semantic consistency of the meta model using the ontology as mentioned above. We design an ontology for meta models, called *meta model ontology*, and the right part of Fig. 4 depicts a part of a meta model ontology, which is a simplified version of [4]. The meta model ontology can give the meaning of the elements of a meta model in the same way as the technique mentioned above. Therefore, a subject domain of the ontology is the domain of meta models. While developing a meta model, a method engineer maps its elements into a part of the meta model ontology. In the example of the figure, she or he maps Data and Message in the meta model into the ontological concepts Data and Event respectively. The relationship "carry" between Data and Message can be mapped into "associate", because "associate" is a relationship between Data and Event in the meta model ontology. The relation among these three elements Data, Message and "carry" is consistent. However, there are no self-relationships on Message, while the meta model ontology has a self-relationship "next" on Event, which Message is mapped into. This can be semantically inconsistent and the method engineer is suggested to add a relationship on Message to keep semantic consistency of the meta model.

By establishing a semantic mapping from meta model elements into the ontology, we can avoid producing semantically inconsistent meta models [2]. The meta model ontology has several inference rules to keep semantic consistency on meta models. In this example, the used inference rule is "If concept A and B are mapped into MA and MB in the meta model ontology and there is a relationship MRAB between MA and MB, then the relationship that can be mapped into MRAB exists in the meta model."

Note that we should explain the stereotypes attached to the domain ontology in Fig. 3. These stereotypes result from the names of concepts of a meta model ontology to clarify the relation between the domain ontology and the meta model ontology. For example, an ontological concept Stop has a stereotype Event in Fig. 3 and the type Event is the same as the concept Event of the meta model ontology shown in Fig. 4.

3 Application to GORA

Goal-oriented requirements analysis (GORA) methods are one of the promising approaches to elicit requirements [19, 23] and are being amplified so as to put them into practice [14]. In this approach, customers' and users' needs are modeled as goals to be achieved by a software-intensive system that will be developed, and the goals are decomposed and refined into a set of more concrete sub-goals. After finishing a requirements elicitation process, the analyst obtains an acyclic (cycle-free) directed graph called *goal graph*. Its nodes express goals to be achieved by the system, and its edges represent logical dependency relationships between the connected goals. We have two types of goal decomposition; one is AND decomposition and another is OR. In AND decomposition, if all of the sub-goals are achieved, their parent goal can be achieved or satisfied. On the other hand, in OR decomposition, the achievement of at least one sub-goal leads to the achievement of its parent goal. Root goals, having no parents in a graph, expresses the needs that the customers would like to fulfill ultimately and the analyst tries to achieve them by combining sub-goals. Figure 5 shows an example of a goal graph to elicit requirements of a seat reservation system of trains, which is a part of a screenshot generated by our GORA supporting tool [16]. In this figure, a root goal N1 "Seat reservation system required" is decomposed into three sub-goals N2, N30 and N4 in AND-decomposition. The arc crossing over edges shows AND decomposition.

In order to construct a goal graph of semantically higher quality, knowledge of a problem domain where the system to be developed operates, so called domain knowledge, is necessary. In Fig. 5, stakeholders and/or an analyst, who are constructing the goal graph, need the knowledge of a reservation business domain and a train service domain, etc.

The example of using our ontological technique is the application of an ontology as a source of domain knowledge for requirements elicitation in the GORA

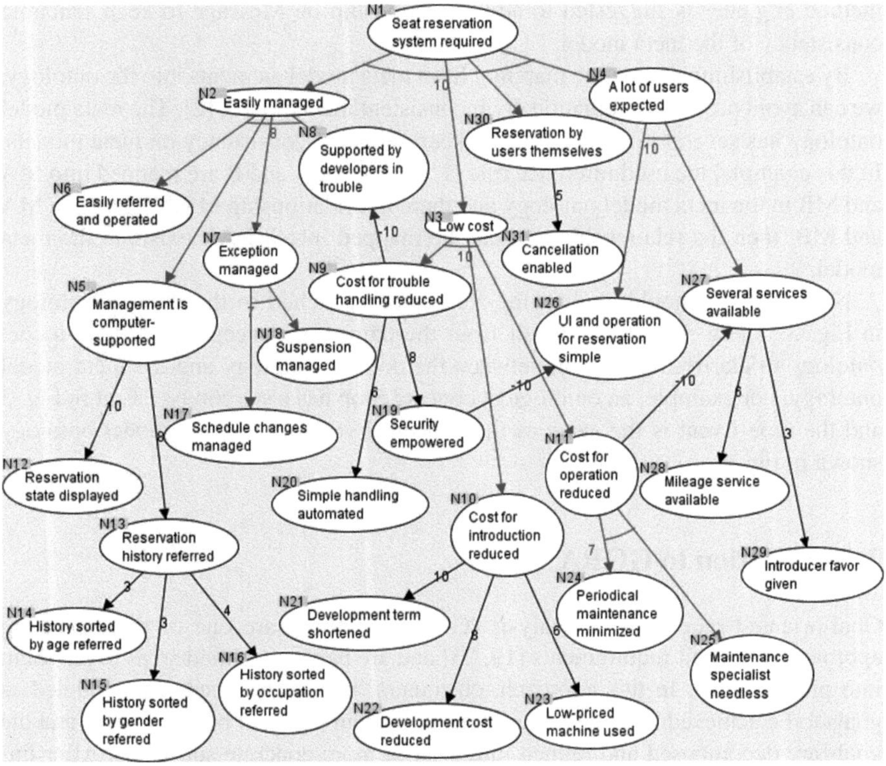

Fig. 5 A goal graph of a train seat reservation system

method. During constructing a goal, when a goal corresponding to an ontological concept of the ontology appears, the supporting tool of GORA shows the other ontological concepts relevant to it by using an inference mechanism, and helps the discovery of new goals and their refinements to sub-goals [18]. Figure 6 depicts how a domain ontology helps stakeholders and an analyst to decompose and refine goals.

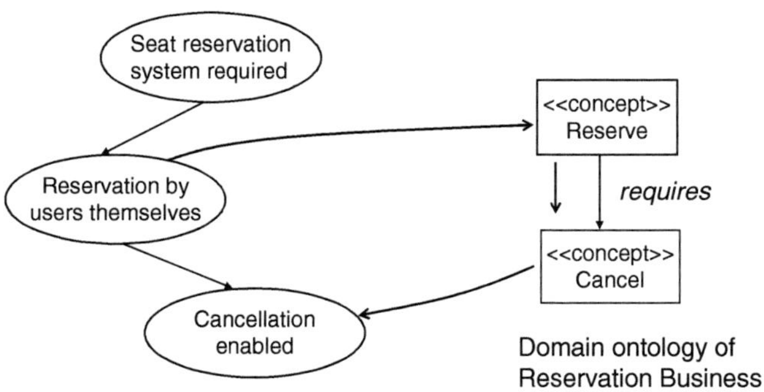

Fig. 6 Using an ontology in GORA

Our supporting tool loads a domain ontology of reservation business, and suggests missing goals as shown in the following steps. First, the tool makes each term in a goal description correspond to concepts in the ontology. Second, it finds missing concepts based on the corresponding concepts and relationships such as "requires" among the ontology. In the figure, the tool extracts the word "Reservation" from the goal "Reservation by users themselves" and establishes a map from the extracted word to the ontological concept Reserve. The tool traces the relationship "requires" between Reserve and Cancel in the ontology, and find that the goal which can be made to correspond to Cancel is missing. And then by the suggestion of the tool, the analyst can add a new goal "Cancellation enabled" as a sub-goal.

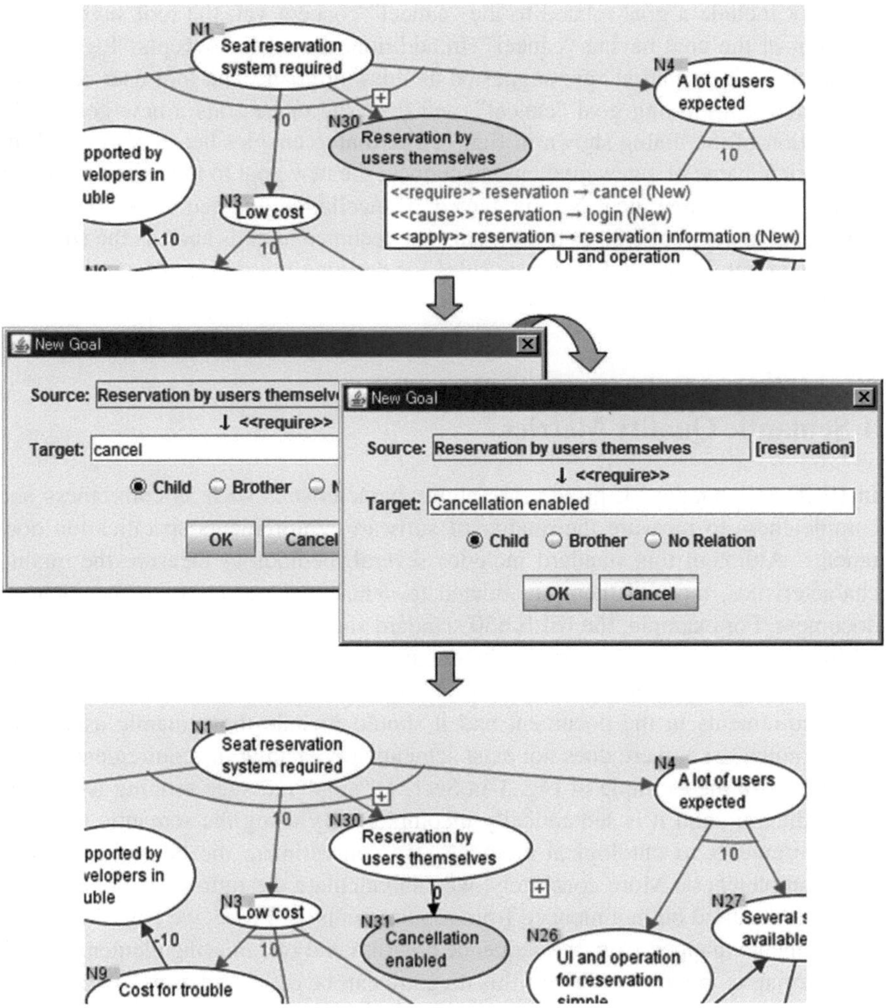

Fig. 7 A supporting tool for goal and ontology oriented requirements elicitation

Figure 7 shows the process for the tool user to add a missing goal to a goal graph. After loading the ontology of reservation business domain and then starting inference, the tool detects the candidates of missing goals. The mark of "boxed +" symbol that is attached to a goal shows that there may be missing goals related to it, and the tool user can refer to the candidates of missing goals by clicking the mark with a mouse. In Fig. 7, our tool tells the user that goal N30 "Reservation by users themselves" may have missing goals because the mark of "boxed +" symbol appears in its upper left area. Clicking the mark allows her or him to see a list of the candidates of missing goals, and as a result three candidates are shown. The ontology used in this example contains the concepts "reservation", "cancel" and a relationship "requires" between them, as shown in Fig. 6. This part of the ontology denotes that "reservation" requires "cancel". Since the current version of the graph does not include a goal related to the "cancel" concept yet, the tool suggests the addition of the goal having "cancel". In addition, the other concepts "log in" and "reservation information" are suggested as missing goals. The tool user accepts a candidate of a missing goal "cancel", and then she or he adds a new goal at the suggestion of the dialog shown in Fig. 7. The dialog enables her or him to fill the appropriate name of a new goal, and to connect the new goal to the existing goal(s). In this case, the new goal N31 is named "Cancellation enabled", and the goal is connected to the goal N30 as a sub-goal. The technical details such as the structure of domain ontologies and inference rules for deriving missing goals are discussed in [18].

4 Semantic Quality Metrics

In IEEE 830 standard [5], there are eight characteristics such as correctness and completeness to measure the quality of software requirements specification documents. Although this standard includes several methods to measure the quality characteristics, most of them are related to syntactical aspects of a specification document. For example, the IEEE 830 standard says that we should check whether all figures, tables, and diagrams in the document are labeled and referred, in order to measure its completeness. In the usual sense, completeness denotes no missing requirements in the document and it should include the semantic aspects of the documents, i.e. there does not exist semantically lacking of requirements in the document. In the example of Fig. 1 in Sect. 1, "stop" message sending is missing in the diagram and it is semantically incomplete. By using the semantic mapping of requirements to ontological elements, we can estimate the degree of semantic incompleteness. More concretely, we can calculate the ratio of the ontological elements required but not mapped from requirements. In Fig. 3, we have 5 ontological elements mapped from the sequence diagram and one missing element "stop". Thus semantic incompleteness of this diagram can be estimated as $1/5 = 20\%$. We can define the other quality characteristics based on semantic aspects using our ontological approach, and readers can find their details in [6].

5 Semantic Version Control

Requirements changes frequently occur after a requirements specification is completed and even during the requirements elicitation step, for various reasons such as changing business goals and improving information technology. In this situation, it is a crucial issue to manage requirements changes. More concretely, to record change histories and rationales, to analyze impacts and change propagations for keeping consistency etc., developers, including requirements analysts, should have various versions of elicited and specified requirements and manage them in their development project. The techniques for version control are significant to support their tasks by using a computerized tool, and in fact, CVS and Subversion are widely used as computerized version control tools for source codes. These tools store a current version of an artifact and the differences (so called delta) between adjacent versions in a repository, so that it can recover the older versions by applying the stored deltas to the current one. However, it is difficult to use these practical version control tools for managing requirements, because they deal with syntactical aspects of text documents and adopt line based management, i.e. the delta is generated line by line. Requirements are modeled and specified not only with natural language texts but also with tables and diagrams, and they are informal descriptions. Handling semantic differences between two versions of requirements is very useful to trace the requirements changes and evolution. The differences in the ontologies mapped from adjacent versions of the requirements represent the semantic differences between these requirements.

Figure 8 illustrates the delta of artifacts (requirements) and ontology delta (differences of the mapped ontological elements). In the figure, Vi ($0 \leq i \leq n$) and Oi stand for the version Vi of the artifact and the ontological elements mapped from Vi

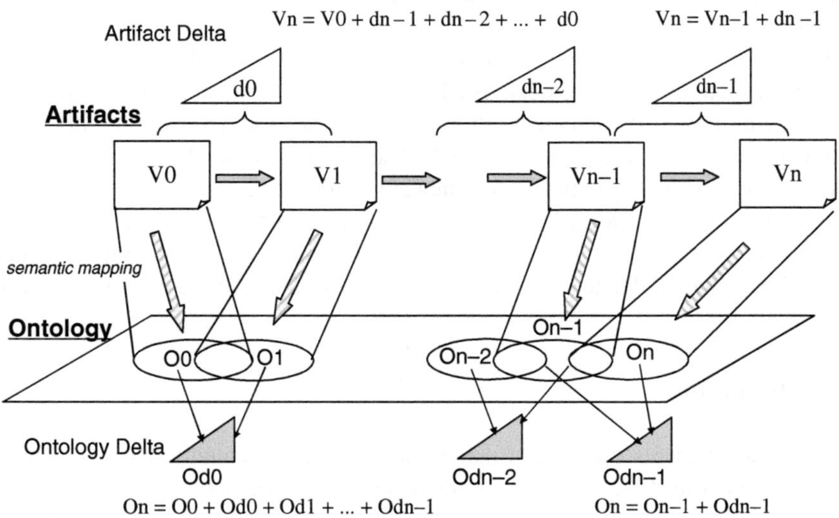

Fig. 8 Difference deltas in a version control

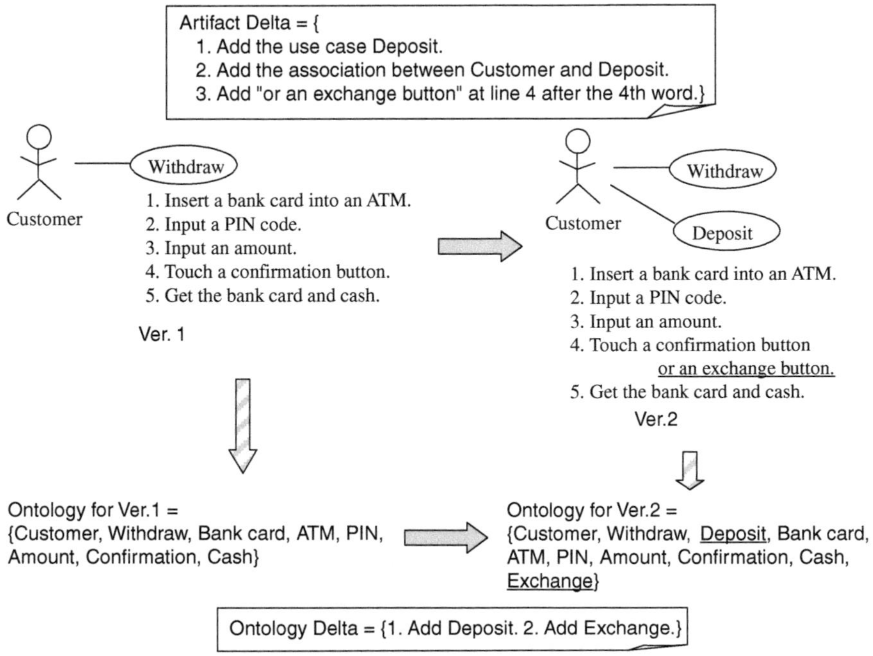

Fig. 9 An example of semantic version control

respectively. The artifact delta dj ($0 \leq j \leq n-1$) is produced as the difference between Vj and Vj+1, while Odj is the difference of ontological elements between Odj and Odj+1, i.e. ontology delta. These ontology deltas allow us to capture the changes of artifacts semantically and reasoning about semantic aspects of their changes can be automated.

Figure 9 shows the simple example. Suppose that we model a banking business and specify it as a use case model. The left hand of the figure depicts a use case diagram having only one use case Withdraw and its use case description with natural language sentences. A requirements analyst adds the use case Deposit and the function of exchange during Withdraw in a newer version Ver.2. As a result, the ontology delta consists of the addition of two ontological concepts Deposit and Exchange. By tracing the ontology deltas, the analyst can find what functions had been semantically added, deleted or modified in which versions of the use case models.

6 Conclusion

This chapter presents the idea of using ontologies as a semantic basis in requirements engineering (RE) so as to automate semantic processing in RE techniques. As mentioned in each section, this idea is not new and it already appears in specific applications such as the support of missing requirements sentences [7] and of suggesting sub-goals in GORA [18], semantics of meta models [2, 4] and a dictionary having domain specific vocabularies called Language Extended Lexicon [8] etc. However, we did not argue these pieces of individual usages of ontologies but the possibilities of ontology usage as a semantic basis throughout RE processes in this chapter. In fact, Sect. 3 presented the support for requirements elicitation and specification activities, i.e. the first and second ones mentioned in Sect. 1. We discussed the techniques for requirements management in Sect. 4, quality assurance of requirements, and in Sect. 5, change management of requirements. As for requirements validation, readers can understand that we also mentioned the technique to detect missing requirements, e.g. checking completeness of requirements specifications, in Sects. 2, 3 and 4. Thus we have illustrated several techniques for the four activities in RE processes, whose common basis is on providing lightweight semantics for RE artifacts using ontologies. In [11] and Softwiki project, the authors designed a Requirements Engineering Ontology called SWORE by collecting ontological concepts such as Functional Requirement, Stakeholder, Scenario, Goal etc., which appeared in the existing RE techniques. The aim of this project seems to be the construction of a common vocabulary of RE techniques for distributed collaborative development of requirements specifications, and is different from ours. Although providing common meaning of terminology of RE techniques is one of the significant benefits of using ontologies, deeper semantic analysis such as inferences on ontologies allows us to develop and manage requirements of higher quality as mentioned in this chapter. Future research agenda are developing more applications in RE processes and constructing a Semantic Repository of Requirements to achieve our idea in practice.

As for the Semantic Repository, we have discussed reusability of semantically annotated requirements in [15] and proposed the unified ontology with the other types of ontologies for implementation structures such as architecture ontology, framework ontology, etc. Furthermore, the technique to retrieve reusable parts of requirements was discussed. We should elaborate these techniques to achieve a practical semantic repository, as shown in Fig. 10.

In a current version of our idea, we use a word or a phrase as an ontological concept. In the example of Fig. 3, we used the single word Stop to denote the concept of a stop action. However, a word itself is less informative and includes too general concepts. Although we can express that a stop action follows a move action, we cannot specify that a stop action and a move action should occur on the same lift in this action causality. We should focus not only on words but also on the connections among the words to represent ontological concepts. The application of Case Grammar is one of the promising approaches [13, 17]. In the case grammar approach, ontological concepts can be defined as case frames as shown in Fig. 11, and the relationships among ontological concepts are considered as the relationships among case frames [22]. In the figure, the slots of case frames are represented with variables, e.g. x, and filled with concrete words which appear in requirements. The same variables in the case frames should denote the same objects. For example, the same word "lift" should be assigned to two occurrences of variable x in the case frames "move" and "stop", and a self-loop of a "stop" message sending is suggested to add in the sequence diagram. The usage of Case Grammar approach is also one of the significant research directions.

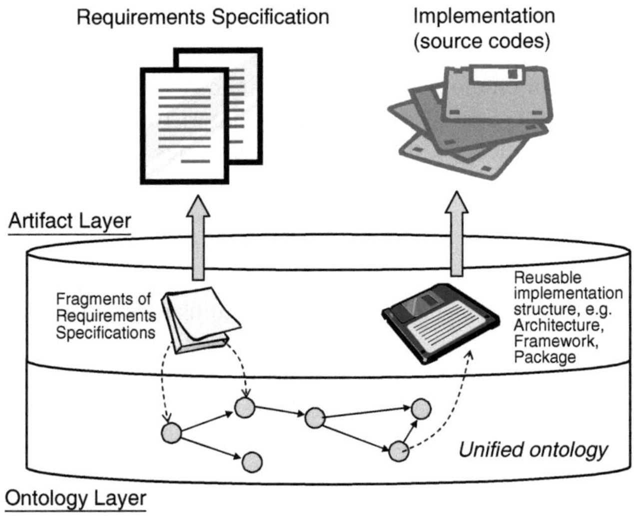

Fig. 10 Semantic repository

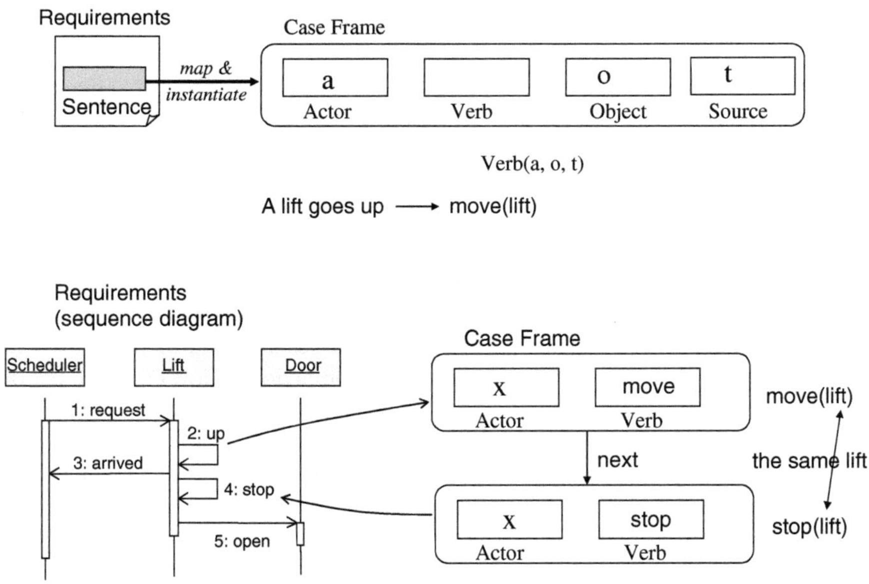

Fig. 11 Using a case frame as an ontological concept

References

1. Brinkkemper S (1996) Method engineering : engineering of information systems development methods and tools. Info Softw Technol 38(4):275–280
2. Brinkkemper S, Saeki M, Harmsen F (1999) Meta-modelling based assembly techniques for situational method engineering. Info Systems 24(3):209–228
3. Gruninger M, Lee J. (2002) Ontology: applications and design. Commun ACM, New York, 45(2):39–41
4. Harmsen F (1997) Situational method engineering. Moret Ernst & Young Management Consultants
5. IEEE (1998) IEEE recommended practice for software requirements specifications. Technical report, IEEE Std. 830–1998
6. Kaiya H, Saeki M (2005) Ontology based requirements analysis: lightweight semantic processing approach. In: Proceedings of QSIC 2005, Melbourne, Australia, IEEE Computer Society, Los Alamitos, CA, pp 223–230
7. Kaiya H, Saeki M (2006) Using domain ontology as domain knowledge for requirements elicitation. In: Proceedings of 14th IEEE international requirements engineering conference (RE'06), Minneapolis, USA, IEEE Computer Society, Los Alamitos, CA, pp 189–198
8. Leite JCSP, Rossi G, Balaguer F, Maiorana V, Kaplan G, Hadad G, Oliveros A (1997) Enhancing a requirements baseline with scenarios. In: Proceedings of the 3rd IEEE international symposium on requirements engineering (RE97), Annapolis, USA, IEEE Computer Society, Los Alamitos, CA, pp 44–53
9. Maedche A (2002) Ontology learning for the semantic web. Kluwer, Norwell, MA
10. Ralyte J, Rolland C (2001) An assembly process model for method engineering. In: Proceedings of CAiSE 2001, Interlaken, Switzerland. LNCS, vol 2068. Springer, Heidelberg, Berlin, pp 267–283
11. Riechert T, Lauenroth K, Lehmann J, Auer S (2007) Towards semantic based requirements engineering. In: Proceedings of the 7th international conference on knowledge management (I-KNOW'07), Toulouse, France
12. Rolland C (1997) A primer for method engineering. In: Proceedings of the INFORSID conference, Toulouse, France
13. Rolland C, Proix C (1992) A natural language approach for requirements engineering. In: Proceedings of CAiSE 1992, Paris, France. LNCS, vol 593. Springer, Heidelberg, Berlin, pp 257–277
14. Rolland C, Souveyet C, Ben Achour C (1998) Guiding goal modeling using scenarios. IEEE Trans Softw Eng 24(12):1055–1071
15. Saeki M (2004) Ontology-based software development techniques. ERCIM News, 58. http://www.ercim.org/publication/Ercim_News/enw58/saeki.html. Accessed 6 May 2010
16. Saeki M, Hayashi S, Kaiya H (2009) A tool for attributed goal-oriented requirements analysis. In: Proceedings of 24th IEEE/ACM international conference on automated software engineering (ASE2009), Auckland, Newzealand, Conference Publishing Services, Los Alamitos, CA, pp 670–672
17. Saeki M, Horai H, Enomoto H (1989) Software development process from natural language specification. In: Proceedings of 11th international conference on software engineering, Pittsburgh, USA, IEEE Computer Society Press, Los Alamitos, CA, pp 64–73
18. Shibaoka M, Kaiya H, Saeki M (2007) GOORE: goal-oriented and ontology driven requirements elicitation method. ER 2007 workshops, Auckland, Newzealand. LNCS, vol 4802. Springer, Heidelberg, Berlin, pp 225–234
19. van Lamsweerde A (2001) Goal-oriented requirements engineering: a guided tour. In: Proceedings of 5th international symposium on requirements engineering (RE'01), Toronto, Canada, IEEE Computer Society, Los Alamitos, CA, pp 249–263
20. W3C Semantic Web Activity. http://www.3.org/2001/sw/

21. Wand Y (1996) Ontology as a foundation for meta-modelling and method engineering. Info Softw Technol 38(4):281–288
22. Watahiki K, Saeki M (2001) Scenario patterns based on case grammar approach. In: Proceedings of 5th IEEE international symposium on requirements engineering (RE01), Toronto, Canada, IEEE Computer Society, Los Alamitos, CA, pp 300–301
23. Yu E (1997) Towards modeling and reasoning support for early-phase requirements engineering. In: Proceedings of 3rd IEEE international symposium on requirements engineering (RE'97), Annapolis, USA, IEEE Computer Society, Los Alamitos, CA, pp 226–235

Goal-Based Domain Modeling as a Basis for Cross-Disciplinary Systems Engineering

Matthias Jarke, Hans W. Nissen, Thomas Rose, and Dominik Schmitz

Abstract Small and medium-sized enterprises (SMEs) are important drivers for innovation. In particular, project-driven SMEs that closely cooperate with their customers have specific needs in regard to information engineering of their development process. They need a fast requirements capture since this is most often included in the (unpaid) offer development phase. At the same time, they need to maintain and reuse the knowledge and experiences they have gathered in previous projects extensively as it is their core asset. The situation is complicated further if the application field crosses disciplinary boundaries. To bridge the gaps and perspectives, we focus on shared goals and dependencies captured in models at a conceptual level. Such a model-based approach also offers a smarter connection to subsequent development stages, including a high share of automated code generation. In the approach presented here, the agent- and goal-oriented formalism *i** is therefore extended by domain models to facilitate information organization. This extension permits a domain model-based similarity search, and a model-based transformation towards subsequent development stages. Our approach also addresses the evolution of domain models reflecting the experiences from completed projects. The approach is illustrated with a case study on software-intensive control systems in an SME of the automotive domain.

1 Introduction

The alignment or fit between business requirements and organizational information systems has been a continuing concern in the business information systems field for over twenty years [36]. The representations, processes, and domain contexts of requirements engineering have been advertised as the bridge from business needs to IS functionality [19]. However, the emphasis shifts from greenfield development towards complex system evolution in a complex and quickly evolving context.

M. Jarke (✉)
Information Systems, RWTH Aachen University, Ahornstraße 55, D-52056 Aachen, Germany
e-mail: jarke@dbis.rwth-aachen.de

S. Nurcan et al. (eds.), *Intentional Perspectives on Information Systems Engineering*,
DOI 10.1007/978-3-642-12544-7_5, © Springer-Verlag Berlin Heidelberg 2010

Managing the fitness relationship between business needs and system functionality is becoming a continuous task. Rolland [36] proposes an explicit management of the fitness relationship as a formal model mapping between business models and system models.

As we are moving into the era of embedded software-intensive systems, the mapping between business goals and software technologies needs to be augmented with a cross-disciplinary mapping within the systems themselves, in particular relating hardware systems (with aspects from mechanical and electrical engineering) with the software systems that control and monitor them. Such tasks are by no means limited to large companies e.g. in the utilities, automotive, or aeronautical fields. In fact, much of the innovation comes from small and medium engineering enterprises (SMEs) who either sell products directly to end customers or supply the big players with innovative designs and components based on inter-disciplinary development projects. The research question addressed in this chapter is therefore how we can extend the idea of fitness to such project-driven cross-disciplinary SMEs.

Important success factors for project-driven SMEs are their flexibility, innovativeness, and customer orientation [4, 11, 21]. For them, requirements engineering activities are part of the offer development where timing and cost constraints are very tight. Pre-planned product line engineering [33] unfortunately does not work for these SMEs without abandoning much of their customer-orientation and flexibility, since they cannot commit to the necessary prerequisite of some domain stability [21]. On the other hand the knowledge an SME has gained throughout previous projects is its core asset and must be reused extensively during later projects [3]. Accordingly, they need means to keep track and internally make available their extensive knowledge [24]. Eventually, this knowledge must be easily adaptable and extensible in order to evolve with new innovations and gained experiences.

The situation is complicated further if the business of the SME is interdisciplinary. A typical example is control system development [1] in automotive design. More and more car control functionality – such as engine management or driver assistance systems – is realized in software on electronic control units [7]. Only this way, quality goals such as comfort, safety, and energy efficiency can be tackled. But the required interplay of theories, methods and tools from control engineering and software engineering, and the resulting interworking of people with different world views and concerns, demands more advanced modeling and management methods.

To address these issues, this chapter presents a *goal- and dependency focused domain model based approach to SME-oriented requirements management*. The approach takes agent goals and their interdependencies as a starting point, building on the *i** framework [45], but elaborates them to a fully model-based domain-specific information management approach. It consists of:

- a simple, but suitably expressive common notation based on *i** that allows to capture the requirements of all disciplines,
- a domain model offering a collection of functional requirements patterns as well as non-functional goals for a particular (sub-)domain and tailored to a particular SME,

- a fast requirements capture process using the domain model as starting point but permitting project-specific extensions,
- a domain model-based similarity search identifying similar finalized projects as sources for reuse,
- a means to enable domain model evolution, i.e.
  - a mechanism to synchronize existing requirement models with a changing domain model (in order to keep similarity search results accurate) and
  - a mechanism to detect candidates for domain model extensions and reductions from the project history, and last not least
- a transformation to subsequent modeling formalisms as a means to quality assurance and a seamless integration into the overall development process.

In summary, our approach adopts a goal and dependency oriented modeling formalism suited to tackle interdisciplinarity and makes specific domain knowledge available as concrete models. This really puts the domain knowledge at the center of support. The suitability and effectiveness of the approach is exemplified by applying it to control systems in the automotive domain.

The chapter is organized as follows. In Sect. 2 the field of control system development is introduced to instantiate the abstract challenges for interdisciplinary, project-driven SMEs for the requirements engineering phase of a combined software and control systems development approach. In Sect. 3 the details of the domain model based requirements engineering approach are presented. The role of the domain model is elaborated especially with regard to how it helps SMEs to address their particular problems. Section 4 discusses related work. Section 5 summarizes the approach and outlines the chances for applying the developed solution to other similar fields.

2 Case Study: Automotive Control Systems Development

Control system functionality, for example in cars, increases the comfort and safety of driving a car or reduces the fuel consumption and exhaust gas emissions [1]. The task of a *controller* is to continuously compare and adapt the current value(s) of some system to some possibly changing desired value(s) [25]. Thereto the controller interacts with the *controlled system* via sensors and actuators. Sensors measure specific values of the controlled system and actuators change input variables of it. Assume the controlled system to be a combustion engine. The controller has to decide on the appropriate amount of fuel as well as the best point in time for injection and ignition reflecting the user's demands (via the accelerator). A typical sensor in this context is the knock sensor to detect self-ignitions that can damage engine components. In this case the controller reacts with adapting the time for ignition. Experiences and knowledge in physics, mathematics, and control theory are required to design a stable controller with good performance.

2.1 Developing Control Systems

For many years, the control systems for vehicle engines were designed by control engineers. However, in the last decade, it has been recognized that massive reductions in pollution and gas consumption as well as advanced driver assistance systems can only be realized if software-based controls are embedded in these systems. These kinds of software-intensive embedded control systems have become a very complex market: a single major supplier sells over 1500 variants of gasoline engine control systems per year [22].

Nonetheless in industrial practice, the development process is still mainly driven by control system engineers. Typically, a controller is developed in five steps [25]. Control engineers have to understand the controlled system, for example the engine, for which a controller has to be developed. Thus, in the first step of the process the controlled system has to be modeled as precisely as possible. This is achieved by building a block diagram of the interactions between the main components and then detailing out these blocks mathematically via, for example, differential equations. The combination of all components and equations therein captures the behavior of the controlled system. This model helps identifying actuating and controlled process variables, i.e. the controlled system's properties, in the second step. In the third phase, the controller's functionality is designed. The fourth step concerns simulating the whole control cycle in crucial situations (model-in-the-loop simulations). If it behaves as expected and demanded, the controller is finally implemented and put into operation in the last step. This includes conclusive hardware-in-the-loop simulations with the real hardware to assess the fulfillment of real-time constraints.

Since recently, the process is supported by rapid control prototyping (RCP) environments [1]. Such a tool chain supports the engineer who can model and especially simulate the whole control cycle to validate the controller design at early development stages without harming a potentially expensive real world device. The Matlab/Simulink (http://www.mathworks.com) environment is most commonly used in this context. Simulink is a graphical programming language on top of the numerical math engine Matlab. It allows the signal oriented (thus, block diagram based) visual capturing of complex systems and provides a large set of libraries with pre-defined mathematical blocks. The environment provides also operational support to derive real-time code from models to run the above mentioned hardware-in-the-loop simulations.

As Fig. 1 shows, software engineers are traditionally involved in the development process only at the implementation phase. They are supposed to efficiently implement the control algorithms on the platform and architecture that have been chosen by the control system engineers. Not surprisingly, software engineers criticize this approach which is purely driven by functional considerations. They argue that a system's structure should follow from the consideration of non-functional goals and requirements. In their view, advanced software techniques have to be used to implement safe, reusable, and efficient solutions.

Interestingly, both disciplines claim to pursue model-based approaches but they have a quite different understanding of the main concept. For control system

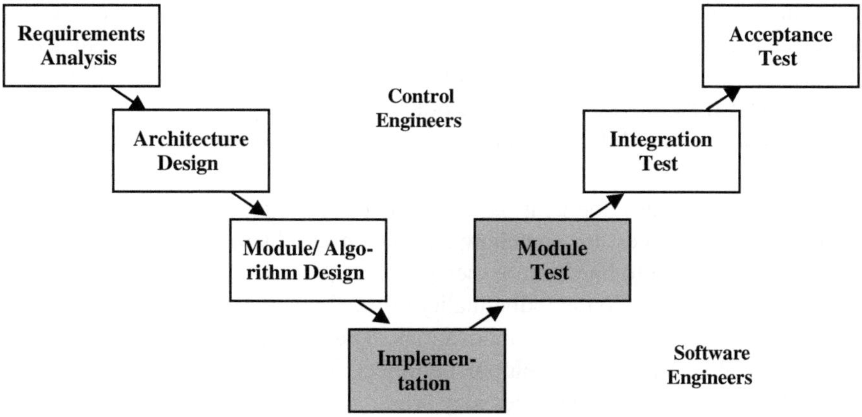

Fig. 1 Development process from control system engineering point of view [22]

development, the model of the controlled system is at the center of interest, in particular to enable simulations as described above. Furthermore at the level of requirements, textual approaches still prevail [15]. In contrast, models within software engineering focus the system to be developed and put these models at the center of the whole development process as envisioned in the model-driven architecture (MDA) promoted by the OMG [29]. Domain-specific modeling languages (e.g. [2, 12]) are intended to be easier to use for domain experts; recent empirical evidence [8] demonstrates that this is indeed the case. Even the Matlab/Simulink environment, most commonly used by control system engineers, can be considered a domain-specific language, but only for the design and implementation level. Besides architectural models, model-based requirement specifications enable a better structuring, traceability and a smarter transition from requirements to subsequent development steps [44].

2.2 SMEs Developing Control Systems

In the control systems development sector, SMEs play an important role as innovation drivers that perform engineering tasks for multiple customers. The process is typically initiated by an engine manufacturer (building engines for cars, boats, power saws, or the like) contacting a number of suppliers to provide an offer to develop a control system for a new engine. By nature, the time frame for the supplier to respond is very short. The manufacturer delivers a specification of the engine and the list of required control functionality. To prepare the offer, the supplier first specifies the requirements on the requested control system from a developer's point of view. In a second step, he prepares a system design in order to calculate the costs for the development of the control system. To keep the development costs low and to win the contract, he must on the one hand reuse as many software artifacts and simulation models as possible from previously developed control systems. On the other hand, if after winning the contract, it is discovered in later design phases that the selected components are actually not reusable, their development from scratch may result in a project loss that can challenge the SME's economic viability. Thus, a careful investigation has to take place quickly.

To summarize the SME and control system related challenges:

- Control system development is a customer- and project-oriented business. Although all engines are somehow similar on an abstract level, they differ in detail, mainly due to hardware issues [7]. This precludes long-term planning of product families due to the individuality of the developed solutions.
- There is a high frequency of innovations. The knowledge changes and grows quite fast. With each new development project, new engine components, sensors, actuators, and construction styles may arise.
- The offer must be developed within a short time frame dictated by the customer. The SME thus must fast and reliably identify reusable components from earlier projects without being able to build on a full product line approach.
- Control systems are realized in software but base on physical features of the controlled system. Its development therefore requires the interdisciplinary investigation of combined software and control requirements and solutions.
- The benefits of model-based approaches during later development stages in both disciplines especially in regard to quality assurance, reliability, and safety [37] need to be taken advantage of.

3 Domain Model Based RE for Control Systems

In this section, our agent and goal-oriented approach to domain model based requirements engineering is introduced in response to the challenges above. The usage of the approach is exemplified for the domain of control systems.

3.1 Agent- and Goal-Oriented Requirements Engineering

The foundation of our approach is a suitable common modeling notation that tackles the interdisciplinary issues. Goal-oriented approaches have proven to be suitable here. "Goals have long been recognized to be the essential components involved in the requirements engineering (RE) process" [43]. Accordingly, they are also suitable as a common ground for different disciplines. A second suitable concept is that of an "agent" [46]. Disregarding any major fundamental distinctions at the detailed level, any stakeholder, environment, legacy, or system-to-be-developed component (irrespective whether physically, hardware, or software motivated) can be represented by an agent and thus be related to other components. Again, this simple concept is amenable for any discipline and suited to prepare a common understanding of a problem.

*i** [45] is a well-known formalism in the requirements engineering field that combines the features of goal- and agent-orientation, and additionally has built-in support for representing non-functional requirements. Furthermore, the formal foundation in the knowledge representation language Telos [26] enables formally sound, automated analysis and transformation support. In detail, *i** supports the notion of *agent* to represent all relevant stakeholders, *dependency* to indicate mutual interactions, and *goal* to capture the internal rationales of stakeholders. The strategic dependency (SD) diagram focuses the stakeholders and their dependencies while the strategic rationale (SR) diagram targets the modeling of internal rationales. Figure 3 mixes the two modeling levels while presenting the requirements of a common rail injection system (see Fig. 2) within a combustion engine.

The common rail is supposed to reliably provide the injectors with fuel; a rail pressure controller must therefore ensure a nearly constant pressure within the rail. The injectors are the disturbances since each injection causes a pressure loss. The controller acts against that by suitably activating the pump.

*i** puts much emphasis on its ability to capture the context of a system to be developed. In our case, the "controlled system" can be considered the most important part of the environment of a "controller" to be designed. In Fig. 3 the "controlled system" is refined into the "rail", the "pump", and the "injector". Is-part-of and inheritance relationships (is-a) can be used as known from object-oriented approaches. Regarding dependencies, *i** distinguishes four different kinds: *task*, *goal*, *resource*, and *softgoal dependency*, the latter suited to capture non-functional requirements. They vary according to the degree of freedom they leave to the dependee. While in a task dependency the depender prescribes the concrete steps, for a goal dependency only a desired situation is specified. Similarly for the resource dependency: it is up to the dependee how to bring the situation (or resource, resp.) about. In control systems development, all these kinds of dependencies apply as well. For example, actuators and sensors can be captured via resource dependencies, see "actuator: pressure valve" and "sensor: pressure" in Fig. 3.

At the strategic rationale level, the types of links on SD level (task, goal, resource, and softgoal dependencies) become modeling elements. They are used to capture the individual goals and processes of stakeholders and systems as well as their relation to external dependencies. Therefore, the SR diagram provides new kinds of links to detail out a complex task (*and*- and *or-decomposition*), to model

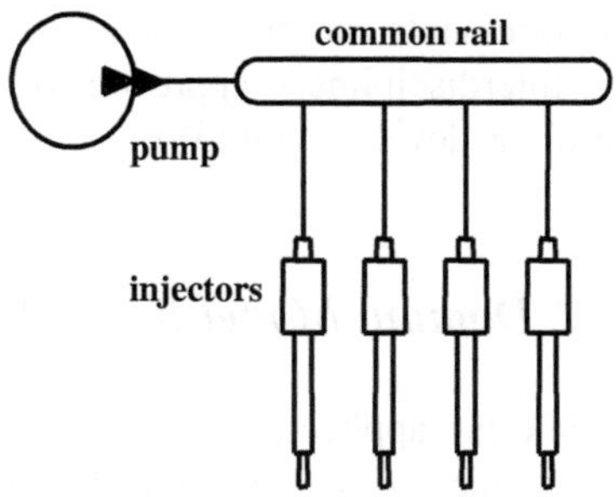

Fig. 2 Schematic representation of a common rail injection system

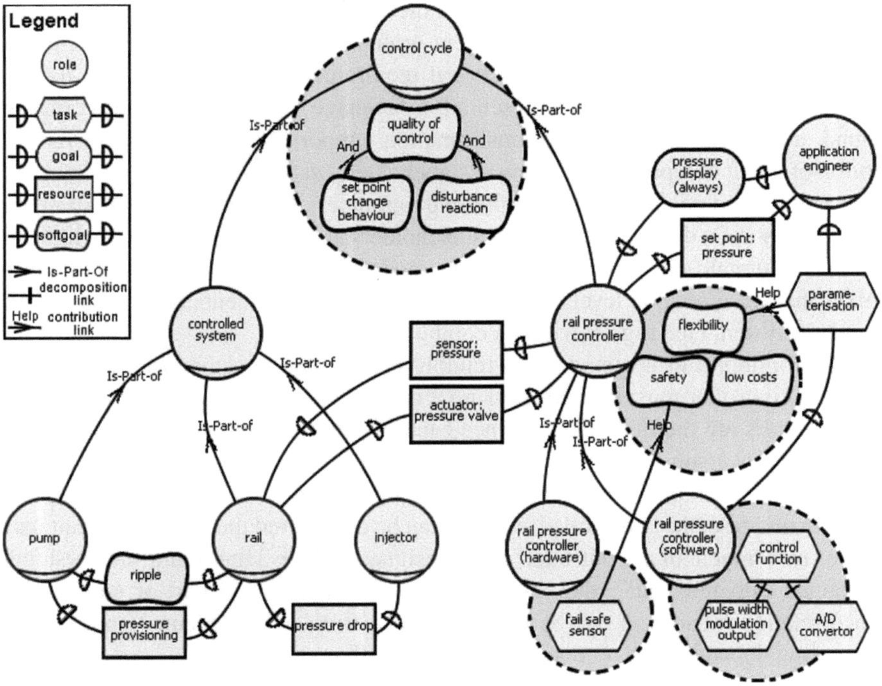

Fig. 3 Common rail requirements example modeled with *i**

alternatives to achieve goals (*means-ends*), and to specify qualitative contributions towards softgoals (*help*, *make*, *break*, etc. *contribution*). Figure 3 shows that "low costs", "flexibility", and "safety" have been recognized as the most important non-functional requirements of the "rail pressure controller". The use of "fail safe sensors" at the "rail pressure controller (hardware)" component is intended to support "safety" whereas the "parameterization" realized by the "rail pressure controller (software)" contributes to the required "flexibility".

In contrast to previous practice in control systems development, this *i** model is able for the first time to capture not only the functional interdependencies of controller and controlled system but also non-functional issues and various additional stakeholders within a combined, model-based view. Due to its origin, software requirements can of course also be represented. Thus, the formalism is suitable as an interdisciplinary approach to requirements engineering in the field of control systems development [38].

3.2 Domain Model Based Requirements Engineering

While the application of the *i** formalism addresses the basic challenges to interdisciplinarity, model-based development and the consideration of non-functional goals, it does not yet address the particularities of the development process employed by SMEs.

3.2.1 Fast Requirements Capture

To address the need for fast requirements capture, the SME is supposed to create one or several specific *domain i* models* that reflect the field(s) the SME is specialized in and that are suitable as an information management infrastructure as well as a starting point for individual models.

As an example, Fig. 4 shows the partial view of the domain model for the combustion engine sub domain [39]. The figure shows the "electronic control unit" omitting all internal details at the center of the picture. The controlled system, i.e. the combustion engine, is modeled in more detail.

The "combustion engine block" is detailed out by internal features regarding for example, the different kinds of "fuel" ("diesel", "gasoline", "gas", "biodiesel"), various types of "cylinder positioning" ("box", "V", "row"), or the "number of cylinders" ("2" to "8"). It is also possible to separate out important components as it has happened with the "common rail" and the "camshaft regulation". The lower part of the figure concerns the details of the "air path" that is important for "exhaust gas after treatment" and "turbo charger" capabilities. Various sensors and actuators connect the engine components to the "electronic control unit" and thus circle around this modeling element. At the upper right, a generic "customer" with some hardgoals and softgoals is also present.

An SME is expected to tailor such a domain model to its particular needs. For Fig. 4, it has been assumed that the SME has particular knowledge in the field of "turbo charging". Thus, the modeling of the "air path" is more extensive than other SMEs would need it. It is easily conceivable that an SME prepares several models of this kind for the various subdomains it is active in. For example, there could also be a domain model for driver assistance systems, electrical engines as well as the combination of combustion and electrical engines as hybrid systems.

The development process at an SME is affected by the existence of a domain model in the following way. Instead of starting from scratch when a potential customer has approached the SME, the engineer chooses a domain model and starts with a copy of it. After eliminating the parts of the model that do not apply for the current project, the engineer can add new elements that are specific to the project at hand. Thus, a requirements model of the new control problem can be established rapidly.

3.2.2 Search for Similar Projects

The next step for the SME is to provide a competitive and reliable cost calculation. To support this activity a domain model based *similarity search* is provided to identify related earlier projects and reusable components [39]. A fully automated identification of reusable software artifacts is not possible. Always a senior engineer is needed to do the technical inspection and to decide if an existing software artifact

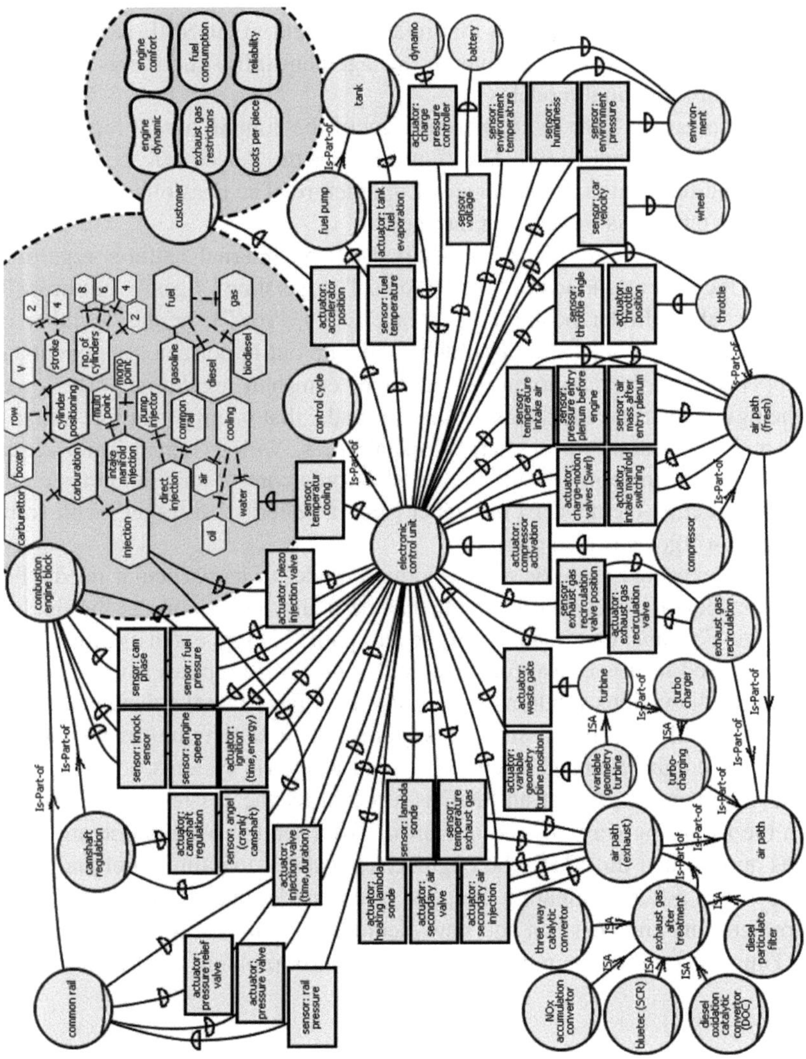

Fig. 4 Combustion engine domain model [39]

suits the new control system. But the similarity search automates the identification of finalized projects containing potentially reusable artifacts and thus reduces significantly the number of finalized projects the engineer has to inspect. This in turn increases the chances that all reusable artifacts are actually found and provides the senior engineer with more time to decide on the actual reusability. Additionally, even if a component is not reusable the project documentation may allow the engineer to better estimate the required efforts and thus also leads to a better cost calculation.

The domain model forms a necessary premise for the similarity search since it ensures consistency of modeling across several projects. Two projects are called similar, if indications exist that parts of the control system software of one project could be reused for the other. An indication is given, if parts of the requirements models of the projects match. Since the requirements models are (via *i**) formalized in the knowledge representation language Telos [26], we can employ for this comparison task the deductive object manager ConceptBase [18] that implements Telos. The selection is based on pre-defined and ad-hoc comparison queries. The pre-defined comparison queries focus on the particular domain model. For example, a query can be formulated that computes the kind of fuel the combustion engine in a particular project uses by identifying all task elements that are parented by "combustion engine block" and are or-decomposed from the "fuel" task element (for Telos details see [39]). This returns a subset of "diesel", "gasoline", "gas", and "biodiesel" (see Fig. 4 upper right, next to "customer") plus potential project-specific extensions. The returned set for the current project can then be compared with the returned sets for earlier projects. Up to now, eleven of such domain model-specific queries are pre-defined for the combustion engine domain model shown in Fig. 4. Additionally, the user can extend this set by ad-hoc queries targeting project-specific extensions. The aggregation of the weighted answers of all queries results in an overall ranking for each project. The projects containing similarities within the highly weighted areas of the new project's requirements model are ranked higher. Accordingly, these are the models the engineer should investigate first.

The requirements model for the concrete customer problem together with the results of the similarity search enable the SME to outline a first solution idea that especially indicates which components can be reused and which ones have to be developed newly. On top of these findings, the SME can produce a reliable and hopefully competitive cost calculation that is sent as an offer to the customer.

3.2.3 Integration with Further Development

Only when the customer accepts the offer of the SME, the development process continues. As elaborated before and in contrast to normal software development, after capturing the requirements, the control system engineers continue the development by building mathematical models. A continuous model-based development approach has to map the requirements to an initial Matlab/Simulink model that then can be enriched with the mathematical equations suitable for the particular problem. By again building on the formalization in Telos, partially automated support for this transformation is provided [40]. During a first manual transformation step, design alternatives are resolved. Here the modeler can make use of all available support for working with i^* models such as label propagation algorithms for computing overall satisfaction of softgoals [16]. The second, automated step generates a Matlab/Simulink skeleton model from the i^* model. Since the conceptual model behind block diagrams and thus Simulink models is rather simple, the matching of concepts is straight forward. Most importantly, various i^* relationships such as is-part-of, decomposition, and means-ends are mapped on the nesting of corresponding blocks. Resource and task dependencies result in signals that are exchanged between components. And goals and softgoals are mapped to model verification or simple model information elements as suitable hints for the developer of the mathematical model. This mapping is encoded in the generic feature of answer formats [18] and thus can easily be adapted to accommodate any other formalism in a different (interdisciplinary) setting. Eventually, an interactive step allows the engineer to incorporate existing hardware and platform components into the skeleton by replacing some of the generic empty blocks. For a concrete SME, there are potentially libraries of sensor and actuator components that are usually combined with a particular hardware platform (such as an RCP system).

Thus regarding the development process, the SME derives the decision for a particular platform from the non-functional requirements on costs, environment conditions, available installation space, safety and reliability constraints, scalability etc. [31]. Accordingly, suitable controller solutions can be considered [10]. Since due to the complexity of real-time constraints often only simulations can reveal the best choice, the engineer might choose to create several different variants (in parallel or iteratively) to be evaluated during the later development that from here on can proceed as usual.

3.3 Experience-Based Domain Model Evolution

The previous section has described the intended process an SME has to follow for a new customer request. In addition to this customer-driven activity, the SME must strategically manage the knowledge and experiences it gains throughout many individual customer projects. The domain model is a suitable means to structure this knowledge and have it influence the development immediately. But the usefulness of the domain model depends heavily on its adequacy for supporting the day-to-day work of the engineers. Neither overly large nor too small domain models are helpful. In the first case eliminating the unnecessary parts takes too much time and in the second case known information needs to be added over and over again. Instead, a domain model must be continuously tailored to the particular needs of the SME. Concrete SMEs will specialize a domain model with regard to the particular methods, tools, and experiences available to them, e.g. particular sensors and actuators. Other sources for changes to the domain knowledge are advances in technology. But the most interesting changes are the ones that result from customer projects over the years. These changes lead to an evolution of the artifacts captured by the domain model. Like Rolland in [34] we established a classification of the various kinds of evolution of the different types of knowledge within a domain model [27].

All these kinds of changes to the domain model are supported in our approach. Initial considerations or externally driven advances can simply be entered to the domain model and are immediately available for use. For project-driven changes, the support is more sophisticated. The indication for changes results here from a number of earlier projects. If a similar project-specific extension has been added several times or if parts of the domain model have always been deleted within the recent past, these are obviously good candidates for extensions and reductions, respectively. While reductions can be identified quite easily, the detection of similar project-specific extensions is much more complicated. The operational support uses a heuristics based approach to compute potential candidates but still relies on manual intervention by an experienced engineer. First details on this are given in [28] but otherwise the issue is subject to current research.

Uncontrolled changes to the domain model can harm the accuracy of the similarity search. Therefore, counter measures have been established. First, the domain model based queries are reformulated to be more robust against changes. This includes favoring object identifiers over names and making more use of the advanced feature of the underlying Telos formalisms (e.g. generic queries [18]). Secondly, limited support for updating earlier projects according to domain model changes is provided. A formerly project-specific extension might need to be slightly reformulated to fit with the current version of the domain model where this extension has been included as a change. Only after such adaptations, the domain model based queries of the similarity search are able to correctly identify the old project as being related [27].

4 Discussion

Figure 5 summarizes the support that our domain model based requirements engineering approach provides. An interdisciplinary methodology allows for capturing control as well as software requirements. Non-functional requirements from both disciplines can be considered. Possible solutions can be investigated irrespective to what is realized in hard- or software. The approach seamlessly integrates with and completes the now fully model-based development approach for control systems. With the support of domain models, the SME is able to capture consolidated engineering knowledge originating in former customer projects. This immediately improves the situation for any new customer. Furthermore together with the similarity search this provides a means to support reuse and to cope with variability while still remaining customer- and project-oriented at the core.

Dedicated work on requirements engineering in the context of automotive software development has been carried out by Geisberger and Schätz [13] by developing AutoRAID, a tool for capturing automotive software requirements. While they also

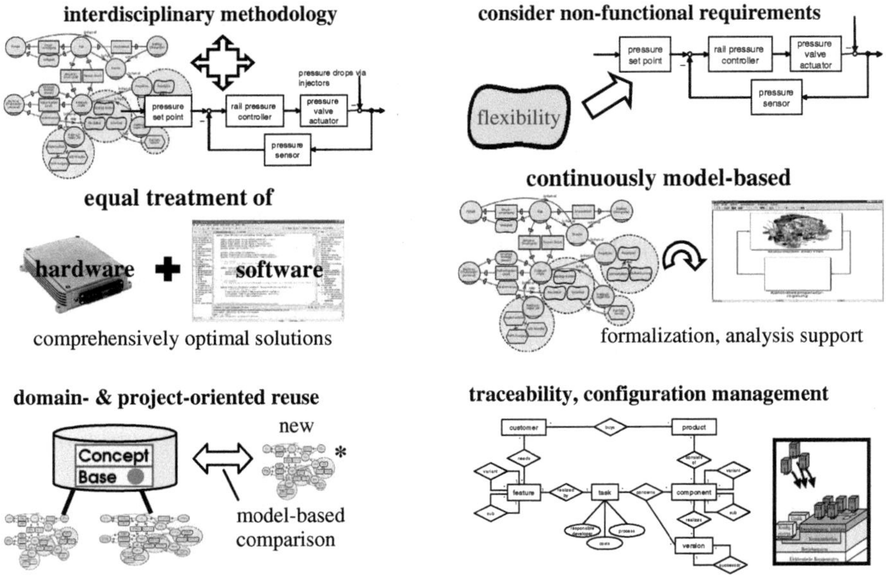

Fig. 5 Contributions of the domain model based requirements engineering approach

put special emphasis on considering the domain by applying a domain-specific language, their approach focuses mostly on functional aspects and does not target small- and medium sized enterprises but larger OEMs. The REMsES project [32] focusses on requirements and architecture artifact co-design but without a particular tailoring to domain or SME specifics. In addition, they also address the embedding of approaches to variability [23]. The latter contribution heavily builds on product line approaches. The more general field of systems engineering explicitly addresses interdisciplinarity, but the available tools are mainly text-based [14]. This critique also applies to SysML [30] since the requirements element here is intended only as a bridge to the text-based tools.

Requirements engineering at small and medium-sized enterprises has explicitly been considered by Kamsties et al. [20]. While they highlight some of the characteristics of software development at SMEs such as overwhelming day-to-day business, large demand for know-how transfer, only one enterprise in their study performed customer-oriented development – the key characteristic addressed by the domain model based approach presented in this chapter. The ReqMan project also targets SMEs [9]. But the emphasis is on how improvements of the development process can be achieved gradually. Additionally, they explicitly want to remain domain independent even though throughout the project they identified the need for considering the domain context.

Jackson [17] discussed the need to investigate and deeply understand the application domain as a major precondition for choosing "close-fitting [problem] frames". But his focus in regard to reuse was on abstract problem frames. Even earlier, Sutcliffe and Maiden [42] argued for the use of generic domain knowledge since in their view it is "doubtful whether tools with embedded domain knowledge could ever keep pace with the development of new systems in changing domains". But generalized domain knowledge seems to rarely benefit the narrowly focused SMEs and means to update the domain model according to experiences in concrete projects have been presented here. Sure et al. [41] investigate the use of ontologies for knowledge management in enterprises. Their approach can be considered heavy-weight in that they expect an explicit ontology engineer to take care of the evolution of the ontology. SMEs rarely have the manpower (or financial scope) for such a position. Instead they need a more pragmatic approach that immediately and tightly integrates with their development practice.

In our approach, design goals, functional requirements, and agents are used mostly as an organizing principle for information management from the perspective of design product reuse. Colette Rolland's long-standing research on requirements process modeling [35] offers an interesting complementary perspective that deserves further attention in our future research. Her Map formalism interprets goals as intentions that can be achieved within the process by alternative strategies where each strategy can have steps from different disciplines; this Map information could be used as an additional aid in the similarity search process presented above, even though it has yet to be determined whether such a strategic process modeling approach is really helpful in the SME context where usually only a few people, who know each other's way of working well, have to cooperate. However, in [36], she additionally points out that the Map formalism can also be exploited as process guidance in the model evolution step to maintain the alignment among the different submodels.

5 Conclusion

In this chapter, a domain-model based approach to requirements engineering for project-oriented small and medium-sized enterprises has been presented. This approach tackles the identified challenges by building on a goal- and agent-oriented model based approach. The few and simple concepts of *i** have proven to be suitable to address interdisciplinarity. The project-oriented development is addressed by a domain model that captures the extensive knowledge of an SME in a particular field and thereby accelerates requirements capture. A similarity search supports the identification of reusable solutions in earlier projects. The necessary evolution of the domain model to maintain its usefulness is considered while still ensuring the accuracy of similarity search results. Support for deriving subsequent development artifacts via semi-automatic transformation finally completes the proposed tool set and contributes towards quality assurance.

The application of the proposed approach has been exemplified for the field of control systems. While the concrete domain model is of course domain specific, the basic ideas behind the approach are applicable to other application fields with similar characteristics. For example, systems for access control and burglary warnings for buildings offer similar characteristics as control systems engineering. It is customer- and project-oriented since each security system is specifically developed for a certain building. Similarly, the construction and set-up of automated manufacturing systems can be considered related as well. Flexible manufacturing systems (FMS) consisting of an arrangement of machines interconnected by a transportation system allow customers to build products in small lot sizes and high numbers of variants at the same time [5]. Again, each installation at a customer is unique. The characteristics of subdomains such as milling and turning or sheet metal processing can exactly be captured by appropriate domain models. Model-based approaches to the configuration of FMS control software have been proposed [6] but up to now do not tie in with requirements engineering nor provide means to incorporate domain knowledge easily. A domain-model based approach to requirements engineering as presented here is thus claimed to be valuable for requirements engineering within customer- and project-oriented, innovative engineering disciplines. This claim needs to be confirmed via additional case studies, for example in the above mentioned fields.

Acknowledgments This research was in part funded by the German Ministry of Education and Research (BMBF) on the project ZAMOMO "Integrating model-based software and control systems engineering", grant 01 IS E04. Thanks to our project partners Dirk Abel, Peter Drews, Frank J. Heßeler, Stefan Kowalewski, Jacob Palczynski, Andreas Polzer, and Michael Reke.

References

1. Abel D, Bollig A (2006) Rapid control prototyping. Springer, Heidelberg
2. Bauer A, Broy M, Romberg J, Schätz B, Braun P, Freund U, Mata N, Sandner R, Mai P, Ziegenbein D (2007) Das AutoMoDe-Projekt. Modellbasierte Entwicklung softwareintensiver Systeme im Automobil. Infor Forsch Entw 22(1):45–57
3. Bjørner D (2009) Domain engineering. Technology management, research and engineering. JAIST, Nomi/Japan
4. BMBF (2007) IKT 2020. Forschung für Innovationen. http://www.bmbf.de/pub/ikt2020.pdf, accessed 2010-05-03. Druckhaus Locher GmbH, Köln
5. Brecher C, Possel-Dölken F, Almeida C (2005) FMS control software with programmable control agents. In: Proceedings of the 3rd CIRP international conference on reconfigurable manufacturing systems, Ann Arbor/USA
6. Brecher C, Buchner T, Cheng Y, Jarke M, Schmitz D (2006) A model driven approach to engineering of flexible manufacturing system control software. In: Rensink A, Warmer J (eds) 2nd European conference on model-driven architecture – foundations and applications (ECMDA-FA). LNCS, vol 4066. Springer, Heidelberg, pp 66–77
7. Broy M (2006) Challenges in automotive software engineering. Keynote. In: Osterweil LJ, Rombach HD, Soffa ML (eds) Proceedings of the 28th international conference on software engineering (ICSE 2006). ACM, pp 33–42
8. Cao L, Ramesh B, Rossi M (2009) Are domain-specific models easier to maintain than UML models? IEEE Softw 26(4):19–21
9. Doerr J, Adam S, Eisenbarth M (2007) Bausteinartige Prozessverbesserung als Schlüssel für erfolgreiches Anforderungsmanagement in KMUs – Erfahrungen aus dem ReqMan-Projekt. Softwaretechnik-Trends 27(1):21–22
10. Drews P, Heßeler FJ, Hoffmann K, Abel D, Schmitz D, Polzer A, Kowalewski S (2008) Entwicklung einer Luftpfadregelung am Dieselmotor unter Berücksichtigung nichtfunktionaler Anforderungen. In: AUTOREG 2008 – Steuerung und Regelung von Fahrzeugen

und Motoren, 4. Fachtagung Baden-Baden, VDI-Berichte Nr. 2009, VDI-Verlag, Düsseldorf, pp 91–102
11. Fiegenbaum A, Karnani A (1991) Output flexibility – a competitive advantage for small firms. Strategic Manage J 12 (2):101–114
12. Fischer G (1994) Domain-oriented design environments. Automated Softw Eng 1:177–203
13. Geisberger E, Schätz B (2007) Modellbasierte Anforderungsanalyse mit AutoRAID. Infor Forsch Entw 21(3–4):231–242
14. Gonzales R (2005) Developing the requirements discipline: software vs. systems. IEEE Softw 22(2):59–61
15. Graaf B, Lormans M, Toetenel H (2003) Embedded software engineering: the state of the practice. IEEE Softw 20(6):61–69
16. Horkoff J, Yu ESK (2008) Qualitative, interactive, backward analysis of i* models. In: Castro J, Franch X, Perini A, Yu E (eds) Proceedings of 3rd international iStar workshop. Recife/Brazil, February 11-12, CEUR Workshop Proceedings 322, CEUR-WS.org pp 43–46
17. Jackson M (1995) Software requirements & specifications. A lexicon of practice, principles and prejudices. Addison-Wesley/ACM, New York
18. Jarke M, Gallersdörfer R, Jeusfeld MA, Staudt M (1995) ConceptBase – a deductive object base for meta data management. J Intelligent Info Systems 4(2):167–192
19. Jarke M, Rolland C, Sutcliffe A, Dömges R (eds) (1999) The NATURE of requirements engineering. Shaker, Aachen
20. Kamsties E, Hörmann K, Schlich M (1998) Requirements engineering in small and medium enterprises. Reqs Eng J 3:84–90
21. Knauber P, Muthig D, Schmid K, Widen T (2000) Applying product line concepts in small and medium-sized companies. IEEE Softw 17(5):88–95
22. Kowalewski S (2006) On the relation between software development and control function development in automotive embedded systems. Invited talk, ARTIST Workshop "Beyond AUTOSAR", Innsbruck/Austria, March
23. Lauenroth K, Pohl K (2008) Dynamic consistency checking of domain requirements in product line engineering. In: Proceedings of 16th international requirements engineering conference, IEEE, Los Alamitos, pp 193–202
24. Lee CC, Egbu C, Boyd D, Xiao H, Chinyo E (2005) Knowledge management for small and medium enterprise: capturing and communicating learning and experiences. In: CIB W99 working commission 4th triennial international conference rethinking and revitalizing construction safety, health, environment, and quality, Port Elizabeth/South Africa, May, pp 808–820
25. Lunze J (2003) Automatisierungstechnik. Oldenbourg, Munich
26. Mylopoulos J, Borgida M, Jarke M, Koubarakis M (1990) Telos: a language for managing knowledge about information systems. ACM Trans Info Systems 8(4):325–362
27. Nissen HW, Schmitz D, Jarke M, Rose T, Drews P, Hesseler FJ, Reke M (2009) Evolution in domain model-based requirements engineering for control systems development. In: Proceedings of 17th international requirements engineering conference, IEEE, Los Alamitos, pp 323–328
28. Nissen HW, Schmitz D, Jarke M, Rose T (2009) How to keep domain requirements models reasonably sized. In: Proceedings of 2nd international workshop on managing requirements knowledge, MaRK @ RE, Atlanta/USA, September 1, IEEE/Los Alamitos, pp 50–59
29. OMG (2003) MDA guide version 1.0.1. http://www.omg.org/cgi-bin/doc?omg/03-06-01.pdf, accessed 2010-05-03
30. OMG (2007) OMG systems modeling language (OMG SysML), V1.0.http://www.omg.org/spec/SysML/1.0/PDF, accessed 2010-05-03
31. Papadacci E, Salinesi C, Rolland C (2004) Payoff analysis in goal-oriented requirements engineering. In: Proceedings workshop on requirements engineering for foundations of software quality, REFSQ, Riga/Latvia, June

32. Pohl K, Sikora E (2007) COSMOD-RE: supporting the co-design of requirements and architectural artifacts. In: Proceedings of 15th international requirements engineering conference, IEEE, pp 258–261
33. Pohl K, Böckle G, van der Linden F (2005) Software product line engineering: foundations, principles, and techniques. Springer, Heidelberg
34. Rolland C (1994) Modeling the evolution of artifacts. In: Proceedings of the first international conference on requirements engineering, IEEE, Los Alamitos, pp 216–219
35. Rolland C (1999) A comprehensive view of process engineering. In: Proceedings of 10th international conference on advanced information systems engineering (CAiSE 98). LNCS, vol 1413. Springer, Heidelberg, pp 1–24
36. Rolland C (2009) Exploring the fitness relationship between system functionality and business needs. In: Lyytinen K, Loucopoulos P, Mylopoulos J, Robinson B (eds) Design requirements engineering: a ten-year perspective. Springer, Heidelberg
37. Schäuffele J, Zurawka T (2003) Automotive software engineering. Grundlagen, Prozesse, Methoden und Werkzeuge. Vieweg, Wiesbaden
38. Schmitz D, Drews P, Hesseler FJ, Jarke M, Kowalewski S, Palcyznski J, Polzer A, Reke M, Rose T (2008) Modellbasierte Anforderungserfassung für softwarebasierte Regelungen. In: Herrmann K, Brügge B (eds) Software engineering 2008. Fachtagung des GI-Fachbereichs Softwaretechnik. Munich/Germany, February LNI P-121. GI, Bonn, pp 257–271
39. Schmitz D, Nissen HW, Jarke M, Rose T, Drews P, Hesseler FJ, Reke M (2008) Requirements engineering for control systems development in small and medium-sized enterprises. In: Proceedings of 16th international requirements engineering conference, IEEE, Los Alamitos, pp 229–234
40. Schmitz D, Zhang M, Rose T, Jarke M, Polzer A, Palczynski J, Kowalewski S, Reke M (2009) Mapping requirement models to mathematical models in control system development. In: Proceedings of 5th European conference on model driven architecture – foundations and applications. LNCS, vol 5562. Springer, Heidelberg, pp 253–264
41. Sure Y, Staab S, Studer R (2002) Methodology for development and employment of ontology-based knowledge management applications. SIGMOD Record 31(4):18–23
42. Sutcliffe AG, Maiden NAM (1993) Use of domain knowledge for requirements validation. In: Proceedings of IFIP WG8.1 conference on information system development process, Elsevier, Amsterdam, pp 99–115
43. van Lamsweerde A (2001) Goal-oriented requirements engineering: a guided tour (invited mini tutorial). In: Proceedings of the 5th international symposium on requirements engineering, IEEE, Los Alamitos, pp 249–262
44. van Lamsweerde A (2004) Goal-oriented requirements engineering: a roundtrip from research to practice (Keynote). In: Proceedings of the 12th international conference on requirements engineering, IEEE, Los Alamitos, pp 4–7
45. Yu E (1995) Modelling strategic relationships for process reengineering. PhD thesis, University of Toronto
46. Yu E (2001) Agent orientation as a modelling paradigm. Wirtschaftsinformatik 43(2):123–132

Intentional Alignment and Interoperability in Inter-Organization Information Systems

Naveen Prakash

Abstract With the emergence of mergers, acquisitions, and collaborative enterprises, the issues of alignment and interoperability in inter-organization information systems have become more complex than before. We propose a two level development approach driven by the intentional level and going to the process model level. Alignment and interoperability requirements are first decided at the intentional level. That is, (a) the intention of the inter-organizational system To Be is properly aligned with intentions of the individual systems that come together, and (b) the intentions of the individual systems must interoperate. Thereafter, at the process model level, process model of the system To Be needs to be properly aligned to its intention and the process models of the participating organizational systems interoperate. We develop a Two-dimensional framework to represent this. This framework drives a development method to support inter-organizational system development. We illustrate this method in a supply chain system example.

1 Introduction

Professor Colette Rolland has worked rather extensively on applying the notion of intention to information systems. This is reflected in her work on process modeling where she proposed the notion of a map [28] as a graph having intentions as nodes and strategies as edges. She also proposed an intentional basis [26] for product lines and families. In requirements engineering, she proposed goal-scenario coupling [27] and developed guidelines for requirements elicitation. In the tool, L'Ecritoire, there was an explicit notion of intention in the natural language interface. Seeing the widespread application of the notion of intention, we propose here to look at alignment and interoperability from the intentional perspective.

N. Prakash (✉)
Department of Computer Science, MRCE, Sector 43, Delhi Surajkund Road,
Faridabad 121001, Haryana, India
e-mail: praknav@hotmail.com

S. Nurcan et al. (eds.), *Intentional Perspectives on Information Systems Engineering*,
DOI 10.1007/978-3-642-12544-7_6, © Springer-Verlag Berlin Heidelberg 2010

Alignment and Interoperability are major problems that have both been recognized for a number of years. The importance of aligning information systems (IS) with business has been considered at two levels. At the top level is strategic business-IT alignment that aims to apply IT in an appropriate and timely way to meet business goals. Empirical studies [7, 15, 21], suggest that *strategic* IS alignment influences business performance. At the second level we have *technical* business-IS alignment that aims to ensure alignment of processes offered by information systems and those of the real business. The issue of alignment has been considered from several perspectives, ERP [6, 20], COTS [16, 18, 22, 27], service orientation [5, 12, 14, 29], and inter-organization information systems [1, 8, 11, 29, 30].

Interoperability [17] is "the ability for a system or a product to work with other systems or products without special effort on the part of the customer." The interoperability problem is well known and can be found in many domains, some examples are: database schema integration [24], interoperability between modeling techniques [10], in meta-modeling platforms [19], of ERP with other systems [3], between heterogeneous information systems [2, 4]. Further, there are a number of application domains where interoperability problems have been faced, in health care systems [9] and in e-governance [13].

Guijarro [13] stresses the fact that there is a need for guidance beyond technical issues. Others [17, 30] suggest a multi-layered model consisting of a business layer, a knowledge layer and an ICT systems layer. Ralyte [25] proposes that interoperability must address business environment and business processes, the organizational roles, skills and competencies of employees and knowledge assets on the knowledge layer, and applications, data and communication components on the ICT layer.

In the last 10–15 years, enterprises have been merging and acquiring new ones, entering into collaborations to offer enhanced customer value, optimizing operations by concentrating on core competencies and outsourcing peripheral services etc. In other words, separate, individual enterprises are coming together to form new enterprises. Such enterprise cooperation imposes its own demands on information systems. Individually developed information systems must cooperate to meet the requirements of the new system and come together to form a cohesive inter-organizational information system.

As we see it, the issues of alignment and interoperability are rather more closely entwined in inter-organizational systems than in traditional intra organization systems. Indeed, the alignment of individual systems to meet the global objective of the inter-organizational system in which they participate requires interoperability of the individual systems. This strong coupling of alignment and interoperability is weaker in intra organizational systems. Accordingly, we attempt to make this coupling stronger.

We propose that inter-organizational systems should be considered at two levels, intentional and process. The former drives the latter. Consider the situation where an inter-organizational system is to be built over systems of different organizations. We believe that the intention of the new system should be a suitable combination of the intentions of the individual systems. For this purpose, we examine the goal hierarchies of the new system To Be with goal hierarchies of each of the older systems, pair wise. The aim is to develop the goal hierarchy of the System To Be from the different system perspectives. The collection of goal hierarchies represents the alignment of the system To Be with the old systems. Since, the old systems are assumed to be aligned then the new system is aligned if the collection of goal hierarchies is aligned.

Now, we need to consider interoperability. Notice that each new goal hierarchy To Be represents only one perspective. However, the system To Be is built when these hierarchies provide and obtain services from one another. This means that we have to identify such points in the goal hierarchies where the goal/sub goal of one hierarchy needs to cooperate with those of the other. Thus, interoperability is intentional in nature.

Once intentional alignment/interoperability is achieved then the process model of the new system is to be developed. This process model must satisfy the goal hierarchy. When this happens then the goals and processes of the system To Be are well aligned. From the perspective of interoperability of processes, the process model To Be is a collaboration between process models of the different collaborating process models.

To sum up our approach, we start with a number of As Is goal hierarchies. We develop the goal hierarchy of the system To Be and the As Is goal hierarchies are extended to To Be goal hierarchies. These latter should align with the To Be goal hierarchies. The To Be goal hierarchies are examined for interoperability and possible collaborations are identified. Once intentional alignment and interoperability are done then we move to the process model level. We again have a number of As Is process models which must align to the process model of the system To Be. For process model interoperability, the points of interaction between the As Is process models are identified to meet interoperability goals at the intentional level.

The layout of the chapter is as follows. In the next section, we argue that in the context of inter-organizational systems, the issues of alignment and interoperability are related to one another. We represent this relationship in a two-dimensional framework of alignment and interoperability. In Sect. 3 we consider intentional alignment and interoperability of the supply chain system. In Sect. 4 we present alignment and interoperability of supply chain at the process level.

2 The Two-Dimensional Framework

The basic assumption underlying our two-dimensional framework is that alignment and interoperability can be considered at two levels, the former driving the latter. This is shown in Fig. 1 by the arrow between the two levels, one elaborating intentions and the other elaborating process models. That is, in developing an inter-organizational system the goals of the system To Be must first be determined. Then it must be ensured that the goals of the individual organizations come together to satisfy these. This is the intentional alignment issue in inter-organizational systems. Further, the points of interaction between the participating systems must

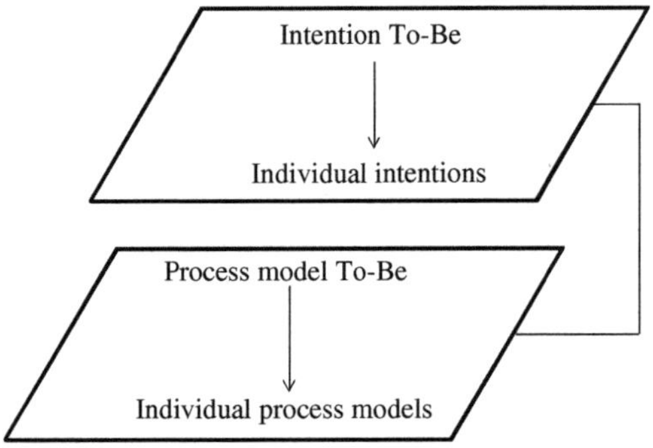

Fig. 1 Interaction between intentional and process levels

be identified. At the intentional level, this implies the identification of goals of the individual organizations that support each other. Thus, we have the goals of different organizations coming together to contribute to the goals of the system To Be.

At the second level, the process level, we must again deal with the process model To Be and the process models of individual organizations. For alignment, it is necessary that the former is in accordance with the goals of the system To Be and the latter modified to play their respective part in the process model. For inter-operability, the goals that interoperate must be supported by interoperability of the process models of the individual organizations.

Now, the two-dimensional framework views alignment and interoperability together. This is shown in Fig. 2. The intention of the inter-organizational system To Be is I, the vertex of the pyramid of Fig. 2. The intentions of the collaborating systems, the As Is intentions are at the base of the pyramid and are denoted by I1, I2, . . ., I*n* respectively. The intention I must be satisfied by the intentions at the base of the pyramid in order for the inter-organizational system to be well aligned. Intentional interoperability is shown in the framework by the link between the base intentions, I1, I2, . . ., I*n*.

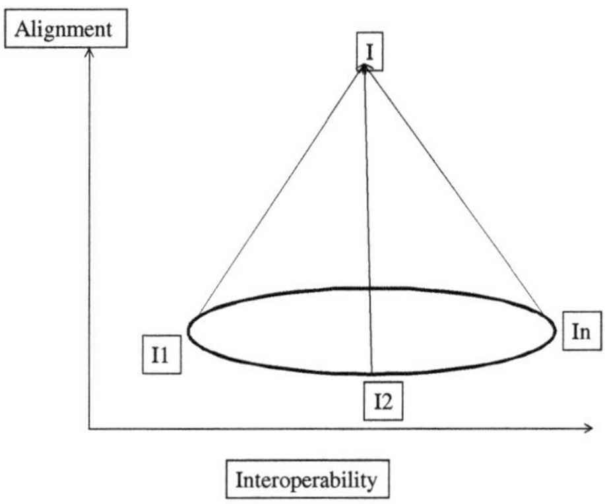

Fig. 2 The two-dimensional framework for intentions

We adopt a similar view for interoperability. Let us replace the intentions of Fig. 2 by process models, P for I and P1, P2, . . ., P*n* for I1, I2, . . ., I*n* respectively. Then by the same argument as for intentions, process model alignment requires alignment of P with the individual ones and interoperability requires interaction between the latter.

In accordance with Fig. 1, the two-dimensional framework of the process level is driven by the intentional two-dimensional framework. Thus, the process model To Be aligns with the system intentions To Be and process model interoperability aligns with intentional interoperability.

Let us now consider the method to be followed in the development of inter-organizational systems. We assume that individual organizational systems are already operational and the problem is to bring them together. Thus, we already have available the goal hierarchies of individual systems as well as their process models. We further assume that these are aligned to organizational needs. We propose the following steps for developing the inter-organizational system:

(a) Build goal hierarchy of the inter-organization system To Be: This hierarchy is a formulation of the intentional requirements of the new system.
(b) Dovetail goal hierarchies of individual systems with that of (a): The goal hierarchy of each individual organization becomes part of the hierarchy of the system To Be. As a result, it is ensured that the intentions of the participating systems and the new one are properly aligned.
(c) Determine cross-goal hierarchy linkages: Since the new system results from interoperability, dovetailed goal hierarchies are examined to determine any cross-hierarchy relationships. These may be in the form of one goal supporting the other.
(d) Modify the process model of each individual organization to satisfy cross-goal hierarchy linkages. In order to participate in the new process model, changes in individual process models may be required to meet cross-goal hierarchy relationships. These changes are to be identified and defined. In this step.
(e) Combine the process models of (d) to form the process model of the system To Be. This is the step that makes the collaboration between systems possible.

In the rest of this chapter, we illustrate the foregoing in the case of a supply chain.

3 The Supply Chain System

Consider the problem of materials management. For an organization, the high level goal of materials management is *To provide material to consumption points when needed*. This goal consists of a number of sub goals (see Fig. 3) like *Obtain material at a good price*, *Ensure quality of material*, *Ensure timely delivery to consumption point*, *Keep proper inventory record*. As is well known, these goals are themselves decomposed till operationalizable goals are reached. From the perspective of alignment, it is necessary to ensure that the design of the system reflects these goals truly

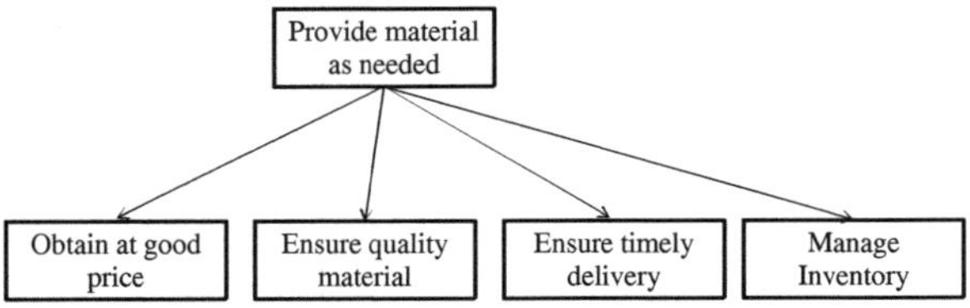

Fig. 3 Goal hierarchy: the user organization

and faithfully. Assume that the system is to be developed from scratch and as such there is no serious interoperability problem.

Now consider a supplier organization that supplies fully assembled systems like computers. It keeps an inventory of system components and whenever it needs additional components, it places an order with component suppliers. The broad goal of this supplier organization is to *Maximize profits*. To achieve this goal there are a number of sub goals as shown in Fig. 4. The supplier organization strives to *Capture a large market share*, *Deliver quality systems*, and *Maintain profitability*. Again, the operationalizable goals shall be reached and the system developed. As before, assume good alignment and no interoperability issue.

Finally consider the component supplier. This organization stocks a range of components that are used as parts. It receives orders, mainly as a retail shop, and supplies against these. The quality of parts ranges from the best to the inferior and the price is commensurate with the quality. A given kind of part is available in many specifications. This organization has its own goal of being an effective retailer. Its sub goals (see Fig. 5) are to *Stock parts in their different specifications* as well as *Stock parts of different quality* and *Do delivery at customer site*. As before let an aligned system be built and let there be no interoperability issues.

Now, when these three organizations work independently then they face certain difficulties. The first needs assured supplies of material and just in time inventory. The second needs an assured market and price realizations, and assured supply of components. The third being a retailer would like to have an assured market. In short, all can come together to form a supply chain.

The supply chain has its own goals as shown in Fig. 6 which is produced following step (a) of the development method outlined earlier. Globally, the supply

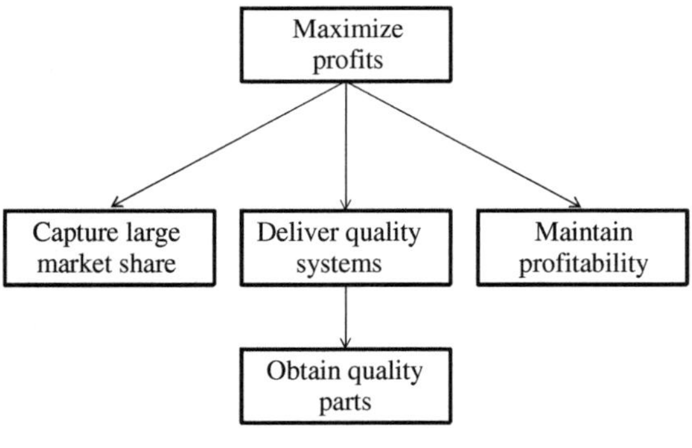

Fig. 4 Goal hierarchy: the supplier organization

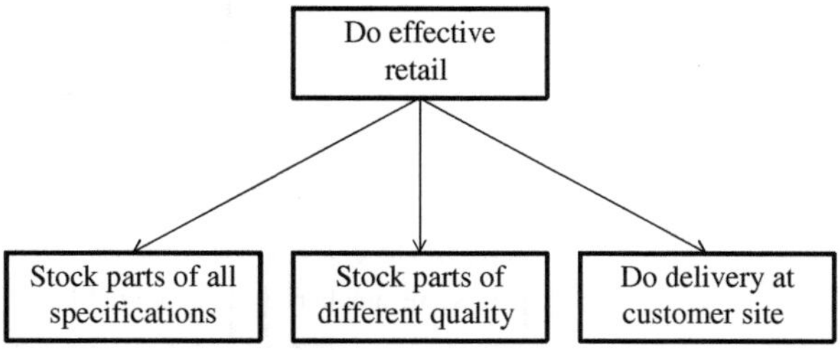

Fig. 5 Goal hierarchy: the component supplier

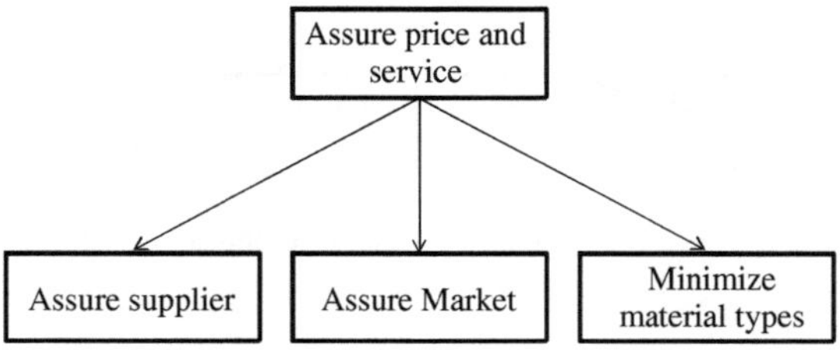

Fig. 6 Goal hierarchy of the supply chain system

chain seeks to provide an assured supply of material at a good price – *Assure price and service*. This goal can be decomposed into its next level, the suppliers must be assured, the market must be assured, and the different part types must be minimized. These three sub goals are shown in the figure. In the formation of the supply chain both alignment and interoperability arise. The former because the supply chain system must align to the needs of the supply chain and interoperability because three different systems are to be brought together. We consider both these issues here.

Now consider the step (b) of dovetailing goal hierarchies with that of Fig. 6. For alignment, it is necessary to ensure that the goals of the collaborating organizations are aligned to the goals of the supply chain. First, consider the user organization. The root goal of Fig. 3 broadly conforms to the root goal of Fig. 6. Therefore, one sees a possibility of alignment. Going deeper, the sub goals of Fig. 3, *Obtain at good price*, *Ensure quality material* and *Ensure timely delivery* can be considered as members of the decomposition of *Assure price and service* goal of Fig. 6. The exact position of these in the goal decomposition hierarchy of Fig. 6 is now to be determined. It can be seen that the sub goal *Assure supplier* of Fig. 6 can be decomposed to include these. The intentional alignment of the user organization and supply chain goals is shown in Fig. 7.

Further the last sub goal, *Manage Inventory* of Fig. 3 remains a private goal of the user organization and does not directly participate in the supply chain. However, it is affected by the *Minimize material types* sub goal of Fig. 6 in so far as there is going to be a change in the material handled. Whereas, this may cause changes in the operations of the organization, it does not present an alignment problem because the supporting IS can gracefully handle a reduced number of material types. Evidently, it is possible to align the goals of the user organization with those of the supply chain.

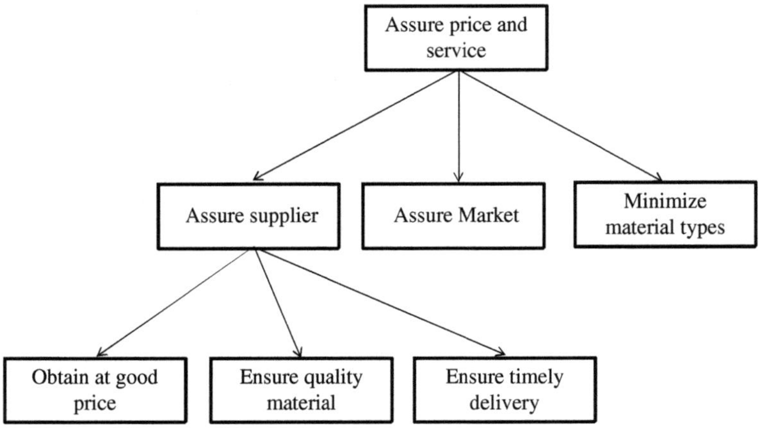

Fig. 7 Intentional alignment of user organization with supply chain

Now consider the supplier organization as in Fig. 4. The root goal *Maximize profits prima facie* does not seem to belong to the supply chain goal hierarchy. However, when viewing its decomposition, we find that *Capture large market share* and *Deliver quality systems* are both relevant to *Assure Market* of Fig. 6. This organization has to assure its own suppliers of parts. Therefore, the sub goal *Obtain quality parts* is relevant to *Assure supplier.* Maintain profitability is an internal goal of the supplier organization and does not really form part of the supply chain. Alignment of goals of the supplier organization with supply chain goals is shown in Fig. 8.

Lastly, consider the component supplier. Alignment of its goals with those of supply chain goals is shown in Fig. 9. The retailer is looking to assure its market and the sub goals *Stock parts of all specifications*, *Stock parts of different quality*, and *Do delivery at customer site* can all be treated as sub goals of *Assure market.*

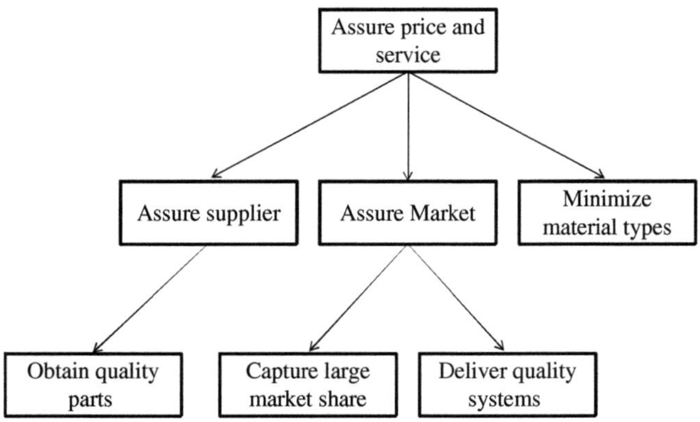

Fig. 8 Intentional alignment of supplier organization with supply chain

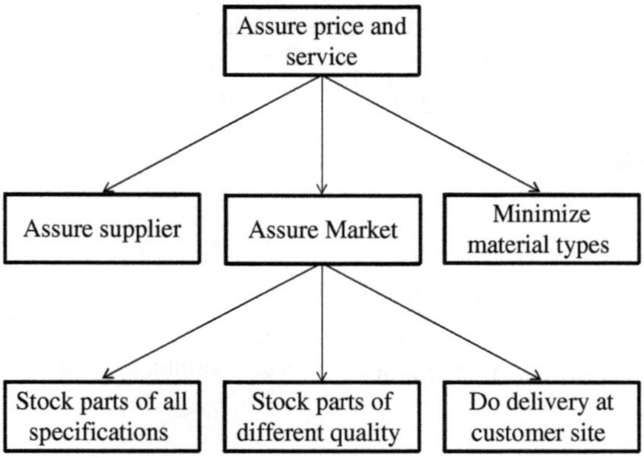

Fig. 9 Intentional alignment of component vendor with supply chain

Thus, as shown in Fig. 8, goals of the component supplier are aligned to those of the supply chain.

It can be seen that alignment is a vertical property; the goals of the collaborative system are at a higher level than those of the collaborating systems and it is necessary for the latter goals to become part of the goal decomposition hierarchy of the former.

Now consider the next step. Intentional interoperability considers interaction of collaborating systems at the level of intentional goal hierarchies. Consider the hierarchies of Figs. 7 and 8. The sub goal *Assure supplier* of the former is related to *Assure market* of Fig. 8 and constitutes a point of collaboration. The former is looking for supplier partners and the latter for client markets. Similarly, in Figs. 8 and 9, *Assure supplier* of the former is related to *Assure market* of the latter.

Now we can move to the process level and follow step (d).

4 The Process Level

In this section we consider alignment and interoperability at the process level by following steps (d) and (e) of the development method. We shall assume that for the user, supplier, and component supplier respectively, the process model is well aligned to their respective goal hierarchies. The process models of each of these are given in Figs. 10, 11, and 12 respectively.

The representation system used has been elaborated in [23]. The basic idea is to represent the process model as a graph whose:

- Nodes are in the form <argument, action>. This corresponds to the notion of a signature found in object orientation and identifies the arguments on which the action occurs.
- Edges between nodes are directed and represent a successor-predecessor relationship between nodes. The properties of the edge are given by two properties,

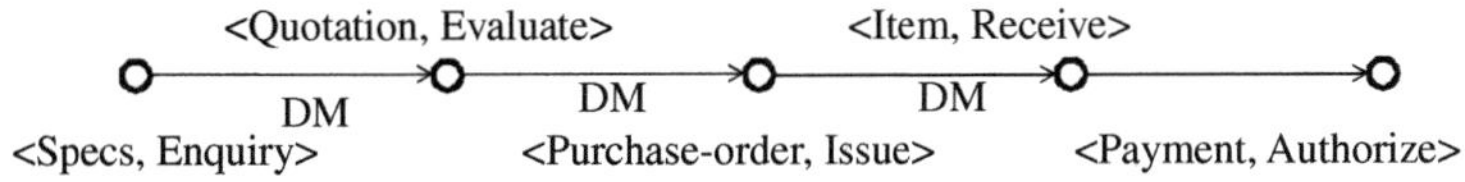

Fig. 10 The user process model

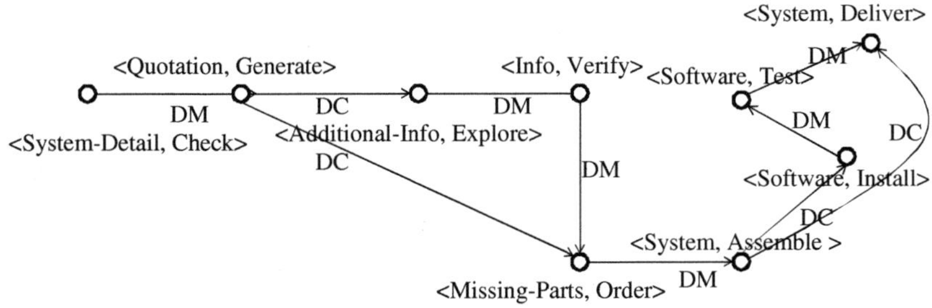

Fig. 11 A system supplier

Fig. 12 The supplier process

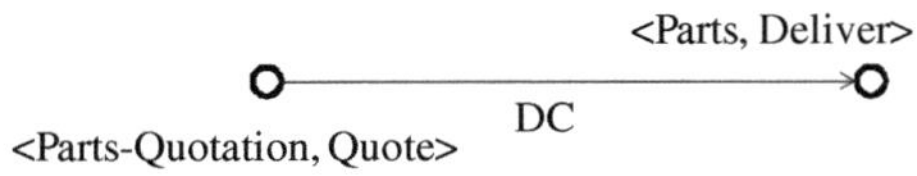

Necessity and Urgency. Necessity identifies whether enactment of a successor node is mandatory after the current node has been enacted or it is optional. Urgency associates a temporal property with the edge and specifies whether the enactment of the successor node is immediately done after the current node is enacted or whether it can be deferred. We have shown in [23] that the deferred necessity is a high level abstraction of the notion of a long running process. It can be used in subsequent development stages to specify a deadline before which the node must be enacted. Combining the two properties, we get four possible properties of an edge as shown in Table 1. These four properties represent a variety of process situations [23], sequence, choice, parallelism etc.

The process model of the user organization asks for quotation enquiries for items meeting specifications, evaluates the received quotations, issues purchase orders to selected vendors, takes delivery of items and finally, makes payment. Each successor node in the figure is necessarily to be enacted but it does not need to be enacted

Table 1 The four edge properties

Abbreviation	Urgency	Necessity
IM	Immediate	Must
IC	Immediate	Can
DM	Deferred	Must
DC	Deferred	Can

immediately upon enactment of its predecessor. This explains the choice of the DM property for the edges in the figure.

The supplier organization receives requests for system configurations, determines that the configuration asked for is indeed realizable and responds with a quotation. If any additional information/clarification is required then it obtains it and verifies it once again. Since it may happen that it has to order system parts that are missing, such missing parts are ordered and the system is assembled together, software installed, if required, and the system is delivered. This process is shown in Fig. 11.

Notice that after <quotation, generate> there are two possibilities, either additional information is to be handled or missing parts are to be ordered. Both these actions can be done after a time delay. Thus, we get Deferred-Can, DC, as the edge property. A similar situation exists after the system has been assembled, i.e. at <system, assemble>. If no software is to be loaded and a bare system is to be supplied then the property is DC as shown in Fig. 9(ii).

Finally, consider a simple supplier process that sends out a quotation and upon receipt of an order delivers parts. The type of dependency is again DM. This is shown in Fig. 12.

Now, the goal hierarchies of supply chain call for interoperability between these process models. The Assure Supplier-Assure market interoperability is between the process models of Figs. 10 and 11. The first point of variation is at <specs, enquiry> of the user organization. Whereas earlier this was self contained in the User process, now it is possible to invoke the supplier for the purchase of systems. In this case, the DM edge in Fig. 10 to <quotation, evaluate>, which was originally DM, shall be changed to DC. The edge from <spec, enquiry> to the Supplier process shall now be introduced and shall also be DC. As a result, this allows a choice between the two courses of action. This is shown in Fig. 13.

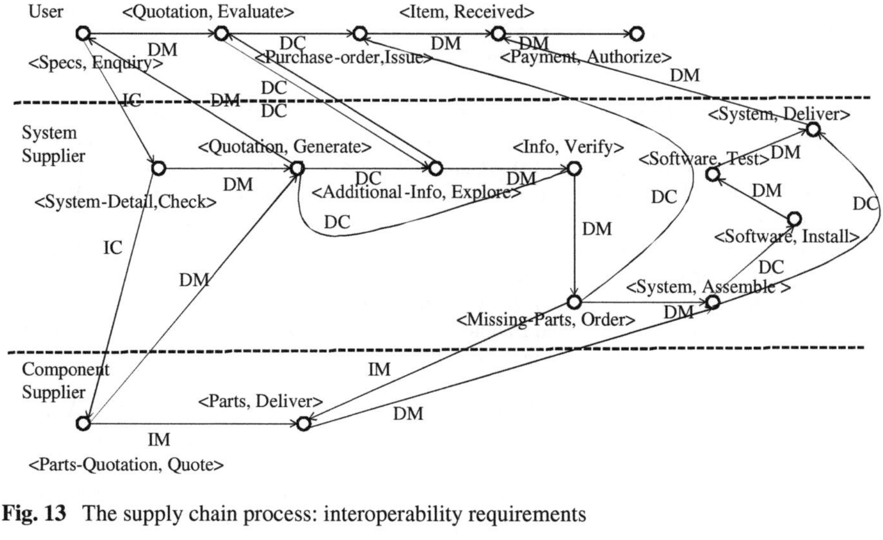

Fig. 13 The supply chain process: interoperability requirements

Similarly, requirements for interoperability are established between the supplier and the process of the component supplier.

5 Conclusion

We have shown that alignment and interoperability of inter-organization information systems are coupled together and a common framework needs to be built for them. This is unlike intra-organization systems where alignment and interoperability are treated as separate problems. Secondly, the requirements of a system are expressed at the intentional and process levels. Intentional requirements identify whether systems can come together to meet the objectives of the collaborative system. Once this is ensured then it is possible to look at what process parts must come together for alignment. This determines the interoperability requirement.

The ideas presented here are being explored in our ongoing work on inter-organizational information systems. We are developing a high level representation system for process models of such systems and studying issues in integrating systems together to meet requirements in the event of mergers, acquisitions, development of virtual organizations and enterprise networks.

References

1. Alaranta M, Henningsson S (2007) Shaping the post-merger information systems integration strategy. In: Proceedings of 40th HICSS, IEEE Computer Society Washington, DC, USA, pp 237b http://www.computer.org/portal/web/csdl/doi/10.1109/HICSS.2007.480
2. Bermundez J, Goni A, Illaramendi A, Bagues MI (2007) Interoperation among agent-based information systems through a communication acts ontology. Inf Syst 32(8):1121–1144
3. Botta-Genoulaz V, Millet P-A, Grabot B (2005) A survey on the recent research literature on ERP systems. Comput Ind 56:510–522
4. Boulanger D, Dubois G (1998) An object approach for information system cooperation. Inf Syst 23(6):383–399
5. Castro de V, Mesa JMV, Herrmann E, Marcos E (2008) A model driven approach for the alignment of business and information systems model. In: Proceedings of Mexican international conference on computer science, IEEE Computer Society, Washington, DC, USA, pp 33–43
6. Chan JO (2005) Enterprise information systems strategy and planning. J Am Acad Business 2:148–153
7. Chan YE, Sabherwal R, Thatcher JB (2006) Antecedents and outcomes of strategic IS alignment: an empirical investigation. IEEETEM 53(1):27–47
8. Daneva M, Wieringa R. (2006) A coordination complexity model to support requirements engineering for cross-organizational ERP. In: Proceedings of 14th IEEE international requirements engineering conference. RE 2006, IEEE Computer Society, Washington, DC, USA
9. Dogac A, Laleci GB, Kirbas S, Kabak Y, Sinir SS, Yildiz A, Gurcan Y (2006) Artemis: deploying semantically enriched web services in the healthcare domain. Inf Syst 31: 321–339
10. Dominguez E, Zapata MA (2000) Mappings and interoperability: a meta-modelling approach. In: Proceedings of ADVIS 2000. LNCS, vol 1909. Springer, Berlin Heidelberg, pp 352–362

11. Fang K, Wu ACH, Tung Yang C (2007) A study of information systems integration with the structuration model of technology as foundation. In: Portland international centre for management of engineering and technology, Portland, OR, USA, pp 1556–1563
12. Fox G, Lantner K (1997) A software development process for COTS based information system infrastructure. In: Proceedings of 5th international symposium on assessment of software tools and technologies, SAST'97, IEEE Computer Society, Washington, DC, USA pp 133–142
13. Guijarro L (2007) Interoperability frameworks and enterprise architectures in e-government initiatives in Europe and the United States. Govt Inf Q 24:89–101
14. Henkel M, Zdravkovic J (2005) Supporting development and evolution of service-based processes. In: Proceedings of the 2005 IEEE international conference on e-business engineering. IEEE Computer Society, Washington, DC, USA, pp 647–656
15. Henningsson S, Svensson C, Vallén L (2007) Mastering the integration chaos following frequent M&As: IS integration with SOA technology. In: Proceedings of 40th HICSS conference. IEEE Computer Society, Washington, DC, USA, p 219b
16. Horowitz BM, Lambert JH (2006) Assembling off-the-shelf components: "learn as you go" systems engineering. IEEE Trans Systems, Man, and Cybernetics – Part A Systems and Humans 36(2):286–297
17. INTEROP (2007) Interop network of excellence IST—508011 presentation of the project. /http://interop-noe.org/INTEROP/presentations. Accessed 30 May 2007
18. Keil M, Tiwana A (2005) Beyond costs: the drivers of COTS application value. IEEE Softw 22(3):64–69
19. Kühn H, Murzek M (2005) Interoperability Issues in Metamodelling Platforms. In: Proceedings of conference INTEROP-ESA 2005: interoperability of enterprise software and applications. Springer, London, pp 215–226
20. Lee J, Siau K, Hong S (2003) Enterprise integration with ERP and EAI. CACM 46(2):54–60
21. Malik K, Goyal DP (2003) IS alignment and IS effectiveness: experiences from Indian industry. In: Proceedings of the Engineering Management Conference, 2003. IEMC '03. Managing Technologically Driven Organizations: The Human Side of Innovation and Change. IEEE Computer Society, Washington, DC, USA, pp 96–100
22. Navarrete F, Botella P, Franch X (2007) Reconciling agility and discipline in COTS selection processes. In: Proceedings of sixth international IEEE conference on commercial-off-the-shelf (COTS)-based software systems. IEEE Computer Society, Washington, DC, USA, pp 103–113
23. Prakash N, Chaturvedi AK (2010) Representing analysis models for alignment. In: Proceedings of RCIS 2010 (to be presented)
24. Rahm E, Bernstein PA (2001) A survey of approaches to automatic schema matching. VLDB J 10:334–350
25. Ralyte J, Jeusfeld MA, Backlund P, Kuhn H, Arni-Block N (2008) A knowledge-based approach to manage information systems interoperability. Info Systems. doi:10.1016/j.is
26. Rolland C (2005) Modelling multi-facetted purposes of artefacts. SoMeT 3–17
27. Rolland C (1998) Carine Souveyet, Camille Ben Achour: guiding goal modeling using scenarios. IEEE Trans Softw Eng 24(12):1055–1071
28. Rolland C, Prakash N, Benjamen A (1999) A multi-model view of process modelling. Req Eng 4(4):169–187
29. Sledge C (1998) Case study: evaluating COTS products for DoD information systems. SEI Monographs on the Use of Commercial Software in Government Systems, SEI
30. van Wendel de Joode R, Tineke EM (2004) Handling variety: the tension between adaptability and interoperability of open source software. Comput Standards Interfaces 28:109–121

Requirements Engineering for Enterprise Systems: What We Know and What We Don't Know?

Maya Daneva and Roel Wieringa

Abstract This chapter presents research progress in Requirements Engineering (RE) for enterprise systems (ES) with a view to formulating current challenges and a promising research agenda for the future. In the field of ES, many RE approaches have been launched and tried out in the past decade, however most of them are over-expensive and their effectiveness is unpredictable. Our goal in this chapter is to make an inventory of the approaches discussed in literature, to evaluate the quality of evidence available regarding whether these approaches actually worked, and to identify promising directions for future RE research efforts. Our results indicate (i) that while there are significant achievements, the primary goal of RE for ES is only partly achieved and (ii) that the field is likely to remain very challenging due to the increasingly more pronounced cross-organizational aspects of RE in ES projects (e.g. cross-organizational coordination, trust). At the same time, the need for practical, efficient and effective RE approaches will grow as the importance of ES in today's extended enterprises is growing.

1 Introduction

For at least a decade, the elicitation, documentation and negotiation of the requirements for systems based on commercial off-the-shelf (COTS) components have been regarded as an important sub-area of Requirements Engineering (RE). An important example of a project dealing with COTS-based system is the implementation of an enterprise solution based on packaged software, or the so-called Enterprise Systems (ES).[1] Typically, ES are large and multi-component systems that

M. Daneva (✉)
University of Twente, Drienerlolaan 5, P.O. Box 217, 7500, EA Enschede, The Netherlands
e-mail: m.daneva@utwente.nl

[1]We prefer to use this more general term over the more traditional "enterprise resource planning (ERP)" because today's ES have an architecture and functionality of a greater variety than traditional ERP systems.

S. Nurcan et al. (eds.), *Intentional Perspectives on Information Systems Engineering*,
DOI 10.1007/978-3-642-12544-7_7,

provide cross-functional services to a business. They often impact data semantics and business processes across more than one functional area of a business and today, they increasingly perform cross-organizational services. This sub-area of RE is becoming even more important as ES bring the vital capabilities for modern companies to network with others in forming extended enterprises [59].

The requirements for ES concern the business processes and the data flows that the ES should support as well as the key information entities in the subject domain of the system. These requirements reflect the needs of organizational units in one or more companies for a system that helps solve coordination and collaboration problems related to processing, for example, a purchase order, a good receipt, a sales order, or managing inventory levels. RE for ES is about composition and reconciliation of conflicting demands [13]. The RE process usually starts with a general set of business process and data requirements, then helps explore standard ES-package functionality to see how closely it matches the ES adopting organization's process and data needs [13]. This typically happens in an iterative fashion and includes (1) in today's cross-organizational case, mapping each partner company's organizational structure into the ES-package's predefined organization units; (2) defining a scope for business process standardization using standard application modules; (3) creating business process and data architectures specific to the extended enterprise based on predefined reusable package-specific process and data models; (4) specifying data conversion, reporting, and interface requirements. Currently, vendors of business software packages and their consulting partners provide standard RE processes for ES projects. In addition, a number of creative solutions were proposed by researchers and practitioners to further reduce the cost of RE-for-ES by avoiding scope creep, involving the right stakeholders, allocating sufficient resources, adopting goal-directed project management practices, and enlisting the vendors' and consultants' support to those problems [13, 28, 41]. Despite these efforts, it is still very difficult to find a match between the flexibility often required by the business and the rigidity usually imposed by the ES-package modules [14, 15]. In this chapter, we set out to identify the need for future research that addresses this difficulty. Our goal is to make an inventory of the approaches discussed in the RE literature, to evaluate the quality of evidence available regarding whether these approaches actually worked, and to identify contemporary currents which shape the future focus of RE research efforts.

The scope of this chapter is restricted to elicitation and modeling/documentation techniques and the main unit of analysis is at the micro level, i.e. projects and organizations, rather a business sector or even a geographic zone (e.g. North America, Europe, Asia). Some good studies that compare RE practices at macro level are presented in [21, 30, 45]. This chapter will not address the matter of industrial take-up of RE practices except in as much as this relates to parts of the RE for ES. For a thorough example of analysis of RE practices, we refer interested readers to [21, 30, 45].

The chapter is organized as follows: We start with a description of the results of a literature review of published research and experience reports in both journals and research-oriented conferences. This is followed by an evaluation of research progress in (i) requirements elicitation, (ii) modeling, and (iii) the impact of a few notable current trends on these two major RE sub-areas. We, then, lay out a set of further research directions that we inferred from our reflection on good recent progress, from examining past failures and from our knowledge about new business developments in the ES marketplace.

2 Identifying Areas of RE Publication Activity

In the RE community, there is a consensus that the main problem in RE for ES is the misfit between business requirements of ES adopters and ES functionality [14, 15, 20, 23]. Both RE researchers and practitioners agree that there is a gap between the functionality required by an organization and functionality offered by the various packages in the ERP marketplace. In the past decade, the RE community came up with a significant number of ideas meant to solve a broad variety of RE issues related to this gap. One reason for this growth in proposals is that an increasingly large number of companies have adopted packaged solutions and many of the adopters started reflecting and reporting on their implementation experiences, including their RE practices. Case studies and experience reports about ES implementations are now being published by companies in virtually any industry sector. In addition, there is much greater awareness of the importance of good RE practices and their adoption.

To illustrate the increase of RE publication on ES, we did a quick search of literature sources in a few prominent bibliographic databases (IEEE Explore, ACM Digital Library, Springerlink), which yielded Fig. 1.

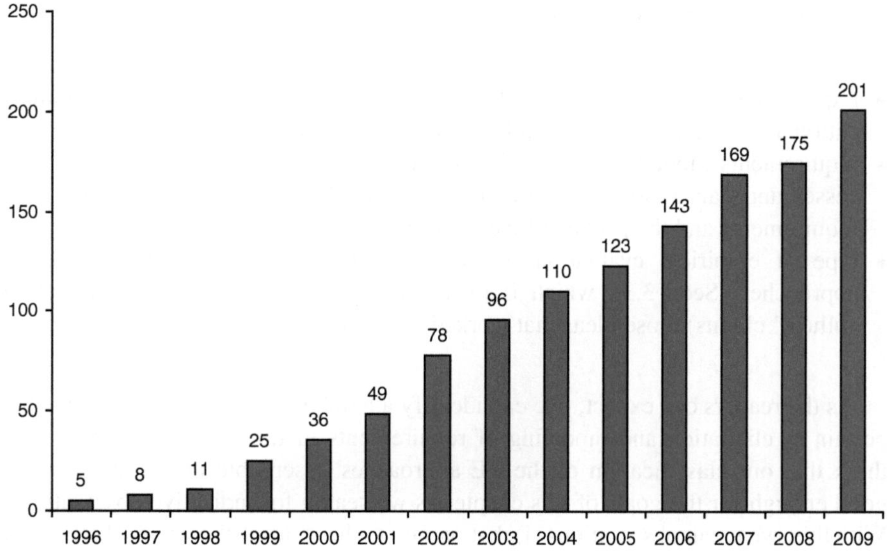

Fig. 1 Number of publications in three bibliographic databases in the last 15 years

Figure 1 indicates the number of papers, that have been published in (RE-related) journals and conferences and that include one of the strings "Requirements Engineering", "ERP", "Enterprise System", "Supply Chain Management System", "Business-to-Business Systems", "COTS", "Customer Relationship Management System" either in their title, or in their abstract. As Fig. 1 indicates, we found that the number of papers published between 1996 and 2010 grew up from 5 to 201. For the purpose of this chapter, we applied the following process of reviewing the content of these publications:

1. We merged the results of the search in the three databases and then eliminated from the resulting list those papers which were only remotely connected to the topics of eliciting and modeling requirements in ES projects.
2. The remaining papers were classified in two groups based on the two RE sub-areas which we deal with in this chapter (namely, elicitation and modeling).
3. We took notes on the key ideas included in the approaches from the papers that we classified in step (2) and on the practical application of the approaches.

We make the note that we did not go further to assess the actual evidence regarding the value of the proposed approaches, because our goals in this chapter are to take a snapshot view of the RE-for-ES field and to complement it with our current knowledge of market changes and, then, shortlist an initial agenda for future research.

Our merging of the search results in each database yielded a total of 110 papers, out of which we considered 53 for inclusion in this chapter. The specific aspects which we identified in these publications and which we selected for discussion in this chapter are listed as follows:

- requirements elicitation (Sect. 3.1), which is concerned with finding, communication and validation of facts and rules about the business,
- requirements modeling (Sect. 3.2), which is concerned with the business processes and data representation and analysis of the gap between the enterprise requirements and the package functionality, and
- type of empirical evaluation of the requirements elicitation and modeling approaches (Sect. 3.3), which is to understand (based on the RE publication authors' claims) those ideas that worked in real-life settings.

As the readers can expect, one can identify a number of overlapping aspects that pertain to elicitation and modeling of requirements in ES projects. However, we think that our classification of the RE approaches observable in the literature, is good enough for the goals of this chapter as we search for indicative observations. With this, we mean observations (i) that pertain to the state-of-the-art in RE research or practice and (ii) that suggest themes worthwhile investing our research efforts in the future.

3 Progress to Date

We checked the published approaches regarding their underlying ideas and assumptions, and the availability of empirical evidence about their effectiveness and the known problems about their use in practice.

3.1 Elicitation Techniques

Our review found that more than 20 requirements elicitation approaches have been proposed and tried out in real life project settings. In our observation, all these approaches are based on domain knowledge, however they differ regarding how they organize domain knowledge and how they create a domain dictionary (e.g. what knowledge sources they use for this). We clustered the elicitation methods in five groups:

1. *Process-mining based methods*, which employ a kind of process-mining technology in support of requirements elicitation activities. Examples of such approaches are presented in [11, 57]. These researchers came up with specialized tools to capture the complete business environments in which the ES will be put in operation. The result of using such a tool is then considered a first sketch of the ES process requirements. The idea of process-mining first surfaced in the 1990s, when Intellicorp, an SAP Development Partner, launched the LiveModel tool capable of identifying all transactions being in use in the current SAP environment in a company. The process models generated through this tool have been used by SAP implementation teams to draft the first version of process requirements in SAP upgrade, consolidation, or migration projects.
2. *Reference-model-based approaches*, which rely on predefined process and data models (termed reference models) and help clarify the questions of (1) what tasks must be performed and what package-embedded business functionality can support these tasks, (2) which organizational units should execute these tasks, (3) what information is needed for executing the tasks in a more efficient way, and (4) what information exchange must happen among tasks and how the package and other applications would support this. We refer to the reference models as to reusable and general descriptions of the commonalities in organizations, business sectors or systems that can be used as a base to derive other models from. In the ES RE field, we distinguish between two types of reference models: (i) software-independent reference models which represent generic descriptions of business processes and data flows in a certain enterprise area (e.g. accounting) or in a certain business sector (e.g. telecommunications), and (ii) ES reference models which are "conceptual descriptions of customizable software" (as defined by [43]). We must note that in RE-for-ES, there is a number of reference-model-based elicitation approaches that proved their market value in the past 20 years. Among the software-independent-reference-model-based

elicitation techniques, the ARIS framework [48] is one of the most popular. It provides RE professionals with a ready-to-use repository of industry-sector-specific business process models, meant to help structuring requirements elicitation interviews and making them more effective. The large consulting companies (e.g. Accenture, Cap Gemini, IBM, and others) have also developed proprietary reference-model-based elicitation approaches which rest on the very same idea as ARIS does. Another example of a business-area-specific elicitation approach is SCOR [31], which proposed an extended reference model of supply chain processes, including the structuring of information exchanged between business processes.

Furthermore, since 1992, the use of reference models has been encouraged by all major ES package vendors (SAP, Baan, Oracle and PeopleSoft). They documented the functionality of their respective packages in the form of ES reference models that also come for free to ES adopters as part of the ES itself. This made it possible, for RE staff and clients engaged in elicitation, to inform themselves quickly about the concerned ES functionality in business terms by navigating from the ES process and data models to the relevant piece of online documentation and to the smallest unit of software functionality, namely the transactions [12].

3. *Quality-model-based approaches*, which focus on the joint elicitation of functional and non-functional requirements by using standard underlying quality models or quality frameworks. The proposals in [6, 17] help building quality models for ES by deploying the ISO/IEC-9026 model, while [49] presents a Fuzzy Quality Function Deployment approach that helps translating functional requirements expressed with linguistic variables into non-functional requirements.
4. *Feature-based approaches*, which draw on the idea of top-down refinement of both functional and non-functional requirements. Similarly to the package-specific-reference-model-based approaches, the feature-based approaches help elicit domain knowledge through the investigation of the specification of the ERP package. These approaches term a function (or a quality attribute of the package) "a feature" [22]. Examples of feature-based approaches are the PORE method [28, 29, 33] and the PAORE approach [22]. When using these approaches, the elicitation analyst first shortlists suitable packages that match the ERP-adopter's requirements, and then elicits and documents in detail the requirements by presenting one concrete package's specification to the clients and by adding those client-specific requirements which are not included in the original package specification.
5. *Constructionist and organization-theory-based approaches*, which consider (i) ES requirements as a specific form of knowledge representation, (ii) the ES as an organizational transformation system, e.g. a system that changes its users' work patterns, and (iii) the ES project reality as socially constructed [2, 4, 24, 39]. These approaches rest on the position that our understanding of the ES requirements can be complete only when we understand the organizational transformation that the ES enables and the effect of the transformation on the

users. As Ramos and Berry explain, the transformation redefines the job of the elicitation analysts in that he/she must be aware of how and when particular pieces of knowledge are created in the RE process in order "to know when to be observing and what to be looking during the observation" [39]. The constructionist approaches generally propose to complement the elicitation techniques that focus on enterprise and system requirements with observation-based techniques (e.g. ethnographic methods) to elicit stakeholders' tacit knowledge and emotional requirements (e.g. values, beliefs). Emotional requirements are deemed [39] as important for the project as enterprise, functional and non-functional requirements are. Based on extensive case study research [39], Ramos and Berry convincingly justify why projects that include emotional requirements are more effective than projects that merely use the elicitation techniques mentioned earlier in the other four classes in this section. Examples of constructionist approaches are proposed in [2, 39]. In [39], the approach provides a list of symptoms and emotional responses which the elicitation analyst should watch for. In [2], the authors provide characterizations of five "roles that an ES can play" for its users. The job of the elicitation analyst is to first map the ES system in the concrete ERP-adopting organization against these roles, and then to structure his/her elicitation efforts based on the characteristics related to the particular role at hand.

It is important to note that most of the authors of the surveyed papers on elicitation techniques (discussed earlier in this section) carried out empirical evaluation research to demonstrate that their proposed techniques meet the goals that have been set for them in the first place. This commitment of RE researchers to the use of empirical research methods as well as the remarkable variety of elicitation techniques motivated us to search for publications that compare the techniques regarding, e.g. their effectiveness, the assumptions about the context that the techniques need to satisfy so that they are useful, or the business goals that can be best achieved by using these techniques. Our search yielded no publication that dealt explicitly with these questions. Instead, we found fragmentary evaluative information in those papers only, which discussed how vendor-provided ES-reference-model-based elicitation compares to process-mining-based elicitation. In all these cases, researchers used the comparison to stress the key limitation of vendor-provided approaches, namely that they are package-specific (and therefore they rarely could be used in projects that implement other packages). We think, therefore, that the search for insights on and improved understanding of when to use which technique, is the next big step in ES requirements elicitation research.

The elicitation techniques also seem to assume that the ES-based solution includes one vendor's product and is implemented in one company. No technique explicitly addresses today's case of cross-organizational ES implementations, in which the solution to be implemented includes more than one package, which may not all be provided by the same vendor and which may not all be used by all partner companies in an extended enterprise. The matter that the setting is cross-organizational poses new challenges, for example, how to elicit the requirements in the face of different partner companies using different ways to organize domain knowledge and to create their domain dictionary. Would it be possible at all for the partners in an extended enterprise to come up with one common way of approaching the requirements elicitation tasks? What kind of coordination models make sense to use so that partner companies coordinate their elicitation efforts? Future research in these areas is needed.

3.2 Modelling Techniques

In our literature review, we made a number of common observations referring to all the surveyed approaches to requirements modeling and documentation in ES projects. First, we found that all approaches are multi-perspective in nature (that is, they use multiple viewpoints to document the ES requirements). This is unsurprising, given the highly complex context where requirements are to be documented, which calls for using viewpoints as a tactics to cope with complexity.

Second, the RE publications agree on that in ES projects, requirements modeling addresses: (i) the selection of a package (and hence, the need to document the domain), and (ii) the alignment of a selected package to the ERP adopter's business (and hence, the need to model the functionality embedded in the package).

Third, the RE researchers give evidence confirming the viability of both top-down and bottom-up approaches to analyzing the gap between enterprise requirements models and system models. These two types of approaches differ regarding the starting point of the requirements documentation process. While bottom-up approaches imply to start from the review of the package specification and proceed with documentation of the domain requirements, the top-down approaches mean to starts from the (solution-independent) domain requirements that are to be further refined by using information about the concrete package functionality. The top-down approaches are preferred in contexts in which (i) modeling is a prerequisite for a package selection exercise, or (ii) it supports a business reengineering effort in an organization. In both cases, the outcomes of the modeling process are solution-independent requirements. The bottom-up approaches suit best those contexts, when the decision on a package has been made and modeling is a part of a business process/ES alignment effort. RE researchers [53] argue that unlike the bottom-up approaches, which target the alignment of a package, the top-down modeling approaches are capable of addressing both the selection of a package and the alignment of a selected package. In our view, regardless the focus of the modeling approaches, they both aid in jointly carrying out problem analysis and solution design activity (that is, joint RE and architecture design).

Fourth, our review indicates one common theme which is inherent to the research on requirements modeling, namely the exploration of the fitness relationship between domain models and system functionality. It is worth noting that those authors, who proposed requirements representation techniques, also investigated the fitness relationship. Their research efforts yielded quantitative models [16, 25, 46, 54] that help understand the fitness relationship and plan actions to preserve it when requirements change. The RE community is especially indebted to Colette Rolland and her team for the number of fitness analysis studies (e.g. [16, 25, 46]) which they carried out in this area.

Fifth, the RE community is united on that it is a good practice to represent both the domain models and the system models by using the same modeling language, because both types of models relate to business issues and in ES projects it is unnatural to segregate them. This position is shared by both researchers [42, 44, 53, 54] and practitioners [5, 12, 13, 36, 48]. Indeed, two of the market-leading packages, SAP and BAAN, provide modeling processes, tools and repositories of (solution-specific) models which describe the package functionality in business terms [12, 36]. SAP-adopting organizations may use the ARIS modeling languages [48], which were used to document the SAP application suite, while BAAN-adopters may use the Dynamic Enterprise Modelling approach [36] which is implied in the BAAN package. Presently, new variants of these modeling techniques have been proposed, e.g. the configurable reference-model approach [38, 44] to smooth even more the gap analysis process and the identification of the best possible configuration options within stated enterprise requirements.

However, the RE community also recognized that not all ERP packages have ready-to-use solution models and, in turn, spent significant efforts to solve the challenges related to this case. In the last decade, Colette Rolland [40] was the first (1999) to develop and evaluate a map representation that is to be applied in both domain requirements modeling and COTS systems modeling. Drawing on her experience, Rolland and Prakash [41, 42] redefined the map representation to cover the special case of ES as a major class of COTS-based projects. In 2000, Illa et al. [19] built the SHERPA method for documenting ES requirements and propose a formal language for modeling the application domain, translating user needs into requirements over the ES products, and for reflecting how concrete ES products adjust to these requirements. In 2002, the UML was customized to the ES project context [26]. In 2003, Arinze et al. [1] proposed an object-oriented framework to ease the gap analysis of enterprise and ES models, and Soffer et al. [53] developed and empirically evaluated the Object Process ERP representation that also is able to capture the so-called "ERP optionality" levels, that is, both the full scope of ES-embedded process and data control options, and the interdependencies among them. Building on it, Soffer et al. developed in 2005 a bottom-up reverse-engineering based modeling approach [54] to solve the problem of aligning a selected package to enterprise requirements. In 2004–2007, Carvallo et al. [8, 17] gave a new dimension to the discussion of requirements modeling approaches in ES by contributing to engineering the COTS (or ES) non-functional requirements. Based on case study research, these authors propose the RECSS method [8], a goal-oriented approach which helps describing enterprise requirements as well as functional and non-functional requirements of the system. By applying this method, requirements analysts can create a goal model of the system environment and also include those external elements that interact with the system. Complementarily to this, the RECSS method also uses a decomposition process through which one can build quality models for the system modules based on the ISO/IEC software quality standard.

Other RE researchers suggested the use of process modelling tiers to manage the complexity of enterprise and ES process modeling [18], the technique of the Requirement Integration Model [32] to account for interdependencies in business workflows, and the Data Activity Model for Configuration approach [34] meant to help align a package to the organization by the joint engineering of data and process requirements. The authors of [3, 52], also proposed ontology-based approaches to the representation and gap analysis of enterprise requirements and package-embedded functionality. For example, Babkin et al. [3] developed a requirements modeling approach that defines four sub-ontologies: ontology of requirements, of main data objects, of business processes and of configuration objects. The first ontology helps the elicitation process, while the other three ontologies are to support business process modeling activities and the activities of data requirements configuration requirements documentation, respectively. It is worth noting that the authors of these approaches [54] posed the question of how their proposals compare with the vendor-imposed modeling approaches (e.g. ARIS [12] and DEM [36]). They found that when using a modeling technique that is not part of the package, there are some extra costs involved in creating the models of the system functionality. Because the modeling approaches are not common standards in the ES field, for RE professionals to use them in a broader practical context, they first have to create a system model of their selected package.

We also make the note that all the proposed modeling techniques have been evaluated as a minimum by their authors by means of empirical research methods. Some techniques, e.g. the event-driven-process chain modeling method of ARIS [56, 58] have been validated by researchers that worked independently from the authors who originally proposed the technique.

Similarly to our survey in the sub-area of requirements elicitation, we also checked whether there are publications that compare the surveyed modeling techniques for their effectiveness. We found three studies [27, 37, 55] that compared business process modeling approaches. In [55] the authors compared them against a set of criteria which are reportedly critical to ES adopters. In [37], the authors compared two variants of the event-driven-process chain modeling technique (which is part of ARIS [12]) regarding perceived usefulness and easy of use from the perspective of modelers, by carrying out an experiment with postgraduate students. In [27], the authors compared business process modeling languages against a five-perspective-meta-model that helps judge the ability of a modeling language to capture the essential elements of the business context and the subject domain. While the authors in [55] indicate when to use which technique, the authors of the other two studies [27, 37] attempted to answer the question which of the compared techniques is better for a specific purpose/RE task.

While analyzing the existing modeling techniques, we also found that all modeling methods make tacit assumptions that might not be realistic in all situations. For example, RE authors seem to still assume that modeling is manifestly more useful than well written textual requirement documents. In our view, reality may question the extent to which this assumption is realistic. RE publications say very little about those contexts in which modeling would yield marginal benefits or be a financial burden and a project "over-kill".

Furthermore, ES requirements modeling approaches have the tacit expectation that the resulting models are sufficiently understandable for those who are to review them and make decisions based on them. Our survey found that understandability of both enterprise and systems requirements models was addressed in very few papers and whenever it was addressed, it was from the perspective of the requirements engineer (also called requirements analyst). This finding agrees with a finding from a recent mapping study [10] that we did on empirical evaluation of the quality attributes of requirement specifications. Therein, we found that understandability was the most frequently researched quality aspect of requirements specifications, yet we found no paper that evaluated understandability of ES specifications. This finding is a surprise as it indicates a paradox: on one side, the authors of modeling techniques do acknowledge the importance of the social aspects in ES projects and the purpose of the models as communication vehicles to help establish a common understanding among stakeholders; on the other side, the RE research community published very little on the extent to which the models, produced by using the proposed modeling techniques, are understandable for the relevant project stakeholders.

Next, the papers which are focused on modeling for the purpose of gap analysis rest on the tacit assumption that the better the fit (that is, the closer the match achieved between business processes and ES solution), the more the value achieved. In reality however, the "aligned" ES solution becomes available for clients at earliest six months after the gap analysis took place and the value that clients receive at that time is far below the expectations. Indeed, the practice shows that only one out of five companies achieves more than half of anticipated benefits [59]. This alone questions the fundamental assumptions behind most gap analysis techniques and makes us think that we should re-evaluate our understanding of "business/ES fit" from the perspective of ES project goals and business value. Most of the ES projects have measurable goals and a gap analysis is rarely performed without considering the business case for the ES project. Therefore, it is worthwhile uncovering the relationship among the concepts of business/ES fit, project goals, and business case. This forms a direction for future research. We think that only when we understand sufficiently well this relationship, could we better leverage the RE community's collective knowledge of business/ES fit and of gap analysis techniques so that it adds more value to RE practitioners and ES-adopters.

Next, most of the papers on modeling techniques do not address the costs involved in using these techniques. Those paper which do so, implicitly assume that the cost and effort needed are acceptable. This assumption might not be realistic in all ES contexts. For example, Soffer et al. [54] indicate that it would cost extra effort to run the OPM modeling process for aligning a package to enterprise requirements, as the analyst first have to create the model of the package functionality. In our view, it's also interesting to understand how much time (e.g. in person hours), it would take to create a model of a specific package component, e.g. accounting, in a company of a specific size. It is also worthwhile knowing how much time it would take to learn a modeling/gap analysis technique and its application process. Answers to these questions are important to make a decision on how to deploy the technique in a particular context. For example, the first author's personal experience suggests that a two-day training on the ARIS modeling technique was not enough for business owners to get comfortable in reading the SAP models without the help of external consultants. In that case, it turned out that hiring a specialist in ARIS-modeling on a permanent basis was much more cost-effective for the ERP-adopter than training all relevant stakeholders on how to use the ARIS methodology.

Last, the published ES modeling techniques tacitly assume that it's possible to scale them up to large projects. Today, this type of projects is, more often than not, cross-organizational, which increases the complexity of ES RE even more. If we are to apply a process-mining or reverse-engineering based approach to such a setting, this assumes that all partner companies in a extended enterprise are prepared to disclose their process and application landscapes (so that the respective tools capture completely their business environments). Assessing how realistic is to assume this means including the concept of trust in the discussion on ES requirements. This alone forms another line of research for the future.

3.3 Did These Techniques Work?

As indicated earlier, many papers on ES elicitation and modeling present empirical evaluations. In our review, we consistently observed that when authors propose a technique, they either provide a detailed account of its application in an industrial setting, or they run a complete action case study research intervention in a company and reflect on their learning from it. Table 1 presents the type of empirical research done in the papers which we cited in Sects. 3.1 and 3.2. In this table, the first column refers to the paper that published a RE-for-ES approach. The second column reports on whether this approach is for elicitation, or for modeling, or for both. The last column indicates the context where the empirical study in the paper has been done. The table shows that RE-for-ES researchers have been actively involved in action research with big companies. Some authors also include empirical research in the IT department of their institution (e.g. studies on ES implemented in a university). The brief indication of empirical studies in the table shows that researchers prefer action case studies for their evaluation. This increases the realism of the study but makes generalizability an important issue to consider.

Table 1 Empirical studies in RE for ES

	Sub-area		
References	Elicitation	Modeling	Context of empirical study
[1]		+	SAP environment
[2]	+		Case study in a BAAN project at six ABB companies
[3]	+	+	Proof-of-concept in SAP CRM project
[8]	+		Proof-of-concept in COTS/Mail server system
[11]	+		Case study in SAP environment
[18]		+	Case study in SAP projects in the power generation sector
[19]		+	COTS projects in Spanish companies
[22]	+		Proof-of-concept in planning sales management project
[26]		+	Case study in SAP environment
[28]	+	+	COTS projects in various UK-based companies
[31]	+		Case study in SAP environment
[32]		+	SAP implementation project at a university in Thailand
[36]	+	+	Case study in Baan implementation projects
[37]		+	Case study in SAP environment
[39]	+		ERP case studies in Portuguese companies
[40]		+	Proof-of-concept in a COTS project
[41]		+	Case study in SAP environment
[44]		+	Case study in SAP environment
[48]	+	+	Case study in SAP implementation projects
[49]	+		A case study in a large ES project in 5 business domains
[53]	+	+	Case study in ES environment
[54]	+	+	Case study in ES environment
[57]	+		Case study in SAP environment

4 Directions for Future Research

4.1 Directions from our Analysis of RE Research

In this section we derive clusters of activities for future research, while reflecting on our findings in Sects. 3.1, 3.2 and 3.3.

Our review confirmed the presence of a multiplicity of RE approaches to ES projects. This is unsurprising, as no one approach is demonstrated to be superior to another. In addition, we observe that the variety of elicitation and modeling approaches brought a variety of empirical studies in which practitioners and researchers have used these approaches and shared their lessons learnt. We consider this use of empirical research methods beneficial to the RE community, especially when the studies are done independently by different researchers and not by the authors of the RE techniques themselves (e.g. [56, 58]), as this means a reduced bias. Moreover, the industrial studies refer to various domains in which ES were implemented and in a variety of business sectors. This is a positive development as well, because it opens up opportunities for cross-case analysis of the lessons learnt. Realizing these research opportunities is a worthwhile endeavor for the future.

Furthermore, today's ES packages no longer compete on business functionality but on quality attributes, that is on how well they meet the quality requirements (or non-functional requirements) of the ES adopters. Finding an ideal match between system configuration options and business processes would not be worth, unless it meets certain performance, availability, security, interoperability requirements (just to name a few). In the literature, we observe a number of publications [8, 9, 49] that acknowledge both the importance of quality requirements and the need to develop systematic approaches to address them in ES projects. However, how to trade-off these requirements, what represents the "right balance" among them, and when it is realistic to achieve the right balance (in intra-company and in cross-organizational settings) is largely unknown. Understanding the challenges this question poses and proposing approaches to counter these challenges represents a viable line for future research. Specifically, we mean understanding the contextual mechanisms that impact the process of joint RE and architecture design in ES projects.

The following two directions are closely connected and motivated by the increased use of ES as cross-organizational coordination support technology and the increased needs of ES adopters to design and redesign ES-supported coordination and collaboration processes within extended enterprises. The first direction refers to making the cross-organizational coordination requirements an explicit part of the requirements elicitation and modeling in ES projects. More in detail, our motivation of the importance of this topic for the future RE research is presented in [14]. In this review we found that with very few exceptions, the elicitation and modeling approaches subsume the coordination requirements into process and data requirements. An overall observation is that all the publications on techniques presented in Table 1 offer very little and fragmentary discussion on coordination, and when they add it, it refers to intra-organizational and not to cross-organizational coordination. We think that while in intra-organizational settings, this might not represent an acute RE problem, in cross-organizational context if we keep using the existing elicitation and modeling techniques as they are, it is likely to be suboptimal because they are not geared to this context. We therefore think that these techniques should be extended (or even completely re-stated) to explicitly handle cross-organizational coordination requirements [14]. The second and related direction for future research is about getting actively involved in empirical evaluation of the existing techniques in cross-organizational contexts. Based on our recent research on cross-organizational ES, we identified seven characteristics of these projects which have implications for ES RE:

1. The projects deliver a shared system which lets the business activities of one company become an integral part of the business of its partners.
2. The projects create system capabilities far beyond the sum of the ES components' individual capabilities, which, allows the resulting system to qualitatively acquire new properties as result of its configuration.
3. The solution-to-be may well include diverse configurations, each of which matches the needs of a unique stakeholder group, which, in turn, implies the presence of coordination mechanisms unique to each configuration.

4. The projects deliver a system which is far from complete once the ES project is over, because a cross-organizational ES solution must mirror rapidly-changing business requirements, and so be adjusted regularly to accommodate current business needs.
5. The resulting solution does not have an identified owner at cross-organizational system level, as the system is shared.
6. These projects may well have a low level of organizational awareness of what RE activities (e.g. eliciting coordination requirements, identifying and analyzing coordination capability gaps, investigation and mapping of coordination mechanisms [14]) are to be used to elicit and model the requirements as completely as possible.
7. The solutions are not "built" in the sense that a master architect envisions the parts and their relationships; rather they evolve into existence and change through their life cycles as new shared pieces of functionality are built, existing intra-organizational systems connect to become shared, and shared parts of the system are disintegrated as soon as needs of sharing processes and data disappear.

We think that these characteristics pose elicitation and modeling challenges which are well beyond those presently addressed in the RE-for-ES literature. For example, these characteristics might make it overall difficult to use predefined business-sector-specific solution-independent reference models, as such models merely can not exist for all various collaborative arrangements that business partners may creatively come up with. In contrast, these characteristics may rather favor the use of constructionist elicitation methods in an extended enterprise settings as they explicitly account for the organizational transformation inherent to cross-organizational ES projects. The point we would like to make here is not that cross-organizational ES are different; it is that the assumptions which we usually make when we elicit and model the requirements in ES projects do not apply. We think that a RE analyst needs to know both (i) the elicitation and modeling vehicles at his disposal and (ii) whether or not the implicit and explicit assumptions about the use of these vehicles match the project settings. We saw in Sects. 3.1 and 3.2 that most of the assumptions we typically make in elicitation and modeling do not apply to a shared ES solution. Therefore, more research effort needs to be put into evaluating our existing techniques and understanding their strengths and possible weaknesses when deployed in a cross-organizational project context.

4.2 Directions from Examining Failures

One observation which we made consistently across the papers in our review is that almost all projects that the papers' authors described were reportedly kinds of successes. This clearly indicates the researchers' practice to learn from success; nevertheless we should not underestimate the benefits of learning from failed projects

[35]. Maybe, because of the prevailing culture to encourage researchers to publish more about the lessons they learn from success than about their learning from failures, in the RE literature we found no study that gives failed examples of using RE techniques in real projects. We must remind that in other disciplines, learning from failures has motivated innovation and we see no particular reason of why learning-from-failed-projects can not be useful for the RE community as well. In the experience of the first author, RE professionals do experience failure but the field does not profit from these failure experiences. The prevailing "we-can-fix-it-later-on" attitude, which is also compatible with the project management practice of compressing deadlines, brings many ES projects teams in a working mode that undermines the role of requirements. If a system fails at the go-life stage, then teams rarely get back to the RE process and look into RE malpractices, discern patterns of failure, and think of what they could do differently the next time. This situation is partly attributable to the prevailing business practice that consultants are contracted for six-month cycles and that, by the time RE mistakes are revealed in a project, they rush to their next project, which may be in another business sector and they may not see an immediate value of the reflection on what they could have done differently should they go through the same project again. Moreover, most of the consulting companies who employ the consultants are focused on securing their next contract engagement in another organization and, therefore, may have little time to spend on accumulating RE knowledge through systematic post-mortems of past projects. We support the position that to start learning from failures, we first need a few published examples of RE malpractice in ES projects. However, these examples are not readily available at the present time and it is a challenge to build up archives of bad examples and failures. By this, we do not just mean a set of poorly specified requirements, e.g. diagrams, or suboptimal gap analyses, but sufficiently documented explanations of why a RE method did not work as originally thought. We think that learning about the mechanisms that are at place and that possibly condition the success and failure of a RE practice will extend our repertoire of knowledge that can assist us in deciding which practice to use in which context. For example, it is well known that business owners in ES projects do not like reading technical descriptions (e.g. data models). However, there are RE teams in (assumingly) mature organizations who apply alternative (more creative) techniques for getting the business data (and conversion) requirements in a way that minimizes that chance of RE failure or even a project failure. What approaches do consultants deploy in getting the data requirements right? We think, these skills could and should be explicated and shared with others.

4.3 Directions from Existing Market Trends

In the last decade, there are a number of changes in the market demands that have implications for RE research for ES. For RE-for-ES to remain an industry-relevant research field, it must be able to keep up with these changes. This section lists some trends, which in our view restate and redefine the known RE-for-ES challenges, or pose entirely new challenges to RE for ES. We make the note that our list below may seem eclectic, reflecting our perception of particularly acute needs.

1. *The increased penetration of free and open source ES (FOS-ES) solutions.* Recent market research reports that ES adopters have become more receptive to FOS-ES [47]. A major reason for this trend is that FOS-ES means reducing licensing costs. In a recession-hit economy, FOS-ES solutions have become a feasible strategy for many small to midsize companies that want to automate their cooperation and coordination process. The technology of service-oriented architecture (SOA) made it possible for these cost-conscious ES-adopters to efficiently embed a FOS-ES-based solution within their processes and application landscapes, and also to customize or improve their systems on ongoing basis [51]. A recent review of the most popular FOS-ERP products is presented in [50].

   This trend introduces some changes that have RE implications [6, 7, 20]. For example, the distance between the user and the developer gets smaller, because the role of the ES adopter is changing from a consumer to a prosumer; this is an active role in which the adopter assumes the process of adapting software, reporting bugs, submitting feature requests, and posting messages to FOS-ES community lists. Based on their willingness to share information, smart prosumers will also provide bug fixes, new features and even entire modules. In this setting, it is expected [20] that the smaller distance between the user and the developer will alleviate the problem of misfit between the FOS-ES functionality to the enterprise requirements. This, however, has not been investigated yet by means of rigorous empirical research methods and we think it is a candidate line of research for the future.

   Moreover, becoming prosumers means to ES adopters a shift from a client viewpoint to a developers' viewpoint, which also means adopting a new mindset and accepting low level of managerial control, as the FOS-ES development is a community-centric activity. Hence, the adopter will have to follow a RE cycle that is influenced by many members of the community, which may incur massive coordination costs. How to create a cost-effective RE process for ES adopters and what coordination-enhancing activities should it include is an open question and warrants future research.
2. *The trend to form vendor-supported community collaborations for ES implementation.* In order to lower the ES implementation cost and shorten the ES project duration for their clients, ES vendors built online communities [47, 60] where ES-adopters can share their knowledge of aligning the respective vendor's package to enterprise requirements For example, two of the major ERP vendors, SAP and Oracle, have built, respectively, the SAP Developer Network and the Oracle Technology Network. The sharing platforms typically are Web 2.0 knowledge repository systems, which facilitate the members of the community to practice RE processes that actively involve case-based reasoning (e.g. exploring past cases, short-listing similar cases and reusing the solutions from the past cases to the particular context in question). Research [60] indicates that these repositories

streamline the collaborative execution of the knowledge-intensive activities in RE-for-ES within and beyond the ES-adopter's organizational boundaries, which can be invaluable in identifying the ways to improve the fit between enterprise requirements and ES functionality. We make the note that despite the collaborative nature of RE-for-ES, the forms of collaborations between the ES-adopters and consultants as well as among ERP-adopters themselves, has received in the RE literature only scant attention. Understanding the forms of collaborative RE-for-ES and the case-based reasoning models that serve best in the alignment of a package to enterprise requirements is a worthy line of research for the future.

3. *The trend to use agile RE approaches.* These have been gaining momentum among RE methodologies and are now entering the realm of ES implementation. More often than before, prominent agile publication venues (e.g. AGILE and XP), report on companies' experiences of introducing agile approaches to ES projects. (We searched the proceedings of these two conferences and found more than 10 papers on agile approaches in ES implementations at large companies). While one might think that the agile philosophy is incompatible with the ES project contexts, these companies experienced agile approaches as a viable option. We do not think that this is surprising, because the agile philosophy's focus on delivering business value and on satisfying clients is appealing to both ES-adopters and consultants who, especially in times of economic downturn, are pressed to demonstrate some specific instances of value of the ES-solution much earlier in the project. Second, at the heart of any agile approach is an assumption that regardless what the requirements might be at the project start, they will not be the same at the project end. It is intuitive to think, therefore, that the longer the project, the more realistic this assumption would be. In most situations, this assumption is realistic in the ES project contexts, notorious for their highly volatile requirements and prolonged duration. We think that the presence of agile approaches has certain implications for ES RE professionals and that it is a potential topic of future research to uncover what these implications are and how we can make a better use of the agile philosophy in RE for ES. In our view, the investigation of these implications is a mandate of the RE community and we should not leave this to the management science community or to the agile community and wait for them to come up with ideas for improving the existing RE-for-ES practices by using agile principles.
4. *The trend to deploy on-demand ES solutions.* The terms Software as a Service (SaaS) or on-demand ES refers to ES functionality being delivered over the Internet from a single application instance that is shared across all users. SaaS ES-solutions are rapidly increasing their share in some ES markets, notably CRM, and also penetrate into various business areas (e.g. financial accounting, human resource management). In uncertain economic conditions, particularly to cost-conscious small and mid-sized businesses, this type of ES solutions yields a number of cost benefits, including no up-front costs, no licensing fees and rapid, easy deployment. More and more companies are moving their mission-critical systems to the SaaS model to realize these benefits.

A SaaS-ES-solution is overall less flexible than on-premises ES in that the ES-adopter can not completely customize or rewrite its code. Because of this, the SaaS-ES-adopters must be prepared rather to change their business process to fit the solution than to align it to enterprise requirements. Also such adopters often face massive coordination effort because they have to integrate hosted software from various vendors with their existing ES solutions and/or legacy applications. How to run an effective RE process for SaaS-ES projects is by and large unknown. We, however, think that further research efforts in this direction are warranted, because SaaS-ES solutions represent an important development in the field.

5 Conclusion

This chapter surveyed the requirements elicitation and modeling approaches in the sub-area of RE for ES. We reasoned about some tacit assumptions these approaches make and why these assumptions might not be realistic in all ES contexts. Based on this we derived directions for future research. We acknowledge that such a survey can bring only a snapshot view on a fast-changing area. However, we think some lessons can be derived from it.

First, RE-for-ES has a long future ahead. ES will stay, though the on-premise ES solutions will have to live with new types of ES, namely FOS-ES and SaaS. The context of these projects gets increasingly more cross-organizational on both the ES adopters' side and the ES vendors' side. That the ES adopters are cross-organizational businesses calls for developing cost-effective approaches for handling requirements for business coordination. ES solutions include hosted and on-premise ES modules provided by multiple vendors, and this calls for cost-effective approaches to the complex problem of aligning the coordination mechanisms embedded in multiple packages to the coordination requirements of the ES-adopters. The elicitation and modeling approaches developed in the RE community in the past decade might only partly serve the needs of the ES projects embracing the current market trends.

Second, our analysis gives us enough evidence that ES implementations have impacted RE research regarding sub-areas as requirements elicitation and modeling. This means that RE researchers (active in non-ES project contexts) who design solutions to problems in those sub-areas should evaluate their proposed solutions regarding how they work in the ES context. In general, if a solution proposal is meant to be industry-relevant, then researchers have to evaluate and generalize its usefulness in various contexts. We think that ES is one significant context, for which such validation evaluations should take place.

Third, we witness that the majority of RE-for-ES techniques have been developed and evaluated by means of empirical research methods. This alone is an achievement, given the inherent difficulties in carrying out this type of research activity.

References

1. Arinze B, Anandarajan M (2003) A framework for using OO mapping methods to rapidly configure ERP systems. Commun ACM 46(2):61–65
2. Askenäs L, Westelius A (2000) Five roles of an information system: a social constructionist approach to analyzing the use of ERP systems. In: Proceedings of 21st international conference on information systems, Association of Information Systems, Brisbane, Australia, pp 426–434
3. Babkin E, Potapova E (2009) Using ontology for implementing enterprise resource planning systems. In: Proceedings of IEEE/ACS international conference on computer systems and applications, IEEE Computer Science, Los Alamitos, pp 67–68
4. Bergman M, King JL, Lyytinen K (2002) Large-scale requirements analysis revisited: the need for understanding the political ecology of requirements engineering. Reqs Eng 7(3):152–171
5. Brinkkemper S (1999) RE for ERP: requirements management for the development of packaged software Baan company. In: Proceedings of 4th international symposium on requirements engineering RE, IEEE CS, Los Alamitos, p 159
6. Carvalho RA (2006) Issues on evaluating free/open source ERP systems, research and practical issues of enterprise information systems, Springer, pp 667–676
7. Carvalho RA, Monnerat RM (2008) Development support tools for enterprise resource planning. IEEE IT Professional 10(5):39–45
8. Carvallo JP, Franch X, Quer C (2008) Requirements engineering for COTS-based software systems. In: Proceedings of the 2008 ACM symposium on applied computing, ACM, New York, pp 638–644
9. Colombo E, Francalanci C (2004) Selecting CRM packages based on architectural, functional, and cost requirements: empirical validation of a hierarchical ranking model. Reqs Eng 9(3):186–203
10. Condori-Fernánsdez N, Daneva M, Sikkel K, Wieringa R, Dieste O, Pastor O (2009) A systematic mapping study on empirical evaluation of software requirements specifications techniques. In: Proceedings of the 3rd symposium on empirical software engineering and measurement, IEEE Computer Science, Los Alamitos, pp 502–505
11. Chiplunkar C, Deshmukh SG, Chattopadhyay R (2003) Application of principles of event related open systems to business process reengineering. Computers Industrial Eng 45(3): 347–374
12. Curran C, Keller G (1998) SAP R/3 business blueprint: understanding the business. Prentice Hall, Upper Saddle River
13. Daneva M (2004) ERP requirements engineering: lessons learnt. IEEE Softw 21(2):26–33
14. Daneva M, Wieringa RJ (2006) A requirements engineering framework for cross-organizational ERP systems. Reqs Eng 11(3):194–204
15. Daneva M, Wieringa R (2008) Cost estimation for cross-organizational ERP projects: research perspectives. Softw Quality J 16(3):459–481
16. Etien A, Rolland C (2005) Measuring the fitness relationship. Reqs Eng 10(3):184–197
17. Franch X, Carvallo JP (2003) Using quality models in software package selection. IEEE Softw 20(1):34–41
18. Gulla JA, Brasethvik T (2000) On the challenges of business modeling in large scale reengineering projects. In: Proceedings of the 4th international conference on requirements engineering, IEEE Computer Science, Los Alamitos, pp 17–26
19. Illa X, Franch X, Pastor JA (2000) Formalising ERP selection criteria. In: Proceedings of the 10th international workshop on software specification and design, ACM, New York, pp 115–122
20. Johansson B, Carvalho RA (2009) Management of requirements in ERP development: a comparison between proprietary and open source ERP. In: Proceedings of the ACM symposium on applied computing (SAC), Enterprise information systems track, ACM, New York, pp 1605–1609

21. Juristo N, Moreno AM, Silva A (2002) Is the European industry moving toward solving requirements engineering problems? IEEE Softw 12:70–77
22. Kato J, Nagata M, Yamamoto S, Saeki M, Kaiya H, Horai H, Watahiki K (2003) PAORE: package oriented requirements elicitation. In: Proceedings of the 10th Asia-Pacific software engineering conference software engineering conference, IEEE Computer Society, Los Alamitos, pp 17–26
23. Kohl RJ (2005) Requirements engineering changes for COTS-intensive systems. IEEE Softw 22(4):63–64
24. Krumbolz M, Maiden NAM (2001) The implementing of ERP packages in different organizational and national cultures. Info Systems J 26(3):185–204
25. Le T, Rolland C (2001) Functional matching in COTS-based development context. Actes du XIXème Congrès INFORSID, Martigny, Suisse, pp 87–110
26. Linvald J, Østerbye K (2002) UML tailored to an ERP framework. In: Tolvanen J-H, Gra M. Rossi M (eds) Second workshop on domain specific visual languages. Companion of the 17th ACM SIGPLAN conference on object-oriented programming, systems, languages, and applications, New York
27. List B, Korherr (2006) An evaluation of conceptual business process modelling languages. In: Proceedings of the ACM symposium on applied computing, ACM, New York, pp 1532–1539
28. Maiden NAM, Ncube C (1998) Acquiring COTS software selection requirements. IEEE Softw 15(2):46–56
29. Maiden NAM, Ncube C, Moore A (1997) Lessons learned during requirements acquisition for COTS systems. Commun. ACM 40(12):21–25
30. Morris P, Masena M, Willikens M (1998) Requirements engineering and industrial uptake. Reqs Eng 3(2):79–83
31. Millet P-A, Schmitt P, Botta-Genoulaz V (2009) The SCOR model for the alignment of business processes and information systems. Enterprise Info Systems 3(4):393–407
32. Mutchalintungkul A, Oonhawat J, Pholpipatanaphong K, Sutivong D, Prompoon N (2006) Experience from applying RIM to educational ERP development. In: Proceedings of 28th international conference on software engineering, ACM, New York, pp 620–624
33. Ncube C, Maiden NAM (1999) Guidance for parallel requirements acquisition and COTS software selection. In: Proceedings of international conference on requirements engineering, IEEE Computer Science, Los Alamitos, pp 133–143
34. Negi T, Bansal V (2009) Integrating process and data models to aid configuration of ERP packages. In: Proceedings of 12th international conference on business information systems. LNBIP, vol 21. Springer, Heidelberg, pp 228–239
35. Petroski H (1992) To engineer is human: the role of failure in successful design. Vintage books, New York
36. Post HA, van Es RM (eds) (1996) Dynamic enterprise modelling: a paradigm shift in software implementation. Kluwer, Dordrecht
37. Recker J, Rosemann M, van der Aalst W (2005) On the user perception of configurable reference process models – initial insights. In: Campbell B, Underwood J, Bunker D (eds) Proceedings 16th Australasian conference on information systems, Sydney, Australia
38. Recker JC, Mendling J, van der Aalst WM, Rosemann M (2006) Model-driven enterprise systems configuration. In: Proceedings of Professional conference on advanced information systems engineering. LNCS, vol 4001. Springer, Heidelberg, pp 369–383
39. Ramos I, Berry D, Carvalho J (2005) Requirements engineering for organizational transformation. Info Softw Technol 47:479–495
40. Rolland C (1999) Requirements engineering for COTS based systems. Info Softw Technol 41(14):985–990
41. Rolland C, Prakash N (2000) Bridging the gap between organisational needs and ERP functionality. Reqs Eng 5(3):180–193

42. Rolland C, Prakash N (2001) Matching ERP system functionality to customer requirements. In: Proceedings of international symposium on requirements engineering, IEEE Computer Science, Los Alamitos, pp 66–75
43. Roseman M (2001) Requirements engineering for enterprise systems. In: Proceedings of 7th Americas conference on information systems, AIS, pp 1105–1110
44. Roseman M, van der Aalst W (2007) A configurable reference modelling language. Info Systems 32(1):1–23
45. Sadraei E, Aurum A, Beydoun G, Paech B (2007) A field study of the requirements engineering practice in Australian software industry. Reqs Eng 12:145–162
46. Salinesi C, Rolland C (2003) Fitting business models to system functionality exploring the fitness relationship. In: Proceedings of conference on advanced information systems engineering. LNCS, vol 2681. Springer, pp 647–664
47. Sang M, Lee MS, Olson DL, Lee S-H (2009) Open process and open-source enterprise systems. J Enterprise Info Systems 3(2):201–209
48. Scheer A-W (1996) Business process engineering: reference models for industrial enterprises. Springer, Berlin
49. Şen CG, Baraçl H (2010) Fuzzy quality function deployment based methodology for acquiring enterprise software selection requirements. Expert Systems Appl 37(4):3415–3426
50. Serrano N, Sarriegi JM (2006) Open source software ERPs: a new alternative for an old problem. IEEE Softw May/June:94–97
51. Smets-Solanes J-P, de Carvalho RA (2003) ERP5: a next-generation, open-source ERP architecture. IEEE IT Professional, July/August:38–44
52. Soffer P, Golany B, Dori D, Wand Y (2001) Modelling off-the-shelf information systems requirements: an ontological approach. Reqs Eng 41:183–199
53. Soffer P, Golany B, Dori D (2003) ERP modeling: a comprehensive approach. Info Systems 28(6):673–690
54. Soffer P, Golany B, Dori D (2005) Aligning an ERP system with enterprise requirements: an object-process based approach. Computers Industry 56(6):639–662
55. Toshiki A, Sommer R (2007) Comparison and evaluation of business process modelling and management tools. Int J Services Standards 3(2):249–261
56. Van de Aalst WMP (1999) Formalization and verification of event-driven process chains. Info Softw Technol 41(10):639–650
57. Van der Aalst WMP, Weijters AJMM (2004) Process mining: a research agenda. Computers Industry 53(3):231–244
58. Van Dongen BF, Jansen-Vullers MH (2005) Verification of SAP reference models. In: Proceedings of international conference on business process management. LNCS, vol 3649. Springer, pp 464–469
59. Ward J (2006) Benefits management. Wiley, Chichester
60. Wu H, Cao L (2009) Community collaboration for ERP implementation. IEEE Softw 26(6):48–55

Requirements as Goals and Commitments Too

Amit K. Chopra, John Mylopoulos, Fabiano Dalpiaz, Paolo Giorgini, and Munindar P. Singh

Abstract In traditional software engineering research and practice, requirements are classified either as functional or non-functional. Functional requirements consist of all functions the system-to-be ought to support, and have been modeled in terms of box-and-arrow diagrams in the spirit of SADT. Non-functional requirements include desired software qualities for the system-to-be and have been described either in natural language or in terms of metrics. This orthodoxy was challenged in the mid-90s by a host of proposals that had a common theme: all requirements are initially stakeholder goals and ought to be elicited, modeled and analyzed as such. Through systematic processes, these goals can be refined into specifications of functions the system-to-be needs to deliver, while actions assigned to external actors need to be executed. This view is dominating Requirements Engineering (RE) research and is beginning to have an impact on RE practice. We propose a next step along this line of research, by adopting the concept of conditional commitment as companion concept to that of goal. Goals are intentional entities that capture the needs and wants of stakeholders. Commitments, on the other hand, are social concepts that define the willingness and capability of an actor A to fulfill a predicate φ for the benefit of actor B, provided B (in return) fulfills predicate ψ for the benefit of actor A. In our conceptualization, goals are mapped to collections of commitments rather than functions, qualities, or actor assignments. We motivate the importance of the concept of commitment for RE through examples and discussion. We also contrast our proposal with state-of-the-art requirements modeling and analysis frameworks, such as KAOS, MAP, *i** and Tropos.

1 Introduction

Colette Rolland is an eminent researcher, mentor and leader in the Information Systems community thanks to a distinguished career that spans more than three

---

A.K. Chopra (✉)
Department of Information Engineering and Computer Science, University of Trento,
Via Sommarive 14, 38123 Povo, Trento, Italy
e-mail: chopra@disi.unitn.it

S. Nurcan et al. (eds.), *Intentional Perspectives on Information Systems Engineering*,
DOI 10.1007/978-3-642-12544-7_8, © Springer-Verlag Berlin Heidelberg 2010

decades. Her plethora of contributions include novel concepts, methods and tools for building information systems, as well as dozens of young researchers who will carry the torch of her ideas for years to come. One of those ideas that has had tremendous impact on the field is the notion that system requirements are stakeholder goals—rather than system functions—and ought to be elicited, modeled and analyzed accordingly [21, 27, 28]. In this chapter, we take this idea one small step farther.

In traditional software engineering research and practice, requirements are classified either as functional or nonfunctional. Functional requirements consist of all functions the system-to-be ought to support, and have been modeled and analyzed in terms of box-and-arrow diagrams in the spirit of SADT [32]. Nonfunctional requirements include desired software qualities for the system-to-be and have been described either in natural language or in terms of metrics. This orthodoxy was challenged in the mid-90s by a host of proposals that had a common theme: all requirements—functional and non-functional—are initially stakeholder goals, rather than functions. Through systematic processes, these goals can be refined into specifications of functions the system-to-be needs to deliver, whereas actions assigned to external actors need to be executed. This view is dominating Requirements Engineering (RE) research and is beginning to have an impact on RE practice.

The main objective of this chapter is to propose a next step along this line of research, by adding the concept of conditional commitment as companion concept to that of goal. Goals are intentional entities that capture the needs and wants of stakeholders. Commitments, on the other hand, are social concepts that define the willingness and capability of actors to contribute to the fulfillment of requirements. Specifically, a conditional commitment involves two actors A and B, where A has committed to fulfill a predicate φ for the benefit of actor B, provided B (in return) fulfills ψ for the benefit A. In our conceptualization, goals are mapped to collections of commitments rather than functions, qualities, and actor assignments.

Our work is motivated by RE frameworks such as i^* [43] which are founded on the notion of actor and social dependencies between pairs of actors; also on Agent-Oriented Software Engineering (AOSE) frameworks such as Tropos [4], where design begins with stakeholder goals and proceeds through a refinement process to identify and characterize alternative designs (plans) that can fulfill these goals. The Tropos framework has been formalized for goals and their refinements [18], but not for goal fulfillment in a multiagent setting where commitments form the primary vehicle for goal fulfillment. We have striven to keep our proposal generic so that it applies not only to Tropos but also other frameworks where there is a need to reason with a collection of agents along with their goals and commitments.

We motivate the importance of the concept of commitment for RE through examples and discussion. We also contrast our proposal with state-of-the-art requirements modeling and analysis frameworks, such as KAOS [10], MAP [29], i^* and Tropos.

Our proposal is intended primarily for the development of socio-technical systems. Unlike their traditional computer-based cousins, such systems include in their architecture and operation organizational and human actors along with software ones, and are regulated and constrained by internal organizational rules, business processes, external laws and regulations [15, 31]. Among the challenging problems related to the analysis and design of a socio-technical system is the problem of understanding the requirements of its software components, the ways technology can support human and organizational activities, and the way in which the structure of these activities is influenced by introducing technology. In particular, in a socio-technical system, human, organizational and software actors rely heavily on each other in order to fulfill their respective objectives. Not surprisingly, an important element in the design of a socio-technical system is the identification of a set of dependencies among actors which, if respected by all parties, will fulfill all stakeholder goals, the requirements of the socio-technical system.

This chapter is structured as follows. Section 2 provides a comprehensive overview on commitments, specifically on their usage in multiagent systems. Section 3 illustrates how commitments can be used with goals to specify requirements, and introduces some reasoning principles. Section 4 exemplifies how the reasoning may be applied in a travel agency setting. Section 5 compares our model to related work. Finally, Sect. 6 concludes with a summary of our approach.

2 Commitments in Multiagent Systems

The concept of commitment spans many disciplines, from Philosophy of Mind, to Psychology, Sociology and Economics. A review of the literature suggests that the concept has only been studied in the later half of the last century (it is true: Aristotle did not discover everything!).

Commitments as a computational abstraction have a long history in Computer Science. Bratman [3] and Cohen and Levesque [9] formulated the notion of an agent's commitment to his intentions. Singh [33] labeled commitments of this nature as psychological commitments, and instead stressed the notion of *social commitment*, that is, commitments among agents. In particular, Singh showed that social commitments are key to modeling communication among agents [34], and consequently to the development of large systems consisting of autonomous, interacting entities—in other words, multiagent systems. In the following, the term *commitment* is used solely in the sense of a *social commitment.*

Singh [35] also elucidated the key ontological aspects of commitments. Since then, commitments have been applied as a basis for flexible interaction among agents [41, 42]; towards the formulation of agent communication languages [17], as an abstraction for business process design [11, 14]; towards a type theory for protocols [6, 24]; towards understanding interoperability among agents [6, 7]; and towards formulating a service-oriented architecture [38]. Aspects related to reasoning about commitments have been addressed in [7, 13, 16, 36]. Commitments have also been recently applied in requirements engineering [39], and for monitoring in conjunction with goals [26].

Below, we characterize multiagent systems especially emphasizing the value of commitments.

2.1 Multiagent Systems

Multiagent Systems (MAS) are *open systems*: *autonomous and heterogeneous* entities known as agents participate in multiagent systems. An agent's autonomy means that no agent has control over it. An agent's heterogeneity means that an agent's internal construction is inaccessible to other agents. An agent may be a human, organization, or some stakeholder projected into the system as software. It is worth emphasizing that socio-technical systems are, first and foremost, multiagent systems.

The purpose of the *system*, specifically, is to provide a basis for coherent interactions among agents in spite of their autonomy. Indeed, the system may be specified independently of the agents [37]. The system itself serves as the specification, from a global perspective, of the legitimate expectations that agents adopting roles in the system would have of each other. In other words, the system is the *protocol* (MAS terminology), or *specification* (RE terminology).

We specify expectations in terms of commitments. An agent that does not fulfill its commitments to others is noncompliant. Compliance balances autonomy. An agent may do as it pleases, but from the system's perspective it may be noncompliant. Example 1 illustrates these concepts.

Example 1. A *housing contract* is a system that specifies the commitments that govern interaction between a tenant and the landlord, both agents. For example, the contract may say that the tenant may not accommodate other persons on the property unless he seeks permission from the landlord. However, the tenant, in noncompliance with the clause, may on occasion host visiting family members. It does not matter whether the landlord knows of the violation; what matters is that from the system perspective, there is a violation.

The question of the basis of compliance goes to the heart of multiagent systems research. The answer lies in how systems (protocols) are specified. Systems specified in terms of control and data flow impose strong ordering and synchronization constraints on interaction; compliance for such specifications amounts to not violating such constraints, as Example 2 shows.

Example 2. Consider a scenario where Alice wants to buy a book from the bookseller EBook. The protocol (the system) they employ specifies that the delivery of the book must precede payment. If Alice pays first, she would be noncompliant with the protocol.

Systems specified in terms of intentional abstractions such as goals and beliefs are brittle because they lead to strong assumptions about an agent's construction [34].

By contrast, system specification approaches based on commitments hit the right balance between over-abstraction (exemplified by goal-oriented approaches) and under-abstraction (exemplified by process-oriented ones). Goal-oriented approaches model desired states of the world without saying who is responsible for doing what in achieving them. Process-oriented approaches, on the other hand, specify specific courses of action that are often violated by the actual actions undertaken by relevant agents. Commitments specify interaction at a high level of abstraction. They signify social relationships between agents and can be inferred solely from the observable communication between agents. Moreover, compliance for an agent simply means satisfying the commitments he has toward others [34]. We elaborate on commitments in the following.

2.2 The Concept of Commitment

A commitment is of the form C(debtor, creditor, antecedent, consequent), where debtor and creditor are agents, and antecedent and consequent are propositions. A commitment C(x, y, r, u) means that x is committed to y that if r holds, then it will bring about u. If r holds, then C(x, y, r, u) is *detached*, and the commitment C(x, y, T, u) holds (T being the constant for truth). If u holds, then the commitment is *discharged* and doesn't hold any longer. All commitments are *conditional*; an unconditional commitment is merely a special case where the antecedent equals T. Examples 3–5 illustrate these concepts. In the examples, EBook is a bookseller, and Alice is a customer; let *BNW* and $12 refer to the propositions *Brave New World has been delivered* and *payment of $12 has been made*, respectively.

Example 3. (Commitment) C(EBook, Alice, $12, BNW) means that EBook commits to Alice that if she pays $12, then EBook will send her the book *Brave New World.*

Example 4. (Detach) If Alice makes the payment, that is, if $12 holds, then C(EBook, Alice, $12, BNW) is detached. In other words, C(EBook, Alice, $12, BNW) ∧ $12 ⇒ C(EBook, Alice, T, BNW).

Example 5. (Discharge) If EBook sends the book (if BNW holds), then both C(EBook, Alice, $12, BNW) and C(EBook, Alice, T, BNW) are discharged. That is to say, BNW ⇒ ¬ C(EBook, Alice, T, BNW) ∧ ¬ C(EBook, Alice, $12, BNW).

Importantly, an agent can manipulate commitments by performing certain operations (technically, speech acts). The commitment operations are reproduced below (from [35]). Create, Cancel, and Release are two-party operations, whereas Delegate and Assign are three-party operations.

- Create(x, y, r, u) is performed by x, and it causes C(x, y, r, u) to hold.
- Cancel(x, y, r, u) is performed by x, and it causes C(x, y, r, u) to not hold.
- Release(x, y, r, u) is performed by y, and it causes C(x, y, r, u) to not hold.
- Delegate(x, y, z, r, u) is performed by x, and it causes C(z, y, r, u) to hold.
- Assign(x, y, z, r, u) is performed by y, and it causes C(x, z, r, u) to hold.

We introduce Declare(x, y, r) as an operation performed by x to inform y that r holds. This is not a commitment operation, but may indirectly affect commitments by causing detaches and discharges. In relation to Example 4, when Alice informs EBook of the payment by performing Declare(Alice, EBook, $12), then the proposition $12 holds, and causes a detach of C(EBook, Alice, $12, BNW).

A deductive strength relation can be defined between commitments [7]: C(x, y, r, u) is stronger than C(x, y, s, v) if and only if s entails r and u entails v. So, for instance, a detached commitment C(x, y, $\top$, u) is stronger than the commitment before detachment C(x, y, r, u).

A commitment arises in a social or legal context. The context defines the rules of encounter among the interacting parties, and often serves as an arbiter in disputes and imposes penalties on parties that violate their commitments. For example, eBay is the context of all auctions that take place through their service; if a bidder does not honor a payment obligation for an auction that it has won, eBay may suspend the bidder's account.

2.3 System Specification: Protocols

Traditional approaches describe a protocol in terms of the occurrence and relative order of specific messages.

The protocol of Fig. 1 begins with EBook sending Alice an offer. Alice may either accept or reject the offer. If she rejects it, the protocol ends; if she accepts it, EBook sends her the book. Next, Alice sends EBook the payment. Because an FSM ignores the meanings of the messages, it defines compliance based on low-level considerations, such as the order in which commitments are fulfilled. Moreover, this type of specification is often inflexible. As illustrated in Example 2, Alice fails to comply if she sends the payment before she receives the book. Note that this drawback applies to all process-oriented specification languages used for specifying rich social concepts such as business processes (e.g. BPMN [2] and BPEL [1]).

In contrast, we build on *commitment protocols* [42], which describe messages along with their *business meanings*. Commitment operations are realized in distributed systems by the corresponding messages. Commitment protocols are therefore defined in terms of the operations introduced above: Create, Cancel, Release, Delegate, Assign, and Declare. We introduce an abbreviation. Let c = C(x, y, r, u). Then, we Create(c) abbreviates Create(x, y, r, u).

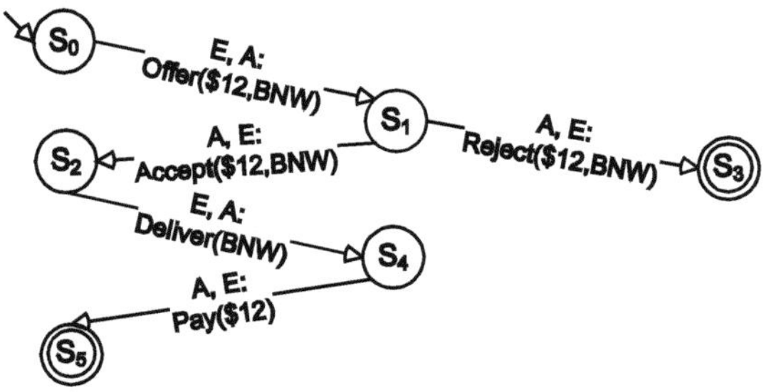

Fig. 1 A purchase protocol as a finite state machine, taken from [7]. Each message is tagged with its sender and receiver (here and below, E is EBook; A is Alice)

Table 1 A purchase protocol expressed in terms of commitments

Domain-specific message	Commitment-oriented message
Offer(E,A, \$12, BNW)	Create(E, A, \$12, BNW)
Accept(A,E,BNW, \$12)	Create(A, E, BNW, \$12)
Reject(E,A, \$12,BNW)	Release(E, A, \$12, BNW)
Deliver(E,A,BNW)	Declare(E, A, BNW)
Pay(A,E, \$12)	Declare(A, E, \$12)

Table 1 shows an alternative purchase protocol specified in terms of commitments. The semantics of domain-specific messages are explained in terms of commitment operations. For example, an *Offer* message is interpreted as a Create operation, whereas a *Reject* message releases the debtor from the commitment.

Table 2 introduces the commitments used in Figs. 2 and 3.

Let us walk through the interaction of Fig. 2, which shows a possible enactment of the protocol described in Table 1. Upon sending Create(c_B), EBook infers c_B; upon receiving the message Alice infers c_B. Upon sending Declare(\$12), Alice infers that \$12 holds. Consequently, she infers that c_B is detached, yielding c_{UB}. When EBook receives Declare (\$12), it infers c_{UB}. EBook finally sends Declare (BNW), thus concluding that its commitment is discharged. When Alice receives Declare(BNW), she draws the same inference.

Notice that Table 1 does not specify any ordering constraints on messages. In effect, *each party can send messages in any order*. Figure 3 shows some additional enactments of the purchase protocol of Table 1. Neither the enactments of Fig. 3(b) and (c) nor the one in Fig. 2 are legal according to the FSM in Fig. 1.

So when is an agent compliant with a protocol? The answer is simple: an agent complies if its commitments are discharged, no matter if delegated or otherwise

Table 2 Commitments used as running examples in this chapter

Name	Commitment
c_A	C(Alice, EBook, BNW, \$12)
c_B	C(EBook, Alice, \$12, BNW)
c_{UA}	C(Alice, EBook, T, \$12)
c_{UB}	C(EBook, Alice, T, BNW)

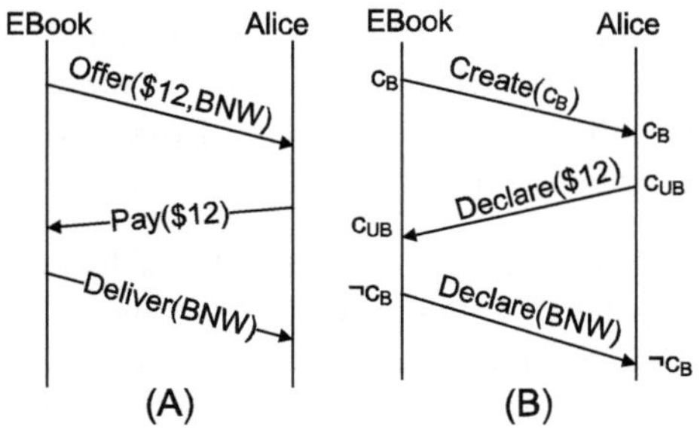

Fig. 2 An enactment of the protocol of Table 1 in terms of (**a**) domain-specific messages and (**b**) commitments. We show only the strongest commitments at each point. For example, because c_{UB} is stronger than c_B, c_{UB} is sufficient

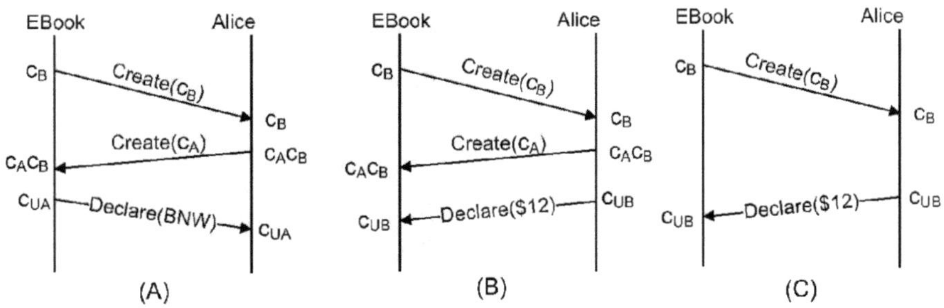

Fig. 3 Three possible enactments of the protocol of Table 1

manipulated. Traditional approaches force a tradeoff: checking compliance is simple with rigid automaton-based representations and difficult with flexible reasoning. Protocols specified using commitments find the golden mean, promoting flexibility by constraining interactions at the business level, yet providing a rigorous notion of compliance.

2.4 Architecture, Interoperability, and Middleware

In the discussion above, we used examples where the commitments are defined over specific agents (for example, Alice and EBook). General protocols can be defined by stating the commitments among roles instead of agents. For example, we can replace Alice with Customer and EBook with Vendor and use the commitments of the previous sections to specify a general protocol for commercial transactions. These generic protocols can then be used in a specific context by binding a specific agent to each role of the protocol.

Protocols are architectural specifications: they specify the interconnections between agents (via roles). Commitment protocols abstract away from considerations of control and data flow, instead focusing on the contractual relationships among agents. This affords agents flexibility in protocol enactment. However, flexibility poses challenges for interoperability: if an agent may send any message at any time, how do we ensure that they will come to the same conclusion about their commitments towards each other? Example 6 illustrates a case of *misalignment*.

Example 6. Assume both Alice and EBook infer c_B. Subsequently, Alice's payment for the book and EBook's cancellation of the offer c_B cross in transit (we are dealing with distributed systems). When Alice receives EBook's cancellation, she considers it as having arrived too late; EBook considers Alice's payment late. Thus, Alice concludes c_UB, whereas EBook does not—they are misaligned.

Interoperability concerns are addressed in [6, 7] via the notion of commitment alignment. Alignment expresses the intuition that whenever a creditor computes (that is, infers) a commitment, the presumed debtor also computes the same commitment. If agents get misaligned, their interaction will potentially break down.

Traditionally, interoperability among services has been captured in terms of whether agents can *send* and *receive* messages in a compatible manner—for example, in terms of (the absence of) deadlocks. Such formalizations of interoperability are useful, but work at a lower level than commitments. Two agents may be aligned commitment-wise, but deadlocked because they are both waiting for the other to act. Conversely, agents may be *live*, but misaligned.

Alignment motivates a middleware that maintains and monitors commitments, and transparently takes necessary actions to maintain alignment [8]. For example, the middleware would transparently notify the debtors when an event occurs that detaches a commitment; otherwise, in a distributed system where different agents have likely observed different events, agents could get easily misaligned. Compare this to what traditional middleware, for example, reliable message queues, do. They send acknowledgments, store messages until they are consumed, maintain message order, and so on, in other words, do the bookkeeping to maintain interoperability. A commitment-oriented middleware would do the bookkeeping at a high level, relegating messages queues to a lower level.

The middleware would ideally be able to monitor goals and commitments, reason about compliance and interoperability, and support adaptations. In essence, the middleware would encode a business semantics and form a common substrate for all kinds of business applications. The middleware would offer a new programming model: it will support writing services directly in terms of goals and commitments, and will alleviate greatly the burden of writing agents.

3 From Goals to Commitments

Let us begin by summarizing the above discussion about commitments.

- Commitments abstract over data and control flow.
- Commitments are a social abstraction—being grounded in interaction, they encode publicly verifiable relationships among agents.
- Commitments support a notion of compliance that enables an agent to act flexibly.
- Protocols, and thus systems, may be specified as the commitments that may arise among the agents participating in the system.
- Commitments may be supported in middleware: this includes monitoring and reasoning for the purposes of compliance and interoperability.

The parallel with the notion of *goals* as studied in RE may already be obvious.

- Goals abstract over data and control flow specifications.
- Goals represent the particular states of the world an agent wants to achieve.
- Goals are also used in reasoning about flexibility and adaptability, especially in terms of the *variants* supported by a goal model.

- Agents may be specified in terms of abstractions such as goals, capabilities, and so on.
- Goals may also be supported in middleware: an agent can monitor its goals and act in order to achieve them.

Goals and commitments are complementary. An agent has certain goals that it wants to satisfy, and in doing so it typically must make (to others) or get (from others) commitments about certain goals. Alternatively, an agent has commitments to others (and a goal to comply), and it then adopts specific goals in order to discharge its commitments.

Thus, there are two things that an agent designer or the agent itself, by introspection at runtime, may do.

First, an agent may induce a protocol—the set of commitments—that are necessary to supports the goals it wants to achieve. The agent would additionally publish the protocol along with the role it has adopted in the protocol, and possibly invite others to adopt the other roles in the protocol or just wait to be discovered. Example 7 illustrates this method.

Example 7. Alice has the goal *BNW*. Alice figures that to get the book, it must interact with a bookseller and pay the bookseller for the book. So Alice induces a protocol with two roles, customer and merchant, with the commitment C(customer, merchant, BNW, payment). She adopts customer, and publishes the protocol as her interface. Eventually, a seller may sell *BNW* to Alice by playing role merchant.

Second, an agent may select a protocol from a repository. This recognizes the fact that protocols are reusable specifications of interaction [14]. Indeed, this is the case with many standardized protocols such as for financial transactions [12]. An agent would naturally want to verify if a protocol selected from some repository were suitable for the achievement of the agent's goals. The agent would also want to verify that if he makes a certain commitment, then his goals support fulfillment of the commitment.

The notion of compliance with a protocol helps decouple one agent's specification from another agent's. For example, a merchant would only care (perhaps modulo other properties deriving from interaction such as trust and reputation) that Alice is committed to payment for the book, irrespective of whether Alice actually intends to pay. In other words, if an agent commits to another for something, from the perspective of the latter, it does not matter much what the former's goals are or how the former will act to bring about the goal he committed to.

We now sketch some elements of the reasoning one can perform with goals and commitments. Given some role in a protocol and some goal that the agent wants to achieve, *goal support* verifies whether an agent can *potentially* achieve his goal by playing that role. *Commitment support* checks if an agent playing a role is *potentially* able to honor the commitments he may make as part of playing the role.

Note the usage of the words *support* and *potentially*. Goal (commitment) support is a weaker notion than fulfillment; support gives no guarantee about fulfillment at runtime. And yet, it is a more pragmatic notion for open systems, where it is not possible to make such guarantees anyway. For instance, a commitment that an agent depends upon to fulfill his goal may be violated.

Goal support We illustrate the basic intuitions with examples.

An agent's goal is supported if the agent has a capability for it (Example 8).

Example 8. Consider Alice's goal payment. Alice supports the goal if she has a capability for it.

An agent's goal is supported if it can get an appropriate commitment from some other agent about the state of affairs that the goal represents (Example 9).

Example 9. Consider Alice's goal BNW. The commitment C(merchant, Alice, payment, BNW) from some merchant supports the goal, but only if Alice supports payment. The intuition is that Alice won't be able to exploit the merchant's commitment unless she pays.

An agent's goal is supported if it can make a commitment to some other agent for some state of affairs (presumably one that the latter would be interested in) if the latter brings about the state of affairs that the goal represents (Example 10).

Example 10. Consider EBook's goal payment. He can support this goal by making an offer to some customer, that is, by creating C(EBook, customer, payment, BNW).

The intuitions may be applied recursively for decomposition in goal trees. Thus for example, if an agent wants to support g, and g is and-composed into g_0 and g_1, then the agent would want to verify support for both g_0 and g_1, and so on.

Commitment support It makes sense to check whether an agent will be able to support the commitments it undertakes towards others.

Commitment support reduces to goal support for the commitment consequent (Example 11).

Example 11. Consider that C(EBook, customer, payment, BNW) holds. EBook supports his goal payment by the commitment; however, if he does not support BNW, then if the customer pays, he risks being noncompliant.

We consider goal and commitment support as separate notions. A reckless or malicious agent may only care that his goals are supported regardless of whether his commitments are supported; a prudent agent on the other hand would ensure that the commitments are also supported.

Reasoning for support as described above offers interesting possibilities. Some examples: (i) [*Chaining*] x can reason that C(x, y, g_0, g_1) is supported by C(z, x, g_2, g_1) if x supports g_2; (ii) [*Division of labor*] x can support a conjunctive goal $g_0 \wedge g_1$ by getting commitments for g_0 and g_1 from two different agents; (iii) [*Redundancy*] to support g, x may get commitments for g from two different agents; and so on.

4 Applying Goals and Commitments

We show how the conceptual model and the reasoning techniques can be used to represent and analyze a setting concerning flight tickets purchase via a travel agency. Four main roles participate in this protocol: travel agency, customer, airline, and shipper. Customers are interested in purchasing flight tickets for some reason (e.g. holidays or business trips), travel agencies provide a tickets-selling service to customers by booking flight tickets from airlines, shippers offer a ticket delivery service.

Figure 4 describes the protocol in the travel agency scenario. The protocol is defined as a set of roles (circles) connected via commitments; the commitments are labeled (C_i). Table 3 explains the commitments.

Figure 5 shows the situation where agent Fly has adopted the role travel agency in the protocol of Fig. 4; the other roles are not bound to agents. Fly has one top-level goal: selling tickets (ticketsSold). In order to support it, three sub-goals should be supported: tickets should be obtained, tickets should be delivered to the customer, and the service should be paid. Tickets can be obtained if the tickets are reserved

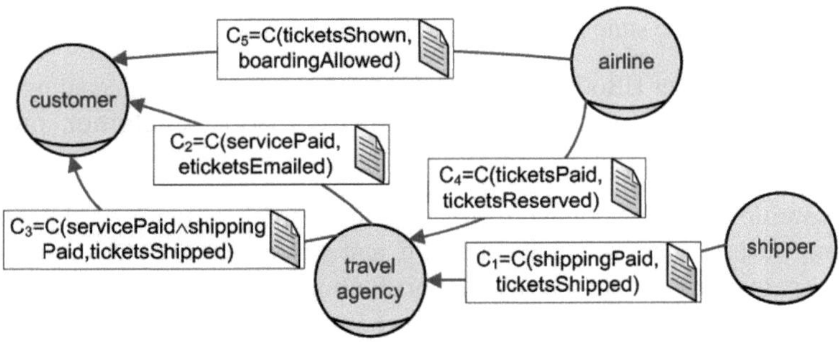

Fig. 4 Role model for the travel agency scenario. Commitments are rectangles that connect (via *directed arrow*) a debtor to a creditor

Table 3 Commitments in the travel agency protocol

Label	Description
C_1	Shipper to travel agency: if the shipping cost have been paid, the flight tickets will be shipped
C_2	Travel agency to customer: if the booking service has been paid, the electronic tickets will be e-mailed
C_3	Travel agency to customer: if the booking service and the shipping cost have been paid, flight tickets will be shipped
C_4	Airline to travel agency: if flight tickets have been paid, tickets will be reserved
C_5	Airline to customer: if tickets have been shown, flight boarding will be allowed

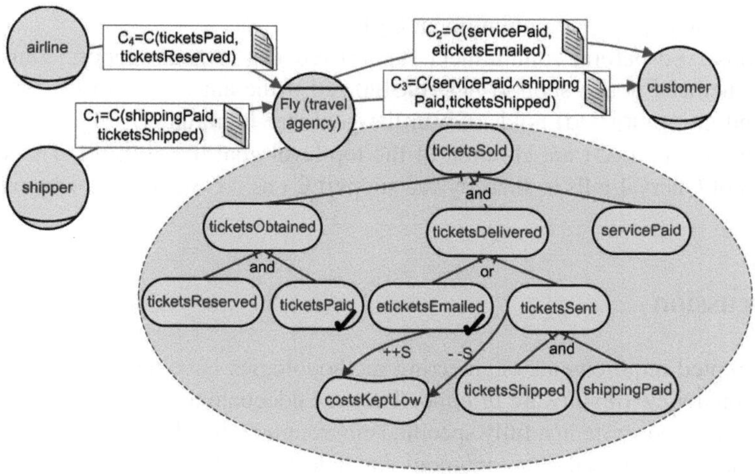

Fig. 5 Visual representation of Fly's travel agency-bound specification

and they have been paid. Fly is capable of goal ticketsPaid. There are two ways to deliver tickets: either electronic tickets are e-mailed or tickets are posted. In order to send tickets via mail, Fly has to ship the tickets and pay for the shipping. Fly is capable of eticketsEmailed. E-mailing tickets contributes positively (++S) [18] to softgoal costsKeptLow, whereas sending via shipping contributes negatively (–S) to such softgoal.

We present now some queries concerning goal and commitment support that can be run against the specification of Fig. 5.

Query 1. Can Fly support goal ticketsSold?

The answer to this query is yes. Fly can support ticketsObtained by using its capability for ticketsPaid and getting C_4 from some airline. Fly supports tickets-Delivered via its capability for eticketsEmailed. Fly can support servicePaid by making C_2 to some customer.

An alternative solution involves sending tickets via shipping. Fly could support ticketsShipped and shippingPaid if it makes C_3 to a customer (which supports servicePaid and shippingPaid) and get C_1 from some shipper (to support ticketsShipped).

Another solution includes supporting both eticketsEmailed and ticketsSent: both C_2 and C_3 are made to the customer.

Query 2. Can Fly support goals ticketsSold and costsKeptLow?

This query adds an additional constraint to Query 1: supporting softgoal costsKeptLow. The only solution is when tickets are e-mailed: eticketsEmailed contributes positively to costsKeptLow and the softgoal gets no negative contribution. Posting tickets does not work: ticketsSent contributes negatively to costsKeptLow.

Query 3. Can Fly support commitment C_3 to customer?

As observed before, commitment support reduces to goal support. Thus, let's check whether Fly can support ticketsShipped if the antecedent of C_3 (servicePaid and shippingPaid) holds. Given the goal tree hierarchy of Fig. 5, the three goals that relate to C_3 are children of the top-level goal ticketsSold. The second solution of Query 1 tells us that Fly can support C_3 as it contains all such goals.

5 Discussion

Goal-oriented requirements engineering methodologies have been conceived with a traditional view of software in mind. They are adequate to design systems where stakeholders cooperate in a fully specified environment, but they are not thought for open systems composed of autonomous and heterogeneous participants.

The MAP approach [29] is describes processes in terms of *intentions* and *strategies*: a map is a directed graph where nodes are intentions and directed arrows represent strategies. A strategy explains how to achieve one intention starting from another intention. Maps have been recently used to define the concept of Intentional Services Oriented Architecture (ISOA) [30], where the authors conceive services in terms of intentional abstractions such as goals. In our approach, we model agents as goal-driven entities. However, we place emphasis on the modeling of the system itself via the social abstraction of commitments.

The *i** framework [43] starts from the identification of the stakeholders in the analyzed organizational setting and model these stakeholders—actors—in terms of their own goals and the dependencies between them. However, as concerns open settings such as socio-technical systems, *i** suffers from two primary drawbacks.

One, dependencies do not capture business relationships as commitments do. Guizzardi et al. [20] and Telang and Singh [39] highlight the advantages of commitments over dependencies for capturing relationships between roles. Both Telang and Singh and Gordijn et al. [19] especially note that dependencies do not capture the reciprocal nature of a business transaction.

Two, the strategic rationale model violates the heterogeneity principle by making assumptions about the goals of others actors. Commitments, by contrast, obviate looking inside an actor; as mentioned above, they completely decouple agents.

*i** has been recently used to describe services [23]; this approach violates agents heterogeneity by making assumptions about other participants' internals. Commitment protocols are more reusable than the goal models of actors [14].

Tropos [4] builds on top of *i** and adds models and concepts to be used in the development phases that follow requirements engineering. Being a derivative of *i**, Tropos suffers of the same problem concerning dependencies. Tropos provides an architectural model for the agents to develop, but exploits a weak notion of agency. Agents are designed and implemented under the assumption that they will cooperate with others. Our proposal differs in that cooperation is guaranteed by mutual interest in a commitment: the agents playing debtor and creditor have their own reasons to interact via commitments, but they don't (and can't) know the other party's motivations. Penserini et al. [25] have extended Tropos to design web services that support the stakeholders' goals. The main limitation of this approach is that it assumes that requirements engineers have a global view on all the actors.

KAOS [10] exploits a system-oriented perspective to specify requirements. Stakeholders are essential to gather system goals, but they are not explicitly represented in KAOS models. Leaf level goals are assigned to agents on the basis of a responsibility principle; van Lamsweerde has also discussed how KAOS requirements models can be mapped to software architecture [40]. KAOS is effective for the development of traditional software systems, but lacks of the proper abstractions to design autonomous and heterogeneous agents in open systems.

Gordijn et al. [19] combine *i** goal modeling with profitability modeling for the various stakeholders to design e-services. In such a way, the authors consider not only the intentions of the agents, but also the economic value of a service. Their approach is less generic than ours: economic value exchanges are a very important criteria but not the only one; moreover, they assume a monolithic system-development point of view which does not suit well in open systems.

Liu et al. [22] propose an *i** extension intended for the design of open systems, and propose some reasoning techniques that can be executed against these models. The authors formalize commitments in a weaker sense—as a relation between an actor and a service, not between actors, as is done in our approach.

Bryl et al. [5] use a planning-based approach to design socio-technical systems. The main intuition behind this work is to explore the space of possible alternatives for satisfying some goal. However, unlike us, they follow goal dependencies inside the dependee actors, thus violating heterogeneity.

6 Conclusion

The power of any technique for eliciting, modeling and analyzing requirements rests on the primitive concepts used to conceptualize them. The advent of goal-orientation in RE twenty years ago brought about a shift from a functional to an intentional view of software systems. The implications of this shift are still being worked out.

This chapter advocates a further shift from an intentional to a social view of requirements for socio-technical systems. The proposal continues along a path originally defined by *i** in Eric Yu's PhD thesis. Our new proposal is founded on the concept of commitment and related social concepts; it calls for a new form of system specification that prescribes a system's course of action more concretely than goal-oriented techniques, but more abstractly than process-oriented ones. We see this proposal as yet another step towards an agent-oriented view of socio-technical systems, their conceptualization, design, and evolution.

References

1. Web Services Business Process Execution Language Version 2.0 (April 2007) http://docs.oasis-open.org/wsbpel/2.0/wsbpel-v2.0.html. Accessed 6 May 2010
2. BPMN: Business process modeling notation, v1.1 (January 2008) http://www.bpmn.org/. Accessed 6 May 2010
3. Bratman ME (1987) Intention, plans, and practical reason. Harvard University, Cambridge, MA
4. Bresciani P, Perini A, Giorgini P, Giunchiglia F, Mylopoulos J (2004) Tropos: an agent-oriented software development methodology. Autonomous Agents Multi-Agent Systems 8(3):203–236
5. Bryl V, Giorgini P, Mylopoulos J (2009) Designing socio-technical systems: from stakeholder goals to social networks. Reqs Eng 14(1):47–70
6. Chopra AK, Singh MP (2008) Constitutive interoperability. In: Proceedings of the seventh international conference on autonomous agents and multiagent systems, pp 797–804, Estoril, Portugal
7. Chopra AK, Singh MP (2009) Multiagent commitment alignment. In: Proceedings of the eighth international conference on autonomous agents and multiagent systems, Budapest Hungary, pp 937–944
8. Chopra AK, Singh MP (2009) An architecture for multiagent systems: an approach based on commitments. In: Proceedings of the 7th international workshop on programming multi-agent systems, Budapest Hungary
9. Cohen PR, Levesque HJ (1990) Intention is choice with commitment. Artificial Intelligence 42:213–261
10. Dardenne A, van Lamsweerde A, Fickas S (1993) Goal-directed requirements acquisition. Science Computer Programming 20(1–2):3–50
11. Desai N, Mallya AU, Chopra AK, Singh MP (2005) Interaction protocols as design abstractions for business processes. IEEE Trans Softw Eng 31(12):1015–1027
12. Desai N, Chopra AK, Arrott M, Specht B, Singh MP (2007) Engineering foreign exchange processes via commitment protocols. In: Proceedings of the 4th IEEE international conference on services computing, IEEE Computer Society, Los Alamitos, pp 514–521
13. Desai N, Chopra AK, Singh MP (2007) Representing and reasoning about commitments in business processes. In: Proceedings of the 22nd conference on artificial intelligence, Vancouver, pp 1328–1333
14. Desai N, Chopra AK, Singh MP (2010) Amoeba: a methodology for modeling and evolution of cross-organizational business processes. ACM Trans Softw Eng Methodol 19(2):6:1–6:45
15. Emery FE (1959) Characteristics of sociotechnical systems. Travistock Institute of Human Relations, London
16. Fornara N, Colombetti M (2002) Operational specification of a commitment-based agent communication language. In: Proceedings of the 1st international joint conference on autonomous agents and multiagent systems (AAMAS), ACM, Bologna, Italy, pp 535–542
17. Fornara N, Colombetti M (2004) A commitment-based approach to agent communication. Applied Artificial Intelligence 18(9–10):853–866
18. Giorgini P, Mylopoulos J, Nicchiarelli E, Sebastiani R (2003) Reasoning with goal models. In: Conceptual modeling—ER 2002. LNCS, vol 2503. Springer, Heidelberg, Berlin, pp 167–181
19. Gordijn J, Yu E, van der Raadt B (2006) E-service design using *i** and e3value modeling. IEEE Softw 23(3):26–33
20. Guizzardi RSS, Guizzardi G, Perini A, Mylopoulos J (2007) Towards an ontological account of agent-oriented goals. In: Software engineering for multi-agent systems V. LNCS, vol 4408. Springer, Heidelberg, Berlin, pp 148–164
21. Kaabi RS, Souveyet C, Rolland C (2004) Eliciting service composition in a goal driven manner. In: Proceedings of the 2nd international conference on service oriented computing, New York, pp 308–315

22. Liu L, Liu Q, Chi CH, Jin Z, Yu E (2008) Towards a service requirements modelling ontology based on agent knowledge and intentions. Int J Agent-Oriented Softw Eng 2(3):324–349
23. Lo A, Yu E (2007) From business models to service-oriented design: a reference catalog approach. In: Proceedings of the 26th international conference on conceptual modeling (ER 2007), Auckland, pp 87–101
24. Mallya AU, Singh MP (2007) An algebra for commitment protocols. J Autonomous Agents Multi-Agent Systems 14(2):143–163
25. Penserini L, Perini A, Susi A, Mylopoulos J (2006) From stakeholder needs to service requirements. In: Workshop on service-oriented computing: consequences for engineering requirements (SOCCER'06) Minneapolis
26. Robinson WN, Purao S (2009) Specifying and monitoring interactions and commitments in open business processes. IEEE Softw 26(2):72–79
27. Rolland C, Souveyet C, Achour CB (1998) Guiding goal modeling using scenarios. IEEE Transac Softw Eng 24(12):1055–1071
28. Rolland C, Grosz G, Kla R (1999) Experience with goal-scenario coupling in requirements engineering. In: Proceedings of the IEEE international symposium on requirements engineering, Limerick, Ireland
29. Rolland C, Prakash N, Benjamen A (1999) A multi-model view of process modelling. Reqs Eng 4(4):169–187
30. Rolland C, Kaabi RS, Kraïem N (2007) On ISOA: intentional services oriented architecture. In: Proceedings of CAiSE 2007.LNCS, vol 4495. Springer, Heidelberg, Berlin, pp 158–172
31. Ropohl G (1999) Philosophy of socio-technical systems. Society Philosophy Technol 4(3): 55–71
32. Ross DT (1977) Structured analysis (SA): a language for communicating ideas. IEEE Trans Softw Eng 3(1):16–34
33. Singh MP (1991) Social and psychological commitments in multiagent systems. In: AAAI fall symposium on knowledge and action at social and organizational levels, Pacific Grove, California, pp 104–106
34. Singh MP (1998) Agent communication languages: rethinking the principles. IEEE Computer 31(12):40–47
35. Singh MP (1999) An ontology for commitments in multiagent systems: toward a unification of normative concepts. Artificial Intelligence Law 7:97–113
36. Singh MP (2008) Semantical considerations on dialectical and practical commitments. In: Proceedings of the 23rd conference on artificial intelligence, Chicago, pp 176–181
37. Singh MP, Chopra AK (2009) Programming multiagent systems without programming agents. In: Proceedings of the 7th international workshop on programming multiagent systems (ProMAS 2009), invited paper, Budapest
38. Singh MP, Chopra AK, Desai N (2009) Commitment-based service-oriented architecture. IEEE Computer 42(11):72–79
39. Telang PR, Singh MP (2009) Enhancing Tropos with commitments: a business metamodel and methodology. In: Borgida A, Chaudhri V, Giorgini P, Yu E (eds) Conceptual modeling: foundations and applications. LNCS, vol 5600. Springer, Heidelberg, Berlin, pp 417–435
40. van Lamsweerde A (2003) From system goals to software architecture. In: Formal methods for software architectures. LNCS, vol 2804. Springer, Heidelberg, Berlin, pp 25–43
41. Winikoff M, Liu W, Harland J (2005) Enhancing commitment machines. In: Proceedings of the 2nd international workshop on declarative agent languages and technologies (DALT). LNAI, vol 3476. Springer, Heidelberg, Berlin, pp 198–220
42. Yolum P, Singh MP (2002) Flexible protocol specification and execution: Applying event calculus planning using commitments. In: Proceedings of the 1st international joint conference on autonomous agents and multiagent systems, ACM, Bologna, Italy, pp 527–534
43. Yu ES (1997) Towards modelling and reasoning support for early-phase requirements engineering. In: Proceedings of the third IEEE international symposium on requirements engineering, Annapolis, pp 226–235

A Method for Capturing and Reconciling Stakeholder Intentions Based on the Formal Concept Analysis

Mikio Aoyama

Abstract Information systems are ubiquitous in our daily life. Thus, information systems need to work appropriately anywhere at any time for everybody. Conventional information systems engineering tends to engineer systems from the viewpoint of systems functionality. However, the diversity of the usage context requires fundamental change compared to our current thinking on information systems; from the functionality the systems provide to the goals the systems should achieve. The *intentional approach* embraces the goals and related aspects of the information systems. This chapter presents a method for capturing, structuring and reconciling diverse goals of multiple stakeholders. The heart of the method lies in the hierarchical structuring of goals by *goal lattice* based on the *formal concept analysis*, a semantic extension of the lattice theory. We illustrate the effectiveness of the presented method through application to the self-checkout systems for large-scale supermarkets.

1 Introduction

Ever-intensifying the dependencies of our society to the information technologies is increasing the *diversity* of stakeholders of the information systems and the complexity of their *intentions* towards the information systems [14]. In requirements elicitation, it is essential to elicit the intentions of diverse stakeholders and reconcile them.

Conventionally, the intentions have been addressed by either stakeholder analysis or goal-orientation.

In stakeholder analysis, a stakeholder matrix is a common technique to identify the dependencies between stakeholders and requirements [5, 7]. The matrix can help clustering the requirements. However, it does not enable to order the priority of the

M. Aoyama (✉)
Nanzan University, 27 Seirei, Seto 489-0863, Japan
e-mail: mikio.aoyama@nifty.com

S. Nurcan et al. (eds.), *Intentional Perspectives on Information Systems Engineering*,
DOI 10.1007/978-3-642-12544-7_9,

requirements due to the lack of the concept of *order* in the model. Another approach is to apply multiple viewpoints in order to identify the different perspectives to a system [6, 10]. However, available techniques mainly focus on the identification of aspects, and are rather limited in the resolution of complex goals.

On the other hand, goal-oriented techniques have been extensively developed in requirements engineering [1, 9, 11, 12, 19]. Goal formalisms and associated techniques and tools to formulate goals are developed. However, those formalisms are based on the single structure of hierarchy. Thus, it is rather difficult to structure the goals of diverse stakeholders due to the lack of a formal model to order a set of goals claimed by different stakeholders.

This chapter proposes a method of structuring and reconciling the goals of diverse stakeholders based on the *goal lattice*, a semantic extension of FCA (Formal Concept Analysis) backed by the lattice theory [8, 17].

Major contributions of this chapter include:

1. Goal lattice, a hierarchical model of goals based on the lattice theory; a formal model of structuring the goals/sub-goals of multiple stakeholders by semantically extending the FCA,
2. A structuring and reconciliation method of goals with the goal lattice by examining the dependencies of goals/sub-goals and stakeholders, and
3. A proof of the model and method proposed by applying them to the self-checkout systems in large-scale supermarkets.

The structure of this chapter is as follows; Sect. 2 explains the problem of structuring and reconciling stakeholder intentions. Section 3 briefly reviews the related works. Section 4 summarizes the FCA (Formal Concept Analysis) and defines the Goal Lattice based on the FCA. Section 5 explains the process and methodology of structuring and reconciling goals with Goal Lattice. Section 6 illustrates the application of the proposed methodology to the self-checkout systems for large-scale supermarket, followed by the evaluation of the approach in Sect. 6. Discussion and conclusion respectively follow in Sects. 7 and 8.

2 Problem of the Structuring and Reconciliation of Stakeholder Goals

Stakeholders and goals play a pivotal role in eliciting requirements. However, requirements tend to be diverse due to the diversity of the stakeholders. Thus, it is necessary to identify the stakeholders of the system, and their intentions towards the system. Intentions of the stakeholders can be first identified as goals for system to be. However, each stakeholder could claim diverse goals. Those diverse goals could depend on one another. Thus, it is highly complicated to identify the goals which are of high importance and influence to the system while ensuring fairness regarding the interests of the stakeholders of the system.

Conventional stakeholder analysis and goal analysis deal with a set of goals or a tree structure of goals. However, it is difficult to structure a set of diverse goals claimed by a set of diverse stakeholders. There is a need to provide a methodology to structure the diverse goals and answer the following questions.

1. Is goal X more important than goal Y?
2. Is goal X dependent on goal Y, that is, if goal Y is met, are all or a subset of sub-goals of goal X met?

It is becoming more important to ensure the fairness of the goals of stakeholders affected by the system, and to comply with the regulations, while those requirements are becoming more complicated. Therefore, it is necessary to provide a methodology to systematically dissolve the interwoven goals and structure the goals with order.

3 Related Works

There are three major disciplines related this work:

Stakeholder Analysis [2, 5, 7]. Stakeholder analysis is a set of techniques to identify the stakeholders, assess the importance and influence of stakeholders, and evaluate the impact and priority of requirements based on the stakeholders. Conventional techniques help to identify the dependencies between stakeholders and requirements with a stakeholder matrix. However, those techniques mostly use heuristic approaches. It is a challenge to systematically identify the dependencies between stakeholders and requirements, and structure the requirements of stakeholders.

Multiple Viewpoints [6, 10, 16]. "Viewpoint" is a subtle model to capture multiple concerns of stakeholders of the system in the requirements acquisition process. There is a large amount of literature on multiple viewpoints in requirements engineering. Most of the literature share the common issues in requirements elicitation; dealing with diverse stakeholders. For example, VOSE (Viewpoint-Oriented Systems Engineering) [6] proposes viewpoint as a composition of actor, knowledge source, and role. In PREView, a viewpoint can be associated with a set of stakeholders [16].

Goal-Orientation [1, 9, 11–13, 19]. Goal-oriented techniques have been extensively studied in the requirements engineering community. Major techniques include KAOS [9], Goal/Strategy Map [13], and i* [19]. Those techniques model goals and their relationship with a graph with some semantic extensions on the edge, and analyze the goals in a top down manner. However, it is difficult for practitioners to deal with the abstract concept of a goal and to find the right goal [13]. Furthermore, we need to deal with multiple stakeholders. Unlike the conventional goal model of a single tree, goals of multiple stakeholders are not clearly related in a single tree. In this chapter, we address the challenge of bottom-up structuring of seemingly un-related goals of multiple stakeholders.

4 The Goal Lattice Model

4.1 FCA (Formal Concept Analysis)

FCA (Formal Concept Analysis) is a formal model based on the *complete lattice of formal concepts* [8, 14, 17]. Here, a concept refers a pair of a set of objects of common attributes and a set of related attributes.

In FCA, the *concept lattice* plays a key role to model the concepts. A concept lattice is a complete lattice with the following order relation defined by the subconcept-subconcept relation:

Definition 1: Order Relation

$$C1(A_1, B_1) \leq C_2\ (A_2, B_2))\ \text{iff}\ A_1 \subseteq A_2\ (\text{iff}\ B_1 \supseteq B_2) \tag{1}$$

Definition 2: Complete Lattice

A *complete lattice* is a lattice with the infimum and supremum under an order relation defined by (1).

By the definition, the concept lattice is a structured subset of objects and attributes under the order relation. Thus, the concept lattice can model a structural of a system of objects in terms of a set of specific relations on attributes of the objects. Thus, it may represent cognitive structure of real-world [15, 17].

The concept lattice can be generated from a *context table* exemplified by Fig. 1(a) and is represented with *Hasse diagram*, a lattice diagram used in FCA, illustrated in Fig. 1(b).

A context table in Fig. 1(a) represents the relationship between objects, stakeholders, in row and attributes, concerns of the stakeholders, in column as the intersection, *X*, in the table. The context table can help to understand the relationships among stakeholders and their concerns. However, it is not possible to hierarchically structure the relationships among stakeholders and concerns, which is the major drawback of the table form, i.e. matrix formalism.

The concept lattice of Fig. 1(b) is generated from the context table of Fig. 1(a) by tracing the relationships in the following manner.

1. Put the top concept, C_{11}, including all objects at the top, ({Manger, IT Dep., End User, Developer}, φ), and the bottom concept, C_{51}, including all the attributes at the bottom, (φ, {Productivity, Cost, Technology, Usability}).
2. Identify the second concept, C_{21} and C_{22}, by adding one element of attribute which is maximally shared by the elements of object, Productivity or Cost.
3. By repeating the step 2 along with the lattice of objects and attributes, then the procedure terminates by reaching to the bottom concept.

	Attributes (M)			
Object (G)	Productivity	Cost	Technology	Usability
Manager	X	X		
IT Dep.	X	X	X	
End User	X			X
Developer		X	X	

(a) Concept Table

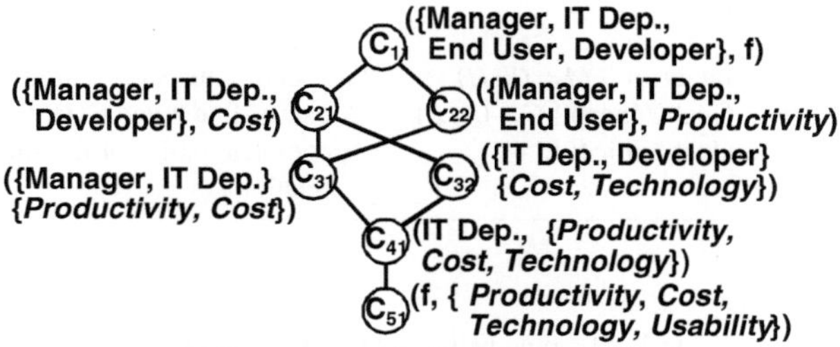

(b) Concept Lattice in Hasse Diagram

Fig. 1 Context table and context lattice

With the abovementioned procedure, the elements of attributes are incrementally added from top to bottom, while the elements of objects are added from bottom to top. Note that the commonality of attributes among the object, that is a subconcept-subconcept relation defined by (1), defines the order of object. As a result, the concept lattice can structure the objects into a lattice. Although the edge of the concept lattice is not associated with an arrow in general, the edge is directed with the order relation by the definition of lattice.

4.2 Goal Lattice

We define the *goal lattice* by semantically extending the FCA. Tables 1 and 2 define the goal lattice and the mapping between the FCA and goal lattice.

Definition 3: Goal Lattice

A goal lattice by a complete lattice of Context K with the order relation; L = ß (K) = ß(G, (S, H), I), where ß (K): = (ß (K), $\leq$) with the infimum and supremum.

To structure the relationship among goals, sub-goals and stakeholders, we assign both sub-goals and stakeholders to attributes. As a special case, a goal may have only one sub-goal. In this chapter, we call such a sub-goal as an *inner* goal.

Table 1 Goal lattice based on FCA

FCA	Goal lattice	Definition of goal lattice
Object: G	Goal: G	A set of entity appearing in phenomena
Attribute: M	Attribute: $M=(S, H)$	A set of attributes of the Object, consisting a set of Sub-Goal (S) and a set of Stakeholders (H)
Context: $K:=(G, M, I)$	Goal Context: $K:=(G, M, I)$: A structure with binary relation I between G and M; $I \subseteq G \times M$	
	Sub-Goal Context: $K_s:=(G, M, I_s)$	
	Stakeholder Context: $K_H:=(G, M, I_H)$	
Extent: $A \subseteq G$	Extent: $A \subseteq G$	Subset of Objects sharing the common Attributes
Intent: $B \subseteq M$	Intent: $B \subseteq M=(S, H)$	Subset of Attributes shared by Extents
Concept: $C=(A, B)$	Goal Concept: $C=(A, B)$	A pair of Intent and Extent
Concept Lattice: L	Goal Lattice: L	A complete lattice of K with the order relation L.

Table 2 Mapping between FCA and goal lattice

Concept	FCA	Goal lattice	Definition
	Object	Goal	Goal is an Object
	Attribute	Stakeholders, Sub-Goals	Sub-Goals of the Goal and associated Stakeholders
	Object and Attribute	Inner Goal	The Goal has a single sub-goal (i.e. the sub-goal meets the goal).

5 A Method for Structuring and Reconciliation of Stakeholder Goals

5.1 Process of Structuring and Reconciliation of Stakeholder Goals

Figure 2 illustrates the proposed goal structuring and reconciliation process consisting of the following steps. The details are explained in the subsequent sections.

Identify Stakeholders. We identify stakeholders with conventional techniques. Here, we identify a number of people in each category of stakeholders, including end-user, developer, IT department, and corporate manager.

Elicit Goals/Sub-Goals. We elicit goals and sub-goals from a group of people in each stakeholder with conventional techniques including written questionnaire and

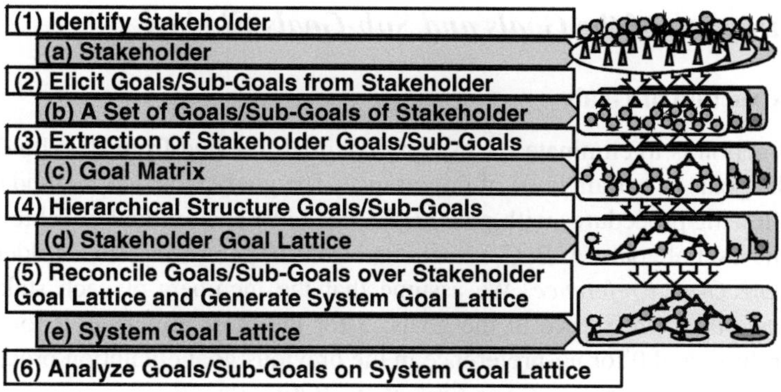

Fig. 2 Process for structuring and reconciliation of goals

interviewing. We expect to get a list of goals and sub-goals which are *not* structured yet. However, we need to ask an individual of each stakeholder group to set the priority of importance, i.e. preference of goals for the subsequent analysis.

Extract Goals Preferred. We found that the raw goals elicited include diverse opinions, some of which might be very exceptional and not preferred by most of the people in the stakeholder group, or preferred by only person in most of cases. From a statistical analysis point of view, such un-preferred goals are considered as exceptions which cause unnecessary complexity in the following structuring and reconciliation process. Therefore, we eliminate a set of exceptional goals from the raw goals.

Hierarchical Structuring of Goals/Sub-Goals. A stakeholder goal lattice is a goal lattice for each stakeholder group. We generate stakeholder a goal lattice from the goals and sub-goals elicited by structuring them with the order relation.

Reconcile Stakeholder Goal Lattices and Generate System Goal Lattice. We generate a system goal lattice by synthesizing stakeholder goal lattices, and reconcile dependencies among the goals and sub-goals while preserving the order relation.

Analyze Goals/Sub-Goals. We propose a set of measures to analyze the importance and dependencies of the goals and sub-goals and the effectiveness of reconciliation of stakeholder goal lattices for the system goal lattice.

In the following section, we explain our key techniques in the goal structuring and reconciliation method along with its steps in Fig. 2.

5.2 Elicitation of the Goals and Sub-Goals from Stakeholders

We assume that we elicit the goals from a group of people in each stakeholder group. For example, we ask people to mark the preferred goals with the order of preference out of a set of goals we listed.

5.3 Extraction of the Goals and Sub-Goals Elicited

5.3.1 Extraction of Goals

Goal extraction is to eliminate the exceptional goals elicited from stakeholders and extract the goals of certain level of importance. The goal extraction method consists of the following procedures with *goal preference table* exemplified in Table 3. Here, we assume a set of goals, A, B, C, . . ., elicited from 10 people in a stakeholder group.

Evaluate Goal Preference. We assume that the members of each stakeholder group grade their preference to the goals; 3 for the most preferred, 2 for second, and 1 for third, and 0 for no-preference in the previous goal elicitation process.

For each goal, calculate Goal Preference Ratio (Pg), the preference order of goals within a stakeholder group.

Table 3 Goal preference table

	Number of preferring stakeholder				
Goal	Most (3)	2nd (2)	3rd (1)	Total score	Pg (%)
A	6	2	2	24	80(=24/30)
B	0	1	0	2	7(= 2/30)
C	2	5	1	17	57(=17/30)
D	1	0	2	5	17(= 5/30)

Definition 4: Pg: Goal Preference Ratio of Goal *X*

$$\text{Pg} = \frac{\sum_{\text{i}} \left(\text{Preference Score of a Goal } X * \text{Number of Member of Stakeholder Group}_{\text{i}}\right)}{\left(\text{Max. Score of Preference} * \text{Total Number of Member in the Stakeholder Group}_{\text{i}}\right)} \quad (2)$$

As indicated in Table 3, we count the number of members within the stakeholder group scoring 3 (most), 2 (second), and third (1) to each goal. By summing up the score multiplied with number of people who graded the score, we calculate a total score; 24 for goal A. Dividing by the max. score of preference 30 (=3 * 10), we can calculate the Pg; 80% for goal A.

Extract the Significant Goals Based on Pg. To extract the goal, we need to set the level of significance as the threshold of Pg. From our experience, we set 10% as the threshold of Pg in this chapter. In Table 3, we can eliminate goal B and extract goal A, C and D. The results indicate that 10% of threshold is low enough to extract enough goals, but high enough to eliminate exceptional goals.

5.3.2 Extraction of Sub-Goals

The next step is to extract sub-goals with the *sub-goal preference table* exemplified in Table 4 through the following process.

Identify the Dependency from Sub-Goals to Goals. With the subconcept-subconcept order relation of FCA, we can identify the dependency from a sub-goal

Table 4 Sub-goal preference (Ps)

		Sub-Goals			
Goal	Preference	1	2	3	4
A	Number of stakeholders	9	5	1	7
	Preference Ratio (%)	90	50	10	70
C	Number of stakeholders	2	1	6	0
	Preference Ratio (%)	25	13	75	0
D	Number of stakeholders	2	0	1	0
	Preference ratio (%)	67	0	34	0

to a goal in terms of the preference of stakeholders. Looking at Table 4, the upper row in each stakeholder indicates the number of people who prefer the goal, say A, and sub-goal 1, 2, 3, ... For example, 9 people prefer sub-goal 1 while they also prefer goal A.

Evaluate the Dependency from Sub-Goal to Goal. We can calculate the preference ratio of a sub-goal Y to goal X by the following definition.

Definition 5: Ps: Sub-Goal Preference Ratio

$$\text{Ps} = \frac{(\text{Number of Stakeholders Selecting the Sub-Goal Y of Goal X})}{(\text{Number of Stakeholders Selecting Goal X})} \tag{3}$$

Looking at goal A in Table 4, the preference to goal A is 90% from sub-goal 1, and 50% from sub-goal 2. On the other hand, it is 10% from sub-goal 3.

Extract Significant Sub-Goals. Similar to the goal extraction, low preference means that the sub-goal is little related to the goal in order to avoid unnecessary complexity among goals and sub-goals. Again, we set 10% as the threshold of Ps in this chapter. In Table 4, the preference of sub-goal 1 to goal A, sub-goal 2 to goal D, and sub-goal 4 to goal D are eliminated.

5.4 Structuring Goals and Sub-Goals by Goal Lattice

Structuring goals and sub-goals is to find the ordered relationships among goals and sub-goals to the set of stakeholders. First, we can find unordered relationships among goals and sub-goals by *goal matrix*. Then, we employ *goal lattice* to order the relationships among goals, sub-goals and stakeholders.

Definition 6: Goal Matrix

A goal matrix is a matrix with a set of goals in the row, and a set of sub-goals and a set of stakeholders in the column.

Table 5 An example of goal matrix

A	B	C	D	E	F	G	H	I	J	K	L	M	N	O	P	Q
	(1)	(2)	(3)	(4)	(5)	(6)	(7)	(8)	(9)	(10)	(11)	(12)	(13)	Manager	Employee	Shopper
A																
B	X	X	X		X			X		X				X	X	X
C						X							X		X	X
D	X						X				X			X		
E	X	X	X		X			X	X	X		X		X	X	X
F		X			X									X		
G																
H	X	X			X				X	X						X
I	X	X		X	X	X	X			X		X	X		X	
J		X	X		X			X	X	X		X	X	X	X	X
Obj 11																
Obj 12																
Obj 13																
Obj 14																
Obj 15																

Thus, structuring goals goes through the following two steps.

Synthesis of Goal Matrix. By combining the stakeholder matrix and sub-goal matrix, we synthesize a *goal matrix.* The goal matrix is synthesized by combining the matrices in Tables 3 and 4, and setting X to the element when the element is non-zero otherwise empty. Table 5 shows a goal matrix synthesized in the case study of self-checkout systems explained in the next section. In Column A, rows A to J represent goals. Columns B to N represent sub-goals (1) to (13) while columns O to Q represent three stakeholders.

Generation of Goal Lattice from the Goal Matrix. Now, a goal lattice is generated from the goal matrix. This process can be automated by FCA tool. Figure 3 illustrates a goal lattice generated from the goal matrix of Table 5 with Concept Explorer [18].

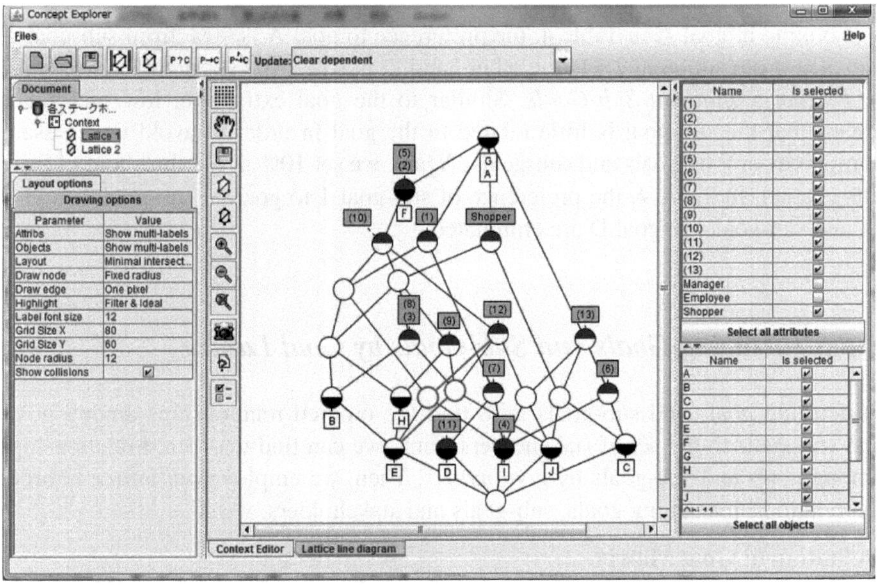

Fig. 3 Goal lattice generated for shopper stakeholder

5.5 Reconciliation of the Structure of Goals and Sub-Goals

To see the whole picture of the relationships among goals and sub-goals against stakeholders as a single structure, we reconcile stakeholder goal lattice and generate system goal lattice as follows.

Definition 7: System Goal Lattice

System goal lattice is a goal lattice of whole system, defining the relationships among goals, sub-goals and all the stakeholders.

Definition 8: Goal Reconciliation

Reconciling goals is to synthesize the goal lattice of each stakeholder while preserving the order relation, and generate *System Goal Lattice.*

Note that by the reconciliation, duplication of the dependencies between the goals and sub-goals, and goals and stakeholders are eliminated, and the system goal lattice can be simplified.

The Goal Matrix in Table 6 represents the context of sub-goal and stakeholders around the goals. We can reconcile three stakeholder goal lattices over three stakeholders in Table 5 and generate the system goal lattice illustrated in Fig. 4.

Table 6 Stakeholders involved in the field study

Stakeholder	Number of participants	Profile of people
Shopper	20	Male/female, age from 20s to 50s
Staff	14	Full-time/part-time employee
Manager	4	Store director, floor manager

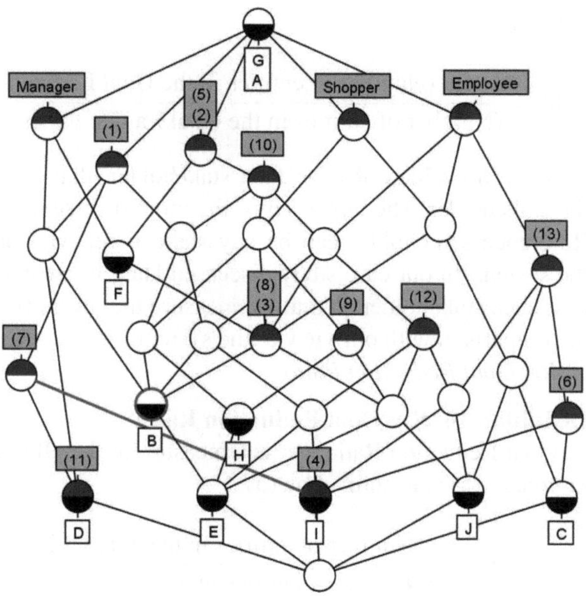

Fig. 4 System goal lattice generated

5.6 Analysis of the Structure of System Goal Lattice

System goal lattice represents the dependencies among goals, sub-goals and stakeholders, and help to understand the structural properties of the systems. Thus, the system goal lattice can be used for the following structural analyses:

1. Analyze the goals and sub-goals from a viewpoint of a specific stakeholder.
   We can identify a set of goals preferred by a specific stakeholder and the sub-goals fulfilling the goals, and high-lighten them on the system goal lattice.
2. Analyze the stakeholders from the viewpoint of a specific goal.
   We can identify the stakeholders who prefer a specified goal or sub-goal, and high-lighten them on the system goal lattice.
3. Analyze the commonality and variability of goals among stakeholders.
   We can identify the commonality and variability of goals among stakeholders.
4. Analyze the fulfillment dependencies of goals among stakeholders.
   We can identify a set of goals of a set of stakeholders and sub-goals fulfilling the goals, and highlight them on the system goal lattice.

5.7 Method for Evaluating the Reconciliation of Goal Lattice

We defined the following two measures for evaluating the effectiveness of goal reconciliation.

Rd: Goal Diversity Ratio

Definition 9: Rd: Goal Diversity Ratio

Goal Diversity Ratio, Rd, is a size measure of the span of goal lattice, which is defined by (4).

$$\text{Rd} = \frac{\text{(Number of entities in the Goal Lattice for a Stakeholder)}}{\text{(Number of entities in the Goal Lattice for the Reference Stakeholder)}} \quad (4)$$

We can evaluate Rd for each stakeholder, that is, the diversity of the goals of the stakeholder. The larger Rd is, the more diverse the goals of the stakeholder are. Reference stakeholder can be any stakeholder who provides a reference view to the system. In our case study discussed later, we select ourselves, developer, as the reference stakeholder so that we measure the diversity of goals of each stakeholder in comparison with our view to the system.

Rr: Goal Reduction Ratio

Definition 10: Rr: Goal Reduction Ratio

Goal Reduction Ratio, Rr, is a measure of the effectiveness of the reconciliation of goals, which is defined by (5).

$$\text{Rr} = \frac{\text{(Number of entities in the goal lattice after reconciliation)}}{\text{(Number of entities in the goal lattice before reconciliation)}} \quad (5)$$

6 Application to Self-Checkout Systems

In 2008, we conducted a field study for the self-checkout system at large-scale supermarkets. Among many industry sectors introducing self-checkout systems, we have chosen the retail industry because of the high complexity of requirements and heavy involvement of shoppers in the checkout systems [3].

6.1 Strategy of Field Study

We set the following two subjects as the goals for our field study:

1. To prove the model and method to structure the goals of diverse stakeholders and relationships among them.
2. To evaluate the effectiveness of the goal reconciliation method in real systems.

6.2 Self-Checkout Systems

Self-checkout systems have been introduced into various industry sectors including banks, hotels, and transportation. However, self-checkout systems in retail are more complicated than in other industry sectors because the systems require heavy shopper involvement including scanning the goods in shopping carts, calculation of the total price, and payment [3, 4]. Therefore, the requirements on self-checkout systems for retail are much more complicated than for other self-checkout systems. Furthermore, the stakeholders concerned by self-checkout systems in the retails industry are diverse.

Successful deployment of self-checkout systems in the retail industry began in the late 1990s. Since then, the introduction of self-checkout systems is spreading across the world.

However, eliciting the requirements for self-checkout systems in the retail industry needs to accommodate concerns of the diverse stakeholders of the systems including, managers' concerns on the cost and return of introduction of self-checkout systems, the staffs' concerns on the change of the relationship between staff and shoppers, and, shoppers' concerns on the waiting-time at check-out, usability of the system, and shopping privacy.

6.3 Identification of Stakeholders

We had the opportunity to observe the activities in a supermarket and to discuss with stakeholders including store managers and staff. From our observations, we identified the following three stakeholders:

1. Shoppers: Expected end-user of self-checkout systems.
2. Staffs working at the checkout system in supermarkets who know the check-out system well.
3. Managers of the store.

Table 6 shows the number of people in each stakeholder group involved in the field study.

6.4 Elicitation and Extraction of Goals and Sub-Goals

We elicited the goals and sub-goals by written questionnaires to the stakeholders. We identified a set of candidate goals and sub-goals listed in Table 7, and asked people to mark them with preference score of 1–3.

Table 7 Goals and sub-goals

Goals	Sub-goals
A. Better quality of services	(1) Avoid long waiting queue at checkout
B. Shorter waiting-time at the check-out counter	(2) Increase the checkout systems available
C. Protecting shopper privacy	(3) Flexible job assignment to the staffs
D. Better shopper satisfaction	(4) Shoppers participation to the checkout procedure
E. Business productivity	(5) High utility of checkout systems
F. Sales increase	(6) Protecting the shopping privacy
G. Better utilization of check-out systems	(7) Avoiding the contact of shoppers to staffs
H. Shorter checkout time	(8) Cut labor cost
I. Less shopper claims	(9) No-hurry at the checkout system
J. Cost cutting	(10) Enabling to handle multiple checkout systems
	(11) Attracting new customer by advanced technology
	(12) Reduce unscheduled cashier re-allocation
	(13) Avoid the claims on handling goods

6.5 Structuring and Reconciliation of Goal/Sub-Goals

Table 8 shows the relation between goals and sub-goals. X represents the dependency between a goal and a sub-goal in the sense that at least one person who selected the goal in the row also selects the sub-goal. For example, the goal A, "Better Service Quality", is associated to three sub-goals; (7) "Avoiding the Contact to Staffs", (9) "No-Hurry at the Self-Checkout System", and (13) "Avoid the Claims on Handling Goods".

Table 8 Sub-goal matrix of shoppers

Goals and number of stakeholders		Sub-goals selected by stakeholders who selected the goal												
		(1)	(2)	(3)	(4)	(5)	(6)	(7)	(8)	(9)	(10)	(11)	(12)	(13)
A	1							X		X				X
B	15	X	X	X	X	X		X			X			
C	11						X			X				X
D	2							X		X				X
E	9	X		X		X			X		X		X	
F	1		X											
G	3		X			X						X		
H	5	X	X			X				X	X			
I	3				X			X						X
J	10			X		X		X	X		X		X	X

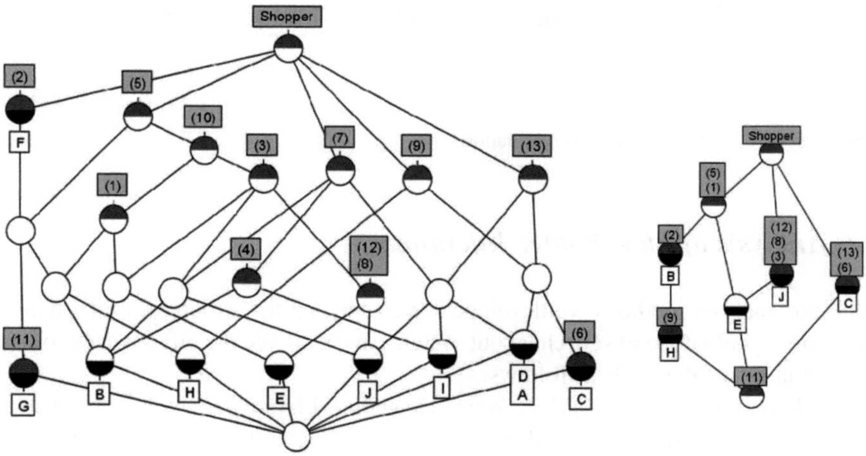

(a) Before Extraction (b) After Extraction

Fig. 5 Shopper goal lattice before/after extraction

Figure 5(a) illustrates the stakeholder goal lattice from the shoppers' viewpoint which is generated from the goal matrix in Table 8 without any reconciliation.

Then, we went through the process (3) and (4) in the goal structuring and reconciliation process illustrated in Fig. 2 and extracted the significant goals and dependent sub-goals. Through the goal extraction, we eliminated goals A, D, F, G and I. By the sub-goal extraction, we eliminated seven dependencies out of 28; B-(3), B-(4), B-(7), C-(9), J-(5), J-(7), and J-(13). As a result, the shopper goal lattice is reduced from Fig. 5(a) to (b).

By merging the three goal lattices of shopper, staff, and manager after extraction and reconciliation, we can generate the system goal lattice illustrated in Fig. 6.

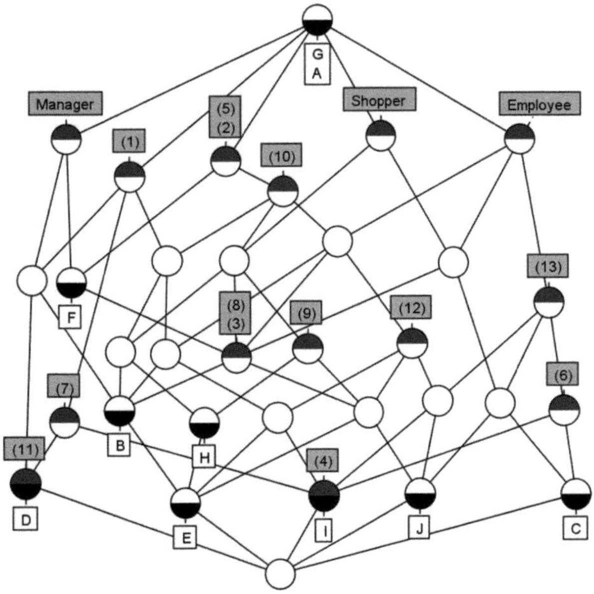

Fig. 6 System goal lattice after reconciliation

6.6 Analysis of Stakeholder Intentions

With the analysis methods we developed, we analyzed the structural properties of the system goal lattice of self-checkout systems and evaluate the effectiveness of the reconciliation of the goals as follows.

Analysis of Goals from Stakeholders' Viewpoint. Figure 7 illustrates the system goal lattice with the highlight of the goals originating from managers; F, B, D, E and J. If we assume that mangers are the most influential stakeholder group, we assume that the goals highlighted in Fig. 7 need to be satisfied first.

Analysis of Commonality and Variability of Goals. By comparing three goal lattices from the three stakeholders of manager, staff, and shopper, we can identify the common goals and variability as illustrated in a Venn diagram (Fig. 8).

While goals B, E, and J are commonly in the interest of three stakeholders, goal I, "Less Shopper Claim", and H, "Shorter Checkout Time" are expressed only by staff and shopper. The variability reflects the intentions of stakeholders well. The contribution of our method is the ability to systematically identify the commonality and variability, i.e. difference in intentions.

Structural Properties of Goals by the Order Relation. By comparing the goals originating from the managers' viewpoint in Fig. 7 with those from the shopper's viewpoint in Fig. 9, the following structural properties can be found.

a) Direct Order Inclusive Relation of Goals: Out of 5 goals from the shoppers' viewpoint, goals B, E, and J are automatically met if the managers' goals are met. This can be also understood from the commonality of goals illustrated in Fig. 8. In order to meet all shoppers' goals, it is necessary to meet goals C and H.

b) Indirect Order Inclusive Relation: Looking at the sub-goals of managers' goals in Table 9, we can identify which sub-goals are met.

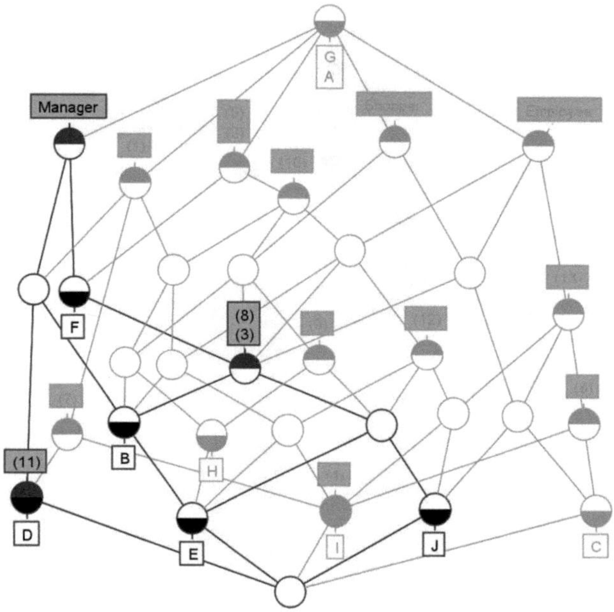

Fig. 7 Span of goals from manager's viewpoint

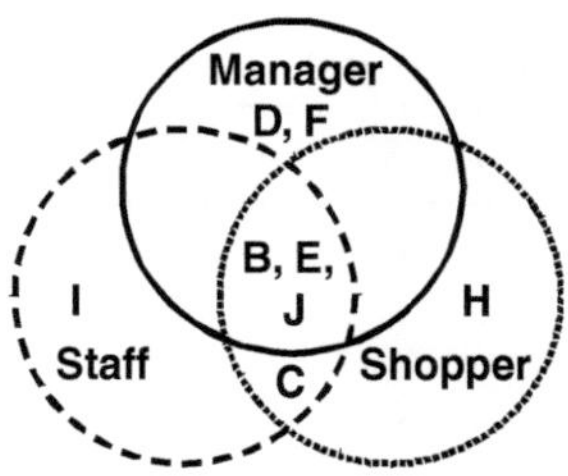

Fig. 8 Commonality and variability of goals

Comparing the sub-goals of goals C and H, which are not met by managers' goals directly, we can find that all the sub-goals of goal H, that is (1), (2), (5), (9), and (10), are included in the union of sub-goals of the goals B and E, which are met by manager. Since all the sub-goals of goal H is met by the sub-goals of goals B and E, goal H is substantially met by the goals of managers. As a conclusion, only goal C remains as the additional goal to be met.

Analysis of the Dependency of Goals. Figure 9 illustrates the same system goal lattice with the highlighting of goals originating from the goal E "Business Productivity". The highlight indicates that meeting the goal E requires meeting goals

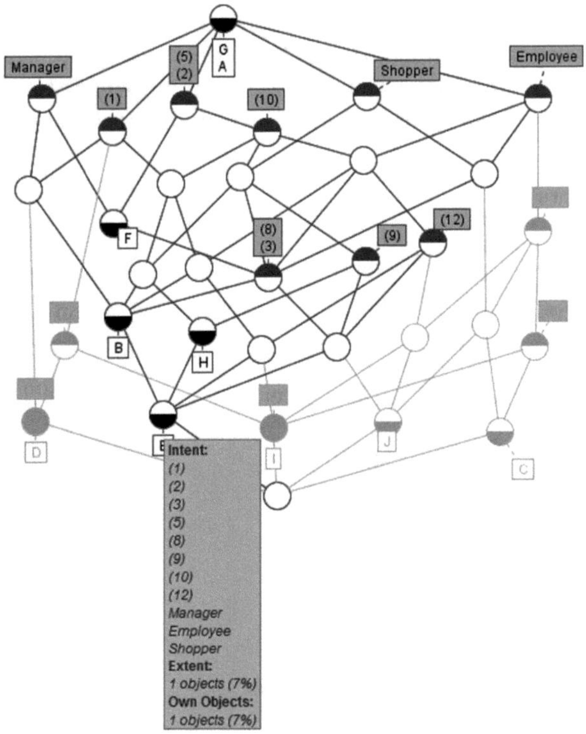

Fig. 9 Goal associated with productivity

Table 9 Manager's goals included and excluded

Goals of manager	Sub-goals included in the goal												
	(1)	(2)	(3)	(4)	(5)	(6)	(7)	(8)	(9)	(10)	(11)	(12)	(13)
B	X	X	X		X			X		X			
D	X						X						
E	X	X	X		X			X	X	X		X	
F		X			X								
J		X	X		X			X	X	X		X	

Goals excluded	Sub-goals included in the goal												
	(1)	(2)	(3)	(4)	(5)	(6)	(7)	(8)	(9)	(10)	(11)	(12)	(13)
C						X			X				X
H	X	X			X				X	X			

B, F and H since at least one of the sub-goals of goal B, F, and H is also sub-goal(s) of goal E. Therefore, the dependency among goals is clearly identified.

7 Evaluation of the Goal Reconciliation

Evaluation of Goal Diversity Ratio. Figure 10(a) shows the Goal Diversity Ratio, Rd, with respect to the number of goals, number of nodes, and number of edges of three stakeholder goal lattices of self-checkout systems. The figure indicates that the shopper's goal lattice presents the widest variety of goals, followed by staff, and manager. Manager's Rd is less than 1.0, which indicates that the manager's intentions are very narrow, i.e. sharp, than any other stakeholders even narrower than reference stakeholder of developer. On the other hand, shopper's Rd is the largest, which indicates their intentions are diverse.

Evaluation of Goal Reduction Ratio. Figure 10(b) shows the Goal Reduction Ratio, Rr, with respect to the number of goals, number of nodes, and number of edges of stakeholder goal lattices. Figure 10(b) indicates that reconciliation is most effective to the shoppers followed by staff, and manager. This result is a dual to the Rd, since the goals of shopper vary most and include the largest space to be reduced in the goal lattice.

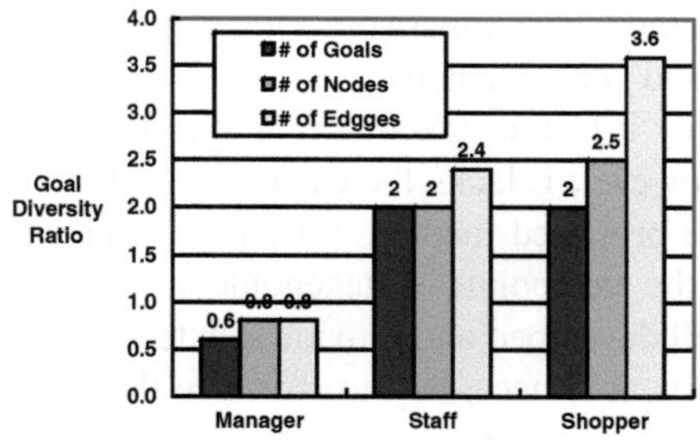

(a) Goal Diversity Ratio

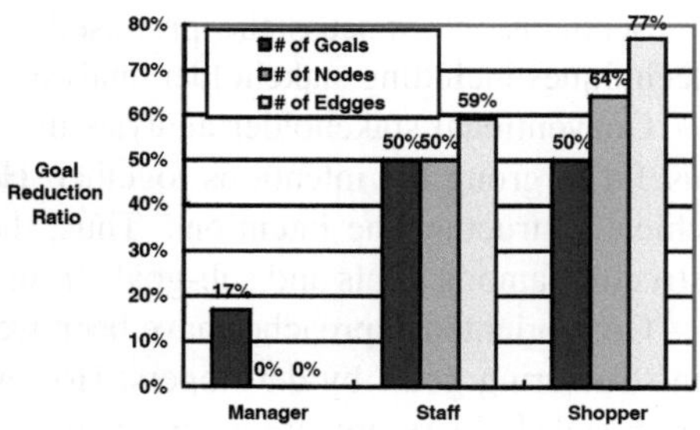

(b) Goal Reduction Ratio

Fig. 10 Evaluation of goal reconciliation effect

8 Discussion

First, we discuss the feasibility of the proposed method from the following viewpoints.

Approach. There are several approaches to stakeholder analysis. However, they are suffering from two major drawbacks:

- Techniques are based on heuristics and lack of mathematical foundation
- Techniques are oriented to developers even though they are targeted to users, i.e. stakeholders.

The proposed technique aims at solving those problems by the following approach:

- The proposed method is based on the mathematical foundation of lattice theory, which is especially appropriate to structure the relationships among entities of goals, sub-goals and stakeholders.
- The proposed method is bottom-up and only requires the information from stakeholders.

As a whole, we can conclude that the proposed method significantly improve the conventional techniques.

Modeling Capability. The proposed method introduced a rather simple semantics in the order relations, i.e. inclusion of attributes, in order to ensure the order relation. This is a two-sided problem. If we introduce more semantics into the model, like many goal-oriented techniques, the model could increase modeling capability, but can be complicated and decidability of order relation may suffer.

Analysis Capability. We developed measures to analyze the structural properties of the goal lattices. Among them, we found that the commonality and variability properties and direct/indirect order relation are especially useful to analyze the structure of goals and prioritize the goals from certain stakeholders' point of view.

Secondly, we discuss the proposed method in comparison with conventional techniques including stakeholder analysis and goal-oriented.

Conventional stakeholder analysis mainly uses the stakeholder matrix which is useful to group the intentions together. However, it lacks the capability to hierarchically structure the intentions. Thus, the proposed method is useful to find the structure among goals and sub-goals from the viewpoints of stakeholders.

Goal-oriented approaches have been well developed and provide rich techniques in structuring goals by developers. However, it is necessary to structure the goals from stakeholders' intentions in a bottom-up manner. Conventional techniques are mostly intended to decompose goals in top-down manner. The presented method relies on the intentions of stakeholders, and generates the structure of stakeholder intentions in a bottom-up manner, which is a major advantage over conventional techniques.

9 Conclusion

We presented a method to structure the intentions of stakeholders in terms of the relation among the goals, sub-goals and stakeholders, to generate the system goal lattice, and to analyze the structural properties of the system goal lattice.

The advantage of the presented method is its mathematical foundation of FCA (Formal Concept Analysis) based on the lattice theory. The presented method enables to elaborate the hierarchical structure among the goals, sub-goals and stakeholders from the intentions of stakeholders in a bottom-up manner.

We demonstrated the feasibility and effectiveness of the presented method by applying the method to self-checkout systems for large-scale supermarkets.

As the conclusion, the presented method enables to systematically elicit stakeholders' intentions in the development of complex large-scale information systems. Unlike conventional techniques, the proposed method employs information from a number of people in a set of stakeholder groups. It is particularly useful to the information systems for public services and consumer products, to which stakeholders are diverse.

Acknowledgments The author thanks to Kayo Suzuki, Tamami Murase, and Nobotu Nakamichi for their collaboration in conducting the case study.

References

1. Anton A (1996) Goal-based requirements analysis. In: Proceedings of ICRE'96, IEEE CS, Los Alamitos, CA, pp 136–144
2. Aoyama M (2007) Persona-scenario-goal methodology for user-centered requirements engineering. In: Proceedings of RE 2007, IEEE CS, Los Alamitos, CA, pp 185–194
3. Avery P (2008) Self-service at supermarkets and grocery stores. White paper. NetWorld alliance. http://www.selfserviceworld.com/white_paper.php?id=72. Accessed 31 Jan 2010
4. Dabholkar PA, Bobbitt LM, Lee E-J (2003) Understanding consumer motivation and behavior related to self-scanning in retailing. Int J Service Industry Manag 14(1):59–95
5. Darke P, Shanks, G (1996) Stakeholder viewpoints in requirements definition: a framework for understanding viewpoint development approach. Reqs Eng J 1(2):88–105
6. Finkelstein A, Kramer J, Nuseibeh B, Finkelstein L, Goedicke M (1992) Viewpoints: a framework for integrating multiple perspectives in system development. Int J Softw Eng Knowl Eng 2(1):31–58
7. Glinz M, Wieringa RJ (2007) Stakeholders in requirements engineering. IEEE Softw 24(2):18–20
8. Hesse W, Tilley T (2005) Formal concept analysis used for software analysis and modeling. In: Formal concept analysis. LNCS, vol 3626. Springer, Berlin, Heidelberg, pp 288–303
9. van Lamsweerde A (2001) Goal-oriented requirements engineering: a guided tour. In: Proceedings of RE'01, IEEE CS, Los Alamitos, CA, pp 249–262
10. Nuseibeh B, Kramer J, Finkelstein A (1994) A framework for expressing the relationships between multiple views in requirements specification. IEEE Trans Softw Eng 20(10): 760–773
11. Rolland C, Souveyet C, Ben Achour C (1998) Guiding goal modeling using scenarios. IEEE Trans Softw Eng 24(12):1055–1071
12. Rolland C, Grosz G, Kla R (1999) Experience with goal-scenario coupling in requirements engineering. In: Proceedings of RE'99, IEEE CS, Los Alamitos, CA, pp 74–81
13. Rolland C, Salinesi C (2005) Modeling goals and reasoning with them. In: Aurum, A, Wohlin C (eds) Engineering and managing software requirements. Springer, Berlin, Heidelberg, pp 189–217
14. Rolland C (2008) Intention driven conceptual modelling. In: Johannesson P, Söderström E (eds) Information systems engineering: from data analysis to process networks, IGI Global, Hershey, pp 16–42
15. Snelting G (2005) Concept lattices in software analysis. In: Formal concept analysis. LNCS, vol 3626. Springer, Berlin, Heidelberg, pp 272–282
16. Sommerville I, Sawyer P, Viller S (1998) Viewpoints for requirements elicitation: a practical approach. In: Proceedings of RE 1998, IEEE CS, Los Alamitos, CA, pp 74–81

17. Wille R (2005) Formal concept analysis as mathematical theory of concepts and concept hierarchies. In: Formal concept analysis. LNCS, vol 3626. Springer, Berlin, Heidelberg, pp 1–33
18. Yevtushenko S, Kaiser T. Tane J, Objedkov S. Hereth-Correia J. Reppe H (2006) Concept explorer: the user guide. http://conexp.sourceforge.net/. Accessed 31 Jan 2010
19. Yu E (1993) Modelling organizations for information systems requirements engineering. In: Proceedings of RE 1993, IEEE CS, Los Alamitos, CA, pp 34–41

Fostering the Adoption of *i** by Practitioners: Some Challenges and Research Directions

Xavier Franch

Abstract The *i** framework is a widespread formalism in the software engineering discipline that allows expressing intentionality of system actors. From the time it was issued, in the mid-90s, a growing research community has adopted it either in its standard form or formulating variations in order to adapt it to some particular purpose. New methods, techniques and tools have made evolve the framework in a way that it may be currently considered quite mature from the scientific perspective. However, the *i** framework has not been transferred to practitioners at the same extent yet: industrial experiences using *i** are not many and have been mainly conducted by *i** experts that are part of that very research community. Therefore, it may be argued that some steps are needed for boosting the adoption of *i** by practitioners. In this chapter, we identify some scientific challenges whose overcoming could represent a step towards this goal. For each challenge, we present the problem that is addressed, its current state of the art and some envisaged lines of research.

1 Introduction

Goal-oriented modelling is a widespread technique in the software engineering community. It is used in broad disciplines like requirements engineering [68] and organizational modelling [39], and in more specific scopes as service modelling [55] and adaptive system modelling [15]. The intentional perspective on systems engineering proposed by C. Rolland [53, 54] had a great impact in the field and largely contributed to this dissemination.

Among these several existing goal-oriented frameworks, methods and languages (e.g., KAOS [13], MAP [53]), the *i** framework [71] is currently one of the most widespread modelling and reasoning approaches. It supports the construction of models that represent an organization and its processes as an intentional network

X. Franch (✉)
GESSI Research Group, Universitat Politècnica de Catalunya, UPC – Campus Nord, Omega building, c/Jordi Girona 1-3, 08034 Barcelona, Spain
e-mail: franch@essi.upc.edu

S. Nurcan et al. (eds.), *Intentional Perspectives on Information Systems Engineering*, DOI 10.1007/978-3-642-12544-7_10,

of actors and dependencies, which may be decomposed into simpler elements. Reasoning techniques allow checking properties and performing some kind of qualitative [29, 35] and quantitative [19] analysis.

The intentional nature of *i** is very clearly explained by Yu: "In *i** modelling, we focus on intentional properties and relationships rather than actual behaviour. By not describing behaviour directly, an intentional description offers a way to characterize actors that respects the autonomy premise. Conventional system modelling which offers only static and dynamic ontologies leads to an impoverished and mechanistic view of the world. Intentional modelling provides a richer expressiveness that is appropriate for a social conception of the world" [72].

Arguably, it may be said that the *i** framework has reached a high maturity level from the scientific point of view, as a result of the intensive work undertook by many research groups, leading to an increasing body of knowledge available through scientific papers and experience reports presented in world-leading journals and conferences. A growing community has been established too, with two clearly visible meeting points: a periodical event, the *i** workshop; and a working space, the *i** wiki [36]. Basic knowledge on *i** is offered through tutorials in scientific conferences and a textbook in which the community research groups provide a comprehensive revision of the state of the art [73]. Last, it may be mentioned the recognition of an *i**-based language like URN as a telecommunication standard [37].

Taking all of this research into consideration, it could be expected that the adoption of *i** by practitioners should had grown the same. Unfortunately, it is clearly not the case. A recent survey of practice [14] does not even mention *i** among current requirements engineering adopted formalisms. Just a few, though valuable, experiences have been reported on the use of the framework and associated tools. We may mention:

- The air traffic control experiences by Maiden et al., see [41, 44] as summary.
- Experiences in Ericsson Marconi Spa about knowledge transfer and process alignment [4, 5].
- The application of *i** for articulating activities around Off-The-Shelf-based and hybrid systems in the Etapatelecom Ecuadorian company [11, 12].

These experiences were basically successful, although they highlighted several obstacles on the adoption of *i** in medium- and large-scale projects. Also, it should be remarked that those experiences have been mainly conducted or at least supervised by expert *i** modellers, being thus uncertain to what extent novice *i** modellers (e.g., the typical profile of a requirement elicitation facilitator) are able to conduct their processes in an effective and efficient way.

Therefore, we strongly argue that the *i** community should dedicate the necessary effort on exploring effective ways to transfer the framework to practitioners, making it more usable in industrial experiences. Efforts are twofold. On the one hand, exploration of scientific issues having to be with the framework that may enhance its usability, improving thus chances of adoption by practitioners. On the other hand, planning and executing strategic community actions not directly related to scientific findings (industry-oriented seminars and tutorials, etc.). Due to the nature of this book, we will focus on the first topic.

This chapter provides an overview of some of the most relevant scientific challenges that shall be overcome in order to attain (at least partially) this knowledge transfer goal. Because of length limitations, we will concentrate on challenges related to the framework's modelling language more than to analysis techniques defined around. For each challenge, after reviewing its context, the problem to be solved and the state of the art, research directions are proposed and justified. As a result, we expect to stimulate research in the community along these directions and thus to effectively help bridging the gap among researchers and practitioners in the use of the *i** framework.

2 Challenge 1: Agreeing on the *i** Metamodel

Context. Since it was first released in 1995, the *i** framework has been adapted to the needs of specific research groups that wanted to represent concepts specific of their application domain, like security [28], temporal precedence relationships [23] or architectural concepts [31]. Furthermore, even the original framework had several variations (GRL for standardization purposes [67], the Tropos methodology on top of *i** [7]) and experienced a natural evolution on time that has led to a slightly modified version available in the *i** wiki [36]. As a result, we may conclude that there is a plethora of variations available in the community, used by several authors with different purposes (see [9] for a summary and more detailed analysis).

Problem. This diversity, although not necessarily pernicious, hampers the progress of the *i** community. When reading a work around the *i** framework, it is necessary first to understand what concrete version of *i** is being used. If the contribution is based on the original framework, sometimes the authors declare which version are they using (lately, it is happening to be the wiki version), but sometimes there is no explicit mention, which usually makes the reader a bit hesitant about details of the proposal being presented. Also it has to be said that the wiki version is currently described as an informal tutorial (a users' guide) without providing such a metamodel. On the other hand, if the work is proposing some new variation, enrichment or customization of *i**, the semantics is sometimes given informally or by using a formalism which is not easy to align with the available descriptions of *i**. Therefore, as some authors explicitly claim [8, 46], a unifying metamodel seems a must.

Challenge. The *i** framework shall include one and only one metamodel; well-established customization strategies for designing variants of this metamodel shall be used.

State of the art. We may find in the literature several approaches of *i** metamodels. Ayala et al. proposed a metamodel [6] that evolved into a more elaborated one by Cares et al. [9], see Fig. 1. It was designed by considering the features of the original Yu's version [71] (which included its own metamodel written in Telos

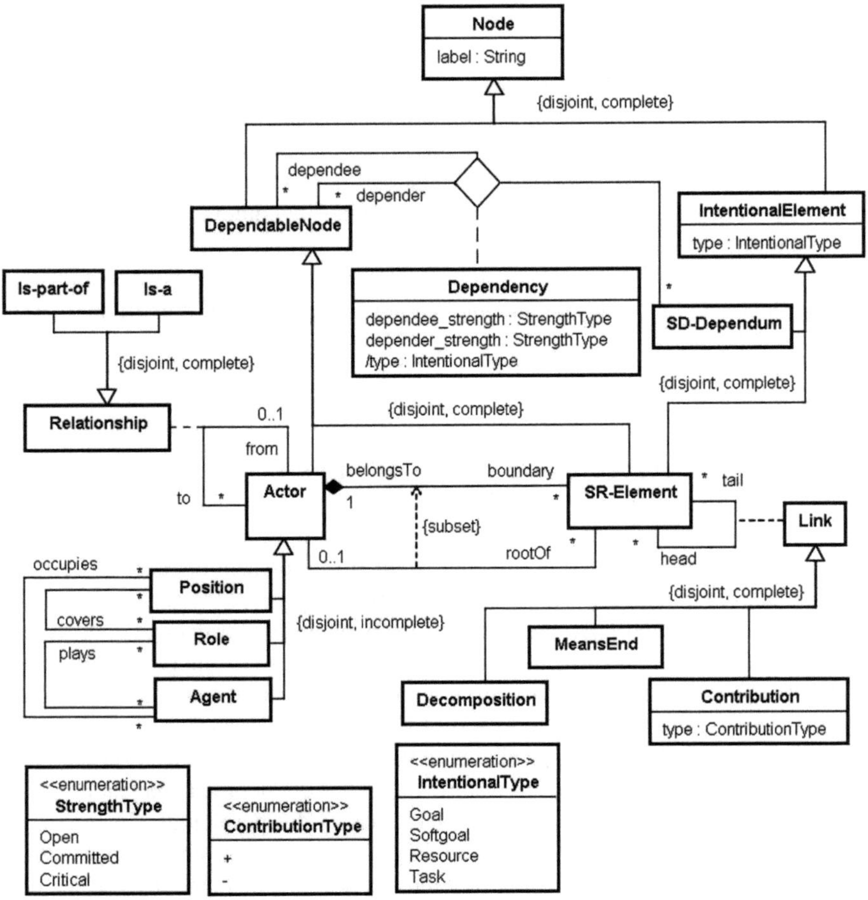

Fig. 1 The *i** metamodel as proposed in [9] (integrity constraints not included)

[45]) and its two most widespread variations, GRL [67] and Tropos [7], proposing a unifying model. It is intended to be reusable too, and several superclasses appear to support this objective. Variations are proposed to be modelled by refactoring although no exploration on the semantic consequences of this process is included. Other approaches with different aim are that of Susi et al. [62] and Roy et al. [57], presenting metamodels not general-purpose as the previous one, but tailored to the specific capabilities of the Tropos associated *i** variation and GRL, respectively.

Research directions. Concerning the metamodel, the community should agree on the final form of the *i** metamodel (probably by upgrading into metamodel the current wiki informal description), and consider it as part of the framework core. Let's call this metamodel "the *i** metamodel". The *i** metamodel should be recognized as standard by all the community, providing then a common vocabulary for the community. We think that the most recent Cares' et al. proposal [9] is an adequate starting point since it is able to express virtually all of the concepts included in the wiki version. Also, it is not oriented to any particular metamodeling technology like EMOF, we think that technology-independence is a good property for this general-purpose metamodel.

As for the customization, we propose that each proposal which needs a particular variant of the *i** metamodel as reference, should formally specify the relationship with the *i** metamodel. To do so, more than a simple refactoring exercise as proposed in [9], a semantically rich definition has to be provided. We may take for instance the formal framework proposed by Wachsmuth [69] and then use the several relationships defined therein (equivalence, enrichment, extension, etc.) to classify the proposed metamodel with respect to the *i** metamodel, providing also the concrete mapping functions that express the differences in a rigorous manner.

One possible immediate application of this notion is to obtain technology-oriented versions of the *i** metamodel. For instance, in [26] it is proposed to use *i** as initial model in a model-driven development process, and a particular version of the metamodel using EMOF defines the form that this departing model may have. In the context proposed here, this EMOF version could be elaborated as a semantics-preserving variation of the *i** metamodel. The mapping from this EMOF-based version to the *i** metamodel would then be completely accurate.

Another technology-oriented version is the iStarML interchange format [10]. This format translates the metamodel proposed in [9] into XML. It is currently used as import/export format in the H*i*ME tool [34] and planned for adoption in a next release of TAOM4E [63]. A natural consequence of agreeing on the *i** metamodel would be to evolve iStarML into a version compliant to this metamodel.

3 Challenge 2: Providing Methodologies for *i** Modelling

Context. In general, modelling is an activity that requires prescriptive methods in order to be repeatable, reproducible and in general, predictable. One could reasonably expect that when facing the same problem, two different (teams of) experts in both the domain being modelled and the modelling framework, working independently, should produce very similar, in some sense "equivalent" models.

Problem. Modelling becomes harder when the level of abstraction of the knowledge to be modelled increases. Therefore, creating a model for the requirements of a system is harder than creating a model of a software architecture. When considering the *i** framework, the modelling activity is harder than ever due to its intentional nature. As Yu states, "The *i** framework is aimed at modelling strategic relationships and reasoning. Such knowledge is not expected to be complete" [71]. In addition, the *i** language itself allows a degree of freedom that creates some uncertainty not only to the novice, but also to the expert, modeller. A summary of recurrent questions include:

- Being *i** models of strategic nature, which elements have strategic relevance enough as to be included in the models, and which don't, and why.

- As a particular case of this situation, which are the conditions that indicate that a model is completely refined.
- In some particular situation, what *i** modelling element is the most adequate. A typical example is: when a task produces a resource, which element must be included: just the task, just the resource, none, or both.

Given an answer as accurate as possible to these and similar questions is the only way to overcome the modelling uncertainty problem.

Challenge. The *i** community shall have available a range of well-defined modelling methods as predictable as possible.

State of the art. The construction of goal-oriented models in general has been subject of interest by the requirements engineering community, for instance Rolland et al. used explored the use of scenarios to drive the discovery of goals [56]. The need of modelling methods for the *i** framework became obvious soon and a major response was the formulation of the Tropos method [7]. Tropos spans four phases of software development, namely early requirements, late requirements, architectural design and detailed design, previous to implementation (in some papers considered a fifth phase) using some agent-oriented infrastructure. The method is not prescriptive inside these four phases and then the modeller still has a great freedom in completing the model. In [27], the authors propose the use of social patterns as a way to elicit the general structure of models. However, still the patterns just provide a general layout of the models.

Other authors propose more detailed methods. In [22] the R*i*SD methodology is proposed for the modelling of Strategic Dependency (SD) *i** diagrams. It is organized into several steps, and intents to be a highly prescriptive procedure. As part of the steps, we may mention: (a) The formulation of two alternative decision trees (under dependum's nature and under responsibility assignment strategy) for determining the most appropriate type of intentional element in a given situation (see Fig. 2), where the transition of one node to a child is based on a question (e.g., in

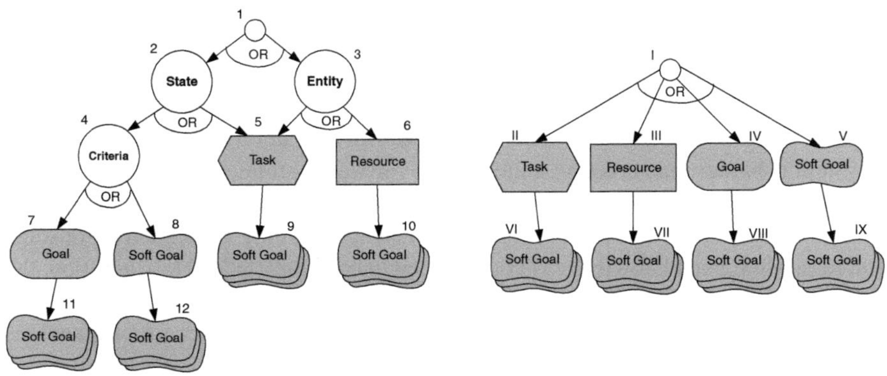

Fig. 2 Decision trees for determining the type of intentional element as defined in [22]

node 1 at the tree at the left: "does the depender depend on the dependee to achieve an entity, or to attain a certain state? If entity, go to 3; if state, go to 2"). (b) The definition of a grammar for fixing the syntax of intentional elements in order to obtain uniform models from the point of view of naming (e.g., a Task's name is of the form: "Verb + (Object) + (Complement)", as in "Answer doubts by e-mail"). (c) The agreement on standard vocabularies for using as lexicon in the intentional models, e.g. the ISO/IEC 9126-1 standard [64] for quality concepts. On the other hand, Oliveira et al. [48] propose *i** Diagnoses, a method that uses questions as a way to elicit the intentional elements that compose the *i** models, e.g. "Why does <<dependee>> collaborate with <<depender>> to have <<goal>>?" and "What if <<goal>> is shared with another actor?". Both proposals claim that the methods produce more predictable models, although no validation supports these claims.

Grau et al. [32] propose the PR*i*M method framed in the business process reengineering problem. Detailed Interaction Scripts describe the current behaviour of the system in a scenario-like style. A set of prescriptive rules transform these scripts into *i** models that act as the basis for an activity of generation of alternatives to be evaluated as part of the reengineering process.

A comprehensive comparative analysis using 12 criteria and including Tropos, R*i*SD, PR*i*M and three other methods (GBM, ATM and BPD) may be found at [30].

Research directions. Given Yu's statement above, it is clear that aiming at designing fully deterministic *i** modelling methods should not be an ultimate goal. But based on the work described above, we may indicate some factors supporting the formulation of more prescriptive methods:

- *Steps.* The method shall consist of a series of well-defined steps and substeps. Remarkably, the model elements that may appear as input and output of each step and their relationships shall be defined in terms of the *i** metamodel.
- *Refinement rationale.* The method shall provide a clear rationale about: (1) whether is it still necessary to refine a given intentional element; (2) which kind of decomposition is needed; (3) which type do the decomposing intentional elements have. The use of questions as proposed in [22, 48] is probably the most comfortable way to proceed for the modeller.
- *Correctness checks.* The method shall provide verifiable means to check that the model being generated fulfils some identified conditions about their structure. The use of metrics [20] could help here.
- *Patterns.* The method shall contemplate the possibility of using knowledge patterns as a way to drive reusability. Patterns could be organized into different catalogues depending on the step where they apply (e.g., social patterns like in [27], but also requirement patterns as mentioned in [61, 70], design patterns, etc.).
- *Vocabulary.* The method shall promote the use of ontologies as a way to improve the accuracy of the models, as well as they consistence of different models over the same domain or system facet. Ontologies of interest may include domain ontologies like the REA enterprise ontology [66], or facet ontologies like the ISO/IEC 9126 quality standard [64] for non-functional characteristics used in

soft goals. General knowledge of ontologies in the agent-oriented field [33] and proposals of representation of ontological concepts into the *i** framework [24] are worth to explore. On the other hand, the methods shall use a consistent grammar to name the intentional elements that compose the *i** models.

4 Challenge 3: Providing Structuring Mechanisms in *i**

Context. Modelling is a stepwise process. Some key elements are identified to build the starting model, and then a series of refinement steps gradually transforms this model into more concrete ones. In the *i** framework, the initial key elements usually are some designated actors (possibly with the main goal that they fulfil) and the most important dependencies among them. Refinement steps may yield to new actors and dependencies, and also to the gradual construction of the Strategic Rationale (SR) *i** diagram of each actor by decomposing their main goal using means-end and task-decomposition links, and establishing the contributions to softgoals.

Problem. This refinement process has not a clear counterpart in the *i** framework. The only structuring mechanism that *i** presents is the concept of actor boundary, that allows separating the declaration of existence of an actor from the rationale that it encloses. But the other refinement steps mentioned above are not supported by the language. Therefore, the final *i** model suffers from several problems:

- *Difficult to reuse.* If a model with some similarities has to be build in the future, reusability is basically copy and paste the designated elements, which is difficult and semantically poor. For instance, if a subpart of an SR diagram is a candidate to be reused, what happens to those dependencies that stem from its intentional elements?
- *Difficult to trace.* Since the model does not keep the stepwise refinement history, the reader is not able to know which elements were introduced in which stages and why. For an intentional framework like *i** is, this is even a more severe drawback because it hides some rationale.
- *Difficult to understand.* Since the model is a monolithic unit except for actor boundaries, the reader has more difficulties than ever to comprehend the full meaning of the system modelled.

Challenge. The *i** language shall include structuring mechanisms for representing the most usual stepwise refinement operations when developing *i** models.

State of the art. There are some lines of research addressing the structurability issue. The two most ambitious contributions at this respect are the incorporation of aspects and services into *i**.

Alencar et al. [3] propose the use of aspects for modelling cross-cutting concerns (see Fig. 3, left). Separation of concerns provides structure to the *i** models, but it does not align with the stepwise refinement process as presented above:

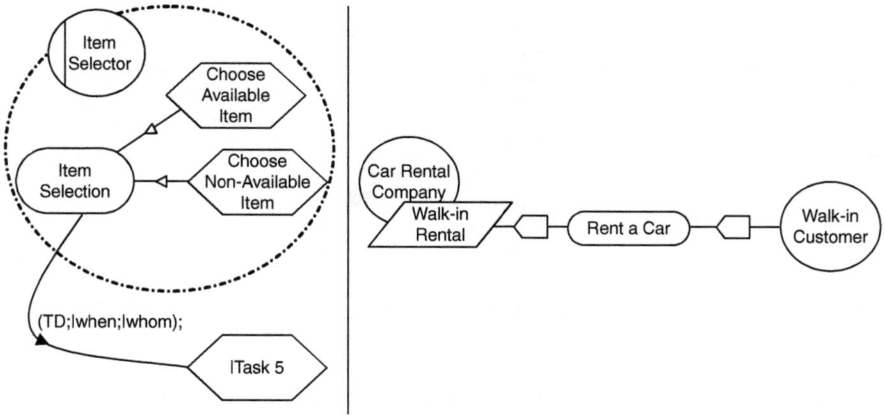

Fig. 3 Structuring *i** models using new constructs: aspects [3] (*left*) and services [16] (*right*)

identification of aspects and modularization of the model is made after the model has been written, therefore the development process is still not recorded. Also, the addition of aspects into *i** results in a framework with more modelling constructs and may eventually require a steeper learning curve.

Estrada incorporates the concept of service into the *i** framework [16] (see Fig. 3, right). This type of modularity unit is closer to the concepts managed in the domain (i.e., business services) and from this point of view fits better than aspects to the natural stepwise refinement process. However it is true that this particular proposal introduces a lot of complexity to the framework, with the fundamental concepts of "service" and "process", and also with the configuration of services inside SR boundaries using a variability-like model with mandatory and optional features combined in several ways. As in the approach above, validation is needed to assess usability of the proposal.

If we consider proposals aligning with stepwise refinement, we still find several proposals. First, we mention the work by Leite et al. [40] that proposes a third kind of *i** diagram to complement the SD and SR diagrams, namely the SA (Strategic Actor) diagram that represents all kind of model actors (roles, positions and agents) with their relationships (plays, occupies, covers, instance, is-a, is-part-of), see Fig. 4, left, for an example. Also, Alencar et al. [1] introduce the concept of alternative for grouping means to achieve an end. This concept is generalized by Franch [21] into the general notion of module that is specialized into different types of SD- and SR-modules (see Fig. 4, right, for example). Remarkably, these three approaches define the introduced constructs in terms of metamodels.

Last, Lucena et al. [43] present a modularization approach that is built on the existing framework without any extension. This means using actors as only encapsulation mechanism. They provide a transformational framework in which transformation rules convert logically connected subgraphs of existing SR diagrams into SR diagrams for new actors.

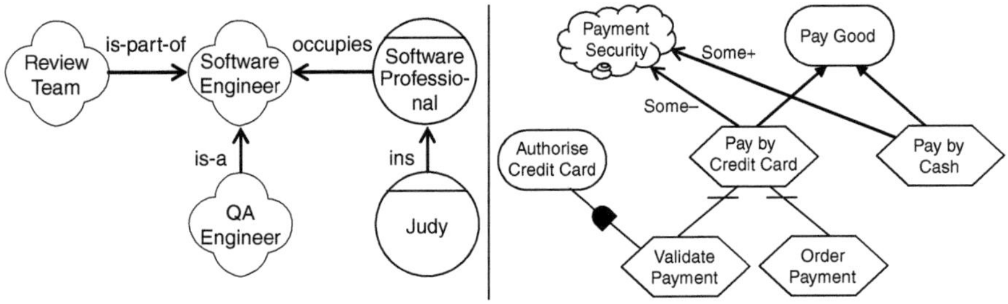

Fig. 4 Examples of structuring mechanisms: SA diagram [40] (*left*) and SR-module [21] (*right*)

Research directions. Basically we foresee two types of structuring mechanisms: domain-independent and domain-dependent.

- Domain-independent. The last three proposals fall into this first category and show a way to go. To sum up, the basic need is: (1) grouping dependencies that are related; (2) grouping related intentional elements inside an SR diagram; (3) defining submodels. Another related work could be analyzing if the aspect-oriented approach could be integrated with them, since both types of modularity constructs seem complementary. However, careful validation about usability of the resulting proposal should be conducted.
- Domain-dependent. The service concept as mentioned by Estrada is one example of concept that may be introduced. If we try to abstract from the service-oriented context to a general, open scope, we could think of introducing a generic structuring mechanism able to be instantiated by any kind of concept, in a way that this instantiation establishes: (1) the kind of *i** model elements that may take part of the module; (2) the relationships that need to be fulfilled.

In both cases, the following issues must be considered:

- Structuring mechanisms exist in virtually all modelling languages; therefore a systematic literature review is needed to learn how they do it, and to try to align to their principles. In particular, the analysis of the UML notion of package seems a must.
- The structuring mechanisms need to be introduced into the *i** metamodel in a non-intrusive way. Then structuring mechanisms become first-class citizens in the framework, whilst not interfering with the semantics of the intentional part.
- There is a need of defining the semantics of: (1) the modules themselves; (2) the module-combination operations (e.g., creation of a new module by the combination of existing ones); (3) the module application operation (i.e., the model that results from applying the stepwise refinement step implied by a module, over an element of the departing model). As essential part of this issue, the classical model merging problem needs to be tackled [58].

- Tool-support is essential. Fundamental capabilities for applying the operations above, for managing a catalogue of modules and for providing views of the model based in the modules are needed.
- Visual representation. Being *i** a notation with a strong emphasis on the visual dimension, an informed decision about the visual representation of modules needs to be made. Work by Moody et al. [46] provides an excellent rationale for making this decision.

5 Challenge 4: Use *i** Models in Later Development Phases

Context. As an intentional modelling vehicle, the *i** framework is used in early stages of the system development. Some of the concepts that appear in *i** models will pervade in later stages, e.g. some *i** actors will act as such in use cases, some resources will appear also in conceptual data models, some tasks will become activities in a behaviour diagram, etc. This suggests for the need of having systematic ways to transform *i** models into other formalisms.

Problem. The transformation of goal models into more elaborate artefacts that appear later in the life-cycle has been tackled in several works (e.g., using the MAP approach to derive data-flow diagrams from goal models [51]). When trying to transform an *i** model into some other kind of model some difficulties arise. Typically the target of this transformation is a UML conceptual model [65], composed at least of a use case specification, a data conceptual model in the form of a class diagram, and perhaps some behavioural model. Sometimes just one of these artefacts is the target.

- Use cases are textual artefacts that reflect communication between actors in a sequential form. The problems that arise are: (1) identifying the appropriate use cases from the *i** model and also the relevant scenarios; (2) identifying the actors that take a part in each use case; (3) inferring the interactions between these actors and write them in the correct order; (4) generating the text itself.
- Data conceptual models are diagrams that include accurate and complete information about classes or entities, their relationships and their attributes. Discovering all of these elements from the *i** model is also a problem since the information that it encloses is not as complete as in data conceptual models (due to its intentional nature).
- Behavioural models like activity diagrams or sequence diagrams include interactions among actors, or activities to be performed, with a flow of control that is not expressed in *i** models.

Solving these problems can be considered a major challenge.

Challenge. There shall be techniques available to make easier (and automate up to a given extent) the transition from *i** models into other types of models.

State of the art. As mentioned above, the main research line related to this challenge corresponds to the transformation of *i** models into UML-like artefacts [50], generally in the context of model-driven development (MDD) [60]. Within the OO-Method MDD methodology [49], Alencar at al. have shown that it is possible to partially infer data conceptual models from *i** models [2]. Actors and their relationships, and resources (both dependencies and internal SR elements), play a fundamental role in this translation. Following the MDD foundations, transformation rules are defined to obtain an initial class diagram that is completed manually (e.g., adding information about multiplicity, not present at *i** models) for obtaining a complete OO-Method class model which can be used in the rest of the MDD process.

Concerning use case generation, Estrada et al. [17] propose a method that covers identification of use cases and actors, and writing of scenarios. Use cases are determined from both the task and resource dependencies that involve the actor that represents the system. The actors at the other end of such dependencies are represented as use case actors. Finally, SR diagrams are used to fill some predefined templates in order to generate the text of scenarios. A similar approach is followed by Santander and Castro [59].

Apart from these kind of models above, *i** has been used in other contexts. Remarkably, Ncube et al. [47] report an extension to the RESCUE process [38] in which a collection of 30 patterns were applied over an *i** model to generate textual candidate requirement statements using the VOLERE template, generating up to almost 600 requirements. As a result of this work, the authors argued that requirements generated from *i** models resulted in a more complete overall requirements specification.

Lucena et al. [42] have gone one step beyond in the development process and they address the generation of architectural models. They combine two levels of refinement, first by modularizing the departing model using the rules described in [43] and then transforming the resulting *i** model into a software architecture model described with the ACME architectural description language [25].

Research directions. As shown above, the transformation of *i** models into other models has been subject of much investigation. However, being a very complex topic, it requires still much work to do. When considering *i** models as the starting point of an MDD process, research is needed with respect to several topics [8]:

- Automating as much as possible the model transformation. It seems clear from previous work that full automation is not feasible since the underlying ontologies cannot be completely aligned. However, the work undertook so far (see above) looks promising and it may be expected that more results will be achieved soon. An important result of these approaches should be the clear statement of the limitations of the proposed methods regarding to automation. Also the possibility of enriching the *i** framework with information that in fact belongs to the target ontology (e.g., order of task in task decompositions [23]) is a point to explore.
- Validating the adequacy of the *i** model before applying the transformations. Since the *i** model is not originally conceived for later transformation, it is

necessary to assess its adequacy, e.g. how well-suited it is for generating classes and attributes in a class model. The definition and application of metrics using the *i*MDF$_M$ method [20] is a possible path to follow.
- Traceability among models. Traceability is a classical problem in MDD methods [52] and as such it needs to be properly managed.

6 Conclusion

In this chapter, we have defended the position of shifting the focus of the *i** community from pure research to a more practical view that may help in transferring the framework to practitioners. For the sake of brevity, we have focused on four challenges that have been described in detail, but several others are out there. These challenges solve some of the drawbacks that the empirical study by Estrada et al. has pointed out [18]. We have focused on scientific challenges, but there are also some other community-oriented issues worth to be considered, among them we may mention:

- Lessons learned. For putting *i** into practice, it is needed to have feedback about its use by practitioners. We think that the facts observed in the experiences mentioned at the introduction of this chapter should be consolidated by all the participants in these and others collaborative experiences, packaged into lessons learned, and the consequences fed back into the community as a main driver for identifying lines of future research.
- Tool support. In our opinion, taking into account the size of the core *i** research community, there is an excess of tools. Given that developing and maintaining such tools has a considerable cost for the research groups, a possible strategic action could be to join efforts for producing a common subsystem at least for the more basic capabilities (e.g., *i** editor) configurable enough to adapt to each group's specificities, importing/exporting models in e.g. iStarML format and with a well-defined API, with a plug-in based infrastructure for enriching its functionality.
- Population for experiments. A great deal of current proposals of modelling variations, analysis techniques, development methods, etc., undergo through a weak validation (if any). The main reason for this probably is the difficulty on getting population enough to run these experiments. A community-oriented view is probably needed in order that the research groups allocate some of their effort in participating in such validations. The *i** wiki may help on implementing this idea.

We hope to see in the next years an increasing effort in these and other topics that make the use of the *i** framework in industrial cases not an exception but a usual practice.

Acknowledgments This work has been partially supported by the Spanish project TIN2007-64753

References

1. Alencar F, Silva C, Lucena M, Castro J, Santos E, Ramos R (2008) Improving the understandibility of *i** models. In: Proceedings of the 10th international conference on enterprise information systems, vol. ISAS-1. INSTICC, Setūbal, pp 129–136
2. Alencar F, Marín B, Giachetti G, Pastor O, Castro J, Pimentel JH (2009) From *i** requirements models to conceptual models of a model driven development process. In: Proceedings of PoEM 2009. LNBIP, vol 39. Springer, Berlin, Heidelberg, pp 99–114
3. Alencar F, Castro J, Lucena M, Santos E, Silva C, Araújo J, Moreira A (2010) Towards modular *i** models. In: Proceedings of 25th symposium of applied computing international conference – RE track. ACM Press, New York, pp 292–297
4. Annosi A, de Pascale A, Gross D, Yu E (2008) Analyzing knowledge transfer in software maintenance organizations using an agent- and goal-oriented analysis technique – an experience report. In: Proceedings of 3rd international *i** workshop. CEUR-WS, vol 322. Aachen, pp 5–8
5. Annosi A, de Pascale A, Gross D, Yu E (2008) Analyzing software process alignment with organizational business strategies using an agent- and goal-oriented analysis technique – an experience report. In: Proceedings of 3rd international *i** workshop. CEUR-WS, vol 322. Aachen, pp 9–12
6. Ayala C, Cares C, Carvallo JP, Grau G, Haya M, Salazar G, Franch X, Mayol E, Quer C (2005) A comparative analysis of *i**-based agent-oriented modelling languages. In: Proceedings of 17th international conference on software engineering and knowledge engineering conference. Knowledge Systems Institute, Skokie, pp 43–50
7. Bresciani P, Perini A, Giorgini P, Giunchiglia F, Mylopoulos J (2004) Tropos: an agent-oriented software development methodology. J Autonomous Agents Multi-Agent Systems 8(3):203–236
8. Cabot J, Yu E (2008) Improving requirements specifications in model-driven development process. In: Proceedings of international workshop on challenges in model-driven software engineering. http://ssel.vub.ac.be/ChaMDE08/wsorganisation, pp 36–40
9. Cares C, Franch X, Mayol E, Quer C (2010) A reference model for *i**. In: Social modelling for requirements engineering. The MIT (in press)
10. Cares C, Franch X, Perini A, Susi A (2010) Towards interoperability of *i** models using iStarML. Computer Standards & Interfaces, doi 10.1016/j.csi.2010.03.005
11. Carvallo JP, Franch X (2009) On the use of *i** for architecting hybrid systems: a method and an evaluation report. In: Proceedings of PoEM 2009. LNBIP, vol 39. Springer, Berlin, Heidelberg, pp 38–53
12. Carvallo JP, Franch X, Quer C (2008) Requirements engineering for COTS-based software systems. In: Proceedings of 23th ACM symposium on applied computing, ACM, New York, pp 638–644
13. Dardenne A, van Lamsweerde A, Fickas S (1993) Goal-directed requirements acquisition. Sci Computer Programming 20(1–2):3–50
14. Davies I, Green P, Rosemann M, Indulska M, Gallo S (2006) How do practitioners use conceptual modelling in practice? Data Knowl Eng 58:358–380
15. DeLoach SA, Miller M (2010) A goal model for adaptive complex systems. Int J Comput Intelligence: Theory Practice 5(2) (in press)
16. Estrada H (2008) A service-oriented approach for the *i** framework. PhD Dissertation, Universidad Politécnica de Valencia
17. Estrada H, Martínez A, Pastor O (2003) Goal-based business modelling oriented towards late requirements generation. In: Proceedings of ER 2003. LNCS, vol 2813. Springer, Berlin, Heidelberg, pp 277–290
18. Estrada H, Martínez A, Pastor O, Mylopoulos J (2006) An empirical evaluation of the *i** framework in a model-based software engineering environment. In: Proceedings of CAiSE 2006. LNCS, vol 4001. Springer, Berlin, Heidelberg, pp 513–527

19. Franch X (2006) On the quantitative analysis of agent-oriented models. In: Proceedings of CAiSE 2006. LNCS, vol 4001. Springer, Berlin, Heidelberg, pp 495–509
20. Franch X (2009) A method for the definition of metrics over *i** models. In: Proceedings of CAiSE 2009. LNCS, vol 5565. Springer, Berlin, Heidelberg, pp 201–215
21. Franch X (2010) Incorporating modules into the i* framework. In: Proceedings of CAiSE 2010. LNCS, vol 6051. Springer, Berlin, Heidelberg, pp 454–469
22. Franch X, Grau G, Mayol E, Quer C, Ayala P, Cares C, Haya M, Navarrete F, Botella P (2007) Systematic construction of *i** strategic dependency models for socio-technical systems. Int J Softw Eng Knowl Eng 17(1):79–106
23. Fuxman A, Kazhamiakin R, Pistore M, Roveri M (2003) Formal tropos: language and semantics. Technical report. University of Trento. http://dit.unitn.it/~ft/papers/ftsem03.pdf. Accessed May 2010
24. Gailly F, España S, Poels G, Pastor O (2008) Integrating business domain ontologies with early requirements modelling. In: Proceedings of RIGiM 2008. LNCS, vol 5232. Springer, Berlin, Heidelberg, pp 282–291
25. Garlan D, Monroe R, Wile D (1997) ACME: an architecture description interchange language. In: Proceedings of conference of the centre for advanced studies on collaborative research (CASCON), IBM, New York, p 7
26. Giachetti G, Alencar F, Franch X, Pastor O (2010) Applying *i** metrics for the integration of goal-oriented modelling into MDD processes. Technical Report ESSI-TR-10-2. Universitat Politècnica de Catalunya
27. Giorgini P, Kolp M, Mylopoulos J, Pistore M (2004) The tropos methodology: an overview. In: Methodologies and software engineering for agent systems. Kluwer Academic Publishers, Berlin, Heidelberg
28. Giorgini P, Massacci F, Mylopoulos J, Zannone N (2005) Modelling security requirements through ownership, permission and delegation. In: Proceedings of 13th IEEE international requirements engineering conference, IEEE CS Press, Los Alamitos, pp 167–176
29. Giorgini P, Mylopoulos J, Nicciarelli E, Sebastiani R (2002) Formal reasoning techniques for goal models. In: LNCS, vol 2503. Springer, Berlin, Heidelberg, pp 167–181
30. Grau G, Cares C, Franch X, Navarrete F (2006) A comparative analysis of *i** agent-oriented modelling techniques. In: Proceedings of 17th international conference on software engineering and knowledge engineering conference, Knowledge Systems Institute, Skokie, pp 657–663
31. Grau G, Franch X (2007) On the adequacy of *i** models for representing and analyzing software architectures. In: Proceedings of RIGiM 2007. LNCS, vol 4802. Springer, Berlin, Heidelberg, pp 296–305
32. Grau G, Franch X, Maiden NAM (2008) PR*i*M: an *i**-based process reengineering method for information systems specification. Info Softw Technol 50(1–2):76–100
33. Guizzardi R, Guizzardi G, Perini A, Mylopoulos J (2006) Towards an ontological account of agent-oriented goals. In: Proceedings of SELMAS 2006. LNCS, vol 4408. Springer, Berlin, Heidelberg, pp 148–164
34. H*i*ME website. http://www.lsi.upc.edu/~llopez/hime/. Accessed May 2010
35. Horkoff J, Yu E (2002) Evaluating goal achievement in enterprise modelling – an interactive procedure and experiences. In: Proceedings of PoEM 2009. LNBIP, vol 39. Springer, Berlin, Heidelberg, pp 145–160
36. *i** wiki. http://istar.rwth-aachen.de. Accessed May 2010
37. ITU-T (International Telecommunication Union, Telecommunication Standardization Sector) (2008) Recommendation Z.151: user requirements notation (URN) – language definition. http://www.itu.int/rec/T-REC-Z.151/e. Accessed May 2010
38. Jones SV, Maiden NAM (2005) RESCUE: an integrated method for specifying requirements for complex socio-technical systems. In: Mate JL, Silva A (eds) Requirements engineering for socio-technical systems. Idea Group, Hershey, pp 245–265
39. Kavakli E (2004) Modelling organizational goals: analysis of current methods. In: Proceedings of 19th ACM symposium on applied computing, ACM, New York, pp 1339–1343

40. Leite J, Werneck V, de Pádua Albuquerque Oliveira A, Cappelli C, Cerqueira AL, de Souza Cunha H, González-Baixauli B (2007) Understanding the strategic actor diagram: an exercise of meta modelling. In: Proceedings of 10th workshop em engenharia de requisitos, Toronto, pp 2–12
41. Lockerbie J, Maiden NAM (2008) REDEPEND: tool support for *i** modelling in large-scale industrial projects. In: Proceedings of CAiSE forum. CEUR-WS, vol 344. Aachen, pp 69–72
42. Lucena M, Castro J, Silva C, Alencar F, Santos E, Pimentel J (2009) A model transformation approach to derive architectural models from goal-oriented requirements models. In: Proceedings of OTM 2009 workshops. LNCS, vol 5872. Springer, Berlin, Heidelberg, pp 370–380
43. Lucena M, Silva C, Santos E, Alencar F, Castro J (2009) Modularizando modelos *i**: uma Abordagem baseada em transformação de modelos. In: Proceedings of 12th workshop em engenharia de requisitos, Valparaiso, pp 33–44
44. Maiden NAM, Jones S, Ncube C, Lockerbie J (2010) Using *i** in requirements projects some experiences and lessons learned. In: Yu E, Giorgini P, Maiden NAM, Mylopoulos J (eds) Social modelling for requirements engineering. The MIT Press (in press)
45. Mylopoulos J, Borgida M, Jarke M, Koubarakis M (1990) Telos: a language for managing knowledge about information systems. ACM Trans Info Systems 8(4):327–362
46. Moody DL, Heymans P, Matulevicius R (2009) Improving the effectiveness of visual representations in requirements engineering: an evaluation of *i** visual syntax. In: Proceedings of 17th international requirements engineering conference. IEEE CS Press, Los Alamitos, pp 171–180
47. Ncube C, Lockerbie J, Maiden NAM (2007) Automatically generating requirements from *i** models: a case study with a complex airport operations system. In: Proceedings of REFSQ 2007. LNCS, vol 4542. Springer, Berlin, Heidelberg, pp 33–47
48. Oliveira A, Leite J, Cysneiros L, Lucena C (2008) *i** diagnoses: a quality process for building *i** models. In: Proceedings of CAiSE Forum. CEUR-WS, vol 344. Aachen, pp 9–12
49. Pastor O, Gómez J, Insfrán E, Pelechano V (2001) The OO-method approach for information systems modelling: from object-oriented conceptual modelling to automated programming. Info System 26(7):507–534
50. Perini A, Susi A (2005) Automating model transformations in agent-oriented modelling. In: Proceedings of AOSE 2005. LNCS, vol 3950. Springer, Berlin, Heidelberg, pp 168–178
51. Prakash N, Rolland C (2006) System design for requirements expressed as a map. In: Khosrow-Pour M (ed) Emerging trends and challenges in information technology. Idea Group, Washington, USA, pp 501–503
52. Ramesh B, Jarke M (2001) Toward reference models of requirements traceability. IEEE Trans Softw Eng 27(1):58–93
53. Rolland C (2007) Capturing system intentionality with maps. In: Krogstie J, Opdahl AL, Brinkkemper S (eds) Conceptual modelling in information systems engineering. Springer, Berlin, Heidelberg, pp 141–158
54. Rolland C, Prakash N, Benjamen A (1999) A multi-model view of process modelling. Reqs Eng 4(4):169–187
55. Rolland C, Samia Kaabi R, Kraiem N (2007) On ISOA: intentional services oriented architecture. In: Proceedings of CAiSE 2007. LNCS, vol 4495. Springer, Berlin, Heidelberg, pp 158–172
56. Rolland C, Souveyet C, Ben Achour C (1998) Guiding goal modeling using scenarios. IEEE Trans Softw Eng 24(12):1055–1071
57. Roy JF, Kealey J, Amyot D (2007) Towards integrated tool support for the user requirements notation. In: Proceedings of SAM 2006. LNCS, vol 4320. Springer, Berlin, Heidelberg, pp 198–215
58. Sabetzadeh M, Easterbrook S (2006) View merging in the presence of incompleteness and inconsistency. Reqs Eng J 11(3):174–193

59. Santander V, Castro J (2002) Deriving use cases from organizational modelling. In: Proceedings of 10th international requirements engineering conference, IEEE CS Press, Los Alamitos, pp 32–39
60. Selic B (2003) The pragmatics of model-driven development. IEEE Softw 20(5):19–25
61. Strohmaier M et al (2008) Can patterns improve *i** modelling? Two exploratory studies. In: Proceedings of REFSQ 2008. LNCS, vol 5025. Springer, Berlin, Heidelberg, pp 153–167
62. Susi A, Perini A, Mylopoulos J, Giorgini P (2005) The tropos metamodel and its use. Informatica 29(4):401–408
63. TAOM4E website. http://sra.itc.it/tools/taom4e/. Accessed May 2010
64. The ISO Organization (2001) ISO/IEC standard 9126 software engineering – product quality. ISO Standards
65. The OMG. http://www.uml.org/. Accessed May 2010
66. The REA Ontology. https://www.msu.edu/user/mccarth4/rea-ontology/. Accessed May 2010
67. University of Toronto. http://www.cs.toronto.edu/km/GRL/. Accessed May 2010
68. van Lamsweerde A (2001) Goal-oriented requirements engineering: a guided tour. In: Proceedings of 5th IEEE international symposium on requirements engineering, IEEE CS, Los Alamitos, p 249
69. Wachsmuth G (2007) Metamodel adaptation and model co-adaptation. In: Proceedings of ECOOP 2007. LNCS, vol 4609. Springer, Berlin, Heidelberg, pp 600–624
70. Yang J, Liu L (2008) Modelling requirements patterns with a goal and PF integrated analysis approach. In: Proceedings of 32nd annual IEEE international computer software and applications conference, IEEE CS, Los Alamitos, pp 239–246
71. Yu E (1995) Modelling strategic relationships for process reengineering. PhD Dissertation, University of Toronto
72. Yu E (2009) Social modelling in *i**. In: Conceptual modelling: foundations and applications. LNCS, vol 5600. Springer, Berlin, Heidelberg, pp 99–121
73. Yu E, Giorgini P, Maiden NAM, Mylopoulos J (eds) (2010) Social modelling for requirements engineering. The MIT Press (in press)

Rights and Intentions in Value Modeling

Paul Johannesson and Maria Bergholtz

Abstract In order to manage increasingly complex business and IT environments, organizations need effective instruments for representing and understanding this complexity. Essential among these instruments are enterprise models, i.e. computational representations of the structure, processes, information, resources, and intentions of organizations. One important class of enterprise models are value models, which focus on the business motivations and intentions behind business processes and describe them in terms of high level notions like actors, resources, and value exchanges. The essence of these value exchanges is often taken to be an ownership transfer. However, some value exchanges cannot be analyzed in this way, e.g. the use of a service does not influence ownership. The goal of this chapter is to offer an analysis of the notion of value exchanges, based on Hohfeld's classification of rights, and to propose notation and practical modeling guidelines that make use of this analysis.

1 Introduction

In order to manage increasingly complex business and IT environments, organizations need effective instruments for understanding their internal operations and strategies as well as their external interactions. Essential among these instruments are enterprise models, i.e. computational representations of the structure, processes, information, resources, and intentions of organizations. Enterprise models may be created on varying levels of abstraction depending on their purpose. A high level of abstraction can be achieved in different ways, e.g. by focusing on essential communicative acts [2] rather than specific message exchanges, by investigating commitments and obligations [11] rather than the way these are fulfilled, or by

P. Johannesson (✉)
Department of Computer and Systems Sciences, Stockholm University, Forum 100,
SE 16440 Kista, Sweden
e-mail: pajo@dsv.su.se

S. Nurcan et al. (eds.), *Intentional Perspectives on Information Systems Engineering*,
DOI 10.1007/978-3-642-12544-7_11,

focusing on the business motivation behind processes. Models on this high level of abstraction are known as business models or value models [13].

Value models have a special characteristic in that they are formulated declaratively without taking into account the order of activities or other forms of activity dependencies. A value model focuses on high level and business oriented objects like resources, actors, and value exchanges. It describes business interaction in terms of intentions and goals, which is a perspective that has been used also in other areas of the information systems field [14, 16]. In contrast, a process model typically includes procedural and technical details including messages and activities as well as control and data flow. The high abstraction level of value models makes them appropriate for representing business cases in a compact and easily understandable way.

A basic notion in value models is that of value exchange, meaning that something of value is transferred between two actors. The essence of this exchange is often taken to be an ownership transfer, i.e. ownership rights on a resource are transferred from one actor to another. However, some value exchanges cannot be analyzed in this way, e.g. the use of a service does not influence ownership. Furthermore, many value exchanges are accompanied by changes of physical states, such as location, which are unrelated to ownership relationships. Thus, addressing only ownership transfers in value modeling will result in impoverished models that exclude important aspects of value exchange and creation. Therefore, there is a need for a detailed analysis of the meaning of value exchanges that will help in the design of rich value models that include not only ownership transfers but also other forms of value exchange and creation. The goal of this chapter is to offer an analysis of the notion of value exchanges but also to propose a notation that makes use of this analysis as well as guidelines supporting the design of value models.

The chapter is structured as follows. Section 2 gives an overview of related research, in particular value modeling and Hohfeld's classification of rights. Section 3 analyses the notion of value exchanges by describing their context and construction in the form of a conceptual model. Based on this analysis, Sect. 4 proposes an extension of the e3value modeling notation and guidelines for designing value models. Section 5 concludes the chapter with a summary of its contributions and suggestions for further work.

2 Related Work

This section introduces two of the main ontologies for value modeling, REA and e3value, as well as Hohfeld's classification of rights, which is used for analyzing basic notions in value modeling.

2.1 The REA Ontology

The REA (Resource-Event-Actor) ontology was formulated originally in [11] and developed further in a series of papers, e.g. [5]. Its conceptual origins can be seen as a reaction to traditional business accounting where the needs are to manage businesses through a technique called double-entry bookkeeping. This technique records every business transaction as a double entry (a credit and a debit) in a balanced ledger.

The core concepts in the REA ontology are resources, events, and actors. The intuition behind the ontology is that every business transaction can be described as events where two actors exchange resources. To get a resource an agent has to give up some other resource. For example, in a purchase a buying agent has to give up money to receive some goods. The amount of money available to the agent is decreased, while the amount of goods is increased. There are two events taking place here: one where the amount of money is decreased and another where the amount of goods is increased. This correspondence of events is called a duality. A corresponding change of availability of resources takes place at the seller's side. Here the amount of money is increased while the amount of goods is decreased.

2.2 The e3value Ontology

The e3value ontology [6, 7] aims at describing exchanges of value objects between business actors. It also supports profitability analysis of the business model created. The basic concepts in e3value are actors, value objects, value ports, value interfaces, value activities and value exchanges, see Fig. 1. An actor is an economically independent entity. An actor is often, but not necessarily, a legal entity, e.g., enterprises and end-consumers. A value object is something that is of economic value for at least one actor, for example a car, Internet access, or a stream of music. (We will sometimes use "resource" as a synonym for "value object".) A value port is used by an actor to provide or receive value objects to or from other actors. A value port has a direction, in (e.g., receive goods) or out (e.g., make a payment) indicating whether a value object flows into or out of the actor. A value interface consists of in and out ports that belong to the same actor. Value interfaces are used to model economic reciprocity. A value exchange is a pair of value ports of opposite directions belonging to different actors. It represents one or more potential trades of value objects between these value ports. A value activity is an operation that could be carried out in an economically profitable way for at least one actor.

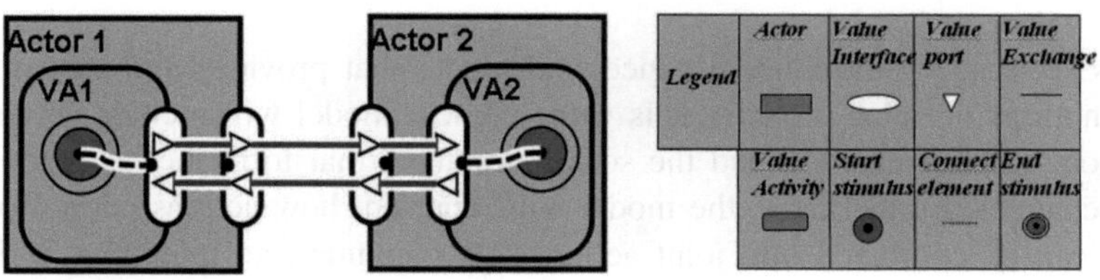

Fig. 1 Basic e3value concepts

2.3 Hohfeld's Classification of Rights

A central component in any value exchange is the transfer and creation of rights. The rights being created can be of different kinds, and it is easy to confuse what rights can mean and how they can be distinguished. In order to clarify the role of rights in value exchanges we will make use of the work of W. N. Hohfeld [8, 9], who proposed a classification identifying four broad categories of rights: claims, privileges, powers, and immunities.

- One actor has a *claim* on another actor if the other actor is required to act in a certain way for the benefit of the first actor, typically by carrying out some action. Conversely, the second actor is said to have a duty to the first actor. An example is a person who has a claim on another person to pay an amount of money, implying that the other person has a duty to pay the amount. Claims always exist within a social structure that is able to monitor and enforce them.
- An actor has a *privilege* on an action if she is free to carry out that action without any interference from a social structure. Some examples of privileges are free speech, free movement, and free choice of marriage partner, which mean that a person is able to talk, move, and choose a marriage partner without interference from the state. Another example is that a person owning some goods has privileges to use the goods in various ways.
- A *power* is the ability of an actor to create or modify a relationship. An example is that a person owning a piece of land has the power to sell it to someone else, thereby creating a new ownership relationship for that piece of land.
- *Immunity* is about restricting the power of an actor in creating formal relationships for other actors. For example, a native people can have an immunity for state legislation concerning their property rights, meaning that the state does not have the power to legislate laws that modify the existing property rights of members of the native people.

Most relationships consist of a combination of several of these rights. For example, if you own a car it means that you have privileges on using it and you also have the power to lend the car or sell it, i.e. creating new ownerships involving other actors.

3 Value Context Model

In this section, we introduce a conceptual model that provides a context for the basic notions of value models. This value context model will include actors carrying out value exchanges and the social structures that form the background of the exchanges. Furthermore, the model will represent how actions carried out by actors can be combined into joint actions that communicate intentions and may result in creating and modifying social relationships. These relationships will be defined in terms of the rights they include. Based on these notions, value exchanges will be modeled as a combination of actions that modify social relationships as well as physical states. The starting point of the model is the OASIS [12] Reference Foundation Architecture for Service Oriented Architecture, which aims at providing a common language for understanding SOA as well as addressing issues involved in constructing, using and owning an SOA-based system. We have chosen this architecture as a basis, since it provides an established foundation for many of the concepts needed to analyze the meaning of value models.

3.1 Actors and Social Structures

3.1.1 Actor

An *actor* is an entity, human, non-human or organization of entities, that is capable of action (taken from [12], Sect. 3.1.1).

The main characteristic of an actor is its ability to take action, which means that an actor can be a human, an organization or even a computational agent. It is not required that an actor be responsible for its actions, as this only pertains to legal entities. Actors, as almost all concepts in the value context model, may exist on a knowledge level as well as on an operational level. According to [4] the operational level models concrete, tangible individuals in a domain, while the knowledge level models information structures that characterize categories of individuals on the operational level. The value context model hence distinguishes between actor types (categories of actors like lawyer, barrister, and teacher) and actors (specific and often tangible concepts like a concrete person).

Actors may be associated to each other through relationships. A relationship may occur spontaneously between two or more humans, as in a friendship. However, many relationships can only occur and exist within the context of some pre-existing social structure. For example, a marriage can only exist within some legal system of a state, and a job position is only meaningful in the context of some organization. In this way, social structures provide a frame or context within which relationships can exist and be meaningful. A relationship typically has different meanings in different social structures, for example a marriage may impose different rights and obligations on the involved actors depending on the social structure in which it exists. Examples of social structures are a company, an association, an NGO, a country, and an international organization.

3.1.2 Social Structure

A *social structure* is a relationship created by a set of actors with the purpose of governing some of their existing and future relationships. A social structure embodies some of the cultural aspects that characterize the relationships and actions among a group of actors (partially based on [12], Sect. 3.2).

Social structures are set up by humans in order to fulfill some purpose, typically to provide value for their environments. For example, the purpose of a school is to educate people, and the purpose of a car manufacturer is to provide actors with cars. A special feature that distinguishes social structures from other kinds of relationships is that they can be actors themselves. The actors who are members of the social structure can be said to have constructed a higher level actor, which is capable of performing its own actions.

3.1.3 Purpose

The *purpose* of a social structure is the value it is intended to provide to its environment (partially based on [12], Sect. 3.2).

Figure 2 summarizes the relationships between actors, social structures, and purposes; it also shows some examples of social structures.

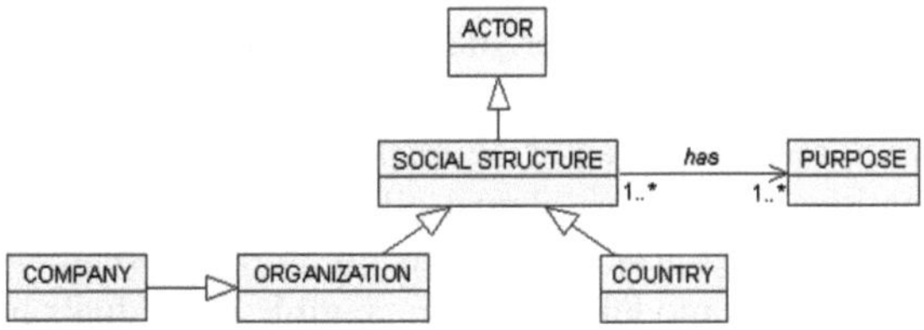

Fig. 2 Actors and social structures

3.2 Actions

3.2.1 Action

An *action* is intentionally carried out by one actor and gives rise to a state change (partially based on [12], Sect. 3.1.2.1).

A distinguishing feature of an action is that it is always carried out with an intention to achieve some effect. Events are similar to actions as they also result in effects, but they happen accidentally or as a result of natural causes, e.g. medical side effects and earthquakes.

In order to achieve a desired effect, it is often required that several actors together carry out a number of actions. One example could be a number of workers that together assemble a vehicle. Another example is a person speaking to another person who listens to what is said. Only when both the speaker has made his statement and the listener has heard and understood it, there will be an effect.

3.2.2 Joint Action

A *joint action* is a coordinated set of actions involving the efforts of two or more actors (taken from [12], Sect. 3.1.2.2).

3.2.3 Communicative Action

A *communicative action* is a joint action in which an actor communicates with one or more other actors (taken from [12], Sect. 3.1.3).

A communicative action is a joint action where information is conveyed from the speaker to the listener. It consists of one speaking action, where the speaker states some content, and a listening action, where the listener acquires and understands the content. While some communicative actions are carried out only with the purpose of transferring information from the speaker to the hearer, many communicative actions also have additional purposes, as analyzed in speech act theory, [15]. Some communicative actions are meant as requests for the listener to carry out some action, while others are meant as promises by the speaker to carry out something. In fact, some communicative acts may on the surface appear as pure assertions by the speaker, while they actually carry another purpose such as a request. For example, if someone states "it is cold in this room", it may look like a straight-forward assertion but is actually a request for the listener to close the open window in the room.

Some communicative actions may ultimately give rise to changes within a social structure through modifying the relationships between actors in that structure or their perceptions of the world. An example could be an employee placing a purchase request to the purchasing department in a company. This request is a communicative action but it will also result in an obligation for the purchasing department to fulfill the request of the employee (given that certain conditions are fulfilled). Thus, the employee's request changes the relationships in the enterprise. In order to clarify the effects of communicative actions we introduce the notion of social action.

3.2.4 Social Action

A *social action* is a joint action that gives rise to social relationships (partially based on [12], Sect. 3.3).

In the next section we will discuss social relationships in more detail, but intuitively they consist of a number of components, including rights, obligations, prohibitions, permissions, and expectations of behavior patterns. In this chapter, we will focus on the formal aspects of social relationships, in particular rights. Communicative actions and social actions are related as a communicative action may count as a social action under certain circumstances. This means that when two actors carry out a communicative action, they thereby also carry out a social action. For example, when an employee places a purchase request to a purchasing department, the two actors carry out a communicative action where the employee informs the purchasing department about her need and asks the department to fulfill it. Under certain circumstances (the employee is correctly authorized, the cost of the request is within budget, etc.) this communicative act will also count as a social act that gives rise to an obligation for the purchasing department to fulfill the request (a social relationship). In this way, an action in one system can count as an action in another system – changing the states of communicating actors can count as changes within a social structure.

3.2.5 Counts As

Counts as is a relationship between two logical systems in which an action, event or concept in one system can be understood as another action, event or concept in another system (taken from [12], Sect. 3.1.4).

Figure 3 summarizes the relationships between actors, actions, joint actions, communicative actions, social actions, and social relationships. In Sect. 3.3 the concept "Counts as" is further modeled and analyzed in the context of how relationships come into being and get their meaning within social structures.

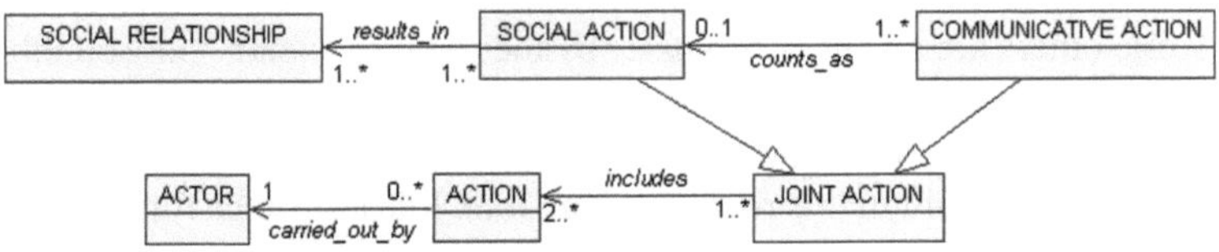

Fig. 3 Actions and social relationships

3.3 Social Relationships

3.3.1 Social Relationship

A *social relationship* is an association between two or more actors, each of whom plays a role in the relationship, that is defined in terms of the rights the actors have in relation to each other.

A social relationship can only exist within the context of a social structure, as it gets it meaning from that structure. For example, a purchase order (a social relationship) is only meaningful within an organization and its surrounding legal environment – if the organization ceases to exist, the purchase order does not have any meaning. Our definition of social relationship can be seen as a specialization of the notion of social fact in [12].

A social relationship involves a number of actors that play different roles in the relationship, for example there are husband and wife roles in a marriage, and buyer and seller roles in a purchase order. A marriage (a social relationship) in one social structure may include two roles: a husband role (male) and a wife role (female) imposing different rights (or equal rights) on the two actors connected through the marriage. In another social structure, a marriage may hold between two partners independently of whether the partners are of different gender or not. Thus, the meaning of a role is dependent on the social structure in which it exists.

3.3.2 Role

A *role* in a social relationship type is a set of rights that an actor playing that role in a relationship has towards the other roles in the relationship (partially based on [12], Sect. 3.2.1).

3.3.3 Right

A *right* is either a claim, a privilege, a power, or an immunity as defined by Hohfeld, see Sect. 2. A privilege or a claim may concern some resource or action, while a power and immunity concern a relationship i.e. power is the right to modify or create a social relationship, while immunity is the right (for an actor) to be excluded from certain social relationships.

An example of these notions is a purchase order (a social relationship) in which the buyer (a role) has a claim (a right) on the supplier (a role) to deliver some product (an action) and the supplier has a claim (a right) on the supplier to pay for the product (an action). Two important types of social relationships are commitments and ownerships.

3.3.4 Commitment

A *commitment* is a relationship between two actors where the rights involved in the relationship primarily consist of a claim, where one actor is obliged to carry out some action for another actor. In other words, one actor is committed to carry out some action for the benefit of another actor.

3.3.5 Ownership

An *ownership* is a social relationship between an actor and a social structure where the rights pertain to some resource. The rights involved in an ownership are primarily privileges (the actor is allowed to carry out certain actions on a resource without any interference from the social structure) and powers (an actor is entitled to create or modify a social relationship). An example is that a person owning a book has the right to read the book and even destroy it but also the right to transfer the ownership to someone else by giving the book away, thereby terminating one social relationship and creating another.

3.3.6 Authority

Authority is the right to act as agent on behalf of an organization or another person (taken from [12], Sect. 3.2.1).

If an actor has the correct authority, some of its actions will count as actions of the organization for which it acts. For example, if an employee at a company writes out a check, it will count as a payment by the company if the employee is correctly authorized.

3.3.7 Resource

A *resource* is any entity of some perceived value that has identity (taken from [12], Sect. 3.3.3). A resource type describes categories of resources.

A similar definition of the term "resource" may be found in REA, see Sect. 2.1 or in the e3value concept of value object, see Sect. 2.2. Examples of resource types are goods, land/real estate, and intellectual property. In some cases relationships can be resources, for instance an invoice (a commitment-relationship between two actors where one actor has to reimburse the other actor) may constitute a resource.

As the meaning and creation of relationships may vary between social structures, we need rules for defining them. In other words, rules model what rights hold for roles and relationships within a given social structure and how these roles and social relationships come into existence in the same social structure. There are three types of rules: meaning rules, derivation rules, and counts as rules.

3.3.8 Meaning Rule

A *meaning rule* defines what rights hold for a certain role in a social relationship relative a social structure.

To be a king (a role) in Sweden (a social structure) entails certain privileges, claims and powers. A privilege may be to use certain castles (but not to give them away so being king of Sweden does not entail an ownership of the castles). Claims include a yearly allowance from the social structure (Sweden), and the powers encompass the right to appoint and dismiss members of court. To be the king of Great Britain entails considerably more privileges and powers compared to Sweden.

3.3.9 Derivation Rule

A *derivation rule* defines how social relationships and roles come into existence. A derivation rule tells which social relationships a social action gives rise to within a certain social structure.

From a modeling point of view, a derivation rule can be seen as a reification of the "results in" association in Fig. 3, which makes the association relative to a social structure. Similarly, the "counts as" association in Fig. 3 can be reified as in the following definition.

3.3.10 Counts As Rule

A *counts as rule* defines what communicative actions count as social actions relative to a social structure.

Figure 4 summarizes the relationships between social structures, social relationships, the various rights that define a social relationship within a social structure, and the rules that define the creation of social relationships.

3.4 Value Exchanges

The notion of value exchange in value models means that something of value is transferred from one actor to another. This exchange often includes a change of ownership, but as the analysis above shows there are also other kinds of right

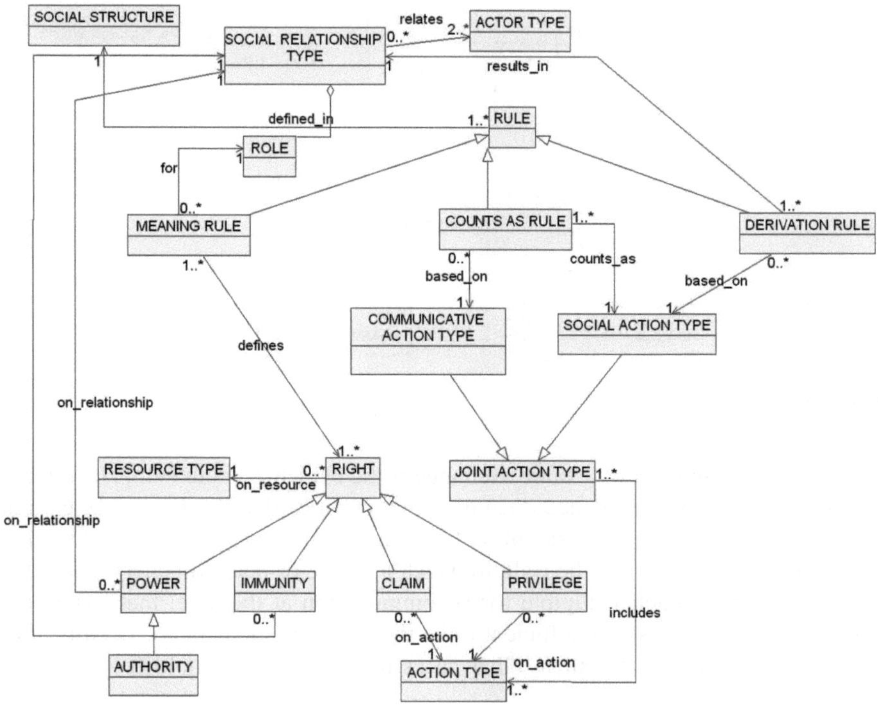

Fig. 4 Social relationships – meaning and creation

combinations that may be created. Furthermore, a value exchange may include actions that are not about creating social relationships, such as the physical transportation of goods.

We suggest that a value exchange is to include three components: social relationship creation, custody provision, and evidence provision. The first component is about the rights an actor gets on some resource. If an actor gets a privilege on a resource, it means that the actor is entitled to use that resource in some way. If she gets a power on the resource, it means that she can create social relationships concerning the resource. For example, in a value exchange where a person borrows a car, she will get some privileges on it, meaning that she can drive it, park it, etc. If she buys the car, she will get the same privileges but also powers on the car, allowing her to lend it to other people or sell it.

The second component of a value exchange is about the custody of the resource [1, 10]. An actor has the custody of a resource if she has immediate charge and control of it, which typically implies physical access. If an actor has the custody of a resource, this does not mean she has rights on it. For example, a distributor may have the custody of some goods, but he is not allowed to use the goods. In a value transfer, there is typically a provisioning of custody to the recipient through which she gets access to the resource. An example is transporting some goods to the recipient.

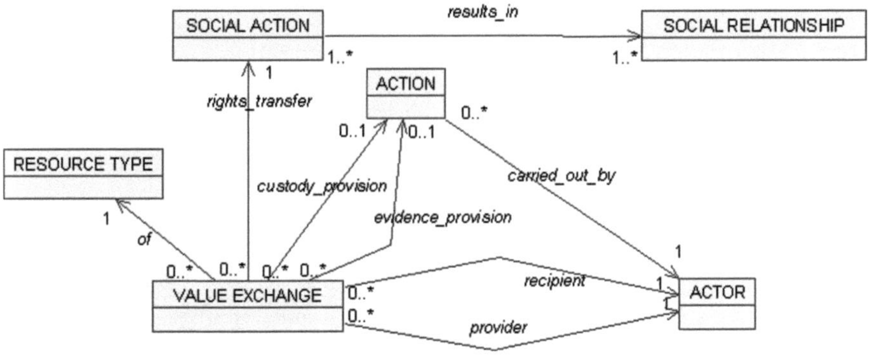

Fig. 5 Value exchanges

The third component of a value exchange is the evidence document [1]. A transfer may include some evidence document that certifies that the buyer has certain rights on a resource. Typical examples of evidence documents are movie tickets that certify that their owner has the right to watch a movie or hotel vouchers that make the owner of the voucher eligible for accommodation at the hotel that issued the voucher. In some cases it is sufficient to be the bearer of an evidence document to use the rights it refers to, but in other cases these rights only hold for a specific person stated in the document.

Summarizing, see Fig. 5 (which is drawn on the operational level), a value exchange can be seen as combining three components:

- The *rights* the buyer obtains on the resource, e.g., the ownership of a book;
- The *custody* of the resource, e.g., the delivery of a book to the buyer;
- The *evidence document*, e.g., a receipt that can be used to prove ownership of a book.

While the first component, the rights, is always considered, the last two components are optional. For example, when buying a piece of land, the buyer is typically not given the custody of that resource. Clearly, evidence documents are not always provided and, furthermore, the provision of custody and evidence documents may be so trivial that it is not of interest to make them explicit. In some complex cases, however, a more detailed analysis is called for since modeling only the transfer of ownership in a value exchange is not sufficient to address important aspects of how value is created and exchanged.

4 Designing Rich Value Models

Most languages for value modeling, including e3value, give meaning to value exchanges by focusing on the transfer of ownership. However, as shown in the previous section, there are also other kinds of rights relevant for value exchanges as well as aspects not related to right transfer and creation. Furthermore, the concept of custody, i.e. what actor has access to a value object, and evidence documents involved in a value exchange, will also be incorporated in the analysis of how value is created in an exchange. In this section, we will discuss how these additional rights and aspects can be taken into account by extending the notation of the e3value language, thereby enabling it to represent richer value models. We will also introduce a number of guidelines assisting a designer in systematically enriching an initial value model that only represents transfers of ownership.

4.1 Notation and Guidelines

In order to represent the meaning of value exchanges, the following notation will be used:

- A value exchange representing the transfer of ownership will be labeled with "O";
- A value exchange representing the granting of a claim will be labeled with "C";
- A value exchange representing the granting of a privilege will be labeled with "Pr";
- A value exchange representing the bestowing of power will be labeled with "Po";
- A value exchange representing the pleading of a claim will be labeled with "PC";
- A custody provision from one actor to another will be shown as a dotted arrow;
- An evidence provision from one actor to another will be shown as a dashed arrow.

In order to support a designer in enriching a value model and making it more precise, we suggest a number of guidelines. These aim at clarifying the kinds of rights involved in value exchanges, the consequences of claims, and the provision of custody and evidence documents.

Guideline 1: *Label existing value exchanges according to the rights involved; possibly split value exchanges in order to get a unique labeling.*

A trivial example of applying this guideline is shown in Fig. 6, which shows a customer buying books from a bookstore. In this case, ownership of books and money are transferred to the customer and bookstore, respectively.

Another example is shown in Fig. 7, where a customer buys insurance from an insurance company. In this case, the customer does not get any privileges to carry out certain actions; instead, she gets a (conditional) claim on the insurance company

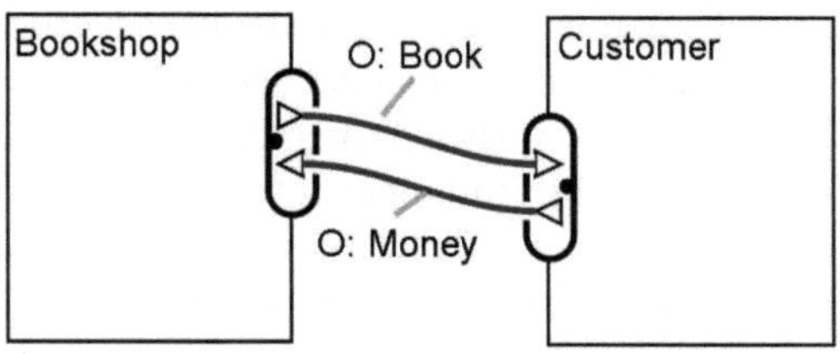

Fig. 6 Bookshop example

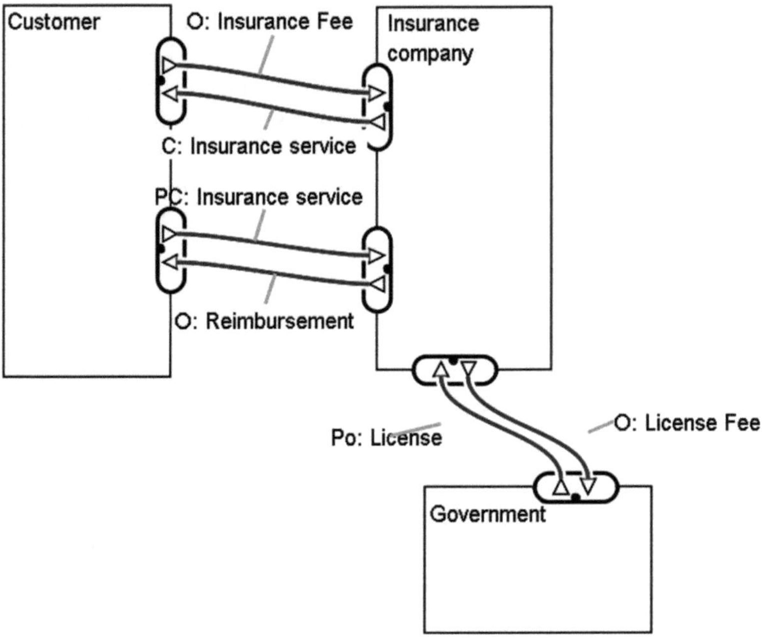

Fig. 7 Insurance example

stating that it is obliged to pay compensation in case of accidents. Thus, the value exchange will be labeled with "C", not "O". Furthermore, the diagram shows a value exchange from a financial supervisory authority to the insurance company. The meaning of this exchange is that the authority gives the company a license, a right, to operate in the insurance market, i.e. a power to establish insurance contracts with customers. Thus, the value exchange will be labeled with "Po", not "O".

Guideline 2: *For each value exchange representing the granting of a claim, introduce a pair of value interfaces including a value exchange representing the pleading of the claim.*

A value exchange representing a claim means that one actor has a duty to carry out some action for the benefit of another actor. However, this action is usually not included in the value interfaces containing the claim granting value exchange. Therefore, the meaning of the claim is not represented in the value model. Another pair of value interfaces has to be introduced in order to make its meaning explicit. These interfaces will include one exchange representing the pleading of the claim, i.e. one actor requesting the other actor to fulfill the claim, and another exchange representing the fulfillment of the claim, which thereby specifies the meaning of the claim. It can be noted that pleading a claim is not about transferring or creating rights but about making use of rights that an actor already possesses, and in this respect it is different from other value exchanges. An example of applying guideline 2 is

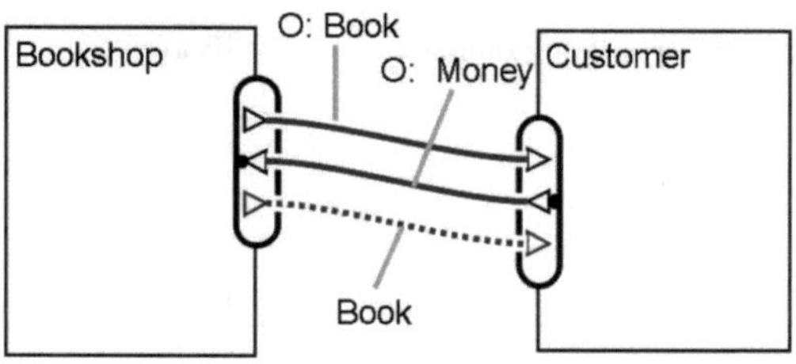

Fig. 8 Bookshop example with custody

given in Fig. 7, which shows that a customer can file an insurance claim (plead a claim) and receive a reimbursement (ownership of money).

Guideline 3: *For each value exchange of goods, introduce optionally an arrow representing custody provision.*

A simple example of applying this guideline is shown in Fig. 8, which extends Fig. 6, showing that a book is physically transported to the customer, thereby giving her custody of it.

Guideline 4: *For each value exchange, introduce optionally an arrow representing evidence provision.*

An evidence document should typically be introduced in a value exchange if the rights that it certifies cannot be proven without showing the document. In some cases it is enough to be the bearer of an evidence document to be eligible to access the rights the document refers to, but in some cases these rights are personal and only hold for the person specified in the document. Only in the former case should the evidence document be included in the value model. In the next section an example where evidence documents are used in the model is introduced.

4.2 The Pawnshop Example

The following example illustrates how to analyze and model a business case using the notation and guidelines proposed above. The business case chosen is that of a pawnshop, which lends money to borrowers on a short-term basis accepting goods as collateral. A pawnshop and a borrower can make business according to a number of value exchanges, in Fig. 9 shown in two different pairs of value interfaces. The first one is when the borrower gets a time limited right to use the money and pays an interest; this is the case where the borrower returns the money and gets the collateral back. The second pair of value interfaces models when the borrower gets ownership of the money and the pawnshop gets ownership of goods, i.e. the collateral; this is the case where the borrower does not return the money and the pawnshop takes the collateral. The diagram also shows that the pawnshop may sell goods to buyers.

The value model of Fig. 9 represents the business case of a pawnshop only partially as it focuses on transfers of ownership, e.g. the role of collaterals is not made explicit. In order to arrive at a richer value model showing a more complete picture

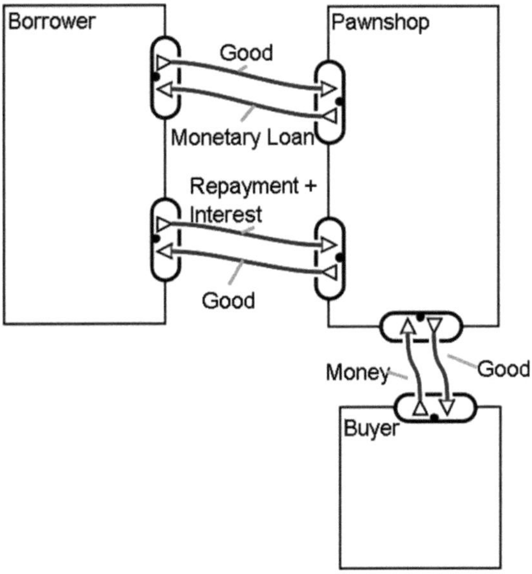

Fig. 9 Pawnshop example I

of the business case, we will analyze the value exchanges and extend the model according to the guidelines proposed.

The first step in the analysis, according to guideline 1, is to identify the kinds of rights involved in the value exchanges. The value exchange monetary loan means that the borrower gets privileges and power rights on the money but also that there is a duty for the borrower to return the money with an interest fee. In other words, the pawnshop gets a claim on the borrower to pay back the loan, which is made explicit in Fig. 10. According to guideline 3, we are also to introduce optional custody provisions. In this case, the borrower gives custody of some goods to the pawnshop as collateral. There is also a duty for the pawnshop to return the goods to the borrower upon request, i.e. the borrower has a claim on the pawnshop, which is also shown in Fig. 10. Thus, the figure shows a partial value model consisting of value exchanges in which the borrower gets a loan, she leaves a good for collateral, the pawnshop gets a claim on the borrower to pay back the loan, and the borrower gets

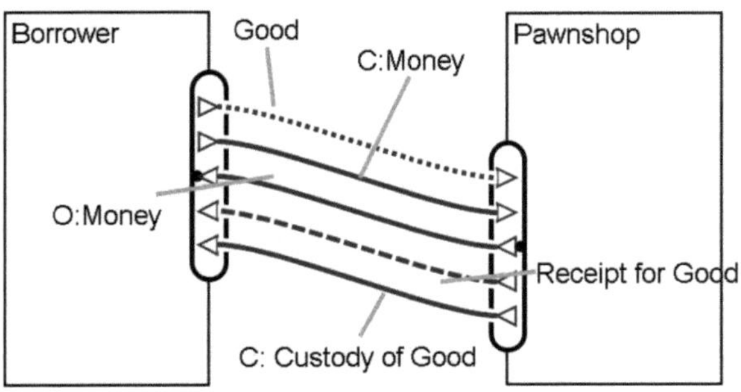

Fig. 10 Pawnshop example II

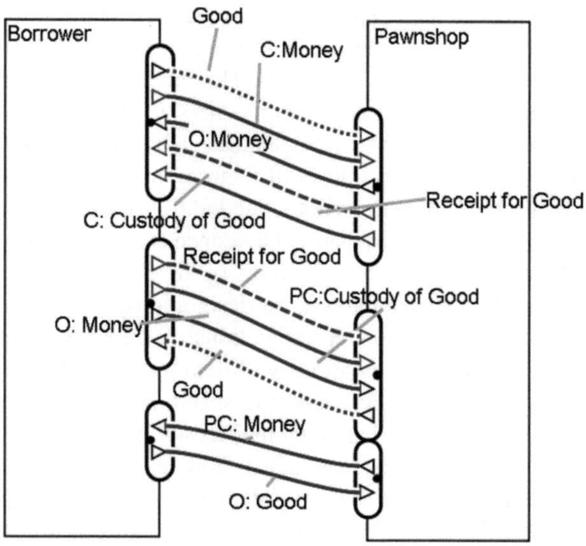

Fig. 11 Pawnshop example III

a claim on the pawnshop to return the good. As proof of having left the good as collateral the borrower furthermore gets a receipt (an evidence document) from the pawnshop, see the dashed arrow of Fig. 10. Notice that in this value model the customer gives up custody of the good and the pawnshop receives the custody, however, it does not get the right to use the good. The pawnshop has in fact an obligation to keep the good safe in case the borrower claims it back. (The part of the diagram in Fig. 9 that also shows that the pawnshop may (re-)sell goods to buyers is omitted in the further analysis in Figs. 10 and 11).

The value model in Fig. 10 needs to be extended according to guideline 2 in order to make explicit the meaning of the claims in the model. The claim of the borrower gives rise to the middle pair of value interfaces in Fig. 11, where the borrower requests her good back (pleading a claim), receives it from the pawnshop (custody transfer) and pays back the loan with an interest (ownership transfer). Similarly, the claim of the pawnshop gives rise to the bottom pair of value interfaces in Fig. 11, where the pawnshop requests its loan to be repaid (pleading a claim) but does not get any money from the borrower and instead takes the ownership of the collateral (ownership transfer). These three value interfaces represent the main logic of the pawnshop business case.

5 Conclusion

Value modeling is an approach for capturing business goals and intentions in the form of value exchanges. Value modeling has many applications and a recent trend is to use value models for defining business services at the enterprise level. In this chapter, we have investigated how to create rich value models that represent the contents and meanings of value exchanges. The contributions of the chapter are theoretical as well as practical. The main theoretical contribution is an analysis of the notion of value exchange using Hohfeld's classification of rights. Value exchanges are not only about transferring ownerships but can also include the transfer and creation of various other rights such as claims to carry out actions and powers to create new social relationships. Furthermore, value exchanges are typically associated with certain kinds of actions not related to rights, in particular the physical transportation of goods and the provision of evidence documents used to identify the rights holder. The main practical contributions of the chapter are notations and guidelines, based on the theoretical analysis, for designing rich value models that are able to provide detailed and precise representations of the values and relationships in a business case. These representations will help to bridge the gap between informal descriptions of business cases and the specification of the business processes needed to realize them. The rich value models will still be on a declarative level and abstract from process issues like control flow and message formats, but they will be more detailed than value models only addressing ownership transfers. This added detail will be a basis for identifying required business processes and their outcomes though not for designing their procedural form.

A topic for future work is to investigate how the rights created in value exchanges will be affected by the type of resource being exchanged. In particular, the exchange of services needs to be analyzed, as services may be viewed as claims themselves [3]. A related issue is how to identify services based on a value model as discussed in [17]. The analysis and proposed guidelines can also be used as building blocks in a more comprehensive methodology for designing value models.

References

1. Andersson B, Bergholtz M, Edirisuriya A, Ilayperuma T, Johannesson P, Gordijn J, Gregoire B, Schmitt M, Dubois E, Abels S, Hahn A, Wangler B, Weigand H (2006) Towards a reference ontology for business models. In: Proceedings of ER 2006. LNCS, vol 4215. Springer, Heidelberg, Berlin, pp 482–496
2. Dietz JLG (2005) Enterprise ontology – theory and methodology. Springer, Heidelberg
3. Ferrario R, Guarino N (2008) Towards an ontological foundation for services science. In: Domingue J et al (eds) Proceedings of future internet – FIS 2008, Springer, Heidelberg, Berlin
4. Fowler M (1996) Analysis patterns – reusable object models. Addison-Wesley, Reading, MA
5. Geerts G, McCarthy WE (1999) An accounting object infrastructure for knowledge-based enterprise models. IEEE Int Systems Appl, Los Alamitos, CA 14(4):89–94
6. Gordijn J, Akkermans JM, van Vliet JC (2000) Business modeling is not process modeling. In: Proceedings of the international conference on conceptual modeling workshops. LNCS, vol 1921. Springer, Heidelberg, Berlin, pp 40–51
7. Gordijn J, Akkermans JM (2003) Value-based requirements engineering: exploring innovative e-commerce ideas. Reqs Eng 8(2):114–134
8. Hohfeld WN, Cook WW (eds) (1919) Fundamental legal conceptions as applied in judicial reasoning and other legal essays. Yale University Press, at Archive.org. http://www.archive.org/details/fundamentallegal00hohfuoft
9. Hohfeld WN, Corbin A (ed) (1978) Fundamental legal conceptions. Greenwood, Westport, CT

10. Hruby P (2006) Model-driven design of software applications with business patterns. Springer, ISBN: 3540301542
11. McCarthy WE (1982) The REA accounting model: a generalized framework for accounting systems in a shared data environment. The Accounting Review
12. OASIS Reference Architecture Foundation for Service Oriented Architecture Version 1.0. http://docs.oasis-open.org/soa-rm/soa-ra/v1.0/soa-ra-cd-02.pdf. Accessed 10 Jan 2010
13. Osterwalder A, Pigneur Y (2010) An e-business model ontology for modeling e-business. In: Proceedings of the 15th bled electronic commerce conference. http://129.3.20.41/eps/io/papers/0202/0202004.pdf. Accessed 20 Jan 2010
14. Rolland C (2007) Capturing system intentionality with maps. In: Krogstie J et al (eds) Conceptual modelling in information systems engineering, Springer, Heidelberg, Berlin
15. Searle J (1969) Speech acts: an essay in the philosophy of language. Cambridge University, New York
16. Soffer P, Rolland C (2005) Combining intention-oriented and state-based process modeling. In: Proceedings of international conference on conceptual modeling – ER 2005. LNCS, vol 3716. Springer, Heidelberg, Berlin, pp 47–62
17. Weigand H, Johannesson P, Andersson B, Bergholtz M (2009) Value-based service modeling and design: toward a unified view of services. In: Proceedings of the 21st conference of advanced information systems engineering (CAiSE'09). LNCS, vol 5565. Springer, Heidelberg, Berlin, pp 410–424

An Intentional Perspective on Enterprise Modeling

Janis Bubenko Jr., Anne Persson, and Janis Stirna

Abstract Enterprise Modeling (EM) has two main purposes: (1) Developing the business, which entails developing business vision, strategies, redesigning the way the business operates, developing the supporting information systems, etc., and (2) ensuring the quality of the business where the focus is on sharing the knowledge about the business, its vision and the way it operates, and ensuring the acceptance of business decisions through committing the stakeholders to the decisions made. In addition, EM has also shown to be useful as a general tool for articulating, discussing, and solving organizational problems. Based on a number of case studies, interviews and observations this chapter defines what is required from EM when adopted for these purposes and intentions respectively. More precisely, it addresses the following types of requirements: documents and models required as input, models that should be developed, requirements on the modeling language, requirements on the modeling process, tool requirements and model quality requirements. The defined requirements are then discussed taking a specific EM method, Enterprise Knowledge Development (EKD) as example.

1 Introduction

Enterprise Modeling (EM), or Business Modeling, has for many years been a central theme in information systems (IS) engineering research and a number of different methods have been proposed. Examples of EM methods can be found in [1–3, 7–10, 13, 16, 35]. Examples of application domains for EM can be found in [5, 6, 12, 17, 29, 31–33].

The application of EM is heavily influenced by a large number of situational factors, one of which is the intention behind its use [20]. We argue that knowledge about these intentions is essential when making decisions about which method, way of

J. Bubenko Jr. (✉)
Department of Computer and Systems Sciences, Royal Institute of Technology,
Forum 100, SE-164 40 Kista, Sweden
e-mail: Janis@dsv.su.se

S. Nurcan et al. (eds.), *Intentional Perspectives on Information Systems Engineering*, DOI 10.1007/978-3-642-12544-7_12, © Springer-Verlag Berlin Heidelberg 2010

working, tool support etc. is appropriate in order for those intentions to be fulfilled. It is important to bear in mind that organizations do not use EM methods only for the sake of using methods. They want to solve a particular business problem and EM is only one of several instruments in that problem solving process.

In this chapter we present a set of requirements on EM methods that are related to intentions that organizations may have when applying EM.

The remainder of the chapter is organized as follows. Section 2 describes organizational intentions of using EM. An example method, Enterprise Knowledge Development (EKD) is used to illustrate some of the requirements. This method is briefly described in Sect. 3. The research approach that resulted in the contribution of the chapter is presented in Sect. 4. Section 5 presents and discusses requirements on EM methods in light of organizational intentions. The chapter concludes in Sect. 6 with a discussion of the results.

2 Enterprise Modeling Intentions

The goal hierarchy in Fig. 1 resulted from interview studies in [22, 27]. It shows common purposes for organizations to use EM. Its initial version contained two main goal hierarchies.

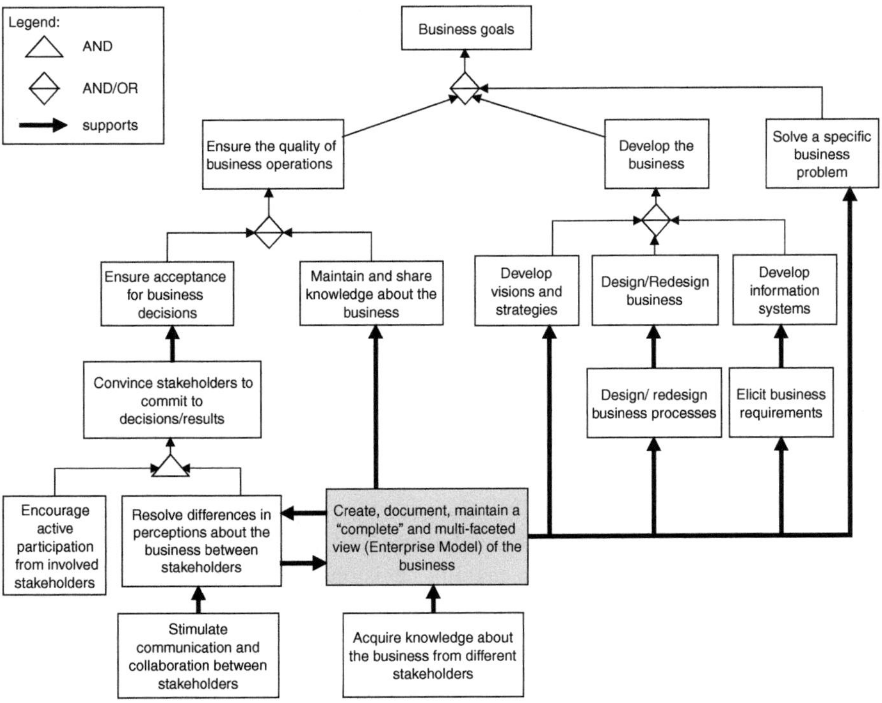

Fig. 1 The intentions of EM, adapted from [20]

One deals with *developing the business*, e.g. developing business vision, strategies, redesigning business operations, developing the supporting information systems, etc. The other deals with *ensuring the quality of the business,* primarily focusing on two issues: (1) sharing the knowledge about the business, its vision, and the way it operates, and (2) ensuring the acceptance of business decisions through committing the stakeholders to the decisions made. We later added a third sub-goal on the top level – *using EM as a problem solving tool*, where EM is only used for supporting the discussion among a group of stakeholders trying to analyze a specific problem at hand. In the following three sections these sub-goals will be discussed in more detail.

2.1 Business Development

Business development is one of the most common purposes of EM. It frequently involves change management – determining how to achieve visions and objectives from the current state in organizations. EM is often used in this process with great success. Some more specific issues can be found in the following interview quotation:[1]

> ... questions like strategies, what type of market to participate in, how is the market structured, which are our clients, who are the other interested parties in the organization, how should we structure our work sequencing, how do we structure our products comparing with the clients, and do we sell everything to everyone. EM also aims to describe the reason for the organization, the goals – to relate them to the strategies, to the business idea. EM continues all the way from the strategies through the processes, through the concepts – in order to arrive at a complete picture, or a picture that fits together. (i1 in [27])

Business process orientation is a specific case of business development – the organization wants to restructure/redesign its business operations.

> One of the main reasons for doing Business Modeling is business process orientation of the organization. In this case you need to describe in some graphical form what business do we have and what business we would like to have. That to my experience is one of the main reasons to hire consultants or to invest in methods and tools and various other things. (i2 in [27])

Also, EM is commonly used in the early stages of system development. See e.g. [4]. A common view among business consultants is that EM is effective for gathering the business needs and high-level requirements.

> In my experience, the most common modeling I have been doing, has been connected in some way to IT development. There has always been a superior decision of doing something in the IT sphere, which has led to the need to understand the business better and describe it much better, otherwise we can't build the right system. That is very often the situation. On the other hand I have not been very much involved in the rest of the IT development. I have just delivered the results – this is the business, this is how it's working, this is the

[1] Note that the quotations from this point onward are excerpts from the interviews. Full transcripts of the interviews are available from the authors on request.

information that needs to be handled. ... That's one situation. ...Another one is business process definition, where the idea as such has been to describe the business in terms of processes. Then other projects have sort of emerged. For example people see that some part of the business should be improved, or this part of the business is not supported by the IT at all. (i2 in [27])

2.2 Quality Assurance

A motivation to adopt EM is to ensure the quality of operations. Two important success factors for ensuring quality, mentioned by interviewees, are that stakeholders understand the business and that they accept/are committed to business decisions. Recently, organizations have taken an increased interest in Knowledge Management (KM), which concerns creating, maintaining and disseminating organizational knowledge between stakeholders. EM has a role to play here as it aims to create a multifaceted "map" of the business as a common platform for communicating between stakeholders. One KM perspective is keeping employees informed with regard to how the business is carried out.

...in those days ... when the company was expanding enormously, they increased by about 100% personnel each year, and it grew very rapidly over the globe. ... So how should we introduce [new people] to the [company E] world and teach [them] how to handle all the things in the [company E] community, etc. It's simply not possible, especially since we don't have good documentation of how we really operate, because everything went on so quickly, that [company E] had to change routines almost every year because of the expansion, etc. So their main motive actually for describing their processes was not to get a lot more efficient, because, maybe rightly, they thought that they were rather efficient, but as a tool to communicate to newly hired personnel, and to show people – this is how we think we are operating, do you have any ideas. (i2 in [27])

Sharing business knowledge becomes instrumental when organizations merge or collaborate in carrying out a business process. One aspect of this is terminology.

I'm thinking about [organization X and organization Y] where they realized that they could use the same data. To be able to do that, they must use the same terms so that they could buy from and sell to each other ... and then it was quite clear that they needed modeling of their business concepts. (i4 in [27])

Most modern organizations consider that the commitment of stakeholders to carry out business decisions is a critical success factor for achieving high quality business operations. Differences in opinion about the business must hence be resolved, requiring that communication between stakeholders be stimulated. The interviews showed that EM, particularly using a participative approach, is effective to obtain such commitment.

... if you want people actively involved and if you want them to go along with what is decided, then they have to be allowed to be involved from the beginning and not get decisions forced on them from management. (i5 in [22])

Active participation leads to commitment. So by creating active participation you make it impossible for people to escape commitment. (i5 in [22])

2.3 *Using EM as a Problem Solving Tool*

In some cases making an EM activity can be helpful when capturing, delimiting, and analyzing the initial problem situation and in order to decide on a course of action. In such cases EM is mostly used as a problem solving and communication tool. The enterprise model created during this type of modeling is mostly used for documenting the discussion and the decisions made.

> [in some cases] you can throw [the models] away – they might just have been a sort of drawing for planning your work and afterwards the value of them is already consumed (i1 in [27])

The main characteristics of this objective are that the company does not intend to use the models for further development work and that the modeling activity has been planned to be only a single iteration. In some cases this situation changes into one of the other EM objectives discussed in Sects. 2.1 and 2.2. This often happens because the organization sees EM as beneficial or the problem turns out to be more complex than initially thought and more effort is need for its solution.

3 EKD – An Example Method

We will use an example method to discuss the requirements on an EM when applied with a certain intention. The chosen method is the Enterprise Knowledge Development (EKD) method, which the authors have been involved in developing, refining and applying since the beginning of the 1990s. This section briefly introduces its modeling language and main principles.

EKD is a result of a strand of research started in the 1980s by Plandata, Sweden [34], and later continued by the Swedish Institute for System Development (SISU). A significant innovation in this strand of EM was the notion of business goals as part of an Enterprise Model, which allowed analyzing the motivational perspective of traditional model component types such as entities and business processes. It was also realized that, considering the multifaceted nature of knowledge that goes into an Enterprise Model, the most efficient way of building such a model is in close cooperation with domain experts and stakeholders. The SISU framework was further developed in the ESPRIT projects F3 – "From Fuzzy to Formal" and ELEKTRA – "Electrical Enterprise Knowledge for Transforming Applications". The resulting version of EKD [3, 16] can be considered to be more or less stable because its modeling language and the overall modeling process has not been significantly changed. Since the 2001, its authors have mainly investigated and developed aspects supporting EKD application in practice, e.g. conducting the modeling process, support for knowledge reuse, and improving model quality. In the next two sections we will briefly present the modeling language and the modeling process as a set of guidelines for a participatory way of working.

3.1 The EKD Modeling Language

The EKD modeling language consists of six sub-models: Goals Model (GM), Business Rules Model (BRM), Concepts Model (CM), Business Process Model (BPM), Actors and Resources Model (ARM), as well as Technical Components and Requirements Model (TCRM). Each sub-model focuses on a specific aspect of an organization (see Table 1).

The GM focuses on describing the goals of the enterprise – what the enterprise and its employees want to achieve, or to avoid, and why. The GM usually clarifies questions, such as: where should the organization be moving; what are the goals of the organization; what are the importance, criticality, and priorities of these goals; how are goals related to each other; which problems hinder the achievement of goals?

Figure 2 depicts a fragment of an EKD enterprise model with its sub-models. Inter-model relationships are depicted by an arrow and a verb that is meant to facilitate the understanding of the relationship between the components.

The BRM is used to define and maintain explicitly formulated business rules, consistent with the GM. Business Rules may be seen as operationalization or limits of goals. The BRM usually clarifies questions, such as: which rules affect the organization's goals; are there any policies stated; how is a business rule related to a goal; how can goals be supported by rules?

The CM is used to strictly define the "things" and "phenomena" that are addressed in the other models. The CM usually clarifies questions, such as: what concepts are recognized in the enterprise; which are their relationships to goals, activities, processes, and actors; how are they defined; what business rules and constraints monitor these objects and concepts?

The BPM is used to define enterprise processes, the way they interact and the way they handle information as well as material. A business process is assumed to consume input in terms of information and/or material and produce output of information and/or material. In general, the BPM is similar to what is used in traditional data-flow diagram models. The BPM usually clarifies questions, such as: which business activities and processes are present in the organization, or should be there to manage the organization in agreement with its goals? How should the business processes, tasks, etc. be performed? Which are their information needs?

The ARM is used to describe how different actors and resources are related to each other and how they are related to components of the GM and BPM. For instance, an actor may be responsible for a particular process in the BPM or an actor may pursue a particular goal in the GM. The ARM usually clarifies questions, such as: who is/should carry out which processes and sub-processes; how is the reporting and responsibility structure between actors defined?

The TCRM becomes relevant when the purpose of EKD is to aid in defining requirements for the development of an IS. This sub-model focuses on the technical aspects of the IS, such as high level requirements and sub-systems, that are needed to support enterprise's goals, processes, and actors. The TCRM usually clarifies questions, such as: what are the requirements for the information system to be developed;

Table 1 Overview of the sub-models of the EKD method [30]

	Goals model (GM)	Business rules model (BRM)	Concepts model (CM)	Business process model (BPM)	Actors and resources model (ARM)	Technical component and requirements model (TCRM)
Focus	Vision and strategy	Policies and rules	Business ontology	Business operations	Organizational structure	Information system needs
Issues	What does the organization want to achieve or to avoid and why?	What are the business rules, how do they support the organization's goals?	What are the things and "phenomena" addressed in other sub-models?	What are the business processes? How do they handle information and material?	Who are responsible for goals and process? How are the actors interrelated?	What are the business requirements to the IS? How are they related to other models?
Components	Goal, problem, external constraint, opportunity	Business rule	Concept, attribute	Process, external proc., information set, material set	Actor, role, organizational unit, individual	IS goal, IS problem, IS requirement, IS component

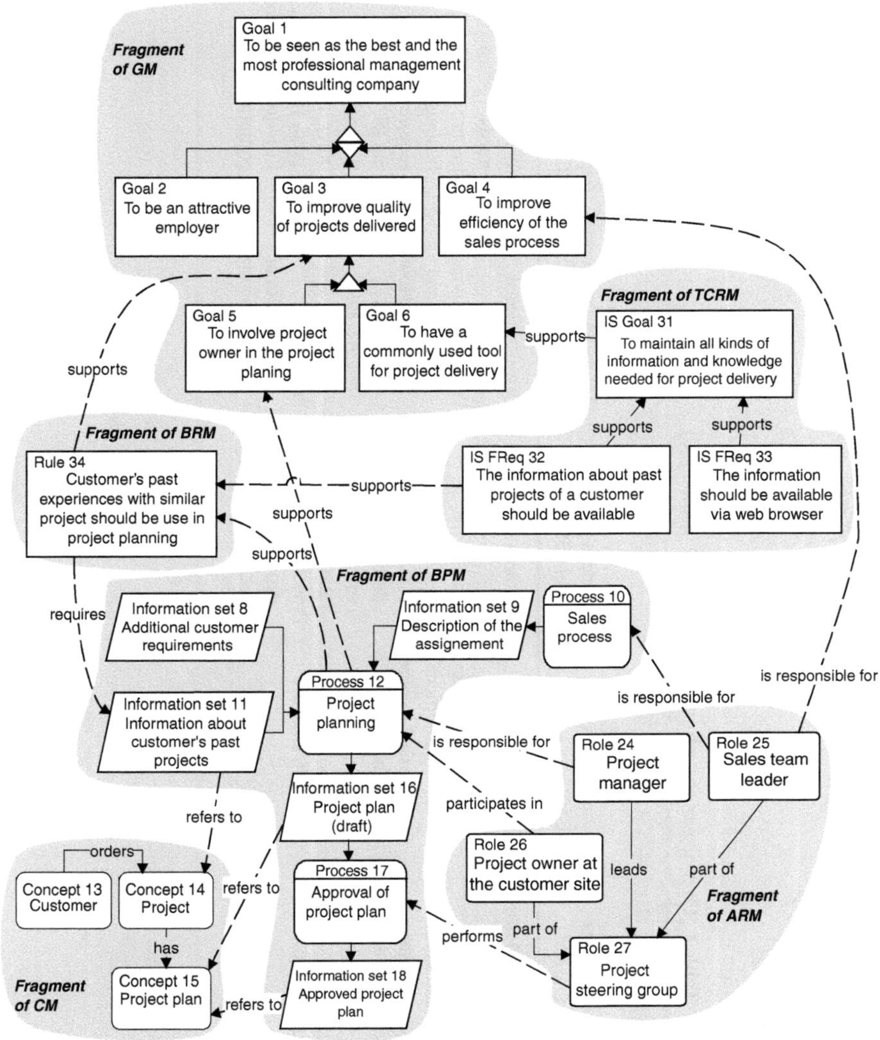

Fig. 2 Fragment of an enterprise model with inter-model links

which requirements are generated by the business processes; which potential has emerging information and communication technology for process improvement?

The modeling components of the sub-models are related within a sub-model (intra-model relationships), as well as with components of other sub-models (inter-model relationships).

EM practitioners and EKD method developers have advocated a participatory way of working using facilitated group modeling (see e.g. [3, 9, 19, 22]). In facilitated group modeling, participation is *consensus-driven* in the sense that it is the domain stakeholders who "own" the model and "govern" its contents, while the facilitator facilitates the process. In contrast, *consultative* participation means that the process is analyst driven. Analysts create models and domain stakeholders are then consulted in order to validate the models. In order for the participatory approach to be applicable the existence of a consensus oriented organizational culture is essential [22] If not, a more consultative approach to participation is advisable.

3.2 The EKD Modeling Process

In order to achieve results of high quality, the modeling process is equally important as the modeling language used. There are two aspects of the process, namely the approach to participation and the process to develop the model.

When it comes to gathering domain knowledge to be included in Enterprise Models, there are different approaches. Some of the more common ones are interviews with domain experts, analysis of existing documentation, observation of existing work practices, and facilitated group modeling. More about the process of modeling can be found in [3, 22, 30].

One aspect that should not be neglected when selecting a participatory approach to EM is the competency of the facilitator. The ability to model is only one, although crucial, part of this competency. The facilitator also needs to be able to effectively facilitate modeling sessions and in large projects also be able to co-ordinate a range of modeling activities. It is also essential that the facilitator is skilled in constructively mediating between different, often conflicting views among the stakeholders. More about EM competency can be found in [23].

4 Research Approach

The research contribution of this chapter is based on a number of research efforts carried out since beginning of the 1990s:

- Development of the EKD EM method;
- Field work applying versions of EKD to a variety of problems;
- Interview studies with Grounded Theory data analysis involving experienced EM consultants and method developers.

The most influential application cases were, for the most part, carried out within international research projects financed by the European Commission. The applications that contributed to this chapter took place in the years 1993–2008. Their processes and their outcome were observed and analyzed.

The synthesis of these analyses is reported in this chapter together with results from interview studies focusing on the intentional and situational factors that

Table 2 Overview of application cases

Organization	Domain	Period in time	Problems addressed
British Aerospace, UK	Aircraft development and production	1992–1994	Requirements Engineering
Telia AB, Sweden	Telecommunications industry	1996	Requirements validation Project definition
Volvo Cars AB, Sweden	Car manufacturing	1994–1997	Requirements engineering
Vattenfall AB, Sweden	Electrical power industry	1996–1999	Change management Process development Competence management
Riga City Council, Latvia	Public administration	2001–2003	Development of vision and supporting processes for knowledge management
Verbundplan GmbH, Austria	Electrical power industry	2001–2003	Development of vision and supporting processes for knowledge management
Skaraborg Hospital, Sweden	Health care	2004–2007	Capturing knowledge assets and development of a knowledge map of a knowledge repository.
SYSteam Management AB, Sweden	Management consulting	2008	Development of a vision for an employee knowledge management portal

influence participatory EM and EM tool usage [20, 22, 27]. An overview of the cases is given in Table 2.

Data from method development, field work and interviews have been analyzed using the EM intentions depicted in Fig. 1 in order to identify requirements on EM application that are related to those intentions.

Apart from these projects, EKD and its earlier versions have also been used in a number of smaller problem solving and organizational design cases at organizations such as e.g. Strömma AB (Sweden), Ericsson (Sweden), Livani District (Latvia), Riga Technical University (Latvia), University of Skövde (Sweden) and RRC College (Latvia).

5 Intentions as the Basis for Defining Requirements on EM

In this section requirements on EM related to the purpose of modeling are described and discussed. Requirements are based on a synthesis of observation data from several research activities (see Sect. 4). The section is organized according to type of requirement: input models and documentation, models to be developed, EM language requirements, EM process requirements, EM tool requirements, and model quality requirements. A summary of requirements is provided in Table 3.

Table 3 Requirements on EM

Purpose of EM	Input models and documentation	Models to be developed	EM language requirements	EM process requirements	EM tool requirements	Model quality requirements
Develop the business						
Develop visions and strategy	Existing models and other business "blueprints"	GM, CM, BPM and ARM as well as inter-model links	Notation that domain stakeholders understand	Participatory	Plastic wall, simple documenting tools	Understandability, correctness, simplicity, flexibility
Design/Redesign the business	Vision and strategy models and other kinds of business "blueprints"	Business oriented models (GM, CM, BPM, ARM, BRM) as well as inter-model links	Notation that domain stakeholders understand, established notation	Participatory involving multiple stakeholder groups	Plastic wall, EM tools that makes it possible to seamlessly move to requirements analysis and IS design	Completeness, correctness, flexibility, integration, understandability, usability
Develop IS	Business oriented models	IS oriented models (TCRM) as well as links with business oriented models	Enough formality and precision to allow modeling of complex facts	Partly participatory and partly analyst driven	Plastic wall, EM tools or CASE tools depending on the development approach	Completeness, correctness, flexibility, integration, usability

Table 3 (continued)

Purpose of EM	Input models and documentation	Models to be developed	EM language requirements	EM process requirements	EM tool requirements	Model quality requirements
Ensure the quality of business operations						
Ensure acceptance for business decisions	Various types of business "blueprints" (e.g. Balanced Scorecard)	Business oriented models (GM, CM, BPM, ARM, BRM) as well as inter-model links	Notation that domain stakeholders understand	Participatory involving knowledge bearers and users	Plastic wall, simple tools, tools for presentation of models to a wider audience (e.g. web-based tools)	Completeness, correctness, integration, simplicity, understandability, usability
Maintain and share knowledge about the business	Business models (GM, CM, BPM, ARM, BRM), inter-model links	"Cleaned" models that make sense to a wider audience	Simple and intuitive modeling language	Partly participatory, partly analyst driven	EM tools with web interface	Correctness, integration, understandability, usability
Use EM as a problem solving tool						
Use EM to analyze and solve a specific business problem	Initial problem statement and other relevant documentation	Business oriented models (GM, CM, BPM, ARM, BRM) & inter-model links	Notation that domain stakeholders understand	Participatory involving multiple stakeholder groups	Plastic wall, simple documenting tools	Correctness, flexibility, understandability

5.1 Input Models and Documentation

In most cases there are some pre-existing documents and even models of different kinds that should be taken into account when planning for an EM effort. It is advisable to show the stakeholders that these are taken into account because this can support the modeling effort by decreasing the stakeholders' need to be overly protective of their respective pet issues. For the modelers these documents and models can shorten the time necessary to get acquainted with the organization and its needs and to help preparing for modeling. Also, the documents and models can shorten the time needed to achieve the desired results since the work does not have to start from scratch. However, the modelers should verify that the documents and models used are up to date and that their use has been approved by the appropriate decision makers.

Develop vision and strategies. In the process of developing vision and strategies all kinds of pre-existing documentation is valuable as input. It is the responsibility of the modelers to carefully select which documentation that can support the modeling process. Sometimes this documentation exists within the organization but sometimes input to the creative process of defining visions and strategies can come from other organizations as well.

Design/re-design the business. One important input to support this goal is existing models and documents that define visions and strategies. If no such input exists, steps should be taken to define visions and strategies before attempting to design the future. In the EKD method parallel development of business processes and their related goals can be carried out.

Develop IS. In order to effectively develop an information system that supports business processes and strategies it is of utmost importance that development is based on models that specify which business processes that are to be supported as well as why and how Enterprise Models can be used to ensure that explicit requirements on an IS are well argued [22] and to review requirements specifications [21].

Ensure acceptance for business decisions. Enterprise Models can, and are, used when describing the arguments for and the effects of business decisions after they have been done. Also, in the process of making decisions enterprise models serve the purpose of documenting decisions and their arguments in a graphical form. This is more effective than taking traditional textual notes, since the notes are visible, throughout the decision-making process, to all stakeholders involved. Experience has shown that this way of working fosters a constructive discussion climate.

Maintain and share knowledge about the business. All kinds of models that have been reviewed and approved have the potential to serve as carriers of knowledge about how the business works and how it is intended to work in the future and why. This is why they can be made accessible to the organization after they have been properly "pruned" to fit their intended audiences. Sometimes the models themselves are too complicated. In this case the models can serve as the basis on which simpler descriptions are created. It is important, however, to always make sure in this case that changes to the original models are correctly reflected in the simple descriptions.

Use EM as a problem solving tool. When EM is used for this purpose the most important input is the initial problem statement. In the preparation of modeling the modelers should also try to identify other relevant documentation that relate to the problem statement and that can support the problem solving process. Also here, models and documents from other organizations and contexts that can inspire the problem solving process are useful.

5.2 Models to be Developed

In this section we use the EKD EM method to exemplify the kinds of models that are to be developed in order to fulfill the different purposes defined. We can hereby illustrate which type of knowledge that is developed in the process of modeling.

Develop vision and strategies. The development of Goal Models is the central output. However, these models often need to be complemented by other types of models in order to ensure the quality of the Goal Models. Examples of such models are:

- BPMs that are developed to drive the definition of goals based on the activities in the process;
- CMs that define or clarify the concepts used in the Goal Models;
- ARMs that describe the responsibilities for the fulfillment of goals and resources to be used in their fulfillment.

In the EKD modeling method the inter-model links between these types of models further support the task of ensuring the quality of the Goals models developed.

Design/re-design the business. This purpose requires that various types of business related models should be developed, e.g. GM, CM, BPM, ARM and BRM. In order to ensure the overall quality of the model set, inter-model links are essential.

Develop IS. Business oriented models should be complemented with IS oriented models, e.g. TCRM. In this context it is important to maintain traceability to business oriented models. In EKD this is achieved through inter-model links.

Ensure acceptance for business decisions. Business oriented models should be developed and linked with inter-model links. The main focus should be on capturing the decisions made by the modeling team explicitly which depending on the nature of the decision can be represented by any of the models, but most commonly this is done using goals model or business process model. It is equally important to specify who is responsible for implementing each decision, which can be visualized by links to ARM components.

Maintain and share knowledge about the business. Here all kinds of models, which convey important messages about how the organization works and why, can be used as input and after cleaning and pruning be made available to the organization. In order for these models to be useful they may be packaged together with information about e.g. how they should be used, in which context they are useful and what are the consequence of applying them. One approach to packaging models is to use organizational patterns and to organize such patterns into a pattern language to support a comprehensive view and to facilitate search and retrieval of models [24].

Use EM as a problem solving tool. Depending on the problem at hand various types of business oriented models are developed here. However, the models themselves are not the essential output. Sometimes the resulting models are quite incomplete and unrefined, but the decisions made based on the modeling process are valuable [22].

5.3 EM Language Requirements

In most cases the modeling project and the problem to be addressed can be modeled by several EM approaches and notations. Even within the meta-model of one modeling language the modelers often define "dialects" and sub-notations, i.e. they add elements of secondary notation such as comments, groupings of modeling components, as well as include modeling components from other languages. During the planning phase of an EM project the main choices the method provider has to make are amongst the following issues:

- The compromise between understandability and formality. Johannesson et al. [11] suggest that the modeling languages that are more understandable by non-experts are less formal and hence the facts are expressed more ambiguously and with less precision.
- The appropriateness of the modeling language for modeling the problem at hand. In some cases what will be done with the models after the modeling project (e.g. integrated with UML models) also influences this choice.
- The acceptance of this language by the stakeholders and the target audience of models, which can be influenced by factors such as education and training, in-house standards for methods and tool usage as well as personal preferences.

Develop visions and strategy. If the modeling project intends to limit with just developing the strategies, then the modeling language should be chosen such that it ensures understandability and involvement of all stakeholders. Most likely the enterprise model will not use all features of the modeling language chosen. For example in initial version of the goal model the sub-goals be arranged in groups rather than linked together with AND/OR operationalization relationships. The BPM might be developed at high level of detail and initially may omit information sets and concentrate on the structural aspects of the process flow. Since the modeling languages and the notation are not closely followed in these projects, the method providers should watch out that it does not deteriorate to a level of informality where the modeling result is not a model anymore but just a drawing. This can happen if the facilitator is inexperienced or gives excessive freedom to the participants.

Design/re-design the business. This objective requires a modeling language and notation that all stakeholders understand, is formal enough to represent the knowledge clearly and unambiguously, as well as is established and known within the organization.

Develop IS. This objective requires using a modeling language that supports clear and unambiguous expression of facts. Furthermore the language chosen should have a meta-model that allows integration with other model types used in IS engineering, such as, for instance, use cases. For modeling business concepts the project might chose to use class diagrams and gradually refine the concepts model into a domain model which can be used in the later stages of the IS development.

Ensure acceptance for business decisions. Similarly to developing the company vision and strategy in this case the modeling language should be understandable by all stakeholders. Since in this case the key focus is on the business decisions, these should be made clearly identifiable in the models. For this purpose the modelers might use additional modeling components such as, for instance, actions. The main purpose of them is to serve as visible reminders about the joint decisions and who should do what in order to implement them.

Maintain and share knowledge about the business. The modeling language chosen should be relatively commonly used, widely accepted by the intended target audience, and since company-wide training in modeling languages is difficult to achieve, intuitive. For instance, in this case models should be expressed by commonly seen languages and notations supported by textual descriptions. Potential misunderstandings of the graphical symbols should also be assessed, e.g. people might easily perceive ellipses as UML use cases or arrows with large arrowheads as UML generalizations.

Use EM as a problem solving tool. The modeling language should fit the nature of the problem – e.g. if the problem concerns an overall identification and analysis of a problem the main requirements for the modeling language are understandability and possibility to use it without extensive training. On the other hand, in some cases the nature of the problem may require a formal modeling language that is able to represent knowledge more strictly.

5.4 EM Process Requirements

It is equally important to select and prepare the right process of modeling to suit different modeling purposes that it is to select the right modeling language. This perspective on modeling has largely been overshadowed by the language perspective, even if the outcome of modeling can never be better than the process that was applied to develop the models. In this chapter we focus on the participation aspect of the process because our research clearly shows that not only the culture of the organization determines whether or not a participatory approach is appropriate. We have also found that different purposes of modeling also influence the choice of approach to participation. More about this is available in [20, 22, 30].

Develop vision and strategies. The development of visions and strategies is a design process where the views of several organizational stakeholders should be taken into account. This ensures that the strategy is possible to implement and that the different goals of the strategy do not contradict each other. One important aspect of this is to make the arguments for the strategy clear to the stakeholders, which in turn enhances acceptance. For this to be achieved a participatory approach is to be preferred, since it enables the stakeholders to listen to arguments and to provide input based on their knowledge about the abilities and shortcomings of the organization.

Design/re-design the business. Depending on the size of the project, this may involve a few or many stakeholder groups. An important quality aspect of an EM that depicts a new design is dependent upon whether or not the design makes sense as a whole and hence is possible to implement [21]. This requires that the different types of stakeholders are actively involved and are given the possibility to learn about other parts of the organization. The individual stakeholder's understanding for her/his role in relationship to the whole organization is essential for the stakeholder's ability to effectively contribute to the overall design. To adopt an analyst driven approach jeopardizes the overall design because it is too dependent on the analyst's ability to understand all complex relationships in the organization.

Develop IS. In the transition between the organizational parts of an IS development process and it's more technical parts it can be effective to adopt a participatory approach. An example situation is when organizational goals are "translated" into overall goals for an IS that needs the acceptance of the organization. When these goals are then further developed into more and more detailed software requirements a more analyst driven approach is appropriate, particularly since the more formal models that are used here can be difficult for the organizational stakeholders to comprehend and validate. Furthermore, an analyst driven approach may drive the formulation of requirements for technology to more realistic ones.

Ensure acceptance for business decisions. To develop visions and strategies and to design/re-design the business are examples of processes that in essence are decision-making processes. In order to ensure the acceptance for business decisions it is most favorable to adopt a participatory approach.

Maintain and share knowledge about the business. In many ways this is similar to EM for designing or redesigning the business – different stakeholder types are to be involved. The specifics of this case require the knowledge sharing purpose of models should be taken in to account, i.e. both knowledge bearers and users should be involved in the EM process. Ideally, representatives of both of these stakeholder types should participate in the process of knowledge capture and packaging.

Use EM as a problem solving tool. Problem solving are in most cases a collaborative process which requires that the creative spirit of the stakeholders and stakeholder groups is supported and that negotiation between stakeholder views is also facilitated. We therefore argue that a participatory approach is superior to achieve these goals. First of all it is more or less impossible to support a creative process by the analyst interviewing a number of stakeholders. Secondly, negotiation processes tend to be more difficult when arguments are relayed through the analyst instead of stakeholders arguing and listening in an interactive setting.

5.5 EM Tool Requirements

Even very simple and short EM projects require some tool support for representing the modeling results during the modeling session. More advanced projects also need tools for analysis, making the project documentation, communication among project participants, and, in some cases, for presenting the modeling result to the target audience. Additional tool requirements can be envisioned for support of collaborative work and for voting on alternatives. An extensive process for choosing and acquiring EM tools in organizations depending on intentional and situational factors in proposed in [27]. In this section we discuss the main choices that the method provider has to make with respect to the tools used in an EM project. More specifically the following issues are to be typically addressed:

- The choice between the "plastic wall" and computerized tool to support the modeling workshop, which is to a large extent by the nature of the modeling activity. If modeling is mainly focusing on creating and capturing new knowledge and communicating among the stakeholders the "plastic wall" is more efficient. If, on the other hand, the main purpose of modeling is to improve and refine an existing model, an EM tool should be used.
- Simple drawing tools (e.g. Visio) vs. more advanced tools with repository support. The factors motivating the usage of more advanced tools are intention to maintain and/or reuse the models for a long time, availability of the tool usage competence, the need to integrate enterprise models with other model types, as well as the need to comply with standards.

Develop vision and strategies. Since the main focus is on supporting efficient knowledge capture of knowledge and communication during the modeling workshop the "plastic wall" should be preferred. After the workshop the models can be documented in a simple drawing tool.

Design/re-design the business. The "plastic wall" should be used for those tasks that require knowledge capture and a more advanced EM tool for analysis and refinement of models. In many cases the enterprise models serve as input to subsequent organizational development, governance, and implementation activities. In these cases the EM tools should be integrated with the IS supporting the business. For instance the MAPPER project proposed an approach a tool for configuring collaborative work support system with Active Knowledge Models (AKM) [15] supported by the Metis tool. More about this is available in [26]. An alternative that allows avoiding the integration is documenting the enterprise model with the tools that will be used for the implementation of the models, even if this requires compromising on the model representation.

Develop IS. The more advanced tools should also be used if the goal is to develop an IS and the team wants to reuse the enterprise models in later development stages for tasks such as requirements management and IS architecture design.

Ensure acceptance for business decisions. The "plastic wall" is suitable for capturing the initial model and making the joint decisions. Once this is done, the models have to be documented possibly with simple tools and presented to the intended target audience, e.g. on the corporate intranet.

Maintain and share knowledge about the business. The tools supporting this intention should be have web-interface and should preferably offer the possibilities to annotating the models with text including collecting user feedback and comments.

Use EM as a problem solving tool. Since after the modeling session the models the models will only serve as meeting minutes, the "plastic wall" should be used for modeling and simple tools for producing the meeting minutes.

5.6 Model Quality Requirements

Quality of enterprise models produced in different projects differs depending on the project objectives and the purpose of models. According to [21] the main criteria for successful application of EKD are that (1) the quality of the produced models is high, (2) the result is useful and actually used after the modeling activity is completed, and (3) the involved stakeholders are satisfied with the process and the result. [14] suggest that the following quality criteria adopted from [18] are applicable to enterprise models:

- Completeness – the degree to which all relevant facts are included in the enterprise model.
- Correctness – refers to how well the enterprise model conforms to the rules of the modeling technique.
- Flexibility – is defined as the ease with which the enterprise model can cope with changes in the modeling domain.
- Integration – refers to the degree of consistency between the different sub-models that constitute the enterprise model.
- Simplicity – refers to the degree of minimal use of modeling constructs for presenting knowledge in the enterprise model.
- Understandability – is defined as the ease with which the concepts and structures in the enterprise model can be understood by the stakeholders.
- Usability – is defined as the ease with which the enterprise model can be used for its intended purpose.

Develop vision and strategies. The main quality requirements are understandability, correctness, simplicity, and flexibility, which are the key factors supporting efficient communication among stakeholders.

Design/re-design the business. The enterprise model presents an organizational design and hence broad range of the quality requirements – completeness, correctness, flexibility, integration, understandability, and usability.

Develop IS. The main quality requirements are completeness, correctness, flexibility, integration, and usability. Referring the choice of the modeling language in this case the understandability for a broad range of stakeholders might be reduced by the need to use a language that allows reaching higher completeness, correctness and integration.

Ensure acceptance for business decisions. The main quality requirements are completeness, correctness, integration, simplicity, understandability, and usability.

Maintain and share knowledge about the business. The main quality requirements are correctness, integration, understandability, and usability. As special emphasis should be put on ensuring that the models are understandable for the target audience without extensive training in a particular modeling approach and language.

Use EM as a problem solving tool. The main quality requirements are correctness, flexibility, and understandability.

6 Conclusion

In this chapter we have defined three main intentions of performing EM:

- Developing the business;
- Ensuring the quality of business operations;
- Using EM as a problem solving tool.

For each of these purposes we suggest a number of requirements regarding different aspects of EM such as input models and documentation, models to be developed, EM language requirements, EM process requirements, EM tool requirements, and model quality requirements. The requirements are based on our experience in developing EM methods, using EM in practice and observing EM practice during more than 17 years. They are not geared towards a specific EM approach and should give guidance in performing the EM process, in selecting an EM language, in selecting tool support, and in ensuring the quality of EM work.

When discussing the application of Enterprise Modeling there is normally not only one question to answer, one problem to solve, or one issue to address. Instead EM must be seen as a multitude of interrelated approaches that are useful in many situational contexts and that potentially can be combined to achieve a high quality result. Determining what kind of situation and context the person responsible for a modeling activity has placed himself/herself into is of utmost importance before starting the, often participative, modeling process and before determining the kind of particular modeling activities to start. This is why interviews with potential stakeholders are so important to conduct before the start of the EM process [22]. Analysis of these interviews will determine which cells of the matrix in Table 3 need to be addressed.

As indicated in the beginning of the chapter, more in-depth research into the practice of EM is needed. Some suggested lines of research to continue what has been reported in this chapter are the following:

Develop more comprehensive guidance for setting up and preparing for EM. The structure depicted in Table 3 is one way of guiding this preparation. A pattern-based way of preparing for EM, particularly focusing on assessing the appropriateness of adopting a participatory approach can be found in [22]. In order to systematize such guidance using the intentions of EM as a basis could be to use the map concept developed by [25].

Develop more easily accessible guidance to support EM users in adopting a participatory approach. Currently the best way to become a decent modeling facilitator is through the learning by doing approach. In the best case a more experienced facilitator can function as a mentor. In any case, it takes a long time. One of the challenges in developing this type of guidance lies in the fact that participatory modeling is heavily influenced by a large amount of situational factors. This means that there are numerous choices to be made in different modeling situations. One potential way of addressing this is to start with the essential advice on what should *not* be done in different situations [28].

Investigate how different modeling domains influence the purposes of EM discussed in the chapter. Different sectors may pose specific requirements on EM. For example, in the telecommunications sector the models are more complex, in the automotive industry the problem domain frequently spans beyond company borders, in the public sector there are multiple stakeholder types with unclear intentions, and so on. The different applications of EM should be supported by reusing the existing knowledge in the area, which emphasizes the need to capture and package it in a reusable form, such as e.g. patterns.

References

1. Bajec M, Krisper M (2005) A methodology and tool support for managing business rules in organisations. Info Systems 30(6):423–443
2. Bubenko JA Jr (1993) Extending the scope of information modelling. In: Proceedings of 4th international workshop on the deductive approach to information systems and databases, Lloret, Costa Brava (Catalonia), Department de Llenguatges i Sistemes Informatics, Universitat Politecnica de Catalunya, Report de Recerca LSI/93-25, Barcelona
3. Bubenko JA Jr, Persson A, Stirna J (2001) User guide of the knowledge management approach using enterprise knowledge patterns, deliverable D3, IST Programme project Hypermedia and Pattern Based Knowledge Management for Smart Organisations, project no. IST-2000-28401, Royal Institute of Technology, Sweden
4. Bubenko JA Jr, Kirikova M (1999) Improving the quality of re-quirements specifications by enterprise modelling. In: Nilsson AG, Tolis C, Nellborn C (eds) Perspectives on business modelling. Springer, Berlin
5. Carvallo JP, Franch X (2009) On the use of i* for architecting hybrid systems: a method and an evaluation report. In: Proceedings of PoEM 2009. LNBIP, vol 39. Springer, Heidelberg, pp 38–53
6. Carstensen A, Holmberg L Sandkuhl K (2008) Supporting collaboration in an extended enterprise with the connector view on enterprise models. In: Proceedings of PoEM 2008. LNBIP, vol 15. Springer, Berlin, Heidelberg, New York, pp 11–126
7. Castro J, Kolp M, Mylopoulos J, Tropos A (2001) A requirements-driven software development methodology. In: Proceedings of CAiSE 2001. LNCS, vol 2068. Springer, Berlin, Heidelberg, New York, pp 108–123
8. Dobson J, Blyth J, Strens R (1994) Organisational requirements definition for information technology. In: Proceedings of the international conference on requirements engineering 1994. Denver, CO

9. F3-Consortium (1994) F3 reference manual, ESPRIT III Project 6612, SISU, Stockholm
10. Fox MS, Chionglo JF, Fadel FG (1993) A common-sense model of the enterprise. In: Proceedings of the 2nd industrial engineering research conference, Institute for Industrial Engineers, Norcross, GA
11. Johannesson P, Boman M, Bubenko J, Wangler B (1997) Conceptual modelling. Hoare CAR (series ed), Prentice Hall International Series in Computer Science, Prentice Hall
12. Kardasis P, Loucopoulos P, Scott B, Filippidou D, Clarke R, Wangler B, Xini G (1998) The use of business knowledge modelling for knowledge discovery in the banking sector, IMACS-CSC'98, Athens, Greece
13. Krogstie J, Lillehagen F, Karlsen D, Ohren O, Strømseng K, Thue Lie F (2000) Extended enterprise methodology. Deliverable 2 in the EXTERNAL project. Det Norske Veritas AS, Norway
14. Larsson L, Segerberg R (2004) An approach for quality assurance in enterprise modelling. MSc Thesis, Department of Computer and Systems Sciences, Stockholm University, no. 04-22
15. Lillehagen F, Krogstie J (2002) Active knowledge models and enterprise knowledge management. In: Proceedings of the IFIP TC5/WG5.12 international conference on enterprise integration and modeling technique: enterprise inter- and intra-organizational integration: building international consensus. IFIP Conference Proceedings, vol. 236. Kluwer, New York
16. Loucopoulos P, Kavakli V, Prekas N, Rolland C, Grosz G, Nurcan S (1997) Using the EKD approach: the modelling component. UMIST, Manchester, UK
17. Lundqvist M, Homquist E, Sandkuhl K, Seigerroth U, Strandesjö J (2009) Information demand context modeling for improved information flow: experiences and practices. In: Proceedings of PoEM 2009. LNBIP, vol 39. Springer, Berlin, Heidelberg, New York, pp 8–22
18. Moody DL, Shanks G (2003) Improving the quality of data models: empirical validation of a quality management framework. Info Systems 28(6):619–650
19. Nilsson AG, Tolis C, Nellborn C (eds) (1999) Perspectives on business modelling: understanding and changing organizations. Springer, Berlin
20. Persson A, Stirna J (2001) Why enterprise modelling? – an explorative study into current practice. In: Proceedings of CAiSE 2001. LNCS, vol 2068. Springer, Berlin, Heidelberg, New York, pp 465–468
21. Persson A (1997) Using the F3 enterprise model for specification of requirements – an initial experience report. In: Proceedings of international workshop on evaluation of modeling methods in systems analysis and design (EMMSAD), June 16–17, Barcelona, Spain
22. Persson A (2001) Enterprise modelling in practice: situational factors and their influence on adopting a participative approach. Doctoral Thesis, Department of Computer and Systems Sciences, Stockholm University, ISSN 1101-8526
23. Persson A (2008) The practice of participatory enterprise modelling – a competency perspective. In: Johannesson P, Söderström E (eds) Information systems engineering – from data analysis to process networks. Idea Group, Hershey, PA, pp 129–157
24. Rolland C, Stirna J, Prekas N, Loucopoulos P, Persson A, Grosz G (2000) Evaluating a pattern approach as an aid for the development of organizational knowledge: an empirical study. In: Proceedings of the 12th conference on advanced information systems engineering (CAiSE). LNCS, vol 1789. Springer, Berlin, Heidelberg, New York, pp 176–191
25. Rolland C (2007) Capturing system intentionality with maps. In: Krogstie J et al (eds) Conceptual modelling in information systems engineering. Springer, Berlin, pp 141–158
26. Sandkuhl K, Stirna J (2008) Evaluation of task pattern use in web-based collaborative engineering. In: Proceedings of the 34th EUROMICRO conference on software engineering and advanced applications (SEAA), EUROMICRO, IEEE, Los Alamitos, CA
27. Stirna J (2001) The influence of intentional and situational factors on EM tool acquisition in organisations. Ph.D. Thesis, Department of Computer and Systems Sciences, Royal Institute of Technology and Stockholm University, Stockholm, Sweden
28. Stirna J, Persson A (2009) Anti-patterns as a means of focusing on critical quality aspects in enterprise modeling. In: Halpin T et al (eds) Enterprise, business process and information

systems modeling, proceedings of the 14th international conference EMMSAD 2009. LNBIP, vol 29. Springer, Berlin, pp 407–418
29. Stirna J, Persson A, Aggestam L (2006) Building knowledge repositories with enterprise modelling and patterns – from theory to practice. In: Proceedings of the 14th European conference on information systems (ECIS). Gothenburg, Sweden
30. Stirna J, Persson A, Sandkuhl K (2007) Participative enterprise modelling: experiences and recommendations. In: Proceedings of CAiSE 2007. LNCS, vol 4495, Springer, Berlin, Heidelberg, New York, pp 546–560
31. Wangler B, Persson A (2002) Capturing collective intentionality in software development. In: Fujita H, Johannesson P (eds) New trends in software methodologies, tools and techniques. IOS, Amsterdam, Netherlands, pp 262–270
32. Wangler B, Persson A, Söderström E (2001) Enterprise modeling for B2B integration. In: Proceedings of international conference on advances in infrastructure for electronic business, science, and education on the internet, L'Aquila, Italy (CD-ROM proceedings)
33. Wangler B, Persson A, Johannesson P, Ekenberg L (2003) Bridging high-level enterprise models to implementation-oriented models. In: Fujita H, Johannesson P (eds) New trends in software methodologies, tools and techniques. IOS, Amsterdam, Netherlands
34. Willars H (1988) Handbok i ABC-metoden. Plandata Strategi. Stockholm, Sweden
35. Yu E, Mylopoulos J (1994) From E-R to "A-R" – modelling strategic actor relationships for business process reengineering. In: Proceedings of the 13th international conference on the entity-relationship approach, Manchester, England

A Goal-Based Approach for Learning in Business Processes

Pnina Soffer, Johny Ghattas, and Mor Peleg

Abstract Organizations constantly strive to improve their business performance; hence they make business process redesign efforts. So far, redesign has mainly been a human task, which relies on human reasoning and creativity, although various analysis tools can support it by identifying improvement opportunities. This chapter proposes an automated approach for learning from accumulated experience and improving business processes over time. The approach ties together three aspects of business processes: goals, context, and actual paths. It proposes a learning cycle, including a learning phase, where the relevant context is identified and used for making improvements in the process model, and a runtime application phase, where the improved process model is applied at runtime and actual results are stored for the next learning cycle. According to our approach, a goal-oriented process model is essential for learning to improve process outcomes.

1 Introduction

Organizations constantly strive to improve their business performance. This has been reflected in efforts made in the area of business process redesign since the early 1990s [5]. Typically, business process redesign initiatives can be characterized on a continuum from radical reengineering [10] to incremental continuous improvements. Various analysis methods can be used in order to identify weaknesses and improvement opportunities in existing business processes. However, the actual task of process redesign still relies exclusively on human reasoning and creativity.

Improving business performance over time is also associated with the concept of organizational learning, defined as the capacity within an organization to improve its performance based on experience [12]. One of the main ideas of organizational learning is that while individuals can learn from past experience, this knowledge has to become shared and applied across the organization to facilitate constant

P. Soffer (✉)
University of Haifa, Carmel Mountain, 31905 Haifa, Israel
e-mail: spnina@is.haifa.ac.il

S. Nurcan et al. (eds.), *Intentional Perspectives on Information Systems Engineering*,
DOI 10.1007/978-3-642-12544-7_13, © Springer-Verlag Berlin Heidelberg 2010

improvement. The knowledge an individual has can be manifested in decision criteria used for selecting a process path at a specific situation or in deviations from a predefined process model in order to solve specific problems. This knowledge is gained through mistakes as well as successful process executions. The knowledge can become shared by others to support organizational learning by embedding it in a process model which evolves over time.

Organizational learning and business process redesign initiatives require in-depth understanding of the current practices. In particular, it should be possible to identify which actions have a positive or a negative effect on business measures in given situations. Relying only on a static predefined process model in order to identify opportunities for improving a process may be limiting or even impossible, since the actual way processes are performed (including ad hoc decisions) is usually not reflected in such models. The actual way in which a business process is performed can be studied using process mining techniques [24]. Process mining analyzes an event log of the information system that supports the process, and produces a model of the process as it is actually performed. Process mining serves various purposes, such as getting a clear and reliable model of the as-is process [24], performing delta analysis, in which the actual process is compared to the predefined process model [2], and analyzing the process with respect to specific performance measures, such as execution time [1]. Process mining can provide an understanding of the as-is process, including specific paths that reflect ad-hoc decisions made in exceptional situations. However, the main emphasis of existing process mining approaches has been capturing the control-flow of the process, namely, the sequence in which activities are executed. Hence, while process mining reflects the common as well as the rarely taken process paths, the situations in which path selection decisions have been made and the extent to which the corresponding executions were successful are not systematically addressed.

This chapter proposes an approach for learning and gradually improving business processes. The approach ties together three elements that comprise the experience gained through ongoing process executions: what actions have been performed, in what situations, and what has been achieved by the process in business terms. The actions that have been performed are the actual process *paths* taken; the situations in which they were performed are the *context* of the process; what has been achieved can be assessed with respect to defined process *goals*.

2 How Goals and Context Facilitate Learning

2.1 The Role of Process Goals

Learning from experience means understanding what mistakes were made (leading to failure) to avoid repeating them, and what was done in successful process executions. Success (or failure) can only be assessed when goals are known and specified.

In this chapter we adopt the notions of business process goals as defined in the Generic Process Model (GPM) framework [19]. GPM is a state-based and goal-oriented view of a process, which relates to two types of process goals: hard goals (or simply goals) and soft goals. Below we discuss these two types of goals and their possible use for process learning.

The hard goal of a process is defined by GPM as a set of stable states at which the process terminates. The goal set is specified by a predicate over values of the state variables of the domain in which the process operates. Since a process is executed in order to bring about some state of affairs in the domain, the predicate expresses the conditions under which this state of affairs is achieved so the process can terminate. The goal is a set of states (rather than a single state), since there might be different specific states that meet the termination condition. For example, a sales process reaches its goal once the order is fulfilled and paid for. This may include different states (e.g., the goods were shipped to the customer, the customer has taken the goods himself, payment was made in advance or upon delivery, etc.).

Considering learning, a process instance (namely, a specific execution of the process) may end up in a state which is in the goal set or in a stable state which is not in the goal set (an exception). In the sales process example, it might be that the customer received the goods, paid with an invalid credit card, and lost contact, so he cannot be located any more. In this case, the state of the process domain is stable, namely, it cannot be changed by actions of the organization, but it is not in the goal set since payment was not received. Learning seeks to avoid exceptional situations or to minimize their occurrence over time.

As explained, the (hard) goal of a process is a set of states, all satisfying the condition under which the process can terminate having achieved what it was intended to achieve. These states might be different from each other in business terms. For example, in the above mentioned sales process it might be considered more desirable to supply goods in two days than in two weeks (although both lead to goal states). Soft goals represent business objectives which differentiate states in the goal set according to how desirable they are. In other words, soft goals define a desirability order relation among states in the goal set [19].

The term "soft goals" is borrowed from requirements engineering, where it relates to desired properties whose satisfaction is not on a binary scale. Similarly, considering business processes, soft goals correspond to performance indicators whose increased values are sought, but they can only be considered successful in comparison to others rather than absolutely. It is possible to define thresholds to performance indicator values, so values above the threshold are considered "good" (e.g., delivery time shorter than one week) as opposed to values below the threshold. Yet, different values of soft goal related performance indicators denote different levels of success even if all values are above the threshold.

Learning in a business process should seek to achieve higher levels of soft goal related indicators over time.

It should be noted that specific soft goals (e.g., minimizing execution time) and their relationships to actual paths have been addressed to some extent by process mining approaches [1, 6]. Here we address soft goals at a generic level, without limiting ourselves to specific ones. This raises two main challenges. First, different soft goals may exist and may even conflict with each other (e.g., quality and cost). Process changes may positively affect one soft goal while negatively affecting the other. Second, soft goals may be affected by more than one process. For example, the quality of a product may be affected by the production process and by the purchasing of raw materials. It follows that considerable attention should be devoted to the precise specification of soft goals with respect to a specific process for learning to be effective.

As explained, learning should assess the level of success of each process execution (process instance) with respect to the defined goals of the process (both hard and soft goals). We refer to the combination of hard and soft goal achievement by a process instance as the *outcomes* of the instance.

2.2 The Role of Context

The success of a process instance can be affected not only by the actual path performed, but also by environmental conditions, not controlled by the process, which we term the process context. Specifically, the context of a process includes the initial state at which the process is triggered (which may hold specific case characteristics, such as customer properties in a sales process) and events in the environment that may occur during its execution. The initial state is specified by values of state variables known when the process is initiated; events in the environment are external to the process domain but affect its state.

Process instances of different contexts may need to be addressed differently (i.e., take different paths) in order to achieve desired outcomes. Alternatively, we may say that if exactly the same path is applied to process instances of different contexts, it might lead to different outcomes. Considering a sales process, a regular customer may place an order and pay once the goods are supplied, while an unknown customer would be required to pay in advance to reduce the risk.

Furthermore, threshold levels of soft goals for determining whether an outcome is "desired" or not may also depend on context. For example, a desired outcome of a broken leg treatment process for an old person would be to be able to walk freely again, while for a young person it would only be considered successful if he never suffers pain again.

It follows that to learn effectively, process instances should be classified according to their context, so that learning could take context into account. However, initial information and external events may relate to a variety of factors, and it is not necessary that all factors indeed affect the outcome of the process. Hence, the challenge faced is to identify the relevant factors that should be taken into account by learning. While some factors may be well known to domain experts and even incorporated into the process model as decision criteria (e.g., regular vs. first-time customer), others may be guessed intuitively by some workers, and some even unknown in advance.

Our learning approach seeks to identify the relevant contextual factors and group process instances into context groups, such that for process instances of a specific context group, similar process paths would imply similar outcomes.

3 Introducing the Running Example

As a running example, demonstrating the concepts introduced in the chapter, we address a production process in a plastic bottle manufacturing firm, illustrated in the BPMN model depicted in Fig. 1. The (hard) goal of the process is to reach a state where customers' acceptance of delivery is achieved. Other states in which the process might terminate (exception termination states) are states where delivery is cancelled due to quality problems and states where the customer rejects delivery (also due to quality problems).

Soft goals defined by the organization include increasing the percentage of deliveries that meet their due dates, increasing machine utilization, reducing waste of raw materials, increasing the quality of the manufactured products, and reducing the overall production costs. These different soft goals could be prioritized and weighted to form one composite soft goal. An alternative approach would be to analyze the dependencies among soft goals and identify a dominant soft goal to be addressed first. Table 1 presents the main causes for poor achievements of the defined soft goals.

As seen in Table 1, the leading reasons for poor business results are quality problems, machine failure and poor technical condition, and the set up operations. Machine maintenance is not in the scope of this process (rather, it is part of its context), and the set up operation is part of the process path. Based on this analysis, we decided to focus on the soft goal of increasing the product quality, which will affect all the other soft goals (including the costs, through reducing material waste).

The contextual variables of the process include the initial case properties and external (uncontrolled) events during the process. Initial case properties include properties of the manufactured product and the customer, intended market of the product (food, medical supplies, chemicals, cosmetics), the main raw material (polyethylene at different density levels, polypropylene), the supplier of the raw material (three possible ones), and the supplier of the pigments (two possible ones), time since last maintenance operation of the machine, and weather (hot or dusty days may affect the machines). There might also be specific requirements made by the customer, such as requirements for the bottle to be resistant to high temperature (in case the customer uses it for storing hot liquids) or to strong chemical solutions. Events that occur during the process are mainly machine failures and quality problems and it is often impossible to tell one from the other.

It should also be noted that contextual variables may affect soft goal thresholds, e.g., higher quality is required if the intended market of the product is the medical supplies.

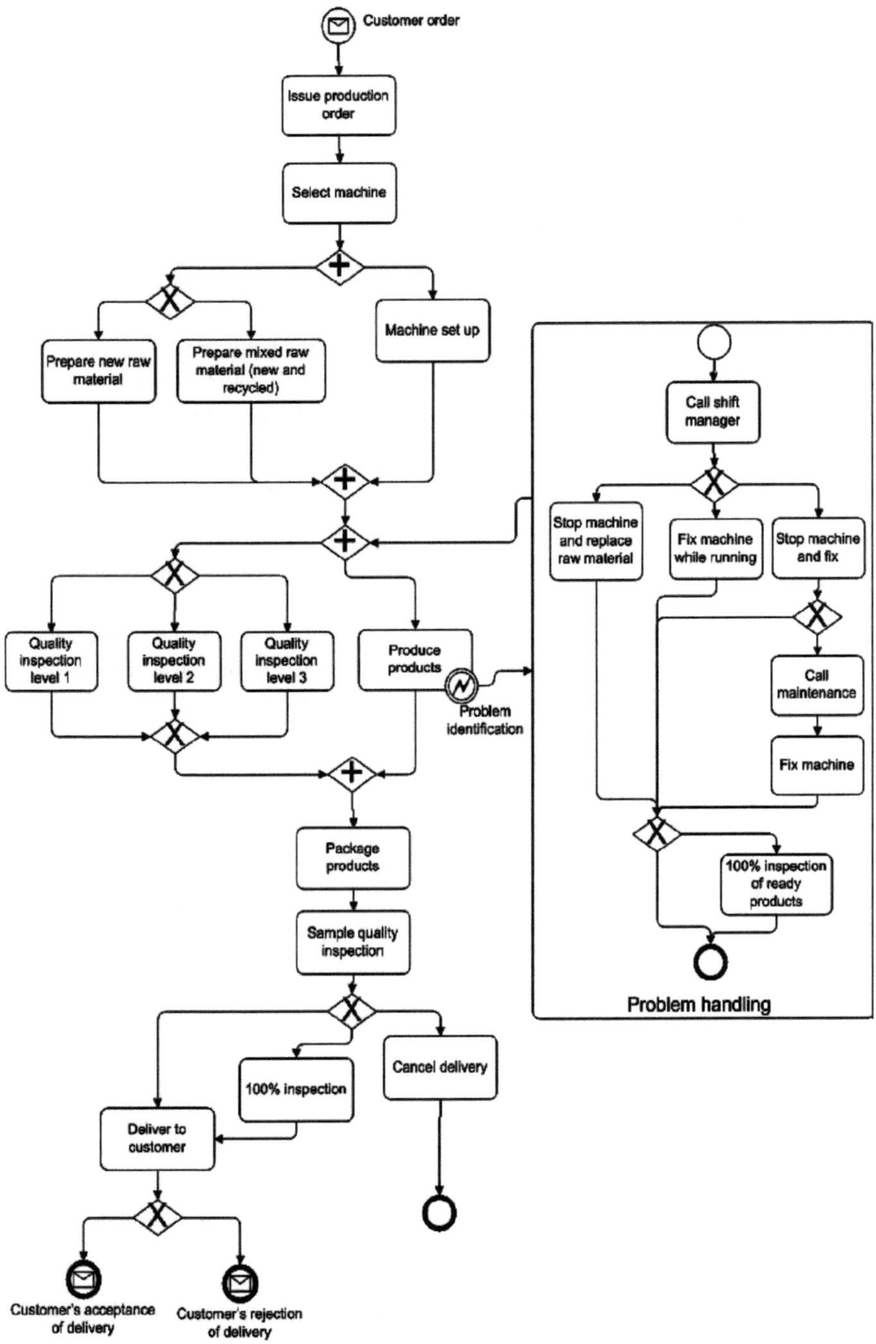

Fig. 1 Plastic bottle manufacturing process

Table 1 Soft goals – reasons for poor achievement

Soft goal	Main reasons for poor achievement
Meeting delivery due dates	Quality problems, machine failure, unskilled workers
Increasing machine utilization	Set up times, quality problems, machine failure
Reducing waste of raw materials	Quality problems, inappropriate machine setup
Increasing product quality	Inappropriate machine setup, poor quality of raw material, poor machine condition, inappropriate quality inspection
Reducing production costs	Raw material cost, raw material waste, labor cost

4 The Learning Approach

The proposed learning approach includes a learning life-cycle, described in Fig. 2. The learning cycle can be initiated when a process has already been performed for a period of time, so some experience has already been accumulated. This experience is stored in an experience base, including data of past process instances: their actual path, their achieved outcome, and their context information. Note that context information includes all the environmental variables, as we cannot tell in advance which ones are relevant.

The life cycle includes two main phases: a learning phase and the application of its results in runtime, which, in turn, produces more experience to be stored in the experience base for the next cycle.

The learning phase includes a step of initial context identification, which yields a definition of context groups. These groups serve as a basis for the generation of

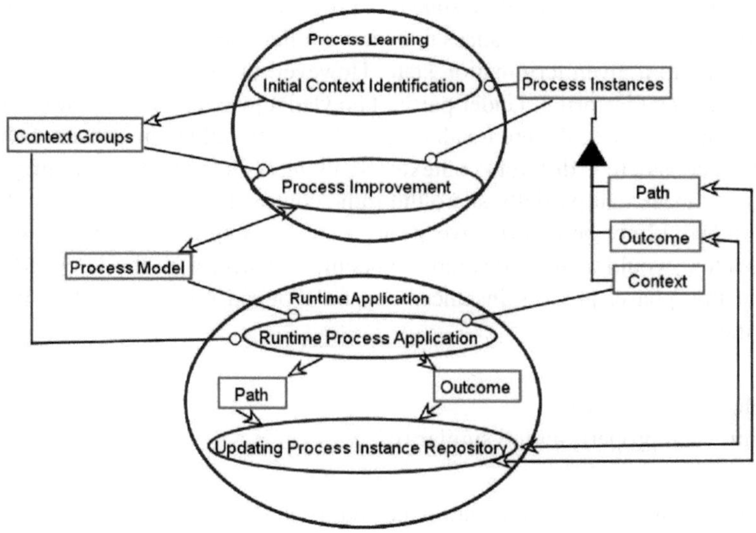

Fig. 2 The proposed learning cycle

improvement recommendations to the process model. Note that these improvements are not automatically deployed. Rather, the analysis yields improvement recommendations which should first be reviewed by humans and only then used for updating the process model.

The runtime phase is an ongoing phase of process execution. Every new process instance is classified into a context group and follows the path recommended accordingly. Its context, path, and outcome data are then stored in the experience base. There might be instances which cannot be classified into an existing context group; they are executed and their data is also stored in the experience base. In some cases, specifically when facing unexpected external events, the process operators may decide to deviate from the process model and take a path which has not been taken before. These are also stored in the experience base. Periodically, when a considerable number of new experiences have been added to the experience base, learning can be applied again, triggering a new cycle. In what follows we provide details about the phases of the learning cycle.

4.1 Context Identification

As explained above, the challenge in identifying context is the huge amount of contextual information that may be available. We seek for classification criteria of process instances that would be effective in determining the best process path at a given situation. This classification should also be meaningful in business terms, so each group of instances can be characterized based on its contextual properties.

Recall, the data of the process instances stored in the experience base includes their actual path, their outcome (or termination state), and their contextual information. The path and the termination state of a process instance constitute its behavior. In a perfect world, process instances that have similar contexts would follow similar paths to lead to a given termination state. However, our knowledge of the process (relevant) context is partial. Under partial knowledge, we may not be aware of contextual variables whose different values may differently affect the process behavior, and can be considered "different contexts". Lacking such knowledge, we may group process instances that partially share the same context but exhibit different behaviors. This would not be an effective strategy for learning the best paths that for a given context would achieve desirable outcomes. Hence, with the knowledge that exists at this phase, process instances can be grouped considering two types of similarities:

(1) Behavioral similarity.
(2) Contextual property-based similarity.

Clearly, these two groupings are expected to be different, since not all contextual properties necessarily affect process behavior, and some properties may have a similar effect. Our interest is to identify a third type of grouping, *context groups definition*, namely, groups of instances whose contextual property-based similarity can predict some behavioral similarity.

Behavioral similarity of process instances can be assessed using some path and state similarity measures. Consequently, process instances can be grouped into clusters of behaviorally-similar process instances, sharing similar paths and similar termination states (outcomes). Each process instance in the experience base would belong to one behavioral similarity cluster.

Contextual property-based similarity of process instances is possible when at least one contextual property of these instances has similar values. The possible number of contextual property-based similarity groupings is combinatorial in the number of contextual properties. Not all these groupings are meaningful in terms of behavior (e.g., grouping process instances based on the color of the customer's eyes would probably be ineffective for predicting behavior of process instances).

Based on these two types of similarity, we define a *context group* as a group of process instances, which are contextual property-based similar, and for which taking similar paths implies achieving similar outcomes.

Note that this definition relates to a situation where the behavior of process instances is fully consistent with respect to their context, namely, there are no unpredicted behaviors or noisy data. Clearly, this is not the situation in real life, where there might be "hidden" variables which cannot be tracked (e.g., distractions of the machine operator) that affect the outcomes of the process. Hence, we cannot assume full predictability of the outcomes given a context group and a process path. However, we may assume that contextual properties have a certain effect and can explain at least part of the variance in the outcomes achieved. Hence, for practical purposes we can formulate the following postulate:

Postulate 1: Consider two groups of process instances, PI_1 and PI_2, so each group includes contextual property-based similar process instances. Now consider $C_1 \subset PI_1$ and $C_2 \subset PI_2$, so the paths taken by instances in C_1 and C_2 are all similar. If statistical tests show that the termination states of C_1 and C_2 are not of the same population, then PI_1 and PI_2 are in different context groups.

Postulate 1 gives us a criterion for excluding two sets of instances from being in the same context group. It can be applied to groups of instances that follow similar paths. However, we may have groups that follow different paths. In that case, we assume the choice of path reflects some implicit domain knowledge used by the process operators. This is reflected in the following postulate.

Postulate 2: Groups of contextually similar process instances form one context group if the distribution of their behavioral similarity categories is similar (not significantly different).

The two postulates can be helpful when some grouping based on contextual properties is available. However, as discussed above, the number of such groupings is combinatorial in the number of known contextual properties. To overcome this difficulty, we employ a learning algorithm, which grows a decision tree whose independent variable is the contextual properties while the dependent variable is the behavioral similarity category of process instances. The algorithm is applied through the following procedure [8].

Step 1: Use existing domain knowledge for an initial classification of process instances based on contextual properties that are known to affect process behavior.

For each partition, separately apply the following three steps.

Step 2: Establish the behavioral similarity of the process instances.

(a) Path similarity categories are formed using a clustering algorithm over path data of the instances. The number of path similar clusters generated is selected according to goodness of fit criteria, such as Akaike Information Criteria (AIC). The clustering algorithm can be applied several times, achieving a series of clustering results with an increasing number of clusters for each clustering set. Finally, the best cluster set is selected as the one that attains the first minima of the ratio of AIC changes.
(b) Categorize termination states to a small number of categories based on a set of predefined rules. The aim is to achieve a coarse grained categorization with a clear distinction between categories.
(c) Combine path similarity categories with termination state categories into behavioral similarity categories.

Step 3: Establish the contextual properties that affect behavior. This is accomplished by training a decision tree algorithm, using the context data as inputs and the behavioral categories as dependent variable (their label). The objective of using the decision tree is to discover the contextual semantics behind each behavioral category. We use a modified Chi-squared Automatic Interaction Detection (CHAID) growing decision tree algorithm to construct the decision tree that represents the context groups and their relationships. CHAID tries to split the context data of the process instances into nodes that contain instances whose dependent variable values (namely, behavioral similarity category) are the same. Each path from the source node to a leaf node in the decision tree represents a different combination of contextual properties. Each leaf node contains a certain distribution of instances among behavioral categories, allowing the identification of the most probable category for that leaf.

Step 4: Form the context groups. Based on Postulates 1 and 2, join tree paths into context groups if the following two conditions are satisfied:

(a) The hypothesis that the process instances in their leaves are of the same population (considering their behavioral similarity categories) cannot be rejected.
(b) If their leaves include behavioral categories that stand for similar paths but different termination states, the hypothesis that termination states for similar paths in both leaves are of the same population cannot be rejected.

Considering our bottle manufacturing running example, one of the difficulties faced is the large number of possible process paths (considering each one of the 14 machines and 40 employees who operate the machines as different paths). Furthermore, the selection of a machine and a worker at runtime is mainly done based on availability, and to a lesser extent on the context, so this choice is not expected to reflect the relevant contextual properties we are looking for. Still, this choice might affect the outcomes. To overcome this, we decided to identify a subset of very reliable employees and use only process instances they participate in for context identification. We also decided not to differentiate paths where different machines were used, but to include the time since the last maintenance operation of the machine as a contextual property.

The identification procedure is applied as follows:

Step 1: An initial classification of the process instances related to whether or not the process faced an event of problem identification. Clearly, this is a contextual variable that affects the process behavior. Hence, we separately performed the following steps to instances where problems were identified and to instances where production was performed without interrupts. We demonstrate the next steps with respect to the group where no problems occurred.

Step 2: Paths were clustered (disregarding machines and workers, as discussed above). The termination states were divided into two groups: (1) instances where the customer accepted the delivery without a need for a 100% inspection, (2) instances where the customer accepted the delivery after a 100% inspection, or where the customer rejected the delivery or where the delivery was cancelled. The combination of path similarity groups and termination state groups included 12 behavioral categories.

Step 3: Applying the decision tree growing algorithm resulted in the tree depicted in Fig. 3.

Each path in the tree (from the root to a leaf) represents a combination of contextual properties relevant for the behavior of process instances. Each node in the tree holds a set of process instances that can be characterized by a distribution over behavioral similarity categories. For example, node 13 stands for process instances related to products in the food and cosmetics market whose size is large and where the customer required resistance of the bottle to high temperatures. Node 12 represents process instances in the medical supplies market with special covers (children proof) where the machine used was not within a short period after its periodic maintenance (hence its maintenance state is not considered as best).

Step 4: Applying postulates 1 and 2. Due to space limitation, we only demonstrate Step 4 with respect to parts of the tree, leaf nodes 8, 9, and 13. The behavioral categories of the instances in all three nodes fall into three path similarity categories (paths 1–3) and two termination state categories, distributed as shown in Table 2.

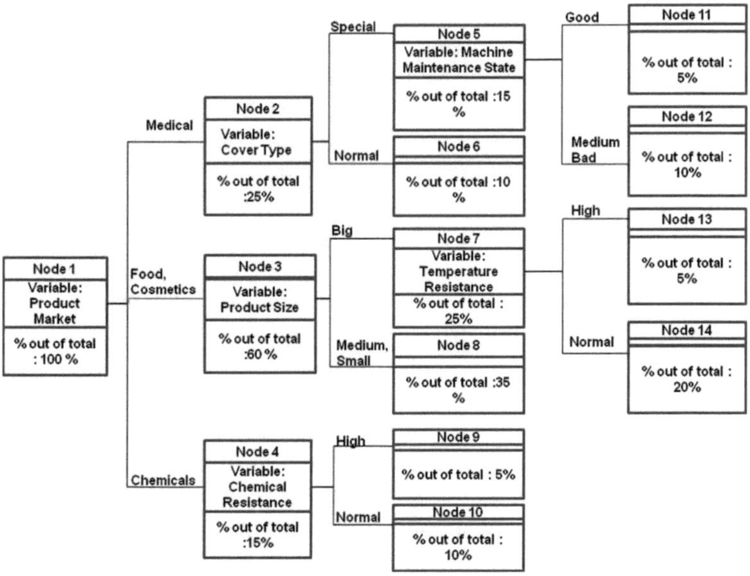

Fig. 3 Context identification decision tree

Table 2 Behavioral category distribution for leaf nodes 8, 9, and 13 (in %)

			Leaf node		
Category	Path	Termination	13	9	8
1	1	Success	13	10	7
2	2	Success	40	40	38
3	3	Success	40	42	43
4	1	Quality problems	3	3	4
5	2	Quality problems	2	2	5
6	3	Quality problems	2	3	3

Based on Table 2, the hypothesis that the instances in all the three leaf nodes are of the same population cannot be rejected, hence condition (a) is satisfied. To check condition (b), Table 3 shows the distribution of termination states for every path in the leaf nodes.

Based on Table 3, paths 1 and 2 lead to significantly different termination states in leaf node 8 as compared to leaf nodes 13 and 9. Hence, it cannot be considered in the same context group.

In summary, while the two conditions hold for leaf nodes 9 and 13, they do not hold for the combination including leaf node 8. Hence, leaf nodes 13 and 9 can be joined to one context group (instances with big products and resistance to high

Table 3 Termination states for paths in the leaf nodes (in %)

Path	Termination	Leaf node 13	Leaf node 9	Leaf node 8
1	Success	82	77	64
	Quality problems	18	23	36
2	Success	95	95	88
	Quality problems	5	5	12
3	Success	95	93	93
	Quality problems	5	7	7

temperature for the food and cosmetics market OR with products for the chemicals market with high chemical resistance requirement), while leaf node 8 is a different group (instances with small or medium products for the food and cosmetics market).

Note that not all the existing and known contextual variables are identified as influencing the behavior (e.g., the supplier of the raw material was found irrelevant).

4.2 Suggesting Improvements to the Process Model

Phase 1 provides a grouping of process instances according to context groups. In addition, these are divided into sub-groups with similar behaviors. However, for improvement purposes a different level of granularity might be needed, both for the paths and for the termination states. The termination state classification for the purpose of context identification aims at creating a clear distinction of different outcomes. Hence, it is at a coarse granularity level, relating mainly to the hard goals of the process and possibly to a threshold over soft goal achievement levels. When attempting to suggest improvements that would affect the business results of the process, a finer granularity level is required, relating to different levels of soft goal achievement. Considering the paths, some distinctions that were disregarded for the context identification (e.g., different machines) must be taken into account, as they might affect the outcomes for a given context.

Process improvement may include three types of action:

1. *Providing criteria for path selection in a given situation.* These would rely on the paths, context groups, and outcomes achieved by process instances in the repository. Considering the granularity level defined as relevant for process improvement, process instances in each context group should again be clustered based on path similarity. These clusters are then ranked based on their average achievement of goals, so the best performing paths for each context groups can be identified and recommended.

   To illustrate path selection recommendations, below are some possible cases concerning our running example.

One situation would be a context group for which a path that uses new material and quality inspection level 3 would yield zero cases of unacceptable quality level (no customer rejects, cancellations, or 100% inspections performed). However, when a certain worker operates the machine, an average 5% defects (which is still acceptable by the customer) is obtained at the sample inspection, while other workers normally have 2% defects. As a result, the specific worker can be trained, or not be assigned to orders of that context group.

As a second example, the current process model includes a decision point where a 100% inspection can be performed (or skipped) after a problem has been identified and solved during production. It could be identified that avoiding 100% inspection at this point significantly increases the probability that the customer would reject the delivered goods. Hence, the process model would be changed so performing such inspection becomes mandatory.

A third example might identify that for a certain group of machines, when the product is for the medical market, the frequency of problems identified during production increases about four months after maintenance activities, while for other machines and other context groups it happens only after six months. This could indicate the need to perform maintenance more frequently for these machines, or to avoid using them for medical products if four months have passed since their maintenance.

2. *Addressing specific questions that might be asked.* Management may have "hunches" about possible causes of poor performance. These can be specifically addressed by analyzing path and performance for all the context groups. For example, in the bottle manufacturing process there are cases of very urgent orders for which the machine set up is done in an accelerated manner. Management wishes to check whether this accelerated set up results in decreased product quality in general or for specific context groups. Specific analysis will try to correlate the time spent for the set up activity with the outcome for different context groups.
3. *Identifying successful deviations from the existing process model as a basis for managerial decision making.* The process instances in the repository may include instances where specific ad hoc decisions were made to deviate from the "normal" process at runtime. For example, there might be cases where special quality inspection instructions were given, not compliant with the existing three levels. Since this has not been repeated enough times to get statistical significance for its results, we can only indicate that such deviations were made and the extent of their success in achieving the process goals. Such indications may be used by management, which may decide to repeat this course of action so more data becomes available for future learning cycles.

It should be stressed that we do not suggest any change to be made automatically to the process model. All the improvement recommendations should be reviewed by humans (managers, domain experts), and the performance of the improved process should be monitored.

4.3 Online Application

Learning can be performed periodically in an off-line manner. At runtime, new process instances are created and executed. The learning results should be applied to these new instances. Each new process instance should be classified to an existing context group so path selection decisions can be made according to the recommended path for the context group according to the improved process model. Some decisions (e.g., assigning a worker or a machine) are usually made based on different criteria (e.g., machine availability). However, the context group may set preferences among possible paths (e.g., prefer a certain machine out of several available for a given context group).

If a process instance cannot be classified to an existing context group (e.g., a new product for a new market or some unfamiliar external event), decisions would be made based on human (managerial) judgment. In all cases, the data of the process instance, namely, context information, specific path, and outcome, will be stored in the experience base repository and serve for future learning cycles.

5 Related Work

This chapter combines three issues that have so far been addressed separately with respect to business processes, namely, goal orientation, context awareness, and actual process paths. We claim that this combination is important in order to achieve learning and improvement over time.

The business process research area has mostly focused over the years on control-flow issues, while goals as the driving force of business processes have not been extensively used. The conceptual basis for the work presented here is the Generic Process model (GPM) framework [21, 22], which relates to goals as a fundamental part of process specification. Relying on Requirements Engineering approaches, GPM distinguishes hard goals of a process from its soft goals [19]. Incorporating goals into process specification enables assessing the ability of a process to achieve its (hard) goal, which is termed the validity of its design [20]. Understanding and explicitly specifying process goals has also been shown to be a key issue for process flexibility [18]. A similar perspective of goal orientation has been suggested by [4], but their approach deals with hard goals only.

Another approach that addresses goal oriented business process modeling is presented in [13], proposing the map representation [16] as an intentional process specification. Map representation has been assigned GPM-based semantics in [19], which highlighted the synergy gained by combining these two.

Context awareness of business processes has recently gained the attention of the scientific community. The main efforts have been devoted to identifying the relevant context of a process, to its representation in a model, and to articulating how it can affect the process execution at runtime. Context identification has mainly been done in a qualitative manner (e.g., using an onion model [17]), while the algorithmic approach used here was first reported in [7, 8]. Context representation in process model has been addressed by [11]. Some representation proposals have been made, but no agreed upon standard has emerged yet. The runtime effect of context is discussed with respect to process flexibility and variability of execution [11, 14]. In addition, context-aware exception handling in workflow systems has been proposed, where the context relates both to the process and to the specific exception [3]. To the best of our knowledge, the effect of context on the outcome achieved by a process and its utilization for learning purposes has not been developed so far.

Actual path discovery has been addressed in the process mining area. Several attempts have been made to use process mining for identifying improvement opportunities in processes. These typically relate to specific performance measures (or soft goals). Examples include [1], who address performance indicators related to time (waiting time, synchronization time) as measured in different nodes of the process model. These measures are local, but can contribute to time-related soft goals if such are defined for the process. Another work [6] relates to an extended set of performance indicators, mostly related to time spent at parts of the process, and to some extent to resource consumption. The focus of these works is on mining technology capabilities rather than on analysis of business goals. As well, context information is not considered; hence learning is only partly supported.

Another related direction deals with adaptable workflow management systems like ADEPT [15]. Such systems allow making ad hoc changes and deviations from a predefined process model at runtime. Research efforts regarding adaptable systems include mining the changes that were made [9] and supporting future changes by employing a case-based reasoning mechanism which retrieves past changes that were made to the process [23]. However, in the absence of goal specification, there is no real assessment of the level of success achieved by past changes in business terms. In addition, the similarity of the situation cannot be fully established without taking context into account. Hence, here too learning is not fully supported.

In summary, while some attempts towards supporting process improvement and establishing a learning process have been made, our work is the first to explicitly incorporate goals and context as a basis for learning.

6 Conclusion

Constantly improving business processes has long been aspired by organizations. From a business perspective, it is clear that improvement can only be established with respect to defined goals. However, organizational goals are usually discussed using high level business terms, while business process modeling and management are addressed at a technical level, and are often not goal oriented. The result of this gap is that attempts made in the business process management discipline to achieve learning are not comprehensive, and can only relate to specific issues one at a time.

The approach presented in this chapter overcomes this gap by employing a goal oriented business process model, which brings the business level goals to the technical level of process specification. Context, which is the third element taken into account, is addressed at the same technical level. Tying these three elements together, this work presents a systematic process for learning and achieving constant improvement. Addressing both hard and soft goals, our approach is expected to reduce the frequency of exceptional terminations of the process and to improve business performance over time.

The learning process we propose draws conclusions from experience gained over time while executing a business process. Comparing this kind of learning to human learning, a major difference is that humans are capable of learning from mistakes they make, by acknowledging a certain decision as a wrong decision that should not be repeated. Humans can avoid repeating a mistake that has only been made once. In contrast, our learning process is statistical in nature; hence it can only draw conclusions after a substantial number of repetitions have been made. To improve the ability of the approach to learn from episodic failures (or successes), other kinds of reasoning mechanisms (e.g., Case-based reasoning) can be used in combination with the one proposed here. Future research will develop a set of learning mechanisms that can be used in combination, so each is applied in different situations. Future research will also experiment with the learning application and validate it in real life processes.

References

1. van der Aalst WMP, van Dongen BF (2002) Discovering workflow performance models from timed logs. In: Han Y et al (eds) Proceedings of the international conference on engineering and deployment of cooperative information systems. LNCS, vol 2480. Springer, Berlin/Heidelberg
2. van der Aalst WMP (2005) Business alignment: using process mining as a tool for delta analysis and conformance testing. Reqs Eng 10(3):198–211
3. Adams M, ter Hofstede AHM, van der Aalst WMP, Edmond D (2007) Dynamic, extensible and context-aware exception handling for workflows. In: Proceedings of OTM 2007 Part 1. LNCS, vol 4803. Springer, Berlin/Heidelberg
4. Andersson B, Bider I, Johannesson P, Perjons E (2005) Towards a formal definition of goal-oriented business process patterns. Business Process Manage J 11(6):650–662
5. Davenport TH (1993) Process innovation, reengineering work through information technology. Harvard Business School Press, Boston, MA
6. van Dongen BF, Adriansyah A (2009) Process mining: fuzzy clustering and performance visualization. In: Proceedings of the 5th international workshop on business process intelligence (BPI 2009), Ulm, Germany
7. Ghattas J, Peleg M, Soffer P, Denekamp Y (2009) Learning the context of a clinical process. In: Proceedings of the workshop on health-care processes (PROHealth 2009), Ulm, Germany
8. Ghattas J, Soffer P, Peleg M (2009) A formal model for process context learning. In: Proceedings of the 5th international workshop on business process intelligence (BPI 2009), Ulm, Germany
9. Guenther C Rinderle-Ma S, Reichert M, van der Aalst WMP, Recker J (2008) Using process mining to learn from process changes in evolutionary systems. Int J Business Process Integration Manage 3(1):61–78
10. Hammer M, Champy J (1994) Reengineering the corporation – a manifesto for business revolution. Nicholas Brealey Publishing, London

11. Modafferi S, Benatallah B, Casati F, Pernici B (2006) A methodology for designing and managing context-aware workflows. In: Mobile information systems II; IFIP international working conference on mobile information systems. MOBIS, vol 191/2005 of IFIP. Springer, Boston
12. Nevis EC, DiBella AJ, Gould JM (1995) Understanding organizations as learning systems. Sloan Manage Rev Winter:73–85
13. Nurcan S, Ettien A, Kaabi R, Zoukar I, Rolland C (2005) A strategy driven business process modelling approach. Business Process Manage J 11(6):628–649
14. Ploesser K, Recker J, Rosemann M (2008) Towards a classification and lifecycle of business process change. In: Proceedings of BPMDS 08. Montpellier, France
15. Reichert M, Rinderle S, Dadam P (2003) ADEPT workflow management system: flexible support for enterprise-wide business processes. In: Proceedings of the international conference on business process management (BPM), Springer, Berlin/Heidelberg
16. Rolland C (2008) Intention driven conceptual modelling. In: Johannesson P, Söderström E (eds) Information systems engineering: from data analysis to process networks. IGI Global Hershey, Pennsylvania
17. Rosemann M, Recker J, Flender C (2008) Contextualization of business processes. Int J Business Process Integration Manage 3(1):47–60
18. Soffer P (2005) On the notion of flexibility in business processes: In: Proceedings of CAiSE 2005 workshops: workshop on business process modeling, design and support (BPMDS'05)
19. Soffer P, Rolland C (2005) Combining intention-oriented and state-based process modeling. In: Proceedings of international conference on conceptual modeling (ER 2005). LNCS, vol 3716. Springer, Berlin/Heidelberg
20. Soffer P, Wand Y (2004) Goal-driven analysis of process model validity. In: Proceedings of CAiSE 2004. LNCS, vol 3084. Springer, Berlin/Heidelberg
21. Soffer P, Wand Y (2005) Goal-driven multi-process analysis. J AIS 8(3):175–203
22. Soffer P, Wand Y (2005) On the notion of soft goals in business process modeling. Business Process Manage J 11(6):663–679
23. Weber B, Rinderle S, Wild W, Reichert M (2005) CCBR-driven business process evolution. In: Proceedings of the international conference on case-based reasoning (ICCBR'05), Chicago
24. Weijters AJMM, van der Aalst WMP (2001) Process mining: discovering workflow models from event-based data. In: Kröse B et al (eds) Proceedings of the 13th Belgium–Netherlands conference on artificial intelligence (BNAIC'01)

Linking Goal-Oriented Requirements and Model-Driven Development

Oscar Pastor and Giovanni Giachetti

Abstract In the context of Goal-Oriented Requirement Engineering (GORE) there are interesting modeling approaches for the analysis of complex scenarios that are oriented to obtain and represent the relevant requirements for the development of software products. However, the way to use these GORE models in an automated Model-Driven Development (MDD) process is not clear, and, in general terms, the translation of these models into the final software products is still manually performed. Therefore, in this chapter, we show an approach to automatically link GORE models and MDD processes, which has been elaborated by considering the experience obtained from linking the *i** framework with an industrially applied MDD approach. The linking approach proposed is formulated by means of a generic process that is based on current modeling standards and technologies in order to facilitate its application for different MDD and GORE approaches. Special attention is paid to how this process generates appropriate model transformation mechanisms to automatically obtain MDD conceptual models from GORE models, and how it can be used to specify validation mechanisms to assure the correct model transformations.

1 Introduction

Nowadays, the requirements engineering (RE) field offers different modeling approaches that analyze complex scenarios and elicit their relevant requirements [20, 29, 43]. Of these approaches, the Goal-Oriented Requirement Engineering (GORE) plays a significant role [19, 21]. However, the way in which GORE models should be used in an automated Model-Driven Development (MDD) process [41] is

---

O. Pastor (✉)
PROS Research Center, Universidad Politécnica de Valencia, Camino de Vera s/n, 46022, Valencia, Spain
e-mail: opastor@pros.upv.es

S. Nurcan et al. (eds.), *Intentional Perspectives on Information Systems Engineering*,
DOI 10.1007/978-3-642-12544-7_14,

very often too vague. An important issue that is still pending is how to properly link the GORE models with the models of specific MDD approaches.

In general terms, for the application of GORE models to software production processes, the specified models must be manually analyzed to obtain the corresponding software representations. As it is reported in [37], the impossibility of applying requirement models directly into a MDD software production process is due to their nature since these models are centered on problem analysis and not on software representation. Unlike requirement models, the models involved in MDD processes are formulated to provide a precise and complete conceptual representation of the intended software systems in order to achieve automatic software generation by means of model compilations.

Thus, we can conclude that for the appropriate application of GORE modeling to MDD processes, an appropriate input for the model compilation processes must be obtained from the defined requirement models (i.e. to generate an MDD conceptual model from a GORE model).

This chapter presents an approach for automatic linking of GORE modeling and MDD processes. It has been elaborated by taking as reference the experience obtained from the integration of the *i** framework and an MDD approach called OO-Method, which has been successfully applied to the industrial software development [34]. From this scenario, we show how the GORE models can be transformed into the corresponding MDD-oriented conceptual models by detailing the following: the customization mechanisms for GORE modeling languages (that are defined to automate the model transformations); the specification of validation mechanisms to assure the appropriate model transformations; and the generation of required transformation rules. All of this is done by a generic process that is based on current modeling standards and technologies to facilitate its application in different MDD and requirement approaches. Finally, we advocate the use of existent open-source tools to support the proposed approach.

The rest of this chapter is organized as follows: Section 2 presents the background related to the *i** framework and the OO-Method MDD approach. Section 3 introduces the process proposed to link GORE modeling and MDD processes. Section 4 presents the related work and a discussion about the proposal. Finally, Sect. 5 presents our conclusions and further work.

2 Background

This section presents an overview of Goal-Oriented Requirement Engineering (GORE) modeling, in particular, the *i** framework, which is used as reference for the presented proposal. The OO-Method approach is also briefly presented, since the experience obtained from the industrial application of this MDD approach has provided the basis for obtaining our linking approach. The OO-Method approach is also used for explanation and exemplification purposes throughout this chapter.

2.1 The i Goal-Oriented Requirements Framework Overview*

Appropriate requirement capturing and elicitation is one of the most important activities in software development, thus the relevance of requirements engineering (RE) to obtain a sound software engineering process. RE clarifies what users want, how they are going to interact with the system, and how the system impacts the business. If these ideas are projected onto the model-driven philosophy, it can be stated that requirement modeling is fundamental in obtaining a sound Model-Driven Engineering (MDE) [18] process for software development. The paper presented in [38] clearly shows the relevance of integrating different modeling approaches to obtain a sound modeling process. This is precisely what we want to achieve with the linking of goal-oriented modeling and MDD-oriented modeling.

In the RE domain, the goal-oriented perspective has provided interesting results at both the industrial [20] and research levels [43]. The Goal-Oriented Requirement Engineering is concerned with the use of goals for eliciting, elaborating, structuring, specifying, analyzing, negotiating, documenting, and modifying requirements [19]. In general terms, it focuses on obtaining the 'what' of the intended systems through the analysis of organizational scenarios. The work presented in [39] shows the relevance of using scenarios for goal modeling, what provides the background for the RE modeling approach considered in this paper.

Among existing GORE approaches, the *i** framework [45] is currently one of the most widespread modeling and reasoning frameworks [20, 29, 43] and is also well documented [25]. It emphasizes the analysis of strategic relationships among organizational actors capturing the intentional requirements. The term actor is used to generically refer to any unit for which intentional dependencies can be ascribed. Actors are intentional in the sense that they do not simply carry out activities and produce entities, but they also have desires and needs.

The *i** framework offers two types of models: the *Strategic Dependency* (SD) model and the *Strategic Rationale* (SR) model. The SD model is focused on external relationships among actors. It includes a set of nodes and connecting links, where nodes represent actors (*depender* and *dependee*) and each link indicates a dependency (*dependum*) between two actors. There are four possible *dependum* elements: *goal*, *resource*, *task*, and *softgoal*. A *goal* in the *i** context is a condition or state of concerns that the actor would like to obtain. A *resource* is a physical or informational entity that must be available for an actor. A *task* specifies a particular way of doing something, which can be decomposed in small sub-tasks. Finally, a *softgoal* is associated to non-functional requirements.

The SR model is a detailed view of the SD that shows the internal actor relationships. In addition to the dependencies that are present in the SD model, the SR model incorporates three new types of relationships: (i) task-decomposition links, which describe what should be done to perform a certain task; (ii) means-end links, which suggest that a task is a means to achieve a goal; (iii) contribution links, which suggest how a model element can contribute to satisfying a softgoal.

2.2 The OO-Method MDD Approach Overview

OO-Method is an MDD approach that separates the application and business logic from the platform technology, allowing the automatic code generation from the conceptual representation of the software systems [34]. The OO-Method production process (Fig. 1) is comprised of three models: the *Conceptual Model*, the *Execution Model*, and the *Implementation Model*. The OO-Method Conceptual Model captures the static and dynamic properties of the system in a *Class Model*, a *Dynamic Model*, and a *Functional Model*. The conceptual model also allows the specification of the user interfaces in an abstract way through the *Presentation Model*. These four models represent the different views of the whole conceptual model, which has all the details needed for the generation of the corresponding software application. The complete definition of the OO-Method Conceptual Model is presented in [35].

The class model is the core of the OO-Method conceptual model; the rest of the models involved are defined starting from elements of the class model. For this reason, the OO-Method class model has been chosen to explain the linking approach presented in this chapter.

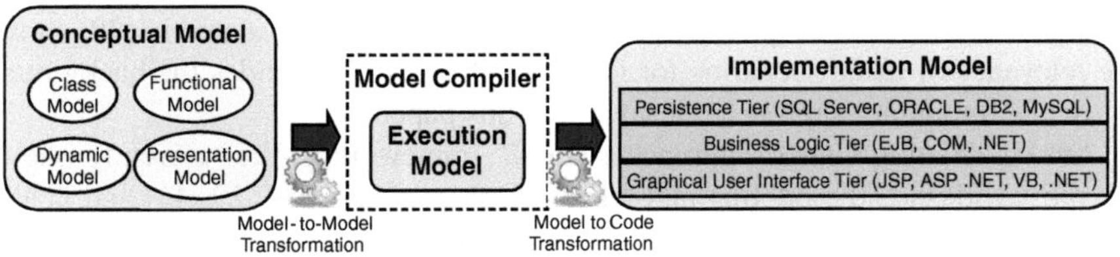

Fig. 1 The OO-method software production process

3 Linking Goal-Oriented and MDD Approaches

Our proposal for linking GORE modeling and MDD starts from the idea that there are two kinds of models that must be coordinated to represent specific parts of the development process: GORE models, and MDD models, which represent the intended systems at the conceptual level. These models are represented by using modeling languages whose abstract syntax is specified by means of metamodels.

For the coordination of these two models, we assume that it is possible to partially infer an *initial MDD model* from both the information that is represented in the GORE model and from extra information that is added when necessary. This MDD model generation is possible if constructs of the MDD modeling language can be inferred from constructs of the GORE modeling language. The constructs involved are represented by the metaclasses of the corresponding metamodels.

It is important to note that we are referring to an initial MDD model and not a complete MDD model because there are aspects related to specific system functionality that cannot be obtained from requirement models. Therefore, these functional

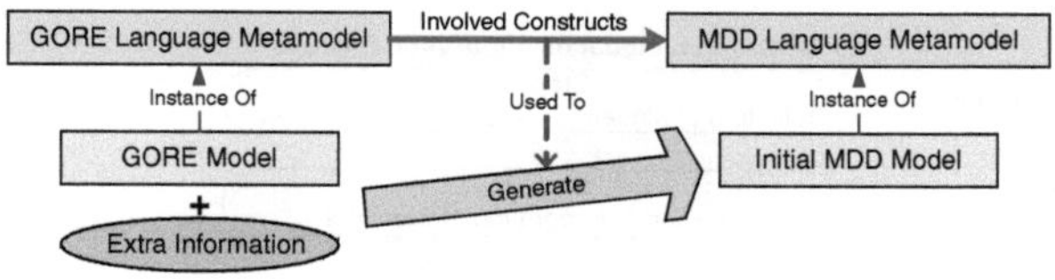

Fig. 2 Basic goal-oriented requirements and MDD linking schema

aspects must be specified later in the refinement of the initial MDD model that is obtained. Thus, the basic linking schema presented in Fig. 2 is the starting point of our proposal. From this initial linking schema, we can state that it is possible to automate the generation of the MDD model by means of well-defined model-to-model transformations, which are based on the metamodels of the modeling languages involved. This automatic generation is possible by using model transformation technologies such as ATL [17] or QVT [31]. However the question of what happens to the required extra information arises. If this extra information is not precisely represented, then the transformation rules cannot be automatically performed. This issue is observed in proposals such as [1, 28]. In these proposals, guidelines to transform goal-oriented models into software conceptual models are defined, but they must be manually applied because of the lack of a proper mechanism to specify the additional information required.

To solve this problem and to provide a well-defined input for the automatic generation of a MDD model, we use metamodel extensions to represent the extra information that is required. For the specification of these metamodel extensions, we use a process that generates them automatically. This process is focused on providing standardized support for the integration of modeling languages, which is the core of our linking proposal.

3.1 Automatic Generation of Metamodel Extensions

The process used for the generation of metamodel extensions (see Fig. 3) is based on an approach that was originally defined in [10] to integrate UML and Domain-Specific Modeling Languages (DSML) [24, 36]. This process proposes that the abstract syntax of a source modeling language can be integrated into a target modeling language through the automatic generation of specific metamodel extensions. The automatic generation of these extensions also provides the information that is essential for performing the interchange of the involved models by means of model-to-model transformations.

The required metamodel extensions are defined by means of a UML profile, which can be used to customize any metamodel that is defined according to the MOF standard [30], and not just the UML metamodel. The articles [4, 9] are good references that explain the different metamodel extension mechanisms and UML profiles, respectively.

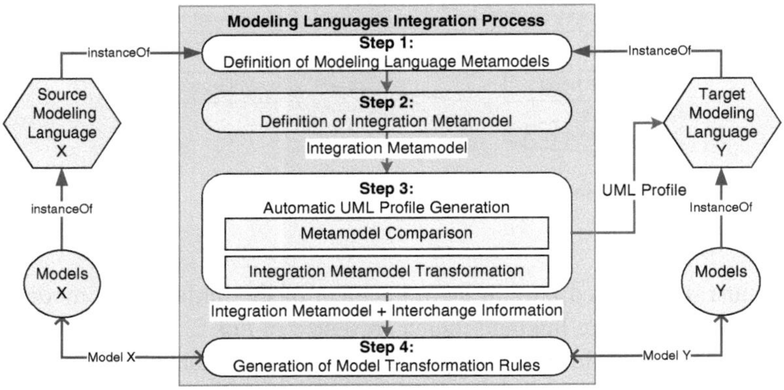

Fig. 3 Integration process application schema

Even though the UML profiles can be applied over any MOF metamodel, we only use the essential subset of the constructs that are defined in MOF for the specification of the metamodels of the modeling languages to be integrated. This subset, which is known as EMOF (Essential MOF), is defined inside of the MOF specification. The decision to use EMOF (instead of complete MOF) is due to the closeness that exists between EMOF metamodeling capabilities and UML profile extension capabilities. This facilitates the generation of UML profile extensions to integrate the particular metamodeling information of a source EMOF metamodel into a target EMOF metamodel [14].

The integration process is comprised by the following steps:

Step 1. Definition of Modeling Languages Metamodels. This step corresponds to the specification of the EMOF-based metamodels [30] that are related to the modeling languages to be integrated. The references [11, 42] provide a good set of guidelines for the definition of these metamodels.

Step 2. Definition of the Integration Metamodel. The Integration Metamodel is the solution defined in [14] to automatically generate metamodel extensions for the integration of two modeling languages. This is an EMOF-based metamodel that is generated from the metamodel of the source modeling language, and its definition includes the mapping information to identify the equivalences between the source and target modeling languages. The Integration Metamodel specification and the systematic approach proposed for its definition are presented in [14].

Step 3. Automatic UML Profile Generation. This corresponds to the mechanism implemented for the automatic generation of modeling languages extensions, which has been presented in [12]. This is a two-step process that not only automatically generates a UML profile from an Integration Metamodel, but also generates mapping information for the interchange of models defined with the integrated modeling languages [10]. The two steps of the UML profile generation are:

- *Metamodel Comparison:* It identifies the metamodel extensions that must be implemented in the UML profile.
- *Integration Metamodel Transformation:* A set of transformation rules that automatically transform the Integration Metamodel into the UML profile that implements the identified metamodel extensions.

Step 4. Generation of Model Transformation Rules. This last step provides the interchange mechanisms to translate models across the different integrated modeling languages. The interchange is based on a set of transformation rules that are generated by using the mapping information obtained in the UML profile generation [13]. These transformation rules can be implemented with model-to-model transformation technologies such as ATL [17] or QVT [31].

3.2 A Generic Process to Link Goal-Oriented Requirement Modeling and MDD Approaches

In this section, we explain the different steps of the proposed linking process. In order to facilitate the understanding, we present the process using a brief linking example that is based on the *i** and OO-Method approaches, which correspond to the GORE and MDD counterparts, respectively. Figure 4 shows the *i** diagram related to this example.

The proposed example represents the reception of work requests (work applications) from potential employees, which is part of a complete case study of a photography agency administration system that was developed in the context of the OO-Method industrial approach (presented in [26]). In order to simplify the example, only a subset of all the *i** and OO-method constructs were used.

Step 1: Definition of the Transformation Guidelines. The first step is to identify those constructs of the GORE modeling approach that are relevant for the generation of constructs of the MDD modeling approach. The identification of the relevant constructs is performed over the metamodels of the modeling languages involved. These metamodels must be EMOF compliant [30] (according to the integration process presented in Sect. 3.1). Then, the set of transformation guidelines that are needed

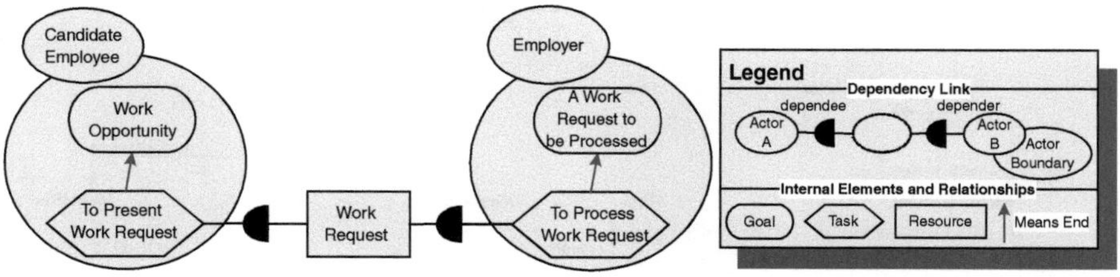

Fig. 4 *i** example model

to obtain the corresponding MDD constructs must be defined from the identified GORE constructs.

For the specification of the involved metamodels, we propose using the Eclipse UML2 tool [6] since it provides automatic generation of EMF metamodels from the defined UML2 metamodels. EMF is the Eclipse Modeling Framework that is based on the EMOF specification. Also, the generated EMF metamodels are tagged with additional information to automatically obtain model editors that have interpreters for the defined OCL rules and that support UML profile extensions.

In the *i** context, there is not a standardized *i** metamodel, and, in general terms, the existent metamodel proposals (such as the one presented in the *i** wiki [16] or in the articles [3, 23]) are not EMOF compliant. However, for the linking example presented here, we can use these proposals as reference for the definition of an appropriate EMOF-based *i** metamodel.

Figure 5 shows the *i** metamodel defined for the example. In this metamodel, the *i** constructs considered are: actors (class *Actor*); dependency resources (class *DResource*); internal goals and tasks (classes *IGoal* and *ITask*, respectively); and dependency links (class *Dependency*). It is important to note that this metamodel is only a subset of a complete *i** metamodel. Some of the differences are that *tasks*, *goals*, and *soft goals* can also participate in a dependency link. Therefore, in a complete *i** metamodel, these constructs must be represented as specializations of the class *Dependency* (the same as *DResource*). The *resources*, *goals*, and *soft goals* must also be represented as internal elements (specializations of *Internal Element*) in a complete *i** metamodel.

The OO-Method metamodel used for the proposed example (see Fig. 6) is also a subset of the complete OO-Method metamodel.

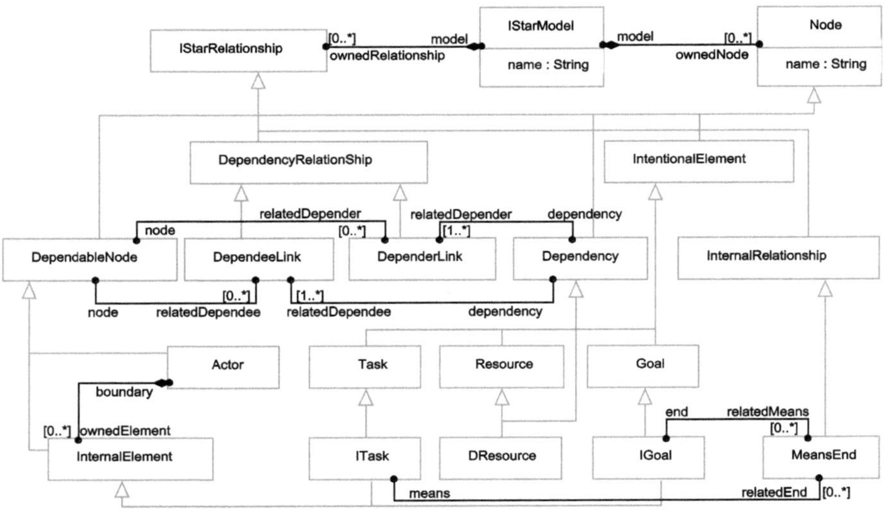

Fig. 5 The *i** metamodel for the example model

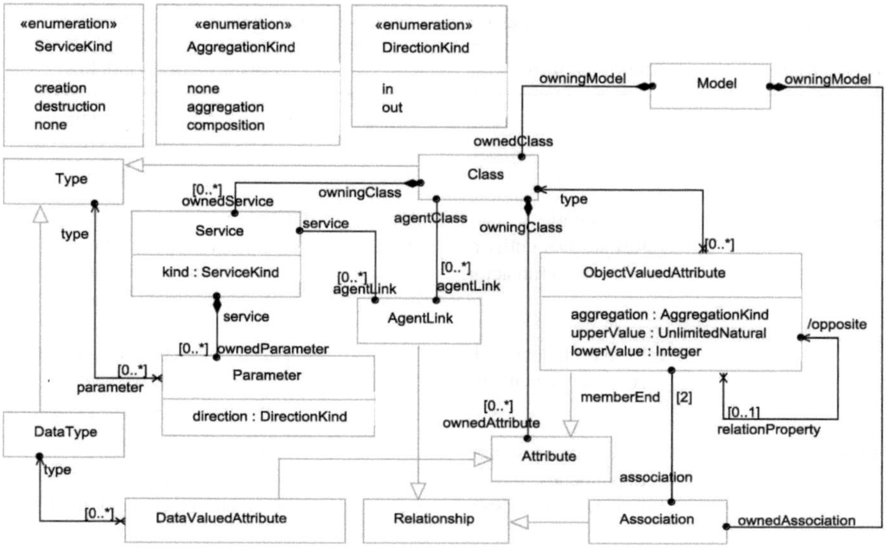

Fig. 6 The OO-method metamodel for the linking example

The presented OO-Method metamodel only includes the essential metaclasses for the definition of classes, attributes, services, associations, and a special relationship that is called *agent link*. This last construct is related to the specification of permissions that a class (of the modeled system) has to execute services of another class. Another particular modeling aspect of the OO-Method class model is the possibility of indicating the services that are capable of *create* or *destroy* instances of the class that owns them. This information is indicated by means of the property *kind*, which is defined in the metaclass *Service*.

Once the EMOF metamodels are properly specified, the relevant *i** construct must be identified, and the guidelines to transform these constructs into the corresponding OO-Method class model constructs must also be defined. Table 1 shows the transformation guidelines involved in the example (the complete list of transformation guidelines for *i** and OO-method is presented in [1]).

Table 1 also shows the additional information that is required by the transformation guidelines, which may not be present in the *i** metamodel. For instance, an *i** resource is transformed into a class or an attribute depending on whether the resource corresponds to a *physical* or an *informational* entity.

Step 2: Definition of MDD Requirement Metamodel. The second step of the linking process corresponds to properly specifying the modeling information that is required by the transformation guidelines in a format that can be processed by model-to-model transformation technologies [5]. To do this, we define a new EMOF metamodel with the information of the identified *i** elements and the additional information that is required. As a result, a specific requirement metamodel for the involved MDD approach is obtained. Figure 7 shows the OO-Method requirement

Table 1 Guidelines for transformation of *i** models into OO-method class models

i* construct	Additional info	Transformation guideline
Actor		Class + Agent Link to the Services generated from the actor's internal tasks
Resource	Physical entity	Class
	Informational entity related to a resource or an actor	A Data Valued Attribute that represents information of the Class generated from an actor or a resource
	Informational entity in a resource dependency	A Data Valued Attribute of the Class generated from the dependee actor
Task	Involved in a resource dependency	A Service of the Class generated from the resource
	If it generates a resource	A Creation Service of the Class generated from the resource
Dependency link	Where the dependum resource and the depender and dependee actors are transformed into classes	Associations are automatically defined among the generated Classes

metamodel obtained for the example, which is defined by considering the information presented in Table 1. In this metamodel, the *i** constructs taken into account are: *actors*, *tasks*, and *resources*.

The defined OO-Method requirement metamodel is considerably simpler than the original *i** metamodel, which facilitates the implementation of model-to-model transformations for generating the OO-Method class model. The additional information introduced in this metamodel is the following:

- Specification of resource kind (attribute *kind* of the metaclass *Resource*).
- Identification of tasks that generate resources (link *producedBy*).
- Identification of tasks that participate in a resource dependency (links *requiredBy* and *providedBy*).

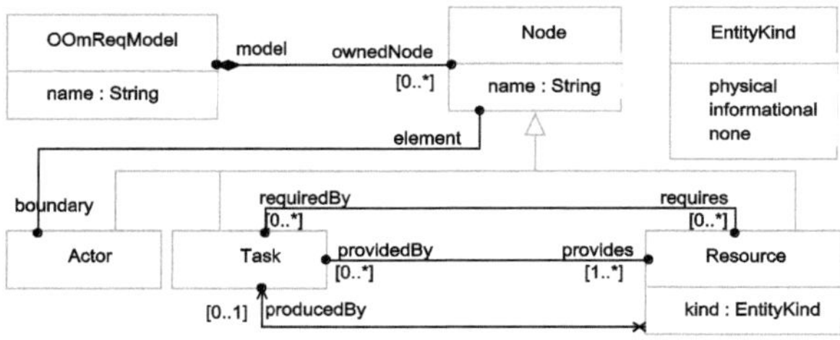

Fig. 7 The OO-method requirement metamodel for the example

To name the links involved in a resource dependency, we consider that the task related to the *depender* actor *requires* the resource for its execution, while the task related to the *dependee* actor is responsible for *providing* the resource.

Thus, at the end of the second step, we obtain two metamodels: the original *i** metamodel (the original GORE metamodel) and the OO-Method requirement metamodel for the generation of the OO-Method class model (the MDD requirement metamodel).

Step 3: Definition of Validation Rules. In this step, syntactical validation mechanisms are specified in order to perform a correct generation of the corresponding MDD models. These validation mechanisms must be defined in the MDD requirement metamodel (generated in step 2), since this metamodel has all the information to perform the model transformations. For instance, in the linking example, an *i** resource is transformed into an attribute or a class, depending on whether the resource is specified as an *informational* entity or a *physical* entity (see Table 1). From this transformation guideline, a possible validation is to assure the appropriate specification of the kind of resource. This validation can not be specified in the *i** metamodel since the information related to kind of resource is not present.

For the specification of these syntactical validations, we propose the use of OCL rules since OCL is also part of the OMG standards for the specification of metamodels; hence, it is defined to work in conjunction with MOF. In addition, the OCL rules can be automatically processed by tools such as [6]. Thus, for the previous validation example, we can define the following OCL rule in the class *Resource* of the OO-Method requirement metamodel:

```
Context: Resource::ValEntityKind ()
Body:         self.kind = Physical or self.kind = Informational
```

It is important to note that the modeling information that is not present in the original GORE metamodel is the critical point to be validated for the correct generation of the MDD model for two reasons: (1) the modeling information that exists in the GORE metamodel has probably already been validated; and (2) the new modeling information is essential for performing the model transformations, and hence, an incorrect specification of this information will produce an incorrect generation of the MDD model.

Step 4: Application of the Integration Approach. The fourth step of the linking approach is to go from the models that are based on the original GORE metamodel to the specific requirement models for the MDD approach that are based on the MDD requirement metamodel. This is because the intention of the linking proposal is to use the original GORE modeling approach for requirement modeling. In the example, this corresponds to going from *i** models that are based on the original *i** metamodel (Fig. 5) to requirement models that are based on the generated OO-method requirement metamodel (Fig. 7).

However, this step is not trivial since the additional modeling information and validation rules that are present in the defined MDD requirement metamodel are not present in the original GORE metamodel. Thus, in this step, the integration approach presented in Sect. 3.1 is put into practice to obtain the required

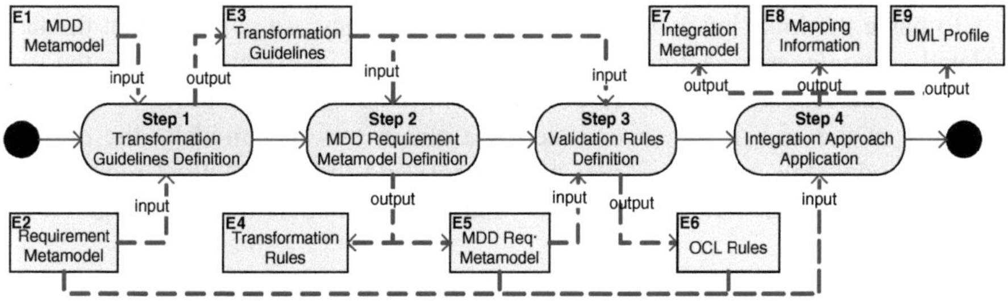

Fig. 8 General schema of the proposed linking process

metamodel extensions for the GORE metamodel and the needed model interchange information. Figure 8 shows the resultant linking schema with the different input and output elements that are related to each step (numbered from E1 to E9).

Figure 8 shows that Step 4 of the process generates the corresponding Integration Metamodel and UML Profile, as well as, mapping information (among the metamodels involved) for the automatic interchange of models.

Figure 9 shows how each one of the input and output elements considered in the linking process are used to link the *i** framework and the OO-Method MDD approach. This figure also shows the generation of traceability information [15, 44], which is necessary to maintain the relationships between the software specification (described in the MDD model) and the requirement specification (described in the MDD requirement model). The generation of this traceability information must be implemented together with the transformation rules for the MDD requirement model.

Figure 10 shows the Integration Metamodel obtained for the example. This metamodel is generated from the OO-method requirement metamodel by applying the systematic approach presented in [10, 14]. This systematic approach is based on taking the OO-Method requirement metamodel (the source metamodel) and performing a set of redefinitions over it to align this source metamodel to the structure of the *i** metamodel (target metamodel). This redefinition allows the automatic identification of the extensions that are required to introduce the modeling needs of

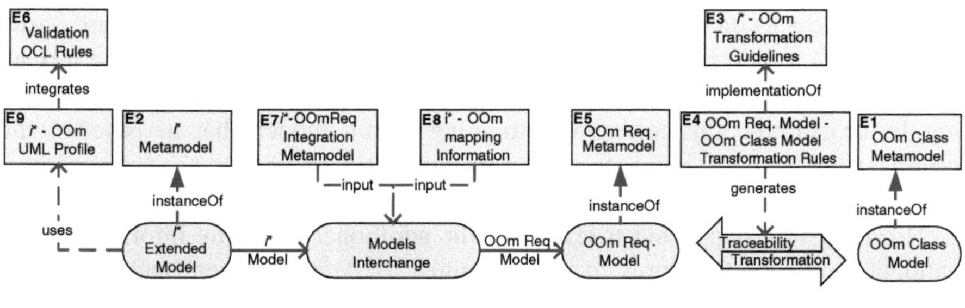

Fig. 9 Linking proposal elements applied to *i** and OO-method

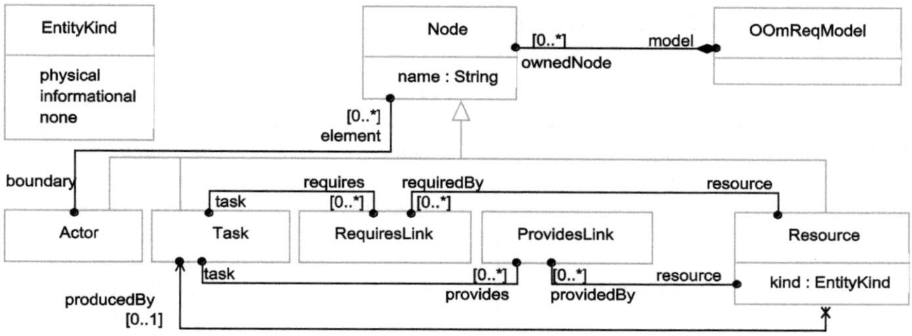

Fig. 10 Integration metamodel for the integration example

the source metamodel into the target metamodel, that is, to extend the *i** framework to represent the information of the OO-Method requirement model.

The resultant Integration Metamodel shows the classes *AffectsLink* and *RequiresLink*, which are not present in the OO-Method requirements metamodel. These classes are defined to perform the correct mapping from the associations *task.requires* and *task.provides* (which are derived from dependency links) to the *i** constructs *DependeeLink* and *DependerLink*. This is done since the mapping can only be performed among elements of the same kind (classes with classes, associations with association, and so on) [14].

There are four conditions that an Integration Metamodel must hold for the automatic generation of the metamodel extensions. These are the following:

- All the classes from the Integration Metamodel are mapped to the target GORE metamodel. This assures that the constructs from the MDD requirement metamodel can be represented from the constructs of the GORE metamodel. Table 2 shows the mapping obtained for the linking example.
- The mapping is defined between elements of the same type (classes with classes, attributes with attributes, and so on).
- An element from the Integration Metamodel is only mapped to one element of the GORE Metamodel.
- If the properties (attributes and associations) of a class A from the Integration Metamodel are mapped to properties of a class B of the GORE metamodel, then the class A is mapped to the class B or a specialization of it.

By applying the automatic UML profile generation to the Integration Metamodel (see Sect. 3.1), the corresponding UML profile that implements the required *i** extensions is obtained (see Fig. 11).

In the generated UML profile, the properties that have no equivalence in the target *i** metamodel are defined as new properties (tagged values) in the stereotypes that extend the metaclasses. In the Integration Metamodel definition and the UML profile generation, specific mappings among the participant metamodels are

Table 2 Integration metamodel and the *i** metamodel mapping

I.M. element	Extended I* element	I.M. element	Extended I* element
Node	Node	Resource	DResource
.model	.model	.kind	(No equivalence)
.name	.name	.providedBy	.relatedDependee (inherited from Dependency)
.boundary	.boundary	.requiredBy	.relatedDepender (inherited from Dependency)
OOmReqModel	IStarModel	.producedBy	(No equivalence)
.name	.name	Task	ITask
.ownedNode	.ownedNode	.provides	.relatedDependee (inherited from DependableNode)
Actor	Actor	.requires	.relatedDepender (inherited from DependableNode)
.element	.ownedElement	RequiresLink	DependerLink
ProvidesLink	DependeeLink	.task	.node
.task	.node	.resource	.dependency
.resource	.dependency	EntityKind	(No equivalence)

generated, which are used to perform the automatic transformation of GORE models into MDD requirements models. These mappings are the following:

1. The mapping between the Integration Metamodel and the extended GORE metamodel. In the example, this corresponds to an extended version of the mapping presented in Table 2, where the elements of the Integration Metamodel that have no equivalence in the *i** metamodel are mapped to the corresponding UML profile elements.

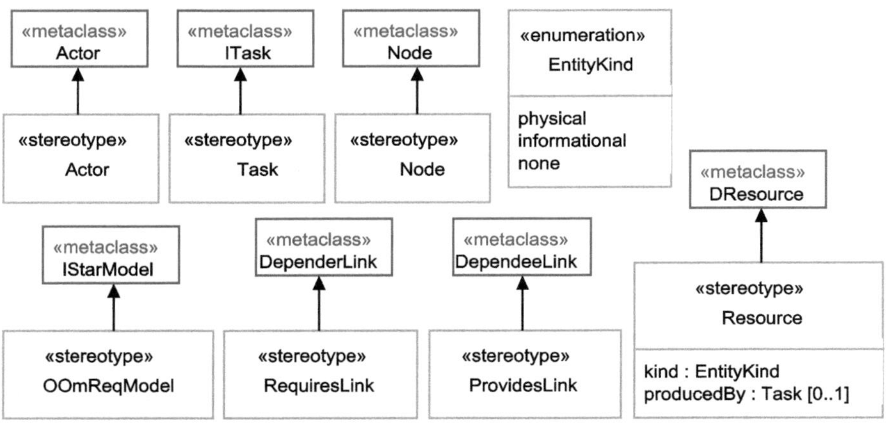

Fig. 11 UML profile generated from the integration metamodel of the example

Table 3 OO-method requirements metamodel and integration metamodel mappings

OO-method req. element	I.M. element	OO-method req. element	I.M. element
Node	Node	Resource	Resource
.model	.model	.kind	.kind
.name	.name	.providedBy	.providedBy.task
.boundary	.boundary	.requiredBy	.requiredBy.task
OOmReqModel	OOmReqModel	.producedBy	.producedBy
.name	.name	Task	Task
.ownedNode	.ownedNode	.provides	.provides.resource
Actor	Actor	.requires	.requires.resource
.element	.element		

2. The mapping between the MDD requirement metamodel and the Integration Metamodel. Table 3 shows the mapping obtained for the linking example.

Finally, the OO-Method class model presented in Fig. 12 is obtained from the example *i** model that is extended with the generated UML profile. In the extended *i** model (see Fig. 12), we considered the resource *Work Request* as a *physical* entity produced by the task *To Present Work Request.*

The generation of the OO-Method class model is performed by means of model-to-model transformation rules that are defined according to the interchange proposal presented in [13], which is driven by the metamodel mappings presented in Tables 2 and 3, and from the transformation guidelines presented in Table 1.

Figure 12 shows that the *i** actors are transformed into classes. The same occurs for the resource *Work Request* since it is a physical entity. The agent relationships are also represented to indicate the permissions that the classes *CandidateEmployee* and *Employer* (generated from the corresponding *i** actors)

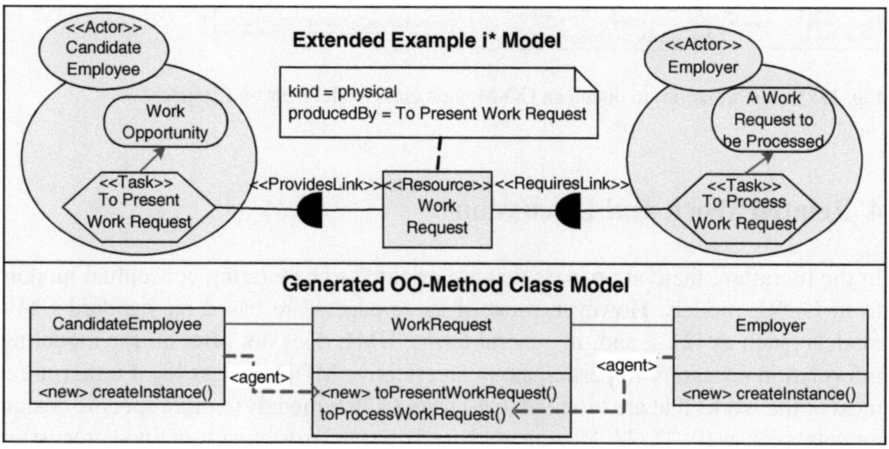

Fig. 12 Extended example i* model and the OO-method class model generated

have over the services of the class *WorkRequest*, which were generated from the defined *i** tasks. The task *to Present Work Request* is transformed into a creation service of the class *WorkRequest* since this service *generates* this resource. The creation services are identified by the tag *<new>* (inferred from the property *kind* of the metaclass *Service* of the OO-Method metamodel). In addition, during the generation of the class model, a creation service is automatically generated for the classes *CandidateEmployee* and *Employer* since, in OO-Method, all classes must have at least one creation service.

Figure 12 also shows that the generated class model has no attribute definition or arguments for the services since this modeling information cannot be derived from the example *i** model. The same happens with the functional specification of the generated services. Therefore, this information must be specified at the design stage in order to generate a complete class model from the initial class model generated. Thus, from the complete model, the final executable application can be automatically obtained through the *OO-Method model compiler* [35].

Figure 13 shows a graphical example of how the transformation of the *i** model is performed. This example shows the transformation of the resource *Work Request* and the task *To Present Work Request* to the corresponding constructs of the OO-Method class model. It is important to note that this transformation is automatically performed by means of the transformation rules; hence, the generation of the intermediate models is transparent. These intermediate models are the instances of the Integration Metamodel and the MDD requirement metamodel.

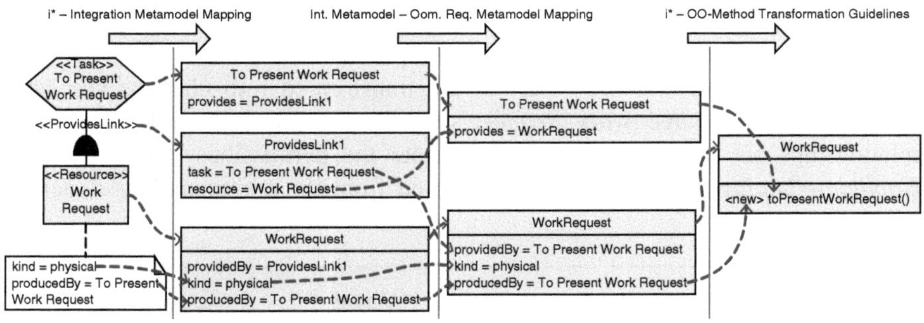

Fig. 13 Transformations to obtain an OO-Method class model from an *i** model

4 Related Work and Discussion

In the literature, there are papers that are oriented to generating conceptual models from GORE models. However, most of these papers are based on standard UML models (such as [21]), and, in general terms, UML does not offer all the modeling information necessary to participate in an effective MDD process [8]. Furthermore, most of the works that are oriented to go from GORE models to more specific design models, such as [2, 22, 28, 40], are not based on standards or well-defined processes, nor do they introduce automation possibilities. Therefore, the application of these proposals must be manually performed [27]. This is not a suitable option because the manual translation of models is a time consuming and error prone task [25]. Hence, automatic linking of GORE models and MDD approaches takes on special relevance for the adoption of new development paradigms and the improvement of development processes.

One important aspect that must be discussed about our proposal is how to identify the subset of GORE modeling constructs that must be considered for the generation of MDD models, since it is very probable that not all the elements of the defined *i** model have to be considered for the development of a software product. In the proposal, even though the constructs that participate in the MDD model generation are identified, this is not enough to assure that only the elements that are related to the software specification participate in the transformation. For instance, in the example, the *i** *Actor* is considered in the class model generation, but in a real *i** model some actors may not be relevant for the intended system, and, therefore, they must not be transformed into classes of the class model. UML profiles provide a suitable solution for this issue since it is possible to indicate that only those stereotyped (extended) elements must be considered in the transformation process. This is an important reason for using UML profiles instead of other metamodel extension mechanisms [4]. Other reasons are that the UML profile has a standard specification [32] and a standardized interchange format (XMI [33]).

Another interesting discussion point of this proposal is the need for defining an Integration Metamodel instead of a direct mapping between the original GORE metamodel and the MDD requirement metamodel. The definition of an Integration Metamodel is performed because a direct mapping does not always provide enough information to automatically identify the required metamodel extensions [10, 12]. Also, a direct transformation is dependent on the extension mechanism selected. In contrast, the Integration Metamodel allows the required extensions to be automatically identified independently of their final implementation.

Some additional benefits of the Integration Metamodel are the following: it automates the generation of the required transformation rules; the required extensions can be validated before its implementation; it allows the automatic generation of the mapping for the interchange of models; and it provides a common interface between the GORE metamodel and the MDD requirement metamodel. This last benefit prevents a change in the original GORE metamodel from affecting the transformation rules that are defined in the MDD requirement metamodel. These benefits are better perceived in real GORE models that are more complex than the presented example.

The Integration Metamodel is also useful for MDD approaches that already have a requirement modeling approach. In this case, the MDD requirement metamodel is the metamodel of the existent requirement approach. The next steps of the process are normally applied over this metamodel, and the differences that may exist with the target GORE metamodel (for instance, the *i** metamodel) are managed by the Integration Metamodel and the metamodel extensions.

5 Conclusion

In this chapter, a proposal for linking GORE models and MDD approaches has been presented. This linking is performed by means of a process that is oriented to obtaining the mechanisms for automatic generation of MDD-oriented conceptual models from GORE models. For the formulation of this process, existent standards and technologies have been used, which facilitates the application of our proposal to different MDD approaches. In addition, existent open-source tools, such as [5–7], can be used to implement the required metamodels and model transformations.

Nevertheless, it is very difficult to find requirement editors that support the standards that are considered in this proposal. For instance, we have not found an *i** editor that is compatible with the MOF specification or that supports modeling extensions, in spite of this chapter shows the relevance of requirement technologies that provide extension facilities to obtain an appropriate linking with MDD approaches. Hence, we believe that appropriate requirement modeling tools that are aligned with the capabilities provided by the current standards and technologies for the specification of modeling languages should be implemented.

We are currently working on the implementation of tools that provide patterns and assistants to facilitate the application of the linking proposal. As future work, we plan to offer a complete *i** metamodel, which can be used as reference for the elaboration of open-source tools that are compatible with the MOF standard.

References

1. Alencar F, Marín B, Giachetti G, Pastor O, Castro J, Pimentel JH (2009) From i* requirements models to conceptual models of a model driven development process. In: Proceedings of 2nd working conference on the practice of enterprise modeling (PoEM). LNBIP, vol 39. Springer, Heidelberg, Germany, pp 99–114
2. Alencar FMR, Pedroza FP, Castro J, Amorim RCO (2003) New mechanisms for the integration of organizational requirements and object oriented modeling. In: Proceedings of 6th workshop on requirements engineering (WER'03), Piracicaba - SP, Brasil, pp 109–123
3. Ayala C, Cares C, Carvallo JP, Grau G, Haya M, Salazar G, Franch X, Mayol E, Quer, C (2005) A comparative analysis of i*-based goal-oriented modelling languages. In: Proceedings of international workshop on agent-oriented software development methodologies (AOSDM'05), at the SEKE conference, Taipei, Taiwan, pp 657–663
4. Bruck J, Hussey K (2008) Customizing UML: which technique is right for you? IBM, USA. http://www.eclipse.org/modeling/mdt/uml2/docs/articles/Customizing_UML2_Which_Technique_is_Right_For_You/article.html. Accessed Feb 2010
5. Eclipse: ATL Project. http://www.eclipse.org/m2m/atl/. Accessed Feb 2010
6. Eclipse: Model Development Tools Project. http://www.eclipse.org/modeling/mdt/. Accessed Feb 2010
7. Eclipse: UML2 Project. http://www.eclipse.org/uml2/. Accessed Feb 2010
8. France RB, Ghosh S, Dinh-Trong T, Solberg A (2006) Model-driven development using uml 2.0: promises and pitfalls. IEEE Computer 39(2):59–66
9. Fuentes-Fernández L, Vallecillo A (2004) An introduction to UML profiles. In: Eur J Informatics Professional (UPGRADE) 5(2):5–13
10. Giachetti G, Marin B, Pastor O (2009) Integration of domain-specific modeling languages and UML through UML profile extension mechanism. Int J Computer Sci Appl 6(5):145–174

11. Giachetti G, Marín B, Pastor O (2008) Perfiles UML y Desarrollo Dirigido por Modelos: Desafíos y Soluciones para Utilizar UML como Lenguaje de Modelado Específico de Dominio. In: V Taller sobre Desarrollo de Software Dirigido por Modelos (DSDM), Gijón, Spain
12. Giachetti G, Marín B, Pastor O (2009) Using UML as a domain-specific modeling language: a proposal for automatic generation of UML profiles. In: Proceedings of CAiSE 2009. LNCS, vol 5565. Springer, Heidelberg, Germany, pp 110–124
13. Giachetti G, Marín B, Pastor O (2009) Using UML profiles to interchange DSML and UML models. In: Proceedings of third international conference on research challenges in information science (RCIS), IEEE Computer Society, Los Alamitos, CA, pp 385–394
14. Giachetti G, Valverde F, Pastor O (2008) Improving automatic UML2 profile generation for MDA industrial development. In: 4th international workshop on foundations and practices of UML (FP-UML) – ER workshop. LNCS, vol 5232. Springer, Heidelberg, Germany, pp 113–122
15. Gotel O, Finkelstein A (1994) An analysis of the requirements traceability problem. In: Proceedings of 1st international conference on requirements engineering (ICRE'94), Colorado, USA, pp 94–101
16. i*: Wiki Web Page. http://istar.rwth-aachen.de/. Last Accessed Oct 2009
17. Jouault F, Kurtev I (2006) Transforming models with ATL. In: Satellite events at the MoDELS 2005 conference. LNCS, vol 3844. Springer, Heidelberg, Germany, pp 128–138
18. Kent S (2002) Model driven engineering. In: Integrated formal methods (IFM). Springer, pp 286–298
19. van Lamsweerde A (2001) Goal-oriented requirements engineering: a guided tour. In: Proceedings of 5th IEEE international symposium on requirements engineering (RE'01), Washington, USA
20. van Lamsweerde A (2004) Goal-oriented requirements engineering: a roundtrip from research to practice. In: Proceedings of 12th IEEE joint international requirements engineering conference, IEEE Computer Science, Washington, USA pp 4–8
21. van Lamsweerde A (2008) Systematic requirements engineering – from system goals to UML models to software specifications. Wiley, West Sussex, UK
22. Liu L, Yu E (2004) Designing information systems in social context: a goal and scenario modeling approach. Info Systems Oxford, UK, 29(2):187–203
23. Lucena M, Santos E, Silva MJ, Silva C, Alencar F, Castro JFB (2008) Towards a unified metamodel for i*. In: Proceedings of 2nd IEEE international conference on research challenges in information science (RCIS 2008), IEEE, Los Alamitos, CA, pp 237–246
24. Luoma J, Kelly S, Tolvanen J-P (2004) Defining domain-specific modeling languages: collected experiences. In: Proceedings of 4th OOPSLA workshop on domain-specific modeling (DSM'04) Nashville, USA
25. Maiden NAM, Jones SV, Manning S, Greenwood J, Renou L (2004) Model-driven requirements engineering: synchronising models in an air traffic management case study. In: Proceedings of CAiSE 2004. LNCS, vol 3084. Springer, Heidelberg, Germany, pp 368–383
26. Marín B, Giachetti G, Pastor O (2008) The photography agency: a case study of the OO-method approach. Technical Report DSIC-II/13/08, Universidad Politécnica de Valencia, Valencia, España
27. Martínez A (2008) Conceptual schemas generation from organizational models in an automatic software production process. Phd Thesis. Universidad Politécnica de Valencia, Valencia, Spain
28. Martínez A, Castro J, Pastor O, Estrada H (2003) Closing the gap between organizational modeling and information system modeling. In: Proceedings of 6th workshop on requirements engineering (WER'03), Piracicaba - SP, Brasil, pp 93–108
29. Nuseibeh B, Easterbrook SM (2000) Requirements engineering: a roadmap. In: The future of software engineering. IEEE Computer Society, New York, USA
30. OMG: MOF 2.0 Core Specification (2006). Doc. number: formal/2006-05-01. URL: http://www.omg.org/spec/OCL/2.0/PDF

31. OMG: QVT 1.0 Specification (2008). Doc. number: formal/08-04-03. URL: http://www.omg.org/spec/QVT/1.0/PDF/
32. OMG: UML 2.2 Infrastructure Specification (2009). Doc. number: formal/2009-02-04. URL: http://www.omg.org/spec/UML/2.2/Infrastructure/PDF
33. OMG: XMI 2.1.1 Specification (2007). Doc. Number: formal/2007-12-01. URL: http://www.omg.org/spec/XMI/2.1.1/PDF
34. Pastor O, Gómez J, Insfrán E, Pelechano V (2001) The OO-method approach for information systems modelling: from object-oriented conceptual modeling to automated programming. Info Systems 26(7):507–534
35. Pastor O, Molina JC (2007) Model-driven architecture in practice: a software production environment based on conceptual modeling, 1st edn. Springer, New York
36. Pohjonen R, Kelly S (2002) Domain-specific modeling. Dr. Dobb's Journal http://www.drdobbs.com/architecture-and-design/184405121. Accessed Feb 2010
37. Rolland C, Prakash N (2000) From conceptual modelling to requirements engineering. Annals Soft Eng 10(1–4):151–176
38. Rolland C, Prakash N, Benjamen A (1999) A multi-model view of process modeling. Reqs Eng 4(4):169–187
39. Rolland C, Souveyet C, Ben Achour C (1998) Guiding goal modelling using scenarios. IEEE Trans Softw Eng (IEEE TSE), Special Issue on Scenario Manage 24(2):1055–1071
40. Santander V, Castro J (2002) Deriving use cases from organizational modeling. In: Proceedings of 10th anniversary IEEE joint international conference on requirements engineering (RE 2002), pp 32–42
41. Selic B (2003) The pragmatics of model-driven development. IEEE Softw 20(5):19–25
42. Selic B (2007) A systematic approach to domain-specific language design using UML. In: Proceedings of 10th IEEE international symposium on object and component-oriented real-time distributed computing (ISORC), pp 2–9
43. Shuichiro Y, Haruhiko K, Karl C, Steven B (2006) Goal oriented requirements engineering: trends and issues. IEICE – Trans Inf Syst E89-D(11):2701–2711
44. Spanoudakis G, Zisman A (2005) Software traceability: a roadmap. Handbook of software engineering and knowledge engineering, vol III. Recent Advancements, World Scientific Publishing, pp 395–428
45. Yu E (1995) Modelling strategic relationships for process reengineering. PhD Thesis. University of Toronto, Toronto, ON, Canada

Testing Conceptual Schema Satisfiability

Antoni Olivé and Albert Tort

Abstract Satisfiability is one of the properties that all conceptual schemas must have. Satisfiability applies to both the structural and the behavioral parts of a conceptual schema. Structurally, a conceptual schema is satisfiable if each base or derived entity and relationship type of the schema may have a non-empty population at certain time. Behaviorally, a conceptual schema is satisfiable if for each event type there is at least one consistent state of the information base and one event of that type with a set of characteristics such that the event constraints are satisfied, and the effects of the event leave the information base in a state that is consistent and satisfies the event postconditions. There has been a lot of work on automated reasoning procedures for checking satisfiability but it is well known that the problem of reasoning with integrity constraints and derivation rules in its full generality is undecidable. In this chapter, we explore an alternative approach to satisfiability checking, which can be used when conceptual schemas are developed in the context of an environment that allows their testing. The main contribution of this chapter is to show that when conceptual schemas can be tested then their satisfiability can be proved by testing.

1 Introduction

A conceptual schema of an information system is correct if the knowledge that it defines is true for the domain and relevant to the functions that the system must perform [11]. The correctness of a conceptual schema must be checked during the requirements validation phase [16, 20–23, 27].

Satisfiability is one of the properties that all correct conceptual schemas must have. Satisfiability applies to both the structural and the behavioral parts of a conceptual schema. Structurally, a conceptual schema is satisfiable if each base or derived

A. Olivé (✉)
Department Enginyeria de Serveis i Sistemes d'Informació, Universitat Politècnica de Catalunya, Jordi Girona 1-3, 08034 Barcelona, Spain
e-mail: olive@essi.upc.edu

S. Nurcan et al. (eds.), *Intentional Perspectives on Information Systems Engineering*,
DOI 10.1007/978-3-642-12544-7_15,

entity and relationship type of the schema may have a non-empty population at certain time. An entity or relationship type is unsatisfiable when the set of constraints defined in the schema can only be satisfied if the population of that type is empty. Behaviorally, a conceptual schema is satisfiable if each event type is satisfiable, that is, there is at least one consistent state of the Information Base (IB) and one event of that type with a set of characteristics such that the event constraints are satisfied, and the effects of the event leave the IB in a state that is consistent and satisfies the event postconditions. A state of the IB is consistent if it satisfies all integrity constraints.

There has been a lot of work on automated reasoning procedures for checking satisfiability, mainly for the structural part of a schema (a representative set of recent papers is [1, 3, 5, 7, 8, 10, 18, 19]). However, it is well known that the problem of reasoning in conceptual schemas including general integrity constraints, derivation rules and event pre and postconditions is undecidable. Therefore, the available automated reasoning procedures are restricted to certain kinds of constraints, derivation rules, pre/postconditions or domains, or they may not terminate in some circumstances.

In this chapter, we explore an alternative approach to satisfiability checking, which can be used when conceptual schemas are developed in the context of a development environment that allows their testing. Essentially, this means that there is a testing language, in which the conceptual modeler writes programs that test a conceptual schema, and a test processor, which is a program able to execute test programs and report on their result.

The main contribution of this chapter is to show that when conceptual schemas can be tested then their satisfiability can be proved by testing. The idea is that the conceptual modeler sets up a test case such that if its verdict is *Pass* then by definition the entity or relationship or event type under test is satisfiable. If the conceptual modeler is unable to set up such test case, then this is not formal proof of unsatisfiability. We show that the unsatisfiability results obtained by testing are not as strong as those obtained by automated reasoning procedures when they are applicable, but in many practical cases testing provides a clue that helps to uncover a faulty schema.

The idea that satisfiability can be proved by testing is similar to that of validating a conceptual schema by prototyping, as was already proposed in the work of the TODOS project [16]. In both cases the main intention is similar: ensuring the correctness of the conceptual schema. The means are only slightly different: in testing we assume that the conceptual schema is directly executable, while in prototyping it is assumed that the prototype is automatically generated from the conceptual schema.

The structure of the chapter is as follows. In the next section, we briefly review the main concepts and the notation used to define conceptual schemas. We also review the main characteristics of test kinds, test cases and test programs needed in this chapter. In Sect. 3 we describe how to test the satisfiability of entity, relationship and domain event types, with examples taken from a fragment of the conceptual schema of the osCommerce system [24], a popular industrial e-commerce system. All of the examples in this chapter are taken from this case study. The full details of the case study can be found in the report [25]. Section 4 summarizes the conclusions.

2 Basic Concepts and Notation

In this section, we briefly review the main concepts and notation of the conceptual schemas under test, and of the testing language.

2.1 Conceptual Schema Under Test

A conceptual schema consists of a structural (sub)schema and a behavioral (sub)schema. The structural schema consists of a taxonomy of entity types (a set of entity types with their generalization/specialization relationships and the taxonomic constraints), a set of relationship types (attributes and associations), the cardinality constraints of the relationship types and a set of other constraints formally defined in OCL [13]. We adopt UML/OCL as the conceptual modeling language, but the ideas presented here can also be applied to schemas in other languages [9, 15]. We are also able to deal with temporal constraints, but for presentation purposes we omit them here. Figure 1 shows a structural schema fragment that will be used throughout the chapter.

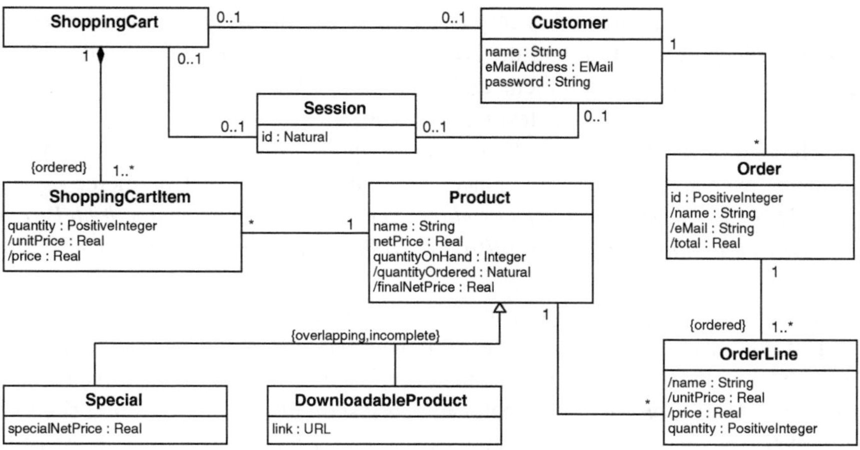


```
context Order::total:Real
  derive: self.orderLine.price->sum()

context Product inv nameIsUnique:
  Product.allInstances()->isUnique(name)

context Session
  inv CustomerCartWhenLoggedIn:
  self.customer->notEmpty() and
  self.shoppingCart->notEmpty()
  implies
  self.customer.shoppingCart=
  self.shoppingCart
```

Fig. 1 Fragment of the osCommerce structural schema

Entity and relationship types may be base or derived. The population of the base entity and relationship types is explicitly represented in the Information Base (IB). If they are derived, there is a formal derivation rule in OCL that defines their population in terms of the population of other types.

Figure 1 includes as an example the specification of two OCL integrity constraints (*Product::nameIsUnique* and *Session::CustomerCartWhenLoggedIn*) and also of the derivation rule of the attribute *Order::total*. See [25] for the whole set of constraints and derivation rules.

The behavioral schema consists of a set of event types. We take the view that an event can be modeled as a special kind of entity, which we call event entity [12]. An event entity is an instance of an event type.

Event types have characteristics, constraints and effects. The characteristics of an event are the set of relationships (attributes or associations) in which it participates. The constraints are the conditions that events must satisfy in order to occur. An event constraint involves the characteristics and the state of the IB before the event occurrence. An event may occur in the state *S* of the IB if *S* satisfies all constraints and the event satisfies its event constraints. Each event type has an operation called *effect()* that gives the effect of an event occurrence. The effect is declaratively defined by the postcondition of the operation. We define both the event constraints and the postcondition in OCL.

For domain event types, the postcondition defines the state of the IB after the event occurrence. It is assumed that the state of the IB after the event occurrence also satisfies all constraints defined over the IB. We deal with executable conceptual schemas, and therefore we need a procedural specification of the method of the *effect*() operation. A method is correctly specified if the IB state after its execution satisfies the postcondition and the IB constraints. UML does not include any particular language for writing methods [2]. In the work reported here, we write those methods using a subset of the testing language.

The example used throughout this chapter uses the minimal subset of domain events necessary to place an order in the osCommerce system: *NewCustomer, NewSession, NewProduct, NewSpecial, NewDownloadableProduct, NewDownloadableSpecial, AddProductToShoppingCart, LogIn* and *Order Confirmation.*

Their detailed specification can be found in [25]. *AddProductToShoppingCart* adds a quantity of a product in the shopping cart of a session (the shopping cart is created if it does not exist yet in the context of the session). Given a shopping cart, *OrderConfirmation* creates the corresponding *Order*. Figure 2 shows the complete specification of the domain event *NewProduct* including its constraint (*productDoesNotExist*), its postcondition and the method of its *effect()* operation.

2.2 The Testing Language

Without loss of generality, in this chapter we will use the testing language called CSTL (Conceptual Schema Testing Language) [26]. A test set of a conceptual schema is a set of one or more CSTL programs. A CSTL program consists of a

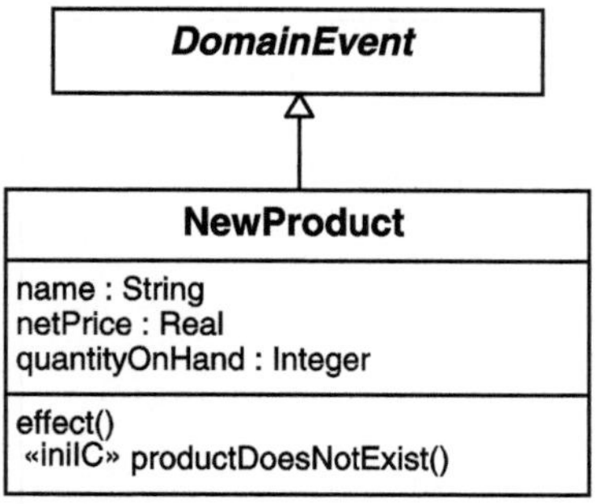


```
context NewProduct::
productDoesNotExist():Boolean
  body: not Product.allInstances()
    -> exists (pr|pr.name = self.name)
```

```
context NewProduct::effect()
  post:(Product.allInstances -
   Product.allInstances@pre) -> one(p:Product|
       p.oclIsNew() and
       p.name = self.name and
       p.netPrice = self.netPrice and
       p.quantityOnHand = self.quantityOnHand)

method NewProduct::effect(){
p:=new Product;
p.name:=self.name;
p.netPrice:=self.netPrice;
p.quantityOnHand:=self.quantityOnHand;
self.createdProduct:=p;
}
```

Fig. 2 Domain event specification example

fixture and a set of one or more test cases. A test case is a set of statements that builds a state of the IB, and executes one or more test assertions. Figure 3 shows a test program that consists of a fixture and two test cases (*confirmOrder* and *productKindsInCatalog*). CSTL also includes other constructs to make easier the task of writing tests.

It is assumed that the execution of each test case of a CSTL program starts with an empty IB state. With this assumption, the test cases of a program are independent each other, and therefore the order of their execution is irrelevant. The fixture is a set of statements that create an IB state and define the values of the common program variables. It is assumed that each execution of a test case starts with the execution of the fixture.

The basic construct of CSTL is the concrete test case. Each concrete test case has a name and consists of a set of statements:

```
test testName {
...
assert ...
}
```

The last statement of a concrete test case is an assertion, but in general there may be several assertions in the same test case. The verdict of a concrete test case is *Pass* if the verdict of all of its assertions is *Pass*. The objective of the conceptual modeler is to write test cases whose final verdict is *Pass*.

In CSTL there are five kinds of assertions, but in this chapter only two are used: asserting the occurrence of domain events and asserting the contents of an IB state, which we briefly describe in the following.

In CSTL, the instances of a domain event type $EventType_1$ can be created with the statement:

$$\texttt{eventId := }\textbf{new}\texttt{ EventType}_1\texttt{(att}_1\texttt{:= value}_1\texttt{,..., att}_n\texttt{:= value}_n\texttt{,}\\ \texttt{r}_1\texttt{:= participants}_1\texttt{,..., r}_m\texttt{:= participants}_m\texttt{);}$$

```
testprogram PlaceOrder{

nc := new NewCustomer
      (name:='John', eMailAddress:='john@john.com', password:='pwd');
assert occurrence nc;
john := nc.createdCustomer;

ns := new NewSession;
assert occurrence ns;
s := ns.createdSession;

np1 := new NewProduct(name:='shirt', netPrice:=20, quantityOnHand:=5);
assert occurrence np1;
shirt := np1.createdProduct;
np2 := new NewSpecial (name:='trousers', netPrice:=80,
                       quantityOnHand:=25,specialNetPrice:=65);
assert occurrence np2;
trousers := np2.createdProduct;

test confirmOrder{
    apsc1 := new AddProductToShoppingCart(quantity:=2,
                                   session:=s, product:=shirt);
    assert occurrence apsc1;
    apsc2 := new AddProductToShoppingCart(quantity:=1,
                                   session:=s, product:=trousers);
    assert occurrence apsc2;
    assert equals s.shoppingCart.shoppingCartItem->at(1).price 40;
    assert equals s.shoppingCart.shoppingCartItem->at(2).price 65;

    li := new LogIn(customer:=john, session:=s);
    assert occurrence li;
    oc := new OrderConfirmation(shoppingCart:= s.customer.shoppingCart);
    assert occurrence oc;
    assert equals oc.createdOrder.total 105;
    assert equals shirt.quantityOrdered 2;
    assert equals oc.createdOrder.eMail 'john@john.com';
    assert equals oc.createdOrder.name 'John';
    assert equals oc.createdOrder.orderLine->at(1).name 'shirt';
    assert equals oc.createdOrder.orderLine->at(2).name 'trousers';
}
test productKindsInCatalog{
    ndp := new NewDownloadableProduct
           (name:='fashionDesigner', netPrice:=43, quantityOnHand:=85,
            link:='http://fashionshop.com/fashionDesigner.zip');
    assert occurrence ndp;
    nds := new NewDownloadableSpecial
           (name:='FashionTipsMagazine', netPrice:=3, quantityOnHand:=15,
            specialNetPrice := 2,
            link:='http://fashionshop.com/tips.pdf');
    assert occurrence nds;
}
}
```

Fig. 3 CSTL program for testing order placement

The statement creates the instance *eventId* of $EventType_1$, and assigns a value to its characteristics (attributes $att_1,...,att_n$ and binary links with roles $r_1,...,r_m$). In Fig. 3 there are ten examples of statements that create an instance of a domain event type.

Once the concrete event *eventId* has been created in a test case, in order to assert that it may occur in the current state of the IB the conceptual modeler writes the following sentence:

```
assert occurrence eventId;
```

The verdict of this assertion is determined as follows:

- Check that the current IB state is consistent. The verdict is *Error* if that check fails (events may not occur in inconsistent IB states). In general, a state of the

IB can be built by means of explicit insertions, deletions and updates and/or by means of the occurrence of domain events. For the purposes of the analysis of the test coverage criteria of complete conceptual schemas we impose that the state of the IB has been achieved by means of the occurrence of domain events, starting from an empty IB. The example of Fig. 3 satisfies this condition.

- Check that the constraints of the event are satisfied. The verdict is *Fail* if any of the event constraints is not satisfied.
- Execute the method of the corresponding *effect()* operation.
- Check that the new IB state is consistent. The verdict is *Fail* if any of the constraints is not satisfied.
- Check that the event postconditions are satisfied. The verdict is *Fail* if any of the postconditions is not satisfied; otherwise the verdict of the whole assertion is *Pass.*

It is often useful to include in a test case an assertion on the current state of the IB. The purpose may be to check that one or more derivation rules derive the expected results, or that a navigational expression yields the expected results or that the effect of one or more domain events implies an expected result in the IB. In CSTL, to assert that the current state of the IB satisfies a boolean condition defined in OCL, the conceptual modeler writes the following statement:

```
assert true booleanExpression;
```

where *booleanExpression* is an OCL expression over the types of the IB and the variables of the test case. The verdict of the assertion is *Error* if the current state is inconsistent. The verdict is *Pass* if *booleanExpression* is true and *Fail* otherwise.

The test program of Fig. 3 contains several examples of assertions about the state of the IB. For example, the statement "*assert equals oc.createdOrder.total 105*" asserts that the total price of the created order in the current state of the IB is 105. The verdict is *Pass* if the valid occurrence of the event *OrderConfirmation* correctly creates the order and the derivation rules of the schema derive its total as expected.

Additionally, CSTL includes the following similar assertions:

```
assert false booleanExpression;
assert equals valueExpression1 valueExpression2;
assert not equals valueExpression1 valueExpression2;
```

3 Testing Satisfiability

In this section, we show how we can check the satisfiability of schema elements by means of testing. We analyze first the satisfiability of base entity and relationship types, then that of derived base and relationships types, and finally that of domain event types.

3.1 Base Type Satisfiability

Satisfiability (or liveliness) is a well known property of base entity and relationship types. A base type is satisfiable (or lively) if it may have a non empty finite population at certain time. In a conceptual schema, a base type is unsatisfiable when the set of constraints defined in that schema can only be satisfied if the population of that type is empty or infinite [17]. In conceptual modeling, it is usually required that all base types be satisfiable [4, 6, 14].

Let T_i be a base type (entity types, attributes and associations) defined in a conceptual schema. The satisfiability of T_i can be checked by means of testing. The idea is to set up a test case TC_j such that it:

- builds a state of the IB having at least one instance of T_i, and
- makes an assertion TA_k that can only *Pass* if the above IB state is consistent (that is, it satisfies all constraints).

If the execution of TA_k gives the verdict *Pass*, then it is experimentally proved that T_i is satisfiable. Note that in a single test case we can instantiate several types and that a single assertion can experimentally prove that all of them are satisfiable.

In the test program of Fig. 3, the fixture creates the customer *john* and the session *s*. It also initializes the online catalog with the product *shirt* and the special product *trousers*. The execution of any of the test cases of the test program example implies the execution of this fixture and ensures that the entity types *Customer*, *Session*, *Product* and *Special* (and also their attributes) are satisfiable.

Moreover, the test case *confirmOrder* adds a shopping cart item with two units of *shirt* and another item with a pair of *trousers*. The shopping cart is created when adding the first item. By this way, the entity types *ShoppingCart* and *ShoppingCartItem* (and also their relationship types, including attributes) are proved satisfiable. The relationship types *ShoppingCart-Session, Session-Customer* and *Customer-ShoppingCart* are also satisfiable when the *LogIn* event occurs (the session is assigned to a customer and the anonymous shopping cart becomes the shopping cart of the customer of the session). The entity types *Order* and *OrderLine* (and their relationship types) become satisfiable when the event *OrderConfirmation* occurs (the order and its order lines are created from the shopping cart). Finally, the occurrence of the instance *ndp* of the domain event type *NewDownloadableProduct* proves the satisfiability of the entity type *DownloadableProduct*.

If a conceptual schema includes a base type T_i that is unsatisfiable, then the conceptual modeler will be unable to set up a test case that builds a state of the IB with at least one instance of T_i, and an assertion that can only *Pass* if that state is consistent. This is not formal proof that T_i is unsatisfiable, but in many practical cases it provides a clue that helps to uncover a faulty constraint.

For example, consider the schema example shown in Fig. 4 (adapted from [4]). The association *Manages* is satisfiable if we do not take into account that *Manager*

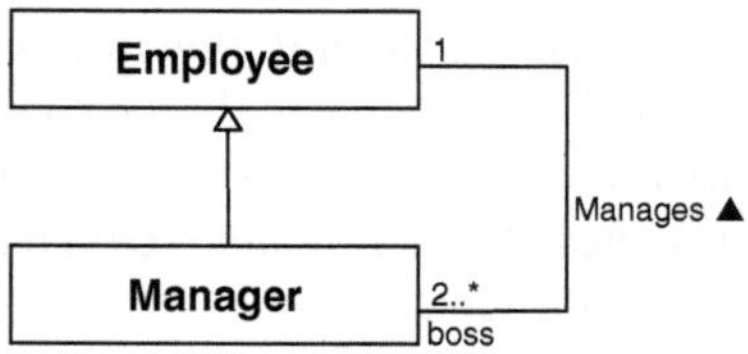

Fig. 4 Schema fragment with types that cannot be satisfied

IsA Employee. However, if we take this inclusion constraint into account then it cannot be satisfied. If the conceptual modeler writes a test case such as

```
test EmployeeWithTwoBosses{
    emily := new Employee;
    john := new Manager (employee:=Emily);
    natalie := new Manager(employee:=Emily);
    assert consistency;
}
```

the assertion will *Fail* because *john* and *natalie* do not have (at least) two bosses. Any change of the instances of the three types will produce the same result, and the conceptual modeler will find out soon that the defined cardinality constraints are wrong.

3.2 Derived Type Satisfiability

Entity and relationship types may be derived. For each derived type, the conceptual schema includes a derivation rule that defines the population of that type in terms of the population of other types. In UML, the derivation rules are written in OCL. Derived types must be satisfiable too [6]. Satisfiability of a derived type means that its derivation rule may derive at least one instance of it at certain time.

The satisfiability of a derived type can be checked by means of testing. The idea is to write a test case that makes an assertion TA_k whose evaluation requires the derivation of at least one instance of that type.

In the example of Fig. 1 there are ten derived attributes. The assertions "*assert equals s.shoppingCart.shoppingCartItem->at(1).price 40*" and "*assert equals s.shoppingCart.shoppingCartItem->at(2).price 65*" (specified in the test case *confirmOrder* shown in Fig. 3) imply that the attribute *ShoppingCartItem::price* is satisfiable and also the attributes *ShoppingCartItem::unitPrice* and *Product::finalNetPrice*. The reason is that the derivation of the *price* of a shopping cart item implies the derivation of its *unitPrice* (its derivation rule expression is *unitPrice*quantity*), and the *unitPrice* of a shopping cart item corresponds to the *finalNetPrice* of its associated product. Similarly, the assertion "*assert equals oc.createdOrder.total 105*" implies the satisfiability of the attributes *Order::total* (its derivation rule is shown in Fig. 1), *OrderLine::price* and *OrderLine::unitPrice*. Finally, the assertions "*assert equals shirt.quantityOrdered 2*", "*assert equals* *oc.createdOrder.eMail 'john@john.com'*", "*assert equals oc.createdOrder.name 'John'*", "*assert equals oc.createdOrder.orderLine->at(1).name 'shirt'*" and "*assert equals oc.createdOrder.orderLine->at(2).name 'trousers'* " make the attributes *Product::quantityOrdered*, *Order::name*, *Order::eMail* and *OrderLine::name* satisfiable.

3.3 Domain Event Type Satisfiability

Domain event types must be satisfiable too. Domain event type satisfiability comprises the properties of applicability and executability defined in [6, 19]: A domain event type Dev_i is applicable if there is a consistent IB state and one instance *d* of Dev_i with a set of characteristics such that the event constraints are satisfied, and Dev_i is executable if Dev_i is applicable and the effects of *d* leave the IB in a state that is consistent and satisfies the event postconditions.

The satisfiability of a domain event type Dev_i can be checked by means of testing. The idea is to set up a test case TC_j such that it:

- builds a state of the IB, and
- creates an instance *d* of Dev_i, and
- asserts the occurrence of *d*.

If the test set includes such test case TC_j, and its execution gives the verdict *Pass*, then it is experimentally proved that Dev_i is satisfiable: applicable (because the initial IB state has been found consistent and the event constraints have been satisfied) and executable (because the new IB state has been found consistent and the event postconditions have been satisfied).

The test program of Fig. 3 exercises the valid execution of all the domain events considered in the example (see Sect. 2.1) and this ensures that these domain events are satisfiable.

If a conceptual schema includes a domain event type Dev_i that is unsatisfiable, then the conceptual modeler will be unable to set ups a test case that builds a state of the IB, creates an instance of Dev_i and asserts its occurrence. Again, this is not formal proof that Dev_i is unsatisfiable, but in many practical cases it provides a clue that helps to uncover a faulty constraint.

For example, related to the schema of Fig. 2, assume that there is a domain event type *RemoveOrder*, whose intended effect is to remove the order to which it is associated. If one of the constraints of the event is:

```
context RemoveOrder::thereAreNoOrderLines ():Boolean
  body: self.order.orderLine->isEmpty()
```

then *RemoveOrder* is not applicable, because an instance of *Order* is always associated with at least one instance of *OrderLine*. Any assertion of the occurrence of an instance of *RemoveOrder* will *Fail*, and the conceptual modeler will find out that either the above event constraint or the cardinality constraint of Fig. 2 is incorrect.

4 Conclusion

We have shown that when conceptual schemas can be tested then their satisfiability can be proved by testing. The idea is that for each entity or relationship or event type in the schema the conceptual modeler sets up a test case such that if its verdict is *Pass* then by definition the type under test is satisfiable. A single test case may prove the satisfiability of several types. If a type is unsatisfiable then the conceptual modeler is unable to set up such a test case, but in many practical cases testing provides a clue that helps to uncover the faulty schema elements.

References

1. Berardi D, Calvanese D, De Giacomo G (2005) Reasoning on UML class diagrams. Artificial Intelligence 168(1–2):70–118
2. Booch G, Rumbaugh J, Jacobson I (2005) The unified modeling language reference manual, 2nd edn. Addison-Wesley, Reading, MA
3. Brambilla M, Tziviskou C (2009) An online platform for semantic validation of UML models. In: Proceedings of ICWE 2009. LNCS, vol 5648. Springer, Heidelberg, pp 477–480
4. Calvanese D, Lenzerini M (1994) On the interaction between ISA and cardinality constraints. In: Proceedings of ICDE 1994, IEEE Computer Society, Washington, DC, pp 204–213
5. Clavel M, Egea M, de Dios MAG (2009) Checking unsatisfiability for OCL constraints. In: Proceedings of OCL workshop MODELS 2009. http://modeling-languages.com/events/OCLWorkshop2009/papers/3.pdf. Accessed 20 Feb 2010
6. Costal D, Teniente E, Urpí T, Farré C (1996) Handling conceptual model validation by planning. In: Proceedings of CAiSE 1996. LNCS, vol 1080. Springer, Heidelberg, pp 255–271
7. Formica A (2003) Satisfiability of object-oriented database constraints with set and bag attributes. Info Systems 28(3):213–224
8. Gogolla M, Kuhlmann M, Hamann L (2009) Consistency, independence and consequences in UML and OCL models. In: Proceedings of TAP 2009. LNCS, vol 5668. Springer, Heidelberg, pp 90–104
9. Halpin TA (2001) Information modeling and relational databases. Morgan Kaufmann, New York
10. Jarrar M (2007) Towards automated reasoning on ORM schemes. In: Proceedings of ER 2007. LNCS, vol 4801. Springer, Heidelberg, pp 181–197
11. Olivé A (2007) Conceptual modeling of information systems. Springer, Berlin
12. Olivé A, Raventós R (2006) Modeling events as entities in object-oriented conceptual modeling languages. Data Knowl Eng 58(3):243–262
13. OMG (2006) Object constraint language. Version 2.0, formal/2006-05-01. http://www.omg.org/spec/OCL/2.0/. Accessed 20 Feb 2010
14. Parsons J, Wand Y (1997) Choosing classes in conceptual modeling. Commun ACM 40(6):63–69
15. Pastor O, Molina JC (2007) Model-driven architecture in practice. Springer, Heidelberg
16. Pernici B, Barbic F, Maiocchi R, Fugini MG, Rames JR, Rolland C (1989) C-TODOS: an automatic tool for office system conceptual design. ACM Trans Inf Syst 7(4):378–419
17. Queralt A, Teniente E (2006) Reasoning on UML class diagrams with OCL constraints. In: Proceedings of ER 2006. LNCS, vol 4215. Springer, Heidelberg, pp 497–512

18. Queralt A, Teniente E (2008) Decidable reasoning in UML schemas with constraints. In: Proceedings of CAiSE 2008. LNCS, vol 5074. Springer, Heidelberg, pp 281–295
19. Queralt A, Teniente E (2009) Reasoning on UML conceptual schemas with operations. In: Proceedings of CAiSE 2009. LNCS, vol 5565. Springer, Heidelberg, pp 47–62
20. Rolland C, Richard C (1982) The REMORA methodology for information systems design and management. In: Olle TW, Sol HG, Verrijn-Stuart AA (eds) Information systems design methodologies: a comparative review. North-Holland, Amsterdam, pp 369–426
21. Rolland C, Cauvet C (1992) Trends and perspectives in conceptual modelling. In: Loucopoulus P, Zicari R (eds) Conceptual modeling, databases and CASE: an integrated view of information systems development, Wiley, pp 27–48
22. Rolland C, Cauvet C, Nobecourt P, Proix C, Coligon P, Lingat JY, et al (1988) The Rubis system. In: Olle TW, Verrijn-Stuart AA, Bhabuta L (eds) Computerized assistance during the information systems life cycle, North-Holland
23. Souveyet C, Rolland C (1990) Correction of conceptual schemas. In: Proceedings of CAiSE 1990. LNCS, vol 436. Springer, Heidelberg, pp 152–174
24. Tort A (2007) The osCommerce conceptual schema. http://guifre.lsi.upc.edu/OSCommerce.pdf. Accessed 20 Feb 2010
25. Tort A (2009) A basic set of test cases for a fragment of the osCommerce conceptual schema. Research report LSI-09-34-R, UPC. http://www.lsi.upc.edu/~techreps/files/R09-34.zip
26. Tort A, Olivé A (2010) An approach to testing conceptual schemas. Data Knowl Eng. doi:10.1016/j.datak.2010.02.002. Accessed 20 Feb 2010
27. Van Lamsweerde A (2009) Requirements engineering: from system goals to UML models to software specifications. Wiley, New York

A Systematic Approach to Define the Domain of Information System Security Risk Management

Éric Dubois, Patrick Heymans, Nicolas Mayer, and Raimundas Matulevičius

Abstract Today, security concerns are at the heart of information systems, both at technological and organizational levels. With over 200 practitioner-oriented risk management methods and several academic security modelling frameworks available, a major challenge is to select the most suitable approach. Choice is made even more difficult by the absence of a real understanding of the security risk management domain and its ontology of related concepts. This chapter contributes to the emergence of such an ontology. It proposes and applies a rigorous approach to build an ontology, or domain model, of information system security risk management. The proposed domain model can then be used to compare, select or otherwise improve security risk management methods.

1 Introduction

During the last two decades, the impact of security concerns on the development and exploitation of Information Systems (IS) never ceased to grow, be it in public or private sectors. In this context, security Risk Management (RM) has become paramount because it helps companies identify and implement security requirements in a cost-effective manner. Indeed, security threats are so numerous that it is outright impossible to act on all of them, because (1) every technological security solution has a cost, and (2) companies have limited resources. Hence, companies need assurance that they adopt only solutions that will provide significant Return on Investment (ROI). This is done by comparing the cost of a solution with the risk of not using it, e.g., the cost of a business disruption due to a successful security attack. In this sense, security RM plays an important role in the alignment of a company's business strategy with its Information Technology (IT) strategy.

É. Dubois (✉)
Centre de Recherche Public Henri Tudor, 29, avenue John F. Kennedy,
L-1855 Luxembourg-Kirchberg, Luxembourg
e-mail: eric.dubois@tudor.lu

S. Nurcan et al. (eds.), *Intentional Perspectives on Information Systems Engineering*,
DOI 10.1007/978-3-642-12544-7_16,

Today there exist literally hundreds of IS Security RM (ISSRM) methods and standards targeted to professionals (see Sect. 3.2 for an overview). They mainly consist of process guidelines that help identify vulnerable assets, determine security objectives, and assess risks as well as define and implement security requirements to treat the risks. By using these methods one reduces the losses that might result from security problems. However, these methods generally offer very little modelling support. Instead, they usually resort to informal documentation in natural language and ad hoc diagrams. This means that powerful abstraction mechanisms, visualisations and automations offered by conceptual modelling techniques are underexploited.

On the contrary, the Requirements Engineering (RE) literature features a number of modelling languages specifically dedicated to security-sensitive contexts.Examples of such languages are Misuse Cases [51] and Abuse Cases [42], which extend Use Cases [7]; Abuse Frames [31–33] derive from Problem Frames [27]; Secure-Tropos [17, 46, 47] originates from Tropos [4] and *i** [57]; KAOS [30] was also extended [29] to deal with security aspects. The main benefit of these languages is to address security concerns in the early phases of IS development. This allows enforcing security *by construction*, which is more effective than doing it after the fact [48]. However, it turns out that these languages lack constructs to properly represent risk, e.g., vulnerable assets, their associated security risks and risk treatments (with the notable exception of [2] which supports a more general notion of risk). Hence, although these languages are useful in eliciting and modelling threats and countermeasures, they are still largely unable to address cost-effectiveness concerns in a satisfactory manner.

These observations could be used as arguments in favour of defining a new, more suitable modelling language. However, defining a completely new notation does not appear to us as a viable option for at least two reasons. Firstly, this would only further populate the already overcrowded jungle of modelling languages. Secondly, we aim at a smooth rather than radical transition from current practice. Existing languages address different complementary views (e.g., scenario-oriented view, goal-oriented view...), all potentially useful for RE. ISSRM actually crosscuts those views and should therefore be related to them. So, as long as this does not make the languages too complex, we rather plead in favour of improving existing languages with a better coverage of the ISSRM domain.

In this chapter, we do not go as far as proposing an extension to an existing language. Instead, we describe an intermediate step which is concerned with answering the following research question: *What are the concepts that should be present in a modelling language supporting ISSRM during the early stages of IS development?* In this, we follow a similar approach as those pioneers who designed IS modelling languages back in the eighties [49, 50]: first identify the key concepts of the subject domain, then design (or adapt) a language to support it.

The remainder of this chapter is structured as follows. Section 2 presents the research method that we have followed for answering this question. In Section 3 we introduce the basic definitions associated with security and risk management and present our survey of the literature. Section 4 proposes a synthesis of the surveyed literature by means of a concept alignment table. The latter is further consolidated into a domain model for ISSRM presented in Sect. 5. Section 6 finishes our work with conclusions.

2 Research Method

Our overall research method (see Fig. 1) consists of four steps:

Step 1 – Concept alignment. We start by investigating the state of the art in ISSRM. Our goal is to identify the core concepts of the domain and harmonise the terminology. The main outcomes are:

- A *concept alignment table* that highlights the core concepts of the surveyed approaches and indicates synonymy or other semantic relationships when approaches use different terms;
- A *glossary* of the terms as found in the sources.

An excerpt of the table is shown in Table 1 (the complete table can be found in [38]). To obtain a comprehensive view of ISSRM approaches, we consider four

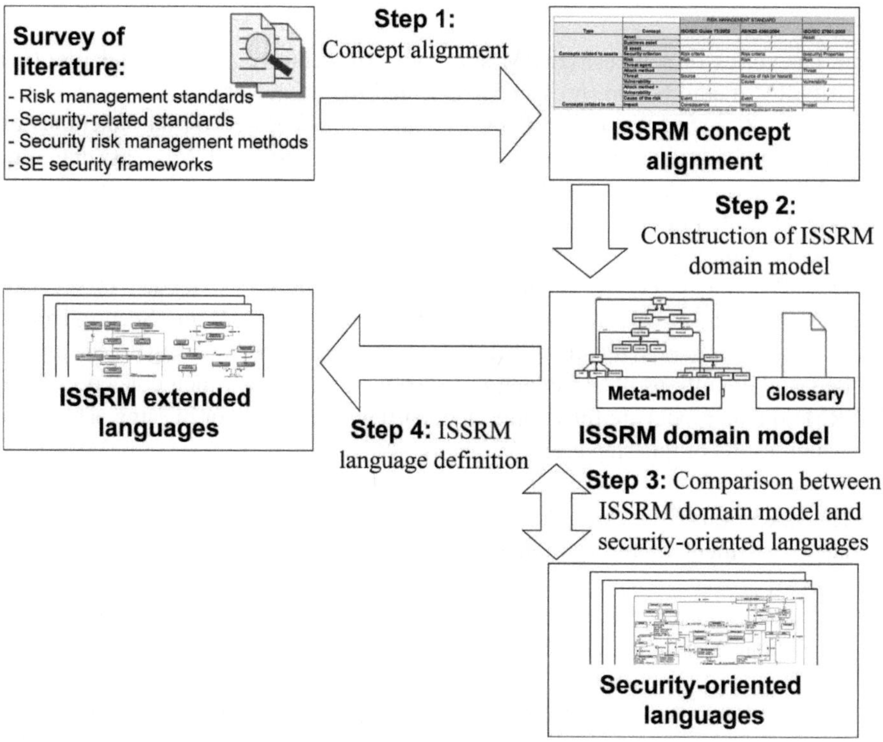

Fig. 1 Research method

Table 1 Alignment of five concepts

References	(1)	(2)	(3)	(4)	(5)
ISO/IEC Guide 73	Risk	Event	Consequence	/	/
AS/NZS 4360	Risk	Event	Consequence Impact	/	/
ISO/IEC 27001	Risk	/	Impact	Threat	Vulnerability
ISO/IEC 13335	Risk	/	Harm	Threat	Vulnerability
Common Criteria	Risk	Threat	Consequence	/	Vulnerability
NIST 800-27 NIST 800-30	Risk	/	Impact	Threat	Vulnerability
EBIOS	Risk	Cause	Impact	/	Vulnerability
MEHARI	Risk Risk scenario	/	Consequence	/	/
OCTAVE	Risk	/	Impact Consequence	Threat	Vulnerability
CRAMM	Risk	/	Loss	Threat	Vulnerability
CORAS	Risk	/	Unwanted incident	Threat scenario	Vulnerability
Haley et al. Moffet and Nuseibeh	Risk	/	Impact	Threat	Vulnerability
Firesmith	Risk	/	Harm	Hazard Threat	Vulnerability

main categories of sources: (*i*) RM standards, (*ii*) security-related standards, (*iii*) security RM methods, and (*iv*) security-oriented RE frameworks.

Step 2 – Construction of the ISSRM domain model. Based on the outcomes of step 1, we define a conceptual model of the ISSRM domain as a UML class diagram, complemented with a glossary obtained by reusing and, when needed, improving the most relevant definitions we found.

Step 3 – Comparison between ISSRM domain model and security-oriented languages. Prominent security-oriented RE languages (KAOS extended to security [29], Abuse Frames [31], Misuse Cases [51], Abuse Case [42] and Secure-Tropos [47]) are confronted with the ISSRM domain model. We investigate the meta-models and definitions of those languages, trying to find out which concepts of the ISSRM domain model are fully supported, partially supported or missing. The main expected results of this step are:

- The validation of the claim that those RE languages overlook RM;
- The assessment of the coverage of each modelling language with respect to ISSRM;
- The identification of the improvements (extensions or revisions) required to make the languages suitable for ISSRM.

Step 4 – Definition of ISSRM language support. As mentioned in the introduction, our final goal is to provide ISSRM-compliant versions of common RE languages. Our aim is to do so by meeting the highest standards in conceptual language definition [20, 45]. Steps 1–3 are intended to guarantee sound and agreed conceptual foundations. But these are not the only criteria. Hence, step 4 will also address the formal definition of syntax and semantics, which facilitates unambiguous interpretation and automated reasoning. We will also take into account "softer", but equally important properties, such as appropriateness of the graphical symbols and structuring mechanisms.

Further motivations for this research method can be found in [11, 40, 41]. The reader should also note that although this process looks rather sequential, steps 1–4 are meant to be conducted in an iterative and incremental way. In this chapter we focus on the first two steps. In the conclusion, we report on the progress made with steps 3 and 4.

3 Survey of the Literature

The survey of the literature is divided into three parts. The first part (Sect. 3.1) delimits the scope of our survey and provides some basic definitions. The second part (Sect. 3.2) is concerned with ISSRM standards, methods and studies. These sources are used as foundations for the ISSRM domain model (which will be described in Sect. 5). The third part (Sect. 3.3) surveys the security-oriented modelling languages. Those are candidate for comparison and extension according to the ISSRM domain model. However, such comparisons and extensions are out of the scope of the present chapter.

3.1 Scope of the Survey and Basic Definitions

The most generally agreed upon definition of risk is the one found in ISO/IEC Guide 73. There, a risk is defined as a "combination of the probability of an event and its consequence" [22]. Following this definition, RM is defined as "coordinated activities to direct and control an organisation with regard to risk" [22]. Depending on the context, RM can address various kinds of issues [24, 54]. For example, risks can be related to the organisation's management (e.g., illness of a key person in regards to the business), finance (e.g., related to investment), environment (e.g., pollution), or security.

In our research, we focus only on *security* RM. Other kinds of risks, such as financial or project risk, are deemed out of scope. The common denominator of the ISSRM approaches is the fact that there are security objectives to reach (or security properties to respect) to ensure reasonable protection of the organisation's assets. Assets are generally defined as anything that has value to the organisation, and thus needs to be protected. However, we will always look at assets related to an organisation's IS, that is, "[a] system, whether automated or manual, that comprises people, machines, and/or methods organized to collect, process, transmit, and disseminate data that represent user information" [56]. Thus, in a given IS context, assets may include hardware, software and network as well as people and facilities playing a role in the IS and therefore in its security, e.g., people encoding data, and arguably such things as air conditioning of a server room. All of these are subject to risks and those risks have to be evaluated with respect to the IS properties that could be damaged. Those properties include *confidentiality*, *integrity* and *availability* of information and/or processes in an organisation [23]:

- *Confidentiality* is the property that information is not made available or disclosed to unauthorised individuals, entities, or processes.
- *Integrity* is the property of safeguarding the accuracy and completeness of assets.
- *Availability* is the property of being accessible and usable upon demand by an authorised entity.

Some other criteria like authenticity, non-repudiation or accountability [23] might be added when the context requires, but they are usually deemed secondary. Summing up, the objective of ISSRM is to protect essential constituents of an IS, from all harm to their security (confidentiality, integrity, availability).

3.2 Risk Management Standards, Methods and Studies

The first family of sources that we review are *RM standards*. Those documents typically contain general considerations about RM and form the basis upon which domain-specific RM approaches are built.

- ISO/IEC Guide 73 [22]: This guide defines the RM vocabulary and guidelines for use in ISO standards. It mainly focuses on terminology, which is of great interest with respect to our research method.
- AS/NZS 4360 [3]: This joint Australian/New-Zealand standard provides a generic guide for RM. The document proposes an overview of the RM terminology and process.

The second family of sources consists of (IS and IT) *security standards*. The selected documents often contain a section on security-specific terminology. Sometimes, some RM concepts are mentioned.

- ISO/IEC 27001 [25]: The purpose of this standard is to act as a reference for establishing, implementing, operating, monitoring, reviewing, maintaining and improving an Information Security Management System (ISMS), that is the part of an organisation that is concerned with information security. The principles and terminology related to IS Management System are provided.
- ISO/IEC 13335-1 [23]: This standard is the first of the ISO/IEC 13335 guidelines series that deals with the planning, management and implementation of IT security. It describes concepts and principles of IT security that may be applicable to different organisations.

- Common Criteria [8]: "Common Criteria" (standardised in version 2.3 by ISO/IEC 15408) provides a common set of requirements on the security functions of IT products and systems, and on assurance measures applied to them during a security evaluation. The first part, entitled "Introduction and general model", is the most relevant with respect to our research scope.
- NIST 800-27 Rev A [53]/NIST 800-30 [52]: Among the series of publications proposed by NIST, the 800-series is about computer security. In this series, NIST 800-27 and NIST 800-30 are in our scope. Terminology and concepts are provided by these standards, which are consistent with each other.

Risk management methods are the third family of sources. In 2004, a CLUSIF[1] study inventoried over 200 security RM methods. We select a representative subset of RM methods based on some recent studies, like the report "Inventory of risk assessment and risk management methods" [13] from ENISA. Most of these methods are supported by software tools, but we will concentrate on their methodological part.

- EBIOS [9] The EBIOS method is developed and maintained by the ANSSI in France.
- MEHARI [6] MEHARI is a RM method developed by the CLUSIF and built on the top of two other RM methods: MARION [5] and MELISA [10], not maintained anymore.
- OCTAVE [1]: OCTAVE is an approach to information security risk evaluation developed by the SEI.
- CRAMM [21]: CRAMM is a RM method from the UK, originally developed by CCTA in 1985 and currently maintained by Insight Consulting.
- CORAS [55]: CORAS is the result of a European project that developed a tool-supported framework for risk assessment of security-critical systems.

Finally, the last family consists of *security frameworks* proposed in the scientific literature. Whereas the previous sources were practitioner-oriented, these are more research-oriented. They originate essentially from the RE literature.

- Haley et al. [18, 19] and Moffett and Nuseibeh [44] propose a framework for dealing with security requirements.
- Firesmith [15, 16] presents a set of related information models that provides the theoretical foundation underlying safety and security engineering. A process to effectively deal with both safety and security engineering is also proposed.

A final remark is about SQUARE [43], a stepwise methodology for eliciting, categorising, and prioritising security requirements for IT systems and applications. Although SQUARE is focussed on security RE and suggests using an ISSRM approach to elicit security requirements, it was not retained in this survey because the first step of SQUARE consists in defining the terminology to be used in

---

[1] http://www.clusif.asso.fr/en/clusif/present/.

the project. Therefore SQUARE does not rely on a pre-defined terminology that we could use.

3.3 State of the Art of Security-Oriented Modelling Languages

Many security modelling languages, or most often security extensions to existing languages, were developed. Existing approaches based on UML have been enriched with security modelling capabilities. In Misuse Cases [51] and Abuse Cases [42], which are extensions of "Use Case" diagrams, the focus is on elicitation of new threats and vulnerabilities that could be exploited by malicious actors. SecureUML [35] extends several UML diagrams. The approach focuses on authorisation constraints and its goal is to automatically generate complete access control infrastructures. UMLsec [28] is a UML profile that allows adding security-related information to UML diagrams. Both SecureUML and UMLsec address security at the design level. They, thus, do not focus on business assets and high-level security requirements.

The KAOS goal-oriented framework addresses security concerns by treating attacks as anti-goals [29]. Anti-goals are the attacker's goals and generate obstacles to security goals. Extensions of the *i** goal-oriented framework [57] also address security problems. For instance, Liu et al. [34] represent attacks as tasks with negative contributions to security softgoals. A formalisation of *i** to deal with security issues is proposed in Secure-Tropos [17, 47]. It suggests, first, to extend the concepts and the processes of *i**/Tropos and, then, to integrate techniques such as security reference diagrams and security attack scenarios. Recently, additional work [12] has been done on representing the notion of vulnerability in *i**. Asnar et al. introduced the Tropos Goal-Risk Framework [2] that addresses RM at three different levels, combining together asset, risk, and risk treatment views. However, the Tropos Goal-Risk framework does not focus on IS security, but supports the concept of risk in general, including project management risk and financial risk, for instance. Finally, Problem Frames extensions were also proposed to handle security issues. Anti-requirements were introduced by Abuse Frames [33]. Abuse Frames are used to delimit the scope of a security problem and thereby are meant to facilitate the analysis of threats and vulnerabilities as well as the elicitation of security requirements. In future work, we plan to confront the concepts of these languages with the concepts of the ISSRM domain.

4 ISSRM Concept Alignment

4.1 Concepts to Consider

The first task of the concept alignment phase is to define the range of concepts to study. In [14], a comparison between the concepts used in various security RE methods was proposed. Our work has a different scope, that is, ISSRM. Here, the core concept to consider is *risk*. Yet, risk is not an isolated concept. A risk (i) depends on the *security needs* placed on the IS *assets* and (ii) is the subject of *risk treatments*. These are the concepts that we include in our first iteration on step 1, but our scope is likely to expand along the way. Conversely, specific usages of our concept alignment table could consider only subsets of it if not all concepts are needed.

4.2 Overview of the Alignment Table

In this section, we analyse the concept of *risk* starting from the definitions found in the sources listed in Sects. 3.1 and 3.2. We focussed on RM standards and security standards; RM methods and RE security frameworks are addressed in [38]. Content-wise, we focus on the notion of risk and its associated components. Risk-related metrics [9, 15, 52] like, for example, its value or its likelihood, are currently not considered.

4.2.1 Risk Management Standards

ISO Guide 73 gives the following definition of a risk:

> **Risk:** combination of the probability of an event and its consequence.

AS/NZS 4360 proposes a similar definition in its glossary:

> **Risk:** the chance of something happening that will have an impact on objectives
> NOTE 1: A risk is often specified in terms of an event or circumstance and the consequences that may flow from it.

Both sources indicate that a risk is composed of two related elements: a cause, called event or "something happening"; and a consequence, also called impact. This consideration is valid in all risk-related domains. To refine our analysis, we compare the above definitions with the ones from the security domain.

4.2.2 Security Related Standards

In ISO/IEC 27001 [25], the concept of risk is not present in the glossary, but in an excerpt of the standard presenting the risk identification step, we find:

> Identify the **risks**.
>
> 1) Identify the assets within the scope of the ISMS, and the owners of these assets.
> 2) Identify the threats to those assets.
> 3) Identify the vulnerabilities that might be exploited by the threats.
> 4) Identify the impacts that losses of confidentiality, integrity and availability may have on the assets.

In ISO/IEC 13335 [23], a risk is defined in the glossary in terms of three related concepts:

> **Risk:** the potential that a given threat will exploit vulnerabilities of an asset or group of assets and thereby cause harm to the organization.

The analysis of both sources [23, 25], and mainly the definition from [23] which is more explicit than the succession of steps presented in [25], shows that these definitions of a risk are compliant with RM standards, because a risk is always composed of a *cause* and a *consequence*. However, the definitions introduce some new concepts: the cause of the risk is presented as the combination of *threat* and *vulnerability*, and the *consequence* is considered as the *impact* or *harm* (see Table 1). The concept of *asset*, which is not analysed in depth in this section, is also introduced as related to the notion of risk. It is defined as anything that has value to the organisation [23]. Common Criteria (CC) [8] defines risk with a finer granularity:

> Threats are categorised as the potential for abuse of protected assets. The CC characterises a threat in terms of a threat agent, a presumed attack method, any vulnerabilities that are the foundation for the attack, and identification of the asset under attack. An assessment of **risks** to security would qualify each threat with an assessment of the likelihood of such a threat developing into an actual attack, the likelihood of such an attack proving successful, and the consequences of any damage that may result. A threat shall be described in terms of an identified threat agent, the attack, and the asset that is the subject of the attack. Threat agents should be described by addressing aspects such as expertise, available resources, and motivation. Attacks should be described by addressing aspects such as attack methods, any vulnerabilities exploited, and opportunity.

Here the cause of the risk is called threat and it encompasses vulnerability, unlike [25] and [23] that define them as related, but separate concepts at the same level. The threat in [8] has multiple sub-components like *threat agent, attack method, attack*, etc. Details of those sub-components can be found in [40]. Threat in ISO/IEC 27001 or ISO/IEC 13335 has thus not the same sense as threat in CC, which is equivalent to the global cause of the risk, encompassing threat and vulnerability. Threat from [23, 25] and threat from [8] are thus not aligned in Table 1. NIST standards also propose a different definition for a risk [52, 53]:

> **Risk:** The net mission/business impact considering (1) the likelihood that a particular threat source will exploit, or trigger, a particular information system vulnerability and (2) the resulting impact if this should occur.

Here, risk is once again defined with the help of three components: *threat source, vulnerability* and *impact*. The concept of threat is defined as the combination of a threat source, its motivation (for human threat) and threat actions, like hacking, social engineering, or system intrusion [52].

The use of the term risk in security related standards is more precise than in RM standards, but remains compliant with the latter. It is thus a mere specialisation of the term. The concept of risk is therefore aligned between the sources in Table 1. However the precision of the components of a risk increases. The consequence of the risk differs only in how it is named (*consequence*, *impact* or *harm*) but the semantics remains largely the same. However, the cause of the risk is presented as a composition of elements, which are different depending on the sources. Differences and equivalences are shown in Table 1.

The concept of *asset* is often mentioned in the definition of risk found in security related standards. It is sometimes associated with *threat* [25], sometimes with *vulnerability* [23] and sometimes with *attack* [8]. In any case, the concept of *asset* plays a role in the definition of risk and should be linked to it. However, due to page limits, we cannot go into such details here. More details can be found in [38].

5 ISSRM Domain Model

The first step of the method has resulted in an alignment of the ISSRM concepts, found in the literature. The second step of the method includes the construction of the ISSRM domain model, presented in Fig. 2. For each concept of the alignment table, a name is chosen. Then, concepts are linked based on the relationships identified in [39]. A glossary is provided together with the domain model, giving a definition for each of its concepts. In this section we introduce the main concepts and their definitions. They are illustrated by examples related to an architecture engineering company [38]. The ISSRM domain model features three principal groups of concepts: (i) *asset*-related concepts, (ii) *risk*-related concepts, and (iii) *risk treatment*-related concepts.

Asset-related concepts describe what are the important assets to protect, and what are the criteria to guarantee asset security. The concepts are:

Asset – anything that has value to the organisation and is necessary for achieving its objectives. Examples: *technical plan; structure calculation process; architectural competence; operating system; Ethernet network; people encoding data; system administrator; air conditioning of server room.*

Note: This concept is the generalisation of the business asset and IS asset concepts.

Business asset – information, process, skill inherent to the business of the organisation that has value to the organisation in terms of its business model and is necessary for achieving its objectives. Examples: *technical plan; structure calculation process; architectural competence.*

Note: Business assets are immaterial.

IS asset – a component or part of the IS that has value to the organisation and is necessary for achieving its objectives and supporting business assets. An IS asset can be a component of the IT system, like hardware, software or network, but also people or facilities playing a role in the IS and therefore in its security. Examples: *operating system; Ethernet network; people encoding data; system administrator; air conditioning of server room.*

Note 1: IS assets are (with the exception of software) material.

Note 2: Sometimes, for conducting a macroscopic analysis, it is necessary to define a system composed of various IS assets as an IS asset.

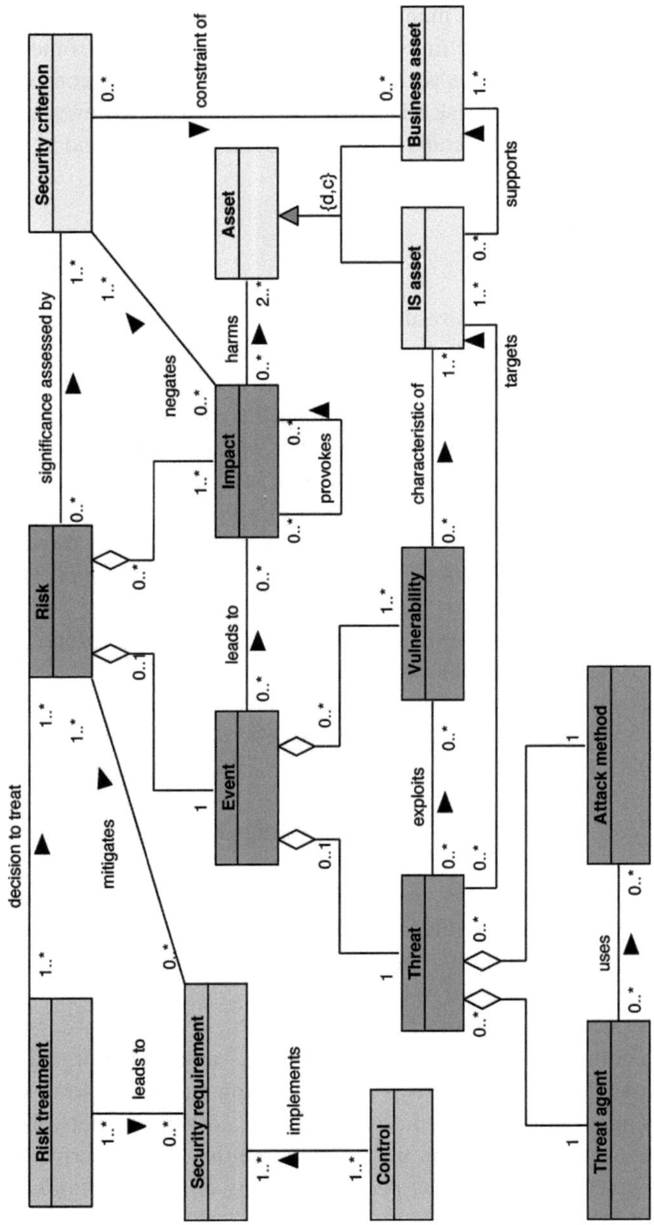

Fig. 2 ISSRM domain model

Security criterion (also called *security property*) – property or constraint on business assets that characterises their security needs. Security criteria act as indicators to assess the significance of a risk. Examples: *confidentiality; integrity; availability; non-repudiation; accountability.*

Note: The security objectives of an IS are defined using security criteria on business assets (e.g., confidentiality of the technical plans; integrity of the structure calculation process).

Our second group of concepts are *risk-related concepts*. They present how the risk itself and its immediate components are defined.

Risk – the combination of a threat with one or more vulnerabilities leading to a negative impact harming one or more of the assets. Threat and vulnerabilities are part of the risk event and impact is the consequence of the risk. Examples: *a hacker using social engineering on a member of the company, because of weak awareness of the staff, leading to unauthorised access to personal computers and loss of integrity of the structure calculation process; a thief entering a company building thanks to deficient physical access control, stealing documents containing sensitive information and thereby provoking loss of confidentiality of technical plans*.

Impact – the potential negative consequence of a risk that may harm assets of a system or an organisation, when a threat (or an event) is accomplished. The impact can be described at the level of IS assets (data destruction, failure of a component, etc.) or at the level of business assets, where it negates security criteria, like, for example, loss of confidentiality of an information, loss of integrity of a process, etc. Examples: *password discovery (IS level); loss of confidentiality of technical plans (business level)*.

Note: An impact can provoke a chain reaction of impacts (or indirect impacts), like for example a loss of confidentiality on sensitive information leads to a loss of customer confidence.

Event – the combination of a threat and one or more vulnerabilities. Examples: *a hacker using social engineering on a member of the company, exploiting weak awareness of the staff; a thief entering a company building thanks to deficient physical access control.*

Note: Event is a generic term, used pervasively in RM and defined as the "occurrence of a particular set of circumstances" [22]. The definition provided in this glossary is specific to IS security.

Vulnerability – the characteristic of an IS asset or group of IS assets that can constitute a weakness or a flaw in terms of IS security. Examples: *weak awareness of the staff; deficient physical access control; lack of fire detection.*

Threat – potential attack, carried out by an agent that targets one or more IS assets and that may lead to harm to assets. A threat is constituted of a threat agent and an attack method. Examples: *a hacker using social engineering on a member of the company; a thief entering a company building and stealing media or documents.*

Threat agent – an agent that can potentially cause harm to assets of the IS. A threat agent triggers a threat and is thus the source of a risk. Examples: *staff members with little technical skills and time but possibly a strong motivation to* *carry out an attack; hacker with considerable technical skills, well equipped and strongly motivated by the money he could make.*

Note: A threat agent can be characterised by expertise, available resources and motivation.

Attack method – standard means by which a threat agent carries out a threat. Examples: *system intrusion; theft of media or documents.*

Risk treatment-related concepts describe what decisions, requirements and controls should be defined and implemented in order to mitigate possible risks. The different risk treatment-related concepts are different levels of design decisions on the IS.

Risk treatment – the decision of how to treat the identified risks. A treatment satisfies a security need, expressed in generic and functional terms, and can lead to security requirements. Categories of risk treatment decisions include:

- *Avoiding* the risk (risk avoidance decision) – decision not to become involved in, or to withdraw from, a risk. Functionalities of the IS are modified or discarded for avoiding the risk;
- *Reducing* the risk (risk reduction decision) – action to lessen the probability, negative consequences, or both, associated with a risk. Security requirements are selected for reducing the risk;
- *Transferring* the risk (risk transfer decision) – sharing with another party the burden of loss from a risk. A third party is thus related to the (or part of the) IS, ensuing sometimes some additional security requirements about third parties;
- *Retaining* the risk (risk retention decision) – accepting the burden of loss from a risk. No design decision is necessary in this case.

Examples: *not connecting the IS to the Internet (risk avoidance); taking measures to avoid network intrusions (risk reduction); taking an insurance for covering a loss of service (risk transfer); accepting that the service could be unavailable for 1 hour (risk retention).*

Note: Risk treatment is basically a shortcut for risk treatment decision, according to the state of the art.

Security requirement – a condition over the phenomena of the environment that we wish to make true by installing the IS, in order to mitigate risks. This definition is inspired from [26]. Examples: *appropriate authentication methods shall be used to control access by remote users; system documentation shall be protected against unauthorised access.*

Note 1: Risk reduction decisions lead to security requirements. Sometimes, risk transfer decisions need some security requirements about third parties. Avoiding risk and retaining risk do not need any security requirement.

Note 2: Each security requirement contributes to cover one or more risk treatments for the target IS.

Control (also called *countermeasure* or *safeguard*) – a designed means to improve security, specified by a security requirement, and implemented to comply with it. Security controls can be processes, policies, devices, practices or other actions or components of the IS and its organisation that act to reduce risks. Examples: *firewall; backup procedure; building guard.*

6 Conclusion

Today, support for security risk management cannot be overlooked anymore, especially during the early phases of IS development. A review of the state of the art indicates that practitioner-oriented standards under-exploit modelling techniques. On the other hand, RE modelling techniques tend to neglect RM, and thereby the cost-effectiveness concerns that are important to practitioners. To improve on this situation, we aim at extending RE languages with ISSRM concepts. In this chapter, we reported on an important step towards this goal: the elaboration of a domain model for ISSRM. This approach is in line with the practices advocated since long time by pioneers of the IS modelling discipline [50].

The proposed domain model extends an earlier version [40]. It consists of a conceptual model (UML class diagram) that highlights the main ISSRM concepts and their relationships, together with their corresponding definitions. Preliminary validation [19] of this domain model has already been performed by practitioners, researchers and standardization experts. We also obtained feedback on usage of the domain model as a teaching artefact for an ISO/IEC 27001 certification. Additionally, encouraging results were also obtained with students involved in a professional Information System Security Management Master programme.

Our on-going work includes enriching the domain model with various metrics commonly used for risk estimation and evaluation [38]. Finally, our current work is progressing according to the steps 3–4 of the research method presented in Sect. 2. With respect to step 3, we started evaluating existing security-oriented RE languages with the intent to later extend them for better supporting ISSRM. At this time, we have analysed KAOS [38], Misuse cases [36] and Secure Tropos [37]. Regarding step 4, en extension of Secure Tropos is under way.

Acknowledgments Thanks to Germain Saval for his help in editing this chapter. And finally, we would like to express our immense gratitude to Colette Rolland for showing us the way.

References

1. Alberts CJ, Dorofee AJ (2001) OCTAVE method implementation guide version 2.0. Carnegie Mellon University, Software Engineering Institute, Pittsburgh, PA
2. Asnar Y, Giorgini P (2006) Modelling risk and identifying countermeasure in organizations. In: Proceedings of the 1st interational workshop on critical information intrastructures security (CRITIS'06), Springer, Berlin, pp 55–66
3. AS/NZS 4360 (2004) Risk management. SAI Global
4. Bresciani P, Giorgini P, Giunchiglia F, Mylopoulos J, Perin, A (2004) TROPOS: an agent-oriented software development methodology. Autonomous Agents Multi-Agent Systems 8:203–236

5. CLUSIF (1998) MARION (Méthodologie d'Analyse des Risques Informatique et d'Optimation par Niveau) available at http://www.clusif.asso.fr
6. CLUSIF (2007) MEHARI 2007: concepts and mechanisms. http://www.clusif.asso.fr/fr/production/ouvrages/pdf/CLUSIF-risk-management.pdf. Last Accessed 21 Feb 2010
7. Cockburn A (2001) Writing effective use cases. Addison-Wesley Longman Publishing Co., Boston, MA, USA
8. Common Criteria version 2.3 (2005) Common criteria for information technology security evaluation, CCMB-2005-08-002. http://www.tse.org.tr/turkish/belgelendirme/ortakkriter/ccpart2v2.3.pdf. Last Accessed 21 Feb 2010
9. DCSSI (2004) EBIOS – expression of needs and identification of security objectives. http://www.ssi.gouv.fr/archive/en/confidence/ebiospresentation.html. Last Accessed 21 Feb 2010
10. Direction des Constructions Navales (1989) MELISA (Méthode d'Evaluation de la Vulnérabilité Résiduelle des Systèmes d'Information). Paris, France
11. Dubois E, Mayer N, Rifaut A, Rosener V (2006) Contributions méthologiques pour l'amélioration de l'analyse des risques. In: Enjeux de la sécurité multimédia (Traité IC2, série Informatique et systèmes d'information). Hermes Science Publications, Paris, pp 79–131
12. Elahi G, Yu E, Zannone N (2010) A vulnerability-centric requirements engineering framework: analyzing security attacks, countermeasures, and requirements based on vulnerabilities. Reqs Eng Journal 15(1):41–62
13. ENISA (European Network and Information Security Agency) (2006) Inventory of risk assessment and risk management methods. http://www.enisa.europa.eu/act/rm/files/deliverables/inventory-of-risk-assessment-and-risk-management-methods. Last Accessed 21 Feb 2010
14. Fabian B, Gürses S, Heisel M, Santen T, Schmidt H (2010) A comparison of security requirements engineering methods. Reqs Eng Journal 15(1):7–40
15. Firesmith DG (2003) Common concepts underlying safety, security, and survivability engineering. CMU/SEI-2003-TN-033 Carnegie Mellon University, Software Engineering Institute, Pittsburgh, PA
16. Firesmith DG (2007) Engineering safety and security related requirements for software intensive systems. In: Companion to the proceedings of the 29th international conference on software engineering (COMPANION'07). IEEE Computer Society, p 169
17. Giorgini P, Massacci F, Zannone N (2005) Security and trust requirements engineering. In: Foundations of security analysis and design III. LNCS, vol 3655. Springer, pp 237–272
18. Haley CB, Laney RC, Moffett JD, Nuseibeh B (2008) Security requirements engineering: a framework for representation and analysis. IEEE Trans Softw Eng 34:133–153
19. Haley CB, Moffett JD, Laney RC, Nuseibeh B (2006) A framework for security requirements engineering. In: Proceedings of the 2nd international workshop on software engineering for secure systems (SESS'06), ACM, pp 35–42
20. Harel D, Rumpe B (2004) Meaningful modeling: what's the semantics of "semantics"? Computer 37:64–72
21. Insight Consulting (2003) CRAMM (CCTA Risk Analysis and Management Method) User Guide version 5.0. SIEMENS
22. ISO/IEC Guide 73 (2002) Risk management – vocabulary – guidelines for use in standards. International Organization for Standardization, Geneva
23. ISO/IEC 13335-1 (2004) Information technology – security techniques – management of information and communications technology security – part 1: concepts and models for information and communications technology security management. International Organization for Standardization, Geneva
24. ISO 14001 (2004) Environmental management systems – requirements with guidance for use. International Organization for Standardization, Geneva
25. ISO/IEC 27001 (2005) Information technology – security techniques – information security management systems – requirements. International Organization for Standardization, Geneva

26. Jackson M (1995) Software requirements & specifications: a lexicon of practice, principles and prejudices. ACM/Addison-Wesley, New York
27. Jackson M (2001) Problem frames: analyzing and structuring software development problems. Addison-Wesley, New York
28. Jürjens J (2002) UMLsec: extending uml for secure systems development. In: Proceedings of the 5th international conference on the unified modeling language (UML'02). LNCS, vol 2460. Springer, pp 412–425
29. van Lamsweerde A (2004) Elaborating security requirements by construction of intentional anti-models. In: Proceedings of the 26th international conference on software engineering (ICSE'04), IEEE Computer Society, pp 148–157
30. van Lamsweerde A, Letier E (2000) Handling obstacles in goal-oriented requirements engineering. IEEE Trans Softw Eng 26:978–1005
31. Lin L, Nuseibeh B, Ince D, Jackson M (2004) Using abuse frames to bound the scope of security problems. In: Proceedings of the 12th IEEE international conference on requirements engineering (RE'04), IEEE Computer Society, pp 354–355
32. Lin L, Nuseibeh B, Ince D, Jackson M, Moffett JD (2003) Analysing security threats and vulnerabilities using abuse frames. Technical report No: 2003/10, Open University
33. Lin L, Nuseibeh B, Ince D, Jackson M, Moffett JD (2003) Introducing abuse frames for analysing security requirements. In: Proceedings of the 11th IEEE international conference on requirements engineering (RE'03), IEEE Computer Society, pp 371–372
34. Liu L, Yu E, Mylopoulos J (2003) Security and privacy requirements analysis within a social setting. In: Proceedings of the 11th IEEE international conference on requirements engineering (RE'03), IEEE Computer Society, p 151
35. Lodderstedt T, Basin D, Doser J (2002) SecureUML: a UML-based modeling language for model-driven security. In: Proceedings of the 5th international conference on the unified modeling language (UML'02), Springer, pp 426–441
36. Matulevičius R, Mayer N, Heymans P (2008) Alignment of misuse cases with security risk management. In: Proceedings of the 3rd international conference on availability, reliability and security (ARES'08), IEEE Computer Society, pp 1397–1404
37. Matulevičius R, Mayer N, Mouratidis H, Dubois E, Heymans P, Genon N (2008) Adapting secure tropos for security risk management during early phases of the information systems development. In: Proceedings of the 20th international conference on advanced information systems engineering (CAiSE'08). LNCS, vol 5074. Springer, pp 541–555
38. Mayer N (2009) Model-based management of information system security risk. PhD thesis, University of Namur
39. Mayer N, Genon N (2006) Design of a modelling language for information system security risk management –elicitation of relationships between concepts and meta-model of each source. Technical report. University of Namur
40. Mayer N, Heymans P, Matulevičius R (2007) Design of a modelling language for information system security risk management. In: Proceedings of the 1st international conference on research challenges in information science (RCIS'07), IEEE Xplore Digital Library, pp 121–132
41. Mayer N, Rifaut, A, Dubois E (2005) Towards a risk-based security requirements engineering framework. In: Proceedings of the 11th international workshop on requirements engineering: foundation for software quality (REFSQ'05), Springer, pp 83–97
42. McDermott J, Fox C (1999) Using abuse case models for security requirements analysis. In: Proceedings of the 15th annual computer security applications conference (ACSAC'99), IEEE Computer Society, pp 55–65
43. Mead NR, Hough ED, Stehney TR (2005) Security quality requirements engineering (SQUARE) methodology. Technical report CMU/SEI-2005-TR-009, ESC-TR-2005-009Carnegie Mellon University – Software Engineering Institute, Pittsburgh, PA
44. Moffett JD, Nuseibeh B (2003) A framework for security requirements engineering. Report YCS 368 Department of Computer Science, University of York, UK

45. Moody DL (2009) Evidence-based notation design: towards a scientific basis for constructing visual notations in software engineering. IEEE Trans Softw Eng 35(6):756–779
46. Mouratidis H, Giorgini P (2010) Extending i* and tropos to model security. In: Yu E, Giorgini P, Maiden N, Mylopoulos J (eds) Social modeling for requirements engineering. MIT (in press), Cambridge, *Massachusetts* (USA)
47. Mouratidis H, Giorgini P, Manson GA, Philp I (2002) A natural extension of tropos methodology for modelling security. In: Proceedings of the agent oriented methodologies workshop (OOPSLA'02)
48. Oladimeji EA, Supakkul S, Chung L (2006) Security threat modeling and analysis: a goal-oriented approach. In: Proceedings of the 10th international conference on software engineering and applications (SEA'06), pp 178–185
49. Olle TW, Hagelstein J, Macdonald IG., Rolland C, Sol HG, Van Assche FJM, Verrijn-Stuart AA (1992) Information systems methodology: a framework for understanding, 2nd edn. Addison-Wesley Longman Publishing Co., Inc. Boston, MA, USA
50. Rolland C (1998) An information system methodology supported by an expert design tool. Elsevier Science, University of Paris
51. Sindre G, Opdahl AL (2004) Eliciting security requirements with misuse cases. Reqs Eng J 10(1):34–44
52. Stoneburner G, Goguen A, Feringa A (2002) NIST special publication 800-30: risk management guide for information technology systems. National Institute of Standards and Technology, Gaithersburg
53. Stoneburner G, Hayden C, Feringa A (2004) NIST special publication 800-27 rev. A: engineering principles for information technology security (a baseline for achieving security). National Institute of Standards and Technology, Gaithersburg
54. The Project Management Institute (2001) Project management body of knowledge www.pmi.org/
55. Vraalsen F, Mahler T, Lund MS, Hogganvik I, den Braber F, Stølen K (2007) Assessing enterprise risk level: the CORAS approach. In: Khadraoui D, Herrmann F (eds) Advances in enterprise information technology security. Idea Group, IGI Global, Hershey, Pennsylvania pp 311–333
56. Wikipedia (2008) Information system definition. http://en.wikipedia.org/wiki/Information_system
57. Yu E (1996) Modelling strategic relationships for process reengineering. PhD Thesis, University of Toronto, Toronto, ON, Canada

Methodologies for Design of Service-Based Systems

Barbara Pernici

Abstract The methodological approaches to service design have started from extensions of conventional design methodologies and are moving towards more specific methods, which consider the complete service life cycle and the flexibility and adaptivity which are inherent in the use of services. In this chapter we discuss how an intentional perspective in service design can be helpful to increase the link between requirements and service construction and to make the development process more systematic.

1 Introduction

The service-oriented approach provides a basis to (re)design business processes for improving business competiveness [1]. In fact, the service-based approach allows developing flexible applications, in which services are composed dynamically to satisfy business goals, taking into account the variability of the context in which services are executed.

Adaptation in the service-oriented paradigm is one of the keywords for realizing flexible services. Adaptation support has been proposed in service-oriented platforms, as a way to support an easier integration of business processes and of existing systems and to provide more flexible and value-added services. Adaptation in services allows varying service execution or service compositions in a process depending on the state of the component services, of the service composition, and of the external context, which might include variable user requirements and variable infrastructural conditions.

B. Pernici (✉)
Politecnico di Milano, Piazza Leonardo da Vinci 32, 20133 Milano, Italy
e-mail: barbara.pernici@polimi.it

S. Nurcan et al. (eds.), *Intentional Perspectives on Information Systems Engineering*,
DOI 10.1007/978-3-642-12544-7_17, © Springer-Verlag Berlin Heidelberg 2010

Adaptivity at the software service level is being studied within the S-Cube[1] (Software Services and Systems) European network of excellence, with the goal of developing advanced design tools and run-time modules which support adaptivity. Service-oriented design has to take into account the fact that software services are strictly related to real world services provided to customers, and that in the consumer perception it is often difficult to separate the software part of a service from the global service provided.

Therefore, coming to service design methodologies, it is more and more important to support the complete service life cycle and to provide methodological guidelines and tools that start from a global consideration of the requirements for the services being designed and developed.

While the initial service-based design methodologies have been derived from consolidated software design methodologies, the need for specific approaches to service design is being developing over time [3, 8].

Yet, even considering the specific characteristics of services during design, most of the proposed methods do not provide specific approaches for the requirements engineering phase.

One emerging approach which proposes linking the requirements engineering phase to the subsequent design phases has been proposed in [6] and further developed in [10], based on the notion of intentions to specify the goals of the business processes in the requirements phases and to design services based on these requirements.

The goal of this chapter is to discuss the specific characteristics of services and service life cycle that motivate different methodological approaches and to illustrate and compare approaches in the first service design phases, focusing on requirements engineering and service design, and on service compositions.

In the following, in Sect. 2 we illustrate the important aspects in designing services and service life cycles, focusing in particular on service compositions. In Sect. 3, we discuss requirements engineering in different service design methodologies, while in Sect. 4 we compare approaches to designing service compositions. Finally, in Sect. 5 future work and possible research directions are presented.

2 Designing Adaptive Services

Service design has been studied from different perspectives and in different research areas. As mentioned in the introduction, the first service design methodologies have been proposed extending the traditional approaches to software development in the literature. In the life cycle illustrated in Fig. 1, which emerged from discussion in the Dagstuhl seminar on Service Oriented Computing [9], some of the characterizing aspects of service development are included. First of all, a provisioning phase is explicitly inserted, thus emphasizing that service provisioning is different from

---

[1] S-Cube project web site: http://www.s-cube-network.eu/.

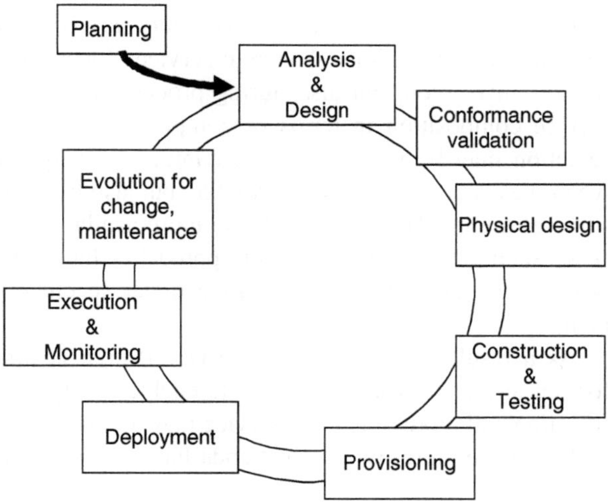

Fig. 1 Service development life-cycle [9]

service deployment and needs to be included in the design phases to guarantee that services are provided according to the requirements also in variable contexts of execution and number of requests. In addition, already in the initial design phases there is a focus on specifying and guaranteeing both functionalities and also the quality of services, and therefore the analysis and logical design phase are followed by a conformance validation phase. Monitoring is essential to guarantee the promised services quality characteristics, but also for evaluating, in the evolution for change phase, whether a service must evolve iterating the design cycle to better guarantee its quality of service, published in service registries and agreed with service consumers [4].

In this chapter, we focus on designing services as service compositions. A service composition is a set of services which are executed according to a number of constraints associated to them. Flexibility during the execution is one of the main characteristics of service compositions.

Most methodological approaches focus on defining an order of execution for services in the service composition, thus creating executable business processes. Service orientation however presents some peculiar characteristics that are fundamental parts of its innovative approach: on one hand, the service composition is not necessarily following a fixed predefined process schema, on the other hand some process characteristics related to the global quality of the service provided by the composed process become important. The quality of service of the process becomes one of its characteristics and the goal of the service provider is to guarantee that the service composition satisfies the promised quality constraints. The service-oriented approach, in order to reach this goal, takes into consideration another important aspect, which distinguishes service compositions from traditional workflow-based processes: the actual services composing the process may vary in different process executions, and also during each of the single executions of the process. In fact, in the literature, there is a distinction between *abstract services*, which compose the process schema, and *concrete services*, which are invoked during process instance executions. Concrete services for a process may be selected before process invocation, but also during process execution, changing dynamically the service composition in terms of component concrete services. Dynamic service selection may be necessary to guarantee global quality constraints, in particular when the execution context is variable, but also to ensure process completion when some of the invoked services are no more available. Concerning adaptivity in process execution, self-management approaches have been proposed for services, in order to guarantee process execution under specified general policies controlling them.

As a result, the objective of service design is first to build process schemas for services compositions, second to enable the dynamic aspects related to service selection and more in general service management.

In the literature, two main trends have emerged in methodologies for process design.

On the hand, the main goal is to design service-based applications starting from consolidated software application design approaches. In [5], the literature is examined comparing approaches that start from a requirements engineering perspective with the ones starting from a business process modelling perspective. In both cases, the goal is to build through a systematic design approach an executable service-based process. While in requirements engineering approaches, process models are derived from the analysis of use cases and scenarios, business process modelling focuses on process modelling notations and on techniques to refine high level business processes into executable processes. Resulting process descriptions may be annotated with quality of service requirements.

However, in these approaches aspects related to the dynamic aspects of service compositions and service management are only marginally considered.

On the other hand, another issue which is considered, e.g. in the methodology developed in [8], is that while a process is considered to be a service composition, the component services and their properties have to be identified and in some case there is a need for developing services to realize the composition. One of the issues studied in this methodological approach concerns the definition of services themselves. In fact, service design is about the identification of the right services, and in their organization in a manageable service hierarchy. Services and their *lifecycle* have to be managed, including their identification, design, development, deployment, discovery, application, evolution, and management. The proposed methodology therefore focuses on defining an iterative and incremental process for service design and development, based on the phases of planning, analysis and design, construction and testing, provisioning, deployment, execution and monitoring. Such phases are related to traditional software development phases, but service identification and construction need to follow specific principles to guarantee that the services are self-contained and easily composable. The main principles are based on *minimizing service coupling* between business processes, on creating highly *cohesive* business processes, on providing services at an appropriate level of *granularity*. These principles are applied throughout the development phases and in particular during the analysis and design phases. The methodology provides general guidelines for service design, while later approaches such as the P2S methodology [2] provide a systematic and algorithmic approach to measure service cohesion and coupling and to derive appropriate granularity levels based on process modelling techniques and the analysis of service interactions to identify candidate services.

However, these approaches, while they focus on specific aspects of service composition, they still lack an analysis at the design time of the dynamic properties which are characteristics of the service approach.

While the first attempts to provide dynamic service composition at run time have been based on managing service invocations to guarantee quality constraints or to heal failures, a more systematic approach to designing service-based application based on an adaptivity paradigm at run time has been proposed within the European S-Cube network on Software Services and Systems. S-Cube is focusing not only on service composition at design time, but also on the adaptive characteristics of service-based approaches at rune time. One of the results of the project is to distinguish clearly among adaptation needs, strategies, and enactment, and to include their consideration during design. In this way the service life-cycle can be extended separating the traditional design phases and the run time service management and adaptation, creating the links between them (see Fig. 2).

In particular, during requirements engineering and design and service construction, the adaptation contexts and strategies need to be defined in conjunction with the service design as described in previous approaches, to enable systematic service adaptation at run time [3]. At run time, to be able to enact adaptation, first adaptation needs are identified, then adaptation strategies are applied.

In the following of the chapter, we focus mainly on the phases which go from the early requirements engineering to service design, considering in particular how the adaptation aspects can be considered at design time to enable run-time adaptation.

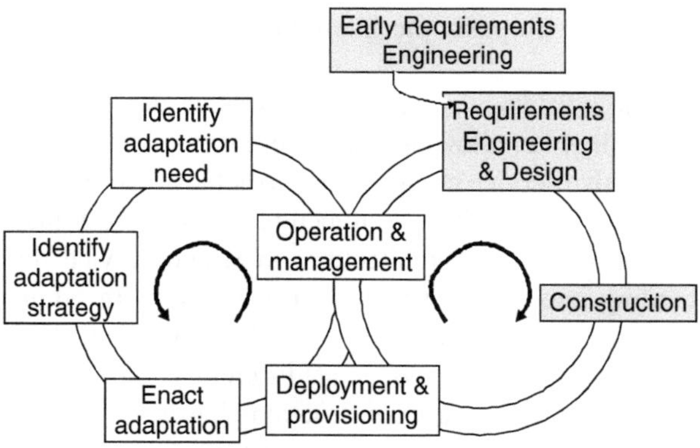

Fig. 2 S-Cube life-cycle of adaptable service-based applications [3]

3 Requirements

In most of the proposed service-oriented design approaches, requirements engineering is the first phase in service design and development. However, in the literature, most authors refer to traditional approaches for this phase.

In the life cycle proposed by Papazoglou [8], the initial phase is the planning phase, in which the business needs are analyzed, the technological landscape reviewed, new requirements are conceptualized and related to existing applications. The planning phase in this proposed approach is very similar to that of traditional software development methodologies.

Also in [5] the adoption of existing approaches in the initial design phase is advocated. Use cases and scenarios are proposed for the initial phases, where initial scenarios are designed and merged and integrated using consolidated techniques. Business process modelling techniques are also considered, but the difficulty of integrating process models in initial phases is analyzed, and process models are described as more adequate for later design stages. However, the use of fragments of process models in conjunction with scenarios might have the advantage of linking scenarios to executable components. Process models can also be annotated with quality of service and information derived from run-time execution which might be useful for composing services at run time. However, while some consideration is given to run-time aspects, there is not a direct link to the run-time adaptation aspects.

An innovative approach for linking business goals and services has been proposed by Colette Rolland and her group, first in [6], then refining this work in [10] to a full fledged service-oriented design approach. The main proposal is to start describing services already in business terms, which makes it easier to transform requirements into executable applications considering the specific characteristics of services and their adaptivity. One of the problems of considering services already in the first design phases is that services are often described in terms of their functionalities, thus focusing on their provided interfaces and operations. The original proposal in [6] is to move from function-driven service oriented computing (SOC) to intention-driven SOC. The intention-driven approach has the advantage of focusing on the purpose, the intention, behind a service, rather than on its functional view.

The advantage of intentional service description is that it allows considering variability, i.e. allowing the representation of alternative variations of a service or alternative service compositions to achieve the same intention.

The classical SOA architecture is therefore transformed in [10] into an ISOA (intentional SOA) architecture, in which service discovery is goal oriented and binding becomes connected to adaptation. In addition, the intention-based service description can be presented at different abstraction levels, thus allowing the description of services at different granularities, which are used then in the subsequent design and construction phases.

In this way, specific characteristics of services illustrated in the previous section can be already considered in the initial design phases, and the derivation of executable processes based on service composition made easier.

Maps are proposed in [10] for modelling intention-driven compositions of services. A central point in this approach is that a service permits the fulfilment of an intention, given an initial situation and terminating in a final situation, when the intention is viewed as a goal for the service (Fig. 3).

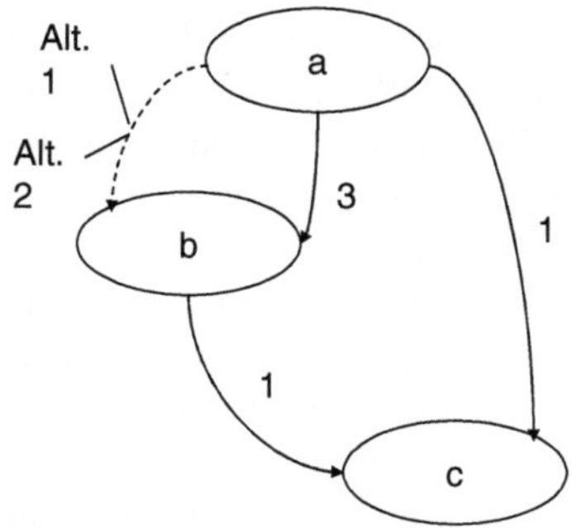

Fig. 3 Business map [10]

A business map allows representing different ways of achieving an intention. An intention can be achieved with several paths in a map from source intentions to targets, and some sections can be mutually exclusive. A hierarchy of maps can be defined to refine business intentions. In this way processes are modelled focusing on intentions and there is no need to focus on "how" a goal is achieved until later stages. Maps are associated with a method to derive intentional services from maps, thus providing an approach which is tailored to the specific characteristics of the service-oriented approach.

4 Designing Service Compositions

The next phase is to derive service compositions that allow the satisfaction of the specified requirements. One of the main goals in this phase is to examine existing services and legacy applications in order to be able to design or redesign processes as compositions of existing services.

In the methodological guidelines of [8], in the analysis phase the objective is to identify aggregations of services in processes and to identify subprocesses to prevent business processes to become unmanageable. Abstract processes are considered in this phase, and a gap analysis is performed to determine which services have to be developed, reused, or repurposed. Only in the design phase granularity and reusability issues are taken into account, as principles for service development. Design is strictly related to service specification, i.e. the ability of representing functional and behavioural aspects of services, as well as policies associated to them. Service compositions are represented with process structures, with abstract process schemas specification, such as in abstract BPEL. Graphical notations can be used in the design phase, such as BPMN. Policies associated to processes and services are mainly in terms of Service Level Agreements (SLA) to specify non-functional concerns, expressed in terms of quality of service constraints.

In synthesis, guidelines are provided to construct abstract process schemas from requirements, taking into consideration the availability of a number of services, possibly derived from a service registry, and annotating the processes with SLAs.

In such an approach the methodological approach to service design prevails, but there is little focus on the potential offered by service-orientation is terms of adaptivity at run time. Some adaptivity is implied by using abstract service descriptions and abstract processes with SLA annotations, however there is a need to better focus on adaptation aspects.

As discussed in the previous section, adaptation can be considered both in the design and in the run-time phases. In the design phase, there is a need to identify adaptive service behaviours and to specify the adaptation strategies that can be applied at run time.

An initial attempt to go in the direction of the life cycle described in [3], is proposed in the PAWS (Processes with Adaptive Web Services) framework proposed in [1]. In PAWS, processes are designed to be adaptive, where adaptation is prepared at design time (Fig. 4).

A process is designed as an abstract process, as proposed in previously illustrated methods, but the choice of the suitable services to be invoked is performed at design time. In fact, for each task a selection of potential services is provided at design time, and interface adaptation and quality of service negotiation for the services

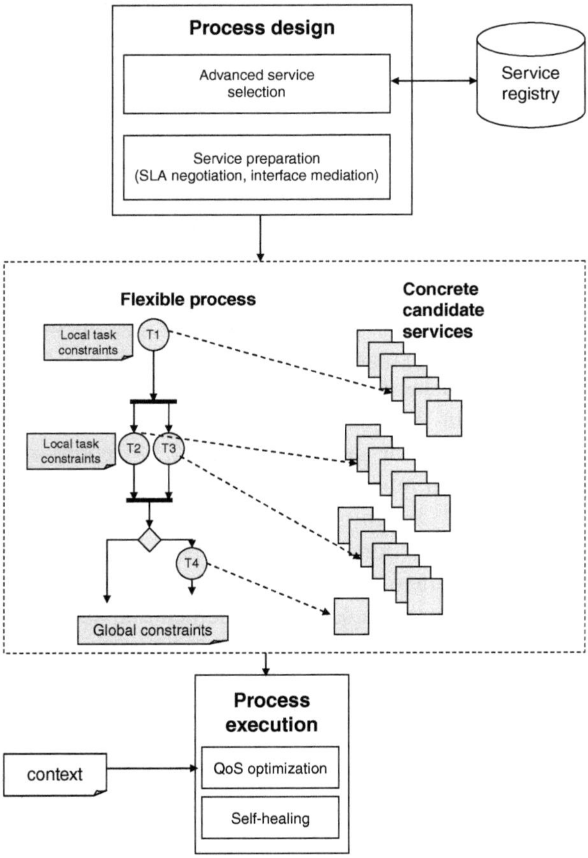

Fig. 4 PAWS, processes with adaptive web services [1]

to be potentially invoked in a process at run time are part of the process design phase.

The process description is annotated with local and global quality of service constraints for the process. In this way, at run time, concrete services can be selected and invoked using QoS optimization techniques, and process self-healing mechanisms can be activated in case of failure.

In this framework, the adaptation may depend also on the context of execution. The context may determine the way in which component services are selected, changing the quality needs for a business process. For instance, the importance of different quality of service dimensions can vary according to the service consumer profile, or also to the context in which the process consumer is operating.

Another direction for designing adaptive processes in the PAWS framework is to extend the process description with variants, thus allowing to model different process fragments which are alternatively selected according to the process and its context of execution. An example is given in Fig. 5, where two different process fragments are defined for different QoS levels.

While service design in PAWS is focused on providing adaptivity mechanisms, it does not provide a way to define different strategies to achieve the process goals through adaptation and to select among strategies at run time, as envisioned in [3].

As seen above, all these approaches have the problem that there is a weak and informal link between requirements expressed in the initial design phase and the following process construction and service specification phases.

The intentional process presented in [10] has instead the advantage of linking goals to processes and then to service design and construction. From the intention maps, compositions of executable services are derived, as shown in Fig. 6.

On the right part of Fig. 6, at the bottom level executable services are represented. The top level represents an agent with controls the achievement of the process goal, while in intermediate levels agents are created to control compositions of services.

As mentioned above, the Maps of [10] do not represent fixed process schemas defined in all details, but allow describing alternative paths and variants. This flexibility can be exploited in operationalizing intentional services into software services.

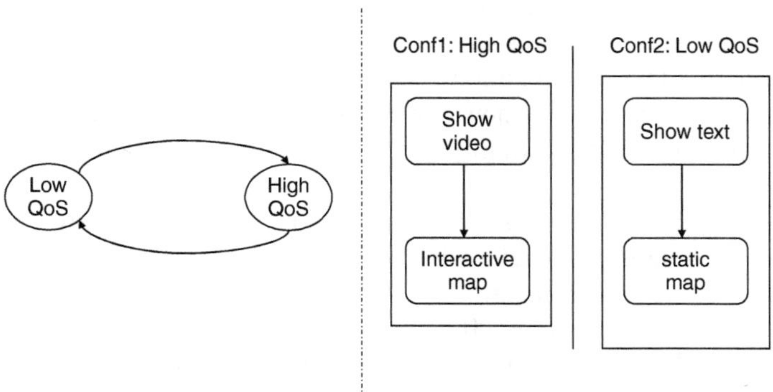

Fig. 5 Context-aware processes [7]

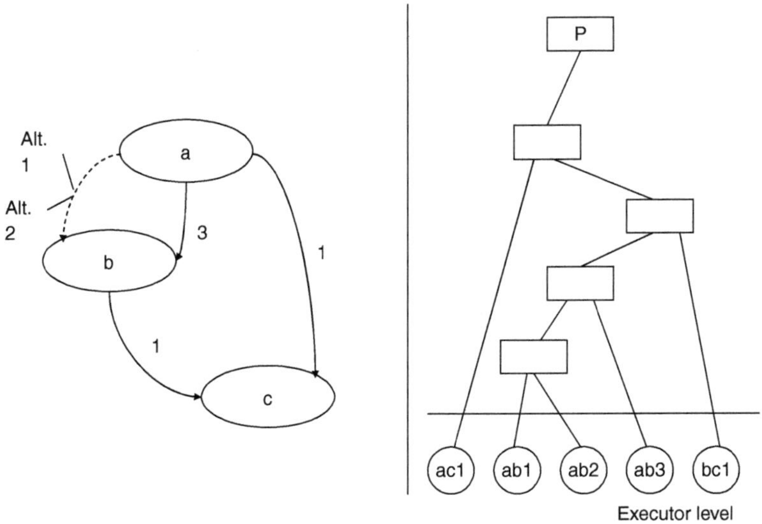

Fig. 6 From intentional maps to enacted services [10]

The intentional services can be mapped to different compositions of services and offer the choice of variants at run time.

As shown in Fig. 6, such variants can be represented in multiple levels, depending on the available alternatives derived from the maps. During execution, a control agent controls the selection and execution of a given composition, which corresponds to a path in a map.

In this way, alternatives available for dynamic service selection at run time are specified, and these alternatives correspond to business goals expressed in the requirements phase.

5 Conclusion

In the present chapter, we discussed some approaches which have been proposed as methodological frameworks for service design.

We illustrated first how traditional software design life-cycles are evolving for service-based applications and how one characteristic aspect of service design is to take into consideration the flexibility of adaptation mechanisms provided by service orientation.

We also discussed how most approaches adopt for service design, in the initial phases of requirements engineering, the same approaches which are applied in traditional software development.

The approach proposed in [10] represents an interesting original research approach which has the goal of preserving the flexibility aspects of services while linking their construction directly to specified requirements, supporting the service construction with a rigorous and formal approach.

Future work should consider this research direction which has the advantage of preserving in service design a general concept of service, linked to business goals, rather than focusing on service-oriented technology already in the initial phases.

Other aspects which have been discussed with respect to adaptivity in this chapter should also be linked to the intentional-based approach.

The quality of service aspects are one of the basis for service selection in related work, and there is a need to relate also business requirements related to quality to service descriptions at the design level, as well as defining the strategies to select the appropriate actions at run time to be able to maintain the quality of service levels specified at design time. The approach of [10], which leaves open the selection of services at run time, could provide a sound basis for adding also QoS considerations at design time in view of run-time adaptation.

Other aspects which should be considered during service design concern the context of use of services. Also in this case the variability elements which can be specified in an intention-based approach can be the basis for defining process variants based on context definition.

Other aspects which need more consideration in IT service-based approach are related to the concept of service in general. In fact, IT services are often used within real world services, and it is sometimes difficult to distinguish between the technological and non-technological aspects of service provisioning and service consuming. A holistic approach to service design should also consider general parameters, which, linking requirements to enactment, consider both characteristics of IT services and those of related real world services. Among the elements to be evaluated is the total cost of ownership of services, including all relevant aspects of service in the complete life-cycle, from design to flexible and adaptive service provisioning.

Acknowledgments The research leading to these results has received funding from the European Community's Seventh Framework Programme FP7/2007-2013 under grant agreement 215483 (S-Cube).

References

1. Ardagna D, Comuzzi M, Mussi E, Pernici B, Plebani P (2007) PAWS: a framework for executing adaptive web-service processes. IEEE Softw 24(6):39–46
2. Bianchini D, Cappiello C, De Antonellis V, Pernici B (2009) P2S: a methodology to enable inter-organizational process design through web services. In: Proceedings of CAiSE 2009. LNCS, vol 5565. Springer, Heidelberg, pp 334–348
3. Bucchiarone A, Cappiello C, Di Nitto E, Kazhamiakin R, Mazza V, Pistore M (2009) Design for adaptation of service-based applications: main issues and requirements. In: Proceedings of fifth international workshop on engineering service-oriented applications: supporting software service development lifecycles (WESOA). Springer LNCS Services Science Subline, Heidelberg
4. Cappiello C, Pernici B (2009) Design of repairable processes. In: Cardoso J, van der Aalst W (eds) Handbook of research on business process. IGI Global, 2009
5. Gehlert A, Danylevych O, Karastoyanova D (2009) From requirements to executable processes – a literature study. In: Proceedings of the 5th international workshop on business process design (BPD 2009), Ulm, Germany. Springer LNBIP, Heidelberg

6. Kaabi RS, Souveyet C, Rolland C (2004) Eliciting service composition in a goal driven manner. In: Proceedings of international conference on service oriented computing (ICSOC). ACM, pp 308–315
7. Modafferi S, Benatallah B, Casati F, Pernici B (2005) A methodology for designing and managing context-aware workflows. In: Proceedings of IFIP international conference on mobile information systems, Oslo. Springer IFIP Series
8. Papazoglou MP, Van Den Heuvel W-J (2006) Service-oriented design and development methodology. Int J Web Eng Technol 2(4):412–442
9. Pernici B (2005) 05462 Summary report on "service design and development". Dagstuhl seminar on Service Oriented Computing
10. Colette Rolland, Manuele Kirsch-Pinheiro, Carine Souveyet, An Intentional Approach to Service Engineering, IEEE Transaction of Services Computing, April 2010 (in press), DOI Bookmark: http://doi.ieeecomputersociety.org/10.1109/TSC.2010.26

Quality Assurance in the Presence of Variability

Kim Lauenroth, Andreas Metzger, and Klaus Pohl

Abstract Software Product Line Engineering (SPLE) is a reuse-driven development paradigm that has been applied successfully in information system engineering and other domains. Quality assurance of the reusable artifacts of the product line (e.g. requirements, design, and code artifacts) is essential for successful product line engineering. As those artifacts are reused in several products, a defect in a reusable artifact can affect several products of the product line. A central challenge for quality assurance in product line engineering is how to consider product line variability. Since the reusable artifacts contain variability, quality assurance techniques from single-system engineering cannot directly be applied to those artifacts. Therefore, different strategies and techniques have been developed for quality assurance in the presence of variability. In this chapter, we describe those strategies and discuss in more detail one of those strategies, the so called comprehensive strategy. The comprehensive strategy aims at checking the quality of all possible products of the product line and thus offers the highest benefits, since it is able to uncover defects in all possible products of the product line. However, the central challenge for applying the comprehensive strategy is the complexity that results from the product line variability and the large number of potential products of a product line. In this chapter, we present one concrete technique that we have developed to implement the comprehensive strategy that addresses this challenge. The technique is based on model checking technology and allows for a comprehensive verification of domain artifacts against temporal logic properties.

1 Introduction

Colette Rolland is a world-known leader in the information systems community well known for her significant contributions, among others, in the areas of method engineering [20–22] and goal-oriented requirements engineering [23, 26, 27]. Her

K. Lauenroth (✉)
Software Systems Engineering, University of Duisburg-Essen, Gerlingstraße 16, 45127 Essen, Germany
e-mail: kim.lauenroth@sse.uni-due.de

S. Nurcan et al. (eds.), *Intentional Perspectives on Information Systems Engineering*,
DOI 10.1007/978-3-642-12544-7_18, © Springer-Verlag Berlin Heidelberg 2010

current research interests include software product lines, respectively variability in process lines. Her interest and her valuable contributions to this relatively new field of research [24, 25] is yet another indication that Colette Rolland is a very active, inspiring and trendsetting researcher – even after having reached the retirement.

Software Product Line Engineering (SPLE) is a reuse-driven development paradigm that has been applied successfully in information system engineering [25], business process modeling [24] and other domains [19]. SPLE explicitly addresses reuse by differentiating between two kinds of development processes [19]:

- *Domain engineering*: During this process, the commonality and the variability of the product line is defined. Furthermore, the reusable artifacts, called domain artifacts, are realized which implement the commonalities and provide the variability required to derive the set of intended products. The domain artifacts include, among others, requirements models (e.g., use case diagrams), architectural models (e.g., component or class diagrams) and test models.
- *Application engineering*: This process is responsible for deriving products from the domain artifacts. Application engineering exploits the variability of the domain artifacts by binding (or resolving) variability according to customer and/or market-specific needs.

The central concept for addressing reuse in product line engineering is the definition of product line commonality and variability. *Product line commonality* refers to parts or aspects of the product line that are part of all products of the product line. *Product line variability* describes the possible variation between the products that belong to a software product line in terms of properties and qualities [17, 19].

Early quality assurance is an important issue in every development project. The quality assurance of variability models has received great attention in product line research [28], whereas the comprehensive quality assurance of other artifacts (e.g. requirements, design, or implementation artifacts) is still an open issue. The product line variability constitutes a central challenge for quality assurance of domain artifacts. Quality assurance techniques from single-system engineering cannot be directly applied to domain artifacts, since the domain artifacts contain variability.

In this chapter, we first illustrate the effects of variability on the quality assurance of domain artifacts (Sect. 2). We will then present different strategies that have been developed for the quality assurance of domain artifacts in the presence of variability (Sect. 3). For each strategy, we will discuss the benefits and the involved challenges.

We will then focus on a particular strategy, the so called comprehensive strategy which aims at checking the quality of all possible products of the product line. This strategy offers the highest benefits, since it uncovers the defects in all possible products. However, the central challenge for the comprehensive strategy is the complexity that results from the product line variability and the large number of potential products of a product line.

Since techniques from single system engineering are not applicable, the development of new or adapted techniques is necessary. As an example for possible adaptation, we will present a quality assurance approach for the comprehensive strategy based on model checking technology in Sects. 4 and 5. A conclusion is provided in Sect. 6.

2 Quality Assurance in the Presence of Variability

This section provides a brief introduction to variability modeling which is a prerequisite for understanding the challenges and solutions for quality assurance in product line engineering.

2.1 Introduction to Variability Modeling

The central concepts for defining and documenting the variability of a software product line are variation point and variant. A *variation point* describes what varies between the products of a software product line. A *variant* describes a concrete instance of a variation point. In case of an online shop product line, for example, the products can vary in terms of the supported interfaces. A product of the product line (i.e. a concrete online shop) could then offer an interface for traditional web browsers while another product offers an interface for mobile phone web browsers.

For the documentation of variability in this chapter, we use the Orthogonal Variability Model (OVM) that has been developed in our group and which offers benefits over other variability modeling techniques. In the following, we give a brief introduction into the OVM together with a small example shown in Fig. 1. For a more detailed introduction into the OVM, we refer to [19].

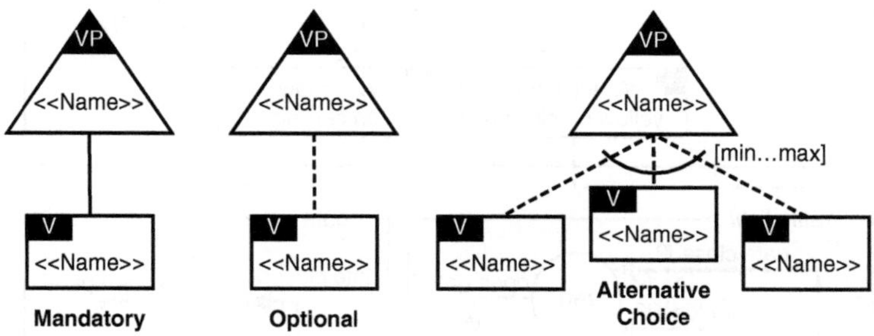

Fig. 1 Graphical notation of the orthogonal variability model

In the OVM, variation points are modeled as triangles and variants as rectangles. We furthermore distinguish three types variability dependencies to document in which way variants of a product line must or can be selected:

- A *mandatory variability dependency* between a variation point and a variant describes that this variant must always be selected when the variation point is considered for the product at hand. A mandatory variability dependency is drawn as a continuous line.

- An *optional variability dependency* between a variation point and a variant describes that this variant can be selected but does not need to be selected. An optional variability dependency is drawn as a dashed line.
- An *alternative choice* is a specialization of optional variability dependencies. An alternative choice group comprises at least two variants which are related to a variation point by optional variability dependencies as shown in Fig. 1. The min, max bounds define how many variants of the alternative choice group must be selected at least (min) and how many variants can be selected at most (max).

In addition to variability dependencies, the OVM allows defining constraint dependencies to document additional dependencies between variation points and variants, e.g. to enforce that two variants of different variation points cannot be selected together.

Variability in the domain artifacts is modeled by using so called artifact dependencies between the elements of the OVM and the domain artifacts. Variants in the OVM are related to variable elements in the reusable artifacts via those artifact dependencies. A simple example of an artifact dependency is shown in Fig. 2 in Sect. 4. Whenever a variant in the OVM is selected for a concrete product, the related elements in the reusable artifacts will be included in the derived artifacts of the product. Elements of the domain artifacts that are not related to a variant in the OVM are considered as a common artifact and are therefore part of every product that is derived.

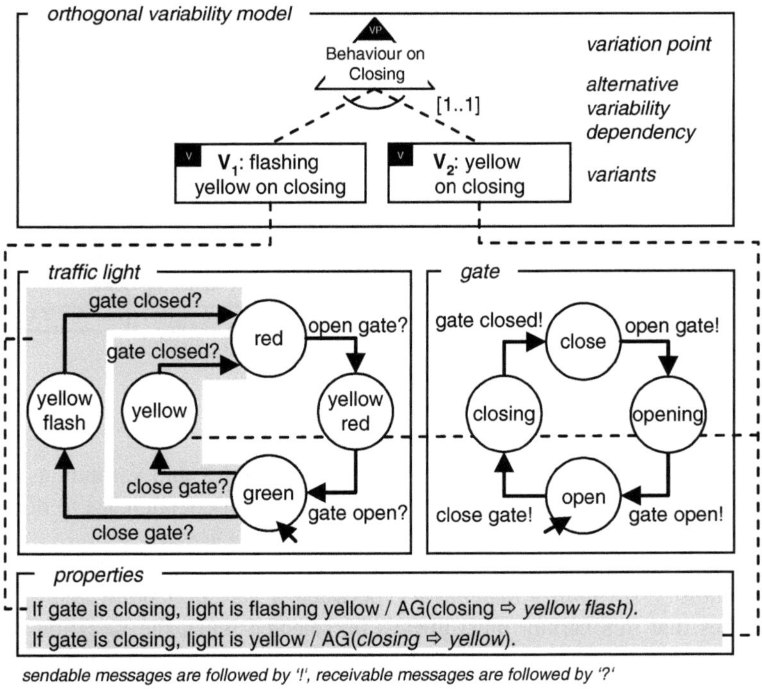

Fig. 2 Simplified example of domain artifacts

2.2 Challenges of Quality Assurance in Product Line Engineering

The overall quality of the product line and its derived products strongly depends on the quality of the domain artifacts. Similar to the development of single software products, defects should be uncovered as early as possible in the SPLE process, as uncovering a fault late in the process can lead to very high correction costs [12]. In product line engineering, this means that defects should be uncovered in domain engineering.

In contrast to the development artifacts that are created in single systems software engineering, the domain artifacts that are created in product line engineering are reused in several products derived from the product line. For instance, a variant can be reused in many different products, or a commonality is reused in all products of the product line. Thus, a high quality of the domain artifacts is desirable. A defect in a domain artifact can affect many products of the product line and thus can become costly to remove, as all those products might have to be corrected [11, 30].

Quality assurance techniques from the development of single software products cannot be applied directly to domain artifacts because these artifacts contain variability. Assume that a domain requirements specification of a product line contains the variable requirement R which is related to the variant v_1 and it contains the variable requirement $\neg R$ which is related to the variant v_2. Using a quality assurance technique from single system development and performing a consistency check of this domain requirements specification would result in the identification of a contradiction, since the requirements R and $\neg R$ cannot be fulfilled together. This means that without the consideration of the variability model, it is not possible to decide whether the detected inconsistency can actually affect any derived product of the product line or not. If the variability model does not allow the combined selection of the variants v_1 and v_2, then the contradicting requirements can never become part of the same specification and therefore will never cause an inconsistency. This simple example already shows that quality assurance techniques for SPLE have to take the product line variability into account.

3 Quality Assurance Strategies in the Presence of Variability

Above, we have shown using a simple example that quality assurance techniques have to take the variability of the product line into account. In order to handle the variability in domain artifacts, quality assurance techniques in domain engineering generally follow three different strategies [15, 18]:

- *Commonality strategy*: Only the common parts shared by all products of the product line are covered by the quality assurance technique.
- *Sample strategy*: The quality assurance technique is applied to sample products that are derived from the product line.
- *Comprehensive strategy*: The quality assurance technique is applied to all possible products of the product line.

In the following, we will discuss these strategies in more detail and present the benefits and challenges for each strategy.

3.1 Commonality Strategy

Quality assurance techniques that follow the commonality strategy aim at checking only the common parts of a software product line. When focusing only on common parts, the variants are typically either (1) ignored during the checking of the reusable artifacts or (2) they are replaced by placeholders that abstract from the variants or simulate them. As an example for the first case, an inspection of a reusable requirements specification for a software product line could focus on common requirements only. As an example for the second case, code fragments of a variant could be replaced by a code fragment that implements some basic behavior or at least guarantees that the code is structurally correct such that it will compile.

The benefits of the commonality strategy are that early testing in domain engineering is enabled and that quality assurance activities can be performed even if no variants have been realized so far.

Techniques that follow the commonality strategy must address the following two challenges:

1. *The effort for creating placeholders has to be kept at a minimum*, since the placeholders are only used for the quality assurance purpose. Creating placeholders usually requires development effort. Thus, the number of placeholders should be kept as small as possible.
2. *An adequate coverage of the domain artifacts has to be guaranteed.* Quality assurance activities should be planned that complement this strategy, since the variants are not covered when following the commonality strategy.

3.2 Sample Strategy

Quality assurance techniques that follow the sample strategy aim at checking a set of sample products of the product line. The basic steps of this strategy are typically as follows:

1. Determine one or more sample products (defined in terms of variants that are selected).
2. For each of the sample products:
   (a) Derive product-specific artifacts by binding the variability in the domain artifacts.
   (b) Apply quality assurance techniques from the single-system development to the derived artifacts.

The benefit of this approach is that existing techniques from single-system development can be used as they are. In order to implement the sample strategy, the following challenges have to be faced:

1. *Selection of representative sample products is necessary.* The sample products should be chosen in such a way that checking those sample products will allow drawing conclusions about the overall quality of the software product line.
2. *Keeping the number of selected sample products manageable.* The number of sample products should be kept as small as possible while guaranteeing a representative coverage of the software product line. Otherwise, the effort for checking the sample products will be infeasible and several redundant checks (e.g. due to commonalities) have to be performed.

3.3 Comprehensive Strategy

The comprehensive strategy aims at ensuring the quality of all potential products of the software product line. A "brute-force" realization [19] of the comprehensive strategy could be as follows:

1. Bind the variability in the reusable artifacts for each of the potential products of the software product line.
2. Apply techniques from the development of single systems to the derived artifacts of each of these products.

The comprehensive strategy is the strategy that leads to the best coverage of the domain artifacts. Although the sample strategy (see the previous sub-section) allows checking all variants of the software product line by determining representative sample products, those variants are not checked in all potential reuse contexts, i.e. they are not checked for all products of the software product line. As an example, it may be the case that v_1 and v_2 have been checked in one sample product and v_2 and v_3 in another sample product and have not exposed any failures, while a product which contains v_1 and v_3 might fail, for instance, due to some undesired feature interactions [16].

Obviously, the number of potential products in a software product line of industry-relevant size prevents any "brute-force" approach from being used for realizing the comprehensive strategy in practice. We illustrate this with a simple example. Assume a set of reusable artifacts that contains 10 variation points each with 2 optional variants. Approximately 1 million possible software products can be derived from these artifacts if there are no further constraints for combining the variants (20 independent variants lead to 2^{20} possible combinations). Industry reports on software product lines with up to tens of thousands of variation points and variants (see [4, 14]) which leads to a much larger set of possible products.

Thus, a significant challenge for realizing the comprehensive strategy is the question how to deal with the complexity that is involved in checking all potential products. One possible approach is to avoid a separate derivation and checking of each product, since checking each product would lead to a large number of redundant checks. Instead, a comprehensive approach should directly check the domain artifacts by taking the variability of the domain artifacts into account. However, the challenge of this approach is to show that every possible product is checked.

In the following section, we present such a comprehensive quality assurance approach that is based on model checking techniques and allows for a comprehensive verification of domain artifacts against temporal logic properties.

4 Towards a Comprehensive Quality Assurance in the Presence of Variability

Automated verification approaches are a common way to address quality assurance in product line engineering [29]. Model checking [2] is a technique for comprehensive quality assurance that facilitates the verification of properties (typically specified in temporal logic, e.g. CTL) of a system (typically specified in a state transition model). In software engineering for single-systems, model checking is an established technique for verifying development artifacts in requirements engineering, design, realization, and test [6] in different domains.

Since product line engineering addresses a set of similar products instead of a single product, model checking of domain artifacts in product line engineering has to be defined as follows:

> Model checking of domain artifacts means to verify that every possible product that can be derived from a domain artifact fulfills the specified properties [10].

In contrast to model checking in single-system development, where a single product is verified against expected properties, model checking in product line engineering has to verify that a whole set of products fulfills the properties specified for each product.

Numerous model checking approaches have been proposed for the verification of single-system specifications [1, 2, 5]. However, model checking approaches from single-system engineering cannot directly be used for the verification of domain artifacts, since they do not consider the variability defined for the product line [9]. We will illustrate this using a simple example.

Figure 2 depicts a simplified example for defining domain artifacts, properties, and the variability of a product line [10]. The example depicts a simplified orthogonal variability model, two I/O-automata and two properties (see [10] for a detailed introduction into the modeling language). The example specifies a simple product line for rail crossing gates which consists of a traffic light and a gate. The traffic light exhibits alternative variable behavior: The traffic light can either show a flashing yellow light or a steady yellow light when the gate is closing. The behavior can be verified with respect to the two variable properties that specify invariants of the product line (the operator AG "always globally" means that these properties must always be fulfilled). The variability is described by the variants of the variability model and by the relationships between the variants and the specification elements.

If one ignores the variability model and applies a model checking approach from single system engineering to the example presented in Fig. 2, the model checking approach would state that both defined properties are not fulfilled by the specified system, since it is possible to reach the states (*yellow flash*, *closing*) and (*yellow*, *closing*) which are counterexamples for the validity of each property.

However, this verification result would be incorrect. The variability model does not allow to derive a product from the domain artifacts for which the property $AG(closing \Rightarrow yellow)$ is specified and which is able to reach the state (*yellow flash*, *closing*), or vice versa for which the property $AG(closing \Rightarrow yellow\ flash)$ is specified and which is able to reach the state (*yellow*, *closing*).

One way to apply model checking approaches from single-system engineering in product line engineering would be to derive every possible product from the domain artifacts and then verify each derived product individually. However, as it has been discussed in Sect. 3.3, such a "brute force" approach is not feasible for product lines of industrial size.

5 Model Checking in the Presence of Variability

In this section, we illustrate the adaptation of a model checking algorithm in order to enable the comprehensive quality assurance of a domain artifact. The verification of the AG operator is shown in [9]. In this chapter, we focus for illustration purpose on the next-time-operator ($EX f_1$) which can be verified easily for single system and only requires minor adaptation for the verification of domain artifacts. The next-time-operator, $EX f_1$ evaluates to true, if there is one path starting at the initial state on which f_1 holds on the next state.

The presented approach is based on the model checking approach from Clarke et al. [2] which is considered as one of the fundamental approaches for model checking. The main idea of the approach is to include the variability information specified in the variability model (as Boolean variables) in the model checking algorithms. During the exploration of the state space, the algorithms consider the variability model to ensure that the current path explored in the state space is valid with respect to the variability model. Algorithms for the verification of other properties are presented in [10].

5.1 Formal Foundations

In this section, we give a brief introduction into the formal foundations of our approach. To reason about the variability model of a product line, the variability model is formalized as follows:

- Each variant of the variability model is represented as a Boolean variable v_i, which evaluates to *true* if the corresponding variant is included in the derived product under consideration.
- The set of all such Boolean variables of an OVM is called V.
- The constraints of the variability model are formalized by a Boolean expression OVM(v) over the variables in V. OVM(v) evaluates to *true* for each valid product of the software product line, i.e., OVM(v) only evaluates to *true*, if the variants included in the derived product under consideration satisfy all variability dependencies and all constraint dependencies.

For more details on the formal specification of the orthogonal variability model, we refer to [17].

For the specification of the behavior of the products of the product line, we use I/O-automata which are an established language for modeling concurrent and distributed discrete event systems [13] and are also used for specifying domain artifacts [7]. The specification of a system typically consists of a set of I/O-automata $C = \{C_1, \ldots, C_n\}$. An I/O-automaton C_i is defined as 5-tuple (Z_i, $z_{0,i}$, $Send_i$, $Receive_i$, T_i) where

- Z_i is the set of states,
- $z_{0,i} \in Z_i$ is the initial state,
- $Send_i$ is the set of sendable messages,
- $Receive_i$ is the set of receivable messages ($Send_i \cap Receive_i = \emptyset$),
- $T_i \subseteq Z_i \times M \times Z_i$; ($M = Send_i \cup Receive_i$) is the transition relation.

For documenting variability in I/O-automata, we define a variability relationship between the transitions T_i of the I/O-automaton and the variants V of the variability model as follows: $VRel_{IO} \subseteq V \times \mathfrak{P}(T_i)$:[1]

- $t \in T_i$ is variable, if t is related to a variant: $\exists(v,T') \in VRel_{IO}$: $t \in T'$,
- $t \in T_i$ is common, if t is not related to a variant: $\forall(v,T') \in VRel_{IO}$: $t \notin T'$.

Without loss of generality, we assume that a transition cannot be related to more than one variant, i.e. $\forall\, (v_1, T'_1), (v_2, T'_2) \in VRel_{IO}$: $(T'_1 \cap T'_2 = \emptyset) \vee (v_1 = v_2)$, since every orthogonal variability model with multiple artifact dependencies between variants and artifacts can be transformed into an orthogonal variability model with a unique artifact dependency. A proof of this claim can be found in [8].

In order to perform the verification of a set of automata, the set of automata is integrated into one automaton by a product construction [14]. Existing single system algorithms for the product construction do not incorporate the variability of the product line. We refer to [10] for a description of an algorithm that incorporates

[1] $\mathfrak{P}(T_i)$ denotes the power set of T_i.

the variability. The result of this algorithm is an extended transition relation that captures the combined behavior of the integrated automata. The extended transition (named as T^*) combines a transition with the variant selection information (V') that is necessary to select a particular transition for a product and is defined as follows: $T^* \subseteq Z \times (\mathit{Send} \cup \mathit{Receive}) \times Z \times V'$.

5.2 Adaptation of Model Checking for *EX f*

5.2.1 Adaption of State Labeling

The model checking approach from Clarke et al. [2] labels each state with the properties that are fulfilled in this state. In variable I/O-automata, the fulfillment of a property may rely on variable transitions. Therefore, the state labeling may include the variant selection which is necessary to fulfill the property. To incorporate the variability, we extend the labeling procedures introduced by Clarke et al. [2] as follows: Let *f* be a CTL expression, let $z \in Z$ be a state of an I/O-automaton, and let V' be a (possibly empty) selection of variants. The state z is labeled with (f, V') (i.e. $(f, V') \in \mathit{label}(z)$), if f_1 is fulfilled in state z for the selection V' of variants.

5.2.2 Adaption of the Verification Algorithm

For the property $EX f_1$, every state should be labeled with $EX f_1$ which has some successor state that is labeled with f_1. Since the transitions in a variable I/O-automaton and the property f_1 can be variable, it is necessary to check whether the variants related to f_1, to the considered transition, and to $EX f_1$ can be selected together. Algorithm 1 shows the calculation of the expression $EX f_1$ for a variable I/O-automaton. The algorithm has two parameters: first, the property f_1 which should be checked and, second, the variant v_{EX} which is related to $EX f_1$. The variant v_{EX} is empty, if f_1 is a common property.

For each outgoing transition of each state of a variable I/O-automaton, the algorithm checks the following. If the reached state z_2 is labeled with f_1 and the combined selection of variants of the property (i.e. v_{EX}), the selection variants of the current transition (i.e. V'), and the selection of variants associated with f_1 in the next state (i.e. V_P) can be fulfilled,[2] then the state z_1 is labeled with $(EX f_1, (v_{EX} \wedge V' \wedge V_P))$ (line (5) and (6)). This label documents that $EX f_1$ is fulfilled if the variants documented by $(v_{EX} \wedge V' \wedge V_P)$ are selected. If the start state z_0 is labeled, a witness for $EX f_1$ has been identified.

[2]The function *SAT-VM(OVM, V')* checks whether there is a selection of variants that fulfils the variability *OVM* and the selection of variants V'.

```
Algorithm 1: Checking EX f1
check EX(f1, vEX){
 for each t = z1nz2 V' ∈ T*{
    for each (f1, VP) ∈ label(z2)
     if(SAT-VM(OVM, vEX ∧ V' ∧ VP))
      label(z1) = label(z1) ∪ (EX f1 ; (vEX ∧ V' ∧ VP))
}}}
```

The correctness of the presented adaption follows from the following observation. The algorithm checks each outgoing transition of each state and all possible labels. Therefore, every possible witness for $EX\,f_1$ will be identified.

The worst case runtime of the presented algorithm is linear in the number of transitions and labels, since every transition is considered only once by the algorithm. For each transition, the algorithm considers each label of the destination state of the considered transition.

5.2.3 Checking the Completeness of Witnesses

The existing single system algorithms for model checking rely on witnesses to show that a property is fulfilled (or not fulfilled) for a given system [3]. This approach is not sufficient for product lines, since a domain artifact represents a set of systems and thus a witness must exist for every possible system. We address this challenge by checking the completeness of witnesses for all possible systems. Algorithm 2 presents the completeness check for witnesses. The algorithm has three parameters: the property *f* and the state *z* for which the completeness check has to be performed, and the variant *v* which is related to the property *f*. The variant *v* is empty, if *f* is a common property.

```
Algorithm 2: Checking Completeness of Witnesses
(1)checkCompletness(f, z, vp){
(2)if(SAT-VM(OVM, vp ∧ (⋀(f, V') ∈ Label(z) ¬V') = false)
(3) output "There is a witness for each product";
(4)else
(5) output "There is at least one product without a witness";
(6)}
```

The algorithm works as follows. It checks in line (2) if the orthogonal variability model can fulfill a variant selection in which v_p is selected and all possible variant selections related to the witnesses for *f* are not selected (i.e. $(\bigwedge_{(f,\,V')\,\in\,Label(z)} \neg V')$). If this is not possible, it is not possible to derive a product which has no witness for the property *f* in state *z*. If such a variant selection exists, this variant selection is an example for a derived product that has no witness for the property *f*.

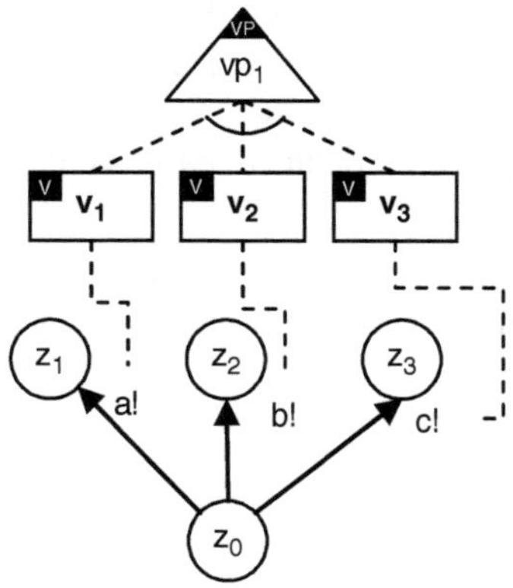

State	Label
Z_0	(EX f_1, v_1) (EX f_1, v_1)
Z_1	f_1
Z_2	f_1
Z_3	$\neg f_1$

Fig. 3 Example of checking the completeness of witnesses

Figure 3 shows an example of the result of model checking $EX\, f_1$ where we assume that $EX\, f_1$ is a common property, i.e. it has to be fulfilled by every possible product. The initial state z_0 is labeled with two labels for $EX\, f_1$, one for the variant v_1 and one for the variant v_2, i.e. there are witnesses for $EX\, f_1$. However, this set of witnesses is not complete. The orthogonal variability model on the left hand side in Fig. 3 defines the three variants v_1 to v_3 as alternative, i.e. exactly one of the three variants has to be selected. Therefore, it is possible to derive a product which only contains the variant v_3 and for this product, there is no witness for $EX\, f_1$ since it is impossible to reach a state from z_0 that is labeled with f_1.

6 Conclusion

In this chapter, we outlined different strategies for assuring the quality of domain artifacts in software product line engineering. It has been observed that a central challenge for the quality assurance of domain artifacts is the variability of these artifacts. The variability prevents the direct application of quality assurance techniques from single-system engineering, since these approaches do not consider the variability of the product line. A common strategy for dealing with the variability is the derivation and quality assurance of sample products with single system techniques. However, the success of this sample strategy mainly depends on the quality of the selected sample products; e.g. they must be representative for all the products. A complete coverage of the product line is thus hard to guarantee in general.

As an alternative, we presented a quality assurance approach that allows a comprehensive verification of domain artifacts and guarantees that all products of the product line provide the specified properties. The approach is based on model checking techniques and considers the variability of the domain artifacts during the verification process, thereby eliminating the need to costly check each product of the product line individually.

In our future work, we plan to examine the extension of further verification techniques (e.g. symbolic model checking) for the verification of domain artifacts in product line engineering. We further plan to include our verification approach in a modeling environment and to perform detailed case studies showing the applicability of our approach.

Acknowledgments This work has been partially funded by the DFG under grant PO 607/2-1 IST-SPL. We would like to thank Ernst Sikora and Nelufar Ulfat-Bunyadi for fruitful discussions on earlier drafts of this chapter.

References

1. Atlee J, Gannon J (1993) State-based model checking of event-driven system requirements. IEEE Trans Softw Eng 19(1):24–40
2. Clarke E, Emerson A, Sistla P (1986) Automatic verification of finite-state concurrent systems using temporal logic specifications. ACM TOPLAS 8(2):244–263
3. Clarke E, Grumberg O, Peled D (1999) Model checking. MIT, Cambridge
4. Deelstra S, Sinnema M, Bosch J (2005) Product derivation in software product families: a case study. J Systems Softw 74(2):173–194
5. Emerson E, Kahlon V (2004) Parameterized model checking of ring-based message passing systems. In: Computer science logic. LNCS, vol 3210. Springer, pp 325–339
6. Grumberg O, Veith H (2008) 25 years of model checking. LNCS, vol 5000, Springer
7. Larsen K, Nyman U, Wąsowski A (2007) Modal I/O automata for interface and product line theories. In: Proceedings of 16th European symposium on programming. LNCS, vol 4421. Springer, pp 64–79
8. Lauenroth K (2009) Konsistenzprüfung von Domänenanforderungsspezifikationen. Phd Thesis (in German). Logos, Berlin
9. Lauenroth K, Pohl K (2008) Dynamic consistency checking of domain requirements in product line engineering. In: Proceedings of IEEE international requirements engineering conference, IEEE, Los Alamitos, pp 193–202
10. Lauenroth K, Pohl K (2009) Model checking of domain artifacts in product line engineering. In: Proceedings of the ACM/IEEE international conference on automated software engineering, Los Alamitos, pp 269–280
11. Lauenroth K, Pohl K (2007) Towards automated consistency checks of product line requirements specifications. In: Proceedings of the ACM/IEEE international conference on automated software engineering, Atlanta, pp 373–376
12. Liu J, Dehlinger R, Lutz R (2007) Safety analysis of software product lines using state-based modelling. J Systems Softw 80:1879–1892
13. Lynch M, Tuttle M (1989) An introduction to input/output automata. CWI Quater 2(3): 219–246
14. Maccari A, Heie A (2005) Managing infinite variability in mobile terminal software. Softw Pract Exper 35(6):513–537
15. Metzger A (2007) Quality issues in software product lines: feature interactions and beyond (invited talk). In: 9th international conference on feature interactions in software and communication systems (ICFI 2007), Grenoble, pp 3–15
16. Metzger A, Bühne S, Lauenroth K, Pohl K (2005) Considering feature interactions in product lines: towards the automatic derivation of dependencies between product variants. In: Feature interactions in telecommunications and software systems VIII. Proceedings ICFI, pp 198–216
17. Metzger A, Heymans P, Pohl K, Schobbens P-Y, Saval G (2007) Disambiguating the documentation of variability in software product lines. In: Proceedings of RE'07, Los Alamitos, pp 243–253

18. Pohl K, Metzger A (2006) Software product line testing. Commun ACM 49(12):78–81
19. Pohl K, Böckle G, van der Linden F (2005) Software product line engineering – foundations, principles, and techniques. Springer, Heidelberg
20. Ralyte J, Rolland C, Deneckère R (2004) Towards a meta-tool for change-centric method engineering: a typology of generic operators. In: Proceedings of CAiSE. LNCS, vol 3084, pp 202–218
21. Ralyté J, Rolland C, Ben Ayed M (2005) An approach for evolution-driven method engineering. In: Krogstie J, Halpin T, Siau K (eds) Information modeling methods and methodologies. IDEA Group, USA, pp 80–100
22. Rolland C (2009) Method engineering: towards methods as services. Software Process: Improvement and Practice (SPIP), Special issue on Software Processes 14(3):143–164
23. Rolland C, Grosz G, Kla R (1999) Experience with goal-scenario coupling in requirements engineering. In: Proceedings of IEEE international requirements engineering conference, Los Alamitos, pp 74–81
24. Rolland C, Nurcan S (2010) Business process lines to deal with the variability. In: Proceedings of the Hawaii international conference on system sciences (HICSS), Hawaii, USA
25. Rolland C, Prakash N, Kaabi R (2007) Variability in business process families. Information Resources Management Association (IRMA)
26. Rolland C, Salinesi C (2009) Supporting requirements elicitation through goal/scenario coupling. In: Conceptual modeling: foundations and applications. LNCS, vol 5600. Springer, pp 398–416
27. Rolland C, Souveyet C, Ben Achour C (1998) Guiding goal modelling using scenarios. IEEE Trans Softw Eng, Special Issue on Scenario Manage 24(12):1055–1071
28. Salinesi C, Rolland C, Mazo R (2009) An ontology of verification criteria in the product line domain. Centre de Recherche en Informatique (CRI), Université Panthéon Sorbonn, Paris, France
29. Salinesi C, Rolland C, Mazo R (2009) VMWare: tool support for automatic verification of structural and semantic correctness in product line models. In: Proceedings of VaMoS 2009, Sevilla, Spain, Essen, pp 173–176
30. Savolainen J, Kuusela J (2001) Consistency management of product line requirements. In: Proceedings of IEEE international requirements engineering conference, Los Alamitos, pp 40–47

Method Engineering: A Service-Oriented Approach

Corine Cauvet

Abstract In the past, a large variety of methods have been published ranging from very generic frameworks to methods for specific information systems. Method Engineering has emerged as a research discipline for designing, constructing and adapting methods for Information Systems development. Several approaches have been proposed as paradigms in method engineering. The meta modeling approach provides means for building methods by instantiation, the component-based approach aims at supporting the development of methods by using modularization constructs such as method fragments, method chunks and method components. This chapter presents an approach (SO2M) for method engineering based on the service paradigm. We consider services as autonomous computational entities that are self-describing, self-configuring and self-adapting. They can be described, published, discovered and dynamically composed for processing a consumer's demand (a developer's requirement). The *method service* concept is proposed to capture a development process fragment for achieving a goal. Goal orientation in service specification and the principle of service dynamic composition support method construction and method adaptation to different development contexts.

Remerciements: La recherche présentée dans ce chapitre n'aurait pu être menée si je n'avais pas eu l'immense chance de rencontrer Colette. Je la remercie très sincèrement pour m'avoir acceptée au sein de son équipe de recherche et aidée tout au long de ma carrière d'enseignant-chercheur. Elle est dans toute la communauté française des chercheurs en systèmes d'information la référence pour la qualité scientifique de ses travaux, pour le rayonnement international de sa recherche et pour sa vision et ses idées novatrices sur notre domaine.

C. Cauvet (✉)
Université Paul Cézanne Aix-Marseille 3, Laboratoire LSIS,
Campus Universitaire de Saint Jérôme, Avenue Escadrille Normandie Niemen,
13397 Marseille Cedex 20, France
e-mail: corine.cauvet@lsis.org

S. Nurcan et al. (eds.), *Intentional Perspectives on Information Systems Engineering*,
DOI 10.1007/978-3-642-12544-7_19,

1 Introduction

In the field of Information Systems (IS) engineering, the years 80–90 have seen the emergence of many IS development methods [11, 16, 18, 33, 35, 36]. Many of these methods have allowed a better control of the complexity, cost and timing of development of IS. They have also provided more rigorous way of working in the development process by introducing particular models, representation formalisms and levels of abstraction. These methods have been widely used in industry and they have contributed to a better understanding of design tasks. Although these methods have now reached a certain maturity, it is clear they are still inappropriate in many contexts, the products they construct are not always satisfactory and they do not support new engineering paradigms such as component-based software engineering or model driven engineering.

In this context, method engineering [1, 13, 27, 38] has emerged as a new research discipline. Method engineering is concerned with the process of designing and constructing methods that fits a project situation. The research field on method engineering is dominated by various approaches that attempt to contribute to an understanding of method development. The instantiation approach [5, 10, 28] aims to construct a new method from meta-method, the configuration approach [14, 15] is based on the existence of a base method that we can adapt to a particular situation, and finally the composition approach [2, 26, 37] uses assembly techniques on method components.

Colette Rolland took an important role in the emergence of method engineering as a specific discipline. The approach presented in this chapter benefit of several results that Colette has produced in this discipline, particularly, the goal modeling approach [31], the component [30, 34] and the service-based [9, 29, 32] engineering perspectives.

This chapter contributes to the method engineering discipline by presenting an approach to method construction that explicitly addresses method components as services (so-called *method services*) and method construction is considered as a service dynamic composition process. This approach makes use of some engineering principles from component-based software engineering (CBSE) and service-oriented engineering (SOE). *Method services* specification are centered on usage concerns (consumer's point of view) and they support adaptation mechanisms to fit project context. In fact, *method services* are considered as available web resources and accessible by a wide range of developers who need methods to solve development problems in particular contexts.

SO2M is a method engineering approach [6, 7], in which a method is constructed "on the fly" by discovering, adapting and dynamically composing existing *method services*. The discovery, adaptation and composition of services are driven by a process of goal satisfaction. This approach differs from the usual definition in which a method is considered as an a-priori fixed set of languages, processes, product models.... Rather the approach supports flexibility in method construction by composing *method services* in different ways according the context.

The chapter is structured as follows: Section 2 introduces the service paradigm and it relates it to the component one, the service paradigm is also discussed in the context of method engineering. Section 3 is an overview of the conceptual elements of SO2M. Section 4 presents the ontology of method, Sect. 5 describes the specification model for *method services* and Sect. 6 introduces the composition process. Section 7 concludes and discusses new challenges for service-oriented method engineering.

2 The Service Paradigm

This section introduces the concept of service, we identify the principles that characterize this concept and compare to the concept of component.

For the majority of computer scientists, both in academics and in industry, the term *service* is associated with those of Web service and service-oriented architecture [22]. However the concept of service can be considered in many ways. The special issue of the Communications of the ACM Journal [4] illustrates the scope and challenges of this area: "The challenges are both the multidisciplinary nature of service innovation, which combines business, technology, social-organizational, and demand innovation as well as the lack of formal representation of service systems".

In this chapter, we consider services as existing method components that can be assembled to deliver a method fragment that satisfy a developer's need. This vision leads naturally to consider services as a particular kind of component. In the next section, we show the essential differences between these two concepts.

2.1 From Components to Services

Recently, several paradigms have influenced IS engineering (ISE) methods, techniques and tools. Component-based software engineering (CBSE) and service-oriented engineering (SOE) can be considered as such paradigms. Some confusion exists between those approaches due to the idea that both utilize some kind of components as fundamental constructs to support the development of IS. Furthermore, both reorganize a portfolio of existing artifacts into self-describing elements, accessible through standard interfaces and that can be assembled together.

Early component-based software engineering has emerged as a new paradigm for supporting software reuse [8, 12]. The basic concept of systematic software reuse is simple [17]: develop systems of components of a reasonable size and reuse them then, extend the idea of "component systems" beyond code to requirements analysis, design models and tests artifacts and also to development process.

Service-oriented engineering involves services as the constructs to bear the development of distributed applications with rapid and easy composition of services. Key to this concept is the service-oriented architecture (SOA) which is a logical

Table 1 Moving from components to services

Criteria	CBSE	SOE
Finality	Software reuse by components integration	Software interoperability by services invocation
Interface orientation	Product-oriented interface	Client-oriented interface
Lifecycle	Deployment/Research	Publication/Discovery
Organization	Assembly and organization with static links	Static and dynamic composition

way of designing software systems to provide services to either end-user applications or to other services distributed over a network, via published and discoverable interfaces [19, 20]. Table 1 provides a summary of major differences between the component-oriented view and the service-oriented one.

CBSE and SOE introduce different points of view about software engineering: CBSE focuses on software reuse and components integration while SOE focuses on software interoperability and services invocation. SOE emphasizes aspects such as autonomy, communication, etc.

Both approaches introduce the notion of interface. However, CBSE and SOE don't consider this notion in the same way: usually, in software components, interface is a set of inputs and outputs while, in services, interface usually is a functional description of what the service can do. Components' interface is a specification of components' behavior that consists of names of semantically-related operations, their parameters and valid parameter types. So interface specification focuses on the product that the component delivers. Components' modeling emphasizes engineering information about components, i.e. information required for implementation, configuration and deployment. For instance, information about communication and data exchange among components is rather relevant for supporting implementation of components. Components access is available when components are deployed, i.e. installed and configured, in a component infrastructure. The interface of services specifies the need a consumer may request from the service. Additionally, an interface may include constraints on the usage of the service that must be considered by both the service and its consumer. Models of services emphasize usage concern, which is what the service is intended to do for a particular consumer. Service providers publish services and make them available (often on the web). Nevertheless, let's note that some advanced components models introduce high-level description of the components [25, 39] while some models of services only consider low-level data [40].

Components and services lifecycles can't be considered in the same way: once produced, components must be deployed by their customers who then have the ability to research in their own components library the one or ones they need; on the contrary, once produced, services are published by their providers. Then, consumers have the ability to discover (dynamically) available services relevant to their requirements. So, usage of components and services is very different; we make use of services via service requests, service discovery and service invocation. In contrast, components are application integrated artifacts. In the first case, an application results from services request while, in the second case, the application consists of components integration.

CBSE and SOE also differ about organizational aspect. Usually, components are statically organized with links predefined at design-time. On the contrary, ser-vices can dynamically be organized with "computed" links. Services possess the ability of engaging other services in order to complete complex transactions. So, service delivery often makes use of composition mechanisms to coordinate several services that together fulfill a consumer's request. Resulting composite services may be used as basic services in further compositions of services. Static and dynamic compositions are one of the major challenges for adoption of the service-oriented approach. Indeed, development of electronic distributed and flexible business applications requires automated composition and integration of services in the current dynamic context of the web infrastructure.

2.2 *Principles of a Service-Oriented Paradigm*

In this section, we define fundamental principles for a service paradigm definition. Each principle is introduced and argued. Impact of each principle on service modeling is presented.

Principle No 1: Goal-oriented specification. We adopt an approach based on usage. In service modeling, we consider that a service exists for delivering a solution to achieve a goal. For instance, in the pedagogic domain, a service can satisfy a learner's goal while in a business domain a service can satisfy a client's problem.

Whatever the domain, we consider that a service is intended to meet consumers' needs, that is what the consumers intend. Then, interface of services should emphasize what a service can do for its consumers. We propose to model services with a goal-oriented specification [3, 24, 31]. This presents two main advantages:

- Goal modeling emphasizes problem-related knowledge rather than solution one. It then induces a separation problem/solution.
- Goal orientation supports service usage specification at a high level of description. Goal orientation emphasizes the "why to use" a service, so goal orientation allows reducing the semantic distance between available services and consumer's requests.

Moreover, goal orientation supports alignment of a service with the domain strategy and processes.

From the provider perspective, each service must have an interface which ex-presses a goal. From the consumer perspective, discovering and invoking a service means expressing a goal.

Principle No 2: Variability and contextual knowledge. Two ways are available to deal with goal satisfaction:

1. Propose one generic solution which can be applied in any case but which is not the most efficient one in all the situations.
2. Propose several solutions, each one being relevant in a specific case.

We choose to adopt the second way: it will allow services to propose the most relevant solution in each case. Then, a given goal can be achieved in different ways. Each way is more or less suitable according to consumers' context. Contextual knowledge is very useful for discriminating the different manners to satisfy the goal. We call "variability" the ability to propose several solutions for one goal.

From the provider point of view, service modeling requires variability specification mechanisms and contextual knowledge capture. From the consumer point of view, a goal expression must be completed with contextual constraints which impact the choice of the solution satisfying the goal.

Principle No 3: Semantic description of services. One of the difficulties for services' consumers when discovering and invoking services is to express their requirements with a specific unnatural language. This induces a gap between consumers' knowledge and services specifications. In order to reduce this gap, we propose to specify services with semantic data and to use "shared" ontologies. Service specification requires knowledge on goals, processes, actors and objects.

From the provider perspective, ontologies should be used for specification of semantic data that describe services. From the consumer perspective, ontologies should be used to express requirements when discovering or invoking services.

Principle No 4: Dynamic adaptation. We consider that a large variety of consumers can access and use a service, so service delivery should support personalization. Thus, services should take into account data about consumers that use them. Usually, those data are expressed in users' profiles. By nature, users' profiles evolve through time and, then, must be considered dynamically.

For the provider point of view, specification of services should weave know-ledge about skills required to correctly use them. For the consumer point of view, a profile should be updated through time for a relevant dynamic personalization.

Principle No 5: Dynamic composition. Some goals being complex, solutions provided by a service may require satisfaction of sub-goals. In this case, a service can delegate satisfaction of these sub-goals to other services.

From the provider perspective, specification of some solutions provided by services must refer to goals which are satisfied by other services. From the consumer perspective, this aspect should be as "transparent" as possible.

Due to goal orientation, variability and contextualization, the dynamic composition can be automatically computed by a service without consumers' contributions.

2.3 *Benefits of the Service Paradigm in Method Engineering*

We consider that the service paradigm defined according the five principles presented in Sect. 2.2 has several advantages with regards to method engineering.

Key to the service concept is the service-oriented architecture (SOA) that supports a logical way of designing systems by providing services to end-users requests or to other services via published and discoverable interfaces. For our concern, this idea suggests to provide and capitalize method fragments constructed by individuals and distributed outside of any one particular organization and then to share and reuse method fragments. By considering methods and method fragments as available services, they are (web) resources accessible by a wide range of developers who need methods to solve development problems in particular contexts.

The service paradigm suggests a goal-oriented modeling of method fragments, thus methods as services emphasize the intention of a developer and consequently they reduce the semantic distance between available methods in a methods base and developer's requests. Against components, services emphasize usage concerns rather engineering aspects. So, a method (or a fragment of method) viewed as a service is selected for the problem it solves rather than the solution it delivers. Furthermore, goal orientation is very suitable to variability specification. In method engineering, variability is related to method flexibility. A service is able to deliver several methods fragments to achieve one goal, each one being relevant in a specific project context. By supporting variability, services allow to achieve method adaptation to particular project situation.

Web-based context leads to relate service description to ontologies. By using the service paradigm in method engineering, we have to address the construction of an ontology for the IS engineering methods domain. Such an ontology is useful for annotating method fragments with semantic on actors, processes and products involved in methods. An ontology of method seems promising for methodological knowledge sharing and management.

Lastly, service orientation leads to a new approach in method constructing: starting from a developer's intention, the problem is to discover, select and compose services to satisfy the intention. The web-based context supports at any time, adding and deleting services. Because the composition of services is realized at execution time, the satisfaction of an intention can benefit all the services available at this time and the selection of the more suitable services can take into account the current context of the intention. The dynamic composition principle issued from service-oriented computing seems to be very powerful to achieve in an automatic way method construction from a methods base.

3 SO2M: An Overview

This section introduces the main elements of SO2M (Service Oriented Meta-Method) (see Fig. 1). SO2M is used to build development methods. Ideally, given a developer's request and a set of *method services*, the composition process would find

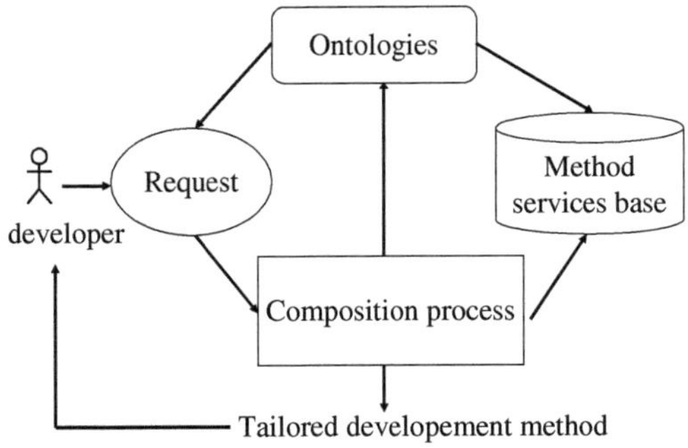

Fig. 1 SO2M overview

a collection of services that achieves the request. Both *method services* descriptions and requests share a common vocabulary specified in ontologies.

The *method services* base contains a set of services called *method services*. A *method service* is a reusable unit that contains one or several method fragments to solve an IS development problem. For example, a *method service* could specify a method fragment to construct a class diagram. The *method services* are described with a semantic service model. The goal orientation emphasizes service usage and customer satisfaction. In our approach, *method services* serve IS developers in carrying out development tasks.

SO2M uses also task ontologies which provide a common vocabulary for specifying both *method services* and developer's requests. There is a need for ontology when applying search and semantic matching for *method services*. Ontologies in SO2M concern the domain of IS engineering. They enable to define a set of terms relating to four dimensions of IS engineering: the goal ontology L_{goal}, the actor ontology L_{act}, the process ontology L_{proc} and the product ontology L_{prod}. These ontologies are inter-dependent; for instance actors from the actor ontology are related to activities defined in the process ontology.

SO2M is based on a composition process that supports the research, the selection and the assembly of services to build dynamically development methods tailored to developer's requirements. The composition process begins with a developer's request. The request allows the developer to specify a goal to achieve. The composition process delivers a composition of services that supports goal realization. For example, the request "Specify requirements" needs a way of specifying information systems requirements. The result may be a method based on an UML use case model or a functional approach. As *method services*, requests are specified with the goal ontology.

4 Ontology of Method

This section presents the ontology of method for describing various aspects related to *method services*. The ontology of method is composed of four sub-ontologies, each one is related to a type of knowledge introduced through principle No 3.

The four ontologies are task ontologies [3] for the domain of IS engineering. These ontologies specify knowledge on IS engineering problems and solutions. They provide a vocabulary to describe engineering activities domain-independently. This independence is essential to describe the services at a method level. The second motivation to use task ontologies is in the possibility to consider developer's needs as problems to solve. Finally, these ontologies play an important role in matching requests and available services.

- The goal ontology (L_{goal}) defines a vocabulary on the IS engineering problems. These problems correspond to tasks appearing in the development process. For instance, "Construct a class diagram" is a classical development task in IS development. IS problems are represented as goals to achieve. L_{goal} provides a hierarchy of goal classes. Instances of this ontology are used to define both the goals of *method services* and developers' requests. Goals are structured with a verb and an object. Figure 2 shows a fragment of the goal ontology L_{goal}.
- The actor ontology (L_{act}) defines roles for the actors involved in IS process development. These roles correspond to functions played by actors within the development. Instances of this ontology are used in service specification to indicate the actors who are concerned by the service.
- The process ontology (L_{proc}) defines a common terminology for the description of the engineering activities (and their organization). This ontology is, in particular, used in service specification to describe the control constructs of processes.
- The product ontology (L_{prod}) defines a common vocabulary for characterizing all the artifacts used and produced during IS engineering. Artifacts correspond to objects necessary during process execution. This ontology is used, in particular, to specify inputs and outputs of the processes.

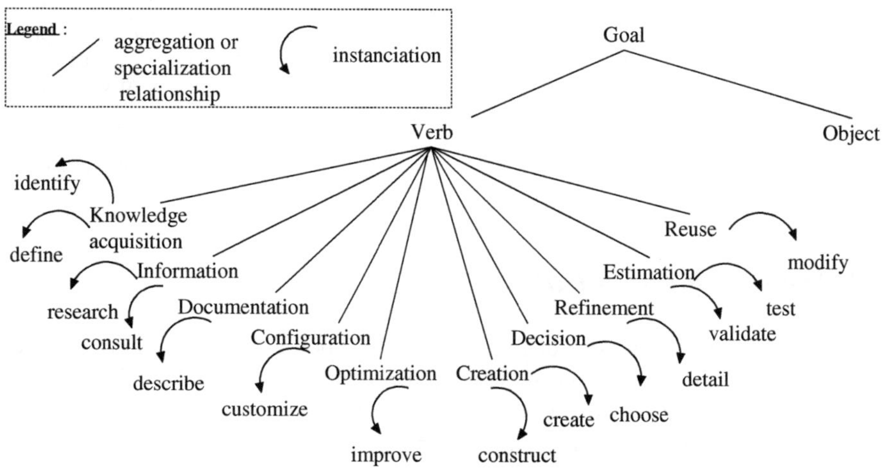

Fig. 2 Fragment of the goal ontology

In method engineering, using an ontology of method presents four main advantages:

- It supports semantic description of *method services*. This ontology provides primitives in terms of which a service provider can describe *method services*.
- It supports request formulation. This ontology defines a vocabulary in terms of which service consumers can ask service needs.
- It supports the research and composition of *method services* with a high degree of automation.
- It reduces the gap between service description available in the service base and consumer's requirements on the service base. In SO2M, the ontology of method provides a common vocabulary which can be used both by the "providers" and the "requesters" of services.

5 The Model of *Method Service*

This section briefly defines major concepts used in *method service* specification. The description of a *method service* contains three parts (see Fig. 3): an identification part, a process part and a resource part. A service delivers a process to achieve a certain goal by using resources. The three parts express service knowledge at different abstraction levels: the identification part emphasizes the development problem that the service solves, the process part characterizes a manner to solve the problem and the resource part provides a reusable process fragment. Identification and process parts aim at describing *method services* in order to enable the automation of *method services* discovery and composition.

Fig. 3 *Method service* specification

Method service
Identification part (goal)
Process part (process structure)
Resource part (reusable process)

5.1 *The Identification Part*

This part defines the purpose of the service. Our approach for designing services is based on a "customer" point of view. So the identification part contains the contextual knowledge of the customer and why the customer (i.e. the developer) takes advantages in using services. Identification part (see Fig. 4) is largely used during discovery and selection of *method services*. The identification part contains two kinds of knowledge: finality and argument.

Fig. 4 Identification part of a *method service*

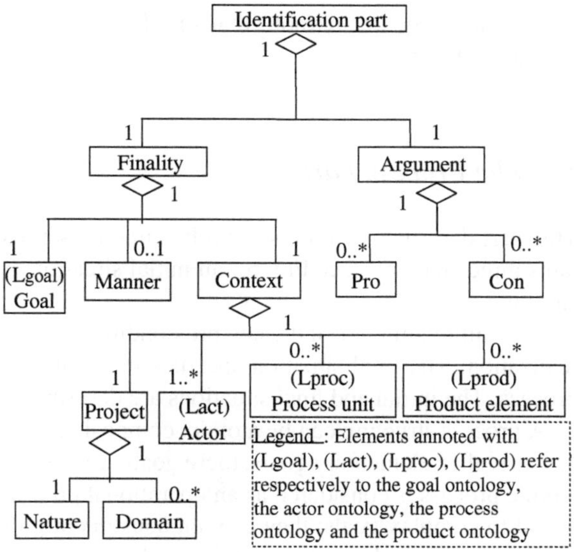

The finality defines the problem that the *method service* solves. The finality is structured with a goal (defined in the goal ontology), a manner and a context. Each goal is defined by a verb and an object. For example, the goal "Construct a class diagram" is defined with the verb "Construct" and the object "a class diagram". The manner defines a way of achieving the goal and the context describes the situation in development project for which the *method service* is suitable. The context is detailed with the project nature, the involved actors, a process phase and some product elements. All these elements refer to ontologies. Finally, the arguments express the advantages (i.e. the "pro" arguments) and the drawbacks (i.e. the "con" arguments) of using the *method service*. So, arguments support service(s) selection within the goal realization process.

For instance, the identification part of the *method service* "Construct a class diagram manually" is presented in Fig. 5. This service helps the developer to construct

-Finality

- **-Goal** : Construct a class diagram
- **-Manner** : manually
- **-Context** :
  - **Project** :
    - **Nature** : Development
    - **Domain** : -
  - **Actor** : Designer, method engineer
  - **Process unit** : Requirement elicitation, design
  - **Product element** : class diagram

-Argument :

- **-pro** : - the suggested process guides class diagram construction
- **-con** : - requires UML skills

Fig. 5 Identification part of the *method service* "construct a class diagram manually"

a class diagram. Let us note that the domain is not indicated, so the service is domain-independent.

5.2 The Process Part

This part describes a process for achieving the service goal. The process part contains three elements (see Fig. 6): an initial situation, a final situation, and a process structure.

The initial situation indicates pre-conditions and artifacts necessary to process realization. The final situation specifies the results and the post-conditions of the process. The initial and final situations are described with process ontology terms.

A process structure can be atomic, composite, simple or decisional. Atomic processes realize elementary goals; these goals are not decomposable into sub goals. An atomic process is considered as an operational process. Composite processes correspond to complex goals; they contain constituent processes organized with control constructs. Control constructs indicate the manner in which constituent processes are executed. In SO2M, constituent processes execution may be in sequence (i.e. in a specific order) or in parallel (i.e. without a particular order). Constituent processes within a composite process may be atomic or simple.

Decisional processes are a specific case of composite processes. Decisional processes propose several alternative decompositions of a goal. Each de-composition

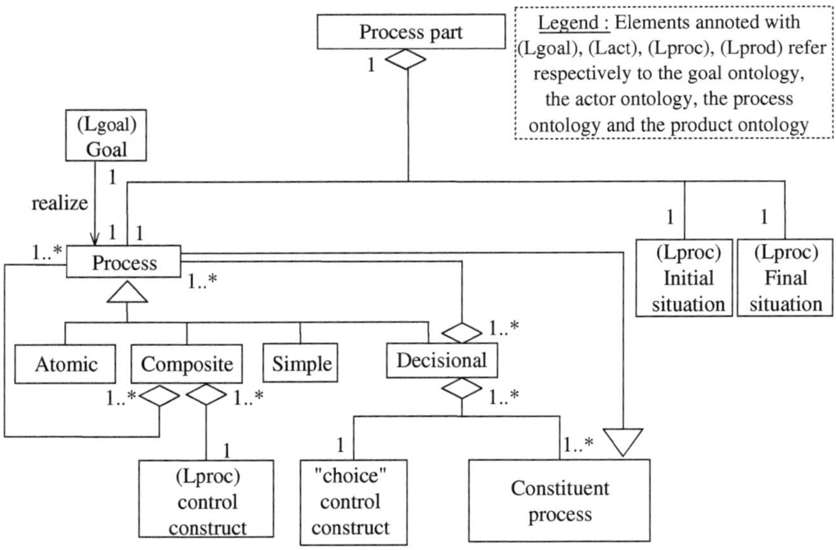

Fig. 6 Process part of a *method service*

-**Initial situation** : class diagram not constructed
-**Final situation** : class diagram constructed
-**Process** :

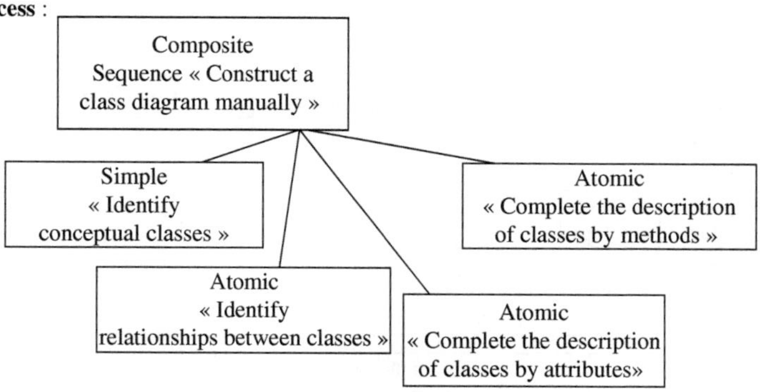

Fig. 7 Process part of the *method service* "construct a class diagram manually"

is characterized by quality attributes that assist developer in making his choice. Decisional processes offer different manners to satisfy the same goal. Decisional processes are suitable for variability. At composition time, the developer has to choose one or several constituent processes to achieve his objective.

Simple processes allow differing process realization in other services. Only at composition time, the simple process is associated to a service supporting its realization. They are a powerful mechanism to achieve flexibility in process specification. They also provide the ability to adapt a process to different contexts. Indeed, at composition time, the simple process will be substitute with the more suitable service.

We illustrate the process part in Fig. 7 with the composite process "Construct a class diagram manually". It has four constituent processes organized in sequence. One constituent process is simple, the other ones are atomic.

5.3 The Resource Part

This part defines the solution offered by the service. The solution is an executable process described in terms of activities and objects. The resource part corresponds to a process fragment, executable by the developer, to achieve his objective within a particular project. This part is composed of resource descriptions and an execution graph (see Fig. 8). Resources correspond to elements which are used or delivered by the process. Resources can be external domain ontologies or development artifacts. The execution graph is a kind of activity diagram including variation points and decision points that represent respectively simple processes and decisional processes defined in the process part.

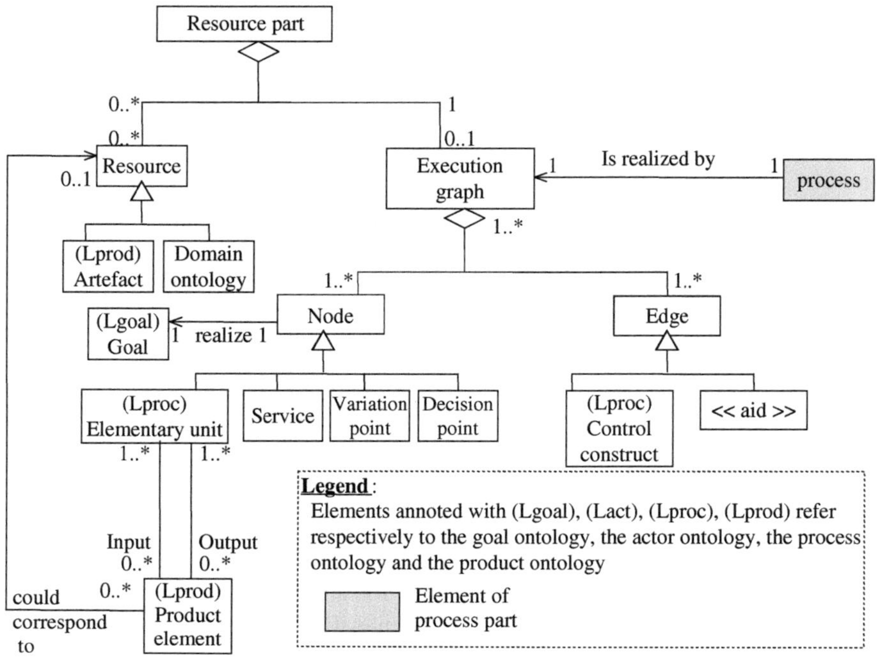

Fig. 8 Resource part of a *method service*

In the execution graph given in Fig. 9, the variation point corresponds to the simple process "Identify conceptual classes" defined in the process part (cf. Fig. 7). At composition time, this variation point will be substitute with the execution graph of the service chosen by the developer. This mechanism enables to generate development methods tailored to developers' requirements.

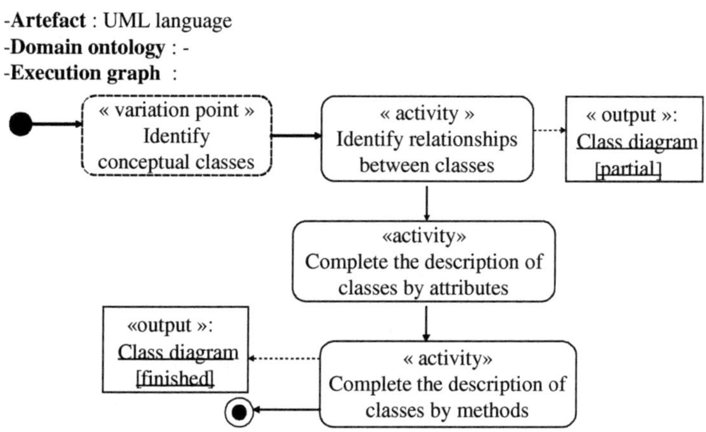

Fig. 9 Resource part of the *method service* "construct a class diagram manually"

6 The Composition Process

This section describes the *method service* composition process. *Method services* are considered as process fragments, so they can be composed to build complex processes. The objective of service composition is to create new processes by combining processes of existing services. Service composition is generated on the fly based on a developer's request. This approach is in contrast to the solutions provided by classical workflow approaches where activities in a process are pre-planned and pre-specified [21, 23].

In SO2M, service composition is seen as an iterative process (cf. Fig. 10). The entry of this process is a request formulated by a developer. The treatment of the request consists in searching, selecting and organizing all the services necessary for satisfying the request. We call "composition graph" (Gc), the graph that specifies all the services and their relationships participating to request satisfaction [6]. The composition process result is a whole development method (or a fragment) defined from the execution graphs of the services appearing in the composition graph. The result is represented by a process graph (Gp). The process graph can be executed in a certain context to elaborate a particular IS [6].

Every iteration in the composition process contains three activities: discovery, composition and refinement. These activities are repeated until the initial request is satisfied with a set of services. The number of iterations varies according to the granularity of the goal in the request. Indeed, the more abstract will be the goal, the more important will be the number of services in the composition graph and the number of iterations in the composition process. It is important to note that simple processes, as constituent of decisional processes or composite processes, initiate new iterations in the composition process. Simple processes lead, at composition time, to explore the service base to find the service the more suitable to realize the process. In this way, at any time, composition takes into account the current state of the services base.

At each iteration the composition graph (Gc) is extended and the process graph (Gp) is refined. Each iteration is driven by a goal. During the first iteration, the goal is the request one. In the following iterations, the goal results from one (or some) simple process(es) defined in a composite or decisional process of a *method service*.

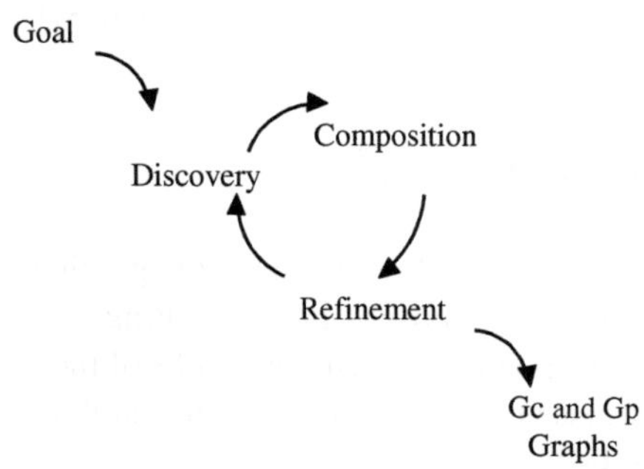

Fig. 10 An iteration in the composition process

Recall that a simple process is an abstract process that can be realized in several manners. The principle of dynamic composition consists in comparing the simple process with potentially matching services. Alternative services may be generated, one or more services can be chosen by the developer according the criteria defined in the *method service* contexts. This type of composition is specified on the fly and requires dynamically structuring and choosing services.

6.1 Discovery

This activity consists of goal definition and service matching. During the first iteration, the goal ontology guides the developer in request formulation. Moreover, the goal ontology allows checking that the formulated request respects the structure of a goal (i.e. a verb followed by of an object). In the following iteration, goals directly result from simple processes.

Service discovery consists in comparing the desired goal with the goal of the method services available in the services base. If the original goal does not correspond to any method service, it is analyzed using the goal ontology and the product ontology. On the one hand, the goal ontology makes it possible to search services which have a similar verb with the goal one. On the other hand, the product ontology enables to analyze the object of the goal. Discovery of services matching the goal may result in service alternative solutions.

6.2 Composition

The composition activity consists in service selection and service composition. Discovery of services matching the current goal may result in alternative solutions. For each solution, service identification description (manner, context and arguments) is available to guide developer's choices. At this stage of the composition process, the chosen services contribute to the initial request satisfaction. These services can be atomic, composite or decisional (i.e. the process part of these services may be an atomic process, a composite or a decisional process). At this stage, these services can be composed in order to achieve the current goal of the iteration. The composition graph is extended with selected services.

6.3 Refinement

Extension of the composition graph leads to process graph refinement. Indeed, refinement consists in substituting the variation points (or decision points) by the corresponding execution graphs of the constituent services. For each process within the services selected in the current iteration, new iterations are initialized according to different situations:

- If the process is decisional, the developer must select one or more simple constituent processes. Quality attributes, defined on each constituent process of the decisional process, guide developer's choices. For all simple processes selected by the developer, a new iteration is initialized with goals corresponding to simple processes. It is important to note that the execution graph of the current decisional service (and consequently of the process graph) comprises a decision point. This new iteration will enable to substitute the decision point of the process graph with the execution graph of the found services.
- If the process is composite, it has one or more simple constituent processes. Similarly to decisional processes, a new iteration is initialized with goals corresponding to simple processes. In this new iteration, the process will search the services which are appropriated to replace the simple processes. It is important to note that the execution graph of the current service (and consequently the process graph) comprises a variation point for each simple process. The following iteration will make it possible to substitute the variation points of the process graph with the execution graphs of the selected services.
- If the process is atomic, either the composition process is finished or it remains variation points or decision points in the process graph and new iterations are necessary.

At the end of the composition process, the process graph does not comprise any more variation point or decision point. The process graph obtained could be carried out to produce particular artifacts in a precise context.

7 Conclusion

In this chapter, we have presented a service oriented approach for building IS development methods tailored to developers' requirements. Development problems are considered as goals to realize and *method services* are self-contained units that provide process fragments to achieve these goals. An ontology of method supports the research and composition of *method services* with a high degree of automation. Furthermore, this ontology provides a common vocabulary which can be used both by the "providers" and the "requesters" of services. Service composition is carried out by an iterative composition process which links dynamically services to generate tailored system development methods.

Even if the service orientation seems promising to answer method engineering requirements, of course, more in-depth research into the practice of service orientation in method engineering is needed.

Based on the work presented in this chapter, we consider that service orientation in method engineering raises new interesting challenges:

The need to develop a community of practice for the domain of IS engineering methods. Such a community should increase service creation and exchanges among people and store and preserve services through a collective distributed and dynamic process. In this context, the ontology of method would get rich dynamically. During service design and request formulation, new terms could be added to the ontology in order to extend knowledge on methods through the community. In this way, knowledge on methods can be shared by "consumers" and "providers" of services through the use of internet based communication technologies.

The need to develop service request languages suitable for IS developers requirements. A service request language and its appropriate run-time support environment is required to allow IS developers to express their needs on the basis of the characteristics and functionality of standard methods whose services are found in service registries. A service request language must provide a formal means of describing desired method attributes and functionality, including both method preferences and practice of the consumer (IS developer) and context and constraints of the project.

The need to address service composition at the semantic level. One of the most challenging areas in method engineering is the process of combining and aggregating several method fragments in order to construct new method fragments. In service-oriented computing, efforts have been made aiming at developing syntactic techniques to automatically compose different services. We argue that goal orientation as a fundamental principle in service specification must be considered as a key concept to address service composition at the semantic level. In method engineering, this kind of composition would help to design new methods more systematically.

References

1. Brinkkemper S (1996) Method engineering: engineering of information systems development methods and tools. J Info Softw Technol 38(4):275–280
2. Brinkkemper S, Saeki M, Harmsen F (1998) Assembly techniques for method engineering. In: Proceedings of the 10th international conference on advanced information systems engineering (CAISE'98). LNCS, vol 1413. Springer, pp 381–400
3. Chandrasekaran B, Josephson JR, Benjamins R (1998) The ontology of tasks and methods. In: Proceedings of the 11th international workshop on knowledge acquisition modeling and management, KAW'98, Banff, Canada
4. Chesbrough H, Spohrer J (2006) A research manifesto for services science. Commun ACM 49(7):35–40
5. Gonzalez-Perez C, Henderson-Sellers B (2006) A powertype-based metamodelling framework. Softw Systems Modeling 5(1):72–90
6. Guzélian G (2007) Conception de systèmes d'information: une approche orientée service. Thèse de l'Université Paul Cézanne, Aix-Marseille 3, Juillet
7. Guzélian G, Cauvet C (2007) SO2M: Towards a service-oriented approach for method engineering. In: Proceedings of international conference on information and knowledge engineering, IKE'07, Las Vegas, Nevada, USA
8. Heineman GT, Councill WT (2001) Component-based software engineering, putting the pieces together. Addison-Wesley Professional, Reading MA
9. Iacovelli, A, Souveyet, C, Rolland, C (2008) Method as a service (MaaS). In: Proceedings of international conference on research and challenges of information systems, RCIS'08, IEEE
10. International Organization for Standardization/International Electrotechnical Commission: Software engineering – metamodel for development methodologies ISO/IEC 24744.

http://webstore.iec.ch/preview/info_isoiec24744%7Bed1.0%7Den.pdf (2007). Cited 5 May 2010
11. Jacobson I, Christerson M, Jonsson P, Oevergaard G (1992) Object-oriented software engineering. Addison-Wesley, Reading MA
12. Jacobson I, Griss M, Jonsson P (1997) Software reuse: architecture, process and organization for business success. Addison-Wesley, Reading, MA
13. Kumar K, Welke RJ (1992) Methodology engineering – a proposal for situation-specific methodology construction. In: Cotterman W, Senn JA (eds) Challenges and strategies for research in systems development. Wiley, New York, pp 257–269
14. Karlsson F (2005) Method configuration – a systems development project revisited. In: Nilsson AG et al (eds) Proceedings of the 14th international conference on information systems development. Springer
15. Karlsson F, Agerfalk PJ (2004) Method configuration – adapting to situational characteristics while creating reusable assets. Info Softw Technol 46(9):619–633
16. Martin J, Odell JJ (1994) Object-oriented methods. Prentice Hall PTR, Upper Saddle River, NJ
17. McIlory M (1976) Mass-produced software components. Software engineering concepts and techniques. In: Buxton JM et al (eds) Proceedings of Nato conference on software engineering, Garmisch, Germany
18. Nanci D, Espinasse B, Cohen B, Asselborn JC, Heckenroth H (2001) Ingénierie des systèmes d'information: merise deuxième génération. Vuibert, Paris
19. Natis YV, Schulte W (2003) Introduction to service-oriented architecture. Technologies, Gartner, Inc.
20. OASIS (2008) Reference architecture for service oriented architecture version 1.0, public review draft 1, 23 Apr 2008. http://docs.oasis-open.org/soa-rm/soa-ra/v1.0/soa-ra-pr-01.html
21. O'Riordan D (2002) Business process standards for web services. Tect, Chicago, USA
22. Papazoglou MP, Georgakopoulos D (2003) Service-oriented computing. Commun ACM 46(10):24–28
23. Peltz C (2003) Web services orchestration: review of emerging technologies, tools and standards. Technical report, Hewlett-Packard Company
24. Prat N (1997) Goal Formalization and classification for requirements engineering. In: Proceedings of the 3rd international workshop on requirements engineering: foundations of software quality REFSG'97, Barcelona, pp 145–156
25. Ramadour P, Cauvet C (2002) Approach and model for business components specification. In: Proceedings of the 13th international conference on database and expert systems, France
26. Ralyté J, Rolland C (2001) An assembly process model for method engineering. In: Proceedings of CAISE'01. LNCS, vol 2068. Springer, pp 267–283
27. Ralyté J, Brinkkemper S, Henderson-Sellers B (eds) (2007) Situational method engineering: fundamentals and experiences. In: Proceedings of the IFIP WG 8.1 working conference. IFIP Springer Series, vol 244. Springer, Boston, MA
28. Rolland C (2009) Endorsement of the book metamodeling for method engineering. In: Jeusfeld MA, Jarke M, Mylopoulos J (eds) Metamodeling for method engineering. MIT
29. Rolland C (2009) Method engineering: towards methods as services. Softw Process Improvement Practice 14:143–164
30. Rolland C, Prakash N (1996) A proposal for context-specific method engineering. In: IFIP WG 8.1 conference on method engineering, Atlanta, Georgie, pp 191–208
31. Rolland C, Salinesi C (2005) Modeling goals and reasoning with them. In: Aurum A, Wohlin C (eds) Engineering and managing software requirements (EMSR), Springer
32. Rolland C, Souveyet C (2009) Service oriented computing: an intentional approach. Trans Service Computing (IEEE-TSC), special issue on REFS (Requirements Engineering for Services), IEEE
33. Rolland C, Foucaut O, Benci G (1988) Conception de systèmes d'information: La méthode REMORA. Eyrolles, Paris

34. Rolland C, Plihon V, Ralyte J (1998) Specifying the reuse context of scenario method chunks. In: Pernici B, Thanos C (eds) Proceedings of CAISE'98. LNCS, vol 1413. Springer, pp 191–218
35. Rumbaugh J, Blaha M (1996) OMT tome1 – modélisation et conception orientées objet, Masson
36. Rumbaugh J, Blaha M, Premerlani W, Eddy F, Lorenson W (1991) Object-oriented modeling and design. Prentice Hall, Englewood Cliffs, NJ
37. Song X (1997) Systematic integration of design method. IEEE Software, vol 14, Issue 2, IEEE Computer Society Press, Los, pp 107–117 Alamitos, CA
38. Van Slooten K, Hodes B (1996) Characterizing IS development projects. In: Brinkkemper S, Lytinnen K, Welke RJ (eds) Method engineering – principles of method construction and tool support. Chapman & Hall, pp 29–44
39. Weinreich RJ, Sametinger J (2001) Component models and component services: concepts and principles. Component-based software engineering, putting the pieces together. Addison-Wesley, Reading MA
40. WSDL Version 2.0 (2007) Part 1: core language. http://www.w3.org/TR/2007/REC-wsdl20-20070626. Accessed 5 May 2010

Collaborative Requirements Engineering: Bridging the Gulfs Between Worlds

Alistair Sutcliffe

Abstract A method engineering approach is described for managing communication in RE processes based on Clark's theory of common ground. The common ground framework is used to evaluate the affordances of different RE representations such as scenarios, storyboards and models. The contribution that representations make to RE activities is reviewed to suggest heuristics for selecting appropriate representations to develop mutual understanding of RE issues between different stakeholders. A meta-model for RE activities is proposed that describes the process of communication and developing mutual understanding driven from abstract and concrete views of the problem domain. The meta-model is applied to management of RE sessions from a method engineering perspective. Application of the framework is illustrated with a case study of health informatics application.

1 Introduction

Design of methods and processes with the accompanying models, representations and tools has been an important influence on RE resulting from Rolland's research over a number of years [22, 25]. In general, Rolland's perspective was one of composing processes which could be executed by individuals or teams; although design of collaborative processes per se was not explicitly addressed in her work. This chapter follows a method engineering approach to RE with a focus on the nature of collaboration and communication in teams and between stakeholders.

Collaboration in the form of viewpoints, negotiations between stakeholders, and management of the RE process has been researched by many authors and is inherent in modelling languages such as i* and RE methods [21]. More recently collaboration among RE teams has received attention [8] to investigate how

A. Sutcliffe (✉)
Manchester Business School, University of Manchester, Booth Street West, Manchester, M15 6PB, UK
e-mail: a.g.sutcliffe@man.ac.uk

S. Nurcan et al. (eds.), *Intentional Perspectives on Information Systems Engineering*,
DOI 10.1007/978-3-642-12544-7_20,

communications are structured within teams and to recommend how CSCW (computer supported collaborative work) technologies might be adapted to improve teamworking. Although RE is recognised to be a multidisciplinary process which draws upon psychology, sociology, anthropology and linguistics, the role of linguistics has been limited to parsing and understanding requirements in natural language statements [23, 24] and formalising requirements statements [4]. More socially oriented discourse theories of language have received less attention. In this chapter a discourse theory of language, common ground [5], is used to motivate a method engineering design for collaborative RE as well as to evaluate the contributions that different representations might make to enhancing mutual understanding with RE teams.

2 Common Ground

The common ground theory or Clark's linguistic theory of discourse [5] describes the process by which mutual understanding is achieved though the process structure of human-human discourse. Briefly, Clark's theory of discourse explains how meaning is constructed by conversation and action which progresses towards a mutually agreed goal, the action ladder and project in Clark's terms. The main tenets of the theory that concern RE are summarised in Fig. 1.

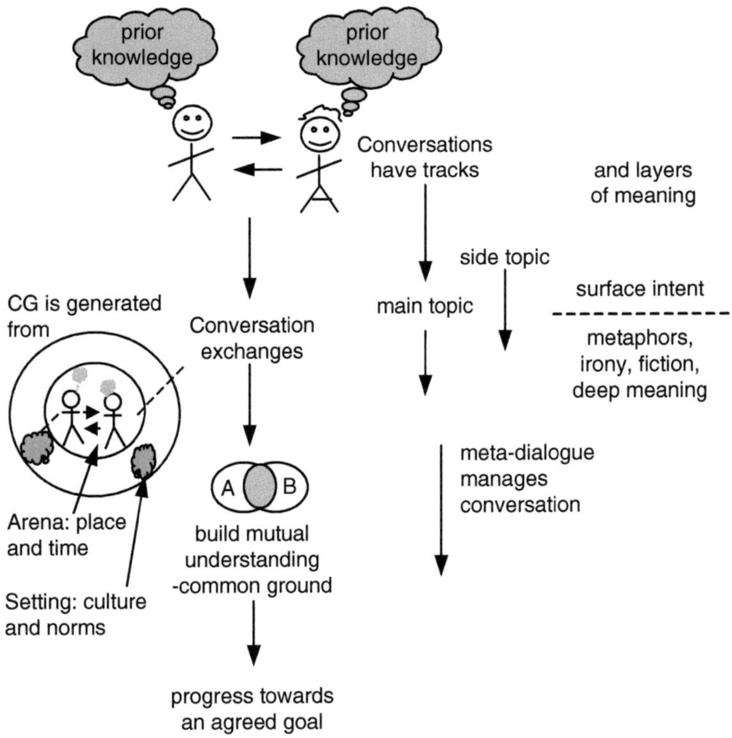

Fig. 1 Summary of common ground concepts

Common ground or mutual understanding is generated from three knowledge sources: (a) knowledge held by the participants about each other and the topic of the conversation; (b) knowledge about the environment in which the conversation takes place, including artefacts in the environment; and (c) shared knowledge about social conventions held by the participants. Conversations have tracks or topics which may be interleaved, for example major and minor topics, and meta-discourse or conversations which control the primary topic-related discourse. Meaning in conversations has different layers; the surface layer is explicit expression, but there may also be layers of tacit meaning which rely on deeper understanding of metaphors and interpretation of puns, irony, jokes and fiction.

Clark's theory explains the establishment of mutual understanding via a process of verbal and non-verbal communication integrated with action in the world, which progresses through stages of increasing understanding (common ground) that move towards a shared goal (the joint project). Shared understanding is helped by the participants' knowledge of each other, past conversations, and the context, referred to as the arena and setting. Brennan and Clark [3] give a set of criteria for effective conversation which has been applied to assessing the effectiveness of computer-mediated conversation (CMC) [15]:

- Co-presence: all participants share the same space and time.
- Visibility: conversers can see each other; inherent in co-presence.
- Audibility: audio communication is supported, e.g. phone conversations.
- Contemporality: messages can be generated and received in the same time interval, i.e. synchronous communication.
- Simultaneity: communication is possible in both directions at the same time, i.e. complete synchronous communication.
- Sequentiality: the order of message generation and receipt is preserved (asynchronous, ordered).
- Reviewability: messages can be re-read, i.e. possible for text but not for audio unless it is transcribed.
- Revisability: messages can be edited, afforded by text but not speech.

These criteria are supplemented with concepts from Media Richness Theory [7] that describe the communication channel/modality and the connectivity in communication (i.e. person-to-person vs. narrowcast vs. broadcast). Representation of participants' identity draws on concepts from Social Presence Theory [29]: explicit visible identities, tokens for identities, assumed covert identities, no identity, etc.

3 RE Representations and Communication Modalities

In this section the affordances of collaborative technologies for supporting RE are assessed using the common ground modalities framework to investigate the types of information and knowledge that can be represented by models, scenarios,

Table 1 Comparison of three scenarios of technology support for collaborative RE

	e-Mail + doc exchange	Video conf + doc exchange	Video conf + interactive docs
Co-presence	x	√	√√
Visibility	x	√	√√
Audibility	√	√	√
Contemporality	x	√	√√
Simultaneity	x	√	√√
Sequentiality	√	√	√
Reviewability	√	x	√
Revisability	√	x	√

prototypes, etc., and how such representations can mediate communication between different stakeholders. Table 1 summarises how communication is supported in three different scenarios of collaborative technology. First, e-mail communication combined with exchange of specifications and other documents is a common mode of collaboration between groups separated by distance. Since communication is asynchronous it enables collaboration across time zones, for example in offshore development. However, asynchronous media such as e-mail do not provide co-presence, and visibility is limited to the documents. Communication is sequential so it does not facilitate formation of common ground through interactive dialogues, although it does have the advantage of allowing time to review and revise documents. Video conferencing, in contrast, provides a richer communication medium for partial co-presence of team members, with synchronous audio and visual communication, although even advanced video conference systems are a considerable degradation from face-to-face communication [17]. The penalty of video conferencing with document exchange is that while it builds common ground between team members, it does not integrate easily with understanding generated from documentation. It is difficult to view and attend to documents during a video conference so reviewability and revisability (of documents and the video conversation) are impaired. In the third scenario, video conferencing technology is enhanced with interactive tools so team members can view and edit documents while conversing. This ideally joins the thread of understanding generated by working on documents with video-mediated conversations; however, maintaining the focus of attention between conversation and working on documents requires careful management; also, review and revision time can be compromised by the time the team spends in synchronous collaborative work. Hence a combination of approaches may be advised. Asynchronous working provides a time to think and reflect which builds understanding of the problem using documentation, while synchronous dialogue builds mutual understanding among team members via conversations.

This leads to investigation of the role of different documents in RE. Since RE representations can experience multiple interpretations [11, 24], it is necessary to briefly describe the representations which will be reviewed:

- Scenarios are considered to be text-based descriptions of systems, expressed in natural language, similar to stories or narrative examples described in Agile methods [2]. Scenarios contain realistic detail about systems, their environment, users, interactions and activities.
- Storyboards and informal sketches are drawings of system designs and the system environment showing realistic layout of objects, artefacts and their context.
- Informal models and notations are models of the system and its environment expressed in a semi-formal diagram language, such as data flow diagrams, object relationships or activity sequence diagrams.
- Formal models and system specifications are expressed in a rigorous mathematically based language, e.g. Z, SCR, KAOS [38].
- Prototypes are software artefacts which present partial implementations of the design system.

The cognitive affordances of these representations are illustrated in Table 2. Clark's communication modalities have been revised with criteria drawn from the cognitive dimensions framework [9] which is more closely oriented toward representations:

- Interaction: how easy it is to point to and manipulate representations during team meetings.
- Comprehensibility: how easily understood a representation is by ordinary users without specific training.
- Testability: how easy it is to challenge and evaluate assumptions and facts expressed in a representation.

Scenarios are reviewable and revisable since text can be scanned and edited, although the ease of revision is enhanced by word processors. Scenarios are easily comprehended, but interaction is limited to indicating particular sections of a narrative. Scenarios, since they express specific instances and examples, are not testable by themselves, although a collection of scenarios can form test cases for specifications [18]. Storyboards and sketches are easy to review but less easy to revise even with software drawing tools, and interaction is limited to pointing to

Table 2 Assessment of RE representations to illustrate affordances for collaboration

	Reviewability	Revisability	Interaction	Comprehensibility	Testability
Scenarios	√√	√√	–	√√√	x
Storyboards and sketches	√√√	√√	√	√√√	x
Informal models/notations	√	√√	√	√	√
Formal models	–	–	–	xx	√√
Prototypes	√√	–	√√	√√	√

and highlighting parts of the sketch. Sketches are possibly easier to comprehend than language-based scenarios, although images can be susceptible to ambiguous interpretation. Storyboards and sketches are not testable in themselves but, as with scenarios, they can provide test cases to validate early requirements with users. Informal models are less reviewable and comprehensible than sketches since even informal notations require some learning, but they have the advantage of easier revision since the format of diagram components enables software tools to facilitate editing. Informal models also facilitate testing since their components have an agreed denotation and dependencies, so associations, links and pathways can be checked for consistency, although not as rigorously as with formal models. Formal notations enable comprehensive testing with model checkers and formal reasoning tools, albeit at the penalty of poor comprehensibility and reviewability for most stakeholders. Finally, prototypes are comprehensible as the behaviour and appearance is visible; furthermore, user interaction facilitates testing and validation of requirements. The penalty lies in poor revisability since this necessitates changing code, although with advanced prototyping languages this cost can be reduced.

Common ground is generated by conversations between stakeholders, augmented by mutual understanding of information expressed in RE representations. Clearly the more generally accessible a representation is, the better it supports the formation of common ground; therefore, not surprisingly, scenarios, storyboards and sketches are effective means of promoting mutual understanding. However, these representations are prone to ambiguous interpretation so understanding between stakeholders may conflict. Informal models can reduce ambiguity by affording easier testing, while formal models can eliminate ambiguity by automated reasoning, although with the disadvantage of more difficult comprehension and limited access across stakeholder groups. An important tenet of Clark's theory is that common ground is generated not only through conversations but also by interaction with artefacts in the world. Hence prototypes promote common ground since mutual understanding is generated by interaction and the consequences of incorrect system actions are visible to all stakeholders, thereby stimulating validation discussions. Finally it is worth noting that informal notations in the design rationale family support common ground by summarising argument and the content of design conversations.

No one representation will suffice to support the development of common ground; rather, a combination is required to support different activities and phases in the requirements process when emphasis might change from discovering information, to negotiation and establishing common views, then testing and checking that specifications conform to goals and known facts describing the world. This leads to the next section, where common ground and RE activities are considered.

4 RE Activities, Representations and Common Ground

The process of collaboration in RE and how this fits within project management more generally are reviewed using the common ground framework. Lessons from CSCW for collaboration, such as shared awareness, activity awareness and role allocation, are applied to RE tasks and processes to suggest how RE might be improved. Activities in the RE road map [16] are reviewed from a common ground perspective while investigating the role for appropriate representations.

4.1 Elicit and Summarise

Elicitation commences with little common ground between the users, domain experts and requirements engineer. This task involves not only capturing information but also making sure that there is a shared understanding about domain facts and user goals. Representations play an important part in summarising information so it can be discussed and checked by all parties. Without representations transient speech in interviews can allow ambiguities and mismatches in understanding to go unchecked. Information representations: sketches, drawings, photographs and video, all help to supplement text and enable elicited facts to be inspected and their meanings evaluated. Scenarios provide records of specific episodes; furthermore, their realism encourages the development of common ground since specific stories and descriptions of the real world are anchored in the users' experience. Similarly sketches, drawings and photographs record reality. However, common ground in RE presents a paradox. The conversation has to progress towards a mutually agreed project: realisation of the users' goals. But this dialogue, as has been increasingly acknowledged in RE, involves exploration of the solution space that might satisfy the users' goals. Specifications inevitably have to be generalised and abstract. While an abstract view of specifications is closer to the personal common ground of software engineers, abstractions tend to be alien to most users. Hence common ground has to be established between abstract and concrete views, which causes a tension that runs through all RE activities. At the elicitation stage, representations will be biased towards the users' common ground and hence tend to focus on specific details in scenarios, sketches, etc., although goal trees may start development over a more abstract view of intentions.

4.2 Analyse and Reflect

The tension between abstractions and specific representations is central to modelling. Generalisations are derived from specific examples, so models arise from scenarios. Unfortunately scenarios impose a constraint on developing abstract common ground, since each scenario focuses on a specific slice of reality. This raises the coverage question: how many scenarios are necessary to capture not only the generalities but also the exceptions in a domain? Increasing the number of scenarios suffers from a law of diminishing returns since the additional detail imposes an information overload on stakeholders. Furthermore, adding more scenarios runs the risk of focusing attention on superfluous detail. There is no ideal solution to the coverage problem, although systems sampling and generative tools can help to increase confidence that models have captured the more important variations [35].

Fig. 2 Combination of representations for common ground in the perspective of RE activities. Two areas of common ground are illustrated, one shared by requirements engineers (RE1, RE2) and user stakeholders (S1, S2), and the other only shared among requirements engineers

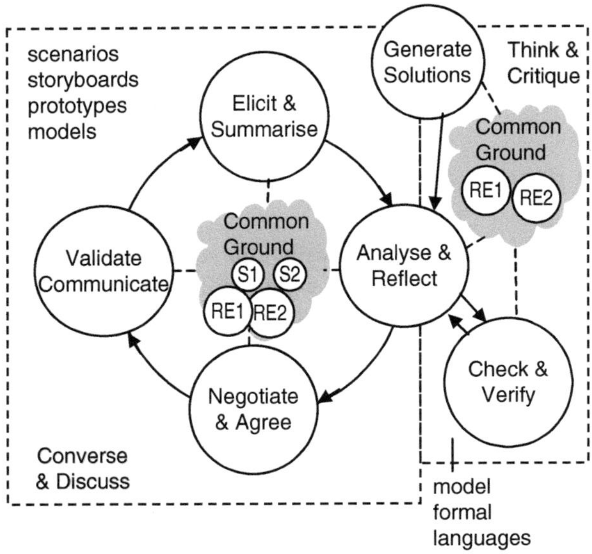

Informal models enable abstract viewpoints to be debated; but models may hide ambiguities and, worse still, assertions may go unchallenged. Models, even informal use cases and data flow diagrams, belong to the realm of the requirements engineer, rather than being part of users' normal discourse. Hence there is a tendency for disjunction to appear between specific and abstract common ground, with requirements engineers focusing on abstractions and users tending to favour the specific. The solution to this dilemma is to juxtapose concrete and abstract representations, for example using scenarios to challenge models and vice versa. This intuition has emerged in some RE methods such as ScenIC [18] where a range of scenarios provide challenges to input process specified in models and then the acceptability of output from system models is evaluated in the light of scenarios of use. This combination of representations helps to bridge the concrete and abstract division in common ground, as summarised in Fig. 2.

4.3 Negotiate and Agree

Negotiating, prioritising and achieving mutually agreed requirements all focus on the process of establishing common ground between stakeholders. Representations have a special role to play in this activity since common ground in conversation is limited by working memory to about five topics or ideas [1, 32]. Working memory is the human equivalent of cache memory; unfortunately its contents are limited, and become lost as they are overwritten by new input. This means we can only process a limited quantity of information at once. However, decisions and negotiations require consideration of many facts and options. Representations overcome the limitations

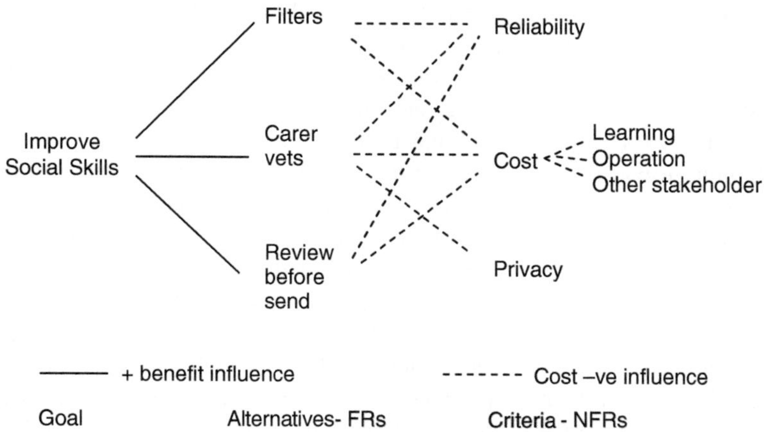

Fig. 3 Design rationale diagram (QOC notation [13], example from [34]) which illustrates the decision space of design solutions to address the user's personal goal to improve his/her social skills in e-mail communication

of working memory since large quantities of information can be inspected at will, so we can read information rather than having to remember it. The representation becomes an external extension to our memory. Representations support negotiation; for example, design rationale [6] (see Fig. 3) presents a set of alternatives (solutions) for a requirements problem (the issue in gIBIS) and criteria through which alternatives can be debated. Design rationale summarises the decision space as the common ground for negotiation.

Other representations, ranging from decision trees to decision tables and ranked lists, all help to summarise the decision space so dialogues can progress towards an agreed common ground. In many cases software tools facilitate the process by comparing many attributes of requirements and proposed solutions, for example House of Quality decision matrixes [10], or goal trees in Analytic Hierarchy Process [12].

4.4 Validate and Communicate

These activities have very different implications for common ground. Validation is the process of establishing that the requirements specification and proposed system design satisfy users' requirements. In this case the external behaviour of the system is the necessary common ground which has to be tested and agreed between developers and users. Hence, in Fig. 2, validation occupies both areas of common ground, discussing the results of walkthroughs, demonstrations and simulations, while reviewing and critiquing the specifications when discrepancies between system behaviour and user requirements have been discovered. Verification, in contrast, addresses checking and proving the correct internal behaviour of the specified system. In this case common ground concerns only the software specialists so formal models and specifications, which are not accessible to users, are appropriate. However, for validation, representations need to support both concrete and abstract views of requirements. Contrasting and integrating representations is part of the answer, but Clark's action ladder points to further lessons.

Common ground is established not only through conversation but also by acting in the world. This is manifest in prototypes where the consequence of action and interaction are immediately apparent. Although interacting with prototypes is a powerful means of analysis, it needs to be combined with specifications and models for causal diagnosis of problems observed during testing prototypes. The causes of incorrect or inappropriate actions need to be traced back to errors in specifications or inadequate requirements. Models can be 'walked-through', and early designs can be mocked-up as storyboards presented as interactive sequences, or designs can be simulated as Wizard of Oz techniques. User hands-on testing, i.e. interaction with RE artefacts and prototypes, plays a vital role in developing common ground since perceiving the consequences of action is a powerful means of promoting understanding. Facts described in a conversation may be accepted uncritically at face value, but it is difficult to ignore the consequences of actions.

4.5 Communicating Requirements

The lessons so far for common ground may be summarised as the following set of principles:

- Iterative cycles or requirements analysis and design exploration build mutual understanding about users' requirements and the space of possible solutions for those requirements.
- Common ground in RE involves integrating the abstract and concrete sub-spaces. Juxtaposing abstract (models) and concrete presentations (scenarios, sketches, storyboards) helps to bridge the gap.
- Interaction with representations and especially prototypes helps to build mutual understanding.
- Negotiation and agreeing common ground requires special representations and tools which support decision making, by depicting the choice space, and facilitating comparisons.

Concurrent use of several representations enables comparisons; for instance, scenarios, drawings, storyboards for specific information, with models, diagrams and text specifications for abstract information, while the decision space is structured using matrices and design rationale. Adding prototypes and simulations for the merits of understanding interaction may seem to be the optimal solution. However, the threads and tracks component of Clark's theory points towards a problem with multiple representations. There is no escape from the limitations of working memory and selective attention. Although multiple representations augment our ability to develop shared understanding, within any one conversation we can only concentrate on a limited quantity of information. The focus of attention within stakeholder groups has to be managed during requirements conversations; furthermore, conversation is only part of the process of generating mutual understanding. This leads to the application of discourse theory and Clark's common ground to management of requirements conversations.

5 Managing RE Conversations

The first principle for establishing common ground is to see the world from the viewpoint of other stakeholders. The ability to imagine the thoughts and intentions of others is probably a unique human attribute, and is known as the theory of mind [14]. Briefly, the theory of mind in social psychology describes our ability to construct models of other people and their intentions. Knowledge of others is first-order theory of mind; this can be extended into a second order as a projection about beliefs other individuals hold about their friends, and so on. Application of the metaphor is simple: project one's imagination into the viewpoint of other stakeholders. The metaphor can be extended to consider the viewpoint of the software machine by treating it as another agent. This can provide a useful perspective for modelling by inquiring what knowledge the software system will need to execute a particular process for achieving a user's goal. A meta-model for managing RE dialogues is illustrated in Fig. 4. This abstracts the basic cycle of conversation and reflection which can be mapped to more specific RE processes illustrated in Fig. 2.

User-stakeholder goals are the starting point for analysis following the accepted GORE-style approaches. Modelling user agents, goals, soft goals and tasks with

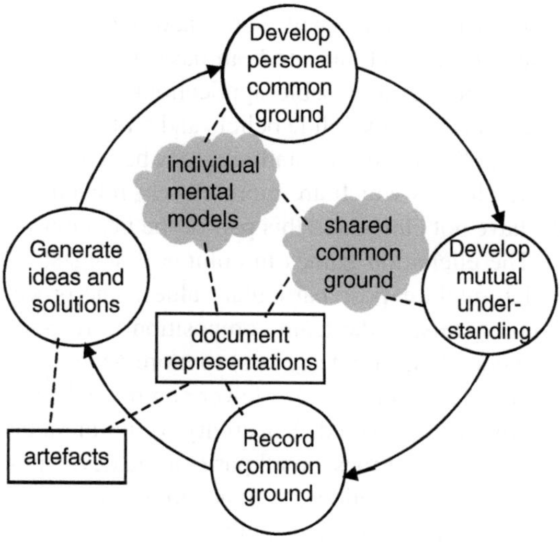

Fig. 4 Meta-model of common ground development

notations such as i* [39] also helps understanding user viewpoints. Clarks's theory draws attention to the fact that mutual understanding is generated during a dialogue set within an arena and setting of mutually understood norms and culture. This background knowledge may be referred to as attitudes, opinions, beliefs and values, a set of linguistically based but ambiguous concepts which shape our intentions, decisions and actions. Attention in RE tends to be driven by modelling and analysis; for example, tracing event flows, decomposing goals or analysing dependencies between agents, tasks and goals. However, there is little guidance about the use of contextual information or the people-oriented issues that are necessary for interpreting models. In spite of the recognition that issues of culture, politics and value clashes often de-rail many system developments, values have not received much attention in RE. I argue that a key component in managing RE conversations is awareness and active analysis of stakeholder values to arrive at a mutually understood and agreed view about what motivates stakeholder goals and why.

5.1 Value-Based Requirements Engineering

The taxonomy of values and their consequences for process guidance are illustrated in Table 3.

Nine upper-level value categories are proposed based on Rescher's theory [20] and investigations from the card-sort experiments and interviews with expert RE practitioners. Six categories accord with generally recognised concepts, some of which have more stable interpretations: trust, morals, aesthetics and security; while sociability and creativity/innovation hide many sub-categories. Some of these are given in the related terms column. Personal characteristics are diverse; personality theory dimensions are used (introvert/extrovert, sensing/intuition, thinking/feeling, judging/perceiving), with some additions. Personality characteristics are closely related to motivations and both have implications for team management in the RE process and customisable applications. Motivations are a placeholder for a more detailed taxonomy, while beliefs and attitudes are a diverse category which includes socio-political, cultural and religious beliefs. These change more rapidly than other value clusters which are more closely related to personal attributes; consequently we have not elaborated this part of the taxonomy.

The elicitation guides in column 3 suggest some potential conversation topics which might expose particular values. The process implications in column 4 vary from organising the team composition in response to aesthetic needs (i.e. include aesthetically aware designers) to more general heuristics for project team management, such as the need for fewer controls when trust is high, or the converse when mistrust is discovered. Sensitivity to moral values indicates the need for honesty, openness and fairness in all parts of the development process. In many cases, especially with motivations, beliefs and attitudes, value analysis may alert the analyst to potential stakeholder conflicts, in which case negotiation will be necessary to

Table 3 Values: elicitation hints and implications for RE process management

Value concept	Related terms	Potential sources	Process implications
Trust	Openness, integrity, loyalty, responsibility, reliability	Relationships with other individuals/ departments, privacy policies	Less control, milestone checks, improved team confidence
Collaboration	Cooperation, friendship, sympathy, altruism	Relationships with others, awareness of others (office politics)	Improved team cooperation, shared awareness
Morals/ethics	Justice, fairness, equality, tolerance	Behaviour towards others, opinions of others' behaviours	Openness and honesty in team
Creativity, innovation	Originality, adventure, novelty	Work processes, problem solving	Creativity, workshops, facilitators
Aesthetics	Beauty, nature, art	Self appearance, reaction to images, shapes, art and design	Team members, designers, storyboards
Security	Safety, privacy, risk	Data management policies, attitudes towards change	Hazard/threat analysis
Personal characteristics	Serious/playful, introvert/ extrovert, systematic/ opportunistic	Self image, personae scenarios, psychological questionnaires	Customisation analysis for personal RE, team conflict management
Motivation	Ambition, achievement	Ambitions, goals, career plans	Stakeholder analysis, rewards, incentives for members
Beliefs and attitudes	Cultural, political, religious topics	Leisure interests, user background, reaction to news events	Stakeholder analysis, team composition, incentives

arrive at a common set of values; alternatively, system configuration/customisation may need to be considered (e.g. different levels of security controls mapped to stakeholders who regard security as very or not important). Values and motivations are used to direct attention during interviews and requirements meetings, and supplement the agenda that would be suggested by goal-oriented RE. They also provide contextual information for interpreting users' goals and assumptions. For example, focusing on motivations before users' goals provides more contextual information on longer-term drivers for users' interests which can then be used to explore more specific goals. Motivations also focus attention on developing a common ground of understanding with individual users which will be important for personalisation (see Table 4).

Table 4 Motivations and their implications

Motivation	Description	Implications
Power	Need to control others, authority, command	Work organisation, responsibility, control hierarchy
Possession	Desire for material goods, wealth	Resource control, monetary incentives, marketing
Achievement	Need to design, construct, organise	Goal oriented, to project aims
Self-esteem	Need to feel satisfied with oneself	Link personal and project goals, praise personal achievement
Peer-esteem	Need to feel valued by others	Team composition, social feedback and rewards, praise
Self-efficacy	Confidence in own capabilities	Confidence building, training, skill matching
Curiosity, learning	Desire to discover, understand world	Extensible systems, self tutoring
Sociability	Desire to be part of a group	Collaboration in work organisation
Altruism	Desire to help others	Cooperation in work organisation

Values direct attention to user beliefs that may either suggest non-functional requirements or perspectives within which to interpret users' motivations and goals. Finally, emotions give useful feedback on users' views which may not be expressed in conversation, so they afford another means of developing common ground by observation of facial expressions, body language and voice tone to detect frustration, anger, pleasure, etc. Agenda-setting heuristics and management of attention to issues within requirements conversations are summarised in Fig. 5.

The heuristics advise on use of the checklists of values and motivations in Tables 3 and 4 as agendas within interviews and other RE activities organised in an iterative cycle of developing mutual understanding.

- Elicit users' and organisation's motivations and values in initial requirements sessions when high-level goals are discussed.
- Analyse motivations in more detail if requirements for personalisation are indicated or to reflect individual needs.
- Goals should be interpreted in the light of user values and motivations; which provide useful consistency checks.
- Motivations and values which have not been cross-referenced to goals during analysis may suggest missing requirements.
- Emotions provide useful feedback on the acceptability of requirements and prototype designs, especially where users are not confident in providing verbal feedback.

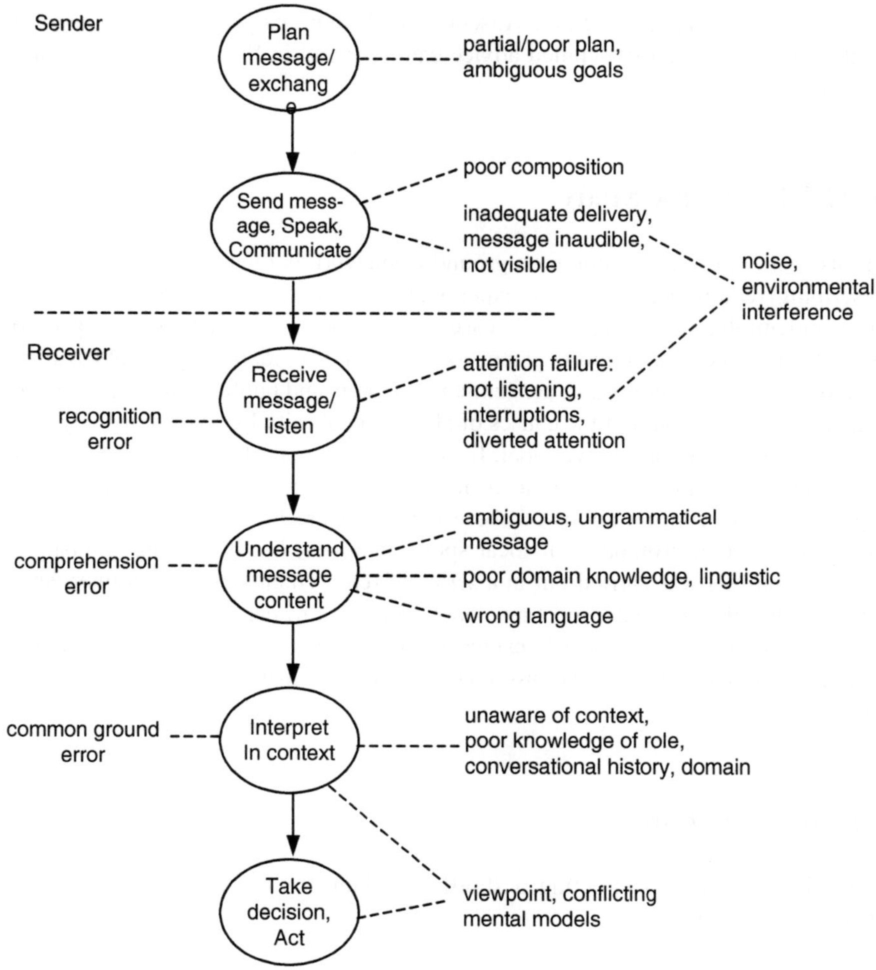

Fig. 5 Discourse sequence model for common ground and attention agenda control

- Analysis of emotional reaction to user values can indicate strong beliefs and hidden social and political agendas.
- Comparing stakeholder values and motivations can help discovering hidden conflicts.

Finally, Clark's theory provides a useful perspective on the difficulties of analysing user values and other such soft issues in RE. Conversations have layers of meaning (see Fig. 1), so stakeholders may not be explicit in verbalising their intentions and beliefs. Value analysis and sensitivity to emotional responses can uncover deeper meanings in tacit expressions; however, such analysis may uncover difficult issues which need sensitive handling. Some issues may be better left unresolved and ambiguous in the early stages of analysis. Further guidance on handling requirements discourse and value analysis is beyond the scope of this chapter, but more detailed advice can be found in Sutcliffe [31] and Thew and Sutcliffe [36].

6 ADVISES Case Study

In this section, use of the common ground framework is illustrated in a case study describing requirements analysis experience in an e-science application to support epidemiological research. The case study reviews requirements analysis for ADVISES, a decision-support system for analysis of epidemiology problems that served two stakeholder groups: academic researchers and public health analysts. For researchers, understanding the causes of childhood obesity by statistical analysis of health records was a high-level goal. In contrast, the goal of public health analysts (PCT: Primary Care Trust) was local health management; for example, identifying where local concentrations of obese children were located and then targeting interventions, e.g. promotion of local sports facilities, healthy eating campaigns, etc. The analysis was carried out in a series of requirements elicitation interviews, observations of stakeholder meetings, observations of research work, and scenario-based discussions of storyboard designs and prototypes. Recordings of the various meetings and interviews were transcribed and analysed using the taxonomy and key issues.

6.1 Value Analysis

Analysis began by constructing a shortlist of hunches based on values directly expressed by the users:

- Being methodical, precise, systematic (personal characteristics).
- Creativity.
- Public profile, collaborations, National Health Service (sociability).
- Users don't collaborate or work together (sociability? trust?).

We used the value and motivation tables to focus attention on these ideas, to unpack the meaning of terms such as 'methodical' for our users, and explore the common ground for understanding shared values, goals and possible design solutions. The users' public profile collaboration appeared to clash with their stated internal approach to work, so we focused attention on this issue.

Following several iterations of analysis making use of both observation and interview data, we developed a deeper understanding of the potential common ground and new ideas about our users' values and emotions:

- Innovation and creativity were important for the researchers, with a strong technical focus and willingness to adopt new software; however, this clashed with the PCT analysts' conservatism and concerns about control.
- Collaboration with outside groups/people is fundamental to our users' way of working. As well as developing new research and tools, academic researchers were motivated by profile-raising for their organisation (achievement and altruism to help collaborators, rather than power). However, they rarely share details of analytical work and display trust and confidence in each others' abilities, which reveals a continuing tension between trust and data security.

The apparent contradiction between internal and external collaboration was explained in terms of differences between working styles (personal characteristics). Security and privacy of data emerged as an important value which was added to the key issues. A common ground value map for the two stakeholder groups is illustrated in Fig. 6.

The PCT users were motivated by service to the community and responsibilities to improve health in the local area, and this implied creative solutions and opportunistic responses to problems. In contrast, academic researchers were motivated by the achievement in scientific research and this necessitated valuing a systematic and methodical approach. Sensitivity to our users' emotional responses has guided the RE process.

Values analysis was influential in shaping our view of user requirements. One illustration is the divergence between the two stakeholder groups. The researchers' values were oriented towards security in data management policies with trust in data analysis processes. They were concerned with accurate, well documented and repeatable scientific processes, indicating non-functional requirements (NFRs) such as reliability, consistency and accuracy in processes, as well as privacy and security for data and results from statistical analysis. Health analysts in contrast were more concerned with creative problem solving, and being responsive to local needs. Privacy and accuracy were not important values, so their NFRs were flexibility, ease of use and rapid response times. The conflicting NFRs were resolved by producing a configurable system, offering the researchers workflows controlling system functions in a consistent and repeatable manner, while the health analysts had access

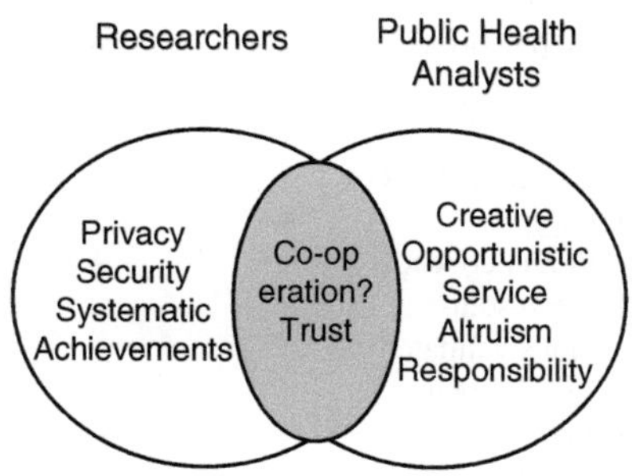

Fig. 6 Value map for negotiating the common ground between the ADVISES stakeholders

to simpler functionality that supported more *ad hoc* analysis. The concerns over privacy and security were agreed as shared NFRs during the requirements process, which developed common ground by using a combination of representations.

6.2 Reflections on Representations and Process

Throughout the requirements process RE techniques and representations were adapted to both project goals and the circumstances at that time. Table 5 summarises the appropriateness of each technique used for identifying the necessary knowledge to drive the requirements process forward.

Early in the project, a combination of interviews, with observation of meetings and working practices, provided rich domain knowledge, and generated ideas which started to shape the project. However, whilst interviews and observation taught us about the more concrete and observable aspects of work, these methods were not effective ways to access tacit expertise about epidemiological workflows and decision making. Instead, the use of scenarios and the domain knowledge workshops were particularly helpful in addressing this gap and understanding how our users considered evidence and made decisions about their data. Once we began the early design work, a combination of scenarios and storyboards worked well, with scenarios proving a particularly effective way to feed users' requirements to the project team, while storyboards and prototypes were useful for exploring designs with users.

Open-ended interviews were effective for initiating the requirements process, since the concept of an interview is widely understood. Interviews elicited both concrete and abstract information, recorded in scenarios of use and lists of goals and domain facts respectively. The stakeholders were comfortable with the presence of an observer/analyst in meetings and this also proved an effective way to get

Table 5 The effectiveness of representations in supporting development of different aspects of common ground

Developing common ground for	Interviews	Observation of work	Domain knowledge workshops	Scenarios	Storyboards	Prototypes
Concrete domain knowledge	++	++	++	+++	+	+
Values and stakeholder CG	++	–	++	++	–	–
User goals	++	–	+	++	++	+
Abstract concepts	+	–	+++	–	–	–
Agreed solutions/validated requirements	–	–	–	++	+++	+++
Requirements specification	++	–	–	++	++	++

background knowledge. However, observations of working practice did not capture much concrete detail and often turned into a dialogue between the requirements analyst and the users, since epidemiology is cognitive-intensive work which involves abstract concepts rather than specific details.

When we first introduced the use of scenarios the epidemiologists found the approach somewhat abstract and felt it was hard to contrive situations that were not grounded in current work. However, as they became more familiar with the method, they were able to think of specific examples of working practices, current problems and how they would like the system to support their investigations. Domain knowledge workshops were intended to capture abstract knowledge about the concepts, terminology and semantics within the users' domain. The workshops placed the epidemiologists in an unusual situation, asking them to discuss aspects of their world that they take for granted. In order to make this task easier, elicitation started with more concrete concepts, e.g. the different types of epidemiological study, and then moved to more abstract questions. This approach worked well, and the epidemiologists commented that they found the workshops interesting and engaging.

Two representations are notable omissions from the case study analysis: informal and formal models. The absence of formal models is not surprising in an iterative user-centred RE process that was closely related to agile development approaches. However, the role of informal models is diverse and needs more explanation. Use cases, data flow diagrams and class diagrams were used but only among the developers. The reasons why these representations were not shared with the users, in contravention of the common ground framework, were twofold. First, the requirements analyst was a bioinformatician and domain expert rather than a computer science-trained requirements engineer; hence her common ground with the stakeholders was not directly supported by models. Secondly, even though the introduction of use cases was encouraged, scenarios and other concrete representations provided sufficient common ground to support development of mutual understanding even for abstract viewpoints on process and data structures. This did incur some penalties in misunderstandings that might have been discovered earlier in the process; for example, the expert researcher workflows were not articulated clearly and use of process dependency diagrams could have focused attention on resolving ambiguities. In data specification, the division of continuous distributions into discrete categories was important for all statistical analyses, yet this remained unshared tacit knowledge for some time. More explicit data modelling may have identified this issue.

In spite of these limitations the use of value-based RE to focus attention on topics which required mutual understanding, coupled with use of multiple representations, served the project well. Storyboards were useful in developing a common ground of design ideas, since alternatives and variations could be deployed quickly within requirements sessions, either by drawing, swapping illustrations or adding post-it notes. Prototypes supported validation by eliciting detailed feedback on design features; however, this was combined with discussion of more abstract concepts, such as workflows for both stakeholder groups and how the system design might be improved to fit different ways of working. Even though the storyboards, prototypes and scenarios were used in separate analysis sessions with academic researchers and the PCT analysts, they formed a common ground understanding of alternative views which evolved into specification of core common functionality of the system, with customised versions for each stakeholder group to meet their needs and values.

7 Conclusion

The contributions of this chapter have been to develop Rolland's vision of method engineering from the perspective of discourse theory and natural language. Application of Clark's common ground as a framework for critiquing representations and techniques throws light on their relative contributions to one of the fundamental problems in RE: how to reconcile abstract and concrete views in system development, so that a mutual understanding of requirements, the software design and domain constraints emerges. Combination of representations has also been researched in Rolland's method engineering [26, 27] to suggest how scenarios and models in particular can improve understanding of requirements. Other examples of using scenarios and concrete representations to challenge models and goals can be found in obstacles analysis for KAOS modelling [37] and scenario-based validation in ScenIC [18].

Use of scenarios, prototypes, and design rationale formed the kernel of the SCRAM method [30]; however, experience demonstrated that too many representations can overload users, resulting in poor focus on key issues [33], in spite of the use of design rationale and scenario walkthrough to structure sessions. So while juxtaposing representations is advantageous, optimal use still poses several research problems. This raises a fundamental question in the method engineering debate: whether it is best to provide users and requirements engineers with a tool-kit of representations and techniques and let them take the decisions on how to use them during the process; or the alternative of trying to provide prescriptive cook-book guidance for different situations. Rolland tended towards the flexible tool-kit approach [19, 26, 28], with which I agree. However, I argue that a theoretical framework, such as the common ground described in this chapter, can give researchers and practitioners useful criteria to compose the RE process and choose representations to suit their particular circumstances.

References

1. Baddeley AD (1986) Working memory. Oxford University, Oxford
2. Beck K (1999) Extreme programming explained: embracing change. Addison-Wesley, New York
3. Brennan SE, Clark HH (1996) Conceptual pacts and lexical choice of conversation. J Exp Psychol: Learning, Memory Cognition 22(6):1482–1493

4. Chantree F, Nuseibeh B, De Roeck A, Willis A (2006) Identifying nocuous ambiguities in natural language requirements. In: Proceedings of 14th IEEE international requirements engineering conference (RE'06), IEEE Computer Society, Los Alamitos, CA
5. Clark HH (1996) Using language. Cambridge University, Cambridge
6. Conklin J, Begeman ML (1988) gIBIS: a hypertext tool for exploratory policy discussion. ACM Trans Office Info Systems 64:303–331
7. Daft RL, Lengel RH, Trevino LK (1987) Message equivocality, media selection, and manager performance: implications for information systems. MIS Quarter 11(3):355–366
8. Damian D, Marczak S, Kwan I (2007) Collaboration patterns and the impact of distance on awareness in requirements-centred social networks. In: Proceedings of 15th IEEE internation-alrequirements engineering conference RE'07, IEEE Computer Society, Los Alamitos, CA
9. Green TRG, Petre M (1996) Usability analysis of visual programming environments: a cognitive dimensions framework. J Visual Languages Computing 7:131–174
10. Hauser J, Clausing D (1988) The house of quality. Harvard Business Rev 5:63–73
11. Jarke M, Pohl K, Jacobs S, Bubenko J, Assenova P, Holm P, Wangler B, Rolland C, Plihon V, Schmitt JR, Sutcliffe AG, Jones S, Maiden NAM, Till D, Vassiliou Y, Constantopoulos P, Spanoudakis G (1993) Requirements engineering: an integrated view of representation, process, and domain. In: Proceedings of the 4th European software engineering conference. LNCS, vol 717. Springer, Berlin
12. Karlsson J, Ryan K (1997) A cost value approach for prioritizing requirements. IEEE Softw 14(5):67–74
13. MacLean A, Young RM, Bellotti V, Moran TP (1991) Questions, options and criteria: elements of design space analysis. Human-Computer Interaction 6(3/4):201–250
14. Mitchell P (1997) Introduction to theory of mind: children, autism and apes. Arnold, London
15. Monk AF, Watts LA (2000) Peripheral participation in video mediated communication. Int J Human-Computer Studies 52:933–958
16. Nuseibeh B, Easterbrook S (2000) Requirements engineering: a roadmap. In: Proceedings of international conference on software engineering (ICSE-2000), ACM, New York
17. Olson GM, Olson JS (2000) Distance matters. Human-Computer Interaction 15(2):139–178
18. Potts C (1999) ScenIC: a strategy for inquiry-driven requirements determination. In: Proceedings of 4th IEEE international symposium on requirements engineering. IEEE Computer Society, Los Alamitos, CA
19. Ralyte J, Deneckère R, Rolland C (2003) Towards a generic model for situational method engineering. In: Proceedings of 15th international conference on advanced information systems engineering (CAISE'03). LNCS, vol 2681. Springer, Berlin
20. Rescher N (1969) Introduction to value theory. Prentice-Hall, Englewood Cliffs, NJ
21. Robertson S, Robertson J (1999) Mastering the requirements process. Addison Wesley, Harlow
22. Rolland C (1998) A comprehensive view of process engineering. In: Proceedings of international conference on advanced information systems engineering (CAISE). LNCS, vol 1413. Springer, Berlin
23. Rolland C, Ben Achour C (1998) Guiding the construction of textual use case specifications. Data Knowl Eng J 25(1–2):125–160
24. Rolland C, Proix C (1992) A natural language approach for requirements engineering. In: Proceedings of the 4th international conference (CAiSE '92). LNCS, vol 593. Springer, Berlin
25. Rolland C, Prakash N, Benjamen A (1999) A multi-model view of process modelling. Reqs Eng 4(4):169–187
26. Rolland C, Salinesi C, Etien A (2004) Eliciting gaps in requirements change. Reqs Eng 9(1):1–15
27. Rolland C, Souveyet C, Ben Achour C (1998) Guiding goal modeling using scenarios. IEEE Trans Softw Eng 24(12):1055–1071

28. Rolland C, Ben Achour C, Cauvet C, Ralyte J, Sutcliffe AG, Maiden NAM, Jarke M, Haumer P, Pohl K, Dubois E, Heymans P (1998) A proposal for a scenario classification framework. Reqs Eng 3(1):23–47
29. Short J, Williams E, Christie B (1976) The social psychology of telecommunications. Wiley, Chichester
30. Sutcliffe AG (1995) Requirements rationales: integrating approaches to requirements analysis. In: Designing interactive systems: DIS 95 conference proceedings, ACM Press, New York
31. Sutcliffe AG (2002) User-centred requirements engineering. Springer, London
32. Sutcliffe AG (2003) Scenario-based requirements engineering. In Proceedings of IEEE joint international conference on requirements engineering, IEEE Computer Society, Los Alamitos, CA
33. Sutcliffe AG, Ryan M (1997) Assessing the usability and efficiency of design rationale. In: Proceedings of human computer interaction INTERACT-97. IFIP/Chapman and Hall, London
34. Sutcliffe AG, Fickas S, Sohlberg M (2005) Personal and contextual requirements engineering. In: Proceedings of 13th IEEE international conference on requirements engineering, IEEE Computer Society, Los Alamitos, CA
35. Sutcliffe AG, Maiden NAM, Minocha S, Manuel D (1998) Supporting scenario-based requirements engineering. IEEE Trans Softw Eng 24(12):1072–1088
36. Thew S, Sutcliffe AG (2008) Value-based requirements engineering. In: Proceedings of 16th IEEE requirements engineering conference, RE'08, IEEE Computer Society, Los Alamitos, CA
37. Van Lamsweerde A (2000) Requirements engineering in the year 00: a research perspective. In: Proceedings of 22nd international conference on software engineering, ACM, New York
38. Van Lamsweerde A, Letier E (2000) Handling obstacles in goal-oriented requirements engineering. IEEE Trans Softw Eng 26(10):978–1005
39. Yu E (1997) Towards modelling and reasoning support for early-phase requirements engineering. In: Proceedings of Third IEEE international symposium on requirements engineering, IEEE Computer Society, Los Alamitos CA

Important Papers by Colette Rolland

1. Ben Achour C, Rolland C, Souveyet C, Maiden NAM (1999) Guiding use case authoring: results of an empirical study. In: Proceedings of the 4th IEEE international symposium on requirements engineering RE 1999, IEEE Computer Society, Washington, DC, USA, pp 36–43
2 Bubenko J, Rolland C, Loucopoulos P, DeAntonellis V (1994) Facilitating 'fuzzy to formal' requirements modelling. In: Proceedings of international conference on requirement engineering ICRE 1994, Colorado Springs, Colorado, pp 154–157
3. Cauvet C, Proix C, Rolland C (1991) Alecsi: an expert system for requirements engineering. In: Proceedings of CAiSE 1991. LNCS, vol 498. Springer, Berlin Heidelberg, pp 31–49
4. Deneckère R, Kornyshova E, Rolland C (2009) Enhancing the guidance of the intentional model MAP: graph theory application. In: Proceedings of the international conference on research challenges in information science (RCIS 2009), Fès, Morocco
5. Etien A, Rolland C (2005) Measuring the fitness relationship. Reqs Eng J 10:184–197
6. Etien A, Rolland C, Salinesi C (2006) A meta-modelling approach to express change requirements. In: Proceedings of international conference on software engineering and data technologies – ICSOFT'2009. Special session on Meta-modelling, Setubal, Portugal
7. Falkenberg FD, Hesse W, Lindgreen P, Nilsson BE, Oei JLH, Rolland C, Stamper RK, Van Assche FJM, Verrijn-Stuart AA, Voss K (1996) FRISCO: a framework of information system concepts. The IFIP WG 8.1 Task Group FRISCO Technical report http://cs-exhibitions.uni-klu.ac.at/index.php?id=445
8. Iacovelli A, Souveyet C, Rolland C (2008) Method as a Service (MaaS). In: Proceedings of international conference on research challenges in information science – RCIS 2008, Marrakech, Morocco, pp 371–380
9. Jarke M, Bubenko J, Rolland C, Sutcliffe A, Vassiliou Y (1993) Theories underlying requirements engineering – an overview of NATURE at genesis. In: Proceedings of IEEE symposium on requirements engineering – RE 1993, San Diego, CA
10. Jarke M, Pohl K, Jacobs S, Bubenko J, Assenova P, Holm P, Wangler B, Rolland C, Plihon V, Schmitt JR, Sutcliffe S, Jones S, Maiden N, Till D, Vassiliou Y, Constantopoulos P, Spanoudakis G (1993) Requirements engineering: an integrated view of representation, process, and domain. In: Proceedings of the 4th European software engineering conference. LNCS, vol 717. Springer, Berlin Heidelberg, pp 100–114
11. Jarke M, Pohl K, Rolland C, Schmitt JR (1994) Experience-based method evaluation and improvement: a process modeling approach. In: Proceedings of IFIP WG 8.1 CRIS conference, Maastrich, The Netherlands, pp 1–27
12. Jarke M, Rolland C, Sutcliffe A, Domges R (eds) (1999) The NATURE of requirements engineering. Shaker, Aachen, Germany
13. Kaabi RS, Souveyet C, Rolland C (2004) Eliciting service composition in a goal driven manner. In: Proceedings of international conference on service oriented computing – ICSOC. New York, NY, USA, pp 308–315

S. Nurcan et al. (eds.), *Intentional Perspectives on Information Systems Engineering*,
DOI 10.1007/978-3-642-12544-7,

14. Lingat Y, Nobecourt P, Rolland C (1987) Behaviour management in database applications. In. Proceedings of 13th international conference on very large databases – VLDB 1987, UK. Morgan Kaufmann Publishers Inc., San Francisco, CA, USA, pp 185–196
15. Nurcan S, Etien A, Kaabi RS, Zoukar I, Rolland C (2005) A strategy driven business process modelling approach. business process management journal. Special Issue on Goal-oriented Business Process Management Journal 11(6):628–649, Emerald
16. Nurcan S, Rolland C (2003) A multi-method for defining the organizational change. J Info Softw Technol 45(2):61–82
17. Papadacci E, Stephanopoli, Salinesi C, Rolland C (2006) NENO process: information systems arbitration process in enterprise architecture project. Information and communication technologies: from theory to applications (ICTTA), Damascus, Syria, IEEE, pp 105–106
18. Plihon V, Rolland C (1995) Modelling ways-of-working. In: Proceedings of CAISE 1995. LNCS, vol 932. Springer, Berlin Heidelberg, pp 126–139
19. Prakash N, Rolland C (2006) System design for requirements expressed as a Map. Information Resources Management Association – IRMA, Software Engineering Track, Washington, USA
20. Ralyte J, Deneckère R, Rolland C (2003) Towards a generic model for situational method engineering. In: Proceedings of CAISE 2003. LNCS, vol 2681. Springer, Berlin Heidelberg, pp 95–110
21. Ralyte J, Rolland C (2001) An approach for method reengineering. In: Proceedings of the 20th international conference on conceptual modeling – ER2001. LNCS, vol 2224. Springer, Berlin Heidelberg, pp 471–484
22. Ralyte J, Rolland C (2001) An assembly process model for method engineering. In: Proceedings of CAISE 2001. LNCS, vol 2068. Springer, Berlin Heidelberg, pp 267–283
23. Ralyte J, Rolland C, Plihon V (1999) Method enhancement by scenario based techniques. In: Proceedings of CAISE 1999. LNCS, vol 1626. Springer, Berlin Heidelberg, pp 103–118
24. Rolland C (1984) Database dynamics. ACM SIGMIS Database, 14(3): 32–43, ACM New York, NY, USA
25. Rolland C (1992) Trends and perspectives in conceptual modelling. In: Proceedings of Indo-French workshop on object-oriented systems, Goa, India
26. Rolland C (1994) Modelling the evolution of artifacts. In: Proceedings of the first international conference on requirements engineering – RE 1994. Colorado, pp. 216–219
27. Rolland C (1997) A primer for method engineering. In: Proceedings of Informatique des Organisations et Systèmes d'Information et de Décision – INFORSID 1997, Toulouse, France
28. Rolland C (1998) A comprehensive view of process engineering. In: Proceedings of CAISE 1998. LNCS, vol 1413. Springer, Berlin Heidelberg, pp 1–24
29. Rolland C (1999) Requirements engineering for COTS based systems. J Info Softw Technol 41:985–990
30. Rolland C (2002) L'E-Lyee: coupling L'Ecritoire and LyeeALL. Info Softw Technol 44: 185–194
31. Rolland C (2006) Aligning business and system functionality through model matching. In: Systèmes d'Information et Management (SIM): 10(3)
32. Rolland C (2007) Capturing system intentionality with maps. In: Krogstie J, Opdahl AL, Brinkkemper S (eds) Conceptual modelling in information systems engineering. Springer, Berlin, pp 140–158
33. Rolland C (2008) Intention driven conceptual modelling. In: Johannesson P, Söderström E (eds) Information systems engineering: from data analysis to process networks. IGI Global, pp 16–42
34. Rolland C (2009) Endorsement of the book "metamodeling for method engineering". In: Jeusfeld MA, Jarke M, Mylopoulos J (eds) Metamodeling for method engineering, MIT, Cambridge, MA
35. Rolland C (2009) Exploring the fitness relationship between system functionality and business needs. In: Lyytinen K, Loucopoulos P, Mylopoulos J, Robinson W (eds) Design requirements engineering – a ten-year perspective. LNBIP, vol 14. Springer, Berlin Heidelberg, pp 305–326

36. Rolland C (2009) Method engineering: towards methods as services. Software Process: Improvement and Practice (SPIP). Special issue on Software Processes 14(3):143–164, Wiley, New York, NY
37. Rolland C, Ben Achour C (1998) Guiding the construction of textual use case specification. Data Knowl Eng J 25(1):125–160
38. Rolland C, Ben Achour C, Cauvet C, Ralyte J, Sutcliffe A, Maiden N. Jarke M, Haumer P, Pohl K, Dubois E, Heymans P (1998) A proposal for a scenario classification framework. Reqs Eng J 3(1):23–47
39. Rolland C, Foucaut O (1978) Concepts for designing an information system and its utilisation in the REMORA project. In: Proceedings of the 4th international conference on very large databases – VLDB 1978. West Berlin, Germany, pp 342–350
40. Rolland C, Grosz G, Kla R (1999) Experience with goal-scenario coupling in requirements engineering. In: Proceedings of the 4th IEEE international symposium on requirements engineering, IEEE Computer Society, Limerick, Ireland, pp 74–83
41. Rolland C, Kaabi (2007) An intentional perspective to service modeling and discovery. In: Proceedings of international computer software and applications conference COMPSAC 2007, Beijing, China, pp 455–460
42. Rolland C, Kaabi, RS, Kraeim N (2007) On ISOA: intentional services oriented architecture. In: Proceedings of CAISE 2007. LNCS, vol 4495. Springer, Berlin Heidelberg, pp 158–172
43. Rolland C, Leifert S, Richard C (1979) Tools for information dynamics management. In: Proceedings of 5th international conference on very large databases – VLDB 1979, Brasil. Rio de Janeiro, Brazil, pp 251–261
44. Rolland C, Nurcan S (2010) Business process lines to deal with the variability. In: Proceedings of Hawaii international conference on system sciences (HICSS), Hawaii, USA
45. Rolland C, Nurcan S, Grosz G (1997) Guiding the participative design process. In: Proceedings of the Americas conference on information systems, association for information systems, Indianapolis, IN, pp 922–924
46. Rolland C, Nurcan S, Grosz G (1998) A Unified framework for modelling co-operative design processes and co-operative business processes. In: Proceedings of international conference on system sciences – HICSS 1998, Big Island, Hawaii, USA
47. Rolland C, Nurcan S, Grosz G (1999) Enterprise knowledge development: the process view. Info Manage J 36(3):165–184
48. Rolland C, Plihon V, Ralyte J (1998) Specifying the reuse context of scenario method chunks. In: Proceedings of CAISE 1998. LNCS, vol 1413. Springer, Berlin Heidelberg, pp 191–218
49. Rolland C, Prakash N (1996) A proposal for context-specific method engineering. In: Proceedings of IFIP WG 8.1 conference on method engineering, Atlanta, GA, pp 191–208
50. Rolland C, Prakash N (2000) Bridging the gap between organisational needs and ERP functionality. Reqs Eng J (REJ) 5(3):180–193
51. Rolland C, Prakash N (2001) From conceptual modelling to requirements engineering. Ann Softw Eng 10(1–4):15–176
52. Rolland C, Prakash N, Benjamen A (1999) A multi-model view of process modelling. Reqs Eng J 4(4):169–187
53. Rolland C, Prakash N, Kaabi RS (2007) Variability in business process families. In: Proceedings of information resources management association – IRMA. Vancouver, Canada
54. Rolland C, Proix C (1986) An intelligent tool for information systems design. In: Proceedings of 19th HICSS international conference, Hawaii, ACM/IEEE
55. Rolland C, Proix C (1992) A natural language approach for requirements engineering. In: Proceedings of CAiSE 1992. LNCS, vol 593. Springer, Berlin Heidelberg, pp 257–277
56. Rolland C, Salinesi C (2005) Modeling goals and reasoning with them. In: Aurum A, Wohlin C (eds) Engineering and managing requirements. Springer, Berlin Heidelberg, pp 189–217
57. Rolland C, Salinesi C, Etien A (2004) Eliciting gaps in requirements change. Reqs Eng J 9(1):1–15

58. Rolland C, Kirsch-Pinheiro M, Souveyet C (2010), An Intentional Approach to Service Engineering, IEEE Transactions of Services Computing, Special issue on REFS (Requirements Engineering for Services) Workshop, April 2010 (in press), DOI Bookmark: http://doi.ieeecomputersociety.org/10.1109/TSC.2010.26
59. Rolland C, Souveyet C, Ben Achour C (1998) Guiding goal modelling using scenarios. IEEE Trans Softw Eng, Special Issue on Scenario Management 24(12):1055–1071
60. Rolland C, Souveyet C, Kraeim N (2008) An intentional view of service-oriented computing. Revue Ingénierie des Systèmes d'Information (ISI), RSTI (Revue des Sciences et Technologies de l'Information) – ISI 13(1):107–137, Hermès, France
61. Rolland C, Souveyet C, Moreno M (1995) An Approach for defining ways-of-working. Info Systems J 4:337–359
62. Rolland C, Stirna J, Prekas N, Loucopoulos P, Grosz G (2000) Evaluating a pattern approach as an aid for the development of organisational knowledge: an empirical study. In: Proceedings of CAISE 2000. LNCS, vol 1789. Springer, Berlin Heidelberg, pp 176–191
63. Rolland, Foucaut O, Benci G (1988) Conception des systèmes d'information: la méthode REMORA. Eyrolles, Paris, France
64. Salinesi C, Rolland C (2003) Fitting business models to software functionality: exploring the fitness relationship. In: Proceedings of CAISE 2003. LNCS, vol 2681. Springer, Berlin Heidelberg, pp 647–664
65. Si-Said S, Rolland C, Grosz G (1996) MENTOR: a computer aided requirements engineering environment. In: Proceedings of CAISE 1996. LNCS, vol 1080. Springer, Berlin Heidelberg, pp 22–43
66. Wieringa R, Maiden NAM, Mead N, Rolland C (2006) Requirements engineering paper classification and evaluation criteria: a proposal and a discussion. Reqs Eng J 11(1):102–107

Index

MIX
Papier aus verantwortungsvollen Quellen
Paper from responsible sources
FSC® C105338
FSC
www.fsc.org

If you have any concerns about our products,
you can contact us on
ProductSafety@springernature.com

In case Publisher is established outside the EU,
the EU authorized representative is:
Springer Nature Customer Service Center GmbH
Europaplatz 3, 69115 Heidelberg, Germany

Printed by Libri Plureos GmbH
in Hamburg, Germany